The
ZUMA
YEARS

The ZUMA YEARS

South Africa's Changing Face of Power

Richard Calland

Published by Zebra Press
an imprint of Random House Struik (Pty) Ltd
Reg. No. 1966/003153/07
Wembley Square, First Floor, Solan Road, Gardens, Cape Town, 8001
PO Box 1144, Cape Town, 8000, South Africa

www.zebrapress.co.za

First published 2013

1 3 5 7 9 10 8 6 4 2

Publication © Zebra Press 2013
Text © Richard Calland 2013

Cover illustration: Dr Jack

PUBLISHER: Marlene Fryer
MANAGING EDITOR: Robert Plummer
EDITOR: Bronwen Leak
PROOFREADER: Lisa Compton
COVER AND TEXT DESIGNER: Jacques Kaiser
TYPESETTER: Monique van den Berg
INDEXER: Sanet le Roux

Set in 10.5 pt on 13.5 pt Minion

Printed and bound by Paarl Media, Jan van Riebeeck Avenue, Paarl, South Africa

ISBN 978 1 77022 088 1 (print)
ISBN 978 1 77022 276 2 (ePub)
ISBN 978 1 77022 277 9 (PDF)

To my own 'Inner Cabinet' of irreplaceable old school friends:
Pete, Cookie, Botty and Luib

Contents

Foreword

Power relationships are in perpetual contest and flux. It's one of the daily wonders of reporting in a new democracy. It is exciting, but sometimes deeply mystifying, as networks shape and reframe continuously. Most of the work I read daily on power and where it lies is guesswork at best and spin at worst.

City Press is proud to be associated with this book because it answers the question of power and its anatomy with some authority. Its author, Richard Calland, is one of South Africa's finest political analysts and astute democrats.

While President Jacob Zuma came to office promising a more open order and responsive administration, it has proved both anaemic and ruthless in its understanding of power and how to exercise it for the greater good.

I remember sitting on a television panel with Justice Malala after the governing ANC's national conference at Polokwane in that unseasonably cold summer of 2007. We were both liberally sipping the Kool-Aid of the moment.

Zuma would be a fresh start, we opined, a needed man of the people after the small-mindedness and intellectual disdain for ordinary people that often characterised the administration of President Thabo Mbeki.

Zuma listened, I said. With the benefit of hindsight, I think I had slipped on blinkers about the corruption charges he still faced. Within a year, those charges had been dismissed in a sleight of hand so shocking I still can't believe it passed without more public opprobrium.

Today, we sit with a hollowed-out National Prosecuting Authority and an impotent Special Investigating Unit. The Hawks are a shallow impersonation of the tough Scorpions in their heyday. The police service is in shambles, as the massacre at Marikana showed us and as headlines reveal every day.

President Zuma can wield power with a scalpel of absolute self-interest. We've seen this time and again. He is a laughing assassin.

But he is a much-loved laughing assassin. At the end of 2012, I sat in the seats of the KwaZulu-Natal delegation at the ANC's Mangaung conference and this time took in another view of President Zuma. In so many ways that Nelson Mandela and Thabo Mbeki were not, he is a man of the people, an emblem of what can be for everyday South Africa.

Jacob Zuma is not a professional or a scholar – most South Africans are not either. He is deeply traditional and even tribal – most South Africans are too. So, while the urban and urbane may turn up their (our) noses at his many wives, his excesses at Nkandla, the presidential estate, and his large convoy of black cars and blue lights, for millions of South Africans, I believe, he is a symbol of an effective transfer of political power. As a feminist schooled by the liberation movement, polygamy does not sit easily with my belief in sexual equality, but I respect that it is a traditional and religious right of many South African men.

He is 'Number One', as we heard in the Guptagate saga, the shorthand term for the cocktail of patronage, favours for friends and cronyism that the Gupta family's Sun City wedding revealed.

Read through the documents that the *Mail & Guardian* and *City Press* have uncovered about the spending at Nkandla and you will see the impact this kind of governance by Number One has had on the state. It is, in many spheres, a play-thing of power and an object for easy enrichment.

This is what self-interest does. The picture is the same in education, where the president needs the support of executive head Angie Motshekga because of the power base she delivers to him.

Counterposed against this heavy hand is another form of governance – governance by no governance at all. In JZ parlance, it is the 'let's talk about it' model, 'and reach a consensus based on no consensus at all'.

In this, President Jacob Zuma is taking a page from one of his most success-ful periods – as peacemaker in the KwaZulu-Natal killing fields, where peace was won through dialogue and inclusion, but as applied power today, the strategy does not work.

In fact, it is what is choking our economy. The president has assembled an economics team near completely at odds with one another. In one corner, you have economic development minister Ebrahim Patel and trade and industry minister Rob Davies, who want a huge, big-spending, industrialised state. In the other are finance minister Pravin Gordhan and planning minister Trevor Manuel, who want balanced books and a modern outward-looking economy. What we have in the end is continued stasis.

This is not a pretty picture. So what keeps me an optimistic South African? Our Constitution and, personally speaking, the enormous freedoms and protec-tions it continues to grant me as a working journalist. There are our courts too, which, despite rhetoric and efforts to eviscerate their independence, remain a powerful centre of righteous governance.

Civil society has, for sixteen years now, been a shining diamond in our demo-cratic edifice. The Treatment Action Campaign ushered in a new era of civic activism when it successfully beat President Mbeki's AIDS denialism. South Africa now has one of the world's largest antiretroviral drug public programmes in the world.

Its noble successor is Equal Education, a lobby group staging a wonderful campaign for decent public education as promised by the Constitution. There are others, too, in which I place my faith for our future. Around the world, politics and power are diffusing into new, less organised forms than we have always understood, and it is quite wonderful to see the trend in South Africa too.

Nineteen years into our democracy, the shape of power is sometimes as we dreamt it, and often not. But it is sufficiently distributed and checked to make ours an exciting, loud and contested democracy. *Amandla?* Who knows where to after our twentieth year of freedom. But right now, this book is your guide.

FERIAL HAFFAJEE
EDITOR OF *CITY PRESS*
JULY 2013

Preface and acknowledgements

This book is the sequel to my 2006 *Anatomy of South Africa: Who Holds the Power?* As Anthony Sampson did with a changing Britain in the 1960s, I am trying to chart the shifts in power and politics during a period of intense social transformation in South Africa's history. Halfway through writing *The Zuma Years*, I looked again at Sampson's 1966 *Anatomy of Britain Today* (written four years after his first book in 1962) and read in the preface his admission that his second book was 75 per cent the same as his first! In contrast, *The Zuma Years* is no more than 2 or 3 per cent the same as *Anatomy of South Africa*. This is partly because I am foolishly ambitious as well as industrious, partly because a lot has changed since 2006 and partly because I take on new aspects of power in South Africa.

So this book features chapters on, for example, foreign policy making and foreign policy makers, not least because it came to my attention that the first book was apparently very popular with the diplomatic corps in South Africa, who would recommend it to new arrivals as an accessible yet sufficiently detailed exposition of the institutions and individuals who run the country. It is also an area of policy making that I am especially interested in and which is scantily covered by the media, commentators and analysts.

There are also new chapters on the universities, the professions, money and politics, the boardrooms, and traditional leaders – all sites of power, social advancement and change (or not, as in the case of the traditional leaders).

Because *The Zuma Years* seeks to provide a contemporaneous X-ray of power relations at the point at which I signed off on the proofs (in mid-July 2013), it is also a hostage to fortune: new events may intercede and change things, perhaps dramatically, and/or people may leave their jobs and move on to new ones. (As if to prove the point, in the week before this book went to print, President Zuma announced a cabinet reshuffle, presumably because he wanted to add further excitement to the final days of the publishing process, as it required various passages to be completely rewritten.) Even the biggest events, however, are unlikely to seriously undermine the rationale of this book – more than anything, if it is successful it will be because it provides readers with the tools to assess for themselves the nature of political power in South Africa in the future. In this sense, it is less of a map and more of a compass.

In my determination to bring South African politics vividly to life, I have sought to emphasise its personal, human side, probably at the expense of hard, dry, empirical analysis – although, thanks to the sponsorship of *City Press* newspaper, I was able to assemble a small team of researchers to assist with this book, which, in turn, means that it covers more ground and digs somewhat deeper, with more evidence and less anecdote, than *Anatomy of South Africa*. I am very grateful to Minette Ferreira, the general manager of *City Press*, as well as the newspaper's editor, Ferial Haffajee, for their willingness not only to support this endeavour but to partner me in it; my thanks and sincere appreciation to them both, and to their colleagues.

Despite the additional research, I have limited the citations and academic references to a bare minimum so as not to clutter the narrative; in a couple of places I have drawn from my own columns in the *Mail & Guardian*. Moreover, there is no attempt to be comprehensive in a scholarly fashion; the examples that are given, and the data that is used, are applied to illustrate a trend and are just that: illustrative. I hope critics will take account of my central purpose when they assess the book's merit: to provide an accessible keyhole into the working life of politics and the politicians – in the broad meaning of the term – who operate South Africa's wheels of power.

In addition to several new chapters, there are a couple of 'losses' from the first book. Although a very able researcher (André Wiesner) did a stellar job in gathering and collating voluminous information, I found that there was too much detail to tell the story of the changes in both the public service and the powerful state-owned enterprises (SOEs), such as Eskom, in this book at this time (although the Conclusion does touch on some of the key issues relating to the state and its power or otherwise in relation to its capacity to deliver public services and respond to public demands). I hope to add a chapter on the public service and SOEs to a future edition, perhaps after the 2014 election, which promises to be the most interesting and keenly contested since 1994, with two to three million new, 'born free' voters entering the electoral marketplace for the first time.

I also dropped the chapter on the media and spin doctors, partly because it would have been inappropriate to express my view that, in Ferial Haffajee, the country has one of the finest, bravest and most principled editors any society could wish for, given that her newspaper provided the funding support for my research team. Her strength of character during the unedifying furore surrounding Brett Murray's *The Spear* spoke volumes of her calibre and commitment to freedom of expression. She is not alone. There are other fine editors, such as Mpumelelo Mkhabela – whom I predicted would rise to the top in my first book, and is now – gratifyingly – editor of the *Sowetan* – as well as my own editor, Nic

Dawes, at the *Mail & Guardian*, where my political column, Contretemps, has appeared since September 2001. By the time this book is out, Dawes will have left his post to take up an exciting appointment in India. He will be greatly missed.

I would like to acknowledge and credit the members of my research team. Jonathan Faull did a superb job compiling and sorting the data for 'The professions' and 'The corporate boardrooms', and providing the initial drafts, as did Matthew MacDevette with the socio-economic data and many of the graphs and charts that are dotted throughout (my thanks to his former teacher, my esteemed colleague at UCT Nicoli Nattrass, for recommending him to me). Matthew went well beyond the call of duty in helping to finalise many of the graphics as publication neared.

Also, with my thanks for the excellence of their work, to Nonhlanhla Chanza ('Parliament' and 'The ANC'); Babongile Mandela ('The traditional leaders'); Cobus Coetzee: ('Foreign policy', 'The foreign policy makers' and 'Money and politics'); André Wiesner ('The unions'); and Chris Oxtoby ('The judges').

Hanne Nyokangi and Ashimizo Afadameh provided additional research for 'The universities' and 'Foreign policy', respectively. Jerry Manako, Adam Armstrong and Lara Wallis conducted additional research at various times.

Mervyn Bennun did a wonderful job researching and drafting 'Appendix 1' (the cabinet biographies), miraculously producing biographies of three new ministers the day after the July 2013 cabinet reshuffle. Sarah Yousaf did an excellent job with 'Appendix 2' (the Constitutional Court biographies).

I am very grateful to all of these people for the contribution they made towards this project.

Some of these researchers prepared drafts of some of the chapters, or sections of them, which I then worked on and embellished. This may account for a few variations in style in the book. But, to be clear: any errors of fact, or egregious unfairness in the analysis, is my responsibility alone.

My particular thanks go to special and trusted friends who read chapters and commented: Judith February, Lawson Naidoo, Nomfundo Ngwenya and Halton Cheadle.

I also wish to acknowledge all the people who lent me their valuable time so that I could pick their brains about the issues I cover in this book. All of them are busy and important people, including several past and present members of the cabinet. Most of them spoke to me on a background basis for ease of discussion, applying the 'Chatham House' rule, which meant that I had to go back to them to secure their agreement to use the quotes that I attribute to individuals. Except where I have provided a specific reference, the source of the comments attributed to any individual is my interview with that person.

Last, my sincere thanks to the team at Zebra Press: Marlene Fryer, for her persuasiveness in getting me to commit to the book, and Robert Plummer, for his skilful as well as patient shepherding of the process. I like people who stay calm under pressure and, while it may well be a prerequisite for his profession, Robert stayed very calm during the fraught final days in the writing and production schedule. Similarly, thanks to Bronwen Leak, not only for her excellent editing, but for maintaining full composure – as far as I could detect – during the dash for the line, editing even faster than I could write, and rescuing my prose as best she could.

Dr Jack has, I hope you agree, produced a very dashing and impactful cover design, for which I am grateful. It presents a South African Mount Rushmore. As I write this preface, former president Nelson Mandela is critically ill in hospital and a nation is preparing to mourn his loss. It is a painful prospect. But it signals the end of a generation, and reinforces the idea that a new generation of leaders must step up and into the big shoes of people like Mandela and the wonderful Archbishop Emeritus Desmond Tutu, while drawing inspiration from them and seeking to apply the principles of great, inclusive, progressive leadership that they have shown the world.

The Zuma Years begins, as did *Anatomy of South Africa*, with Trevor Manuel, a fine leader committed to public service, who is one of only two cabinet ministers (the other being Jeff Radebe) to span all the cabinets since 1994. He has, therefore, served presidents Mandela, Mbeki, Motlanthe and Zuma, and has been one of the predominant faces of the changing landscape of power in modern South Africa.

Thereafter, I explore the new Presidency, and the impact of the man who heads it, identifying the new key players and institutions. From thence I move to Zuma's 'coalition' cabinet, noting its changes in ideological outlook and ethnic composition. Two chapters on foreign policy making and makers follow, for the reasons I mention above.

Then I look at Parliament through the eyes of the leadership of the Right2-Know campaign – thereby giving a sense of the state of 'civil society', which has changed significantly in recent years – and also those of a leading opposition member of Parliament, who, like his equivalent in *Anatomy of South Africa*, ANC MP Johnny de Lange, is a fine parliamentarian.

I then tackle the big political formations: the African National Congress (and within that exploration, its relationship with one Tripartite Alliance partner, the South African Communist Party); the unions (the analysis of which includes an attempt to explain the current dilemmas and divisions in the Congress of South African Trade Unions, and its relationship with the ANC); the opposition, which has largely coalesced and amalgamated around the Democratic Alliance since 2006 and, thanks to changes in the face of its leadership, is in a much stronger position to challenge the ANC in the 2014 election; and traditional leaders, who hold power over a large percentage of South Africans, but about whom the middle class know very little.

The judges, or 'the last frontier' as I like to call them, are examined in depth, focusing on changes in the face of their own leadership, the chief justice, and the body that appoints judges, the Judicial Service Commission.

Money and politics represent a toxic cocktail, as evidenced by the interconnections and hidden networks presented in Chapter 12.

In the final section of the book, I explore some of the drivers of power and the establishment, looking for evidence of change in the boardrooms, the professions and the universities from where come the professional classes, who are always significant players in defining the character, ideology and leadership of both the public and private sectors.

Although I am naturally prone to optimism, and although I still remain positive about South Africa's ability to rise to its challenges, it has not been so easy to remain so hopeful in recent times. Indeed, *The Zuma Years* concludes on an uneasy note, on the basis that the logic of the evidence that this book presents is inescapable and must now be confronted for what it is and what it means for the future.

RICHARD CALLAND
CAPE TOWN
JULY 2013

Abbreviations and acronyms

ACDP: African Christian Democratic Party
AMCU: Association of Mineworkers and Construction Union
ANC: African National Congress
ANCWL: African National Congress Women's League
ANCYL: African National Congress Youth League
AU: African Union
AZAPO: Azanian People's Organisation
AZASO: Azanian Students Organisation
BAT: British American Tobacco
BEE: black economic empowerment
BLA: Black Lawyers Association
BMF: Black Management Forum
BRIC(S): Brazil, Russia, India, China (and South Africa)
BUSA: Business Unity South Africa
CA: chartered accountant
CALS: Centre for Applied Legal Studies
CASAC: Council for the Advancement of the South African Constitution
CBD: central business district
CCMA: Commission for Conciliation, Mediation and Arbitration
CEC: central executive committee
CEPPWAWU: Chemical, Energy, Paper, Printing, Wood and Allied Workers Union
CIPC: Companies and Intellectual Property Commission
CODESA: Convention for a Democratic South Africa
CONTRALESA: Congress of Traditional Leaders of South Africa
COP: Conference of the Parties
COPE: Congress of the People
COSAS: Congress of South African Students
COSATU: Congress of South African Trade Unions
CPUT: Cape Peninsula University of Technology
CTA: Certificate of the Theory of Accounting
CTICC: Cape Town International Convention Centre
CWU: Communication Workers Union
CWUSA: Creative Workers Union of South Africa
DA: Democratic Alliance
DASO: Democratic Alliance Students Organisation
DENOSA: Democratic Nursing Organisation of South Africa

DG: director general
DGRU: Democratic Governance and Rights Unit
DIRCO: Department of International Relations and Cooperation
DPME: Department of Performance Monitoring and Evaluation
DRC: Democratic Republic of the Congo
DTI: Department of Trade and Industry
EDD: Economic Development Department
EPA: economic partnership agreement
EU: European Union
FAWU: Food and Allied Workers Union
FFP: Freedom Front Plus
GCBSA: General Council of the Bar of South Africa
GCIS: Government Communication and Information System
GDP: gross domestic product
GEAR: Growth, Employment and Redistribution
GNU: Government of National Unity
GPA: Global Political Agreement
HSRC: Human Sciences Research Council
IBSA: India-Brazil-South Africa
ID: Independent Democrats
IDASA: Institute for Democracy in Africa
IEC: Independent Electoral Commission
IFP: Inkatha Freedom Party
IMF: International Monetary Fund
ISS: Institute for Security Studies
JSC: Judicial Service Commission
JSE: Johannesburg Stock Exchange
KZN: KwaZulu-Natal
LSSA: Law Society of South Africa
MDC: Movement for Democratic Change
MEC: member of the executive council
MK: Umkhonto we Sizwe
MP: member of Parliament
MPL: member of the provincial legislature
NADEL: National Association of Democratic Lawyers
NALEDI: National Labour and Economic Development Institute
NCACC: National Conventional Arms Control Committee
NCOP: National Council of Provinces
NDC: National Disciplinary Committee
NDP: National Development Plan
NDPP: national director of public prosecutions
NEC: national executive committee
NEDLAC: National Economic Development and Labour Council
NEHAWU: National Education, Health and Allied Workers Union

NEPAD: New Partnership for Africa's Development
NGO: non-governmental organisation
NGP: New Growth Path
NHI: National Health Insurance
NIPP: National Industrial Participation Programme
NNP: New National Party
NP: National Party
NPA: National Prosecuting Authority
NPC: National Planning Commission
NUM: National Union of Mineworkers
NUMSA: National Union of Metalworkers of South Africa
NWC: national working committee
OCJ: Office of the Chief Justice
ODAC: Open Democracy Advice Centre
PAC: Pan Africanist Congress
PAIA: Promotion of Access to Information Act
PAWUSA: Public and Allied Workers Union of South Africa
PBF: Progressive Business Forum
PCAS: Policy Coordination and Advisory Service
PEC: Provincial Executive Committee
PFP: Progressive Federal Party
PIC: Public Investment Corporation
PICC: Presidential Infrastructure Coordinating Commission
PIMS: Political Information and Monitoring Service
POPCRU: Police and Prisons Civil Rights Union
PPP: purchasing power parity
PSC: Public Service Commission
PWC: PricewaterhouseCoopers
R2K: Right2Know
REC: Regional Executive Committee
SAA: South African Airways
SABC: South African Broadcasting Corporation
SACCAWU: South African Commercial, Catering and Allied Workers Union
SACOIR: South African Council on International Relations
SACP: South African Communist Party
SACTWU: Southern African Clothing and Textile Workers Union
SACU: Southern African Customs Union
SADC: Southern African Development Community
SADF: South African Defence Force
SADNU: South African Democratic Nurses Union
SADTU: South African Democratic Teachers Union
SAFPU: South African Football Players Union
SAHRC: South African Human Rights Commission
SAICA: South African Institute of Chartered Accountants

SAIIA: South African Institute of International Affairs
SAIRR: South African Institute of Race Relations
SAMA: South African Medical Association
SAMWU: South African Municipal Workers Union
SANDF: South African National Defence Force
SAPS: South African Police Service
SARS: South African Revenue Service
SASAWU: South African State and Allied Workers Union
SASBO: South African Society of Bank Officials, now the Finance Union
SASCO: South African Students Congress
SATAWU: South African Transport and Allied Workers Union
SAYCO: South African Youth Congress
SCA: Supreme Court of Appeal
SCOPA: Standing Committee on Public Accounts
SIPs: Strategic Infrastructure Projects
SOE: state-owned enterprise
SRC: student representative council
TAC: Treatment Action Campaign
TISA: Trade and Investment South Africa
TRC: Truth and Reconciliation Commission
UAE: United Arab Emirates
UCT: University of Cape Town
UDF: United Democratic Front
UDM: United Democratic Movement
UFS: University of the Free State
UJ: University of Johannesburg
UKZN: University of KwaZulu-Natal
UN: United Nations
UNHCR: United Nations High Commissioner for Refugees
UNISA: University of South Africa
UNSC: United Nations Security Council
UWC: University of the Western Cape
Wits: University of the Witwatersrand
WTO: World Trade Organization
ZANU-PF: Zimbabwe African National Union-Patriotic Front

1

From Mbeki to Zuma

Trevor Manuel ought to have known better. Perhaps it was the early hour of the 6 a.m. flight from New York to Washington that had made him forget, or maybe it was his state of mind, but South Africa's long-standing minister of finance had neglected to turn off his cellphone before take-off. As the plane began to descend into Ronald Reagan Washington National Airport, Manuel's phone began to simultaneously ring and beep angrily and persistently, causing consternation and irritation among his fellow passengers and the United Airlines stewardesses.

'The thing was ringing off the hook and I couldn't turn it off,' Manuel recounts now, with a deep-throated chuckle. 'Everyone on the plane was looking at me.'

At home, in South Africa, everyone was looking *for* him. It was Monday 22 September 2008. The news that Manuel had resigned as minister of finance had just leaked, and the rand 'fell out of bed', to use Manuel's own phrase.

After waiting for sufficient time to pass until it felt decent to start answering his phone as the plane taxied towards the terminal building, Manuel took his first call. It was Thoraya Pandy, his long-standing, loyal media liaison officer. She was desperate to speak to him. The previous day, as Manuel had departed for the United States, Pandy had responded to press inquiries by saying that Manuel had no intention to resign.

Now, an actual letter of resignation, dated Saturday 20 September and signed by Manuel, was out. Pandy had not lied, even though she knew that the letter existed: Manuel did not wish to resign and he had no intention of leaving his post as the world's longest-serving finance minister, a fact of which he was proud. But his boss, Thabo Mbeki, had just been deposed in the most dramatic of palace coups and Manuel thought there was an important point of constitutional law at stake.

Indeed there was. At around midnight on the Friday, the national executive committee (NEC) of the ruling African National Congress (ANC) had decided, amidst scenes of unprecedented rancour, to 'recall' Mbeki as president. It was a stunning fall from grace for the man who had dominated the politics of the ANC for the better part of two decades, eleven of them as president of the ruling party and nine as president of the Republic of South Africa.

1

Out with the old

Precious few insider accounts have been written from within the ANC or the governments of Mandela and Mbeki since 1994, a fact that continues to disappoint. Mightily disingenuous though it is in places, with its cloying sycophancy towards Mbeki, Frank Chikane's *Eight Days in September*[1] does at least capture both the drama of Mbeki's political downfall and the constitutional issue that had so enervated Manuel in the hours leading up to his departure that weekend in 2008.

Though undoubtedly motivated by his loyalty to Mbeki, after having served the latter's presidency as director-general and cabinet secretary, Chikane's account reveals the NEC's clumsy disregard for the Constitution, as well as the ruthlessness of its decision. It was an NEC now dominated by bloodthirsty Zumarites so eager for revenge and in such a 'foul mood', as it was reported to Chikane at the time, that it was unwilling to take into account the many constitutional considerations that arose from its decision.

In South Africa's system of government, the president is elected not directly, but by the National Assembly. It is the first thing that a newly elected Parliament must do after its members are sworn in after a national election – at which point, peculiarly, the person elected as president ceases to be a member of Parliament (MP). Thus, reason would suggest that, having put the president into office, only the National Assembly should have the right to remove him or her – indeed, the Constitution makes provision for such action.[2]

So, for the ruling party to say to Mbeki 'we want you to go and go immediately' was to ignore Parliament's role completely. On one reading – certainly Chikane's – it speaks volumes about the Zuma faction's attitude to such constitutional rules. On another, it is a simple expression of realpolitik: the ANC put him into Parliament, ergo the ANC can remove him from office. Why waste time when you can cut out the (institutional) middleman?

What really rankled Chikane was the NEC's refusal to permit Mbeki to complete his immediate duties and to leave office with grace. Mbeki was due to speak at the United Nations (UN) that week – where Manuel was headed, along with then minister of foreign affairs Nkosazana Dlamini-Zuma – and at an important summit of African leaders a week later, but was told by the ANC leadership that he must leave office immediately.

To Chikane, this 'brought us close to the definition of a coup d'état'. In the thirty-six hours that followed the late-night decision to recall Mbeki, the ANC leadership's attitude was hard-line and uncompromising: he must leave immediately. It is an ANC stalwart, Chikane, not an opposition politician or a pesky journalist or commentator, who makes the point that 'the lines between parliament and party were again blurred and parliament was used as if it were a representative of the ruling party rather than elected representatives of the people'.

At the centre of the controversy was Baleka Mbete, who had once been an Mbeki favourite, but who had slipped well down the pecking order during his decade in the top job, partly due to her foolishness in cheating the system to get herself a driver's licence in 1997. Having not lost her hunger for power – far from it, in fact – Mbete had rebuilt her political career, this time under the wing of Jacob Zuma and as a leading member of the anti-Mbeki coalition that had formed in the run-up to the organisation's famous national conference in Polokwane in December 2007, when Zuma toppled Mbeki as president of the ANC and Mbete was elected on the Zuma slate as the ANC's new chairperson.

For Mbete, revenge was a dish best served cold. She had bided her time in the political wilderness, while, with cunning relish, building new alliances amidst the growing number of Mbeki enemies. She was also now the Speaker of the National Assembly, a position that was a key milestone in her political rehabilitation, but which bored her to death.

Instead of ensuring that Parliament's constitutional role was properly protected, it was Mbete who signed the letter informing Mbeki when precisely his term as president would cease – at 11 a.m. on Thursday 25 September 2008 – despite the fact that there had been no parliamentary resolution dealing with the president.

In other words, Mbete was using her power as Speaker to enforce a decision of the ruling party whose NEC she chaired.

If ever one wanted a lesson in conflict of interest and in the inappropriate use of public office, this would be it. It was a consideration that was apparently beyond Mbete's grasp, most probably because of her simple lack of principle, which has remained a constant and perhaps defining feature of the Zuma era and one that this book is forced to return to time and again.

Here, perhaps, Mbeki was hoist by his own petard. Mbeki had played fast and loose with the Constitution during his time in office. The principal charge is that he used institutions of state – especially those responsible for the criminal justice system, such as the National Prosecuting Authority (NPA) – to prosecute not felons, but his own political enemies.

Zuma was one such political enemy, or so he had become. The story of the decline of their erstwhile comradely association from the days of exile and struggle against apartheid is a long and complex one, and not for the telling here. The decline of the ANC's commitment to principle did not begin and end in September 2008. That was merely the denouement; the start of the new order, when power really changed hands and an old new establishment was replaced by a new new establishment.

The decay began under Mbeki, despite attempts by Chikane and other acolytes to present Mbeki as a victim who lost 'his presidency at the height of its glory'.

This revisionist view of history, incidentally, led his closest allies, such as Ronnie Kasrils, Essop Pahad and Chikane himself, to reassure Mbeki that he would win the presidential election at Polokwane, even minutes before the outcome was announced and despite the mountain of evidence that the tide had turned against Mbeki among the delegates and, probably, within the organisation as a whole.

Mbeki was now being forced to pay dearly for the decisions he thought he had to take to make sure the centre would hold (with reference to his favoured poem, 'The Second Coming'). Of course, it didn't, and since then things have slowly and inexorably continued to fall apart. To all intents and purposes, this is what this book is all about. One can almost hear Mbeki reciting Yeats's poem, of which he is so fond, while reading this.

Yet, this is not a history book. Like its predecessor, *Anatomy of South Africa: Who Holds the Power?*, which I wrote in 2006, it does not attempt to present a comprehensive account of any of the events to which it refers. Instead, it is concerned with power in South Africa and its changing face.

What those 'eight days in September' showed was how dominant a political force the ANC had become – that it could remove a president within forty-eight hours, notwithstanding the constitutional rules, and that the country could, seemingly, emerge relatively unscathed, although this might not be so true now, just a few years on. Mbeki could, of course, have resisted and used those rules to try to hang on to power. But he knew the game was up and he understood that although the National Assembly had elected him, he owed his political power to the ANC and not to Parliament, and that once the party's support for him had evaporated, so he too should go quietly rather than force an ugly constitutional crisis. Even though some of his closest advisors and political allies, such as Mojanku Gumbi and Alec Erwin, wanted to challenge the decision in the courts, Mbeki knew it would have brought further rancour and division.

Trevor Manuel was very clear in his mind: Mbeki had appointed him and if Mbeki left, so too should the cabinet. As he prepared to depart for the United States that September weekend, it was not yet known when exactly Mbeki would cease to be president – Mbete had not yet cut her swathe through the Constitution. So he left behind a signed letter of resignation so that if Mbeki had to leave rapidly, the letter would be in place. For Manuel, it was a matter of principle: he would not continue to serve as minister of finance until a new president appointed him.

The letter remained under wraps, but as Manuel winged his way across the Atlantic, the ANC's leadership insisted that the president resign by 7 p.m. on Sunday evening, which he agreed to do. Mbeki announced the fact of his resignation over the South African Broadcasting Corporation (SABC) in a short televised address at that exact hour, just as his letter of resignation was being delivered not to Parliament, but to an ANC NEC meeting in Midrand, at their insistence.

At lunchtime the following day, Manuel's resignation letter was leaked. That the markets reacted so dramatically to this event was an indication of two things. First, that Manuel was regarded as a respected, competent and safe pair of hands – ironic, given that his appointment as the first black finance minister in 1996 had caused a correspondingly negative flutter in market indicators. Manuel, as much as Mbeki, was an embodiment of the new establishment that had emerged during the years before and after the turn of the century. It is used to discredit him by his detractors, but Manuel's soberness and composed hand at the tiller of macroeconomic and budgetary authority were key elements of the new establishment's power and self-confidence.

Second, the markets' reaction to Manuel's resignation showed just how precarious their confidence in the new establishment was. Things had changed. The mood had changed. The country was changing.

The anatomy of power was being tested, and shaken.

In with the new

Although this is a sequel to *Anatomy of South Africa*, and even though some of the same parts of the political system are covered, this is a very different book. So much has changed; so many significant events have interceded – from the president all the way down.

There has been a changing of the guard, but not just at the top. In the early months of the Zuma administration, a very curious thing came to my attention. As I attended meetings in the ordinary course of my work in and around politics and with government officials and ministers, I started to notice how people kept referring to 'the old government' or even 'the old days'. And they tended to say it coldly, even with hostility. On occasion, I found myself wondering if they were referring to the *really* old days – the pre-1994 days of apartheid. But no, they weren't. They were referring to the Mbeki administration. And it was as if the Democrats had succeeded the Republicans, or the Tories had come in to replace Labour.

It was quite extraordinary. The ANC may have been re-elected in 2009, but it was not behaving as if it had. The desire of the new administration to distinguish itself from its predecessor was palpable, explicit. Sometimes it was new ministers or new officials who were speaking, which made a certain amount of sense; sometimes it wasn't, which made less sense.

This is a theme I return to in Chapter 3, where I deal with the cabinet. As I say there with greater elaboration, the Zuma administration operates like – and should be viewed as – a sort of coalition government. Whereas Mbeki ruled firmly, from the centre, pulling his party and his government with a centrifugal velocity, Zuma uses a 'big-tent approach'. His cabinet contains conservatives and nationalists, social democrats and Marxists, with a few moderates thrown in for good measure.

The ANC has always been a broad church. It has always had two great traditions – the one nationalist, the other socialist (or close variants of the two). Its great leaders, without exception, not only straddled the two traditions, but also pulled them together. To do so required strength as well as political dexterity, cunning as well as fortitude.

Zuma lacks enough of both. He is too weak and makes too many mistakes. At best, he is a mediator, not a leader. He leads in so far as he accumulates and retains power, and he understands the ANC so well that he can do so.

Thus, the first of the many big changes in the years since my first look into the anatomy of power has been the collapse of the ANC's leadership and, therefore, the collapse of the ANC.

This is not to say that the ANC is not still very powerful – after all, as already noted, it removed a president and did so with scant, if any, regard for the Constitution. But its power is now more diffuse, less focused, far less coherent and, therefore, far more vulnerable. It is, in short, a more erratic organisation now, less predictable in many ways. Whereas before, two plus two equalled four, now it could amount to almost anything.

Julius Malema is a consequence of this, not its cause. Distinguishing cause and effect in South African politics is never easy. With the rise of Malema it has proved to be even trickier. Malema is a symptom of a greater malaise.

But what exactly is he? It was only when sitting in a bar in Cambridge in 2010, well into the Malema saga, that it finally dawned on me, and it needed the prompting of an expat South African to elicit the epiphany. The Brits that were present were asking me about Malema, as so many had over the past few years. I was attempting to explain, using words such as 'populist' and 'opportunist' – words that can properly be attached to this angry young man – when Jeremy Baskin, who played a noble part in the trade-union movement prior to 1994, interjected with a very simple observation: 'Malema's a fascist.'

And indeed he is. Certainly, his political 'register' is that of fascism, and so is everything he represents. He may use the language of economic emancipation, with his talk of 'economic freedom' and his 'man-of-the-people', revolutionary T-shirt-wearing bravado, but he is a fascist. For a while no one else seemed to see it that way, and it was only in 2012 when, finally, the South African Communist Party (SACP) referred to him as 'proto-fascist' that the broader progressive movement began to call it what it is.

Earlier, admittedly, it was the SACP – yes, the communists, even allowing for the fact that the SACP's leadership is no more (or less) than social democrat – who exposed Malema's call for the nationalisation of the mines for what it was:

a crude, opportunistic, populist positioning for influence and attention. An alien coming to earth for the first time, but armed with a Political Ideology 101 textbook, would have been forgiven for presuming that it would be the SACP calling for nationalisation. That it was not, and that it was they who were the most eloquent opposition to Malema's call, tells you all you need to know about Malema's true intentions and his real place in the ideological spectrum.

The rise of Malema and the right within the ANC is the big story of the years since *Anatomy of South Africa* and since 2006. The idea of a right wing within the ANC is, admittedly, a hard thing to grasp, not least because the notion of a right wing means different things to different people. I explore the issue in greater depth in Chapter 7 on the ANC, save to say at this point that by 'right wing' I mean more than just 'nationalist'. The ANC has always, as I say, had nationalist tendencies – tendencies whose tools of analysis were primarily race- rather than class-based, and whose primary occupation was the transferral of power from white to black. But what has emerged from these tendencies is a category of political thought and action that is profoundly conservative in its core content – that is to say, non- or even anti-progressive, in that it does not share the same progressive values that the rest of the ANC has always held dear: notions of collective rights (rather than individual material accumulation); of gender equality; of tolerance towards difference, whether 'minorities' or sexual orientation; and of political economy, that there should be fair distribution of wealth as well as opportunity to amass it.

A watershed

A great deal seems to have happened in the seven years since 2006: Polokwane and the victory of Zuma over Mbeki in late 2007; the brutal 'recall' of Mbeki less than a year later; the 'political solution' that enabled Zuma to evade serious corruption charges, which were dropped on the eve of the national election in April the following year; and the successful hosting of two mega global events in successive years – first the FIFA World Cup in 2010 and then the 17th UN Climate Change Conference of the Parties (COP17) in Durban in 2011.

And then came 2012.

The year 2012. A watershed for South Africa. Our *annus horribilis*. The year of the three Ms: Malema, Marikana and Mangaung.

Malema, thrown out of the ANC, only to bounce back as the ultimate provocateur, leapt into the abyss of despair and disarray that followed the Marikana massacre of 16 August. It was a day of great shame for the new democratic South Africa, and it fanned the flames of discontent and violence, highlighting once again a lack of leadership in the ANC and – a game-changing factor – division within the trade-union movement. As I explore in Chapter 8, Marikana was a watershed moment not just for the National Union of Mineworkers (NUM), but for the ANC-aligned Congress of South African Trade Unions (COSATU) and for modern industrial relations in South Africa. The massacre had myriad consequences for the country's reputation, not least in the eyes of those who make decisions about its suitability as an investment destination.

Whether Marikana altered the outcome of the ANC national elective conference process that culminated at Mangaung in late December 2012 is hard to say. Certainly, Marikana was a wake-up call for the ruling party and its Triple Alliance partners, COSATU and the SACP. Rightly, it shocked the hell out of a lot of people inside the Alliance, though it also provoked defensiveness. It is clear that Marikana was an assault upon the establishment and its sensibilities, and so perhaps it should come as no surprise that some elements of the establishment – most notably the safety and security cluster, especially the police, who were most obviously liable for the terrible events at Marikana – were resistant to any sense of the tragedy's bigger meaning: that the social compact of the mid-1990s had finally broken down.

This did not happen overnight; it had been a long time coming. Its roots lie in the Mbeki years. It cannot be laid only at Zuma's door, though his style of leadership did, I would argue, speed up the process of decay. Could Marikana have happened under Mbeki? Perhaps, but my instinct is that Mbeki's political antennae and his understanding of the socio-economic dynamics of his country would have enabled him to anticipate what lay ahead. The processes that Mbeki and his trusted lieutenants instigated and maintained, often over-elaborate as they were, often mischievous in that they were designed to control or co-opt, would have provided the government with a better early warning system.

What was the 1990s social compact? Well, its constituent parts were, to my mind, as follows: first, and perhaps foremost, the 'one-nation' leadership of Nelson Mandela. Second, the commitment to negotiation and to multi-stakeholder dialogue. Third, the system of collective bargaining that it spawned, and which was to a large degree codified in the far-reaching Labour Relations Act of 1996. Fourth, the fierce determination to govern from the centre, with a fiscal rectitude to match. Fifth, and profound in impact, that all of the above benefited in a very fundamental way from the capacity of the ANC and COSATU to act together as a sponge to absorb socio-economic pressures, such as those that presented themselves at Marikana and where, self-evidently, the 'new' ANC and COSATU were unable to prevent the tragedy from occurring.

Whether explicitly or otherwise, the remaining chapters of this book return to these five reference points because they represent a significant part of the changing political climate. There are plenty of democracies around the world where an event as painful and as brutal as Marikana would have brought down the government. In South Africa, however, not even the minister of police has resigned or (yet) been called to account.

Indeed, though it may have caused many thinking members of the ANC to pause for deep reflection about where the country is heading and about the government's leadership, Marikana did not apparently do any harm to Zuma's political future – at least not in the immediate aftermath, because less than four months later he romped home to a decisive victory in the ANC's five-yearly national conference at Mangaung, having, with the able assistance of the party's secretary-general, Gwede Mantashe, cooked the membership books of the ANC sufficiently adroitly that Kgalema Motlanthe's challenge was dead well before the actual conference in the Free State provincial capital in December 2012.

Increasing electoral competition

Against the backdrop of the end of the 1990s social compact and the turmoil and confusion of the Zuma years, the opposition, led by the Democratic Alliance (DA), continued to make serious inroads. In *Anatomy of South Africa*, I was willing to dismiss the opposition's chances on the basis that 'until the one party with any serious capacity – the DA – changes both its leader and its strategy, it will be unable to exert any serious influence on politics in South Africa'.

Well, the DA did change its leader and appears, to an extent, to have changed its strategy. As to the latter, more in Chapter 9. With regards to the former, I was having a meal one night in the excellent Lebanese restaurant on Sea Point Main Road, the Cedar Café, when a gentleman came over and introduced himself as one of former DA leader Tony Leon's best friends. 'You know,' he said, 'Tony resigned after he read your book. You pushed him over the edge.' This observation is partly corroborated by what Leon himself says in his autobiography.

I am entirely indifferent as to whether what I had to say about Leon's leadership and his 'boys' club' that dominated power within the party had anything to do with Leon's decision to relinquish his position as leader in 2006, but it is certainly true that power has greatly shifted within the DA. On its 2011 local government campaign billboards there was not a 'boy' in sight, only 'girls'. Three of them, in fact: the new leader, Helen Zille; a newly anointed parliamentary leader, Lindiwe Mazibuko; and a fresh recruit, Patricia de Lille, the then leader of the Independent Democrats (ID), who is now mayor of Cape Town.

While the official opposition – the DA – has got stronger and more influential and powerful, so civil society's influence has arguably diminished. In *Anatomy of South Africa*, I described how in many ways the non-governmental organisation (NGO) community had more power and influence than the opposition during the Mbeki years. While Mbeki and his cohorts were swift to swat away the complaints of the DA and other opposition parties, dismissing them when necessary as 'white parties' or simply ignoring them, the ANC was apparently more easily stung by criticism from NGOs such as the now defunct Institute for Democracy in Africa (IDASA).

But the NGO landscape was changing significantly even then – in many respects, for the worse. Most local NGOs were engaging with issues of democracy and governance, and human rights were suffering badly as a result of a funding crisis brought on partly by the 2008 global economic crisis that had led to the cutting of overseas development budgets in developed countries, and partly due to an analysis of South Africa's democracy and development circumstances, which concluded, lazily and superficially, that things were 'good enough'.

Tell that to human rights organisations monitoring police conduct or the treatment of prisoners, let alone the workers at Lonmin's mines in Marikana and the rest of the unemployed or working poor of South Africa. Diplomats based in the embassies of Sweden, Norway and Denmark, for example, understood the concerns expressed by locals; most of the time, they appreciated that South Africa is often not what it seems and that if you scratch beneath the surface you will find a profoundly precarious society, perpetually on the brink of some kind of crisis.

But in their capital cities, different points of reference were employed: relative to Afghanistan, Mali or North Sudan, South Africa is both 'developed' and 'stable'. When you're having to cut the social services budget of your own nation, and feeling a lot less rich than you used to, then cutting the democracy and governance budget to South Africa and treating it as a middle-income country – despite its brutal disparities of wealth – probably seems like an entirely reasonable thing to do.

The implications for local NGOs have been severe.

Take my former employer, IDASA, with whom I worked for sixteen years, from 1995 to 2011. We had boomed during the early years of the century, expanding our work to meet demand in Africa, to the point where, in 2006/07, our budget had doubled from around R60 million a year to R120 million, as had the staff complement – from 60 to 120. Then 2008 came and, after a short lag, in 2010 the money started to dry up. IDASA was one of the larger NGOs, and often the object of jealousy from other organisations. The bigger you are, the harder you fall. So, in 2011, we decided to contract dramatically, retrenching 60 of those 120 staff, as the budget fell to around R50 million.

It may not have been just cuts in development aid that caused the decline; other factors may include feeble board oversight and a lack of clarity around our core messages and our brand (for which I take my fair share of the responsibility), with mission-creep quickly following on from a pragmatic need to 'follow the funding'. When donors smell blood, they run for the hills, as word gets round that organisation X is in trouble.

IDASA was not alone, far from it. Other big organisations with strong fund-raising track records, such as the Treatment Action Campaign (TAC) – the doyen of donors during the late 1990s and the early 2000s, as it fought Mbeki's mad HIV/AIDS denialism – and the Institute for Security Studies (ISS), have struggled badly of late. As a result, the NGO sector's power and influence has declined. There is no longer such a strong watchdog presence in Parliament or over politics.

New organisations have sprung up, however, and I remain hopeful that South Africa's civil society will remain vibrant and robust. I deal with one example of a new formation – the Right2Know Campaign – in Chapter 6 on Parliament. Other new organisations, such as Equal Education, Section 27, the Social Justice Coalition, the Socio-Economic Rights Institute, and Ndifuna Ukwazi, have emerged in the past six or seven years, either as children or disciples of the techniques and strategies of the TAC, the organisation that pioneered a new form of activism under the leadership of Zackie Achmat, combining social mobilisation and campaigning with parliamentary advocacy, media presence and constitutional litigation. Indeed, it can be no coincidence that nearly all of these new, progressive NGOs were founded in or around 2008 – the year in which Mbeki was thrust out of office, taking HIV/AIDS denialism with him.

Dissecting South Africa

Whereas *Anatomy of South Africa* covered the body politic, this anatomy digs deeper to examine, as Anthony Sampson did with his anatomies of Britain in the 1960s, a changing society. Sampson was concerned with class and with examining whether Britain was becoming a more meritocratic society. He wanted to explore whether Britain's old establishment was loosening. Was it easier to climb up the social ladder, to enter the grand old professions, or did your accent or your old school tie still matter?

This book has a similar preoccupation. How do people get to where they are in modern South Africa? How did Mazibuko become parliamentary leader of the DA at just thirty-one? How did Mogoeng Mogoeng become a member of the Constitutional Court, let alone chief justice, given his modest judicial record and inexperience? How, for that matter, did Zuma ascend the greasy pole of ANC politics to become president, despite his lack of formal education? And what about Malema – how did he rise? On the back of his formidable charisma and resilience alone?

Given the appalling state of public education, how do young, working-class South Africans rise up the ladder? Or rather, can they? Does it depend on a streetwise-ness that formal education can't provide or do political connections matter more? The Zuma 'vibe' has been decidedly anti-intellectual, which is not surprising given Zuma's own approach and background. The dumbing-down of the past few years has arguably given greater licence to those who believe that advancement should be about whom you know and your political loyalties rather than your professional merits.

This book wrestles with these questions and tries to shed some light on the answers. Whereas *Anatomy of South Africa* relied heavily on my direct personal experiences in and around politics in the decade from 1995 to 2005, this book relies more on research and data gathered by me and by the researchers that have assisted me. In this, it does not attempt to be exhaustive or comprehensive.

The notion of 'change' (or 'transformation') is often used and spoken about in South Africa, but it is rarely explored or explained. Change is often used in a one-dimensional sense to refer to race and the broad-based black economic empowerment (BBBEE) understanding of change. A more careful assessment of what is meant by change and how to measure it is needed. Otherwise, it plays into the hands of populist nationalists, who wish to exploit a 'numbers-game' approach to change based on whether racial representation is increasing or not. Understanding what 'real' transformation means is a demanding but necessary task for everyone.

This is why the core theme of this book is access – to the 'establishment' and to the networks and ladders that lubricate the necessary opportunities. Who has access? And has this changed over time?

But what is meant by this notion of 'establishment'? In making sense of South Africa's establishment, we must consider what it is and how it operates. The term was coined by British journalist Henry Fairlie, who, in September 1955 in the London magazine *The Spectator*, defined that network of prominent, well-connected people as 'the Establishment', explaining:

> By the 'Establishment', I do not only mean the centres of official power – though they are certainly part of it – but rather the whole matrix of official and social relations within which power is exercised. The exercise of power in Britain (more specifically, in England) cannot be understood unless it is recognised that it is exercised socially.[3]

Whereas with the old English establishment it was necessary, for example, to have been to Oxford or Cambridge in order to join the British civil service or political office, Sampson, in the conclusion of his final book, *Who Runs This Place? The Anatomy of Britain in the 21st Century*, describes the anti-establishmentarian politicians as belonging to a more established and formalised network:

> ... for all its 'toffery' it has never been formalised or structured in any specific way. The politicians who gained popularity in opposition to the establishment,

those who represented 'the people' and the 'common folk', often belonged to close-knit networks of effective communication and mutual support. As such the modern anti-establishment is more formalised than the traditional establishment.[4]

Access to the establishment in South Africa may not be the same as in England, and the route to political power is far less clear. Under Mbeki it was often opaque, but once one dug a bit and applied one's mind, there was a degree of clarity as well as rationality – a certain method to the madness. Now, it is more medieval as well as labyrinthine; far more based on patronage in the cruder sense of the word, as this book seeks to explain.

The state of the nation

In order to examine the establishment and pathways to it, one needs to have in mind the broader socio-economic context. What is the state of the nation? To what extent is power, in a broader sense, changing? Is its face changing, too, as well as the body politic?

Table 1.1 gathers selected indicators of social and economic progress and shows how they have changed since the early 1990s. Broadly speaking, the following two conclusions can be made from the data in the table. Firstly, living conditions in South Africa have improved since the advent of democracy. Adult literacy, under-five mortality, access to water, levels of sanitation and rates of poverty have improved. Notably, the proportion of people living on less than two dollars a day, an internationally accepted measure of poverty, has declined either from 16.2 per cent in 1996 to 2.7 per cent in 2011 (if one considers South African sources) or from 39.9 per cent in 1995 to 31.3 per cent in 2009 (if one considers World Bank data). This is encouraging; however, we do see an approximately 15 per cent decrease in life expectancy between 1990 and 2010. The ravaging effects of HIV/AIDS, the prevalence of which increased by 17 percentage points between 1990 and 2011, doubtless explains much of this.

The second conclusion that can be drawn is that access to the benefits that come with employment has been squeezed. Income inequality has worsened. Our Gini coefficient, which measures the extent of such inequality (0 indicating perfect equality and 100 indicating that one person owns all the wealth), has worsened by 6.6 points. Meanwhile, the income share of the top 10 per cent of earners has *risen* by 6.6 percentage points, and the share of the bottom 20 per cent has declined by 0.9 percentage points. Indeed, South Africa now enjoys the dark accolade of being the most unequal society in the world. While we have slightly improved our Human Development Index score (a composite of life expectancy, education and income per capita), our global ranking among our

Table 1.1: Performance of key socio-economic indicators

		1990	1994	1995	1996	2000	2006	2009	2010	2011	2012	Performance (1990/1994/2000 to most recent year)
Life expectancy at birth[i]	X	62	61	60	59	55	51	52	52			15.4 % worse
Under-five mortality rate (per 1 000)[i]	✓	62.3	60.9	61.8	63.4	74.1	75.8	61.3	52.6	46.7		25 % better
Adult literacy[i]	X	76.2%			82.4%	84.8%			89.3%			13.1 % points better
School enrolment, secondary (% gross)[i]	✓	66.1%	79.7%			85.3%	95.0%	93.8%				27.7 % points better
Access to improved water source*[i]	✓	83%	83%	84%	85%	86%	90%	91%	91%			8 % points better
Proportion of population with access to improved sanitation**[i]	✓	71%	72%	72%	73%	75%	77%	79%	79%			8 % points better
HIV prevalence (%)[i]	X	0.5%	0.8%	4.9%	6.9%	14.8%	17.3%	17.2%	17.3%	17.3%		16.8 % points worse
Human Development Index (HDI)[i]	X	0.615				0.616			0.615	0.619		0.004 points better
HDI rank (emerging markets)[i]	X					107				123		16 places worse
People living on less than $2/day (%)[i]	✓			39.90%		43%	35.74%	31.33%				8.6 % points better
People living on less than $2/day (%)[ii]	✓				16.20%	18%	10.50%	6.30%	4.40%	2.70%		13.5 % points better
Unemployment rate (expanded)[ii]	X		31.50%		35.60%	35.5%	36.1%	32.4%	35.8%	36.9%	36.2%	4.7 % points worse
Unemployment rate (official)[ii]	X		20%		21%	26.7%	23.1%	23.6%	25.2%	25.7%	24.9%	4.9 % points worse
Gini index[i]	X			56.59		57.77	67.4	63.14				6.6 points worse
Income share of highest 10%[i]	X			45.09%		44.93%	57.54%	51.69%				6.6 % points worse
Income share of lowest 20%[i]	X			3.57%		3.06%	2.45%	2.70%				0.9 % points worse

*Tap or pump, for example. **Protected pit latrines or flush toilets, for example. [i]World Bank Group.[5] [ii]South African Institute of Race Relations (SAIRR)[6] emerging-market peers has slipped. Finally, and worryingly, the unemployment rate, which considers both formal and informal employment, has worsened by approximately 5 per cent.

From a distance, then, it seems that South Africa has been able to improve the material living conditions of the average South African, but has failed to secure meaningful improvements in access to economically productive activity, both formal and informal.

But what if we look closer? The above shows an extremely broad picture, after all, and may mask more specific, potentially important changes that have taken place since 1994.

Let us consider transformation. An extremely important question, after all, is how the prospects of black (broadly defined) South Africans have changed. Within this realm, substantial improvements have indeed been made. The percentage of black (African, coloured and Indian) employees involved at the management and professional levels increased dramatically from 1996 to 2011.[7] The proportion of executive and senior management positions inhabited by black individuals rose from 8 per cent in 1996 to 34 per cent in 2011, an overall increase of 325 per cent. This proportion increased from 10 to 38 per cent, meanwhile, for middle managers, and from 32 to 52 per cent for those involved in junior management or professional positions.

Black ownership of the Johannesburg Stock Exchange (JSE) has also risen, predominantly among Africans. If one considers individual South African ownership – that is, ownership of shares excluding state and foreign bodies – between 2000 and 2010, African holdings increased from 16 to 25.8 per cent, Indian holdings increased from 2.5 to 3.7 per cent, while coloured holdings decreased from 4.7 to 3 per cent. During the same period, white ownership of the JSE declined from 76.5 to 66 per cent.[8] Black ownership of shares in JSE retirement funds also increased from 23 per cent in 1995 to 37 per cent in 2010, while white ownership declined from 77 to 63 per cent.[9]

While such trends indicate the opening up of certain forms of economic activity to certain black South Africans, overall, racial disparities in economic power are still very much in evidence. For example, while annual average household income increased by 210 per cent for Africans, 277 per cent for coloureds and 212 per cent for Indians between 1996 and 2011, white households enjoyed a 235 per cent increase over the same period and an average income that, in 2011, was more than five times that of Africans, almost three times that of coloureds and approximately one and a half times that of Indians.[10] Also in 2011, net private ownership of assets – that is, assets owned minus private debt – per capita for white individuals was more than ten times that of African individuals, almost seven times that of coloured individuals and approximately two and half times that of Indian individuals.[11]

Figure 1.1: Proportion of net disposable income by race, 1996–2011[12]

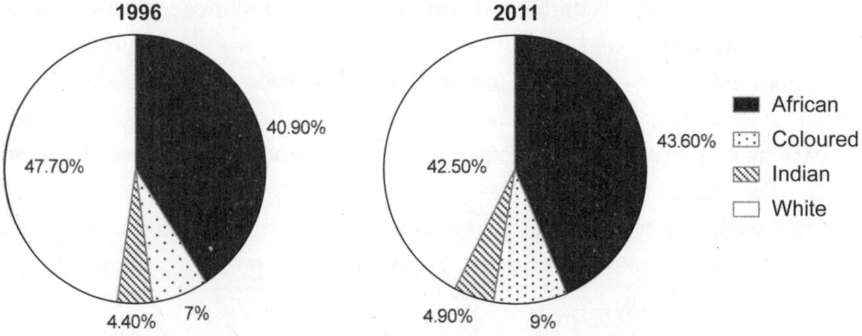

For example, as Table 1.2 shows, half of African individuals earn less than R2 500 per month, while half of white South Africans earn more than R10 000 per month.

Figure 1.1 provides more evidence of the relatively muted change in the status quo. The share of total net disposable income held by white individuals declined by only 5.2 per cent between 1996 and 2011, owing mostly to the increased shares of African and coloured individuals. Further, we must remember that, despite an increase in the relative share of Africans, per capita income levels within this group are the lowest in the country.

Table 1.2: Monthly income by race (ZAR), 2011 (includes social grants)[13]

	Bottom 5%	Median	Top 5%
African	520	2 383	15 000
Coloured	800	3 033	19 500
Indian	1 400	6 800	24 000
White	1 750	10 000	40 000
Total	600	3 000	20 000

For example, as Table 1.2 shows, half of African individuals earn less than R2 500 per month, while half of white South Africans earn more than R10 000 per month.

So there seems to be an absolute increase in average welfare and ownership among black South Africans, with very little relative gain in economic power. While the pie is growing, white South Africans are still enjoying the largest portions of it.

Let us turn now to unemployment – after all, job creation has long been a key pillar of government policy. And if the broader economy has not been significantly reshuffled in relative terms, perhaps there has been meaningful change in the employment prospects of previously disadvantaged groups that, over time, will see them increasing their relative economic power. As was stated earlier, the unemployment rate has actually *increased* since the mid-1990s. According to the official definition, it now stands at around 25 per cent. But who has borne the brunt of this worrying trend? In short, who are the unemployed? The first thing to note is that they are young. Indeed, the official unemployment rate among 15- to 24-year-olds is well above the average, currently standing at 51.5 per cent, while the rate for 25- to 34-year-olds is 29.3 per cent. Secondly, they are slightly educated. Those that have entered but failed to complete secondary schooling represent the largest share of the unemployed (47 per cent) and, further, suffer the highest rates of unemployment among all other groups (32 per cent) – strangely, even those with less schooling.[14]

Figure 1.2: Unemployment rates and numbers by race, 1994–2012[15]

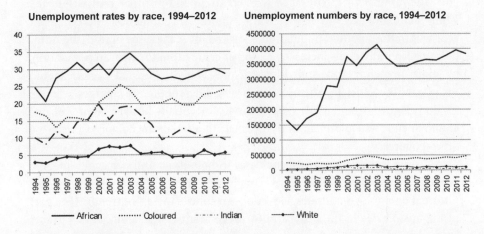

Thirdly, as Figure 1.2 shows, the unemployed are black. Unemployment is worst among Africans, both absolutely (in terms of numbers) and relatively (as given by the unemployment rate). While all groups save for Indians have suffered a general increase in the rate of unemployment, especially since the 2008 global economic crisis, African and coloured populations seem to suffer a pernicious combination of large and growing numbers of unemployed. And while both absolute and relative levels of unemployment among Africans seem now to be declining, the above figures do not take into account the full story.

The official unemployment rate considers those of working age who have actively looked for work within the four weeks prior to being surveyed. However, and importantly, it does not include those who are willing and able to work but have given up hope of finding employment. These individuals can be referred to as 'discouraged workseekers', and are defined by Statistics South Africa thus:

A discouraged workseeker is a person who was not employed during the reference week of the survey, wanted to work/start a business but did not take

active steps to find work during the four weeks prior to being interviewed by
Stats SA, provided that the main reason given for not seeking work was any
of the following: no jobs available in the area, unable to find work requiring
his/her skills, lost hope of finding any kind of work.[16]

Such discouraged workseekers arguably represent an important piece of the
unemployment puzzle; their addition may provide a fuller, if more tragic, idea
of the true extent of joblessness in South Africa. From 2001 to 2012, the number
of discouraged workseekers grew by 34 per cent overall. Worryingly, this increase
is wholly focused within the African demographic. Indeed, between 2001 and
2012, the number of discouraged workers declined by 76 per cent within the
white population, by 53 per cent within the Indian population and by 47 per
cent within the coloured population. However, over the same period, the numbers of such individuals increased by 50 per cent within the African population,
by approximately 733 000 individuals. If one adds discouraged workseekers to
the pool of the 'officially unemployed', a very different picture emerges.

Both Figure 1.3 and Table 1.3 present a substantially bleaker picture of unemployment, particularly among Africans, but also among coloureds, than the
official figures.

So while we have witnessed increases in household and per capita income
across all races since 1994, we have actually seen an increase in both formal and
informal unemployment rates. How do we reconcile these two trends? One part
of the answer lies in the provision of social grants. The value of such grants
increased from 2.9 to 3.5 per cent of gross domestic product (GDP) between fiscal
years 2003/04 and 2010/11; the proportion of the population receiving grants,
meanwhile, increased from 8 per cent in 2001 to 29 per cent in 2011.[17] As pointed
out earlier, income figures include contributions from social grants. Unsurprisingly, those worst affected by unemployment are also those most heavily
dependent on such grants. Approximately 50 per cent of both coloured and
African households list grants as a source of income, while this figure is 29 per
cent for Indians and Asian households and 11 per cent for white households.
Moreover, only 59.7 per cent of African households list salaries, wages or commission as a source of income, while this figure hovers between 70 and 75 per cent
for the other groups. In fact, African households are placed last in relation to all
sources of income save for remittances and social grants. Indeed, 19 per cent of
these households report remittances as a source of income, while this figure is
less than 10 per cent for all other groups. It seems that, being the group with least
access to employment opportunities, members of African households have to
rely on a combination of the state and transfers from other individuals (family
members, for example) to survive.

Figure 1.3: Unemployment numbers (including discouraged workseekers) by race, 2001–2012[18]

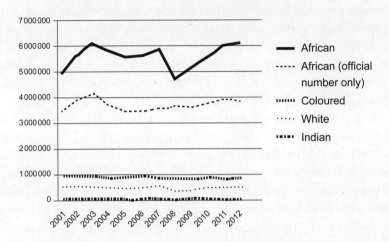

Table 1.3: Numbers and rates of unemployment by race, official (O) vs alternative (A) calculation, 2012

		Number	Rate (%)
African	O	3 839 000	28.7
	A	6 040 000	38.8
Coloured	O	464 000	24.0
	A	544 000	27.0
Indian	O	50 000	9.5
	A	59 000	11.0
White	O	117 000	5.7
	A	138 000	6.6
Total	O	4 470 000	24.9
	A	6 781 000	33.5

Alternative calculation refers to official numbers of unemployed + discouraged workseekers (D). Alternative rates were calculated thus: (O + D) × 100 ÷ (economically active + D)

So what does all this mean for the ruling party, and for the changing landscape of power in South Africa? Well, crucially, it points to a dangerous stuttering of progress within the ANC's core African demographic. Not only are the vast majority of this group not reaping the gains of a 'transformed' South African economy, but there is an alarming increase in the number of Africans who are not only unemployed, but who have become so disillusioned with their prospects that they no longer believe they will find work. Such disillusionment may manifest itself in a loss of faith in the broad church of the ANC – seeds of this are already evident – and may finally break the long-standing, near-unconditional allegiance to the ruling party that many South Africans have hitherto demonstrated.

This provides succour to the largest opposition party – the DA – but also to the likes of the Economic Freedom Fighters, Malema's new political party.

An establishment under pressure

This is a powder keg. South Africa is not alone in facing a rising number of pro-tests, driven by an angry young populace. But its history of violence – both from the state and from within society itself – is cause for alarm. As I was researching this book, I met with a source who has a long history of working in the intelligence service. Apart from his disquieting stories about the state of the intelligence services today, which he is acquainted with because he conducts training programmes for them, his analytical antennae are alert to the broader socio-economic and political context, like any good intelligence operative's would be.

I went to see him because I was still harbouring the hope that I could produce a chapter on the intelligence services (which, alas, was not possible). He confirmed the disarray that the State Security Agency is in. The consequences are grave, both for accountable governance – with loads of inadequately skilled and poorly managed operatives running around – and for ensuring government is properly prepared to understand, as well as respond to, internal threats to stability (for example Marikana).

The key to a good intelligence service, my source explained, is its ability to understand what the national strategic purpose is, and to act as an intermediary between those responsible for leading it in government and those on the ground. A very serious problem arises when there is a lack of clarity around the national strategic purpose. If there is uncertainty or confusion, as there is now, then the operatives will be all at sea and unable to deliver on their mandate. The failure to articulate and communicate a national strategic purpose must lie at the very top of government, with the president – ironically, given that Zuma is a professional spy and ran the ANC's intelligence arm for many years in exile, it is his failure in leadership that is the root cause of the current weakness in the intelligence service.

There are other factors, however, that contribute to institutional weakness. In the case of the intelligence service, for example, the greatest cause for concern is the failure to adhere to the requirement of filling in a standard form, my source informed me. Form-filling? Doesn't sound very James Bond; *007, with a licence to form-fill*. But, for accountability and coordination purposes, every operative is supposed to fill in a form for every single assignment explaining what the mission was and what they did. Yet, when training them, my contact discovered that few of the State Security Agency operatives knew about the form, let alone how to complete it.

Institutional shortcomings aside, my intelligence source wanted to talk about political risk and the ability of the establishment to absorb socio-economic pressures – a subject close to my own heart. As we chatted, he leant forward, took my notebook and drew three triangles of varying sizes: one for Ethiopia, one for Zimbabwe and one for South Africa. Echoing in part the analysis of Roger Southall, editor of the biannual academic publication *New South African Review*, my source took me back to the 'elite deal' that was made in the 1990s, whereby the National Party (NP) and the white capital-owning class gave up political power to the ANC, provided that their property rights and other economic assets were protected. Part of the deal, my source was now suggesting, was that the ANC would be given the opportunity to 'uplift' the poor, calculating, no doubt, that this would help keep the lid on the powder keg.

The problem, of course, is that upliftment has not happened, or not with sufficient pace and not in a way that has substantially advanced the interests of the working class. My source added an inverted triangle to the bottom of the Ethiopian triangle, creating a diamond shape in contrast to the pyramid shape of the South African triangle. Whereas South Africa tried to create work for the poor, Ethiopia, he stressed, created 'productive work' for the poor, whereby a vast number of people were given fifty hectares of land to create a sustainable economic base for their own self-advancement, thereby creating a massive new 'middle class'.

The logic of this would suggest that South Africa's failure to break from an old paradigm means that it is in some respects doomed. Drawing a line across the bottom section of the Zimbabwean triangle, with arrows pointing outwards, he suggested that Robert Mugabe faced a fork in the road when the Movement for Democratic Change (MDC) emerged, initially at least with a working-class orientation, and he used state force to suppress its power. Marikana and the emergence of the breakaway Association of Mineworkers and Construction Union (AMCU) was an equivalent moment, when the state resorted to brutal force to suppress a new and potentially dangerous adversary. Resorting to state power, to keep hold of power, was inevitable at that point.

Thus, the original 'elite compact' or 'elite compromise', to use the academic phraseology of Southall and others, is breaking down: the ANC is no longer able to 'control' the working class by uplifting it effectively. What happens if and when the broader working class begins to lose even more confidence in both the ANC and COSATU?

In the most recent edition of the *New South African Review*, Southall charts the history of the elite compromise and what he now calls South Africa's 'fractured elite' – referring to the split between the political and corporate elites.[19] He suggests that while the composition of the political elite is relatively easy to identify, it is far harder with the corporate elite, and, rightly, that wealth does not always translate into power. My sense is that he overestimates the ease with which one can dissect the political elite – which has become considerably muddier and more diffuse during the Zuma years – and underestimates it in the case of the corporate elite. This book attempts to shed a little more light in both directions.

The difficult journey, which Southall certainly does not embark on, is identifying and understanding the overlaps between the two (which I attempt in Chapter 12 on money and politics). Adopting the words of the original elite theorist, C. Wright Mills, whose approach Southall engages with, like America in the 1950s, South Africa has an 'uneasy coincidence of economic, political and military power'.[20] While neither the fundamental structure of corporate ownership nor the landscape of the main professions may have transformed substantially since 1994, despite changes in the composition of the corporate boardrooms, which Chapters 13 and 14 examine, the common interest in a stable economic environment in which business can make money drives an uneasy coincidence of economic, political and state security power in today's South Africa.

It is anything but neat and tidy; but, warts and all, this is South Africa's contemporary establishment, and it is not inconsistent with Southall's view that there is a 'disjuncture between the major concentrations of power within the political and corporate elites', which 'allows considerable space for other less powerful forces within society … At the middle level of power, notably at provincial and local levels, ambitious factions jostle for influence, money and tenders, whilst opposition parties, trade unions and civil-society groups lobby the ANC and government, around matters of class, sectional, and general interest within an untidy but lively democracy.'[21]

As the irrepressibly ebullient but admirably realistic ANC minister Yunus Carrim put it to me: 'The overlaps between factional power struggles within the ANC, executive power in municipal government and local tenderpreneurs are very dangerous and destabilising.' This confusing picture of modern South Africa, painted in greater detail in the chapters that follow, is one of formal political connections and informal networks; of the overlap between political power and corporate interests, big and small; of gangsterism alongside entrepreneurialism; and of naked power exerting its influence by exploiting weaknesses in the state.

What does this mean for the changing face of power and, specifically, for 'establishment' power? One of the things I have learnt in the nineteen years since I came to South Africa is that for every good and reasonable question there are always at least two perfectly good and reasonable answers.

So, has a new, new establishment been formed? In other words, has the new establishment of the Mbeki era been replaced with a different one that is the child of the Zuma era?

Yes and no.

Anatomy of South Africa reached the following conclusion about the new establishment that had formed by 2006:

> The more things change, the more they stay the same. In a way, therefore, the Quixotic challenge for the new establishment is to ensure that the more it changes, the more it really does change. In response, parallel developments – new networks of power inside the new establishments and new social movements in civil society outside of the establishment – will compete for hegemony. The one represents a new elite, with powerful vested interests in the current trajectory of politics and the economy. The other represents an excluded poor majority, with an increasingly angry determination to challenge the new establishment. Set within the elegant superstructure of a much-admired and much-vaunted new constitutional order, the most important institutions – parliament, NEDLAC and the Constitutional Court – will be the sites of a massive tussle for influence and power. The outcome cannot be predicted for the following reasons: the lines are not yet clearly drawn; and there is a complex array of crossovers, creating intermingling interests and agendas. Some of the members of the new elite remain committed to social transformation – a new euphemism, in some quarters at least, for socialism. The most powerful capitalists – new and old – are installed within the new establishment and, although they are dominant, they are not yet hegemonic. There is a new anatomy of power in South Africa, and decisively so. Whether it is an anatomy that befits the 'New South Africa' and serves the majority is equally a matter of debate. A new establishment has formed, but its roots are shallow and its physiology largely untested. The power play has barely started. The battle for conclusive control of power has just begun; the new anatomy is anything but settled.[22]

And so it proved: the new anatomy *was* anything but settled. Since then, power has been contested – and has shifted – in many institutions of state and society. The old new political establishment was forced out of power by the Zuma coalition of the willing and the wounded. But the challenge for the new new establishment is precisely the same as for the previous one: to ensure that there is real transformation in society. Without it, the dangers are now there for all to see. Marikana was a murderous depiction of what could lie ahead.

This book is partly an examination of whether power is changing in ways that will preclude social disintegration – what Mantashe is speaking of when he refers to 'anarchy' – and the disintegration of the state, and which will preserve the dream of the rainbow nation created by former president Nelson Mandela and Archbishop Emeritus Desmond Tutu, and the vision of a just and equal society articulated in the Constitution.

With Cyril Ramaphosa, one of the architects of the constitutional settlement and one of the most obvious beneficiaries of the first version of BEE that made him one of the richest members of a small new club of black captains of industry, returned to public life, can the social compact of the 1990s be rebuilt? Can the modus operandi of South African political life that we saw during the transition to democracy and the golden age of reform that followed as the last century closed – of dialogue and negotiation – be restored?

Or, alternatively, will the new anatomy of power precipitate disintegration or increase its likelihood? Should this book really be entitled *Anatomy of a Crisis: The Rise and Fall of the New South Africa*?

2

The Presidency

Thursday 16 August 2012 was a typical late winter's day in Rustenburg. The weather was clear and pleasantly warm, like most winter days on the Highveld. In the muggier Maputo, an afternoon storm threatened. As the wily South African president and former long-standing head of the ANC's intelligence wing, Jacob Zuma, sat at a Southern African Development Community (SADC) heads of state meeting in the humid Mozambican capital, a massive storm of an entirely different nature – of a political and socio-economic character – was heading his way. It was one that he could not see coming.

When a moment of national crisis arrives, for a head of state there is only one thing worse than being at home to greet it, and that is not being at home. The SADC meeting was dragging on. Zuma's own concentration was waning as a series of new heads of state introduced themselves and felt inclined to offer small, and in some cases not so small, speeches, thus prolonging the proceedings even further.

Just over 600 kilometres west of Maputo, members of the South African Police Service (SAPS) were, for reasons that at the time of writing remain inexplicable, opening fire on a group of striking Lonmin platinum miners.

Thirty-four people were shot dead, and South Africa changed forever.

It was Zuma's 9/11 moment. Most people have seen the footage of George W. Bush being told by his chief of staff, Andrew Card, about the attack on the World Trade Center on 11 September 2001, as the president sat listening to a class of Grade 2 learners being taught to read by an earnest and energetic teacher.

The seven members of the White House Press Corps who were watching, later recalled their surprise: no one ever interrupts the president of the United States. Zuma's own chief of staff, Lakela Kaunda, faced the same dilemma that Card must have faced. Of course, the situation was different – Zuma was not under any threat – but it was obvious that it was huge.

The text message from the media staffer back in Pretoria who first relayed the news to presidential spokesperson Mac Maharaj, who had accompanied Zuma to the SADC summit, said that more than fifty miners had been killed.

Maharaj's immediate reaction was to inform Zuma without delay. He spoke to Kaunda, who told him that Zuma was in with the other heads of state and that she could not interrupt. So they sent a note in to Zuma, who then requested

SADC chair Armando Guebuza to permit his release from the meeting so that he could return to South Africa immediately.

According to one of Zuma's staff, Guebuza 'pleaded' with Zuma to stay until the new heads of state had finished their introductions. Out of respect for his host, and fastidious as he is about protocol, Zuma agreed to stay and let Kaunda know as much.

Realising that back home the media would be eager to hear from the president and would be impatient for his return, Maharaj knew the political significance of getting back as soon as possible. When Kaunda told him that Zuma had decided to stay for the remaining inaugural speeches, Maharaj asked how many were left. When told, he informed colleagues in Pretoria that 'we've got to wait for five fucking new heads of state!'

The reason for Zuma's tardy return to South Africa – his respect for SADC protocol – was not made known at the time, as Maharaj chose not to brief the media about what had transpired.

Zuma was certainly criticised back home. British newspaper the *Guardian* reported:

> Critics say that in the hours after the bloodshed at the Marikana platinum mine in the north-west of the country, Zuma was slow to return to South Africa from a summit in neighbouring Mozambique. By the time he did reach the mine, it was 'too dark' to address the angry mineworkers ... The South African press has accused Zuma of misjudgment in his handling of the shootings. An editorial in the *Times* said: 'Being a leader comes with a responsibility and in this case the president, or his advisers, failed to read the mood. Sometimes a leader needs to suspend protocol and take charge of a situation in his country. Zuma's absence from the "crime scene" gave others space.'[1]

As it was, they were only able to take off from Maputo after 6 p.m., but as soon as the president's jet landed at Waterkloof Air Force Base in Pretoria, his convoy sped straight towards Rustenburg.

How a president responds to a crisis not only shapes both public and media attitudes, but also tells us about his presidency as a whole. Maharaj knew that this was a big moment and that the public's and the media's demands would be testing. He needed to be alongside his principal when he arrived at the Lonmin corporate lodge – a strange choice of venue, under the circumstances – to address the media.

But fate would intervene, and Maharaj would not be alongside Zuma at the press conference. He was still making his way across the West Rand, after his driver got lost in Pretoria after leaving Waterkloof. This is the sort of thing that can happen; the small mishaps that can have untold wider implications. For Zuma's performance at the press conference was anything but convincing. The moment called for reassurance, for a sense that government was in control and that the president was properly seized of it. But more than anything, it required a dose of humanity – to capture and reflect the public's sense of outrage and concern that so many lives could be lost in such an apparently barbaric way. South Africa got none of this from its president that night. Instead, Zuma was wooden, paralysed like a rabbit caught in the headlights.

Our collective outrage was expressed by the ANC traditionalists, who were shaking with anger. Thabo Mbeki's former spokesperson, Bheki Khumalo, recalls being called and told to 'turn on your television now' and his 'profound upset and anger that such a thing could be happening in democratic South Africa'.

For businessman and ANC stalwart Sipho Pityana, now the chairman of the Council for the Advancement of the South African Constitution (CASAC), it was a day that 'filled me with horror and I was forced to ask myself: is this 2012 or 1985 or even 1976?' After Pityana contacted me and alerted me to what had happened, I drafted a statement for CASAC that called for the immediate appointment of a commission of inquiry. It read:

> Even if the protesters were violent, even if they shot at the police first, it is impossible to think that it was in any way necessary or lawful for the police to then shoot dead so many of the protesters. Understandably, people are talking of a 'rogue state'. Quite apart from the tragic loss of life, South Africa's international reputation will undoubtedly be harmed.

And harmed it was. First of all, by the terrible events and the shocking television footage of police officers shooting at a group of apparently unarmed striking miners who were charging towards them. And secondly, by the events of the weekend that followed, as first the injured miners who had survived were arrested and charged with murder on the basis of an obscure, ancient legal provision, and then were released as the charges were dropped twenty-four hours later.

Clearly, the South African government had lost its head. That was the world's reaction, anyway. Messages came in from around the globe: what on earth is going on there?

The state had imposed its might on the strikers. The power of the police had been given grotesque expression. But where was the president? Why had his government not intervened to prevent the Marikana massacre?

It was, if nothing else, a failure of intelligence-gathering on the one hand, and of dialogue and negotiation on the other. Asked whether they think something like Marikana could have happened under Mbeki, numerous people acquainted with both leaders answer a straight 'no'.

All the president's men, and women

'We know the president gets advice. We just don't know who he gets it from.'
~ Senior official in the Presidency, comment to the author, late summer 2013

Why could Marikana not have happened under Mbeki? Because Mbeki had more refined structures and better advisors – a large kitchen cabinet that included his own private group of intelligence operatives, innocuously named the Presidential Support Unit. From the moment that Mbeki became deputy president in 1994, he began building up the Presidency, recognising that if he was to lead government properly when he one day became president, he would need the capacity around him to do so effectively.

The result was the inception and then development of the Policy Coordination and Advisory Service (PCAS), which was led by the brilliant Joel Netshitenzhe, whom I described in *Anatomy of South Africa* as the second most powerful person in South Africa after Mbeki himself. Tellingly, I suggested that Mbeki's legal advisor, Mojanku Gumbi, had, with her greatly expanded role, become one of the five most powerful people in the country. I'll deal with Zuma's own legal advisor, Michael Hulley, shortly, not because he is one of the five most powerful people in the country – although he undoubtedly exerts significant influence of a different sort – but because of what his appointment says about Zuma's penchant for conflict of interest or, rather, his lack of any self-awareness and apparently flagrant disregard for the constitutional principle of accountability. Keeping himself away from criminal prosecution has been Zuma's overriding objective for a number of years, and until the case against him is finally comprehensively buried, nothing will change in this respect.

Comparisons between Zuma's presidency and that of his predecessor, Mbeki, are as inevitable as comparisons between the men themselves – and, from the point of view of the system of government and its operational integrity, no less apposite. As I researched the Mbeki presidency for *Anatomy of South Africa*, I gratifyingly found myself speaking to a group of hard-working experts whose sense of service to the people of South Africa, as well as to their president, was sincere. I was deeply struck by this discovery and it made me think differently about Mbeki, who was not easy to like. Certainly, my respect for him grew the more I got to know about him. He had surrounded himself with a group of able, capable people. Although prone at times to surprising levels of paranoia –

probably ingested from the president himself – they were nonetheless decent and approachable people.

This time round, things are both the same and very different. How so? There are still sincere and capable people in the Presidency, but they are no longer around the president as such. The kitchen cabinet has been smashed. A key element of the transition from Mbeki to Zuma, and of the 'Polokwane effect', was the overhaul of the Presidency. Part of the motive for the restructuring was positive – to create two new wings that would provide for national planning on the one hand, and oversight of government performance on the other – but another part was negative: to prevent a repeat of the 'imperial' Mbeki presidency, in which the president was able to 'overcome' his ministers through the sheer force of his organisational capacity.

Of course, Mbeki's kitchen cabinet and the PCAS fitted the style and aptitude of the man: Mbeki not only wanted to read each and every document that came in front of cabinet, he wanted them 'gutted' by the PCAS, with no stone left unturned. Zuma has no such inclination, and the transition team, led by key members of COSATU and the SACP, were determined that the new incumbent of the West Wing of the Union Buildings would have no such opportunity. The intellectual resources of the new Presidency would be housed not in the West Wing, which is occupied primarily by the president and his private office, but in the new National Planning Commission (NPC) secretariat and, to an even greater degree, in the new Department of Performance Monitoring and Evaluation (DPME).

So, when Zuma is feeling curious and wants the answer to something, he has to turn to one or other of his new structures. Staff from both the NPC and the DPME tell me how, every now and then, they get an urgent call from the private office of the president, always from Zuma's right-hand woman, Kaunda, requesting information or answers. It's usually urgent and they have to jump.

Yet Zuma *does* get advice from other sources, as a senior official in the Presidency told me when we crossed paths at an entirely unconnected seminar in early 2013. This person, whom I had never met before, said: 'Richard, when is your new book coming out? You see, we know the president gets advice. We just don't know who he gets it from. And I'm hoping you're going to tell us in your book.'

I hope they're not holding their breath. No one seems to know. In an attempt to find the answer, I seek out journalist Ranjeni Munusamy, who probably knows Zuma better than most, having, at times, been close to him. 'I found common cause with JZ,' she tells me. 'I was cast out like him.' This is a reference to her at times chequered journalistic career, which hit rock bottom in 2003 after she was forced out of her position as a political correspondent at the *Sunday Times* and then subpoenaed to give evidence in front of the Hefer Commission that had been appointed by then president Mbeki to investigate allegations that, among others, the then national director of public prosecutions (NDPP), Bulelani Ngcuka, had been an undercover spy for the apartheid regime.

Ngcuka was close to Mbeki; both – so the conspiracy theory goes – were out to get Zuma. Though her defence is that she was drawn like a mouse to cheese to the story, when well-known intelligence operative Moe Shaik passed her information about Ngcuka, the allegation against Munusamy was that she acted in a partisan fashion: as an accomplice in the plot to undermine Ngcuka and, thereby, ward off the threat to Zuma that Ngcuka's persistent investigation of him represented.

Thinking back to those days, when her reputation was being dragged through the mud, it is not hard to see how Munusamy and Zuma would indeed have found common cause. She was subjected to some absurdly holier-than-thou commentary from some of her colleagues in the media, as well as an unhealthy dose of sexism from the political establishment, which at times treated her like an errant schoolgirl who had got herself mixed up in something rotten with the 'big boys'.

In fact, Munusamy is one of the country's smartest and most able political journalists, to which her writing in the online *Daily Maverick* now attests. Like all of us, she has human fallibilities, but her treatment as a latter-day journal-istic version of Joan of Arc to be burnt at the stake seemed, even at the time, ridiculously harsh.

Zuma had received equivalent treatment, times a thousand. Munusamy had watched his fall from close quarters. As a cub reporter, along with Kaunda who was at the *Natal Witness*, Munusamy would travel to Ulundi in her home prov-ince of KwaZulu-Natal to report on the provincial government in which, in the first democratic period of 1994–99, there were just three ANC ministers: Zuma, Zweli Mkhize and S'bu Ndebele. Zuma's role as a peacemaker in the troubled province, which was wracked by violence between ANC and Inkatha Freedom Party (IFP) followers in the years leading up to 1994 and which simmered for some time thereafter, is now the stuff of legend – and where his reputation as a great mediator derives from.

Zuma was rewarded for his good work in KwaZulu with an appointment to deputy president in Mbeki's 1999 government. He was reappointed after the 2004 election, but then Mbeki sacked him in 2005 after the Schabir Shaik corruption trial, in which evidence emerged of the 'generally corrupt relationship' between Zuma and Shaik (in the words of the prosecution, not, as was often misreported, Judge Hilary Squires, who presided over the case).

Before her own forced departure, Munusamy was covering the Presidency for the *Sunday Times*. 'I was following JZ around to cover some of his work as deputy president,' she recalls. 'After he was fired he was so alone. Everyone around him scattered. Sometimes I would go to visit him just to keep him company.'

Then came the rape allegations, and many of the remaining friends and support-ers slipped away into the shadows. 'There was an eerie feel around him,' recalls Munusamy. Even the ANC dropped him, pretty much. It gave him little support and left him to make all his own arrangements. In the 2006 local government elections, he played no role at all, as the ANC leadership ordered him to stay away.

In due course, Munusamy became involved as webmaster in the infamous Friends of Zuma website – infamous, not only for attracting an eclectic and at times bigoted group of followers and online commenters, but also for viciously attacking the integrity of the victim/complainant in the rape trial, with whom Zuma admitted having unprotected sex even though he was fully aware of her HIV-positive status despite his having an 'avuncular' relationship with her, as she was a long-standing friend of the family.

Munusamy smiles ruefully when I raise the Friends of Zuma and explains that it came into being as a 'vessel for people to rally around JZ and express their support'. I'm interested in who the real – core – friends were, and are. 'Various businesspeople,' she says, 'mostly from KZN', and cites individuals such as Sifiso Zulu (who was recently paroled after serving nine months of a three-year prison sentence for killing two people in 2008 after his car jumped a red traffic light), Vivian Reddy and Sizwe Shezi (who chairs the Jacob G. Zuma RDP Education Trust, which attracted controversy in 2012 after revelations that a donor to the trust – EduSolutions – had won a lucrative government tender), as well as SACP secretary-general Blade Nzimande (who is now in the cabinet as minister for higher education and training). Munusamy was never paid for her work on the website; she did it as a labour of love.

The actual trustees of the Friends of Zuma Trust were Shezi (on behalf of Zuma's 'close associates', as Munusamy delicately puts it), Fikile 'Slovo' Majola, the general secretary of the National Education, Health and Allied Workers Union (NEHAWU) (because COSATU was supportive and eager at that point to put some muscle behind Zuma's counter-attack against the Mbeki establish-ment) and Don Mkhwanazi (on behalf of KwaZulu-Natal black business). The geography of this support is illustrative of the general landscape of Zuma's political career – or, at least, his return from the political dead.

'Zuma was a victim, and he united a bunch of other victims into a negative coalition,' says Munusamy. 'But it fell to pieces soon after Polokwane.' Zuma and Nzimande, whom Munusamy worked for as media liaison officer after his appoint-ment in Zuma's first cabinet in 2009, are no longer so close, for example. Nzimande was a sort of 'useful idiot' for Zuma, always taking on extreme positions, but has now been pushed away after he became too pushy and his usefulness diminished.

Munusamy herself is now quite critical of Zuma. Much of her reporting and analysis these days reflects poorly on him. What did she like about him before and why has she changed her tune? Munusamy gives a long, detailed and rather interesting account of her childhood in Dannhauser, KwaZulu-Natal, where her father worked as a barber. She recalls sitting and watching him work, and her hurt when she had to leave after a white customer objected to her presence. She watched the 'death' of her hometown, and so when Zuma spoke with 'real passion about rural development, I thought he meant it, but not now. I realise now that it was a line; he planted the seed that he was the "peoples' president".'

She began to keep her distance during the rape trial, which had become an increasingly ugly spectacle thanks to the attitudes of many of Zuma's supporters outside the courtroom. 'I was one of the first people he told about the circumstances of the rape,' she recalls. 'It was hard for him, because of his position. It was humiliating for me to listen.'

After his acquittal, Zuma began what Munusamy now calls his 'march to power', whereupon 'all sorts of weird characters began to attach themselves to him, and I began to worry that what I had imagined would be his political approach would not happen in reality'.

However, she still believes that, despite everything, deep down Zuma's commitment to rural upliftment is 'authentic', but so are his personal shortcomings. 'Money and women,' says someone else who has worked closely with Zuma, echoing an ANC member whom I know well and who knew Zuma well when he was in exile, who put it this way: 'Money and women, yes, we knew about the women, but it was money that was always the real problem.' The first source elaborates: 'He has a sense of entitlement to both. On money, that he is owed it. On women, that they are there to be appreciated.'

This is not a book about Zuma. It is a book about the changing face of power during the Zuma years. While the character and world view of the president is relevant, just as significant is his relationship with the institution he inhabits: the Presidency. So, back to my original point of inquiry: who advises Zuma and who does he listen to?

Kaunda and Zuma go back a long way, to the early 1990s, when she, like Munusamy, was a junior KwaZulu-Natal reporter. She went to work for him in the mid-nineties, then returned to journalism until he became deputy president and he brought her in as his spin doctor. She did well, running a crafty counter-campaign to Mbeki on issues such as HIV/AIDS. When Zuma went to the Great Lakes and played a positive role in the peace negotiations, 'she found alternative ways for him to shine,' says Munusamy. And she is good at projecting him as a leader in touch with the common man.

Now Kaunda is head of his private office – effectively his chief of staff – and very much his gatekeeper. She is one of the most powerful individuals in the country, by virtue of her proximity to Zuma and the role she plays.

Zuma still listens to Mkhize, a rising star in the ANC and a potential future leader, who now holds a powerful position as the keeper of the purse (treasurer-general) in the ANC's national executive. He is a medical doctor, measured and decent, and as such really struggled with his support for Zuma during the rape case, which was a 'horrible experience' for him, according to Munusamy. After it was revealed that Zuma had fathered a child with Sonono Khoza, daughter of businessman and soccer impresario Irvin Khoza, early on in his tenure as president, it was Mkhize who was dispatched by the ANC to speak to Zuma about his conduct.

There is a sense, though, that Zuma's interests in office are narrow. They are essentially about retaining power in order to avoid the alternative; in Zuma's case, prison. He is, in both ideological and policy terms, a vacant space – a medieval ruler surrounded by a dry moat, in which various interest groups, organisations and factions jostle for space and domination.

In this sense, the Zuma era is a far cry from the iron grip of the Mbeki presidency, which tried to manage and control everything. One of Zuma's most influential advisors, Lindiwe Zulu, puts it this way: 'I do know that people went to Mbeki worried, because here is a person who is an intellectual, who reads. You could not go there waffling and not knowing what you are saying.'

Which rather suggests that with Zuma you can. 'Mbeki's character was not so easy. He did not laugh easily. The two are completely different from each other. Zuma creates the comfort around the place; it is just in his nature,' Zulu adds. 'I am able to argue with my principal, because he has the patience and the ear to listen. I don't think twice about going to the president. I don't think, "Oh gosh, what is he going to be thinking of today, what is his mood?" I will go with my list.'

But, again, this is hardly surprising, as Zuma's interests are far less extensive than Mbeki's ever were, constrained as they are by his own limited horizons. He has no major policy ambitions, no great ideological frame of reference, no grand idea à la the African Renaissance and, therefore, no sense of vision.

I raise this with the man whom Zuma appointed to communicate his presidency to the nation: Mac Maharaj. We meet the day after Zuma's 2013 State of the Nation address on 14 February. Maharaj sits demurely in one of the vast chairs that adorn the lobby of Cape Town's 15 on Orange Hotel, looking every bit like a Bond villain, an Indian Blofeld minus the cat. He has invited me to a 7:30 breakfast. I had been surprised by the timing: clearly he wasn't interested in listening to SABC radio's coverage of the address, which was airing as I hurriedly parked my car outside the plush hotel. I thought back to some of his predecessors: Mandela had the elegant, distinguished Parks Mankahlana; Mbeki, the impeccable, adroit professional Bheki Khumalo. Both would have been listening intently to the radio, perhaps calling in themselves or arranging for a loyal

ANC activist to do so, to defend the Presidency, instead of having breakfast with someone like me.

But Maharaj is not that sort of spin doctor. He may look a lot younger – in fact, in his elegant grey paisley shirt, with carefully coiffured hair, he looks damn good – but he is close to eighty. You'd hardly expect to see him running around with a cellphone attached to one ear, a BlackBerry in his free hand and a pager buzzing insistently on his belt. Or, apparently, listening to the radio.

Neither will you see him tweeting every five minutes, nor updating Zuma's Facebook page. No, Maharaj is a presidential spokesperson from another age. As I wrote when he was appointed: 'If Maharaj is to be of any use whatsoever he will have to be for Zuma what that old bruiser Bernard Ingham was to Margaret Thatcher, Joe Haines was to Harold Wilson, and Alastair Campbell was to Tony Blair: an internal enforcer. In other words, an old-style press secretary.'

But there is little or no evidence that he has lived up to that expectation.

Instead, a rather more laissez-faire attitude seems to be the order of the day. 'There is a hell of a lot in this presidency, I suppose in any presidency, that is unclear or unstructured,' says Maharaj. 'Having worked under Mandela, I can say that structure is important, but every president must find his way past the structure, in order to find his own style.' It sounds chaotic, to the point of being anarchic. But what I think he means is that the human being has to find an accommodation within the institution that he is required, by high office, to inhabit.

What is curious about the management of Zuma the politician is that there seems to be such scant attempt to 'package him' or to improve the package. His annual State of the Nation addresses are exercises in rhetorical mediocrity. 'He is a slow reader,' admits Maharaj, which makes things harder, though he insists that there has been a 'radical improvement in his delivery. He is definitely improving it himself. The way he is on the plane. He is studying his documents, correcting words.' Kaunda writes the speeches, he confirms: 'Lakela clears them. She has the speed and the nuance.'

There is no apparent attempt to make the best of him or to improve him. Why not train him to use an autocue? Mbeki was willing to do so, and although he never looked entirely comfortable with it, it greatly improved the quality of his communication, because you could see his face as he was no longer looking down at his speech, like Zuma does. Trevor Manuel was superb at mastering the autocue, and his successor, Pravin Gordhan, is getting there.

You don't have to be a great intellectual with a sophisticated grasp of the intricacies of policy to be a great leader with a strong brand and the ability to communicate clearly and powerfully. Ronald Reagan was the prime example of this. Indeed, at one point, I suggested that Zuma might be South Africa's Reagan – expressing simply what his government was doing, so that the maximum number of people could understand it. But neither Maharaj nor anyone else seems interested in getting Zuma into shape. And, besides this, Maharaj seems singularly unsuited to his role: he clearly hates the media, with plenty of battles of his own with the *Mail & Guardian* and others; and he is inclined towards secrecy, probably because of years of underground activism. At his age, it may be hard for the leopard to change its spots.

Maharaj believes that the critical positions in the Presidency are the director-general and the chief of staff. Under previous presidents, the director-general was also the chief of staff. But these days the roles have been separated, with the former journalist Kaunda fulfilling the role of chief of staff and Cassius Lubisi that of director-general. Kaunda is the chief gatekeeper and speechwriter. Virtually every major speech that Zuma gives is written by her – which is an onerous responsibility.

Lubisi is an experienced public servant and knows the regulatory environment very well. He has headed a provincial education department, so 'he's been at the coalface', notes a senior official in the Presidency. This, says another, is what differentiates him from his predecessor, Chikane, who, although trusted by Mbeki, had no experience in the public service to speak off. 'Lubisi is very practical and especially in this era of trying to improve performance and basic administration, his outlook and experience is very useful,' my source says. 'And he is very passionate about improving public service.'

Maharaj says that Jakes Gerwel (Mandela's director-general) commanded by absorbing Mandela's style, and Chikane by absorbing Mbeki's. Lubisi, he suggests, is a 'calm presence, doesn't rush around, doesn't rush to judgement; he is easy to get on with; he is firm when he needs to be'. I am interested to learn from Maharaj that Lubisi also has 'impeccable struggle credentials' from Pietermaritzburg, where he was one of that firebrand-warrior-of-the-townships Harry Gwala's young lions. 'I joke with him,' Maharaj says, 'about how in the old days if the main speaker was late, Cassius would hold the crowd together. Now he is a measured presence, with a quiet leadership.'

Mbeki had no one around him who was willing to say, 'No, Mr President, you are wrong'. Does Zuma have such people? 'This president has a different problem. Too many people looking at his body language and guessing about what they think will make him happy and then doing it. I think it's a huge problem,' Maharaj replies.

How does one get around it? 'You can't get round that except if we confront the issue of patronage – which can be either good or bad. We don't discuss it as a reality. What are the regulations that we can put in place?'

He, not I, raises, as an example of his point, Nkandla, the president's controversial homestead, on which around R250 million of public money is said to have been spent. 'How much of it is ministers and officials doing their own damn thing? I find it difficult to believe that this was the president saying "Yes, close down the public clinic and move the resources to my home". Knowing him as I do, I don't believe he would agree to that, and I don't think it can have been put to him like that.'

Maharaj then tells me something really noteworthy: he suggested to Zuma that he, Maharaj, go down to Nkandla and take a look for himself, 'through the bunker and the whole damn thing. And the president says to me, "Go on, it's a good idea." But I didn't.'

Why not? 'To a certain extent, what I am telling you in this example, [it] isn't going to help me in my job to know more, because I have to ask a different question, is this a matter on which I stand or fall? If I find something significantly unacceptable, will I say goodbye?'

'So you didn't want to put yourself in that position?' I ask.

'No. I would have had a crisis.'

This is extraordinary. Maharaj, whose seniority in the ANC and his own proud record as a liberation fighter would have enabled him to stand up to Zuma, could not bring himself to do so because he was afraid of what he might find if he looked too hard. Perhaps he is not the first spin doctor who has turned the other cheek in order to avoid knowing too much about his or her principal, but it is still a pretty astonishing admission. And it answers my question: Zuma does not have anyone who can say 'no' to him, because if Mac can't, then no one can.

And the consequences are unsettling. I am surprised to find myself quoting self-confessed socialite, businessman and 'sushi king' Kenny Kunene – who infamously ate sushi off naked women at his fortieth birthday party – but on the day that I was finalising this chapter, he wrote with such clarity and singularity of purpose, in an open letter to Zuma: 'When they speak to your face, Mr President, they tell you your imperial clothes are very stylish. When they talk to me, and feel they are safe from your army of spies, most of them admit that you, the emperor, have no clothes.'[2]

Number One

In recent times, public servants have taken to referring to their president as 'Number One', with thinly disguised contempt, and amusement, after the phrase appeared in the absurd investigation into the unlawful landing of the Guptas' private jet at Waterkloof Air Force Base in April 2013. It was yet another public-relations disaster for Zuma and his administration, in which he looked weak and beholden to a rich foreign family, who had clearly been highly successful in wheedling their way into his affections, probably through secret donations to him and/or the ANC.

Incredibly, the inter-ministerial 'investigation', such as it was, concluded that officials and not ministers, still less the president, were responsible, ignoring the concept of political accountability in so doing. Bruce Koloane, the Department of International Relations and Cooperation (DIRCO) official and chief of state protocol who authorised the landing, told the ministerial investigators that he had felt under pressure from 'Number One'.

Not surprisingly, the ministers did not trouble themselves to explore this line of inquiry. After all, justice minister Jeff Radebe's job was to clean up the mess, not make it worse for his boss. But 'Number One' has stuck, though it is used less with awe than with disdain. As Kunene put it in his letter:

> The Gupta issue alone should be the last straw for many South Africans. But the extent of how much the Gupta family controls you, and by implication this country, has not even begun to be understood. It's amazing how terrified most people in the ANC are to speak about this reality, because they truly fear you. Even if you're not in government, tenders are used to inspire fear among people of influence. Thank God my livelihood is not dependent on tenders. I'll save you the trouble of trying to find out if I have any tenders so you can cut me out of them. I don't have any.[3]

Zuma sets the tone from the top. And he came into office with grave doubts about his probity, after serious corruption charges were dropped without proper explanation shortly before the 2009 election. Somewhere there is a smoking gun. When Ngcuka originally decided against pursuing the charges against Zuma back in 2003, he said there was a *prima facie* case against Zuma. The hope was that this would be damaging enough, and that Zuma's career would be over. In order to get to that point, the prosecutorial authorities would have had to carefully consider the evidence that existed against Zuma. Somewhere there must be a document that sets it out – the basis for and against bringing charges.

It is possible that this and other evidence might have to be disclosed during the judicial review proceedings that the Democratic Alliance has brought against the NDPP, claiming that the latter's decision to withdraw the charges against Zuma was irrational and unlawful. When the hearing takes place, perhaps as soon as late 2013, dynamite might be uncovered that could yet explode the Zuma presidency. Or, as the evidence emerges, or threatens to emerge, a critical mass inside the ANC could tell Zuma to step aside. We shall see. Zuma's power is not quite what it seems.

One of his key advisors is, therefore, his lawyer, Michael Hulley. Conveniently for them both, Hulley is now employed part-time as the presidential lawyer – paid for by the state. It may be that Hulley is assiduous in ensuring that when he advises Zuma as Mr Zuma, and not as Mr President, he notes the times of the consultation and bills Zuma for his own account. Or it may not. It may be that we are all paying for the defence of Jacob Zuma.

One of the consequences of this sort of bizarre, and to my mind totally inappropriate, appointment is that Zuma has no sense of conflict of interest. And, of course, were he to ask his lawyer to advise him on it, what would Hulley's response be? Well, that would depend on which hat he and/or his client is wearing.

Conflicts of interest such as this lie at the heart of the Zuma presidency. They gnaw away at the integrity of the governance system. Take, for example, the failure to appoint an NDPP. Since his first attempt – Menzi Simelane – was declared by the Supreme Court of Appeal and then the Constitutional Court to be irrational and therefore unlawful – because of doubt about Simelane's own probity, given his role as director-general of justice in the suspension by Mbeki of Vusi Pikoli as NDPP following Pikoli's decision to prosecute then police commissioner and ANC stalwart Jackie Selebi, which led to the Ginwala Commission of Inquiry describing Simelane as an unreliable witness – Zuma has failed to make a permanent appointment (as at July 2013).

Many experts believe that this has led to the inevitable decline in the morale of the National Prosecuting Authority and, in turn, its string of poor results in key cases, such as the prosecution of the policemen responsible for shooting dead service-delivery protester Andries Tatane.

If the DA wins its case, then the NDPP will be required to reconsider prosecuting Zuma. Is it in Zuma's interests to have a strong, independent-minded NDPP? Or rather a lackey beholden to him or simply too incompetent to do the job required of him or her?

Trevor and the NPC

Trevor Manuel tells people now that there was no way he was going to accept minister of finance again. The truth is, there was no way the victors of Polokwane would have let him stay on. Nevertheless, he'd had a wonderful innings, but he was uncertain about returning. In the February before the 2004 election, Manuel did not even want to sign the ANC nomination form, because he thought he should perhaps go. He was worried about what lay ahead.

But he has a profound sense of public duty and public service. He could walk into any number of private-sector jobs or international institutions, as he has a very good global reputation. But he sticks with his duties in government, though he often asks himself why he bothers, because much of what goes on these days pains him greatly.

Manuel tells me that he 'wanted some clarity about things' in the run-up to the 2009 election, which is Manuel-speak for negotiating what happened next.

Zuma had approached him, saying 'I want you to stay; it will be something new. Please don't ask me to discuss it, it would be unfair to others, but we will work it out.' So come the election, Manuel knew that he was going to be minister of national planning and that was good enough for him.

It was a challenge he relished. To be the architect of South Africa's first National Development Plan (NDP) no doubt appealed to Manuel's sense of self-fulfilment and the need that we all have to leave something of a legacy. 'I had to get into the place and start it all,' he recalls. 'There was just a ministerial office but not much space for staff in the West Wing. The idea was that we would move across to the East Wing.' Naturally, Manuel wanted to take some of his most trusted and favourite staff with him. 'I had to sit with PG [Pravin Gordhan, the new minister of finance] and figure who I would need.' Key ministerial staff went with him: his aide and his PA, Dumisa Jele and Patti Smith, and his protectors. He also took the rump of PCAS, which in the fullness of time would be split up – some going to the DPME and some staying at the NPC.

The NPC was the left's idea. So either Zuma has a good sense of humour or else he wanted to stick one up the nose of COSATU and the SACP by appointing Manuel as its minister. I ask Manuel about the attitude of the left. He is contemplative: 'Those things will never go away. The ANC is a forgiving organisation. I get on exceedingly well with that grouping. When they take the posture that they do, my view is that it's a feature of life, but you don't lose sleep over these things.'

In reality, it got nasty. As Barbara Hogan, minister of health in Kgalema Motlanthe's interim cabinet, and initially minister of public enterprises in Zuma's 2009 cabinet, recalls: 'Manuel's dignity was removed by nasty stuff and perpetual attacks by COSATU.' And veteran COSATU strategist Neil Coleman, who was part of the team that was put together to handle the transition from Mbeki to Zuma, says that 'Zuma did not back Trevor up. He hung him out to dry and let COSATU attack him.' For Coleman, the question of whether the NPC was going to be a real power was not a done deal. The calculation, he suggests, was that Manuel would be 'neutralised and would be a lot less powerful in that position'.

In other words, the Polokwane victors, or those on the left, who had, and still have, a lingering animus towards Manuel stretching all the way back to the sudden imposition of the Growth, Employment and Redistribution (GEAR) plan in the mid-nineties, accepted that the government had to have Manuel – that Zuma was not going to drop him entirely – and so it became about how and where his power could be contained.

But Manuel has a thick skin and, once appointed, he simply got on with the job. 'Establishing the commission was a fascinating journey,' he recalls now. The NPC promptly drafted a green paper on the model of the commission and its work, based on that of India's Planning Commission. Manuel would be the chair: 'I tested that with the president and deputy president – the Indian prime minister is the chair of their Planning Commission, but is a titular head, but it lends the commission more gravitas.'

The fight between COSATU and Manuel now shifted to new terrain. To their mind, Manuel was trying to establish himself as a prime minister, using the national planning mandate to run government out of the Presidency, right under Zuma's nose.

Manuel sees it differently: 'We started debating it. I had tested the thing in the ANC and – funny story – swine flu hit me, in July 2009, and I wasn't able to present it to Parliament. JZ then said, "Hold on, I don't think we should proceed with this green paper, as I don't want other ministers there – they will defend their turf." It was reported that my imperial powers were clipped ... It was anything but that.'

As one of the original architects of the idea of a national planning entity tells me now, if anything, it was because Zuma 'got very nervous of it and pushed it out of government'. As a semi-detached commission, comprised of part-time commissioners, it was easier to control and to manipulate: that was Zuma's thinking and he was adamant, despite being pushed by the leadership of the SACP and COSATU to think again.

So, in 2010, the NPC advertised for commissioners and appointed twenty-five, including Cyril Ramaphosa as deputy chair. 'It was an iterative process within the ANC,' says Manuel. 'We said we don't want just ANC people. So we have someone like Bobby Godsell, who is a member of the DA. And some quite disaffected by the ANC, someone like Jerry Coovadia.'

Zuma had to give the okay because it was his commission. The inaugural meeting took place on 11 May 2010, just over a year after the election and where-upon the plan-building process commenced. Interestingly, Manuel says, 'what people will tell you, if you look to the Chinese National Development and Reform Commission or the Malaysian, is that the first plans they put out were garbage. It was the second or third plans that made the difference.'

It was a tedious process. Most of the commissioners had not worked together before and so Manuel had to shepherd them along, being as inclusive and accommodating as possible – perhaps too much so, his critics might say. Neva Makgetla, a senior strategist in the Presidency, for example, says of the NDP: 'it's a good initial effort, but it's too big-tentish ... It should have set out the big issues, the big fights, and then identified choices, instead of which it uses language that tries to please too many people.'

That sounds about right for a Zuma plan. Yet, as part of the deal that saw him return to public life on the Zuma ticket at Mangaung, Ramaphosa persuaded the president to put the NDP at the top of the ANC's policy tree for the next five years. In the run-up to the conference, the NDP, which had been unveiled on 11 November 2012, was just another piece of paper. Its future was uncertain. It still is, but now, at least, the NDP has been adopted as ANC policy and, moreover, as the overarching policy under which all else will fall.

It will remain highly contested territory. Its inevitable conflicts with other policy documents, such as the New Growth Path (NGP), are being put under the spotlight and the differences exaggerated by people who have either not read the documents properly or have malign intent. Clearly, there are different points of emphasis and myriad issues of detail that are still to be worked out in terms of the execution of the plan. But what the NDP offers is a clear vision of the future and one that different parts of society can rally around.

However, while the ANC's adoption of the NDP was good news for Manuel and his team, they recognise that they have to sell it to the nation and secure full political traction for it. COSATU is waging war against it, primarily because the NDP invites a loosening of labour-market regulations as part of its prescription for youth unemployment – a sacrifice that the unions are unwilling to contemplate, since it would constitute a retreat from their greatest gain since democracy, the Labour Relations Act of 1995.

Meanwhile, much will depend on political leadership. Will Zuma continue to back the NDP or will he zigzag on it according to the expedient needs of the day, as he does on most policy issues? The hope, and expectation, is that Ramaphosa will take responsibility for leading its execution when he assumes the deputy presidency of the country after the 2014 general election. On his broad shoulders sits a weighty responsibility. Manuel's work is pretty much done. Only Radebe has served uninterrupted in cabinet from the very start of the democratic era. Manuel's has been a slow and reluctant departure from government, but I would be surprised to see him return to the cabinet after the election.

Without his focus and sense of conviction, there is a danger that the NPC will wither on the vine. It has few actual staff, though it was recruiting in early 2013 to bolster its complement for the task of communicating the NDP and engaging with a wide range of stakeholders, who will be needed to build support and understanding of its 2030 vision. How much power it will exert beyond 2014 is far from clear. Without strong leadership and support from the president – or, when the time comes, the deputy president – the NPC is likely to diminish in power over time.

National Planning Commissioners

Bobby Godsell	Elias Masilela	Jerry Vilakazi	Noluthando Gosa
Jennifer Molwantwa	Mike Muller	Mariam Altman	Chris Malikane
Vivienne Taylor	Marcus Balintulo	Vuyokazi Mahlati	Malekgapuru Makgoba
Joel Netshitenzhe	Anton Eberhard	Bridgette Gasa	Thandabantu Goba
Phillip Harrison	Ihron Rensburg	Jerry Coovadia	Karl von Holdt
Mohammed Karaan	Tasneem Essop	Pascal Moloi	Vincent Maphai

Instruction to deliver: The DPME

My appointment to interview Sean Phillips, director-general of the DPME, is at 7:30 on a glorious February morning in Pretoria. The Union Buildings always seem like an oasis of calm, even at midday in the baking summer sun. The buildings are situated high above Pretoria and you can drive past them, but few cars seem to make it up the hill to do so. And when you enter the buildings themselves, the lack of congestion is still noticeable and the 'where is everyone?' question continues to nag. At this time of the morning, the serene effect is even greater. It's partly the architecture – Herbert Baker's masterpiece.

The Presidency is spread between the twin towers of the East and the West wings. The president's private office is in the West Wing. Both have enormous central courtyards and huge stone staircases. The gentle red-brick stonework cools the air and calms the mood. The overall effect is like entering a really tasteful spa. At any moment one expects to see a white-dressing-gown-clad kugel emerge from one of the doors and stroll along the wide corridors in search of her next massage or facial.

The establishment of the DPME was one of the big reforms of the Zuma administration. It was a long time in the planning. Although its roots can be traced to Polokwane, the seed of the idea had been knocking around for a while before then. Moreover, the concept itself was not invented in South Africa; as Phillips reminds me, there is a lot of academic literature from the 1960s that tries to measure the impact of overseas development aid, with development agencies seeking to justify the expenditure of taxpayers' money in foreign lands. In the 1970s and 80s, it began to spread to government, just as the management theory of results-based management emerged in the corporate world.

As Phillips says, 'The latest theory is that the centre of government – usually the presidency or prime minister, but sometimes the treasury – should try to drive a process of strategic planning and results-based impact, asking questions such as: What is our theory of change? Where do we want to get to? What do we need to do to get there?'

Tony Blair set up a delivery unit in 10 Downing Street, Phillips tells me, as he gets up and wanders across his vast office to the bookshelf to retrieve a copy of *Instruction to Deliver: Fighting to Transform Britain's Public Services* by Michael Barber, who headed the Number 10 delivery unit for four years (2001–5). Since the purpose of government is to get things done, the preface to Barber's book says that it is a 'story not so much of the "what?" of public service reform, but of the "how?"'.[4] Phillips tells me I can keep the book – clearly a job lot of them were provided to the South Africans on one of their study visits to the UK – and I dutifully open it later in the day on the flight back to Cape Town, and find it to be a surprisingly good read, with little of the management-speak that I feared it would contain.

Phillips himself is fluent in such language, no doubt from his time away from the public service in the private sector, but he skilfully avoids swamping me with it, communicating with admirable precision and clarity the purpose and modus operandi of the DPME (after twelve years in the public service, Phillips took a few years off to run a management consultancy). The international shift towards results-based management has been accompanied by the idea of 'evidence-based policy making', which helps drive the evaluative process, the idea being that if you have a properly researched reason for doing something, then it should be easier to track the impact. 'The ANC leadership, including President Zuma, were aware of these developments internationally and how results-based management can be a tool of modern government, having met with people from the World Bank and perhaps with Michael Barber himself,' Phillips tells me.

The establishment of the DPME also flowed from a general recognition that government policy making was good, but implementation was poor. While Mbeki's PCAS was also concerned with impact and trying to measure success and failure, the DPME, according to Phillips, is more focused: 'PCAS was doing some of the kinds of things we're doing, but working on a lot of things. What is different is that we have got into it in a much more systematic fashion, with a lot more detail in the Presidency's work with departments, [through the] performance agreements [between the president and individual ministers] and delivery agreements [between groups of ministers who need to work together to achieve an outcome].'

The performance and delivery agreements are pivotal: linking activities to outputs, to use the language of logical frameworks (a planning tool favoured by many development aid agencies globally), with the intention being to drive a much more precise and focused approach to public-service delivery. These obviously have to be handled delicately: ministers, after all, have to sign a piece of paper committing them to deliver particular targets. Some ministers have published their performance agreements with the president and some haven't, and the DPME has made all the delivery agreements public on its website. 'Our view was to encourage transparency,' says Phillips, choosing his words carefully. 'Frankness is essential to the whole model,' he adds. 'The literature internationally emphasises the importance of transparency … you have to be frank about where you are. The assessments have to go public, in our view, and help the democratic constitutional system of accountability to work better.'

According to Phillips, Zuma keeps on saying 'we need to do things differently', which in Phillips's book is about making government more business-like, because in the private sector it is routine to use data to try to improve so as to remain competitive, whereas the management culture in the public sector does not have this 'continuous improvement' instinct – a shortcoming that is not unique to

South Africa, he quickly adds. Moreover, the managers are not good at using their discretion; the system has not broken free from being very centralised and rules-based.

'Change management is always very tough, with lots of resistance,' says Phillips. 'You need leadership from the centre, but you need to bring people along with you, otherwise you impose but create resistance.' The key players in this process are Treasury and the Forum of South African Directors-General.

A couple of months later, I get to know one of Phillips's deputy directors-general, who explains to me how important individual relationship-building was, and is, to the process. Often, he has to sit down with his opposite number in the line departments to reach agreement about the monitoring and evaluation process.

Political cover is important. The DPME is based in the Presidency, but institutionally South Africa opted for a model that gives the DPME less power than in other countries, such as Indonesia or Malaysia, where the equivalent unit has legal authority over the other ministries and departments, and has a 'super-minister' presiding over it.

Says Phillips: 'We've had to do it more collectively than in other countries. On the strengths side, we've got cabinet-level agreement for everything we've done, rather than having a super-minister telling everyone what to do. It's better to try to get buy-in than to be dictatorial. The downside is that we've not been able to move as fast or as far as we could if we were able to move with more authority.'

The minister of the DPME, Collins Chabane, is relatively young and, although close to Zuma and trusted by him, is not familiar with the inner workings of national government and so has had to tread relatively lightly. In the early days, there were stories that Chabane was not being taken seriously, especially by long-standing ministers such as Nkosazana Dlamini-Zuma, who regarded him as a bit of a lightweight. From the officials in the DPME, however, or at least those whom I have spoken to, there are only positive words for their minister – perhaps because he trusts them and lets them get on with it, stepping in only when they need political cover.

According to one official, Chabane's approach is 'refreshingly hands-off. His attitude seems to be "I trust my director-general and I will let him get on with it". When we need him, he responds very quickly.'

Phillips has been 'neither surprised nor disappointed' by the extent to which the Presidency can push reform. But what is emerging is a picture of considerable success in establishing the DPME and its fourteen macro-level outcomes, led by eleven outcome facilitators (who manage the fourteen outcomes), who are all appointed as specialists at deputy director-general level. They are the engine room of the new system. I have met several of these people, for various reasons,

The fourteen DPME outcomes[5]

1. Education: Improved quality of basic education
2. Health: A long and healthy life for all South Africans
3. Safety: All people in South Africa are and feel safe
4. Employment: Decent employment through inclusive economic growth
5. Skills: A skilled and capable workforce to support an inclusive growth path
6. Economic infrastructure: An efficient, competitive and responsive economic infrastructure network
7. Rural development: Vibrant, equitable and sustainable rural communities with food security for all
8. Human settlement: Sustainable human settlements and improved quality of household life
9. Local government: A responsive, accountable, effective and efficient local government system
10. Environment: Environmental assets and natural resources that are well protected and continually enhanced
11. Internal and external relations: Create a better South Africa and contribute to a better and safer Africa and world
12. Public service: An efficient, effective and development-oriented public service and an empowered, fair and inclusive citizenship
13. Social protection
14. Nation-building and social cohesion

in recent years. All of them have greatly impressed me – with their expertise and experience; but also with their sincerity, and diligence and determination to make progress in delivering better, more effective government to the people of South Africa. If you want to understand South Africa's government, warts and all, across all the big policy areas, talk to these people, as they are eleven of the most important and influential men and women in South Africa.

And there are some tangible accomplishments now: the DPME has rolled out two rounds of a new Management Performance Assessment Tool (MPAT), which is essentially a self-assessment tool to permit departments to assess their own performance against thirty-one management standards, under four key performance areas (KPAs), with a traffic-light system from red to green according to whether there is non-compliance with legal and regulatory requirements, partial compliance, full compliance or full compliance *and doing things smartly*. The key performance areas are:

1. Strategic management
2. Governance and accountability
3. Human resource management
4. Financial management

In the latest round, for approval by cabinet in August 2013 and which was being finalised as I completed this book, 156 national and provincial government agencies had conducted the MPAT, involving the examination of 20 000 documents by the DPME. In summary, according to this measure, government is generally doing all right with regards to planning, poorly with regards to financial management (50 per cent non-compliance), moderately on governance and accountability, and very poorly with regards to human resource management (75 per cent non-compliance).

The DPME will be presenting the results to cabinet in August and will publish the report thereafter. As in 2011/12, with the first round, it will publish the detailed results for each national department, but leave it to the discretion of the premiers to publish the results for their individual provincial departments. What is commendable about this approach is the transparency in relation to the publication of the results, because in an election year, the conclusions of the latest MPAT could be politically disadvantageous for the ruling party.

The report, for example, shows that the Western Cape is by far the best-scoring provincial government on governance and accountability (see Figure 2.1). Indeed, ahead of the finalisation of the report by cabinet, this piece of information had already leaked after the DPME shared the draft report with their provincial counterparts, and a DA tweet did the rounds bragging about the Western Cape's showing. You can see the headline on the media release, or even the roadside advertisement hoarding: 'President Zuma Announces Western Cape is the Best-Run Government in South Africa!'

The officials concerned with the report tell me that Phillips told them to proceed, that cabinet had approved the MPAT process, and that the DPME needed to be frank and open about the results. During an era when the Zuma administration is often criticised for being secretive or oversensitive, the commitment to transparency that this approach entails should be recognised and rewarded.

Nonetheless, this, I suspect, is where Chabane will earn his salary: by backing his director-general and his excellent team of officials, and sticking to the course that has been set.

The latest report also notes that not all government agencies and departments are taking the process seriously and that the next step will be to persuade them to do so. What is clear is that the report will provide a large amount of food for thought – for example, on the issue of senior management service continuity, since instability at the top of departments was found to be a major contributor to poor performance.

The other next step will be to align the fourteen outcomes and the reporting and evaluation under each of them with the Medium Term Strategic Framework (MTSF), which is a core piece of government planning made every five years.

Figure 2.1: Provincial and national rankings on KPA indices

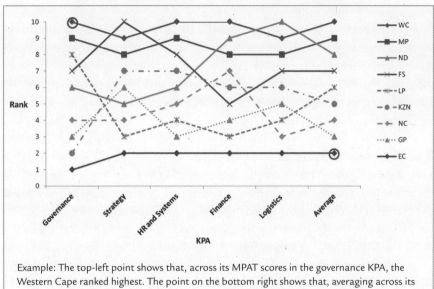

Example: The top-left point shows that, across its MPAT scores in the governance KPA, the Western Cape ranked highest. The point on the bottom right shows that, averaging across its MPAT scores for all the KPAs, the Eastern Cape was ranked eighth, after Gauteng's seventh. North West province has been omitted from this graph, as its data is incomplete.

The last one was produced in 2008, so for the first four years of the Zuma administration they have been out of step – something that is due to be rectified when cabinet meets for its annual lekgotla in mid-2013 and starts considering the next five-year MTSF (2014/15–2019/20).

Parliament has not yet taken the opportunity presented by the DPME's work or risen to the challenge of establishing an oversight committee over the Presidency, though things are beginning to change, says Phillips, as certain portfolio committees pay more attention to their outputs, such as public service and energy. 'Initially they didn't know what to do with us,' says one of Phillips's deputy directors-general, 'or how to handle the negative news. But that is changing slowly.'

Finally, of course, alignment between the NPC and the DPME's outcomes will be crucial to give full effect to 'joined-up government'. The idea is that each five-year MTSF will be a building block towards the 2030 vision of the NPC, which will operate as a superstructure under which the outcomes will be housed. Phillips believes that the Presidency now plays a much more powerful role in planning than before 2009, when, despite PCAS, Treasury held the reins. 'There is always the tendency to be territorial, but the majority of people in Treasury want to see an improvement in performance, as does SARS [the South African Revenue Service], which collects money for government to spend, but we are not getting the results that are needed from the public expenditure. Actually, Treasury's been very supportive.'

Most tellingly, according to one DPME official, Number One has been making more use of the DPME's reports, with more requests coming from his private office. To what purpose is yet unknown. And, indeed, the proof of the pudding will be in the eating for the DPME: is its intricate management process compelling government to deliver more effectively and, over time, will its impact be known and acknowledged?

The Presidency: More or less powerful?

Early on in the Zuma presidency there was conflict between the different power centres within government. This was inevitable. The restructuring had weakened the Presidency – certainly the president's ability to engage with policy and political decision-making – and Treasury. There were new kids on the block, such as the NPC, the DPME and the new Economic Development Department (EDD).

A cabinet-level source told me that 'about two months in, Trevor and EP [Ebrahim Patel, minister of economic development] could barely speak. It was a bit of a joke, with PG [Pravin Gordhan] in the middle. There was so much acrimony. Rob [Davies, minister of trade and industry] and EP are very close and they just wanted Trevor out. Things stagnated and stagnated and stagnated. This was the problem with the Zuma presidency – by the time of the first lekgotla, there was simply no economic policy and he would just let things drift.'

This account is confirmed by two other well-connected sources, one of whom worked closely with Manuel and describes the period as being 'a complete mess, with no clarity, and turf wars'. 'If I were the president,' he says now, 'I would leave the macroeconomics to Treasury and give the micro to Economic Development.'

Patel and Manuel's animus goes back a long way, to the United Democratic Front (UDF) days; I've been told by someone who knows them both that Manuel once punched Patel on the nose (he should have picked on someone his own size ...). There was also 'massive conflict between EP and PG', according to my cabinet-level source. 'EP presented his plan, and Treasury overreacted, for understandable reasons, in trying to hang on to Trevor's legacy.' A crisis meeting was called. 'JZ got us together,' recalls one cabinet minister who was present, along with Patel, Manuel, Gordhan, Hogan and Davies. '"You've got to make economic policy," Zuma told them, which I thought was a bit scandalous,' says the source, who diagnoses the underlying problem like this:

There has been a complete breakdown in how you make decisions in recent years. In the lekgotlas, you have every minister, sometimes directors-general, presenting their wonderful reports on what they achieved and what they were going to do. It would go on and on for three days. And this is what happens in the ANC's NEC now as well. Zuma does not say, 'We've got this view here, and that one, and here's my decision'. There is no management of decision-making. The one that speaks the loudest gets the nod. People just rabbit on, with tomes of PowerPoint ... in fact, it's death by PowerPoint. The level of incoherence in decision-making is frightening; there is no intellectual depth. There is no leadership. I have seen Mbeki chair and steer the conference to decision-making. Nothing like that happens. In cabinet, for instance, when one minister opposed someone's appointment to head a state-owned enterprise, Zuma allowed the discussion to go on for three hours; he was rubbernecking; he was too scared to say anything. Finally, Kgalema could not stand it any more. Usually he never speaks, but he stepped in to force a decision to be taken. When there are dissenting voices, no one is able to reconcile them.

But Zuma came in with a reputation as a 'great reconciler', I protest. That was his unique selling proposition. And after Mbeki's hauteur, it seemed like it might be welcome balm. 'No,' says my former cabinet ministerial source. 'He's Mr Nice Guy, which means he's nice to everyone ... but doesn't take them on. That is a problem. He is not a reconciler.'

In his brilliant book *The New Machiavelli: How to Wield Power in the Modern World*, Tony Blair's long-term prime-ministerial chief of staff, Jonathan Powell, uses Machiavelli as both the standard and the narrative backdrop for his distinctive, unrivalled account of Blair's premiership. The decision for a head of a cabinet-based government, says Powell, is 'not between Cabinet government and no Cabinet government but between a weak leader and a strong one'.[6]

'The difference,' argues Powell, looking back at Margaret Thatcher's term as prime minister as a point of reference for his assessment of Blair's leadership, 'between her and her predecessors was not the degree of her commitment to Cabinet government but that she was a strong prime minister who knew her mind and could get her way.'[7] This is the key question in Machiavelli's view, 'whether the Prince is strong enough, if occasion demands, to stand alone, or whether he needs continual help from others'.

With Zuma, there is no evidence of such decisive leadership. Talking to a range of sources, it is clear that he exerts his power in other ways, instilling fear where necessary, by the means he has at his disposal; principally, through his control of the security establishment and his use of patronage, rather than through his decision-making or force of argument.

'Thabo brutally slew everyone; he let people run his course; that's a different thing,' adds my source, who is hardly known as one of Mbeki's greatest admirers.

But distance – and an inferior alternative – apparently make the heart grow fonder.

'Zuma is a chameleon,' explains someone else who has worked closely with him. 'He is very adaptable and can adapt to whomever he is talking. As soon as he walks out of the room he forgets what he has said or promised. He seduces people very easily, convinces them that he cares for them, creating the impression that they really mean something to him. You need to study him close up and see him in action to see how fickle he really is.'

This is the objective reality of the Zuma years. A president who, like Ronald Reagan, is not much interested in policy detail, and who, although far from stupid, because he is a wily political operator of the highest order, lacks the sophistication and the education to engage with policy at anything more than a headline level. Zuma is the first South African president since Paul Kruger not to have enjoyed a university education. He cannot be faulted for that; and it is all too easy to slide into the complacent snobbery that many of his detractors both inside and outside the ANC do. Yet, all the available evidence suggests that this is a president that is not on top of the issues and that, moreover, and unlike Reagan, does not have the kitchen cabinet and enough of the necessary highly skilled advisors to provide him with the support he needs.

Thus, the paradox of the Zuma years is this: the president is less powerful, because of who he is, but the Presidency is perhaps more so, because of structural changes. However, since so much of the Presidency's political and institutional heft is drawn directly from the president himself, his individual weaknesses, of which there are many, are exaggerated by the absence of a strong team around him. Zuma is afforded little protection from himself.

Perhaps that is deliberate on the part of the ANC. After all, it spat out a president who was very powerful – a philosopher king who read everything and looked over the shoulder of everyone in his cabinet. Indeed, as we shall see, a distinctive feature of the shift from Mbeki to Zuma was about the ANC reclaiming greater control over government, from the top down.

Zuma has no such inclination or aptitude. But he can't set the right tone because of the constraints imposed on him by his chequered past, which continues to hang over him and may yet return to bite him and even force him from power. He cannot shake it off; and while that particular sword of Damocles hangs over him, it informs everything he does, including the way he governs.

And the Presidency cannot impose a message, narrative or theme from the top. The truth is simple: you can't surf without a wave, and since Zuma is out of his depth, there's very little his spin doctors can do to rescue his reputation or build a stronger brand. Most of his government know it. Most of his party know it. The Presidency does the best it can under the circumstances, which, in fact, is not at all badly: the NPC and the DPME are two important institutional reforms. The NPC has come up with a first National Development Plan that, despite its critics, could yet be the rallying point the country needs. And the DPME is making great strides in building real accountability for performance inside government itself, even though it is going to need to have serious and sustained political support and leadership to back up its technocratic excellence.

In spite of, rather than because of, President Zuma, the Presidency still exerts significant power, and even though its institutional character has changed remarkably in the short period of time since 2006, it remains the pivotal governmental actor.

3

The cabinet

'Zuma doesn't read.'

Those are the exact words one of his cabinet ministers uses when he describes to me what serving in a Zuma cabinet is like.

It is very different from Mbeki's era. Then, the president read everything. Often he knew as much about the particular portfolio as the minister, which made preparation essential. It meant ministers could not 'wing it' and had to 'know their stuff'. Zuma's personality, his leadership style and his inability to lead on issues of substance have changed the nature of the Presidency and the cabinet. Yet, structural changes within the Presidency have also diminished the power of the president himself to lead government – certainly from a policy-making and implementation perspective. The dissolution of the Policy Coordination and Advisory Services, the advisory structure that served Mbeki so well, was one of the first casualties of the Zuma administration and substantially weakened the Presidency as an institution. The PCAS was its intellectual heart. Its closure left a void that has not been filled.

Mbeki's presidency, as well as his style and aptitude, kept everyone very much on their toes. Mbeki dominated his cabinets – even though there were strong individual members, such as Trevor Manuel, Kader Asmal and Nkosazana Dlamini-Zuma – because of his preoccupation with detail and, to put it simply, his control freakery. Mbeki would sit and listen and then cut to the chase, raising some point of detail about the matter, often drawing on the minister's own documents and quoting them back to him or her.

Zuma just sits and listens. Then, typically, in the words of one of his ministers with whom I spoke, 'JZ will look at the minister and say, "So when will that happen? When can I come to you and see that you have achieved what you say you are wanting to achieve?" And then he will give that smile of his, sometimes with that chuckle of his.'

'It's not very sophisticated,' adds the minister, 'but it has a certain effect. His way is not to engage intellectually with the policy or the diagnosis, but with the practical solution.'

That is the way of non-ideologues (as well as non-intellectuals); they seek to turn their weakness into strength by focusing on practical matters. Politically, this can come across well with the broader public who hear: 'I just want to get things done.'

The result with Zuma is that, because he doesn't read the cabinet documents or the briefs that are prepared by the cabinet secretariat, or at least not in great detail, he relies heavily on his instincts. This, in turn, has significantly altered the relationship between the president and his cabinet.

Compared with Mbeki, Zuma gives his ministers far longer leashes. On the one hand, they have more space to operate, in that they don't have a president looking over their shoulders and immersing himself in their portfolios.

On the other hand, they rarely get his full backing, so they never really know if their place is secure, which makes taking tough and potentially unpopular decisions harder and leads to indecision.

The 'Zuma way' tends to be an advantage to those ministers who are confident and brave and decisive, who have a clear vision and a sense of purpose, and who are willing to run with the space they have – such as the minister for higher education and training, Blade Nzimande, or health minister Aaron Motsoaledi, or economic development minister Ebrahim Patel.

But are they running in the same direction? Do they have a common purpose, clearly, carefully and powerfully articulated by Number One? Not according to one member of Zuma's first cabinet. When asked about the Zuma administration, this former cabinet minister told me: 'It's sweet anarchy. The centre doth not hold.'

Despite the adapted deployment of Mbeki's favourite rhetorical question – will the centre hold? – this minister was not an Mbekite by any means and, in fact, places the blame firmly at Mbeki's door: 'No, he is a major part of the problem, because by being so stubborn in insisting on another term [as ANC president], he literally opened the door for Zuma and this very inchoate coalition of forces, the consequences of which we are now living with on a daily basis in government.'

The constitutional role of the cabinet

In 1867, the great political essayist Walter Bagehot described the role of cabinet in *The English Constitution* thus:

> The efficient secret of the English constitution may be described as the close union, the nearly complete fusion, of the executive and the legislative powers ... A cabinet is a combining committee – a hyphen with joins, a buckle which fastens, the legislative part of the state to the executive part of the state. In its origins it belongs to the one, in its functions it belongs to the other.[1]

Although the South African governance system now differs greatly from the British, with its brilliant, overriding Constitution and Bill of Rights, it has retained the core element, which is that the cabinet is the primary executive authority and is accountable to Parliament. Moreover, the legislature and the executive overlap in the cabinet. Because the former is so overshadowed by the latter, the cabinet is a crucial institutional receptacle of political power in the new South Africa.

The Constitution describes who is in the cabinet, how they are appointed and whom they are accountable to. Thus, the cabinet consists of the president, as head of the cabinet, a deputy president and ministers; they are appointed by the president, who 'assigns their powers and functions' and 'may dismiss them'; and they are 'accountable collectively and individually to Parliament for the exercise of their powers'.

It is a classic statement of a liberal democratic parliamentary democracy. As head of the cabinet, the president is really a prime minister, and the ministers are (in the great majority) drawn from Parliament, to whom the cabinet, including the president, is accountable. This can be contrasted with a presidential system, where the legislature (Parliament) and the executive (departments and Presidency) are elected separately, and, although the latter can be called to account by the former, there is no overlap in functions, authority or personnel.

This is especially important for understanding the power relations between the legislature and the executive: in parliamentary systems, the executive is always far more powerful than the legislature, and there is a mountain of academic literature to back up this assertion. In both, the president or prime minister is very powerful: in the presidential system, he or she draws particular succour from the fact that he or she has been directly elected; in a parliamentary system, the power of the prime minister is entrenched by the built-in power he or she can exercise over the legislature through his or her control of the majority party. These are crucial themes that I will return to in the coming chapters on Parliament and the ANC itself.

But what exactly does the cabinet do and how does it operate? Its narrow role is as a political decision-maker. At its fortnightly Wednesday-morning meeting in the Union Buildings (sometimes, if Parliament is in session, it will meet in Tuynhuis in Cape Town, the presidential building next to the National Assembly), it makes and reviews policy, and forms *political* judgements on the issues that emerge, which it does with the help of cabinet memoranda.

These are prepared by the cabinet secretariat in close consultation with the responsible line-function department and are supposed to be circulated the Friday before the cabinet meeting. In most cases, however, the cabinet secretariat operates far more as an administrative body, with memoranda drafted by the minister and his or her staff.

Before the memoranda make it to the cabinet meeting, numerous drafts are subjected to technical revisions, as well as budgetary and implementation considerations that arise. This occurs through an intricate process of inter- and intra-departmental committee meetings, which culminate in a review by the appropriate cabinet cluster committee. Some policy proposals, however, do go directly to cabinet.

Where there is a labour consideration, then the proposal will have to go through the National Economic Development and Labour Council (NEDLAC). In Mbeki's days, the PCAS of the Presidency would have critiqued the policy and its memorandum, but the Presidency's capacity to do so now is comparatively far more limited.

As a result of the absence of strong input from the Presidency, matters may still arrive at cabinet in a far from polished form. And there may still be tough political decisions to be made as well.

The political judgement is the culmination of a non-technical process that usually runs parallel to the technical side of policy making. This is more organic and less structured, and will include engagement with a wider group of some-times non-governmental stakeholders, including the ANC's allies COSATU and the SACP, although now that the SACP is more heavily represented in cabinet, this is a lesser consideration nowadays.

Cabinet-making

'Cabinet-making is probably the most important part of a Prime Minister's job, but the scope is not perhaps as great as might appear from outside. Political rivals cannot easily be demoted, discontented followers must be pacified: left and right must be balanced: the heads of the most important departments cannot be constantly changed: and the number of first-class men in parliament does not give unlimited choice.'

~ Anthony Sampson, *Anatomy of Britain Today*[2]

Apart from the gender exclusivity of the point about 'first-class men in parlia-ment', Sampson's observation about cabinet-making in Britain in the mid-1960s is almost completely applicable to cabinet-making in South Africa now. As a result of the nature of his victory and the disparate and ideologically unruly coalition of forces that Zuma put together at Polokwane, his job in choosing a cabinet was complicated, with lots of plates to spin and interests to balance, as well as favours to return.

As a result of his approach to policy making and the relative weakness of his kitchen cabinet and presidency as a whole, cabinet ministers under Zuma arguably have more power individually and collectively than under Mbeki. This makes any cabinet choices extremely crucial.

So what was the 'grand plan' post-Polokwane regarding the transition from Mbeki to Zuma and how did the forces who helped Zuma come to power think they would be able to shape a more inclusive presidency? There had been *some* forward planning – after all, Zuma had the better part of two years to prepare, although he may well have spent most of that time fretting about corruption charges and related legal battles than thinking through the intricate options for his first cabinet in the event that he avoided prison and made it to the West Wing – but these things tend to get left to the last minute, because apparently the information will inevitably be leaked and you don't want to unnecessarily extend the period between leaked news of a likely cabinet appointment and the actual appointment.

Thus, on the day of Zuma's inauguration, he and his closest political advisors in the Alliance were still in deliberations. As Trevor Manuel tells me: 'The custom since 1999 is that everyone, both current ministers and ones that are about to be appointed, are called and everyone is put into one big room at the presidential guesthouse in Pretoria to wait.'

The ANC leadership had been celebrating the inauguration at Montecasino in Sandton and had to travel late in the evening to Pretoria; most ministers got there at about 11 p.m. Ministers were called in from midnight. Some were there until the early hours.

'Gwede Mantashe, JZ and Kgalema [Motlanthe] were sitting there, having conducted their final discussion and negotiations,' recalls Manuel. 'It's a very strange arrangement. Once you're done you're escorted out through another door, so that you don't go back into the big room and have to face your colleagues having been either delightfully surprised or bitterly disappointed.'

One of the ways Zuma dealt with the challenge of putting together a cabinet when he had to take into account so many considerations was simply to increase its size. Mbeki's 2004 cabinet had 29 ministers. Zuma's has 35 (by way of comparison: the UK's cabinet is currently 24, India 33, Brazil 27, and the United States 15). Six new ministries were created, one way or another: economic development; education was split into two – basic education and higher education; the Presidency (formerly held by Mbeki's henchman and long-time right-hand man Essop Pahad) was split into two – national planning and performance monitoring and evaluation; women, children and disabilities were moved from the Presidency to form a new ministry; rural development – Zuma's pet subject; and tourism, which was split from environmental affairs (something that officials within the department had long been calling for, due to the obvious conflicts between the needs of tourism and environmental protection).

The real inflation, however, came in the ranks of deputy ministers. Whereas Mbeki had 18, Zuma created 14 more to a reach a total of 32. In the words of one of Zuma's cabinet ministers appointed in 2009: 'Far too many ministers, all to do with patronage. A completely bloated government.'

Sometimes deputy ministers do real work, if they have a busy portfolio with a minister pulled in many directions, such as international relations, or if the minister is hopeless or lazy. (Before his well-earned promotion to cabinet in July 2013, deputy minister Yunus Carrim's hard work in backstopping successive ministers at the Department of Cooperative Governance and Traditional Affairs comes to mind.)

Most times, however, deputy ministers are appendages, a drain on the taxpayer, whose main function is to provide the president with more opportunities for keeping people happy and dispensing patronage.

There were also name changes: housing became human settlements, foreign affairs became international relations and cooperation, mining became mineral resources, defence became defence and military veterans, and intelligence became state security.

Some of these were merely cosmetic, but others were indicative of a fresh approach. Governments are forever tinkering with such things, hoping that the nomenclature will prompt new thinking and a new respect from the public.

What was extraordinary was how the new Zuma administration differentiated itself from its predecessor, as if a new party had won power.

The changes were substantial: not just new names and new ministers, but new advisors and new administrative needs and changes. 'There was a long transition,' one of the cabinet ministers remarked to me, 'and a great deal of time was wasted.'

The real craftsmanship required of Zuma was first of all to find the right balance in his cabinet between different sorts of characters and skills – what one might call the political alchemy of the cabinet – and second, to pick the right individuals for the particular portfolios. Given the myriad political debts that Zuma had to repay, and the ideological diversity of the anti-Mbeki coalition that he had assembled at Polokwane and which now had to be converted, picking a cabinet was not going to be a simple task.

Although the final decisions about the composition, in terms of who would get which post, were left to the last minute, the consultations in the lead-up to the April 2009 election and the 'transitional planning' that went into setting up Zuma's administration were not insubstantial, resembling those one might expect when, say, the Republicans prepare to replace the Democrats in the White House, or when Labour supplants the Tories in 10 Downing Street.

The discussions included representatives from some of the main Polokwane protagonists, namely COSATU and the SACP, as well as, of course, the new ANC secretary-general, Gwede Mantashe, and the by now 'interim' president of the country and ANC deputy president, Kgalema Motlanthe.

Much of the negotiations were concerned with structural considerations: the establishment of the National Planning Commission and the creation of the new economic development cabinet portfolio. The cases for these changes were put almost entirely by the SACP and COSATU, but with a huge ally in Mantashe, who of course was in a position to wear all three hats (SACP, COSATU and ANC).

The primary goal of this left-of-centre group was to create a new capacity for central planning – a fondly held traditional instinct of the left, based on the belief that for the state to cope with the other centres of power in society and in the economy, it needs to have a robust grasp of the planning trajectory and its stake in the economy – and to do so without further adding to the power of the Presidency but, ideally, diminishing it. There had been some inevitable horse-trading. The left wanted an economic policy-making ministry. 'There was a process of wheeling and dealing,' says Neil Coleman, a member of the transitional task team that handled the transition from the Mbeki era to the Zuma era. 'For instance, the decisions about who would be the minster of national planning and who would be the minister of economic development were two sides of the same coin.' If anything, the left were keen to see Manuel, long their bête noire and the architect in chief of economic policy during the Mbeki years, fall on his sword or be considerably weakened.

The choice of Manuel as minister of national planning was, therefore, a highly controversial one. Coleman believes it was never presented to COSATU general secretary Zwelinzima Vavi as a trade-off: 'It was presented as a fait accompli, although in general Zuma did consult more widely than Mbeki would have done.'

There was an eagerness to avoid a repeat of the Mbeki era with its 'imperial presidency' beyond the reach of the ANC and its Alliance partners. After all, the whole point of Polokwane was to defeat not only Mbeki the individual political leader, but also his aloof style in exercising executive and policy-making power.

Having made progress with the structural questions, the core group, assisted by the transitional task team, turned to the question of who would fill the positions, at which point Zuma drew his cards closer to his chest. He was smart enough to know that while he was duty-bound to confer with a number of people, and to take some account of their wishes, the choice was his alone. He also knew that selecting a cabinet is the most important vesting of power that a president or prime minister undertakes.

There were certain unavoidables. The SACP had been punting the idea of a state or presidential council – or some such structure – to sit between the president and the cabinet. It had been discussed and, they thought, agreed to at the ANC's 2008 Alliance meeting, at which an interesting document entitled 'The Alliance at a Crossroads' was tabled, in which the argument for restructuring the executive branch of government was presented.

This idea was directed towards both the primary goal of limiting or controlling presidential power and a secondary, but barely less important, concern: the need to control or limit the power of the National Treasury.

In the first fifteen years of democracy, South Africa's government, not untypically for many governments around the world, was dominated by the pivotal role that Treasury played at its heart. Trevor Manuel had been the finance minister since his appointment in 1996 as South Africa's first black minister of finance.

Neither Zuma nor Motlanthe was much attracted by the idea of a state council. Both distrusted the intentions of Blade Nzimande, the secretary-general of the SACP. As a leading member of Zuma's Polokwane coalition, Nzimande had to be in the new cabinet; that much was clear. But his ambition either to be a member of a new state council comprising perhaps three to four ministers without portfolios – a sort of politburo to guide policy and strategy from the heart of government – or to take one of the 'Class A' portfolios – such as foreign affairs, finance, home affairs or defence – was to be thwarted. Zuma knew all too well that he would need to keep Nzimande in his place; and so the latter had to be satisfied with minister of higher education and training.

After all, Zuma had to make sure that he did not give the left too much. Like any ANC president, he had to balance the two great ideological tendencies of the organisation: its nationalist and socialist wings. Giving too much to COSATU and to the SACP especially would provoke the rage of the nationalists, who Zuma hoped to placate with juicy positions in the security cluster, thereby serving both their needs and his own ethnic chauvinism – what critics quickly painted as the 'Zulufication' of government.

There was also some straightforward horse-trading. Aside from Nzimande, the SACP also got its deputy secretary-general, Jeremy Cronin, into cabinet as a deputy minister (he got transport, which made sense as he'd served for many years as the chairperson of the transport portfolio committee in Parliament). COSATU, meanwhile, got their new ministry – economic development – and secured its occupancy with their man Ebrahim Patel, an experienced unionist with an international profile and a reputation as a clever, hard-nosed negotiator.

When trying to explain Zuma's cabinet to diplomats, I often resort to comparisons with a northern European coalition government – such as those that have been frequent in the Netherlands, Germany and, in recent years, Scandinavia.

Zuma's 2009 cabinet was a coalition consisting of COSATU, represented by Patel; the SACP, with several representatives; 'hard' nationalists, such as Nathi Mthethwa (police) and Jeff Radebe (justice), and related Zuma-loyalist securocrats, such as Siyabonga Cwele (state security); and 'soft' nationalists (Christian

Democrats, in the language of northern Europe) who had joined the anti-Mbeki campaign, such as Tokyo Sexwale (human settlements, subsequently sacked) and Lindiwe Sisulu (defence, now public administration).

The rump was represented by either hard Zuma loyalists, such as Sicelo Shiceka (cooperative governance, since deceased), S'bu Ndebele (transport, now correctional services) and Collins Chabane (performance monitoring and evaluation), or centralists with no fixed ideological abode, such as Aaron Motsoaledi (health) and Gugile Nkwinti (rural development).

Only eight of Mbeki's last cabinet (i.e. those who were serving members of his twenty-nine-minister-strong cabinet when he resigned in September 2008) survived to serve in Zuma's first cabinet: Naledi Pandor (education), Marthinus van Schalkwyk (tourism), Nosiviwe Mapisa-Nqakula (home affairs, then correctional services), Membathisi Mdladlana (labour, subsequently sacked), Makhenkesi Arnold Stofile (sport, also sacked), Sisulu (housing), Radebe (transport) and Manuel (finance).

Unlike Mandela and Mbeki, who were apparently loath to reshuffle their cabinets unless they absolutely had to (the death of public works minister Stella Sigcau in 2006, for example), Zuma reshuffles relatively often. So far he has done so on four separate occasions. In the October 2010 reshuffle, two ministers were reassigned, seven were replaced and seventeen new deputy ministers were appointed. In the second reshuffle on 24 October 2011, two ministers were removed, two were reassigned, two deputy ministers were promoted to ministers, two deputy ministers were reassigned and two new deputy ministers were appointed. On 3 October 2012, after the election of Nkosazana Dlamini-Zuma as chairperson of the African Union (AU) Commission, one minister was reassigned to a new portfolio and one deputy minister became a minister. On 9 July 2013, three ministers were removed, their replacements including two promoted deputy ministers, and two ministers swapped jobs. Three new deputy ministers were appointed. One deputy minister was removed, three were appointed, and one was reassigned.

By the end of October 2011, just six of Mbeki's last cabinet survived to serve in Zuma's by now bloated thirty-five-member cabinet: Pandor, Van Schalkwyk, Manuel, Mapisa-Nqakula, Sisulu and Radebe. In just three years, the character and personnel, as well as the ideological hue and political alchemy, of the cabinet had changed dramatically, even though the same political party was in power.

Ethnic mix: 'Zulufication'?

As I mentioned in *Anatomy of South Africa*, after Mbeki announced his new cabinet in 2004, the first caller to SAfm radio complained about the 'Xhosa Nostra'. He or she would have had no such complaints when Zuma announced *his* cabinet in 2009.

Zulu-speakers now dominate, particularly in the main security cluster. There are six ministries in the justice, crime prevention and security cluster, four of which are headed by Zulu men. In addition, Zuma appointed the controversial and colourful Bheki Cele, a fellow Zulu, to police commissioner in 2009, but he was later fired in the wake of corruption allegations concerning the granting of leases for police buildings in Pretoria. It quickly became apparent that Zuma was determined to keep the key security portfolios close to home. As the former head of ANC intelligence, and given his own difficulties with the law, one would expect nothing less from him.

In addition, there can be little surprise at Zuma's appointment of a number of Operation Vula stalwarts to positions in the security cluster and beyond, including Moe Shaik (who, before his departure from government, served as chief of South Africa's secret services), Siphiwe Nyanda (Zuma's minister of communications until his dismissal), Nathi Mthethwa (minister of police), Pravin Gordhan (minister of finance), Raymond Lala (one-time head of SAPS intelligence), Solly Shoke (current chief of the SANDF) and Mac Maharaj (presidential spokesman).[3]

Except for the removal of Fikile Mbalula as the deputy minister of police, this cluster has hardly been affected by the four cabinet reshuffles. After all, the president is not likely to mess with a cluster that is full of his friends and remains crucial to his retention of office.

Zuma's response to accusations of 'Zulufication' is to accuse those who count the number of Zulus he has brought into cabinet of being 'politically shallow' with nothing else to say. He is quick to point out that Siyabonga Cwele, his minister of state security, was appointed by former president Motlanthe, 'who is not a Zulu'.

How exactly does Zuma's cabinet compare with Mbeki's? Table 3.1 shows the shift in the ethnic mix of the cabinet.

Table 3.1: Shift in the ethnic mix of the cabinet, 2004–2013

Language/ethnic group	Zuma's cabinet,* 2013	%	Mbeki's cabinet,† 2004	%	% shift
Coloured	4	11.11	3	6.25	+4.86
Indian	2	5.56	4	8.33	−2.78
Sotho/Sotho & Pedi	6	16.67	4	8.33	+8.33
Swazi	0	0	1	2.08	
Tsonga	0	0	1	2.08	
Tswana/Tswana & Pedi	4	11.11	0	0	
Venda/Shangaan	1	2.78	2	4.17	−1.39
White	3	8.33	8	16.67	−8.33
Xhosa	6	16.67	18	37.50	−20.83
Zulu	10	27.78	7	14.58	+13.19
Total	36		48		

* Ministers only   † Ministers and deputy ministers

As can be seen, there has been a substantial increase in the number of Zulu ministers under Zuma, though not perhaps as much as the 'Zulufication' scaremongers would have us believe. If anything, it is *where* this Zulu contingent is dominant rather than *how large* it is that says more about Zuma's priorities and politics.

Cabinet cluster committees

The primary task of government is to get things done. Cabinets, especially ones as large as Zuma's, may inhibit rather than enable. As a result, many countries, including South Africa, organise cabinet subcommittees – or cluster committees, as they are known in South Africa. These tend to meet every two weeks, sometimes more frequently, and ministers prioritise attendance. 'You can't miss those,' one advisor told me. They are very important locations of decision-making, less cumbersome than the full cabinet and with more detailed documentation. The cluster committees deal with political questions, as well as key questions of policy implementation. They are also the scene of vibrant tussles between ministers and their directors-general.

Under Mbeki, the committees were not much smaller than the cabinet itself – the social sector committee, for example, had twenty cabinet ministers and eight deputies – and, despite the efforts of Mbeki and his advisors, they were generally not regarded as especially useful in streamlining government and making its decision-making more effective.

Long-time cabinet minister Kader Asmal, who served in the Mandela and Mbeki cabinets of 1994–1999 and 1999–2004 respectively, was not enthusiastic about the cluster committees in general, and neither is Trevor Manuel, though most of the other cabinet members are more positive. Asmal once made the point that the cluster committees are 'an attempt to strengthen "joined-up government", but unless the budget is allocated to the clusters – which it is not – then it can't be joined-up decision-making'.

As Coleman tells me about his time at the centre of the transitional task team secretariat preparing the Zuma administration for government, 'we inherited this cluster system, and its purpose was to ensure coordination and integration of policies and it had failed badly, because of a contestation of power – with the key actors being the Presidency and Treasury – which was a key economic power centre in government.

'So the Polokwane manifesto anticipated substantial change in economic policy and the big thing that worried them [the outgoing Mbeki regime] was a reconfiguration of government, because the experience so far had been that you could have radical policy proposals from the ANC, but they made zero difference at the level of the state because they were effectively sabotaged, especially at the level of the Presidency and Treasury, something that was worsened by the very different levels of development at the various ministries and in certain clusters.'

One of the big things I discovered in my research for *Anatomy of South Africa* was the notion of the 'two ANCs': one in government and one outside government. This still pertains, despite Coleman's best hopes, though the balance of power has undoubtedly shifted in favour of the ANC outside government. The question is, how much?

ANC nationalists would see this strategy of trying to ensure that the broader ANC – including its Alliance partners, COSATU and the SACP – has a stronger hand on the tiller of government as inappropriate meddling in the affairs of the ANC by its Alliance partners; they would see the 2008 'Alliance at a Crossroads' document as proof that COSATU and the SACP are trying not only to infiltrate but to dominate the ANC.

Hence the contestation for state power that will endure so long as the ANC Alliance remains an Alliance of three.

The planned reconfiguration of government, outlined in the 'Alliance at a Crossroads' document, was intended to link the presidential or state council with the cluster committees: senior ministers who chaired the clusters would then constitute a 'council of ministers' – in effect, creating 'super-ministers'.

'The key figures of the old regime mounted a massive rearguard action and shifted focus to the planning commission and chipped away at this idea of a council and systematically undermined it and it lost out,' says Coleman. 'One of the things that they did was to lobby within the ANC on the basis that it would be humiliating to more junior ministers.' Coleman concedes that it might have had that effect.

Instead, Zuma went for the outcomes approach, establishing the Department of Performance Monitoring and Evaluation in the Presidency in an attempt to achieve the same thing through a different method, one that to Coleman's mind is 'much less effective'.

Looking now at who chairs the various clusters (see Table 3.2), it is clear that seniority is not the deciding factor; the original idea of having the most senior ministers heading the clusters and serving on an overarching council was obviously abandoned. Most notably, with typical obfuscation, Zuma sought to weaken Treasury's reach by appointing a newcomer, Nkwinti, as chair of the economic policy cluster, and not the finance minister, Gordhan.

While the cluster committees are now smaller than they were under Mbeki and, according to one insider, 'play a far more focused role', they have not made the 'great leap forward' – to coin a phrase – in government coordination and, more significantly, in wrestling power away from the Presidency and Treasury that was envisaged by the transition team.

Instead, they have become new sites of policy contestation. Manuel, for instance, is conspicuous by his absence on the economic policy cluster. Some of the cluster committees are dysfunctional. Zuma picked then home affairs minister

Table 3.2: Ministerial clusters and members, 2013[4]

Cluster/Ministry	Minister
INFRASTRUCTURE DEVELOPMENT	
Chair: Transport	*Ms Elizabeth Dipuo Peters*
Deputy Chair: Public Enterprises	*Mr Malusi Gigaba*
Communications	Mr Yunus Carrim
Cooperative Governance and Traditional Affairs	Mr Lechesa Tsenoli
Economic Development	Mr Ebrahim Patel
Energy	Mr Ben Martins
Finance	Mr Pravin Gordhan
Human Settlements	Ms Connie September
Public Enterprises	Mr Malusi Gigaba
Public Works	Mr Thulas Nxesi
The Presidency: National Planning Commission	Mr Trevor Manuel
Transport	Ms Elizabeth Dipuo Peters
Water and Environmental Affairs	Ms Edna Molewa
ECONOMIC SECTORS AND EMPLOYMENT	
Chair: Rural Development and Land Reform	*Mr Gugile Nkwinti*
Deputy Chair: Science and Technology	*Mr Derek Hanekom*
Agriculture, Forestry and Fisheries	Ms Tina Joemat-Pettersson
Communications	Mr Yunus Carrim
Economic Development	Mr Ebrahim Patel
Finance	Mr Pravin Gordhan
Higher Education and Training	Dr Blade Nzimande
Labour	Ms Mildred Oliphant
Mineral Resources	Ms Susan Shabangu
Public Enterprises	Mr Malusi Gigaba
Rural Development and Land Reform	Mr Gugile Nkwinti
Science and Technology	Mr Derek Hanekom
Tourism	Mr Marthinus van Schalkwyk
Trade and Industry	Dr Rob Davies
HUMAN DEVELOPMENT	
Chair: Basic Education	*Ms Angie Motshekga*
Deputy Chair: Health	*Dr Aaron Motsoaledi*
Arts and Culture	Mr Paul Mashatile
Basic Education	Ms Angie Motshekga
Health	Dr Aaron Motsoaledi
Higher Education and Training	Dr Blade Nzimande
Labour	Ms Mildred Oliphant
Science and Technology	Mr Derek Hanekom
Sport and Recreation	Mr Fikile Mbalula

SOCIAL PROTECTION AND COMMUNITY DEVELOPMENT	
Chair: Social Development	*Ms Bathabile Dlamini*
Deputy Chair: Public Works	*Mr Thembelani Nxesi*
Cooperative Governance and Traditional Affairs	Mr Lechesa Tsenoli
Environmental and Water Affairs	Ms Edna Molewa
Human Settlements	Ms Connie September
Labour	Ms Mildred Oliphant
Public Works	Mr Thulas Nxesi
Rural Development and Land Affairs	Mr Gugile Nkwinti
Social Development	Ms Bathabile Dlamini
Transport	Ms Elizabeth Dipuo Peters
Women, Youth, Children and People with Disability	Ms Lulama Xingwana
INTERNATIONAL COOPERATION, TRADE AND SECURITY	
Chair: Defence and Military Veterans	*Ms Nosiviwe Maphisa-Nqakula*
Deputy Chair: International Relations and Cooperation	*Ms Maite Nkoana-Mashabane*
Defence and Military Veterans	Ms Nosiviwe Maphisa-Nqakula
Finance	Mr Pravin Gordhan
International Relations and Cooperation	Ms Maite Nkoana-Mashabane
State Security	Dr Siyabonga Cwele
Tourism	Mr Marthinus van Schalkwyk
Trade and Industry	Dr Rob Davies
Water and Environmental Affairs	Ms Edna Molewa
GOVERNANCE AND ADMINISTRATION	
Chair: Home Affairs	*Ms Naledi Pandor*
Deputy Chair: Public Service and Administration	*Ms Lindiwe Sisulu*
Cooperative Governance and Traditional Affairs	Mr Lechesa Tsenoli
Finance	Mr Pravin Gordhan
Home Affairs	Ms Naledi Pandor
Justice and Constitutional Development	Mr Jeff Radebe
Public Service and Administration	Ms Lindiwe Sisulu
The Presidency: Performance Monitoring and Evaluation and Administration	Mr Collins Chabane
JUSTICE, CRIME PREVENTION AND SECURITY	
Chair: Justice and Constitutional Development	*Mr Jeff Radebe*
Deputy Chair: Police	*Mr Nathi Mthethwa*
Correctional Services	Mr S'bu Ndebele
Defence and Military Veterans	Ms Nosiviwe Maphisa-Nqakula
Home Affairs	Ms Naledi Pandor
Justice and Constitutional Development	Mr Jeff Radebe
Police	Mr Nathi Mthethwa
State Security	Dr Siyabonga Cwele

This table was updated after the July 2013 cabinet reshuffle, and it assumes that the three new ministers will take the positions of their predecessors.

Nkosazana Dlamini-Zuma to chair the governance and administration cluster committee, but according to a Presidency source, she 'never convened a single meeting'. Dlamini-Zuma is widely credited with providing the leadership needed to help turn around a dysfunctional department (home affairs), but according to my source she was 'sulking because she was not given responsibility for one of the twelve [now fourteen] outcomes that the Presidency set for the administration's term' and effectively refused to cooperate with colleagues in cabinet.

The SACP and the 'left' in cabinet

Zuma's original 2009 cabinet had twelve members who were active in the structures of the SACP or had been members of the SACP during the struggle against apartheid. Some, like the late Sicelo Shiceka, had served in the structures of both the SACP and the trade-union movement.

Mbeki's 2008 cabinet had seven and eight members with an SACP and trade-union background respectively. Only Sydney Mufamadi served in the structures of both the SACP and COSATU.

What with Zuma's four reshuffles, as of July 2013 his cabinet has eighteen SACP members, many of whom serve either in the party's central committee or its politburo. Others are just ordinary members, though it is not clear if they are still card-carrying and active, as they do not hold high-profile positions within the SACP.

COSATU members or those with a trade-union background include Patel, Susan Shabangu, Mildred Oliphant, Edna Molewa, Connie September and Thulas Nxesi, though it is important to note that the closeness of the relationship between the individual minister and the unions varies greatly from person to person.

The economic policy cluster in particular has come under fire. Made up of twelve ministries, it is chaired by the minister of rural development and land reform, Gugile Nkwinti. Of the twelve ministers, eight have backgrounds closely associated with either the SACP or COSATU: Gordhan, Patel, Nzimande, Shabangu, Oliphant, Carrim, Rob Davies and Tina Joemat-Pettersson.

Aside from their ideological disposition, the choice of people to fill the economic policy positions raised the eyebrows of some in the ANC and especially irritated the nationalist wing, who commented that the cluster had an over-representation of minorities. Indeed, when Zuma announced that Gill Marcus would become Reserve Bank governor, analyst Duma Gqubule complained that 'minority' incumbents in economic portfolios, such as Manuel (planning commission), Gordhan (finance), Patel (economic development), Davies (trade and industry) and Barbara Hogan (public enterprises, since replaced by Malusi Gigaba), already demonstrated the ANC's 'lack of confidence' in 'blacks of African descent'.[5]

Economic development: A new centre of power in cabinet?

Post-Polokwane, the ANC's Alliance partners wanted to get full value for their support for Zuma. With good reason, they saw it as their big moment. Having been marginalised for so long under Mbeki, they were determined to milk the cow for all it was worth institutionally and policy-wise. Perhaps they got greedy or were too ambitious. What they ended up with was the NPC and a super-economic policy ministry in the form of the Economic Development Department. As noted, these two new institutions became the subject of intense horse-trading.

A senior official in EDD tells me: 'If you read the economic planning litera-ture, you'll quickly realise that it has to be either a super-ministry or else in the Presidency. Economic development couldn't be in the Presidency because the planning commission was there. This was the balancing act. They were worried about investor confidence, so they had to give Trevor something that was grand enough, but also something for the other main constituency, COSATU.'

Zuma is 'a good mediator and so he knew to give someone something, some-thing that makes everyone a bit unhappy, but not too unhappy, because they know the other side is also a bit unhappy'.

It reminds me of my days as a practising lawyer, when my pupil-master in London taught me that the definition of a good compromise outside court 'is one where each side walks away equally unhappy'.

The EDD official has some regrets about how things have turned out, recall-ing a discussion at the pre-Polokwane policy conference in mid-2007. Part of the thinking back then was that you would have a super-ministry for economics to take over macroeconomic policy and strategy and to trump Treasury in the process, and also to better coordinate the implementation of economic policy, much of which happens through line ministries such as energy. Now, however, he reckons that having both new institutions 'makes no sense'.

The original idea was to break up the line ministries into smaller ministries – such as splitting energy and mineral resources – and to have them both report to the super-ministry. What actually happened was the worst of all worlds: split ministries, but no super-ministry. The nascent EDD did not have the power of an overarching ministry and so, initially, conducted itself – *had to* conduct itself; it had no other option – like an NGO, a think tank, within government.

For example, I witnessed an early meeting convened by the EDD in Parliament to share the findings of a study on wealth and equality that Haroon Bhorat and Charlene van der Westhuizen had produced for them.[6] It contained important insights – about how, since 1994, economic growth had simply served to make the rich richer, and increase the inequality gap – but the meeting was sparsely attended, with about a dozen or so MPs dozing on the red leather seats of the new

Committee Room and a few policy wonks from NGOs and think tanks listening intently.

My impression then was that the EDD was going to struggle to impose itself on government and the body politic. But, while its longer-term impact is anyone's guess, it has probably been more effective than many suspected judging by its performance in the first months of the Zuma administration.

Apart from dispersing economic policy-making power more widely across government and thereby away from Treasury, what was the EDD supposed to achieve? To EDD deputy director-general Neva Makgetla, it has a coordinating function: 'When DTI [Department of Trade and Industry] or whoever can't figure out how to coordinate or who to talk to across government, we step in and try to help. We do the alignment stuff. That's the gap we fill. Everyone could see there was a problem there.'

The role that Patel has seized for the EDD as the secretariat to the Presidential Infrastructure Coordinating Commission (PICC) is an example of such a coordinating role, in relation to the Strategic Infrastructure Projects (SIPs). As a Treasury source pointed out to me, the SIPs are mainly building on existing plans, not really bringing more money, but rather coordinating (and EDD's budget remains modest at R722 million out of an annual overall government budget of R1.15 trillion). According to my source, during the first phase of the SIPs, 'EP has done well ... He has built a "storyline", with regional focus areas, drawing out the links between water and energy for example, and bringing people around the table who need to work together to sequence and coordinate.'

Interestingly, a source in the Presidency suggested to me that the creation of the PICC simply illustrated the inability of government to use its existing structures properly to ensure coordination. 'Why can't the cabinet cluster committee do its job? Instead, because of the arguments and the fault lines in the committee, another structure has to be created.'

The PICC role also exposes the department's limitations: the complexity of the R10-trillion-over-ten-years SIPs plan stretches the capacity of the small EDD staff to breaking point; and getting the projects to sequence correctly, across geographical, sectoral and departmental lines and different spheres of government (national, provincial and local), is an enormously complex process, but one that is vitally important for the country's future economic strength, both in terms of job creation and having the necessary modern infrastructure to be competitive.

For this reason, Coleman says, the early days were important in realising that although introducing new ideas and shaking old ways of thinking about the economic policy-making paradigm were 'critical', Patel 'realised that he had to establish some institutional power, because economic policy would be contested indefinitely'.

Having been the EDD's first director-general, Coleman recalls 'one of the things EDD had to do was to have a strategic plan – basically what are the programme structures and funding – and who determines that ultimately is Treasury. They sabotaged the process from the word go. They spun it out and spun it out, and tried to bleed EDD dry.'

It was the start of a war of attrition that continues to ebb and flow.

Fortunately, Patel had an ally in Davies, the left-leaning minister for trade and industry, who was willing to transfer the Industrial Development Corporation from the DTI to the EDD, providing the latter with both the institutional capacity and the funding that it so sorely needed, as well as 'a hand in the economy'.

Although they have had their differences, Davies and Patel continue to enjoy what one insider calls 'a constructive relationship'.

The EDD also took over responsibility for the competition authority – one of the most efficient and effective areas of government and, potentially, an ideal entry point into the economy from a social democratic, interventionist perspective.

Patel made full use of the competition laws when challenging Walmart's takeover of South African retailer Massmart in 2011. Indeed, according to David Lewis, the former chairman of the Competition Tribunal and who, as a former advisor to the union movement and current head of COSATU's Corruption Watch, can hardly be described as anti-union, Patel may have abused the process by using it to put bargaining pressure on Massmart.[7] At the Cape Town launch of his interesting book, *Thieves at the Dinner Table*, Lewis repeated his assertion that Patel had a tendency to use the competition law as a 'bargaining instrument', which threatened the independence of the competition authorities and left him with a 'vague feeling of disquiet'. Remarked Lewis: 'Competition law is a very indirect lever of economic policy.'

Just as interesting, as insightful political analyst and public intellectual Mcebisi Ndletyana has argued, the response to the Walmart transaction exposed the ideological fissures and lack of policy coordination within the cabinet. Ndeltyana noted that while Patel (along with Rob Davies and Tina Joemat-Pettersson) sought to oppose the takeover of Massmart, Deputy President Motlanthe went out of his way to welcome it, on the basis that it showed confidence in the South African economy.[8]

The transaction was a godsend to Patel, as it would have been for any frustrated revolutionary. Here was one of the world's biggest companies – to his mind, the embodiment of American capitalism with all its worst anti-labour attitudes – coming to his own backyard. At a time when he was struggling to give COSATU a return on its investment in the Zuma coalition (an investment that secured the union movement his new seat in cabinet), taking on Walmart provided a welcome opportunity to reassert his pro-union credentials and boost his profile both at home and internationally as a radical opponent of free-market capitalism.

Patel has gone through four directors-general since 2009. Coleman was succeeded by Richard Levin, Saleem Mowzer and, more recently, former ANC MP Jenny Schreiner. He is not the easiest person to work with. Someone who has worked closely with him told me that 'if you want to understand EP, then read the [Walter Isaacson] biography of Steve Jobs'. I think this was a thinly veiled reference to Patel's obsessive-compulsive disorder or, put simply, his unrelenting desire to control everything.

He works extremely hard – a workaholic, according to those who have worked with him (one of whom reminded me of the legendary tale about how Patel's wife once turned up at the department to find out where he was) – but does not delegate well, essentially because he finds it hard to trust anyone to do things as he would like them done. As someone who has worked in his department suggested to me, 'Patel's strength would be as an advisor. He's not someone who's particularly into it or good at being a minister, but is very good at coming up with good ideas ... and despite his personality he's done really well ... and people should stop seeing him as a COSATU puppet and viewing and judging him as such.'

The EDD's principal policy contribution has been the New Growth Path (NGP). Like the NPC's National Development Plan (NDP), it was probably important for the ministry, as a new kid on the block, to lay down a distinctive policy marker.

Indeed, for the NPC, it was essential: after all, the NPC was created to produce the NDP. The EDD had no such imperative, at least not formally. But the fact remained that unless Patel was able to come up with a document that articulated an alternative vision, the old economic policy paradigm would have remained untouched and, therefore, hegemonic within government.

For Makgetla, one of the architects of the NGP, it 'has a single perspective, even though there was lots of horse-trading in there too. Every national policy document so far has had a great deal of detail, much of which gets forgotten. So, the main thing is, what do you take away from it?'

Interestingly, considering the policy wonk that she is, Makgetla is actually asking about the power of its message, rather than the detail of its policy proposals. In other words, will it make a difference?

The Growth, Employment and Redistribution (GEAR) plan, she says, had a clear message whether you liked it or not: cut the budget, 'which was not so great'. The Accelerated and Shared Growth Initiative for South Africa (ASGISA) was 'all about infrastructure'.

With the NGP, Makgetla says, the message is that 'employment and equity are important'. It's a simply expressed mantra, but, given South Africa's growing political risk and social instability, a vital one.

'What do you take away from the NDP?' she asks. 'It may take a while,' she concedes, for it to settle down and for people to digest it. And she is not being adversarial when she asks rhetorically: 'But what does it mean to talk about implementing "it"?' Which is a fair point, although one that could also be made about the NGP.

The NDP 'says virtually the same thing' as the NGP, according to Makgetla. 'The only thing it adds is exports ... which I don't really like as it plays into a particular paradigm, but it's not such a big deal.'

I would agree. Certain parts of the press, especially *Business Day*, have invested time and effort in exposing what they claim is a contradiction between the NGP and the NDP. The two documents may not be perfectly aligned, but that is not to say that they are mutually exclusive. Far from it: Manuel was unusually diplomatic in what he said about the NGP in the NDP, bending over backwards, it seemed to me, to make it clear that the two visions could operate together.

When the NGP was published, COSATU immediately attacked it. I was surprised at the time. After all, Patel was *their* man; this was supposed to be *their* economic policy shift. Had he not consulted with them beforehand? Or had he 'gone native', contaminated by cabinet culture and negotiated into compromises that were not to the taste of his sponsors?

'It did quite a lot of damage,' admits Coleman. 'The NGP – what is it?' he asks rhetorically in order to begin his explanation of what happened. 'It is a product, an animal, which is the result of that balance of forces in the state. Its own incoherence reflects the government's incoherence, which reflects the president's own incoherence.

'This is about where the real power lies in state and society: if the contestation is confined within the state and your key conservative power centres are in the state, the only way to take it on is to throw it open to society.'

Which takes us back to Zuma's lack of leadership. Makgetla maintains that Zuma is more responsive to the broader society, but as the head of cabinet, he is unable to follow through.

'What happened with the NGP was that the Treasury vetoed vetoed vetoed in cabinet,' says Coleman. 'What they were doing was whittling away ... to the extent that they undermined the fabric and coherence of the document.

'That's EP's style – he's a negotiator. He will always look how far he can push the boundaries of his negotiation, whereas Zweli [Vavi] negotiates in the street as well as the boardrooms.'

National Treasury: Still a government within a government?

In *Anatomy of South Africa*, I presented National Treasury as a 'government within a government', with a strong, cohesive and capable 'Team Treasury' led by an experienced, devoted minister, Trevor Manuel, who was given the full backing of his president (Mbeki). Team Treasury was very loyal to its minister. Is this still the case? If you accept Coleman's analysis, Treasury remains powerful, notwithstanding attempts to weaken it by diffusing economic policy making through the restructuring of government.

To find the answer, I seek out long-standing Treasury official Andrew Donaldson. We meet at a café near Parliament, just days before the national budget speech in February 2013. Surrounded by the hubbub of a busy, trendy Cape Town eatery in Buitenkant Street near the District Six Museum, Donaldson is an island of calm composure; careful and parsimonious in his language, he doesn't look like he would be easy to ruffle, which is probably a useful attribute in someone so close to the national budget-making process, with its frenetic annual rush towards the finishing gate of Budget Day.

Donaldson has been in Team Treasury since 1993 and is now deputy director-general responsible for public finance. Structurally, he tells me, Treasury has not changed much since the substantial institutional modifications that were made at the end of the last century, when the departments of finance and state expenditure merged. Since then, however, there has been a substantial expansion, especially in terms of appointing more economic analysts and investigators in response to corruption, something that Gordhan is very big on.

In addition, the technical-assistance capacity has grown, which includes financial management support to other parts of government. For example, the municipal infrastructure development programme has expanded, as Treasury works more and more with the country's municipalities – where it believes things can 'get done'. Indeed, if there is a leitmotif that has emerged so far during the 'Gordhan years', it is that in order to satisfy the need to spend better, Treasury has strengthened its capacity to get involved in other areas of government with the hope that its presence will drive efficiency and drive out corruption.

'Ironically,' says Donaldson, 'the capacity was not really there when the left criticised us, in response to GEAR [the strategy that replaced the more Keynesian Reconstruction and Development Programme that was the ANC's mantra when it first came into power in 1994]. Now, that criticism is quieter, though we do have more intellectual horsepower ... though not as big as some might think,' he adds quickly.

'We struggle to recruit good people; much depends on who ends up where, and it can be good luck just as easily as good planning. When big reforms are on the cards it is important to have the right people. So having capacity in health economics is important now, whereas treasuries don't have much to say about the justice or security system, for example.'

The National Health Insurance (NHI) plan is an interesting case study. First mooted in the run-up to Polokwane, commentators who bothered to examine the numbers thought it would never get off the ground. The potential costs of a national, comprehensive healthcare scheme seemed prohibitive in the extreme. It looked like a pipe dream to the members of the SACP-dominated committee that developed the idea and succeeded in getting it confirmed as ANC policy amidst the cacophony of Polokwane.

Treasury was especially sceptical. Talking to Treasury sources at the time, I well remember them pooh-poohing the idea. Health can't even get the basics right, they said, never mind roll out such an ambitious scheme – one that, if it comes to be implemented, will not only potentially revolutionise South African healthcare but – and this is rare to the point of being unique – do so in a cross-class way, by requiring the healthcare system to serve both the rich and the poor.

But the Department of Health has got its act together, under the excellent leadership of Motsoaledi, who has built on the stabilising work of Hogan (who was minister of health during the Motlanthe 2008–09 interim administration) after a brutally corrosive decade of madness under Manto Tshabalala-Msimang.

'Personalities do matter,' concedes Donaldson. 'Pravin has a good long-standing relationship with the minister of health and health is a very tough issue fiscally and financially everywhere in the world.' As a result, Treasury is keeping its beady eye on things. But, as Motsoaledi rights the ship, with the assistance of an equally capable and sensible director-general, rebuilding the department's ability to do the basics right and to get the country's public health system functioning better in the face of massive odds and terrible conditions in many parts of South Africa, so Treasury has opened its mind to the possibility that the NHI, now halfway through a series of pilots, might actually be doable.

When corporate leaders or others with a stake in the economy get anxious about the policy direction of the ANC, I often point to the NHI as an indication of how slowly things move. This is partly because of the ANC and its structures, but also because the ANC is not the government. The ANC can commit to policy X, but the government's own processes will have a major impact on whether X happens or happens in the form, and at the pace, that was anticipated.

In this, National Treasury exerts a major influence, not least because its medium-term budgeting approach – with 'medium-term budget statements' setting three-year plans every October – provides an inherent stability to budgeting and, thereby, policy execution. 'There are always more opportunities for us to get involved, more than anyone else, and we can bring an overall coherence and perspective on things that other departments don't need to have,' explains Donaldson.

On the change from Manuel to Gordhan, Donaldson is instructive: 'Trevor's great strength was his focus on the big fiscal issues – fiscal management kept at bay lots of pressures – expenditure and resistance from lobbying – and so by 2008 we had reached a fiscal surplus.' Gordhan is, says Donaldson, 'a different personality and it is a different era: now we have to deal with service-delivery challenges, rising levels of discontent and a dysfunctionality in many parts of government that must be addressed'.

Minister of trade and industry Rob Davies talks to me about Treasury's 'night-watchman' role during the Mbeki era, in which 'the minister of finance was supposed to veto everything [on the basis that] macro policy was held to be the key to everything'. Davies believes that Treasury still has a 'powerful apparatus and does a very significant job in terms of the way it positions itself, which these days is much more about taking a longer-term view and [being] a little less sensitive to the daily machinations of the market'.

Gordhan has a very different style from Manuel and is eager to make more of Treasury's capacity to get involved, even though there is a danger of overpromising, by helping provinces to build schools, for example. The dynamic between the centre and the municipalities is not straightforward and there are concerns within Treasury itself that trying to do too much from the centre will get Treasury into trouble, as it is based on short-term imperatives – doused in naivety, some would say – and over the longer term might end up making things worse.

Treasury, says Donaldson, has always defended the idea that managers should be held accountable, but it is 'hard to defend decentralised management when so much is going wrong'.

But for big infrastructure projects Treasury seeks to exert more influence these days. This started, says Donaldson, with the big infrastructure programmes that were necessary to host the 2010 FIFA World Cup. 'Often there was very weak capacity in the responsible departments or even in parastatals and not much of a tradition of rigorous project appraisal that is so well established in advanced economies, for example. The World Cup required major projects that had to be completed on time. So we set up a small unit to drive the project-management process. Now there is an expectation that the whole procurement-management system needs to be overhauled, but we are not so sure how easy it is to manage that centrally.'

At this point we are interrupted to be told that the risotto we'd ordered for lunch had been chosen from the wrong menu and that the 'right' menu did not have risotto on it – news that is treated equably, almost cheerfully, by Donaldson, from whom I take my cue.

On infrastructure, I open up another front: nuclear. There is a pause. And some rumination. 'The numbers will speak for themselves,' says Donaldson. 'The NPC is opening up the choice between gas and nuclear, and there is a lot of wariness about international partnerships. The renewables programme has really got going, and after two successful IPP [independent power producer] rounds, a whole new industry has been built almost overnight. But where the next major baseload capacity should come from: we really do need to do the arithmetic before decisions are taken.'

The relative success of the renewables programme is something that Donaldson refers to again, as an example of effective government performance to set against all the other evidence of dysfuntionality and underwhelming performance, when I write to him three months later seeking 'good news' to convey to a group of investment-fund managers I am meeting with in London. I am struggling, after many years of greater optimism, to find positive things to say about South Africa's economic and political trajectory.

He's right; and it's certainly evidence, by the way, that at the heart of government, in the economic policy-making departments, there is a critical mass of new thinking about the virtues of a 'green economy' approach. But I wonder about his 'the numbers will speak for themselves' line. After all, that's pretty much what Treasury said about the ill-judged arms deal fifteen years ago, when it advised cabinet that the country could not really afford it and that the decision depended on the cabinet's 'appetite for risk'.

On my way to London for the meeting with the fund managers, I happen to bump into one of the commissioners of the NPC, who tells me that, again, although we can't afford nuclear, the pressures – and inducements – from international sources could tip things in a particular direction. He tells me that Zuma met three times with Russian president Vladimir Putin during the first few months of 2013. They, and the French, are pushing hard for South Africa to switch to nuclear, which will provide Treasury with a new test of its power and its ability to ward off undue influence. We shall see.

Instead of referring back in time to the arms deal, I look ahead and ask Donaldson about the NDP instead, which he describes as 'a monster of a document that has a lot of good ideas but is far from being internally coherent ... It's become a bit of a religious text, it's what we believe in, but actually reading it and interpreting it is a different thing altogether.' To my surprise, given the animus that has apparently animated the relationship between Gordhan and Patel, Donaldson offers the view that 'the NGP is a much tighter document' and, although he says he broadly agrees with my suggestion that the conflict between the NDP and the NGP is exaggerated by *Business Day* and others, there is, he says, a 'bit of truth in it [but only because they are] so complex and interconnected that there are going to be disputes about some things'.

Donaldson reminds me that 'there was a bit of political game-playing'; that

'EP had the international advisory board, with [Joseph] Stiglitz, to give it heft'. But he then introduces an important and sobering note into our discussion by asking: 'What have we really got to show for getting strategy going?'

This is the big question, not just for the country but for the Zuma administration as it approaches the 2014 election. Donaldson admits that 2012 was a 'wake-up call for the current account and in terms of the labour environment', which means, he argues, that 'there is a much soberer sense of needing to work together than before. The change in the objective conditions …,' he pauses and gives an embarrassed snigger, for this is, as he knows, exactly how the left speaks, 'means we can't just muddle along with unresolved policy issues; we need to take industrial policy and labour-market processes much more seriously. We're on the route to nowhere if we don't work together properly.'

The PICC, in which Patel is central, represents another clustering of influence, one that complicates matters further for Treasury. But it is clear that the process has reached the stage that unless Gordhan and Patel, and their respective departments, find each other, coordination between the ministries will be impossible, and projects will get stuck. As I noted earlier, the cabinet committees have not helped resolve such problems; the cluster committee on economic policy has not helped; and departments also have their own internal issues, says Donaldson, citing 'the tensions within DTI between the BEE and the industrialisation lobbies, or different perspectives on trade policy'.

Fragmentation within DTI is a problem. Can Treasury sort this kind of thing out? Taking me back to his earlier point about intellectual horsepower and its limitations, Donaldson points out that 'there has never been the great engine of minds in Treasury that is sometimes portrayed, capable of influencing everything. In reality, the budget sets broad parameters, while departments or provinces have considerable discretion about priorities and programmes. And even on issues that are pressing and where there is general agreement, such as supporting the DTI's Special Economic Zone programme, or the commitment to develop a bio-fuels industry, there are challenges in getting the technical work done and other departments are waiting for us.'

When the NPC was established, inevitably Manuel took a few of his people from Treasury with him – most notably, Kuben Naidoo. But, as testimony to their commitment to their work, most of Team Treasury has stayed, notwithstanding their sense of loss over losing a long-standing minister whom they were loyal to.

The first few months after Gordhan's appointment in 2009 were the hardest. Staff had to get used to a new leader. There were many mutterings – some of which revealed the sense of loss, because they were often either unfair, cosmetic or even petty. For example, one of Manuel's closest staff at Treasury told me that when she arrived to park her car at around 7 a.m. in the underground car park beneath Treasury in Pretoria, if Manuel was not away, his car would already be there, whereas now, she lamented, Gordhan would 'stroll in' a good while later.

But, like professionals, most of them have adjusted. And certainly, most of them have come to respect Gordhan for being the no-less-committed, hard-working and honest servant of the public as his predecessor. Table 3.3 shows key staff changes at senior-management level within the National Treasury since 2006. As can be seen, there was significant reshuffling following Mbeki's recall. Since then, staff turnover has been relatively low, save perhaps for 2011/12.

Perhaps the most significant departure was that of Director-General Lesetja Kganyago in 2011, as he left before a successor had been found. There were some concerns about this, and also that his successor (Lungisa Fuzile) might be more attuned to the interventionist, fiscally less-prudent persuasions of the likes of Patel than to the need to maintain fiscal and monetary discipline.

Does Zuma have Gordhan's back? Not perhaps as much as Mbeki had Manuel's. But they do go back a fair way and are certainly reasonably close. Gordhan is reported to have been an underground member of the SACP for twenty years and his connections with Zuma are said to have begun after Zuma's release from Robben Island in 1973.[9]

Gordhan was emboldened by winning election to the ANC's NEC at Manga-ung, and as 2013 unfolded there were signs that he was beginning to exert Treasury's influence on policy making more assertively – for example, by proceeding with the much-needed new measures to incentivise youth employment. Treasury, despite the hopes of those who saw it as a conservative government within a government under Mbeki, remains the pivotal player at the heart of the South African government. What has changed, perhaps, is that it is no longer the *only* big player. Like so many things, the picture is now more cluttered and less clear.

Conclusion: The balance of forces

So, how are the forces balanced in government now? Where does the power re-side? 'You have EDD and DTI on the progressive end of things,' explains Coleman. 'The big asset for them is that they represent the official policy perspectives within the ANC and the Alliance. They have that legitimacy. Then you have Treasury plus the planning commission, and the Presidency I suppose, on the other side of the fence, and there their key asset is the fact that they wield power, with a very entrenched bureaucracy, a culture with key personnel and an established modus operandi.'

I spoke with Coleman before the publication of the final NDP in spring 2012 and its endorsement and elevation at the ANC's national conference in Mangaung. He is now the architect of COSATU's attack on the NDP. The ANC's endorsement of the NDP represents a major defeat for COSATU; Coleman can no longer

Table 3.3: Changes in senior management of National Treasury, 2006–2012

Position	Occupier 2006–2007	2007–2008	2008–2009	2009–2010	2010–2011	2011–2012	2012–2013
MINISTER OF FINANCE	Trevor Manuel	→	Pravin Gordhan	→	→	→	→
Deputy Minister of Finance	Jabu Moleketi	→	Nhlanhla Nene	→	→	→	→
Director-General	Lesetja Kganyago	→	→	→	Lungisa Fuzile	→	→
Head(H): Corporate Services	Najwah Allie-Edries	→	Marion Mbina-Mthembu	→	→	Stadi Mngomezulu	→
H: Public Finance	Andrew Donaldson	→	→	→	→	→	→
H: Budget Office	Taz Chaponda →	Kuben Naidoo	→	Matthew Simmonds	→	→	→
H: Tax, Finance and Intnl Econ.	Ismail Momoniat	→	→	→	→	→	→
H: Economic Policy	Christopher Loewald	→	→	→	→	Fundi Tshazibana	→
H: International and Regional Econ. Policy	(post not yet in existence)			Mmakgoshi Phetla-Lekhethe	→	→	→
H: Intergovernmental Relations	Lungisa Fuzile	→	Kenneth Brown	→	→	→	→
H: Asset and Liability Management	Phakamani Hadebe	→	Lungise Fuzile	→	→	Thuto Shomang	→
H: Specialist Functions	Coen Kruger	→	→	→	→	→	→
H: Office of Accountant-General	Freeman Nomvalo	→	→	→	→	→	→
Number of changes		1	5	2	1	3	

Source: South African National Treasury Annual Reports, 2006/07–2012/13.

position it as not being ANC policy. It supersedes Polokwane, and so the Patel–Davies axis is weakened. Their plans remain government policy, but they must find a way of cohabiting underneath the roof of the overarching NDP.

Besides, as Coleman says of the EDD's institutional adversaries in government, 'they have control over the budget and that gives them a flying start. Their main strategy is to bog things down. Delay can only work in their interests – in policy change and implementation. You can have the NGP and new industrial policy, but if the key decisions have not been taken about resources – IPAP [the DTI's Industrial Policy Action Plan] is completely under-resourced, for example – key decisions around the exchange rate, for example – Treasury has a very keen interest in ensuring that the debate continues for as long as possible.'

According to Coleman, 'Treasury had become hegemonic in the Presidency in the old regime ... they were Siamese twins.'

Where is the key progressive centre? This is the question that keeps Coleman awake at night. 'It is in the Alliance, but it is fragmented,' he admits. *Plus ça change*. Polokwane was about recalibrating the relationship between the ANC and government; as always, for the Alliance partners this was, therefore, also about ensuring that the agenda of the SACP and COSATU is taken up by government. It is the task of Sisyphus. Given the nationalist tendencies of the ANC's right wing, which deeply opposes the leftist 'entryism' of the SACP and COSATU – with its cross-over membership that enables members of the leadership structures of its two Alliance partners to enter ANC structures and influence their future course – there will always be resistance.

The cabinet has to find its own course. The question is whether in doing so it reflects the balance of forces in the Alliance or carves its own path. Because Zuma had to give some power to those who brought him victory at Polokwane, both the SACP and COSATU now have the representation and political space in the cabinet that was denied them under Mbeki. The Zuma years have been ostensibly kind to them.

Yet it is a chimera. With the opposition to Mbeki 'there was a glue', says Coleman. 'Post-Polokwane, things fell apart.' He describes the coalition as the 'walking wounded', remnants of the fight against Mbeki, 'and therefore inherently incohesive. There was no progressive centre of power to drive the agenda in government in May 2009 and onwards.'

Considering the adverse circumstances, the general view in an around government is that Patel has done surprisingly well to push a progressive agenda and develop an institutional platform from which to do so, with an emphasis on employment and equity in government. But he has to fight for every inch of space, and there is absolutely no guarantee that Zuma will remain loyal and retain him or the EDD after 2014.

With Zuma you never know. Team Treasury has held largely firm at the centre of government, while all around chaos has reigned. The Presidency is weaker than it was under Mbeki in terms of its grasp of policy and its ability to lead politically. The effect is that Zuma's coalition cabinet, hustled together in classic Zuma style, without a clear, negotiated programme of action – like a 'normal' coalition government would negotiate before entering office – has to negotiate everything as it goes along, which is no way to govern.

Characteristic of the Zuma years, the face and political character of the cabinet has changed, with individual ministers having sought to exploit the weaknesses of the president's leadership. The consequent lack of clear common purpose has weakened the cabinet's collective power and rendered government even less able to meet the challenges of the day.

When one considers, pound for pound, the individuals that make up the cabinet, it may actually be stronger now than under Mbeki. But collectively, poor leadership and a failure to scrutinise departmental memoranda, a function that used to be undertaken by the Presidency's Policy Coordination and Advisory Service, weaken them. As a member of Zuma's first cabinet recalls: 'It was pretty brutal, not collegial at all; cabinet members were very brutal with each other. But there was also no attempt to intellectualise and understand the issues. Trevor [Manuel] became another Kader Asmal, reading everything [across departments] including all the [departmental] memos and he fought hard battles with everyone.'

Postscript: An all-women cabinet

In *Anatomy of South Africa*, I offered what I hoped would be an amusing excursion from real life when I selected a 'Fantasy Left Cabinet', in the spirit of 'fantasy football'. Headed by President Zwelinzima Vavi, it is somewhat interesting to reread now. Only four of my fantasy fifteen actually made it into Zuma's cabinet, which may or may not be telling: I had Gordhan as finance minister (who's been more moderate in office than one might have expected), Patel at trade and industry, Nzimande at foreign affairs and Davies at telecommunications.

There was, however, a very serious structural problem with my fantasy cabinet, which I was completely – and shamefully – oblivious to, and which was later kindly pointed out to me by my friend the then deputy ambassador to Norway, May-Elin Stener. My cabinet was comprised only of men.

So much for my feminist credentials.

This time, in an attempt to right the wrong, I have selected an all-woman cabinet for your consideration, review and improvement. The issue of gender equality has risen even higher up the political agenda since Zuma came to power, partly because of his own obvious shortcomings in this regard – his polygamy

Table 3.4: Gender breakdown of the current cabinet, 2013
(63.9 per cent male, 36.1 per cent female)

Minister	Department	
1. Ms Tina Joemat-Pettersson	Agriculture, Forestry & Fisheries	F
2. Ms Matsie Angelina Motshekga	Basic Education	F
3. Ms Nosiviwe Maphisa-Nqakula	Defence & Military Veterans	F
4. Ms Grace Naledi Mandisa Pandor	Home Affairs	F
5. Ms Cornelia 'Connie' Carol September	Human Settlements	F
6. Ms Maite M Nkoana-Mashabane	International Relations & Cooperation	F
7. Ms Mildred Oliphant	Labour	F
8. Ms Susan Shabangu	Mineral Resources	F
9. Ms Lindiwe Sisulu	Public Service & Administration	F
10. Ms Bathabile Olive Dlamini	Social Development	F
11. Ms Elizabeth Dipuo Peters	Transport	F
12. Ms Bomo Edna Molewa	Water & Environmental Affairs	F
13. Ms Lulama Xingwana	Women, Youth, Children & People with Disabilities	F
14. Mr Jacob Gedleyihlekisa Zuma	President	M
15. Mr Kgalema Motlanthe	Deputy President	M
16. Mr Paul Mashatile	Arts & Culture	M
17. Mr Yunus Carrim	Communications	M
18. Mr Solomon Lechesa Tsenoli	Cooperative Governance & Traditional Affairs	M
19. Mr Sibusiso Ndebele	Correctional Services	M
20. Mr Ebrahim Patel	Economic Development	M
21. Mr Ben Martins	Energy	M
22. Mr Pravin Jamnadas Gordhan	Finance	M
23. Dr Pakishe Aaron Motsoaledi	Health	M
24. Dr Bonginkosi Emmanuel 'Blade' Nzimande	Higher Education & Training	M
25. Mr Jeff Thamsanqa Radebe	Justice & Constitutional Development	M
26. Mr Trevor Andrew Manuel	Minister in the Presidency for National Planning	M
27. Mr Collins Chabane	Minister in the Presidency for Performance Monitoring, Evaluation & Administration in the Presidency	M
28. Mr Nathi Mthethwa	Police	M
29. Mr Malusi Knowledge Nkanyezi Gigaba	Public Enterprises	M
30. Mr Thembelani 'Thulas' Nxesi	Public Works	M
31. Mr Gugile Nkwinti	Rural Development and Land Reform	M
32. Mr Derek Andre Hanekom	Science & Technology	M
33. Mr Fikile April Mbalula	Sport & Recreation	M
34. Dr Siyabonga Cyprian Cwele	State Security	M
35. Mr Marthinus van Schalkwyk	Tourism	M
36. Dr Rob Davies	Trade and Industry	M

for one thing; the circumstances that led to the rape charge (namely, that Zuma had unprotected sexual intercourse with a young woman half his age, whom he knew to be HIV-positive and over whom he had a long-standing avuncular role) of which he was found not guilty in 2005, for another – and partly because a number of brutal rape stories, including that of Anene Booysen in early 2013, have demonstrated the depth and extent of gender-based violence in South African society and the nature of the social crisis.

I have tried to pick progressive women (broadly defined), to link to my previous fantasy cabinet, but I have also sought to make this a cabinet of 'all the talents' – as they say in Europe when trying to escape the strictures of party politics – one which befits the national emergency in gender-based violence that would bring this government of national unity into power.

As such, it is a cabinet with an ANC majority, but with representatives from other parties. I have discarded ANC women whom I regard as not progressive or competent enough (think Baleka Mbete or Angie Motshekga), and included some opposition women even though they may be more liberal than progressive. I have also cast my net wider than current politicians, to catch some of the 'talents' from other fields, such as business and civil society.

It's a strong team. Better balanced, I think, than the current real cabinet, and with no obvious weak links.

It is headed by a very strong, independent woman, whom I respect very much and who is largely responsible for where and who I am now, given that it was she who hired me at IDASA in 1995.

President: Mamphela Ramphele. Because she soars above day-to-day politics and the partisanship of party political leadership (and the insurmountable challenges in leading Agang that I elsewhere in this book predict she will struggle to rise to), I have little doubt that Ramphele would provide the clarity of vision and leadership that South Africa needs to help restore its reputation in the world, while grasping the big nettles in the domestic arena.

Deputy president: Nkosazana Dlamini-Zuma. With a non-ANC president, the ANC has to have the deputy presidency, and I have 'recalled' the African Union Commission chairperson on the grounds that it is a national emergency and that her country needs her. As deputy president, she would lead the national campaign to end gender-based violence – I can't think of anyone stronger to head such a daunting initiative. Accordingly, though ironically, I have cut the position of 'minister for women' from this all-woman cabinet. Dlamini-Zuma would also lead on African diplomatic relations, for obvious reasons given her experience on the continent, leaving Ramphele to focus on the G20 and South Africa's relations with the Western powers, with her minister of international relations concentrating on South–South diplomacy and the country's role in BRICS (the Brazil, Russia, India, China and South Africa grouping).

Finance: Gill Marcus. Time to bring Marcus back into government, after several years away, first in academia at the Gordon Institute of Business Science and latterly as a much-respected, independent-minded governor of the Reserve Bank.

International Relations and Cooperation: Lindiwe Zulu. Her various apprenticeships complete, this hard-working, ambitious woman, a key advisor in the Zuma presidency, as smooth as she is smart, is ready for a top job in government and would be the perfect person to reboot South Africa's foreign-policy vision and to drive its stake in BRICS.

Defence: Sue Rabkin. Out of the shadows, please, Sue. South Africa's longest-serving special advisor, she has held the position to all four of the ministers who have held this 'Class A' portfolio since 1994, and knows more about the inner workings of the defence force than just about anyone. (Not sure I can see her in a general's uniform though.)

National Planning in the Presidency: Sheila Barsel. Admittedly from left field, literally. The veteran SACP activist and thinker, who still serves on its politburo, and one of the brains behind the NHI scheme, gets a chance to apply a fresh approach to national development planning and to ensure that Ramphele gets a run for her money on key long-term strategic decisions about the future direction of the country.

Performance Monitoring and Evaluation and Standards in Public Life in the Presidency: Thuli Madonsela. The courageous, forthright Public Protector gets a chance to set new standards in public life, from the very heart of government, with an emphasis on ethical standards rather than management-speak.

Public Service and Administration: Lindiwe Sisulu. At the time of writing, she was just getting into her stride in this vital portfolio. She has the toughness required to handle the public-sector unions and to drive corruption out of the public service.

Basic Education: Helen Zille. In this national-emergency coalition cabinet, the DA's leader needs a top position, and what could be more important than sorting out the national emergency in schools?

Further Education: Naledi Pandor. She's an open-minded, essentially progressive politician with a natural inclination towards thinking and learning (though it was suggested mischievously to me by an ANC ministerial colleague of hers that as a coloured person married to a Xhosa man she would make the ideal ANC candidate for Western Cape premier).

Intelligence Services: Thenjiwe Mtintso. Time to sort out the spooks. Former ambassador to Cuba and long-standing SACP politburo member, Mtintso has the experience, the toughness and the savvy to do the job. A good all-round addition to the cabinet.

Public Enterprises: Maria Ramos. As a former director-general of finance and CEO of Transnet, she knows government and its state-owned enterprises like the back of her hand. After a few years in the private sector as CEO of ABSA, Ramos is now even better equipped to lead this vital portfolio, and gets the nod just ahead of Cheryl Carolus.

Trade and Industry: Cheryl Carolus. After a varied and largely successful career outside of national government, as high commissioner to the UK, head of South Africa's tourism agency and, latterly, as chair of the South African Airways board, Carolus is well placed to take over this significant portfolio.

Health: Barbara Hogan. Hogan was brought into government in 2008 by her close friend Motlanthe, and had an immediate remedial impact on the department, after years of madness under Manto Tshabalala-Msimang. Unfortunately, Zuma moved her to public enterprises in 2009, but her good work was continued by the admirable Dr Aaron Motsoaledi. Now that his gender disbars him, time for the incorruptible Hogan to resume her reforming role.

Police: Thandi Modise. She had a difficult few years as ANC deputy secretary-general and her time as premier of the North West province has not added greatly to her reputation. Nonetheless, I have a high regard for Modise's innate integrity and commitment to human security. She is tough and streetwise, as she will need to be to sort out the police force.

Transport: Patricia de Lille. She chaired the parliamentary Portfolio Committee on Transport for several years in the late 1990s and early 2000s, and has a good understanding of the sector, not least from her recent mayorship in Cape Town, as well as an instinctive grasp of the needs of the ordinary working-class people for whom public transport is a daily headache.

Home Affairs: Fatima Chohan. Part of the team that turned this dismal depart-
ment around, as deputy minister, Chohan now deserves promotion to the top job.
Despite her rather hackish performance on the Judicial Service Commission,
I have full confidence in her intelligence and progressive values.

Economic Development: Neva Makgetla. One of South Africa's best progressive
economists, she is currently deputy director-general of economic policy in the
EDD, having worked at NALEDI (the National Labour and Development Institute) and then COSATU in the 1990s and early 2000s, before Mbeki appointed
her to his policy kitchen cabinet in 2006. She had previously been shunned for
fear that she was too left-wing.

Human Settlements: Janet Love. Currently a human rights commissioner and
director of the enduring Legal Resources Centre, she is well versed in the duties
that the constitutional right of access to adequate housing places on government
and now gets the chance to make progress in a challenging portfolio.

Water, Minerals, the Environment and Energy: Tasneem Essop. Currently a
national planning commissioner and head of the World Wide Fund for Nature's
Global Climate Deal Network Initiative, Essop is well equipped to lead South
Africa's negotiating team and to drive the green-economy agenda in government as the head of a new super-ministry that brings together water, energy,
environment and minerals.

Science and Technology: Olive Shisana. The current head of the Human Sciences
Research Council (HSRC), the government-funded think tank, was director-
general of the national Department of Health in the 1990s during its pre-Manto
days and led a number of important reforms, including the anti-smoking legislation that is widely regarded as a success. These days, she is a great enthusiast
for the NHI scheme that is struggling to gain full traction inside government,
given uncertainty about its funding model, and BRICS. With her commitment to
science and innovation, Shisana would be an ideal appointment to this portfolio.

Social Welfare and Development: Adila Hassen. The energetic, activist leader of
Section 27 gets a chance to serve the poor in government.

Disabled: Masingita Masunga. An award-winning activist for the disabled,
Masunga gets the opportunity to implement some of her ideas for improving
the lives of the disabled.

Correctional Services: Jenny Schreiner. Schreiner is an experienced public servant and SACP central committee member, who has held leadership positions in respect of prison reform in the past.

Telecommunications: Nozipho January-Bardill. The cosmopolitan politician-turned-businesswoman, and former diplomat, would lead this portfolio into a new visionary phase, armed with her experience as head of group corporate affairs at MTN.

Cooperative Governance and Traditional Affairs: Nomboniso Gasa. It's a portfolio that needs urgent attention and the former gender-equality commissioner and long-time activist will bring a strong gender-rights approach to traditional leaders and some much-needed rigour into national governmental oversight of provincial and local spheres of government, including getting tough with the ANC factionalism that is corroding the probity of municipal governance.

Tourism: Lindiwe Mazibuko. The DA parliamentary leader gets a taste of national government in an important sector for job creation. Mazibuko will be a persuasive and passionate salesperson for South Africa abroad.

Justice and Constitutional Development: Yvonne Mokgoro. The former Constitutional Court judge has recently turned herself into something of a public administrator, working behind the scenes in the Office of the Chief Justice. In this portfolio, she can drive reform of the courts' administration and, with her human-rights and constitutional credentials, there will be no worries about executive interference in the independence of the judiciary.

Labour and Youth Employment and Training: Joyce Moloi-Moropa. The up-and-coming SACP treasurer will bring a pro-worker stance to a newly structured portfolio.

Public Works: Futhi Mtoba. It might look like an odd appointment to bring an accountant into this portfolio, but it's certainly one that needs a good audit and the CEO of Deloitte is no stranger to prospering in a male-dominated arena. She will bring some real-world business acumen into the cabinet as well.

Land Affairs and Agriculture, Fisheries and Forestry: Lynne Brown. This is an important portfolio that needs someone who can make land an economic development strategic policy issue, not an emotive political one. Working with farmers and big companies like Massmart/Walmart, the former Western Cape minister for economic development has the drive and talent to make it happen in an enlarged portfolio that combines land affairs with agriculture, fisheries and forestry.

Arts, Culture and Sport: Pregs Govender. The South African Human Rights Commission deputy chair and gender activist, and former ANC MP, gets an opportunity to steer art and culture in South Africa so that it can stimulate and serve a national strategic goal of equality, while balancing modernity with tradition. (I've merged sport into arts and culture because I've always regarded sport as high culture and an art form in its own right.) It's a good portfolio to end with. You can sense whether a nation is at ease with itself through its art and cultural proclivities (and its sport). As the controversy over *The Spear* showed, South Africa has a long way to go.

This is a large cabinet in terms of numbers – just like the real-life one – and far larger than many others around the world. Arguably, it makes decision-making cumbersome and diffuses accountability, making it harder for the president to assert him/herself across such a wide range of portfolios. It is also expensive. Accordingly, in this fantasy government there are no deputy ministers. The buck stops with the minister and the minister alone.

4

Foreign policy

As she walks across the large colonial hallway of Tuynhuis, the president's Cape Town office next to Parliament, Ambassador Lindiwe Zulu crosses paths with Collins Chabane, the minister in the Presidency responsible for performance monitoring and evaluation. It is 13 February, the day before the president's 2013 State of the Nation address. The sun is shining and everyone powerful in government is in town.

'Good morning! Are you the Kitchen Girl?' Collins asks cheerily as he sees her. She laughs loudly, as is her wont. She knows exactly what he is referring to; the previous Friday, the *Mail & Guardian* had run a piece identifying Jacob Zuma's key advisors, or 'kitchen cabinet'.

'People like me know all about what being a kitchen girl is like,' she throws back at him as they pass, she teetering a little as her high stilettos sink into the plush red carpet, the svelte Collins swiftly bustling onwards towards the cabinet meeting room.

Zulu heads the other way, to the left, towards the mountain, down a short corridor and then up a narrow staircase to an even narrower corridor where her temporary office is located. It's obviously temporary because, from my vantage point on the two-person sofa inside, it has precious little in it, apart from Zulu's laptop bag, iPad and handbag.

I've been looking forward to seeing Ambassador Zulu again. (South Africa seems to have adopted the American approach to public office, which is that you retain your title even after you have left office.) Her name keeps cropping up in conversations and in documents.

I first met her in the 1990s, when she was a member of the Gauteng Provincial Legislature. She was young – in her mid-thirties – certainly considerably younger than most of her fellow ANC members of the provincial legislature (MPLs), and far smarter and more modern too. As the Deputy Speaker, she had a vision for the legislature that far outstripped anything else in the other eight provincial legislatures, which is why the Gauteng legislature ran so fast and so far ahead.

My memory of her from those days was as one of the most impressive young ANC people I had encountered and someone who was as authentically democratic in her political instincts as she was crisp and forthright in her points of view.

Since then, she has built up a formidable CV, working in the Department of

International Relations and Cooperation (DIRCO) as special advisor to then foreign minister Nkosazama Dlamini-Zuma; and as ambassador to Brazil – a significant posting.

Zulu is now Zuma's chief advisor on foreign affairs, but my gut tells me she is more than that. I have a hunch that she is becoming to Zuma what Mojanku Gumbi was to Thabo Mbeki: one of his most influential lieutenants.

Perhaps one of the most striking findings of *Anatomy of South Africa*, especially to anyone not close to the inner workings of the Mbeki presidency, was the presentation of Gumbi as one of the five most powerful people in South Africa. Advocate Gumbi, originally appointed as legal advisor to the president, had ended up years later representing Mbeki in meetings with Robert Mugabe in Zimbabwe and captains of industry at home.

Her job title had elongated over time. She had earned her place alongside Mbeki through her devotion to duty and her loyalty. Unlike Zulu, however, Gumbi was not an ANC person. Her background was the Azanian People's Organisation (AZAPO), which contributed to Mbeki's trust in her. She was absolutely no threat whatsoever; she had only his support and patronage to go on. Without that, at least so far as her position in government was concerned, she was nothing.

So any comparison between Zulu and Gumbi has its limits. Zulu is on the ANC's national executive committee, and has been since the national conference in Polokwane in 2007. She was elected for a second term in Mangaung in December 2012, in thirty-sixth place in the list of eighty. This gives her additional power, vested in her strength within the organisation itself.

'Politically,' Zulu tells me, 'this is very important. When I speak, I can speak not only with the president's authority, but with that of the ANC.'

Take Swaziland, she says: 'COSATU are pushing it, and they are right to. Because I am not part of DIRCO I don't have to worry [about longer-term diplomacy]. The Mangaung resolutions on Swaziland are much stronger and so when I meet with the king of Swaziland I say, "Your Majesty, the ANC has taken the position".'

This is extraordinary stuff. Sitting demurely on the two-person sofa in the colonial surrounds of Tuynhuis, with glorious Table Mountain looking down imperiously, I pour coffee and let what she has just told me sink in. 'Did you meet with the king of Swaziland alone?' I ask.

Yes, she says; twice, both times alone – just her and the king. Twice since Mangaung, armed with the tough new resolution that was passed by the ANC at its national conference in December 2012.

Imagine how that went down with the Swazi royalty. Zuma likes protocol. But he also knows how to play power politics. What better way to show who's boss in this relationship than to send one of my advisors to meet with you?

A woman, at that. Alone.

It tells us a lot about Zuma. And it also tells us a lot about Zulu, and how much she is trusted by the president and how much influence she has.

But the other point is this: Zulu clearly sees no difficulty whatsoever in using the ANC to buttress her position in such circumstances. She goes to meet with the head of state of a neighbouring country, but does so not only as the advisor to the president of South Africa, but as an elected member of the ANC's top decision-making body, its NEC. She knows, as we must all acknowledge, that the liberal nicety about the division between state and party means little these days in South Africa, and under Zuma the overlaps are even greater.

Foreign policy begins at home

One of the oldest clichés is that foreign policy begins at home. As with most clichés, there is a large grain of truth in this. Thus, in order to understand the way in which a country positions itself, especially when the global community is so obviously closely attached and the interests of nation states so interdependent in a globalised economy, it is essential that the drivers of policy at home – those, at least, that impact on foreign policy – are understood.

Navigating the murky waters of a country's foreign policy is not the easiest of expeditions to undertake. However, for the purposes of getting a grasp on how a country relates with the outside world, such an exploration is necessary.

As the Zuma era emerged and then unfolded, so foreign relations took on a different hue. Under Mbeki, there was considerable international interest in South Africa's foreign policy – partly because Mbeki himself paid a lot of attention to it and was a well-known figure on the international stage, with a substantial reputation as an international diplomat, and partly because South Africa continued to 'punch above its weight' in international affairs.

While Mbeki sometimes confused diplomats with his rhetorical flourishes and his convoluted or obscure reasoning, over time more seasoned watchers of South Africa's foreign policy making were able to make sense of things, not least because it was evident that foreign policy was controlled by a very small group of people.

Mbeki's attitude to Zimbabwe made for many a bad headache, and South Africa's record as a member of the UN Security Council (2007–08) surprised and even shocked some commentators. For example, South Africa controversially opposed, in league with Russia and China, the condemnation of human rights abuses in Myanmar and Zimbabwe, further sanctions against Iran over its nuclear programme and the inclusion of the issue of climate change on the Security Council agenda.[1]

Yet, despite this, the general view of South African political risk was relatively measured and comfortable.

When Zuma appeared on the horizon, and then toppled Mbeki, the political-risk analysts had to recalculate; Zuma was a far lesser-known commodity. Apart from his forays into Great Lakes peacemaking, not much was known about his attitude towards international affairs and little if anything could really be discerned from his domestic-policy positions because these were generally regarded as an 'ideology-free zone'.

Moreover, the stakes rose as South Africa's domestic conditions weakened. For those of us who are either self-proclaimed or regarded as 'political analysts', increased political risk is good for business. In the immediate aftermath of Marikana in August 2012, for example, the requests to postulate poured in – often from investment banks with increasingly twitchy clients. I did telephone conferences for the likes of Citibank and UBS; where usually the number of asset-manager clients who would likely call in would be as few as twenty, in the febrile post-Marikana mood, it increased to sixty or seventy.

Although the post-Mbeki concerns were primarily about domestic policy, there were also questions about foreign policy. Moreover, it was – and is – clear that perceptions about South Africa in the international investor community are often informed by how the country positions itself on global matters and foreign affairs, and also how agile and articulate its foreign policy makers and diplomatic representatives are in addressing concerns and reassuring investors.

Thus, those that make and deliver foreign policy wield significant influence over events that impact on South Africa at home, as well as abroad.

Foreign policy: The background and trajectory
In building South Africa's foreign policy in recent years, a great deal of attention has been paid to strengthening economic ties with major emerging markets, especially the so-called BRICS grouping comprising Brazil, Russia, India, China and South Africa.

South Africa's foreign policy has, therefore, largely been driven by its economic interests. Interestingly, there is no evidence to determine concretely how domestic private business interests shape the direction or manner in which South Africa engages other states in terms of this economic interest. Instead, insight must be gleaned from cases that come to light, such as the MTN Iran matter, where Turkcell brought proceedings in a US court alleging that MTN had used its influence with the South African government to help win a trillion-dollar licence to operate a GSM cellphone system in Iran, ousting Turkcell from the lucrative market in the process. When the allegations arose in early 2012, MTN appointed former UK law lord Lennie Hoffmann to head an internal inquiry into the allegations, which included bribery of key government officials in Iran. Hoffmann, in turn, commissioned me to write a report on South Africa's foreign policy and to assess whether or not there was reason to believe that MTN did influence South African foreign policy as a part of its courting of the Iranians.

Hoffmann's report is unequivocal in its conclusion: there is no evidence to support the allegations, either in respect of the bribery or the assertions about foreign-policy influence.[2] I had had little difficulty in reaching the same conclusion, which was essentially that, under Thabo Mbeki, South Africa's foreign policy was set fairly and that there was no evidence that it could have been, or was, redirected by MTN.[3]

However, I did note that 'it is important to recognise that a major driver of Mbeki's foreign policy was the need to find new markets for South African business and South African products and services. Iran represented, and was regarded by Pretoria, as a significant opportunity in this regard. As deputy foreign minister Aziz Pahad said in May 2006:

Iran has been an important oil supplier to South Africa. Our companies are now moving into Iran with new investments ... we try to say to our private sector that Iran is an important country, which after these tensions, it will continue to play a major role in the region and that it is vital for our private sector to begin to understand the potentials there.[4]

'And in 2005, Ambassador Martin Slabben, South African department of foreign affairs Director for Gulf Relations, was said to be "thrilled" by the Iranian government decision to award the contract to MTN.[5]

'The other major driving force behind South African foreign policy during the period 1997–2007 was the commitment to South-South relations, based partly on political solidarity but also on common economic interests. "South-South" relations refers to diplomatic and economic relations between countries of the "global South", as opposed to Western, developed nations; it is now an established term of art, used by diplomats, policy makers, academics and commentators when referring to economic, trade, technological, diplomatic and political co-operation between developing countries and/or emerging economies.

'In South Africa's case, a distinct element of this was Pretoria's self-regard in terms of its potential role as a mediatory force in international relations. After South Africa's transition to democracy, it assumed the status of leader in the Non-Aligned Movement and was considered a middle power because of its involvement in "international 'bridge-building' and multilateralism".'[6]

One reason that may account for South Africa's uncoordinated approach to issues of foreign policy may be the fact that there is little synergy between the institution that oversees South Africa's domestic and international economic affairs (the Department of Trade and Industry, DTI), that which oversees its international relations in general (DIRCO), and the Presidency.

During the Mbeki years, intra-government institutional relations were absolutely clear: foreign policy, like domestic policy, was run out of the Presidency. The fact that one of Mbeki's key advisors – perhaps *the* key advisor – his long-time friend and confidant Aziz Pahad, also happened to be deputy minister for foreign affairs throughout the whole of Mbeki's presidency did not make any difference: Pahad influenced Mbeki directly, and this influence played out through the decisions that Mbeki took as president rather than through Pahad's executive authority as deputy minister of foreign affairs.

Apart from the issue of coordination among government departments and institutions, there are also question marks about the way in which the chief implementers of foreign policy 'in the field' – namely, South Africa's ambassadorial representatives – are selected and then prepared for their important role.

Research shows that, while in some instances ambassadors have been appointed on the basis of experience in foreign relations, more often than not they have been appointed solely on the basis of domestic politics. Ordinarily, this should not be so much of a problem, because ambassadors act on the instructions they receive from DIRCO. However, it becomes a challenge when DIRCO is not in total control of all aspects of foreign policy or does not have sufficient technical capacity.

The aftermath of Polokwane and the defeat of the über-diplomat

Zuma's administration followed a long period dominated by what international-relations thinker and commentator Chris Landsberg called the 'über-diplomat', Thabo Mbeki. While Zuma's foreign policy has largely followed Mbeki's articulation of ANC foreign policy, it has had to operate within a markedly different global and domestic context: a post-financial-crisis world dominated by new emerging powers and, domestically, a post-Polokwane political term with new party power relations and players.

Zuma's first statement post-Polokwane, on 8 January 2008, showed then how the new ANC leadership would continue with foreign policy as drawn up by Mbeki prior to the ANC conference: 'We need to continue our work with like-minded governments and organisations to develop international institutions, rules and norms that will contribute to a more equitable world order. We must consolidate South–South relations through, among other things, continued engagement with India, Brazil and China.'[7]

Although the country's focus on South–South relations, trade and a continuation of an African-orientated agenda remains on the surface a further representation of continuity rather than change, behind the scenes new individuals have been jostling for influence over the country's foreign policy.

Moreover, beneath the surface there have been shifts in emphasis. Firstly, there is Zuma's desire to define his foreign-policy leadership style as different from that of his defeated political opponent. Independent Newspapers' Peter Fabricius calls it 'continuity, but a change of emphasis'. Secondly, there has been a stronger attempt to position South Africa within a new changing global order, by siding with BRICS nations and pursuing Chinese trade while pushing for its own trade and political interests in the region and on the continent.

And, thirdly, there has been a move to balance Zuma's own political interests – by delivering rewards for those who supported him at Polokwane and securing support (especially in the provinces) for political survival at Mangaung, primarily through appointments as ambassadors and advisors.

South Africa overseas: The appointment of ambassadors

South Africa has 103 embassies, 14 consulates and 64 honorary consulates abroad.[8] South Africa's hybrid system of government means that the president wears two constitutional hats: one as state president, the other as head of government.[9] When the president appoints ambassadors under section 84(2)(i) he does so as head of state and, accordingly, may do so without having to expressly exercise his power 'together with other members of the cabinet' as he must do when exercising authority as head of the national executive (section 85(2)). There are plenty of slots to fill, so there is ample opportunity for dispensing patronage and sending difficult people and enemies to Siberia – in some cases almost literally.

While for most 'foreign policy begins at home', in Zuma's case foreign policy begins with the need to shore up support in the provinces.

Since his great victory at Polokwane in 2007, Zuma has posted several ANC political leaders to far-flung countries after they were either rocked by scandal, had a bumpy stint in government or were discovered to constitute a possible future threat to the ANC's stability and/or Zuma's leadership. Sometimes these postings will reflect Zuma's need to manoeuvre within the ANC or its broader political alliance – for example, sending Malema's former secretary-general, Vuyiswa Tulelo, to Chicago as consul-general in 2012.

In 2011, the *Mail & Guardian* noted: 'Zuma recently sent a number of political outcasts to diplomatic missions abroad, in keeping with his policy of not alienating potential political opponents.'[10] The newspaper listed a number of Limpopo leaders who had been trained and were waiting to be posted to head up diplomatic missions. Former Limpopo finance and treasury member of the executive council (MEC) Sa'ad Cachalia was appointed ambassador to Qatar, while Stan Mathabatha, from the Limpopo Enterprise Development Agency, was appointed ambassador to Ukraine, Armenia, Georgia and Moldova. Cachalia and Miriam Segabutla were both advisors to Limpopo premier Cassel Mathale after they were appointed to the provincial cabinet in 2009.

From the Western Cape, former premier Ebrahim Rasool was shipped to Washington DC in late 2010. Rasool's appointment to the US followed volatile infighting in the Western Cape ANC that led to his removal as premier in July 2008. A month later, Rasool was appointed as special advisor to then president Kgalema Motlanthe after Mbeki was recalled.

Even after this, infighting in the party's provincial structures continued and by November 2009 the ANC in the province had charged Rasool, along with Max Ozinsky, with bringing the party into disrepute. The ANC's charges had been dropped by 2010 and Rasool was sent to the US capital. Trouble, however, followed Rasool over the 'brown envelope' scandal, and in 2011 the *Mail & Guardian* ran an article about rumours that he might be recalled.[11] But earlier knowledge about it didn't prevent the ANC or Zuma's administration from deciding against his initial posting.[12]

Zuma has also appointed former ANC Western Cape spokesperson Shaun Byneveldt as ambassador to Syria and former provincial minister for social development Kholeka Mqulwana to Australia.

After a cabinet reshuffle in 2010, Zuma sent four sacked ministers, one high-ranking official and an ousted premier to embassies abroad. Noluthando Mayende-Sibiya, the fired minister for women and children and people with disabilities, went to Egypt, while labour minister Membathisi Mdladlana was sent to Burundi, public works minister Geoff Doidge to Sri Lanka and minister of sport and recreation Makhenkesi Arnold Stofile to Germany. Zuma's highly regarded director-general in the Presidency, Vusi Mavimbela, went to the embassy in Harare, Zimbabwe, after Zuma decided that the alchemy was not quite right and that he needed a closer ally as director-general. Former North West premier Maureen Modiselle was appointed high commissioner to Trinidad and Tobago after she was removed as head of the provincial government.[13]

Zuma similarly dealt with staunch Mbeki supporters early in his administration by sending former minister of social development Zola Skweyiya to the high commission in London and former correctional services minister Ngconde Balfour to Gaborone, Botswana. Balfour resigned only a year later.[14] Another Mbeki loyalist, former health DG Thami Mseleku, who was despised by the Treatment Action Campaign for his uncompromising execution of the controversial HIV/AIDS denialist policies of Mbeki and his eccentric health minister, Manto Tshabalala-Msimang, was appointed high commissioner to Malaysia in 2010.[15]

Zuma's administration has also appointed two controversial former newspaper columnists. Mohau Pheko was appointed to the embassy in Canada even after she left the *Sunday Times* under a cloud and accusations of plagiarism.[16]

In 2008, Jon Qwelane had written in his *Sunday Sun* column that homosexuality was wrong and a degradation of the country's values and traditions. In 2010, he was appointed to Uganda, where homosexuality is illegal and gay men have been executed. In 2011, the Johannesburg Equality Court found him guilty of hate speech, but even then the Zuma administration refused to recall him, DIRCO announcing publicly that they didn't see any problem with Qwelane's appointment.[17]

Arguably, Zuma's actions have further politicised the diplomatic service. Though, as former deputy foreign minister (2004–10) Sue van der Merwe points out, the making of 'political' diplomatic appointments is commonplace around the world and is often strategically justified, as in the case of Skweyiya, who was given the blue-chip posting in London – a 'perfectly appropriate and defendable political appointment, given his seniority within the movement', says Van der Merwe.

Although Van der Merwe is no longer formally in government, she continues to contribute to international trade as a member of the Portfolio Committee on Trade and Industry in Parliament and, informally, to diplomacy – often as a sounding board for DIRCO officials or home-coming diplomats, or, her special forte, foreign diplomats based in South Africa.

Van der Merwe knows the service well because, for the six and a half years she was in office, her job was to 'keep the shop in order' while her fellow deputy minister of foreign affairs, Aziz Pahad, travelled the world conducting South Africa's high-end diplomacy. At least, as she puts it now, that was 'what President Mbeki said he wanted me to do in the five seconds we spoke at the time of my appointment'.

As she had been his parliamentary counsellor to the president based in the Presidency, Mbeki knew he could trust her. And she remains an Mbeki loyalist in many respects. She is not by any means a typical ANC politician: with her cut-glass English accent and pearls, she could easily be mistaken for a grand dame of the southern suburbs, lunching for a living. Instead, she is a long-standing member of the ANC's NEC, re-elected at the Mangaung conference in December 2012.

She is also a long-time member of the NEC's subcommittee on foreign relations. Part of her role has been, and continues to be, to spend plenty of time with foreign diplomats, who come to know and respect her, recognising that she can provide what DIRCO often can't – because of undue caution or diplomatic protocol, or simply being overstretched – namely, reliable information about the state of thinking within the ANC and the government.

Because of her knowledge, charm and – let me be candid at the risk of being sexist – good looks, which in the mainly male foreign diplomatic corps is a considerable competitive advantage, she is much sought after for meetings, as well as for the numerous cocktail parties and other functions held at the various embassies and high commissions in the leafy Pretoria and Cape Town suburbs of Waterkloof and Bishopscourt respectively.

Despite what the Constitution implies, Van der Merwe says that the president does not make ambassadorial appointments alone, but in practice in consultation with the minister of international relations. She accepts that there has been an increase in political appointments in recent years.

A couple of days after I talked with Van der Merwe, one of the more 'bizarre appointments that have been made' – as a DIRCO source put it – was reported to have been sent home from China after being found wandering the streets of Shanghai naked at night. Lassy Chiwayo was appointed consular-general to China in 2012, removing him from the troubled Mbombela Municipality in Mpumalanga where he had served as mayor. Chiwayo stood for ANC provincial chairman in 2008, but lost to current Mpumalanga premier David Mabuza. Chiwayo instituted investigations into alleged corruption in preparation for the 2010 FIFA World Cup, but was replaced as mayor in 2011. During these investigations, key witnesses were assassinated, while Chiwayo was treated for severe stress.

What better solution than to send him to represent the country in one of the most powerful cities of the twenty-first century? I ask Van der Merwe why this sort of appointment happens and why someone like Chiwayo is not simply discarded. 'It's not how the ANC works,' she replies drily. But she does acknowledge that appointments of this nature, or of an overt political patronage type, do 'create a tension within the department [DIRCO] when they see prime positions going to political appointees'.

For some career diplomats, it is 'terrible', she concedes.

It also leads to some confusion. Political appointees are supposed to serve one term and then come back. Yet often they don't; they can end up serving two, three or more.

As Van der Merwe says, 'Some of these appointees don't know if they will become career diplomats or be offered a second posting ... that's another problem.' They will ring up Van der Merwe and ask, 'Can I ask for another term?' 'Some of them end up serving four terms,' she says. 'And I don't know how that works.'

Sometimes a politician will transition into the diplomatic service almost by osmosis. Thenjiwe Mtintso is a case in point. The SACP stalwart and former Umkhonto we Sizwe (MK) leader was initially appointed as ambassador to Cuba in 2007 because of her stature in the organisation, but once her term expired in 2010, she was given another ambassadorial posting to Italy.

In terms of rank and pay, each ambassadorial position comes with a ceiling. Brazil, London and India will typically be chief directors. Sometimes deputy DGs are deployed to ambassadorial positions – they keep the pay grade, but do not get the expense allowances of the higher public-service ranking.

Yet many ambassadors are directors or even deputy directors – relatively low in the public-service ranking – in 'Uruguay or somewhere', Van der Merwe says with a barely concealed edge of disdain. However, perversely, Dumisani Kumalo remained at the modest director level in New York at the UN for eighteen years, despite the seniority of his posting and the high level of influence he enjoyed thanks to Mbeki's willingness to rely on his judgement when deciding on South Africa's position on UN resolutions.

What of the opposition? I was aghast when I heard that Tony Leon, the former leader of the Democratic Alliance, had been appointed as ambassador to Argentina. Buenos Aires is one of my favourite cities. It's a plum job. What on earth did he do to deserve that?

I was so disillusioned I penned a caustic, ironic open letter in my *Mail & Guardian* column, Contretemps:

Dear Tony (if I may),
I would like to congratulate you on your appointment as South Africa's next ambassador to Argentina. But I can't. I am struggling to summon the good-will to do so. I had not anticipated arriving at this point of extreme envy, but Buenos Aires is such a delicious city. I simply cannot help myself; the truth is this: I want your job (which is really not a phrase I ever expected to utter –). What did you do to deserve such a succulent posting? After all, Ngconde Balfour got Botswana. He is a far better cricketer than I suspect you will ever be: what on earth did he do to deserve Gaborone? In fact, now one looks at it afresh, the Democratic Alliance seems to do rather well out of these diplo-matic appointments. Your fellow parliamentary sniper, Douglas Gibson, got Thailand; Sandra Botha, for a while leader of the DA in Parliament, got the Czech Republic – Prague, another of the world's great cities.
Admittedly, another former DA MP, Sheila Camerer, got Bulgaria, and Sofia is hardly in the Prague-Bangkok-Buenos Aires league for exotic enter-tainment and café society, but Bulgarians should not be underrated; they can be terribly good fun.
So, one is back to the fundamental question: how did you, of all people, land this job? Clearly, I have been going about things in entirely the wrong

way – carefully choosing my words, articulating a delicate sense of empathy, striving for balanced commentary that did justice to the constitutional imperative of accountability and oversight while recognising the challenges of being in power.

Instead, I should have been adopting a completely different tone when dealing with the ruling class and the ANC establishment. Your approach – acidic, sarcastic, snobbish, scoffing, condescending, unforgiving, smug, patronising, sneering, but otherwise totally reasonable – has prevailed.

Silly, naive me; and well done you.

I mean, it is not as if they – the new administration – need you out of the way, do they? You had reclined into submissive semi-retirement.

The fat biography in the bag; the increasingly genteel and elegantly penned journalistic missives from the election front; your apparent conversion to the Zumaresque modality of collective leadership; and the paternalistic columns of recent weeks – surely this gentler, softer Leon had nothing to do with your appointment? Though it sticks in the craw, I have to hand it to you. Buenos Aires. Congratulations. I have, at last, seen the errors of my ways. Forget democratic socialism and social democracy, egalitarianism and social transformation: I shall join the forces of (neo)liberalism that you expounded with such unforgiving ferocity. I am, now, a true convert.

Yours etc.[18]

Leon did not, apparently, see the funny side of this. Or perhaps he just takes himself too seriously to have been able to do so, because when I bumped into him at the British High Commission party on the eve of the state opening of Parliament in February the following year (2010), he shunned my greeting of 'Good evening, Mr Ambassador'. It was a variation on an earlier theme when as DA leader he once told me to 'fuck off'. However, once he had stepped down we had exchanged pleasantries on more than one occasion at the Sports Science Institute gym in Newlands and, bearing him no ill will, despite what he claims was my modest role in his decision to give up the leadership of the DA (on account of what I had to say about him in *Anatomy of South Africa*), I was looking forward to a thawing of our relationship, because Leon does have an enjoyably sharp wit – though not, clearly, one that extends to himself.

More space for foreign policy making at home

Despite the obvious problems of his approach to diplomatic appointments, as always with Zuma, his overall approach to policy created new space for debate. When Mbeki was ousted in Polokwane, party members welcomed more openness. Foreign policy has also become a more openly contested space within the

Alliance. Examples of a more robust internal foreign-policy debate included the occasions in June 2008 when the ANC publicly pleaded with ZANU-PF to adhere to Southern African Development Community (SADC) guidelines,[19] and in December 2008 when Sisisi Tolashe, secretary-general of the ANC Women's League, said that 'the political crisis of Zimbabwe has come to a point whereby no peace loving person can keep quiet and say nothing especially when you see the depth of its effects on ordinary Zimbabweans especially women and children'.[20]

Other critical voices were heard from COSATU on Zimbabwe and Swaziland as late as 2011, and from the ANC Youth League on Botswana and Zuma's dealings with Libya and foreign policy.

Zuma has been quick to side with new allies in southern Africa that were previously sidelined by Mbeki, most obviously Angolan president José Eduardo dos Santos. Zuma made his first trip as ANC leader to Luanda in 2008, and his first state visit was not to a traditional Western trading partner but rather to Angola, a developing country in the middle of an economic boom. Although South Africa has visited the European Union, France and the UK during Zuma's administration, BRICS countries have attracted some of the biggest delegations.

By January 2009, one of Zuma's most trusted lieutenants, Ebrahim Ebrahim, had laid the groundwork for what was to become the Zuma administration's style of foreign policy when he told the *Sunday Independent* that, in respect of Zimbabwe, 'Mbeki has failed. He has not achieved the government of national unity. It's gone back to SADC now.' He said he is 'not sure what the government is going to do, but I would advise that if one of the parties doesn't want Mbeki, then he should be replaced by someone who is acceptable to all parties. That's what I'm prepared to say to [ANC leader Jacob] Zuma.'[21]

The Zimbabwean Global Political Agreement (GPA) was Mbeki's last big diplomatic victory before he was removed from the Union Buildings by the ANC. In June 2009, Ebrahim, by then deputy minister of foreign affairs, told the *Sunday Independent* that Zuma's administration would take 'a different tone ... more critical of Mugabe'. He believed Mbeki's GPA was 'a flawed agreement and the onus should be put on SADC, who put the agreement together initially, to ensure that Mugabe upholds the agreement'.[22]

Again, in July 2011, he said: 'President Zuma is prepared to have open confrontation with Mugabe.'[23] Certainly a clear shift from Mbeki's 'quiet diplomacy'.

Despite Zuma's attempts to distance himself from Mbeki's ANC, the party's loyalty to Mugabe remains. In December 2011, ANC secretary-general Gwede Mantashe offered ZANU-PF the ANC's support during the coming 2012 Zimbabwean elections: 'Our relationship is steeped in blood, the ANC wishes to affirm her commitment as a trust-worthy neighbour.'[24] He continued: 'That is government. We are liberation movements. The government was appointed by SADC to mediate, and we are liberation movements that have a history.'[25]

But back in 2009, Zuma was determined to distance himself from Mbeki's foreign policy as much as party policy allowed and his apparently fresh, firm stance on Mugabe delighted the UK and other European nations that had long been frustrated by Mbeki's approach. He talked to the idea of going back to a 'human-rights-based' foreign policy. DIRCO's white paper on foreign policy, released in 2011, recalled these ideals with its term 'the Diplomacy of Ubuntu'. The white paper stated: 'South Africa's unique approach to global issues has found expression in the concept of Ubuntu ... It recognizes that it is in our national interest to promote and support the positive development of others.'[26]

However, as Nomfundo Ngwenya, now a National Treasury chief director on policy towards the BRICS and, specifically, the development of a BRICS bank, says: 'It's an overstatement to say that the "Diplomacy of Ubuntu" places South Africa's foreign policy in a human rights tradition of foreign policy.'

Rather, she says, 'the idea refers to greater political and economic cooperation that is mutually beneficial [hence the term ubuntu], instead of a traditional Realist approach to foreign policy that maximises benefits for one party based on national interest'.

Other insiders are less polite. One long-time ministerial advisor in government describes ubuntu as 'absolute rubbish ... we'd never heard of it in exile'.

Other commentators were quick to deride the idea. Senior lecturer in the political science department at the University of Pretoria and former chief director of trade policy at the DTI Mzukisi Qobo[27] claimed that the idea of 'ubuntu diplomacy' was stillborn, fizzling out in DIRCO's own white paper. He wrote in the *Mail & Guardian*:

> There are no solid ideas or compelling substance that defines this new diplomacy ... Fundamentally, the paper fails to project a clear purpose for South Africa's foreign policy or to unveil new instruments and tools that would lend strong meaning to the alignment between foreign policy and key domestic priorities ... Each page reminds us that things will stay the same. The rhetoric has just changed its inflection. Anyone who expects to see new ideas under [minister of international relations and cooperation] Nkoana-Mashabane is sure to be disappointed.[28]

Economic relations

In May 2009, Zuma addressed Parliament for the first time as the president of South Africa. He said government must 'ensure that our foreign relations contribute to the creation of an environment conducive to sustainable economic growth and development'.[29]

Chris Landsberg replied: 'This is the closest we have to a foreign policy doctrine of the Zuma government.'[30] Economic relations, especially to new emerging economies like China, India and Brazil, has become the key foreign-policy pillar in the Zuma administration, as evidenced by the Dalai Lama debacle. Shortly after the Dalai Lama was denied a visa to South Africa during the brief Motlanthe administration in 2009, the new foreign minister, Maite Nkoana-Mashabane – a 'left-field' appointment in the Zuma cabinet – promised Parliament that if he applied again, his application would be approved.[31] However, two years later, the Zuma administration stalled the Dalai Lama's next visa application.[32] Mkuseli Apleni, DG for home affairs, admitted in an affidavit to the Cape High Court that South Africa's membership in BRICS and Deputy President Kgalema Motlanthe's Chinese visit, as well as Pretoria's One China policy, would have made it difficult to decide in favour of the Dalai Lama. He said he was wary of a falling-out with China similar to that experienced by other countries (like France and Australia) that had granted the Dalai Lama a visa.[33]

IBSA: The 'other BRICS'
South Africa was caught on the back foot when the BRIC (Brazil, Russia, India and China) grouping was first formed. Back in 2009, South Africa was still placing its main bets with IBSA – the India-Brazil-South Africa axis that had been an Mbeki brainchild – as a way to bring about change to multilateral institutions and the 'international architecture'.[34]

Ayanda Ntsaluba, DG of DIRCO at the time, optimistically told the media in August 2009 how South Africa's ministers were looking to forge ahead and get Brazil and India to help 'create synergies between IBSA and BRIC [note the lack of an 'S' at that time] given the participation of both India and Brazil in the BRIC formation'.[35]

The BRIC grouping was the creation of Jim O'Neill from Goldman Sachs, who referred to it in a 2001 economics paper about the wealthiest developing nations. He sketched a scenario called 'Building Better Global Economic BRICs' and painted a picture of how the BRIC nations would overtake the wealthiest G6 nations by 2050 in terms of GDP.[36]

In June 2009, India and Brazil attended the first BRIC summit in Yekaterinburg, Russia, where the political group was formalised for the first time. 'Many commentators saw the "historic event" as a trump by Russia's President Dmitry Medvedev over the US, bringing four big emerging powers together under the Russian umbrella into a new global force,' *Business Report* wrote.[37]

South Africa was initially left out of the grouping and worked hard during 2010 to lobby old IBSA partners, and also China, to include South Africa as its 'Gateway to Africa' partner. In late October 2009, Ntsaluba had said, 'Brazil, Russia, India and China are trillion dollar economies. South Africa is not a trillion dollar economy ... [but] South Africa has certain strategic advantages ... a significant place on the continent and is also a significant player among the formations of the South.'[38]

South Africa joined BRICS at the turn of 2010/11 – a quiet time in the country's news cycle. This meant our new membership was met with positive coverage, and a lot of it, though sceptics such as Qobo remained unconvinced: 'Three years ago, before Zuma ascended to power, it was unthinkable that South Africa's foreign policy would ever be dictated by another country, or that the government would easily sell its soul in exchange for maintaining a commercial relationship with a country ... When South Africa lobbied to be allowed into the Bric (Brazil, Russia, India and China) club, it was a sign that its foreign policy was undergoing a prolonged crisis of confidence. Opportunistically, China took up South Africa's cause and ensured the country's acceptance into this elite club of economically influential emerging economies. It is partly this debt that South Africa is repaying today – at the cost of its values.'[39]

Other commentators chimed in: 'Since the end of the Mbeki administration, there has been concern about the lack of clear sense of leadership, inspirations and purpose in the South African foreign policy,' said Wits University's Jan Smuts Professor of International Relations Gilbert Khadiagala. 'Jacob Zuma's administration has favoured a more institutional approach and it is debatable whether the Department of International Relations and Cooperation (Dirco) has seized this opportunity to lead.'[40]

5

The foreign policy makers

Under President Zuma, advisors and other foreign policy makers matter a lot more than before. Zuma's influential foreign policy advisor, Lindiwe Zulu, puts it like this: 'With Mbeki, it was all about him and his approach to foreign affairs. He was very hands-on. Whereas this presidency is more hands-on domestically. He says that "it is all very well to look good internationally but not good for us to be looking bad internally" ... He allows the Department of International Relations and the DTI to have the space to run with the projects that they need to run with.

'Therefore, the role of the advisor is very important because it means I need to have a really strong understanding of what the projects and programmes are and a strong link with the relevant departments – for example, my work as part of the president's team on Zimbabwe ... with DIRCO and DTI, with Treasury in the case of Zimbabwe, and to some extent with Intelligence.'

'So I cannot not get on with DIRCO,' Zulu says of her relationship with the department. 'I have to call inter-departmental meetings.' Fortunately, she worked for a number of years in the department, including as advisor to former foreign affairs minister Dlamini-Zuma and as the chief director of west and central Africa. She used to sit on the inter-ministerial committee; she knows the bureaucracy of DIRCO and 'who to call' on any given issue.

'This president says that "I need the departments to have the institutional memory",' she adds. In practical terms, this means that people who were previously excluded from key meetings are now included. Unless it's a meeting of the principals, i.e. Zuma and his counterpart, he will want others to sit in. In Mbeki's case, with the occasional exception of Gumbi or Aziz, he would often prefer to meet with his opposite number alone.

This new approach has created some awkward situations. 'We had to make the parties comfortable,' says Zulu, citing the case of Zimbabwe. 'Formerly, the ambassador used not to be part of the meetings. But now we ask him to sit in because he needs to be informed and to be able to sustain things when we [the presidential envoys] leave.'

Zulu meets with Zuma weekly: 'He tells me, "I am giving you Zimbabwe to work on", and he normally gives me the things that are a bit of a big challenge,' Zulu chuckles, clearly relishing the responsibility that he gives her, 'such as Zimbabwe and the DRC, where I must work carefully with the minister of defence.'

I ask about relations with Intelligence. Mbeki had his own private intelligence service, run out of the Union Buildings, as I revealed in *Anatomy of South Africa* – the innocuous-sounding Presidential Support Unit, which could have been a group of typists, but was in fact a small team of spooks whose job it was to run around the world gathering intelligence and then to report back to Mbeki so that he could second-guess the official intelligence service.

Zulu responds: 'This president expects us to meet very closely with Intelligence. He gets his normal reports from them. He wants to see institutional capacity. If you have all these high-level things, he asks, "What will happen lower down?"'

Zulu is clearly a pivotal link between the Presidency, DIRCO and other key agencies such as the State Security Agency. 'My role,' she adds, is that 'I must look for the potholes' – which is a wonderfully crisp summary of the role of any high-level political advisor anywhere in the world.

The Zuma administration's focus on economic growth as a key component of South Africa's foreign policy has brought with it new individuals, ministers and outside state players, who are all part of a contest for control over foreign policy. They include:

- DIRCO leaders like Ebrahim Ebrahim (Zuma's own Aziz Pahad and chair on foreign policy within the party) and cabinet minister Maite Nkoana-Mashabane as a close confidante;
- DTI minister Rob Davies and his department's new desks that mimic those of DIRCO;
- National Treasury and minister Pravin Gordhan's influence on BRICS, EU and Southern African Customs Union (SACU) matters; and
- public enterprises minister Malusi Gigaba, a key bagman for Zuma in the party's politics, but also in charge of a ministry at the helm of 'state capitalism'.

You will also find business leaders like empowerment giant Iqbal Survé, political families, ANC leaders and party funders all scuffling for influence over foreign policy.

In May 2009, the media and analysts expected Zuma not to have the same focus and direct involvement in foreign policy as Mbeki had. Reports said responsibilities were to be delegated down to Deputy President Kgalema Motlanthe. But figures show Zuma left the country twenty-six times in his first year of office, compared to Mbeki's twenty-two times in his first year.[1]

When Zuma announced his cabinet, many were surprised by Nkoana-Mashabane's appointment as minister of DIRCO. Before then, she was MEC for housing and local government in Limpopo. Baleka Mbete, ANC chairperson and deputy president in Motlanthe's government, and party heavyweight Lindiwe Sisulu were the favourites to get the job.

Mbete has since played a key role in ANC party international relations, especially using her good relationship with Nigeria's Goodluck Jonathan. Sisulu was given the barely less-weighty position of minister for defence (until her 'demotion' to the pivotal portfolio of public service and administration in 2012).

The media assumed Zuma's relatively junior choice for a minister of foreign affairs reflected his administration's domestic focus. 'Maite Nkoana-Mashabane is the big newcomer, and seen as an unusual choice. However, she serves on the party's powerful national working committee and is no stranger to the diplomatic scene,' *Business Day* reported.[2] 'One of the biggest surprises was the appointment of former Limpopo local government MEC and former ambassador to India, Maite Nkoana-Mashabane, as minister of international relations and co-operation,' said *Independent Online*.[3]

Nkoana-Mashabane wasn't a complete novice to international relations. She had accompanied Zuma and Ebrahim to most international political-party engagements in 2008 and early 2009. With hindsight, she was clearly being groomed for the position. She had also been an ambassador for a decade, to Malaysia (1995–99) and India (1999–2005).

Within the Presidency itself, Zuma appointed advisors who were to assist him with foreign policy, economic policy, intelligence and security, but also mediation in Zimbabwe and elsewhere in the region and on the continent.[4] They were leading spook Welile Nhlapo as national security advisor; Mandisi Mpahlwa as economic advisor; Charles Nqakula as political advisor (a Mbekite who had switched to Zuma in the run-up to Polokwane); Lindiwe Zulu as international relations advisor; Bonisiwe Makhene as legal advisor; and Mac Maharaj as part of the special envoy team for Zimbabwe. Nhlapo and Mpahlwa were subsequently redeployed within foreign affairs.

People in power: The president's men and women

Welile Nhlapo: National security advisor
Although used by Mbeki on security issues, Nhlapo has had close ties to Zuma as an international mediator. They worked together in Burundi, where he was part of a technical team assisting Zuma's mediation efforts in the Great Lakes region. Nhlapho also served as South Africa's representative to the African Union mission in Burundi and, before that, as ambassador to Ethiopia.

Before his appointment as Zuma's national security advisor in 2009, Nhlapo served as ambassador to the US in Washington during the Mbeki and Motlanthe governments. In June 2011, he was appointed 'South Africa's Special Representative to the Great Lakes Region' at DIRCO, a position formerly held by Mbeki confidant Dumisani Kumalo since shortly after Zuma took up office in May 2009.

Kumalo represented South Africa at the UN during Mbeki's term and at the UN Security Council during South Africa's first term. He resigned after he was recalled and joined the University of South Africa (UNISA) as an academic at the Thabo Mbeki African Leadership Institute, telling friends how 'nice it is to be in a think tank, such a luxury to be able to say and write what you like', which was ironic given the, at times, vitriolic attitude he had displayed towards such think tanks during his long tenure as UN ambassador under Mbeki.

Regarding Nhlapo's appointment, the Presidency said: 'The appointment is aimed at further boosting and strengthening South Africa's cooperation and relations with countries in the Great Lakes, which includes Burundi, Uganda, Tanzania, Democratic Republic of Congo, and Rwanda.'[5] Stability in the DRC and the Great Lakes region is important to South Africa's economy, but Rwanda has been a thorny issue for South Africa since June 2010, when Rwanda's former army chief, Faustin Kayumba Nyamwasa, was nearly assassinated in Johannesburg. Nyamwasa, who had received refugee status after arriving in South Africa in early 2010, was shot outside his security-complex home in Atholl.

Nhlapo's appointment as Special Representative to the Great Lakes Region in June 2011 was said to be purely for intelligence and security reasons. And there may well have been good reasons to deploy an intelligence operative of such seniority and experience as Nhlapo, who was head of Mbeki's 'private spooks' team, the Presidential Support Unit, which reported directly to Mbeki on issues of geopolitical or regional security or of strategic significance or interest to him personally.

Earlier in the year, Nhlapo had been in Libya and Zimbabwe as part of Zuma's 'envoys to represent him in Libya and Zimbabwe on missions to find solutions to political conflicts and stalemates'.[6] The minister of state security, Siyabonga Cwele, and the deputy minister of international relations, Ebrahim Ebrahim, had accompanied him. (Zuma has also sent Cwele to Sudan on missions, reinforcing the notion that Zuma – who headed the ANC's intelligence division in exile for many years – sees foreign policy making and intelligence gathering as intertwined.)

Mandisi Mpahlwa: Economic advisor

Mpahlwa was appointed economic advisor after underperforming in cabinet as minister of trade and industry from 2004 to 2009. His tenure is probably best represented by the bungling of the National Lottery between 2006 and 2008. Just a year into his position as economic advisor, Zuma's presidency was rocked by a series of resignations. In July 2010, Collins Chabane, minister in the Presidency, announced Mpahlwa was to take over as ambassador to Russia. 'His mandate is to work towards further deepening relations with Russia, which is part of the Brazil-Russia-India-China (BRIC) axis, an important partner for South Africa economically and politically,' read a statement put out by the Presidency.[7]

'It was felt that given the importance of Russia, we needed a seasoned cadre to represent the president and the national interest in that country,' said Chabane.[8] However, according to *Business Day*, Mpahlwa's move was more likely due to speculation about 'inactivity and stagnation in the Presidency' than anything else.[9] Other newspapers like the *Sunday Independent* reported that Zuma didn't trust certain advisors in the Presidency because of their closeness with Mbeki, and it is clear that during the early months of Zuma's reign, the Presidency was wracked with paranoia.

Despite being regarded as an 'Mbeki man', for a time Mpahlwa was also Zuma's sherpa or point man for G20 and G8 interfaces, as well as for the New Partnership for Africa's Development (NEPAD), before he was replaced by George Nene. But, one by one, Mbekites have been removed from positions of influence close to the Presidency. So while some, such as Tito Mboweni in Mangaung in 2012, have begun to make comebacks, in terms of advisors, most have now been cleared out by Zuma.

Charles Nqakula: Political advisor

Since Mbeki's former minister of defence, Nqakula, was appointed as political advisor to Zuma, he has largely been tasked with international relations, especially within the region.

He was part of the South African facilitating team sent to Zimbabwe to ensure credible elections in 2012 – subsequently postponed to 2013 – and the adoption of a new constitution. The team consisted of Nqakula, Lindiwe Zulu and spokesperson Mac Maharaj.

Although also assigned to mediatory talks in the Madagascar conflict, Nqakula served largely as a support to former Mozambican president Joaquim Chissano, who was leading the process, before DIRCO deputy minister Marius Fransman took over from Nqakula and secured a victory for South Africa's diplomacy.[10] Nqakula is considered a relatively good negotiator and was previously involved with the Burundi talks, led by Zuma.

More recently, he was tasked with drumming up support among African countries for the election of Nkosazana Dlamini-Zuma to chairperson of the AU Commission. Zambian president Michael Sata reportedly embarrassed Nqakula by interrupting him and telling the media that Nqakula was there not to congratulate Sata for his election victory, but to ensure support for Dlamini-Zuma.[11]

Zuma has since appointed Nqakula as presidential envoy to South Sudan to assist South Africa's involvement in securing Africa's newest nation.

Lindiwe Zulu: International relations advisor

As I noted in Chapter 4, Zulu is a close confidante to Zuma, both in the Presidency and on the ANC's NEC. They first met when Zuma headed the ANC office in Swaziland and Mozambique during apartheid. Zulu was born in KwaZulu-Natal, grew up in Swaziland, studied journalism in Moscow and was an Umkhonto we Sizwe operative in Angola.[12]

Before she was appointed as international relations advisor to Zuma, she worked as the South African ambassador to Brazil. She returned to South Africa to assist the ANC with communications in the run-up to the national election in 2009.[13]

Zulu has been at the forefront of Zuma's foreign policy, outspoken and some-times taking the lead in negotiations, especially with regards to Zuma's 'tougher stance' on mediation in Zimbabwe. In May 2011, Zimbabwean newspapers were filled with reports about Zulu's so-called 'reckless and inflammatory' behaviour during mediation. State newspaper the *Sunday Mail* wrote: 'It is understood that before the formal complaint, Vice-President John Nkomo had last week also raised concerns about Ms Zulu's conduct to President Zuma. Sources say Mr Zuma agreed that indeed "the girl's wings should be clipped".'[14] Jonathan Moyo, Zimbab-we's former minister of information, even went so far as to brand Zulu an 'enemy'.

Zulu seems to be secure in her political standing. Charles Molele of the *Mail & Guardian* wrote after an interview with her: 'Zulu laughed out loud when I put it to her that making such statements in a politically-charged environment ahead of the ANC's conference in Mangaung could be a career-ending move.'[15]

This followed her criticism of Julius Malema's statements on Zimbabwe and Botswana. She had told the *Sunday Times* that the ANC must act against Malema if it was to regain the respect of neighbouring countries. 'I was in Zimbabwe not so long ago and people there were saying: "What's wrong with you? What's hap-pening? Tell us whether the Youth League is the one in charge so that we can talk to the Youth League and not you." You don't like getting to places and getting such statements. I feel they should be disciplined. We can't keep talking about this discipline in corners … there were issues that the ANC agreed upon in as far as comrade Malema is concerned. I sit here and ask myself: "Where is that pro-cess? Does [Malema] really understand the impact of some of his utterances?"' she said.[16]

She also voiced her opinion when Malema called for a 'regime change' in Botswana. The *Daily Maverick* wrote: 'The League's Botswana plan has caused red faces all round in the ANC government, with Zuma's advisor on international affairs Lindiwe Zulu complaining that foreign diplomats had been calling her, asking whether the league was articulating ANC policy, and if not, why the ANC could not rein it in. She called for disciplinary action to be taken.'[17]

When Zulu testified during Malema's disciplinary committee hearing, she related how ambassadors from the Netherlands, the US and Sweden had all sought clarification from her as to whether the ANC saw Malema's utterances as interfering with Botswana as a sovereign country. At a SADC summit, a Botswana official had jokingly asked if South Africa planned to remove the Botswana government from power.[18] Zulu told the committee how the Chinese government had also sought clarification on Malema's utterances in relation to China's role in South Africa's economy and the ANC's stance. She did admit, however, that Malema was correct to say the African Agenda was in decline, but that it was more due to the collective failure of the AU and the SADC.[19]

She also criticised Archbishop Emeritus Desmond Tutu in October 2011 for speaking against the government's handling of the Dalai Lama's visa applications. Zulu told the *Mail & Guardian* that Zuma 'has been consistent' on foreign-policy matters. 'His consistency is derived from the policies and resolutions of the ANC. His positions are also informed by decisions taken by regional structures such as SADC, the AU and COMESA [the Common Market for Eastern and Southern Africa]. He consults others before acting. He is driven by the quest for peace, security and political stability on the African continent,' she told the paper.[20]

Despite her resoluteness, when Zulu pushed Zimbabwean leaders to clear up the remaining issues before elections could be held, her remarks in June 2011 and the reaction that followed showed that Zuma's team did not (and still doesn't) have a sure grip on ZANU-PF. She told the media that all Zimbabwean parties were in agreement that elections would not be held in 2011 but, immediately after, a ZANU-PF spokesperson refuted it.

Zuma's team has also struggled with unwillingness from SADC members to take a firmer position on Zimbabwe. In June 2011, member states of the SADC troika only 'noted', and did not 'endorse', the Livingstone communiqué,[21] pushing negotiations out to the August summit in Luanda, Angola.[22]

Zuma apparently took a tougher stance on Zimbabwe at the Luanda summit, reportedly telling members that 'he would become personally involved in ensuring the full implementation of the GPA and would secure meetings between Zimbabwe's political leaders and the security sector chiefs'.[23] Zimbabwean newspaper *Daily News*, which allegedly had a copy of the report, said that Zuma blasted the principals for making no progress on the items they had agreed to and blamed ZANU-PF for many of the disruptions to the process.[24] But despite Zuma's tough stance at the Luanda summit, no outcomes were ensured and once again the SADC left with no clear solutions.[25]

People in power: DIRCO

Maite Nkoana-Mashabane: Minister

Soon after Nkoana-Mashabane was appointed as minister, US diplomat Raymond L. Brown tried to make sense of Zuma's cabinet. In a diplomatic cable from Pretoria to Washington DC he wrote: 'The ANC [read Zuma] wants to retain Limpopo Province's loyalty. This will be a key goal as the ruling party seeks to ward off opponents in the 2011 election and as the ANC prepares for its next party congress. Several of the senior players in Zuma's government hail from Limpopo, which is a strategically important province that helped sway ANC members to Zuma at the December 2007 ruling party congress.'[26]

Zuma secured a key ally within Limpopo party politics when he appointed Nkoana-Mashabane. She, deputy minister of arts and culture Joe Phaahla and others like Collins Chabane were (and still are) critical in lobbying support for Zuma in the province and were, therefore, essential for his survival at Mangaung in 2012. These ministers and their support base lobbied hard in November 2011 to replace Premier Cassel Mathale as ANC provincial chair in the run-up to the provincial ANC conference in December 2011.[27]

This wasn't the first time Nkoana-Mashabane rallied support for Zuma. Back in 2007, the Congress of South African Students (COSAS) and the ANCYL used the funeral of her husband, Norman Mashabane, to rally support for Zuma. The *Mail & Guardian*[28] reported how it was carefully orchestrated and how supporters only listened when Zuma stepped in.[29]

At the end of that year, Nkoana-Mashabane was elected at the bottom of the ANC NEC list at Polokwane and made it to the national working committee of the ruling party. Seventeen months later, Zuma selected her to be minister. 'Her appointment was one of the biggest surprises of Zuma's cabinet, given her relatively junior status in the party and lack of prominence in the foreign policy community. However, in contrast to her predecessor, she brought formal diplomatic experience,' wrote former diplomat and Pretoria academic Yolanda Spies. 'Her affable approach to the civil servants she now headed and the foreign diplomatic corps in Pretoria, immediately set her apart from the notoriously abrasive Dlamini-Zuma.'[30]

That is one view of her. There are others, which paint an entirely different picture. Said one DIRCO insider to me: 'The minister is a complex character and at times very difficult to work with. She is not much loved in the department, to be honest.'

A former minister told me: 'There was shock and horror in the [foreign affairs] department when she was appointed ... and I am not sure she has ever fully won their confidence.'

It is certainly true that during her first months in office, civil society praised

Nkoana-Mashabane for her openness and consultative manner during DIRCO's work on the white paper. She was on something of a charm offensive, arranging a series of 'outreach' visits to universities and other institutes.

Nkoana-Mashabane has sought to enhance domestic understanding of, and engagement in, foreign policy making through her appointments. She appointed Eddy Maloka, then CEO of the Africa Institute of South Africa (AISA), as her special advisor 'due to his strong academic background, [and] vast experience in working with the State, Civil Society and International Organisations'.[31]

She also brought in two former Limpopo civil servants to spearhead public diplomacy and media relations: Clayson Monyela, who was the minister's provincial spokesperson when Nkoana-Mashabane was MEC for local government and housing, and Saul Kgomotso Molobi, who served as spokesperson for the government agency Trade & Investment Limpopo.

During her first budget speech, and again in 2010, Nkoana-Mashabane promised to establish a 'foreign policy council'. In 2010, she told Parliament: 'We are currently in the process of consulting our stakeholders on the need for the establishment of a foreign policy council. This will serve as an avenue for our non-state actors to interface with DIRCO on our foreign policy development and implementation.'[32]

And again, in May 2011, Deputy Minister Marius Fransman told Parliament on her behalf: 'This will be an advisory council on international relations, to again strengthen our resolve to make our foreign policy as inclusive and participatory as possible.'[33] An advertisement asking members who wanted to be part of the South African Council on International Relations (SACOIR) to come forward was put out only in late 2011, and at the time of writing the body still had not come into being.

A US diplomatic cable from the embassy in Pretoria mentions comments made by a key ANC member on foreign policy soon after Nkoana-Mashabane's appointment. Professor Iqbal Jhazbhay, a member of the ANC NEC subcommittee on international relations and its newly formed ANC International Relations Rapid Response Task Team, described Nkoana-Mashabane to US embassy officials in Pretoria as 'warmer than Dlamini-Zuma' and 'nicer to work for', continuing that 'she did not need to be a great leader because she will continue the same policies'. However, the cable noted: 'There also are rumours that she is a "screamer" and difficult to work for. Yolanda Kemp Spies said she was a horrible High Commissioner, but still not as difficult as Dlamini-Zuma.'[34]

This side of her came to light in September 2011, when Nkoana-Mashabane refused to let airport personnel in Oslo, Norway, search her handbag or let it pass through an X-ray machine. This caused her to miss her flight to Bulgaria, costing the South African taxpayer R235 343.[35]

(Further to the topic of expenditure, Nkoana-Mashabane admitted in a written reply to Parliament that she had spent more than R10 million of public money on fourteen chartered flights between 1 April 2010 and 30 June 2011, and took twenty-six other commercial flights to the cost of R2 million.[36])

In mid-2011, there was speculation about Trevor Manuel being nominated to fill vacant positions in international financial institutions – specifically, the International Monetary Fund (IMF) and the World Bank. Finance minister Pravin Gordhan indicated that he and the government were thinking about it, and conferring with allies in the global South, such as India and Brazil, concerned that they might consider Manuel too close to the Western powers from his long tenure as finance minister.

Gordhan said in May 2011: 'For too long, the IMF's legitimacy has been undermined by a convention to appoint its senior management on the basis of their nationality. In order to maintain trust, credibility and legitimacy in the eyes of its stakeholders, there must be an open and transparent selection process, which results in the most competent person being appointed as Managing Director, regardless of their nationality.'[37]

A few weeks later, on 11 June 2011, Manuel and Gordhan addressed the media, saying that Manuel would not be vying for the IMF job. 'It is important to understand that decisions take place in the context of world politics; against that backdrop, I have decided not to avail myself,' Manuel said.[38] What he meant was that as the tradition of appointing a European to the IMF job was likely to continue, his candidacy would be stillborn. The former French finance minister, Christine Lagarde, was subsequently appointed.

The speculation and confusion around who is responsible for nominating South Africans to positions at international institutions led to cabinet deciding that only DIRCO and its minister would have the honour,[39] a not insignificant victory for Nkoana-Mashabane, who had been miffed at the hype around Manuel's possible nomination, envious no doubt of his special place in the mainstream media's affections.

Nkoana-Mashabane's relationship with Manuel is not a good one. During the COP17 international climate-change conference in Durban in December 2012, I happened to run into Ruth Kagia, the then country director of the World Bank in Pretoria, whom I had become friends with over previous years. A straight-talking, no-nonsense Kenyan, Kagia appeared genuinely shocked as she recounted an incident that she had witnessed earlier that day. Manuel had arrived a few minutes late to a closed meeting between South African ministers and senior diplomats and visiting ministers, giving Nkoana-Mashabane an opportunity to chide him fiercely for his discourtesy. 'It was really embarrassing for Trevor,' Kagia recalled. 'She did not hold back and gave him the full two barrels. I really felt for him.'

The Manuel/IMF debacle is an example of how Nkoana-Mashabane has been increasingly asserting her power as a minister since taking office, affirming it through the president. 'She certainly is a favourite of JZ,' says another member of the ANC NEC with inside knowledge of foreign affairs. 'He thought that she did a very good job in India as high commissioner. She travelled with him a great deal in the run-up to Polokwane.'

For another example of where Nkoana-Mashabane's power comes from, one need only look to the question of who was to lead South Africa at COP17. In July 2011, the *Mail & Guardian* reported tensions between DIRCO and the Department of Environmental Affairs (DEA) over who was to take responsibility for the running of the conference. Up until then, the international norm was for the host country's environmental department to lead the content of the conference, while the foreign affairs department dealt with the logistics of the event. But confusion crept in when Zuma instructed DIRCO to take the lead.[40]

The conflict between the two departments led to disruptions and delays in the preparations, causing many diplomats to express their private concerns to me, fretting that South Africa was going to 'mess up' through a lack of focus and organisational efficiency. In August 2011, the two ministers finally tried to put an end to speculation about the rift between them. Nkoana-Mashabane told the media: 'In South African vocabulary, there is no such thing as a turf war. There is one president of COP17, and she is Maite Nkoana-Mashabane. And there is one leader of the South African delegation to COP17, which is the environmental minister. South Africa is on track for COP17, if not ahead of schedule.'[41]

Zuma has also let Nkoana-Mashabane play a more prominent role than Mbeki allowed his foreign affairs minister to do. On nineteen occasions in her first year as minister, she was the most senior South African delegate.[42] In Durban, she emerged with both her and South Africa's reputation intact, saving the conference from ignominious failure thanks to a prolonged final weekend session where the 'clock was stopped' on the formal negotiations, permitting informal negotiations to continue.

'With tempers rising and the talks minutes from being abandoned, the chair, South African foreign minister Maite Nkoana-Mashabane, ordered China, India, the US, Britain, France, Sweden, Gambia, Brazil and Poland to meet in a small group or "huddle". Surrounded by a crowd of nearly 100 delegates on the floor of the hall, they talked quietly among themselves to try to reach a new form of words acceptable to all,' reported the *Guardian* newspaper.[43]

As a result of the last-minute deal, whereby the words 'agreed outcome with legal force' were substituted into the agreement to continue to negotiate a new Kyoto Convention in the coming years, the Durban COP17 was saved. (While the EU had pushed hard for a new treaty, India had strongly resisted such a 'legal outcome'. The phrase 'agreed outcome with legal force' was a sufficiently ambiguous compromise that satisfied both parties.)

This deal avoided the embarrassment of the Kyoto Treaty dying on African soil and thus boosted Nkoana-Mashabane's own reputation internationally.

Notwithstanding this, the jury is still out on her term as minister. Government and ANC-insider critics complain about the lack of vision. 'We still don't have a definition of "national interest" to work with,' one senior defence ministry official told me in the context of the South African troop deployment to the Central African Republic and the DRC. 'It makes it hard for us to be clear about why we are there,' the source added. From Defence's perspective, there is a hierarchy that is very different from DIRCO's: first, the SADC region; then the African Union; and lastly, the rest of the world, including BRICS.

Another ANC insider described Nkoana-Mashabane as 'unworldly', no doubt in comparison to Thabo Mbeki.

Ebrahim Ebrahim: Deputy minister

Some deputy ministers are about as much use as a chocolate teapot. They are there to make up the numbers, beneficiaries of patronage. Ebrahim Ebrahim, or 'Ebi' as he is widely known, is no such person. As Zulu puts it: 'Ebi is one person who can see the president whenever he feels like it.'

Imprisoned on Robben Island, kidnapped in Swaziland and tried for treason, Ebrahim has links with Zuma that go back to the 1980s, when he was stationed in the frontline states and joined MK. Zuma headed Swaziland and Mozambique at the time and was a leader in the ANC's intelligence network.

Ebrahim crossed paths again with Zuma in July 2002, when he resigned from Parliament to take up the position of senior political and economic advisor to the deputy president. Before then, Ebrahim had chaired Parliament's foreign affairs committee and joined the Joint Standing Committee on Intelligence. He has headed the ANC's international affairs committee since 2006.

As Zuma's political advisor, Ebrahim assisted with conflict resolution in Rwanda and the DRC, and in Palestine and Israel. He was also part of efforts in Nepal, Bolivia, Kosovo and, closer to home, Burundi.[44]

Ebrahim has been an intellectual base to Zuma on foreign policy, but very rarely travels the globe. He undertook only twenty-three flights abroad between April 2010 and June 2011, very little compared to the foreign minister herself. Since Zuma's election to the leadership of the ruling party in December 2007, Ebrahim has been at the helm of foreign policy, more so than during Mbeki's strict reign. In that sense, and because he is so close to Zuma, comparisons with Mbeki's long-standing confidant, Aziz Pahad, make sense. Like Ebrahim, Pahad was deputy minister of foreign affairs, but exerted a disproportionate amount of influence over foreign policy because of his personal relationship with the president, which enabled him to 'leapfrog' the minister of foreign affairs in his dealings with Mbeki.

In the office of deputy minister of DIRCO, Ebrahim has continued to give guidance on South Africa's foreign policy relating to the Middle East and North Africa regions,[45] and to communicate to the country the administration's decisions on the continent, in the region and in South–South blocs like BRICS.[46]

In 2011, Ebrahim took the lead to explain the administration's position on Libya and the UN Security Council vote on resolution 1970 of 27 February 2011 and resolution 1973 of March the same year.[47] He wrote several op-eds for the *Sunday Independent* and other newspapers, and gave lectures at universities like the University of Zululand and the University of Venda, among others.

On Libya and the UN he said: 'The current situation in Libya is as a result of the failure to transform the global system of governance. Powerful states remain dominant and imposing over the powerless. This does not augur well for an international system founded on the principles of international peace and security that underpin the UN as an institution. It is precisely for this reason, amongst many, that we believe we are correct in calling for the reform of the institutions of global governance.'[48]

Underestimate Ebrahim at your peril; he is a gentle, often taciturn man. But he is tough and clear-minded. While 'keeping shop' in Pretoria, Ebrahim has taken issue with some countries' human rights records. He summoned and gave the Myanmar ambassador what Steven Gruzd called a good 'dressing-down' on the house arrest of Aung San Suu Kyi.[49] He also took on Iran during a bilateral visit by the head of Iran's human rights council, Mohammad-Javad Larijani. He said Iran's use of the death penalty is excessive, he questioned the country's persecution of religious minorities and he asked for clarity on the stoning of Sakineh Mohammadi Ashtiani.[50]

But he has been quiet on China's human rights record. With regards to China, South Africa knows on which side its bread is buttered.

Marius Fransman: Deputy minister
Fransman was appointed on 2 November 2010 as DIRCO's second deputy minister – more than a year after the Zuma administration took up office. The former teacher and influential Western Cape ANC leader was first elected to Parliament in May 2009 as chairperson of the Portfolio Committee on Higher Education and Training. Before then, he had been a provincial minister in the Western Cape government and a key ally of the South African ambassador to the US, Ebrahim Rasool, who was Western Cape premier at the time.

Fransman was elected to chair the ANC in the Western Cape in 2011 and has been commended largely for calming divisions between Mcebisi Skwatsha and Rasool supporters and racial divisions within the party.[51] Infighting had led to the ANC in the province being disbanded for eighteen months, adding to the 2009 election defeat and an only somewhat mildly better showing in the 2011 local elections.[52]

Fransman had no knowledge of international relations prior to joining DIRCO. His appointment plays into perceptions that Zuma has used DIRCO appointments, especially those of ambassadors, to calm provincial rivalries in the ANC and consolidate national support. Fransman was important to Zuma's ambitions in Mangaung in 2012 as he is seen as a buffer against the youth league in the Western Cape.

Fransman does not believe that his appointment to a national ministry has affected his ability to keep a hold on the province. Soon after he became Western Cape ANC chair, *City Press* asked Fransman if he would continue at DIRCO or would rather focus on rebuilding the ANC. 'There are ministers who are also chairpersons, so that can't be a big issue. In fact, the portfolio helps to reach people extensively,' he replied.[53]

Fransman's role in DIRCO has been largely marked by his involvement in mediation efforts in Madagascar. His first 'diplomatic coup' was convincing all parties to sign a roadmap to peace. He told *City Press* soon after: 'We were unstinting in our position and clarified the views of the Southern African Development Community. The process previously favoured one of the parties. Also, we affirmed that Madagascar is a sovereign state and that the current process is a political one, not a judicial one.'[54]

He took an approach South Africa has used before in negotiations with Zimbabwe: 'parking' difficult issues in order to move negotiations forward. 'This means that issues like former president Marc Ravalomanana being found guilty of abuse of office will be dealt with later,' he explained to *City Press*.[55] This approach couldn't, however, prevent a fallback in 2012, when Ravalomanana failed to return to his country when he was threatened with arrest.[56]

In February 2012, Fransman's South African–led mediation was hit with another blow when the *Sunday Independent* reported on leaked US documents that described how South Africa had possibly violated arms rules when it supplied anti-riot ammunition and gear to forces loyal to Ravalomanana. These arms, some originally from China, had bypassed South African customs and were collected in a private jet hired by Ravalomanana, according to the leaked document.[57]

In January 2013, however, Ravalomanana's long-term rival, interim president Andry Rajoelina, agreed not to contest elections in May, falling in line with a plan by mediators from SADC and the EU. It was a major breakthrough in the negotiations, and another feather in Fransman's cap. Ousted leader Ravalomanana, a wealthy businessman, had already agreed not to stand again, saying in December 2012 that he wanted the country to rebuild itself.

Fransman has also been roped into fielding questions from the press as the DIRCO minister has decreased her weekly appearances at a press conference in Pretoria. His predecessor, Sue van der Merwe, still plays a critical role in fostering relations with ambassadors in Pretoria.

Jerry Matjila, Director-general

Matjila was appointed DG nearly two years into Zuma's term. His predecessor, Ayanda Ntsaluba, resigned in April 2011 after trade unions threatened to go on strike if a forensic audit into the 'tyrannical and oppressive' administration was not undertaken.[58]

Before liberation, Matjila was the ANC's representative first in the Scandinavian countries and then later in Japan and North East Asia. In the early 1990s, he served as high commissioner to India, which was around the same time Nkoana-Mashabane was serving as a diplomat in that country. Prior to his appointment to DG, Matjila served as ambassador to the EU (2001–06) and the UN in Geneva. He has led South African delegations in IBSA engagements, chaired the South African team at the Forum on China-Africa Cooperation and coordinated the country's engagements at the India-Africa Dialogue Forum.[59]

Matjila's appointment was groundbreaking: he was the first former diplomat to be appointed DG. Curiously, previous DGs for foreign affairs have been recruited from elsewhere in government. Ntsaluba, for example, came from the health department after former foreign affairs minister Nkosazana Dlamini-Zuma lobbied then president Mbeki for more than a year to appoint him. The DG position had been vacant from 10 January 2002 to October 2003, after Sipho Pityana resigned due to an acrimonious relationship with the minister.

Matjila has largely continued to operate behind the scenes since his appointment in mid-2011. Ntsaluba often fielded questions and held weekly media briefings, but these have now to a large extent been taken over by the garrulous Fransman.

Nkosazana Dlamini-Zuma, AU Commission chairperson

In August 2011, a SADC leaders' summit in Angola endorsed Dlamini-Zuma as their candidate to take on Jean Ping as chairperson of the AU Commission. Although Pretoria diplomats like Nqakula lobbied for months behind the scenes, Nkoana-Mashabane only formally announced Dlamini-Zuma's candidacy on 18 January 2012 in Bela-Bela.[60]

In the week before, South African diplomats and ministers criss-crossed the continent to convince especially francophone countries to vote against the Sorbonne graduate from Gabon, even though they might publicly support Ping (a favourite of their biggest donor: France).[61] South Africa lost, with twenty-four votes 'for' and twenty-five 'against', while Ping didn't get the two-thirds to secure re-election.

Eddy Maloka, Nkoana-Mashabane's special advisor, downplayed the fallout from the vote, telling the *Mail & Guardian* that votes for Dlamini-Zuma had come 'from all over and the great unifying issue was the fact our African institutions and their leadership must in the future be both accountable for their performance and impervious to foreign interference' (alluding to France). In the same article, Petrus de Kock of the South African Institute of International Affairs (SAIIA) said that South Africa's celebrations afterwards 'imparted a sense that they [South African diplomats] at least achieved their purpose of changing the dynamic in the [AU] Commission'.[62]

Finally, in July 2012, AU members voted in favour of Dlamini-Zuma, who won 60 per cent of the votes to become the first woman to head the AU Commission.[63] She is now clearly in a very important position, both continentally and also in terms of Africa's relations with the rest of the world.

One of the many delicate diplomatic dilemmas that Dlamini-Zuma will have to finesse is how she plays her hand in relation to South Africa. Other states will be watching her like a hawk to see if she is unduly favourable in her dealings with her home country and its interests. On the flip side, she will no doubt be eager to ensure that she does not overcompensate, to the cost of Pretoria, which in turn must be hopeful that Dlamini-Zuma will be an ally in the AU.

Even more intriguing, in terms of domestic politics, is whether her sojourn at the AU will harm or further her prospects. While there was little truth in the rumour that Zuma was eager to support his former wife's candidature in order to get her out of the way ahead of Mangaung in December 2012, she is a highly respected politician within the ANC, to the extent that many are tipping her to return from Addis in time to secure a 'middle way' victory as president of the ANC in 2017, overtaking the new deputy president, Cyril Ramaphosa, to seize power.

As with sport, sometimes being 'out of the team' can further one's prospects as others come in and fail. If she succeeds at the AU, absence may make the heart grow fonder, or it may simply cut her off from domestic ANC politics and weaken her broad-ranging support across the party.

People in power: Economic diplomacy and state capitalism
The turf war over who controls economic policy has not left South Africa's foreign policy untouched. Three ministers, specifically Pravin Gordhan at finance,

Rob Davies at trade and industry and Malusi Gigaba at public enterprises, have a constant impact on the country's foreign policy.

Their importance, position and power may increase as South Africa strives for better regional economic integration and an African free-trade zone, along with an intensified approach to the pursuit of state capitalism and a foreign policy positioned more directly towards benefiting nationalist interests, which would set South Africa up to compete with investors from the West, China and Brazil within Africa, notwithstanding its involvement in BRICS as a political and economic grouping.

A paper prepared by the neoliberal SAIIA argues that 'the sound African political landscape dominates decision making, both political and economic in Southern Africa' and 'political instability in South Africa, specifically the lack of a political centre in the African National Congress (ANC) and the presence of the two ideological frameworks/economic models is a strong driving force that will shape the future of SACU [Southern African Customs Union]'.[64]

The report also remarks, 'South Africa's foreign policy ambitions could see Pretoria playing a development partner role on the continent [such as the South African Development Partnership Agency (SADPA), which was established in 2012, and state-owned enterprises, such as Eskom or Transnet]. It could use the revenue pool funds towards this purpose.'[65]

National Treasury, for instance, plays a major role in the BRICS engagement, since key issues on the agenda relate to finance and the economy. Treasury also refocused a chief director's function in order to drive South Africa's role in the formation of a potentially significant new international development institution, the BRICS Bank, with Dr Nomfundo Ngwenya, a former South African Secret Service official with a specialisation in emerging economies and a PhD from the University of Cambridge, filling the role in 2012 ahead of the March 2013 BRICS summit in Durban – a big moment for South Africa.

Pravin Gordhan and Treasury

National Treasury is a pivotal part of government, and although less powerful than under Mbeki, it is still a 'government within a government'. This extends, in part at least, to international affairs. For example, Gordhan's mandarins took the lead in the country's G20 engagements and were the main drivers behind regional relationships and capacity to deal with SACU.[66]

And when, in 2010/11, Swaziland's coffers were hit by a 60 per cent reduction in its income after SACU cut 60 per cent of the funds flowing into the country, South Africa's Treasury came to the rescue. Gordhan announced a R2.4 million loan to King Mswati's Central Bank of Swaziland from the South African Reserve Bank, to be paid in three instalments in August and October 2011 and February 2012.

Gordhan laid down fiscal and financial reforms that Swaziland had to adhere to – similar to the sorts of conditions the IMF might itself have imposed – including tabling in Parliament the Public Finance Management Bill by October 2011, implementing the Fiscal Adjustments Roadmap by February 2012, protecting the peg between the lilangeni and the rand, agreeing on priority spending programmes as contained in the Staff Monitored Programme that was agreed upon between the government of the Kingdom of Swaziland and the IMF, implementing acceptable financial reporting, and finalising and implementing an auditing bill.[67]

Gordhan endured severe criticism in the weeks following this announcement. Civil society, the media and even Alliance partners like COSATU criticised the minister and the government for granting the loan. The *Mail & Guardian* reported that Zuma and the ANC might be in a conflict of interest by granting the loan, as the party's investment vehicle had significant business interests in Swaziland.[68]

At a media briefing shortly after the announcement, Gordhan told the press: 'Will this loan encourage genuine change? We hope so.' He later added: 'In light of the current dialogue between the two countries, the government of Swaziland will give renewed impetus to these by broadening the dialogue process to include all stakeholders and citizens of the Kingdom of Swaziland.'[69]

Despite all the minister's reassurances, Swaziland refused to agree to the terms, diminishing the credibility of using loans to force democratic and fiscal reform in the region. October 2011 passed without any agreement being signed and, by February 2012, Swazi authorities had still refused to agree to some conditions.[70]

Despite these setbacks, Finance Minister Gordhan has played a key role within South Africa's foreign relations and especially with regards to reforming SACU and the European Free Trade Area negotiations.

He has also been pivotal in reconsidering SACU's funding model, whereby South Africa divides almost all its customs revenue to the BLNS (Botswana-Lesotho-Namibia-Swaziland) countries. South Africa and Gordhan consider this funding model unsustainable, while BLNS countries, led by Botswana, went outside the SACU framework to sign agreements with the EU.

Rob Davies, the DTI and economic diplomacy

'The success of its economic diplomacy will determine the extent to which South Africa can achieve its domestic priorities ... For South Africa to meet these priorities, its economy must be able to participate competitively in the global marketplace,' a May 2011 DIRCO white paper on foreign policy notes.[71]

In June 2007, cabinet decided South Africa needed to train its diplomats to be more fluent in economics. It instructed the then Department of Foreign Affairs' diplomatic academy to develop a curriculum. This followed cabinet's endorsement of a document entitled 'Strengthening of Economic Diplomacy and the Challenges of Co-ordinated Marketing of South Africa Abroad'.

Between November 2009 and July 2011, the academy trained 302 international relations officials, while 90 civil servants from other departments who deal with foreign affairs attended workshops. The deputy director of the academy, Maud Dlomo, wrote in the *Sunday Independent* in August 2011 that 120 more DIRCO officials were to be trained in the latter part of 2011. The academy was also training civil servants from provincial governments and selected metros.[72]

Except for DIRCO's focus on training of embassy staff and civil servants, Minister Rob Davies and the DTI have largely spearheaded South Africa's economic diplomacy. This has led to some tensions between the two departments in the past.[73]

Since 2009, Davies and his department have played an increasingly important role in establishing relations with fellow BRICS countries, reforming SACU and creating a regional and African free-trade zone, while attracting new investment.

DTI officials are deployed to some embassies, while desks within the DTI have been set up to mirror DIRCO structures. The DTI's capacity overseas, however, is limited. By August 2011, only 26 out of 124 South African embassies and consulates around the world housed a DTI official, according to Dlomo.[74]

In 2010, South Africa had no commercial attaché in the key African country of Angola, even though it was in the middle of a commodities boom. 'The type of Brazilian state-business co-operation that is at play in Angola is simply absent on the South African side. There is no trade and commercial attaché in Luanda. The post of ambassador has been open since last year and is unlikely to be filled before the end of this year,' wrote Lyal White and Nomfundo Ngwenya in *Business Day*.[75] Ngwenya, head of the South African Foreign Policy and African Drivers Programme at the SAIIA, told a rapt Cape Town audience at an SAIIA event in 2010 that it was inexplicable that Zuma should travel to Luanda in his first months as president, rebuild the relationship with President José dos Santos and Angola, but then fail to appoint an ambassador, thus wholly undermining the good work done during the visit.

In June 2011, General Godfrey Ngwenya was appointed ambassador to Angola, a move that will likely strengthen economic ties. Nomfundo Ngwenya (no relation) is hopeful: 'It's a very powerful message to send to a country when you appoint the former chief of your defence force as ambassador. It may also be significant that he underwent his military training in Angola and he might have very close relations to the president and the ruling party.'

The DTI's Trade and Investment South Africa (TISA) programme is responsible for encouraging direct investment into South Africa, increasing exports and managing the DTI's network of representatives in South Africa's embassies and consulates.

TISA lists forty-two embassies and consulates where it has some sort of representation. The majority of these missions have a marketing officer, but in the Netherlands, for example, all posts are vacant. To Abuja, Nigeria, however, the DTI posted Nse Johnson as trade secretary.[76]

Deputy Director-General Pumla Ncapayi is at the heart of TISA, implementing South Africa's trade and industrial policies. TISA's head since June 2011, Ncapayi holds a diploma in trade law and policy from the Geneva, Switzerland, based World Trade Organization (WTO) and was previously DTI's project leader for Asia. She has also worked as a director responsible for bilateral agreements with European countries.[77]

Davies himself leads interactions between the other BRICS countries and South Africa, as well as trade negotiations with the EU and SACU. He also champions the establishment of free-trade zones and supports the idea of trading within BRICS without the use of the US dollar or the euro.[78] Fluent in Portuguese, Davies wastes no time during negotiations and press conferences correcting translators while speaking.

Davies was one of the strongest advocates of South Africa joining BRICs and moving eastward, away from its traditional trade dependency on Europe. 'The emerging economies, led by Brazil, Russia, India and China (BRIC), are new sources of global economic growth, trade and investment flows. According to the International Monetary Fund, these countries will account for 61% of global growth in three years' time. It is also projected that developing countries' share of world trade will double during the next 40 years, from 37% in 2007 to 69% in 2050,' Davies wrote in the *Mail & Guardian* in 2011.[79]

In August 2010, he had defended China in Africa in an interview with the *Financial Times*, saying China's expansion in Africa 'can only be a good thing', because it will increase competition for resources and influence in the continent. 'We don't have to sign on the dotted line whatever is shoved under our noses any longer; we now have alternatives and that's to our benefit.' Accompanying Zuma on a visit to China at the time, Davies said an appropriate response to Western critics who accuse China of pursuing neocolonialist power in Africa is that 'it takes one to know one'.[80]

Since taking up office at the DTI, Davies has led a hard-line stance on the EU and especially in trade negotiations with Europeans. As early as 2008, as deputy minister, Davies accused the EU of being afraid of losing its foothold on the African continent and of trying to prevent this at all cost, primarily by hooking African states into economic partnership agreements (EPAs). He said that African nations should rather focus on emerging economic powers, such as China and India, rather than on the EU.[81]

'There is a huge gap between what Europe says its intentions are and the true picture,' Davies told the Inter Press Service, IPS. 'Brussels claims that the EPAs will promote integration and development in the region and that it has no mercantilist intentions with the EPAs. This is not the case. Firstly, the ACP [Africa, Caribbean, Pacific] region has been divided into six different configurations. This does not contribute to unity.'[82]

Davies's tougher stance on EPA negotiations has since caused tensions between SACU member countries, South Africa and the EU. Botswana, Lesotho and Swaziland signed agreements with the EU outside SACU, while South Africa refused.[83]

'South Africa doesn't want the EPA to create a climate where the SACU is undermined. In fact South Africa is in favour of even deeper integration in SACU. We don't want to see it as only a form of convenience for transfers of revenue,' Davies told a Business Unity South Africa (BUSA) meeting in 2009.[84]

In 2011, Davies had to deal with increasing tensions within SACU. A troubled global economy saw small member countries like Lesotho and Swaziland lose more than 70 per cent of their revenue, while Namibia and Botswana also took a serious knock. Davies wrote in the *Mail & Guardian*: 'The recent global economic crisis, which led to a sharp contraction in the size of the revenue pool, is a sober reminder that continuing dependence on a volatile source of finance carries enormous risks. Our objective for the review is to establish an arrangement that offers greater predictability in the sharing of revenue and supports our work on regional industrial and infrastructure development.'[85]

Based on SACU's revenue-sharing formula figures for 2011/12, Botswana would get R9.7 billion, Namibia R8.1 billion, South Africa R4.5 billion, Swaziland R3.3 billion and Lesotho R3.1 billion of the customs revenue.

'How is it that a country like South Africa, which accounts for more than 90% of the union's GDP, gets only 15.6% of customs revenue, whereas Botswana, which accounts for 4% of the GDP, gets 34%? It irks South African treasury and trade officials, to say the least. "Why should South African taxpayers subsidise richer Botswana when our own people don't have public services?" they argue,' wrote Roman Grynberg in the *Mail & Guardian* in July 2011.[86]

South Africa is committed to revising the division-of-customs-revenue formula and SACU to form the basis of a larger African free-trade zone by 2013. This feeds into South Africa's foreign relations and economic ambitions, as DTI director-general Lionel October said in June 2011: the establishment of the free-trade zone by 2013 would 'absolutely' enhance South Africa's weight within the BRICS group of emerging markets. 'We will no longer be a pimple,' he said.[87]

A proposal by an Australian consultant to radically reconstruct the division model was rejected at a SACU meeting. History is on the side of the smaller nations dependent on SACU funding, as the union has only changed its model three times in the past 100 years.

Grynberg has accused Davies and South Africa of being increasingly insular-looking. He pointed to when Davies and two other ministers opposed a R16.5 billion takeover from Walmart. Davies submitted to the Competition Commission that Walmart would kill local production. Despite this, the foreign direct investment was approved.[88]

Malusi Gigaba and state capitalism

In June 2011, public enterprises minister Malusi Gigaba surprised business when he replaced board members of state-owned enterprises Eskom and Denel with new non-executive directors.[89] He appointed Zola Tsotsi as Eskom chairman and Zoli Kunene to Denel – both had interests and companies with business interests in these sectors.[90]

This bold intervention signalled the start of Gigaba as a more assertive leader within the Zuma administration and also at the helm of SOEs – a key driver of Chinese/Brazilian-style state capitalism that government has since been flirting with – placing him at the centre of the country's foreign policy, a fact he himself was aware of.

'We have said that each entity must develop an African footprint. They must invest in infrastructure in SA and [the rest of] Africa so their revenue streams are not limited to what they can achieve locally,' Gigaba told the *Financial Mail* in July 2011.[91]

He recited a planned R110 billion to be spent on rail expansion, Eskom's R450 billion on power generation, Passenger Rail Agency of South Africa's R86 billion on passenger rail, South African Airways' expansion plans and Denel's repositioning as examples of how South African SOEs could prepare to expand into the continent.

The newspaper commented: 'Gigaba's new thinking is "in its infancy" and he has no actual examples ... but reaching into the rest of Africa to provide infrastructure will put SA parastatals in direct competition with the Chinese, whose financing model – African governments pay for infrastructure through agreements to extract minerals – has proved most attractive.'[92]

Gigaba alluded to a closer relationship with the other BRICS countries, especially China and Brazil, in its expansion into Africa, while he as minister would play 'a frontline role'.

'It is a kind of economic nationalist vision reminiscent of that of the old National Party, which used SOEs to build industrial capacity and provide jobs for whites left landless through industrialisation or other reasons. But if it works, even partially, the commercial opportunities, particularly for black-empowered enterprises, will be huge,' wrote seasoned political journalist Carol Paton.[93] But she also sounded a note of caution: 'If commercial and growth opportunities are the upside of Gigaba's dream, corruption and cronyism are certainly the downside.'[94]

An example of how Gigaba has been at the forefront of the country's economic diplomacy is when he visited Europe and the US in mid-2011 to promote Transnet to possible investors.[95] And in August 2011, Gigaba, together with Rob Davies, held a 'Connecting Africa' conference in Durban, where continental trade corridors and infrastructure projects were discussed. By February 2012, Zuma had announced a more infrastructure-heavy model placing SOEs and Gigaba at the centre of the new state-capitalism approach.

In February 2012, Gigaba argued in *Business Day* that South Africa needed to restructure the way it managed its SOEs. He suggested all SOEs should be managed under one umbrella ministry, streamlining their management and securing better economic growth. 'This is no call for a Chinese or any other model, but a call for a Proudly South African model that takes into consideration our own experiences and developmental aspirations,' he wrote.[96]

Earlier, in January, Gigaba had suggested to the *Sunday Times* that a super-ministry was needed to give him power over the Development Bank of South Africa, the Public Investment Corporation (PIC), Transnet and Eskom, among others. Since the PIC is currently one of the few substantial state agencies that fall under Ebrahim Patel's Ministry of Economic Development, this proposal pits the right-of-centre nationalist Gigaba against the leftist Patel. Gigaba argued that policy needs to stay with portfolio departments (while his department runs the SOEs' operational side), opposing Trevor Manuel's proposal of stripping Gigaba's powers as minister to appoint CEOs of these government entities.[97]

Gigaba came second in the Mangaung 2012 ANC NEC election, which boosts his power inside the ANC as well as shows his popularity, and so as his political star continues to rise there is every chance that he might get his way after the 2014 national election.

Outside players

Mbeki and AU peacekeeping

After 2008, when the ANC recalled him from office, Mbeki disappeared from the front pages of newspapers. For nearly two years he was treated as a mere ghost politician as journalists turned their attention to the new Congress of the People (COPE), Zimbabwe, HIV and foreign policy.

But throughout these two years, Mbeki continued to play a pivotal role in foreign relations on the continent, even outside the realm of the South African government. In mid-2011, Mbeki granted interviews to the *Sunday Times* in which he raised questions about the NATO-led strike in Libya and the French's involvement in Ivory Coast.

His mediations in South Sudan and negotiations with the AU had racked up so many air miles by 2011 that the government decided to bump the former head of state to commercial airlines. Now that Dlamini-Zuma has secured the position of AU president, there is a likelihood that Mbeki's role in foreign relations on the continent will increase, as he and Dlamini-Zuma have always been close and hold each other in high regard.

The ANC and foreign policy making

Foreign policy has become a more openly contested space within the Alliance during Zuma's leadership. Due to successful lobbying by organisations such as the Southern African Liaison Office run by Joan Brickhill, COSATU became increasingly critical on issues of foreign policy during the Mbeki era, especially with regards to Zimbabwe and Swaziland. Under Zuma, the trade union federation has sustained its stance, extending its public criticisms to issues such as Zuma's dealings with Libya and the ANCYL's public intervention on Botswana.

At the beginning of his term, Zuma allowed individuals to be openly critical of foreign-relations issues, especially in 2008, when it served the purpose of distancing the new party leadership from Mbeki.

The ANC's party-to-party relations have also impacted on the Zuma administration's foreign policy, especially the party's controversial Progressive Business Forum (PBF). As Chapter 7 shows, the PBF now enjoys a central place in the ANC's institutional arrangements and plays a vital role in its financial sustainability. Not long after I paid the visit to the PBF that I record in that chapter, I bumped into Daryl Swanepoel at Café 41 in Pretoria, the lunchtime hangout of many senior ANC and government people. Swanepoel looked a bit awkward, but nonetheless introduced me to his lunch companion: a Chinese man. I asked what he was doing in South Africa and Swanepoel, somewhat guiltily I thought, told me that they were setting up a Chinese branch of the PBF.

Aside from fund-raising and its own financial interests, the ANC is generally eager to impose itself more on policy, including foreign policy.

There has been a significant shift in government-ANC relations, at least in some areas. As Zulu puts it: 'I am seeing the ANC being much better organised. We don't want a situation where the tail is wagging the dog. Before, the ANC was dependent on the officials at foreign affairs. Now, the ANC has organised itself.'

On Zimbabwe, for example, Zulu says that 'ZANU-PF used to say "we don't need to worry about those ones" [the ANC]. But now, the SG [ANC secretary-general Gwede Mantashe] has said "they have created these things – MDC1 and MDCM[98] – and you have to be as fair as you can to all the role-players".'

Certainly, the new chair of the subcommittee on foreign affairs, Obed Bapela, has breathed new life into the subcommittee, which met three times in the early weeks of 2013 after he was elected to the position at the ANC's national conference in Mangaung in December 2012. Ebrahim Ebrahim was the previous chair. Says one insider: 'Ebi was not strong at admin and the subcommittee was not very energetic or effective.'

Left out of cabinet in 2009 after a short stint as deputy president, Baleka Mbete has been very useful as a party relations officer and has had significant impact on the country's foreign policy. Her strong relationship with Nigeria's Goodluck Jonathan has come in handy for South Africa to calm tempers between the two African powerhouses. In July 2011, she represented the ANC at the South Sudan independence celebrations, but not before she met with Jonathan in Nigeria.[99] She also led the ANC delegation at the Continental Consultative Dialogue on the Impact of Climate Change on Women held at DIRCO's O.R. Tambo building in Pretoria.

Civil society, academics and SACOIR

Civil society and academics were full of optimism when Nkoana-Mashabane came to office in 2009. SAIIA's Tom Wheeler wrote of a new relationship and of greater openness, and of how their inputs were listened to in the writing of DIRCO's white paper on foreign policy.

This optimism, however, has wilted as DIRCO has dragged its feet since 2009 to establish a permanent platform to engage. Only on 20 November 2011 did DIRCO advertise for members of the South African Council on International Relations to be nominated. The members are to be from civil society, academia, business and labour.

In December 2011, Nkoana-Mashabane said in an answer to a parliamentary question that SACOIR, which will function under DIRCO, 'will serve as a consultative forum for South African non-state actors and government experts to interact with my Department on the development and implementation of South Africa's foreign policy'.[100] It will be a platform to publicly debate international relations, to 'review' the country's foreign policy and its implementation and to advise the minister.[101]

As noted earlier, at the time of writing SACOIR had still not been constituted, prompting the George Soros foundation, the Open Society Foundation for South Africa, to launch its own civil-society-led version of the US Council on Foreign Relations – the South African Foreign Policy Initiative. However, at the time of writing, it, too, had failed to make any progress towards fruition, and foreign policy making in South Africa continues to be a largely exclusive domain, with little or no public debate or participation.

People in power: Business interests

Business delegates and state visits

'One of the most talked about and arguably controversial tools used by the South African Government to pursue commercial diplomacy is business delegations accompanying the President on his official state visits to other countries. Although not a new phenomenon, these have become more prominent since President Zuma assumed office in 2009,' wrote Catherine Grant, former BUSA executive director, in July 2011. She tracked how the number of business delegates joining Zuma on state visits had dramatically increased.[102]

In 2009, Zuma mandated BUSA to officially work with the DTI's TISA to draw up lists of business delegates to accompany him on his visits across the continent, the South and the world.

On Zuma's first state visit, to Angola, altogether 124 business delegates, the biggest delegation yet at the time, accompanied him. They were from agriculture, financial services, infrastructure, mining, oil and gas, tourism and transport.

The number of delegates grew. From 213 in a March 2010 trip to the UK and 226 in June 2010 to India, the number rocketed to 371 in August 2010 when the president visited China.[103]

Previously, DIRCO had a very limited relationship with business and seldom consulted with the National Economic Development and Labour Council, BUSA or any grouping in the business sector. BUSA's Nomaxabiso Majokweni had stressed the importance of business's involvement in multilateral engagements like IBSA and BRICS. 'Within the IBSA umbrella, the business forum is one of the most influential and critical components as, without business, the utility of the entire endeavour will be drastically reduced,' she wrote in City Press in 2011.[104] In March 2013, a BRICS Business Council was launched at the BRICS summit in Durban.

Grant explains how business delegates are chosen to join state visits and other engagements: BUSA has a database of individual businesspeople who have indicated their interest in state visits. Generally there are no restrictions and people are registered on a first-come, first-serve basis; however, to certain events only specific companies are invited. Host countries, along with South African missions, play a role in determining which sectors are important to them and the arrangements. Once the right sectors have been identified, TISA and BUSA jointly send out invites. The DTI prefers Rob Davies to lead briefings of business delegates, while parallel sessions often may report back to Zuma during trips.

Usually businesspeople pay for themselves, although government does support emerging and youth business leaders. There is little monitoring to quantify the results or true benefits of state visits to business delegates, and there is 'little strategic thought given to planning of state visits,' writes Grant. She also questions whether some business delegates join state visits to seek business opportunities in the respective countries or 'to support President Zuma for domestic political reasons', as they only attend one or two events.[105]

In her research, Grant found that during different visits different business leaders would take the leading role. In Angola, a strong former-MK contingent that is now in business took the lead, while in India, although Patrice Motsepe officially took the lead, the Gupta brothers were influential there and in the UK. During Zuma's visit to the UK in March 2010, Ambassador Zola Skweyiya's wife, Thuthukile – a businesswoman herself and a former ambassador to France – meddled in who got invited to banquets, events and a match at Wembley Stadium.[106]

According to BUSA delegates, Iqbal Survé still has plentiful access to power and especially to Zuma and Nkoana-Mashabane on official state visits. Survé leads the most empowered company in South Africa, Sekunjalo. It has stakes in fishing, biotechnology, media and motors, among others. It is also not a stranger to political influence. In 1999, the Sekunjalo Breakfast Club was launched to enable networking between the public and private sectors. When Zuma came to office in 2009, Sekunjalo noted on its website that the company was approaching 'an interesting period' with 'interesting changes in the political landscape'.[107]

It seems Sekunjalo has been able to secure sound relations and/or patronage through its subsidiary Premier Fishing. It paid R100 000 for private security at Nkoana-Mashabane's home between 2010 and 2011.[108] When Nkoana-Mashabane failed to declare this in the Members' Interest Register, the *Mail & Guardian* raised questions about the nature of the relationship, prompting Sekunjalo spokesperson Kaveer Bharath to tell the newspaper that the minister and Survé are 'close family friends'.[109]

Whatever the relationship, Sekunjalo has proved to be as useful to DIRCO as it has been to Survé, as his business empire has grown throughout the African continent. I interviewed him on 13 March 2013, just a day before he was due – so he told me – to travel to the United Arab Emirates (UAE) to try to secure the release of Dr Cyril Karabus, who had been convicted in absentia in the Middle East state on charges of manslaughter and falsifying documents after the death of a three-year-old cancer patient, and sentenced to three years in jail. Unaware of the charges and sentence, Dr Karabus was arrested in Dubai in August 2012, while in transit on his return to South Africa from Toronto, Canada, where he had attended his son's wedding.

Survé told me that he was taking a small group of Muslim businessmen to the Middle East to talk with the UAE government about the Karabus case. Within days of his visit, it was announced that a medical review committee had absolved Karabus of all blame associated with the patient's death and, on 21 March 2013, the decision to release Karabus was confirmed by a UAE court.

Seventy-seven years old at the time of his arrest, Karabus is an emeritus professor at the University of Cape Town (UCT), a specialist paediatric oncologist and, most importantly it turns out, a long-time family friend of the Survés.

DIRCO spokesman Clayson Monyela said the South African government had taken various measures to plead Karabus's case: 'We see this as a vindication of what the professor was saying all along. We as government also feel vindicated.' Monyela thanked everyone who had been involved in the matter, but did not mention Survé by name.[110]

What Survé had to offer, and what business was done, to lubricate the wheels of UAE justice and send them spinning in a different direction will probably only emerge later. But what one can be sure of is that DIRCO and South African business relationships are not one-way streets.

A trend that started under Mbeki has entrenched itself under Zuma – and not necessarily for the worse, as evidenced by the Karabus case. Diplomacy, by its very nature, often involves smoke and mirrors. In most countries, discerning who holds the power and exerts the most influence is never a straightforward matter.

What is clear in South Africa's case is that, whereas under Mbeki's presidency all roads led to and from the Union Buildings, under Zuma 'the foreign policy makers' are a diverse and at times eclectic bunch of people, and so South Africa's foreign policy making inevitably reflects a diverse range of world views and interests. Neat, strategic coherence may, therefore, continue to be elusive.

6

Parliament

Being a great parliamentarian: A surprisingly exciting job
The first time was especially nerve-wracking. Walking out of arrivals at O.R. Tambo International Airport to be whisked away by a person whose identity he did not yet know – a source who had promised him information so alluring that it was worth flying all the way from Cape Town.

It turns out that the life of an opposition MP in South Africa can be quite exciting – if you have a penchant for a John le Carré–type lifestyle, that is. And if you want to do your job properly and effectively. For DA MP David Maynier it has become 'a way of life' – one in which, 'forced underground, you have to conduct yourself like an investigative journalist'.

Maynier has received a variety of threats since he took on this role. 'You're taking an enormous risk,' his fiancée had told him the previous night. She was worried. He was too. As he stepped out into the dry Johannesburg air and felt the slight pinch in his lungs and the tightening in his chest that high altitude causes in those of us who live by the sea, his heart was pumping for reasons other than the need to get more oxygen to his brain.

The questions circulated in his mind: Who is this guy really? Will he even pitch? Who are his real bosses? Will he have the documents he says he has? Will I be able to use them? What the hell am I doing?

Suddenly, a car drew up and with barely a second's thought Maynier got in. Instinctively, he sensed all would be well. And it was. The source's identity was now revealed. Though he was required, immediately, to dismantle his cellphone before being driven off to an undisclosed, secret venue, Maynier was no longer so fearful that he was putting his life in danger.

Such sources have been crucial for the role that Maynier now plays in Parliament: that of watchdog-in-chief over matters of defence and state security. Or, to put it even less elegantly, royal pain-in-the-butt to the government and the ruling party.

To be a great parliamentarian in South Africa – and in my view Maynier is a great parliamentarian – requires a special kind of resourcefulness.

Despite his boyish looks, Maynier is tougher than he seems. This is, after all, the man who charmed Lindiwe Sisulu – one of the ANC's tenacious leaders, who is no pushover in any situation and who, as well as being 'very smart and very hard-working', according to Maynier, 'also has a sharp sense of humour'.

Maynier pursued her – politically, that is – for three years, unrelentingly, from the time he took up his seat in the National Assembly in 2009 as the opposition party's shadow minister of defence and military veterans. Sisulu had just been appointed by President Zuma to serve as defence minister.

For all her attributes as a politician and strengths as a minister, Sisulu is not always inclined towards transparency. Maynier had to dig and dig to get information about a number of important defence projects. They fought hammer and tongs. At one point, Maynier challenged Sisulu on the number of flights she had taken on luxury Gulfstream jets chartered by the defence department while she was defence minister. Maynier claimed there were 203; Sisulu claimed only 35; Sisulu's successor, Nosiviwe Mapisa-Nqakula, subsequently revealed that there were actually 229. Sisulu sent Maynier an electronic calculator as a present. He responded by sending her a custom-made luxury comfort pillow – which was 'suitably pink, with feathers' – to use when flying commercial.

Even though Sisulu subsequently told Maynier in Parliament to sit his 'flea-infested body down', Maynier says this was 'not personal and it was incumbent on me to calm people who on social networks do not understand the repartee, and though it may have been unparliamentary it was not hate speech, as some people had suggested'.

'I think we have a similar sense of humour. The public does not get to see this side of things,' explains Maynier. 'The fact that behind the scenes there is collegiality between MPs of different parties. There is also a lighter side. And, frankly, there needs to be some levity.'

Lobbying Parliament

In contrast to Maynier, Nkwame Cedile probably is as tough as he looks. A large-framed man, probably in his late thirties or early forties, he has a big paw and a firm grip, which he squeezes tighter as I reach in my mind for his name.

'You're looking for who?' he asks.

'Nkwame Cedile,' I reply.

'Well, you've found him.'

I'm in Community House, Woodstock, Cape Town. I haven't been here for a while. It takes me back to when I first came to South Africa in early 1994, working for the ANC. Most of the 1994 campaign planning was undertaken in the simple rooms of Community House; this is where I attended my first meeting of the ANC Western Cape campaign's 'white voters committee' – one hell of a striking irony for someone fresh off the boat from England who'd come to South Africa during the dying days of apartheid and hadn't expected to discover racial segregation in the ranks of the ANC (though for electioneering purposes it made perfect sense to segment the campaign along the lines of the main racial groups).

Now Community House is home to a small collection of non-governmental organisations, as well as the Labour Research Service that has long been housed here. The Right2Know (R2K) campaign offices are on the second floor, which is why I am returning to Community House. R2K has been at war with the ANC for over three years, fighting the Protection of State Information Bill, better known as the 'secrecy bill', that caused so much controversy locally and among dismayed overseas investors and other observers intent on looking for signs of an emerging authoritarian streak within the ANC.

Cedile's toughest moment during the whole painful, drawn-out secrecy-bill affair was not the thinly veiled threats he received from the ANC or the public accusations that he and other R2K campaigners were 'foreign agents', but the moment when he had to ask Helen Zille to take off her T-shirt or leave.

As he admits this to me, I contemplate what it must be like to have to ask the robust Western Cape premier and DA leader to remove her top ... given how fond Zille is of wearing her royal-blue DA T-shirt at virtually any opportunity. But the occasion was not, recalls Cedile, 'appropriate'. It was an R2K campaign meeting in Gugulethu, the famous Cape Town township, in early summer 2011. Thousands had turned up – 'far more than we expected,' he recalls.

The campaign was really working: it was joining the dots between the secrecy bill and its threat of greater state control of information – with the deeply unattractive prospect of more cover-ups of corruption – and the daily concerns of ordinary people. Making that link was R2K's greatest accomplishment thus far. As an early campaigner for the right to information and the founder of one of the leading organisations in the R2K campaign – the Open Democracy Advice Centre (ODAC) – I was profoundly impressed by R2K's strategy and its achievements. I had seen campaigns for the right to know gain massive public support in India, with tens of thousands marching on the streets of Rajasthan, but I had always harboured substantial doubts about whether anything like that level of popular support could be garnered in South Africa, even though at ODAC we had worked hard to assist communities and social movements such as Abahlali baseMjondolo by making access-to-information requests relating to housing, water and other socio-economic issues under the Promotion of Access to Information Act (PAIA) passed in 2000.

So when I participated in a march to Parliament on 27 October 2010, I was impressed with the turnout of 2000 or so people wearing the bright red R2K T-shirts, and especially impressed that R2K organisers Cedile and Murray Hunter had succeeded in getting such a range of grass-roots organisations to join the campaign. It wasn't just the chattering classes and the professional NGOs like ODAC, IDASA and the Institute for Security Studies, but a much broader coalition of groups, which gave it far greater political strength.

As I note in Chapter 1, civil society has in some respects weakened in recent

years, in particular the democracy and human rights sectors. While Equal Education has emerged as a powerful campaigning organisation, and R2K itself has
been dynamic and effective, other important organisations such as IDASA have
closed. Few organisations, if any, pay much specific attention to Parliament –
except for the Parliamentary Monitoring Group (PMG), which, I am proud to
say, I founded with fellow NGO parliamentary observers Alison Tilley (then of
Black Sash) and Advocate Susannah Cowen (then of the now defunct Human
Rights Committee) in 1995. PMG continues to provide invaluable reports of the
proceedings of parliamentary committees (in the absence of any official records).[1]

The ANC must be delighted by the plight of organisations such as IDASA.
Well, some parts of it at least – the parts that don't much care for real debate, that
treat NGOs as 'foreign agents' and that are so intellectually insecure that they
run for cover at the first whiff of anything approaching a fact-based exchange
of views.

Of course, in the case of the R2K campaign and the secrecy bill, the 'debate'
was toxic from the word go. From the government side, it was run and relentlessly
pursued by the securocrats who have a much greater hold over such matters
since Zuma came into power. Cedile reminds me that the *Mail & Guardian*, with
a simple bit of technological investigation, revealed that the documents given to
the ANC members of the National Assembly ad hoc committee that considered
the secrecy bill were authored by a Dennis Thokozani Dlomo, then an intelligence
advisor to minister of state security Siyabonga Cwele.

Cwele accused the R2K campaigners in Parliament of being 'paid proxies' of
'foreign spies', and referred to them as the 'Right to Lie campaign'. Incidentally,
Cwele subsequently rewarded Dlomo in 2012 by appointing him acting director-
general of the State Security Agency (a position he still holds at the time of
writing, notwithstanding stories emerging in the press about probity[2]).

Hunter says that 'they pushed the idea that we were "obsessed with openness"'
and, as the public war of words worsened through 2010 and 2011, so the claims
about the R2K campaign became more and more vitriolic.

But when I ask Cedile who had the power in the battle between R2K and
Parliament, he surprises me at first: 'Parliament is a powerful institution.' As he
proceeds, however, I realise that he is paying careful respect to the institution – it
is, after all, the primary democratic product of the struggle for freedom. And
Cedile is of an age where that still matters a great deal; for any black person who
fought against apartheid, the victory – expressed in the form of universal suffrage
and a Parliament that free and fair elections deliver every five years – is something that should be treated with respect.

But he is quick to qualify his initial statement: 'Powerful, but vulnerable
as well.'

'To what?' I ask.

'They are nervous about perceptions. Look how they announced the secrecy bill during the World Cup [in mid 2010]. Look how quick they are to remind people, through the media, that "we liberated you". They were nervous, jumpy and called us names. And a new phenomenon emerged – impressing those in power.'

Doing the right thing in Parliament

On a Sunday morning, David Maynier is often to be found at the big table inside Melissa's coffee shop at Constantia Village, perusing the morning papers with his breakfast. This is where I meet him to discuss the state of South Africa's national Parliament.

On this occasion, in late summer 2013, he is sitting outside when I arrive, reading Frank Chikane's second volume, *The Things That Could Not Be Said*, which had just come out. He is obviously a political junkie: I had not yet even seen the book on sale anywhere, but Maynier was already halfway through it. We discuss the importance of such 'insider accounts'. For Maynier, 'it is especially valuable in terms of gaining a greater understanding of how the intelligence community in government operates'. For me, the so-called political analyst, democracies need such insider accounts to give sustenance – or constructive contradiction – to the 'outside' analysis that we all trade in.

Defence and national security is the beat that Maynier has made his own, though in fact it was his second choice. Maynier initially wanted state security, something that he notes is 'subject to very – and this is putting it delicately – limited democratic control', but as a new entrant to Parliament after the 2009 election he had to accept his second choice: the defence portfolio.

It does not seem to have held him back or harmed his prospects. Indeed, he has stamped his authority on it – ever since, he says, he called a press conference on 2 August 2009 after receiving information that showed South Africa was either selling or about to sell conventional weapons to a series of what Maynier calls 'rogue states'.

Initially, Maynier set his sights on a very important part of South Africa's new democratic institutional machinery – the National Conventional Arms Control Committee (NCACC).

Established by the National Conventional Arms Control Committee Act of 2002, the NCACC was created in order to provide regulatory oversight of trading in conventional arms by South Africa. Pursuant to the Act, no person may trade in conventional arms or render foreign military assistance unless that person is registered with the Directorate Conventional Arms Control and is in possession of a permit issued by the NCACC.

While the NCACC scheme essentially involves ex post facto reporting – i.e. there is no legal requirement to get the permission of the committee prior to sale – the presence of the NCACC and its obligation to provide quarterly reports to Parliament[3] help ensure that careful consideration is given to arms sales so that South Africa's reputation is not sullied by weaponry being used by purchasers against their own citizens or for offensive purposes.

The DA press release presented by Maynier on 2 August 2009 claimed that

> dodgy deals that have been 'authorized' by the NCACC include:
> - selling glide bombs that could be used to deliver nuclear, chemical and biological weapons to Libya;
> - selling multiple grenade launchers to Libya;
> - selling multiple grenade launchers to Syria; and
> - selling thousands of multiple grenade launchers and upgraded assault rifles to Venezuela.
>
> The dodgy deals that are 'pending' authorization by the NCACC include:
> - attempting to sell thousands of aviator G-suits to Iran;
> - attempting to sell thousands of sniper rifles to Syria; and
> - attempting to sell millions of rounds of ammunition to Zimbabwe.[4]

It was the press conference that 'launched my political career', Maynier says now, although he adds, in appealingly self-deprecating fashion, 'largely, or at least to some extent, because I had no idea what I was doing, in that I convened the press conference and revealed the information in the parliamentary precinct but not in the chamber of Parliament itself and so I did not have parliamentary privilege'. Did he not realise this, I ask? 'Frankly, I felt so strongly about the issue and I was so determined to put it into the public domain ... I did not bother to think it through.' He had taken advice on the 'line and the message', but not legal opinion per se.

There was all manner of speculation, put out by national intelligence, that he might be prosecuted, and it was not long after that he did have to retain attorneys and not long before he was 'advised about what to do in the event of my arrest'.

It was a baptism by fire, albeit one of his own choosing. If you can't stand the heat, don't go into the kitchen. 'It was an extremely stressful period and, frankly, [it] terrified my parents. But I had no doubt through the whole saga that I was doing the right thing.'

Parliamentary power: Structural and political limitations

But how does Parliament – as an institution – do, or not do, the 'right thing'? This question is fundamentally about power and how power is or is not utilised within the institution and between it and other institutions, most particularly the executive arm of government.

Parliament performs two main functions that determine the nature of its primary relationship with the executive and, therefore, its power or lack of it: legislative process and executive oversight. In turn, four factors are likely to determine the extent to which these two opportunities for meaningful exercise of parliamentary power over the executive play out: first, the Speaker and Deputy Speaker; second, the electoral system and the structural and political impact this has; third, the parliamentary committees and their chairs; and fourth, the ruling party and its whippery.

The Speaker and Deputy Speaker

Arguably, the Speaker – whose primary role is to chair the sessions of the National Assembly, but who quite obviously plays a managerial role as the head of the institution – despite the importance of his position, in terms of both its ceremonial frontage and its procedural authority, does not wield a huge amount of influence. As I will later suggest, the parliamentary committees at least have the potential to exert serious oversight over the executive. Compared with the committees, at their best and most effective, the Speaker's role is relatively limited. In my opinion, it is more by omission than commission that the Speaker exerts a negative influence over the balance of power between institutions of governance.

For example, when news broke that thirteen South African soldiers had been killed in the Central African Republic in March 2013, Parliament was conspicuous by its absence. Surely this was the moment to recall Parliament – which happened to be in Easter recess – to perform its constitutional function by 'providing a national forum for public consideration of issues' (section 42(3))? But Speaker Max Sisulu was silent. He did nothing. He is, to put it bluntly, a very lazy politician. As chief whip of the ANC in the late 1990s, he was notorious for wandering in mid-morning. One of his then advisors told me he would call Sisulu some mornings only to discover that he was still at home. I am not sure a great deal has changed. Since he became Speaker after the 2009 election, once again overlooked for executive appointment – despite his aristocratic name he has never been in the cabinet – he has done nothing to stamp his authority on Parliament, which as an institution meanders along.

As for the Deputy Speaker, former mayor of Cape Town Nomaindia Mfeketo, the less said the better. She has courted controversy from the word go with a number of partisan rulings.

The electoral system

When assessing the power of Parliament, it is important to focus on the power of the individual member of Parliament. In the South African electoral system, with a 'pure' proportional representation system and no constituencies, the seat in Parliament is 'owned' by the party and not the MP. The effect of this is that it gives an obvious controlling power to the party managers, especially the chief whip. They have complete power over the MP, who is in Parliament only because he or she was chosen to be on the party's electoral list and not because he or she was chosen by the local branch and then voted into Parliament by a majority of his or her constituency. Whereas in a constituency-based system an MP can say, 'I am here representing the voters of X and Y, was voted in by them and am accountable to them', he or she cannot say that in a proportional representation system, where the voters pick a party.

This is compounded by the socio-political and socio-economic realities of South Africa and its political class at this point in time. MPs earn a good salary, but many are playing catch-up with their careers; many will have little or no pension provision; they are supporting a wider family or group of people; they have no other career to fall back on and they are too old to contemplate retraining. They therefore need to hold on to their membership of Parliament.

The parliamentary committees

As I recounted at length in *Anatomy of South Africa*, the engine room of Parliament is now the portfolio committees. The most exciting development in the evolution of the South African Parliament since 1994 was the creation of the parliamentary committee system, which, at its best, is as strong as virtually any other Parliament in the world. The committee system is underwritten by the Constitution, which is unusual but helpful. Sections 55–57 of the Constitution provide for the role of committees: Parliament must create mechanisms to hold the executive to account; the committees have the authority to receive evidence and summon witnesses; they must facilitate public participation in the parliamentary process.

The system has been driven by the ambitious and talented men and women who were not selected as members of Mandela's government and who realised they would have to create an alternative career path within Parliament.

Hence the rapid evolution of the parliamentary committee system: the machinery of the new South African democratic Parliament. Blade Nzimande, Pravin Gordhan, Gill Marcus and Johnny de Lange, to name but four pre-eminent examples, led the education, constitutional affairs, finance and justice committees respectively into pastures new in the first democratic Parliament of 1994–99.

Strong – or *stronger* – Parliaments have combated the international trend towards executive dominance with the development of solid committee systems. Within the general public, not a lot is known about the committees and how they operate. They do not sound sexy and they do not attract television or radio coverage. But they are generating the heat as the real engine room of Parliament.

For the opposition parties, the exponential growth in both the number and the potential influence of the portfolio committees – each one 'shadowing' a national government department – presented great opportunities but also considerable challenges, not least how best to cover the ground adequately.

As the DA has grown in electoral support, so, of course, have its numbers in Parliament increased. Endowed now with sixty-seven seats in the National Assembly (having won almost 17 per cent of the votes in the 2009 election), the DA is better able to focus the efforts of its MPs than previously, when they inevitably were more thinly spread and had to take on a wider range of portfolios.

Thus, an MP such as Maynier is able to focus on defence and state security by limiting his parliamentary committee membership to the Joint Standing Committee on Defence and the Portfolio Committee on Defence and Military Veterans. He also currently sits on two ad hoc committees dealing with two specific and very important and controversial bills: the General Intelligence Laws Amendment Bill and the Protection of State Information Bill (the so-called secrecy bill to which this chapter returns later).

'My political business has expanded to state security in the sense that I serve on these two ad hoc committees,' says Maynier. It is interesting that he speaks in such terms. I wonder how many other MPs would do so. How many would think of their parliamentary role in terms of a career path?

It's an important point. As an institution, Parliament is only as strong as its members. If they merely see Parliament as a place to clock in and pick up the pay cheque, as many voting fodder members of the ruling party clearly do, then it's unlikely to encourage diligence or fortitude or expertise. If, however, the individual MP thinks, 'I can make a name for myself here or make a real difference', then the opposite may apply.

The individual qualities or otherwise of MPs, especially the committee chairs, as well as their level of motivation, matter greatly, above all in terms of how they perform in the parliamentary committees.

The role of the committee chairperson is critical to the new Parliament's well-being and relevance. There are twenty-six portfolio committees, one for each government portfolio. As veteran ANC MP and portfolio committee chairperson Johnny de Lange says, 'The strength of the committee depends on the strength of the individual who is chairing it, and the hegemony of the committee, especially among the ruling party members. If you have a weak chairperson who is scared of the opposition, then he or she is more likely to close things down. But if you [take] on the issues, then the ANC can show that it has the ideas. People in the opposition realised it was not the plenary, where you can talk nonsense and get away with it. We knocked the socks off of them on the issues.'

He points to the fact that many of the early chairpersons – Gordhan, Nzimande, Raymond Suttner, etc. – were intellectual giants with a culture of open debate. They were confident in their own ideas and therefore willing to have robust debates in their committees. The quality of the discussions flourished and, by osmosis, so did Parliament.

In terms of the current chairs, one can make a number of observations. First, they are a mixed bag in terms of experience – an important factor – with some who have been MPs since 2004, 1999 and even 1994. There are approximately fifteen former chairpersons who made it to a fourth term in Parliament, representing a relatively high degree of continuity, something committees need if they are to develop both strong conventions and their own institutional memories.

Second, the majority have 'struggle credentials' of some kind, as one might expect – from the anti-apartheid youth movement and ANC underground structures to involvement in the UDF, trade unions and the SACP. Some, like Vincent Smith, the 'shark-eyed filibuster supreme' (as I described him for his role in shutting down parliamentary oversight of the arms deal in 2001), have been rewarded with chairmanships.

Third, the current chairs are fairly highly qualified in terms of further education, and those with matric have made attempts to study further, usually through Parliament's Capacitating Programme in partnership with the University of the Western Cape.

Nonhlanhla Chanza is one of the most seasoned and expert parliamentary watchers around. Having worked for several years for IDASA's Political Information and Monitoring Service, she is now the parliamentary liaison officer for the Law Society of South Africa. She says that she has 'not witnessed major changes in parliamentary performance since 2006, particularly in terms of how Parliament performs its roles, especially that of holding the executive accountable'.

Chanza is, however, concerned by the fact that so many committee chairs get promoted to higher office. She notes that almost all cabinet reshuffles have resulted in some senior MPs, usually committee chairs, moving to the executive branch of government. When Mbeki was recalled as president in 2008, several ministers resigned from their positions, prompting the appointment of several committee chairs into ministerial positions. The 2009 general election also resulted in some chairs being appointed to cabinet, as have Zuma's subsequent cabinet reshuffles.

Besides changes in committee chairpersonship, Chanza has also observed that ordinary members are often moved from one portfolio committee to another. 'There is simply no guarantee that a member will serve a certain committee for the duration of the election term,' she says. 'Considering that it takes time for one to be fully conversant in issues, it is concerning to me that such changes continue to occur without due regard on the impact this might have on the work of the committee. While I cannot say what impact this has [been], I have been to many meetings where some MPs ask questions which they should already have answers to. Others simply don't ask questions and hardly contribute to the deliberations, and I have always wondered if this has got to do with ignorance of the issues under discussion. There needs to be a better way of controlling the movement of members between committees.'

The most powerful parliamentary committees

Standing Committee on Public Accounts
In contrast to the portfolio committees, whose oversight responsibilities have to compete with their law-making obligations, Parliament's Standing Committee on Public Accounts (SCOPA) is purely an oversight body. It is charged with the task of checking that public expenditure has occurred in the manner intended and with full value to the public. In this, its role interlocks with the constitutional mandate of the Auditor-General, one of the chapter nine constitutional watchdog institutions.

The work of SCOPA is extremely technical, and the experience and expertise of MPs are therefore disproportionately valuable to this committee. Chanza's view is that SCOPA has for the most part been the most 'feared' parliamentary committee by public officials, especially during the public hearings on the audited financial statements. 'This was once admitted to even by a senior government official while before the committee,' she recalls. 'I don't doubt that other officials share similar sentiments, as no government department has so far managed to escape tough questioning from committee members.'

SCOPA was 'hot, hot' when it had Mandla Mbili as its ANC whip. The late MP was very outspoken, speaking his mind on issues, interrogating the answers from officials and remaining consistent throughout. He even stood up for Parliament and the committee when the then minister of defence, Lindiwe Sisulu, refused to appear before SCOPA to account for her department's successive qualified audits. He strongly rejected the ANC chief whip's explanation, which sought to imply that SCOPA had no right to call the minister to appear before the committee. He also disputed the chief whip's version of events, who told the media that the question of whether the minister would appear before SCOPA was never discussed by the ANC caucus.

It was not surprising when Mbili was removed from SCOPA in 2010. In one round-table discussion hosted by IDASA, the current chair of SCOPA, Themba

Godi, mentioned a new tendency to fill committees with junior ANC members who cannot hold senior party members in government accountable.

Arguably, SCOPA has never recovered from the arms-deal saga in the early 2000s, when the ANC infamously imposed itself on the committee and forced out Andrew Feinstein, who had led the ANC study group on SCOPA which was then asking difficult questions of the executive in relation to the purchase of US$10 billion worth of weaponry.

Appointed in 2005, the independent-minded Godi, a member of the Pan Africanist Congress (PAC) then (he subsequently formed his own party, the African People's Convention, in 2007), has carefully rebuilt SCOPA and its modus operandi to the point where it has regained much of its pre-arms-deal credibility. However, notwithstanding Godi's skilful chairing, as the case of Feinstein and the arms deal showed, much still depends on the attitude of the ANC contingent and, in turn, the ANC whip on the committee.

'Obviously,' notes Chanza, 'the departure of Mandla Mbili from the committee had a huge impact on it, but this did not entirely stop SCOPA from having robust interactions with departments.'

Unlike with many other committees, members of SCOPA come highly prepared to meetings. This could be due to the intense briefings they receive from the Auditor-General and the preparations they have thereafter. They are attentive to detail and easily spot and reprimand officials for even grammatical errors in reports. Most importantly, members speak to the issues as highlighted by the Auditor-General. Party politics matters a little less than usual, as the committee members find common cause through the technical nature of their parliamentary responsibility – which is to assess whether public money has been spent as it was intended.

'Committee members across party lines seem determined to find answers to how the money was spent, whether the spending was justified and whether the public received value or not,' says Chanza. 'Government officials know that they have to come prepared when appearing before SCOPA and that their responses will be interrogated by its members.'

Like all parliamentary committees, its effectiveness suffers from Parliament's lack of a proper mechanism to monitor the implementation of the resolutions of the house by government departments, something that is a perpetual concern for Godi. Often the shortcomings that SCOPA identified in one year will crop up again the following year, having not been properly addressed by the relevant national department or government agency. In most cases, committee members will reprimand officials for their failure to fix the problems identified in the previous financial year. But this does not always result in a better financial performance. In other words, even in the case of a relatively well-performing parliamentary committee, there are structural limitations to its influence.

'What I noticed from monitoring the committee is that the work on a single report gets divided among committee members,' comments Chanza. 'One member will lead the committee's interrogation of a particular issue during the engagement with the department. Another member will take over and lead on another issue. Other members will ask additional questions on that particular issue. I think this ensures that there is always one member within the committee who masters a particular issue and can always take on the department and engage it.'

'This,' she adds, 'is not what things are like in other committees, where you find that only a few members will seem informed about the issues under discussion while others will remain quiet for the rest of the discussion. SCOPA's way of doing things also relieves the burden from the chair, as he does not need to be the only one to prepare for meetings.'

Portfolio Committee on Justice and Constitutional Development

The justice committee, as it is generally referred to, has always been the exception to the rule. As such, it is a very fine example of the point made earlier: that strong chairpersonship, combined with a commitment to creating institutional remedy and a convention of oversight or law-making diligence, is crucial to the power and influence of a committee.

Under Johnny de Lange – who chaired the justice committee during its formative period in the 1990s – the committee was active and diligent, passing more than 100 pieces of legislation and amending dozens of others. De Lange was an energetic, determined chairman and, as I argued in *Anatomy of South Africa*, a great parliamentarian.

In the intervening period since my first book, he enjoyed a few years in the executive, as deputy minister of justice. As always, he made the most of the situation and was as diligent as the limited role of deputy minister permitted. The truth is, I suspect, that while De Lange's golfing handicap lowered, so, too, did the quality of Parliament.

Regrettably, there have been too few great parliamentarians since 1994 for the institution not to miss someone like De Lange.

Branded an Mbekite, De Lange was removed from his government position after the 2009 election and is now once again a committee chair, this time in a portfolio which he initially knew very little about – water affairs. Unsurprisingly, he is making the most of it and enjoying the challenge of an area of policy that is vital for the long-term sustainable development of the country (water shortages are likely to become the new version of Eskom 'brownouts').

Meanwhile, his erstwhile stamping ground – the justice committee – continues to be reasonably effective, partly also because it has enjoyed continuity of membership. A small, cosy club of MPs has dominated for many years, and comprises John Jeffery from the ANC (recently appointed deputy minister), Dene Smuts and

Debbie Schafer from the DA, Steve Swart from the African Christian Democratic Party (ACDP) and eccentric one-off Mario Oriani-Ambrosini from the IFP.

Knowledgeable yet prone to cynicism, willing to listen to intelligent outside input but slow to suffer fools, this group is amusing to engage with, as I have done from time to time on various issues.

Vexing though their short-temperedness may be to outsiders making submissions to the committee, my own view is that they take their responsibilities very seriously and are committed parliamentarians who work hard and pay the difficult issues full attention, even if they constantly appear to be wandering in and out of meetings or busy on their BlackBerrys. Each of them is approachable and more than willing to be disturbed after hours on their cellphones. One cannot complain about this sort of accessibility and lack of grandeur.

For her part, Chanza has observed that 'party politics appear to matter less than [in] many other committees and decisions are generally reached through consensus. The committee rarely has to resort to a vote. There are often robust engagements with the justice department and all other bodies who appear before it. There are also lively discussions even among committee members.'

It also helps that some have legal qualifications, Chanza says, especially when faced with legal minds from the department. 'They don't leave any stone unturned and their interrogation focuses on issues even if it's the minister before [them].'

John Jeffery, or JJ as he is generally known, plays the leading role amidst the ANC members and liaises with the minister, Jeff Radebe. He will usually do the ANC leadership's bidding on any given matter and, when the political stakes are high, will kowtow to the executive. On ordinary legislative affairs, however, he will encourage the committee to play a full role, permitting the opposition MPs to contribute, often teasing them mercilessly or employing his idle brand of sarcasm.

'It's unfortunate that the chair, Luwellyn Landers, will always be associated with the role he played as the ANC's main man during the consideration of the Protection of State Information Bill,' notes Chanza, for, despite his political hinterland, Landers is actually a gentleman, who handles himself and those that appear before his committee graciously.

Portfolio Committee on Police
Under the chairmanship of Sindisiwe Chikunga, this committee consistently grilled and reprimanded South African Police Service management, including then national police commissioner Bheki Cele and police minister Nathi Mthethwa. Almost always, says Chanza, SAPS management was taken to task over everything that is wrong with the service and even 'the [Richard] Mdluli matter was not left off the hook ... The SAPS management were made to account for their decisions

or lack thereof. The chair was always on fire, sometimes leading the grilling of officials.' The well-connected Mdluli had been suspended, finally, as head of the police's powerful intelligence division, following his arrest on serious charges.

Judith February, who at the time led IDASA's parliamentary monitoring programme, concurs: 'Interestingly, she [Chikunga] started out inexperienced but seemed to have a desire to do the job she was tasked with. We had a meeting with her at the start about the release of crime stats behind closed doors ... she seemed willing to listen to our argument that there was no reason for it to happen behind closed doors, that the public should hear the interaction with the minister and where it happened was important – i.e. that it should happen at Parliament, as the democratic space was important, as opposed to it happening at some hotel' (as was Mthethwa's preference).

However, in June 2012, Chikunga was promoted to deputy minister of transport. Some saw this as a manoeuvre to get her out of the way as she was just too vibrant. The police committee is now chaired by Annelize van Wyk, a floor-crosser from the United Democratic Movement (UDM) and, before that, a National Party MP. After a hesitant start, she appears to also be taking a firm line, including writing a strong op-ed piece in the press after the brutal police murder of Mozambican Mido Macia in February 2013.

Portfolio Committee on Defence and Military Veterans
Chanza corroborates the notion that Maynier's number one committee has been more effective than most. 'The committee had its moment in 2010,' she says, 'when it was deliberating on the Defence Amendment Bill. It took some tough decisions when faced with the minister's [Lindiwe Sisulu] refusal to hand over a report which members argued was essential for its deliberations.' It even suspended its deliberations on the bill, but later caved in under pressure.

By this time, the Speaker, Max Sisulu, had already failed to show the committee the support it needed, and the ANC had issued a statement that appeared to criticise it. The chair of the committee, Nyami Booi, was swiftly removed from his position. Standing up to powerful members of the ANC is clearly a 'career-limiting move' – to use the euphemism that is often applied among ANC folk.

Maynier's admittedly partisan view is that 'at least in the Portfolio Committee on Defence, the new chairperson, Stanley Motimele, who replaced Booi, is there to ensure no oversight – it is patently obvious. I described him in a parliamentary debate recently as the minister's parliamentary valet. He has performed extremely well and ensured absolutely no oversight of the executive.'

Maynier adds, 'I thought Booi was a very good chairperson. History will show that he stood up to the minister.'

February agrees, recalling a particular tale: 'The committee was about to meet in secret. We wrote demanding that it continue to meet in public. [Booi] did not reply immediately. And so when I was due to be on Radio 702's David O'Sullivan drive-time show on the matter, I called Booi and asked him, "What shall I tell O'Sullivan? Open or closed?" He thought about it and said, "Open". In other words, he was responsive and willing to stick to principle.'

It was ultimately Booi's attitude to Minister Sisulu's lack of attendance before the committee that led to a stand-off and his firing. Not long after he was fired, Gwede Mantashe was in Parliament saying MPs should not upset ministers. In this model of democratic centralism, a committee's role is not to exercise any oversight.

So real scrutiny and oversight is almost non-existent. In Maynier's view: 'The defence force is a state within a state – beyond parliamentary oversight and scrutiny. In my time, the chief of the defence force and the service chiefs have not once appeared before the committee to account. I have asked many times.'

In addition, says Maynier, the committee has never been briefed on the military preparedness of the defence force – a point that was perfectly amplified in March 2013 as I was drafting this chapter, when thirteen South African National Defence Force (SANDF) soldiers were killed on duty in the Central African Republic, under circumstances that, at the time of writing, were riddled with confusion about the nature and purpose of their deployment and how it served South Africa's national interest.

Moreover, the committee's programme is decided by the parliamentary management group, Maynier adds, which includes the ANC's chair of caucus and chief whip, and they 'decide the programme without any consultation'.

Despite these political obstacles to parliamentary strength, when I ask Maynier to give me his 'league table' of successes since becoming an MP, he is briskly positive, encouraging, once again, the idea that if you are dogged and resourceful, Parliament can be a useful site of power and executive oversight.

Exhibit A is the NCACC, which was in the middle of a 'meltdown' (to use Maynier's word, one that is entirely justified) in 2009, when Maynier first turned his attention to it. When I had reason to examine the work of the NCACC – as a result of a commission from Lord Hoffmann on behalf of MTN in respect of the corruption claims that had been made against them by their rivals Turkcell, MTN having pipped Turkcell to the post in winning a highly lucrative new cellphone licence in Iran in the mid-2000s – I found that there was a 'black hole' in the NCACC's reporting to Parliament between 2005 and 2008.

There is no clear or satisfactory explanation for why there was this three-year gap in formal reporting, although it is possible that reports were prepared but classified and therefore not made publicly available. Indeed, the reports that *are* available are generally only now in the public domain as a result of proceedings brought by ODAC pursuant to the Promotion of Access to Information Act of 2000 on behalf of the Ceasefire Campaign, leading the pressure group to claim:

> The NCACC's annual reports are extremely bland. They report no issues that the Committee had to consider. They give no details of policy with regard to process or principle in the consideration of applications for arms exports or of matters of transparency. While they give country-by-country statements of the types of conventional arms exported and the value of the exports, they give no more than is required in terms of the Act; there is evidently no commitment to proactive transparency.[5]

The reporting of the NCACC has been erratic and, in some respects, lacking in transparency – the opposition DA has to push hard in Parliament for the required reports.[6] Nonetheless, for a long while, the NCACC was a reasonably functional structure and, under the chairmanship of the esteemed former human rights lawyer, the late professor Kader Asmal, established itself during its founding period as a serious new institution.

This needs some qualification. Asmal himself was not beyond criticism: despite seeking to develop a strong culture of oversight, he excluded Parliament from the ambit of the NCACC's work or, at the very least, made it hard for Parliament to play the role that the legislation intended of it (as the recipient of disclosures made to and by the NCACC).

Arguably, therefore, the positive impact of the NCACC was its direct influence on the executive arm of government: Asmal was respected and his independence of mind was to some extent feared by his colleagues in the ANC and in the cabinet. The very presence of the NCACC, despite its limitations, no doubt exercised a restraint on the government – something the government sources I spoke with when conducting my own research for the Hoffmann-MTN committee tended to confirm.

The NCACC wobbled as a result of the transition from Mbeki to Zuma and the inter-party conflict related to that transition. 'What we have seen over time, under Jeff Radebe, is a strengthening of the political component of the NCACC itself, evidenced by regular reporting,' asserts Maynier. Annual and quarterly reports have been submitted. 'One also saw a strengthening of the Directorate of Conventional Arms Control,' he adds.

Radebe? Really? I suggest that Radebe is as 'pragmatic as they come' – which is a euphemism for unprincipled, of course – so why would he bother? Radebe has 'simply complied with the legislation – no more, no less than that,' replies Maynier. He points also to decisions that the NCACC has taken, or not taken, in the past, which have caused unnecessary embarrassment to South Africa's international reputation. The Zuma administration is trying to put such matters to rest.

The role that Parliament has played in this process of bringing improvements in NCACC reporting 'are small, but important wins,' says Maynier.

The ruling party in Parliament

In a Westminster system, Parliament is always at a disadvantage when compared with the executive arm of government, which has by comparison all the resources and people, and all the political weight. As I described in *Anatomy of South Africa*, it is very hard for backbench MPs in such a system to stand up to their seniors – those holding positions in the cabinet – especially when the electoral system compounds the problem by giving the political bosses – which would by definition include those cabinet ministers as part of the leadership of the party – even more power.

The national executive committee of the ANC is elected (see Chapter 7), but when it meets, those cabinet ministers who were not elected onto the ruling party's chief decision-making body attend as observers. They may lack power and influence within the ANC – finance minister Pravin Gordhan, for example, was not an elected member of the NEC for the first three years of his time at Treasury; he was only elected onto the NEC at Mangaung in December 2012 – but they are still a part of the party's leadership.

So when a backbench ANC MP wants to stand up to a cabinet minister, it requires particular courage. And courage tends to come with experience. So, the younger you are, the newer you are to Parliament, the less likely you will be to have the courage and the means to do so.

Beyond the weekly ANC caucus meeting held on Thursday mornings, the ANC members of a particular committee meet as a 'study group', often prior to the committee's meeting on an issue or a bill, which is sometimes attended by the minister and sometimes by the director-general, 'which is absolutely wrong' in Maynier's view. (Incidentally, the 'study group' is always a key place to lobby if you want to influence a parliamentary committee.) In the case of the secrecy bill, R2K pointed out that at key moments Cecil Burgess and Luwellyn Landers, both members of the ad hoc committee, were getting their instructions directly from the executive. As Judith February explains: 'Burgess and Landers were both weak and pliable. They abrogated their responsibilities as members of Parliament completely.'

The minister is an MP and a member of the ANC caucus. What appears to happen, however, particularly when dealing with legislation, is that the director-general will brief the ANC study group on which amendments are acceptable and which are not. 'It subverts the legislative process completely', as Maynier puts it.

In the case of the secrecy bill, there was little real debate within the ANC study group of the ad hoc committee. But there was some level of debate within the NEC. Cedile claims that ANC secretary-general Gwede Mantashe intervened in order to ensure that the secrecy bill was discussed in the NEC that happened to be meeting the weekend before a vote in Parliament due to take place the following Tuesday, 20 September 2011. Mantashe was concerned that the bill had not gone 'through the right procedures in the ANC' – code for the NEC losing control of it to the executive, which in this case was hell-bent on passing a potentially draconian bill that in its early forms would have had a hugely chilling effect on the constitutionally enshrined right of access to information. It may have been an afterthought – too little, too late – but it showed the ANC's traditional centre-ground was waking up to the fact that its hawks in government were causing unnecessary political grief for the party.

At the NEC meeting, former intelligence minister Ronnie Kasrils – who had been minister of intelligence between 2004 and 2009, when the bill was first conceptualised, with very different intentions and legal content – spoke up against the bill, as did veteran Pallo Jordan. But their voices, as has so often been the case for the 'sensible left' in recent years, were not heard or heeded. The ANC is a different party now. Its core values have been diluted by the waifs and strays of political life. As evidence of this, its parliamentary party is now full of political 'mongrels', to use a rather ugly expression.

Two fine examples are the two aforementioned ANC MPs who were the R2K campaign's main antagonists in Parliament: Cecil Burgess and Luwellyn Landers. Both have come to the ANC from other parties: Burgess in 2005, having entered Parliament just a year earlier as a member of the newly formed Independent Democrats – he wasted no time in jumping ship and finding greener pastures, leaving the ID at the first available opportunity, namely the floor-crossing window in September 2005; Landers in 1994 from the National Party, which he had served in government as a deputy minister in PW Botha's last administration in the 1980s – a fact that the incorrigible veteran IFP MP, Koos van der Merwe, was all too happy to remind the house of during one of the more irascible debates on the secrecy bill in November 2011.

These two had little difficulty doing their new party bosses' bidding. Landers had been a champion of PAIA when it was passed in 2000, yet here he was fighting every inch in defence of a secrecy bill that would denude PAIA in significant and dangerous ways.

Whereas Landers was mild-mannered and moderate in his albeit misguided approach, Burgess was especially dismissive of R2K and hostile. He became known as 'Vetkoek' (a starchy Afrikaner snack, like a dumpling, that is well known across South Africa) by members of the R2K campaign, because of his protective concerns about the food brought to the parliamentary committee meetings.

There is no hard and fast rule, and most committees are happy to share their food with any visitors who are attending in order to make submissions or simply to observe. The R2K campaign set great store by always being present when the secrecy bill was being debated: it was a key element of their lobbying strategy, and something that many NGOs and other civil-society organisations fail to do, or are unable to do, because of Parliament's location in Cape Town and resource constraints.

Many of the R2K members who attended the parliamentary committee hearings were 'bussed in' by Cedile and Hunter; and they were often 'very glad of the committee snacks', as Hunter put it. But Parliament was not always a warm host. On one occasion, Burgess was overheard through his microphone whispering to the committee secretary, 'The food is out for the MPs only'. This led Matilda Groepe, a dynamic campaigner who has attained almost legendary status within R2K, to coin the nickname 'Vetkoek' for Burgess and it stuck, turning the large, grey-bearded MP into a figure of derision for the campaign.

The ANC whippery

The ANC chief whip and his team of whips are a key part of the parliamentary machinery and a critical site of power and its application. If cabinet is the buckle, then the chief whip is the belt and braces. In parliamentary systems, chief whips are there to marshal the troops and maintain party discipline. The position generally tends to attract charismatic people with real political clout – though the ANC's chief whip until his sudden removal in June 2013, Mathole Motshekga, fell short on both counts; he imposed his power through more basic methods, which meant he was widely disliked even by his own side.

The ANC whips in the National Assembly are mainly responsible for ensuring that ANC MPs execute their parliamentary duties in accordance with the decisions of the ANC caucus. The current list of whips is indicative of the type of person that prospers in the parliamentary system and rises to a position of some power within the ruling party caucus. As with the committee chairs, it is unsurprising to find that many have a history of involvement in the struggle: whether student or youth politics, anti-apartheid underground structures, the SACP, the UDF, the MK Military Veterans Association or the trade unions. Older MPs are likely to have worked in underground structures and lived in exile; some may have played a role in the activities of the UDF. Young MPs' struggle credentials come from involvement in the Congress of South African Students, student representative councils or the ANC Youth League.

The list also shows that some of these MPs are relatively new to Parliament, joining either in 2004 or 2009. There are some ANC whips, however, who joined in 1994 and are now well versed in its institutional nooks and crannies.

The whips are distributed around the various parliamentary committees and play a crucial role in holding the line and ensuring that the rank-and-file backbench MPs stay disciplined. Alpheus Maziya, the ANC whip in the Portfolio Committee on Defence, for example, will object to a question put by an opposition MP to a government minister or official and instruct the minister or official not to answer, according to Maynier. 'I protest, but in most cases the question is not answered,' he says.

Maynier adds that 'the average ANC member on a committee rarely reads the documents and is almost always unprepared and is, therefore, by and large supine and vulnerable to manipulation by the executive'. This is something that I myself have observed whenever I have sat in on a parliamentary committee meeting, except for the justice committee, which, as noted above, is run by a small group of experienced and relatively voluble MPs.

The ANC whips see it as their prerogative to censor the opposition, which is another way of impressing those higher up in the ruling party. Former chief whip Motshekga is, in the words of one veteran backbench ANC MP, 'a complete apparatchik, an utter hack ... and technically useless to boot'. His replacement, Stone Sizani – who was, surprisingly, taken from his position as chair of the rural development portfolio committee just as (or perhaps because) he was getting into his stride on the emotive subject of land reform – will have to re-motivate the ANC backbenches in the run-up to the 2014 election.

The parliamentary class of 2009

I am not sure that censoring the opposition is such a 'new phenomenon', as Cedile has suggested to me. When 229 of the ANC's 257 MPs voted in favour of the contentious Protection of State Information Bill, *City Press* editor Ferial Haffajee tweeted: 'Who stole the ANC? Who were those heckling, disingenuous people? Those cavaliers who killed free expression today? Who are ANC members of Parliament?'

All good questions, but not new.

Under Mbeki, Parliament became more docile, more willing to roll over in front of the executive. Structurally, it was bound to happen: the South African electoral system weakens the position of the MP in a fundamental way. As I have already noted, he or she is elected not by a constituency, but by virtue of being on a list compiled by his or her political party. Accordingly, MPs are beholden primarily not to the electorate but to their party and its bosses.

The Constitution itself reinforces this: if you lose your membership of the party whose list you appeared on at election time, then you automatically lose your seat. It's a pretty hefty sword of Damocles: one foot wrong and the whip's office will bring it crashing down and you will be out.

This, inevitably, encourages party loyalty. ANC members never vote against the party. They will tell you that there is robust debate behind the scenes – and once upon a time there was – but in recent years it has become blatantly clear that this is not true.

Initially after Zuma overthrew Mbeki at Polokwane, Parliament enjoyed a 'Prague Spring', as Judith February called it at the time. But the moment soon passed – perhaps because the new Parliament that was sworn in after the 2009 election was so inexperienced.

And so what of this current batch of MPs, the class of 2009?

By the time the 1994 Parliament's term ended, more than a quarter of the original 400 members had left Parliament. Put differently, in 1994, 252 MPs represented the ANC in the National Assembly. In 1999, this number increased to 266; 136 of the original 252 MPs elected to the National Assembly on the 1994 ANC ticket returned to Parliament. By the end of the second Parliament, in 2004, 102 of the MPs elected in 1994 remained. If one removes from this group those MPs who sit in cabinet but who do not engage in the day-to-day proceedings of the legislature, the figure drops to 75.

How many members of the 2009 Parliament are new to the institution, in particular the National Assembly? Table 6.1 shows the state of play as at 5 May 2009.

What are the implications of this high turnover?

In his State of the Nation address to Parliament after the 2009 election, Zuma announced that the fourth Parliament (2009–14) would be an 'activist' Parliament. Since then, Parliament's leadership has made a number of public statements aimed at positioning it as an 'activist' institution. There is, however, so far no evidence to suggest that Parliament has performed its duties differently or with new robustness or levels of energy – the golden period of the first Parliament of 1994–99 is but a faded memory now.

Chanza cites a number of examples in support of this proposition. In 2011, the Portfolio Committee on Public Enterprises had to consider amendments to the Companies Act of 2008. The committee had passed the bill in 2008, but it was later discovered that it was riddled with various grammatical and technical errors, 'such as inconsistencies, incomplete sentences, misalignment and ambiguities'. The committee spent the week of 18 January 2011 holding public hearings on the amendments.

The errors were attributed by some analysts to a lack of expertise within the committee, but this could also be a reflection of Parliament's weak legal capacity, which needs to be strengthened as recommended by the Independent Panel

Table 6.1: MPs in the 2009 Parliament

Political party	Seat	Old MPs	New MPs
ANC	257*	130	127
DA	67	23	44
COPE	30	4	26
IFP	18	12	6
UDM	4	2	2
ID	4	3	1
ACDP	3	3	0
FFPLUS	4	4	0
APC	1	1	0
PAC	1	1	0
MF	1	1	0
AZAPO	1	0	1
UCDP	2	2	0
Total	393†	186	207

* The ANC actually has 264 seats, but only 257 were filled as at 5 May 2009.
† Note that Parliament's official list as of 5 May 2009 only had 393 members of Parliament. This number may have increased to 400 as the remaining ANC MPs took up their seats.

Assessment of Parliament that was appointed in December 2006.[7] Amusingly, the then Speaker, Baleka Mbete, told the panel at its first meeting that she wanted to 'bring all the problem children together to assess Parliament'. Although it was tabled in 2009, Speaker of Parliament Max Sisulu has not lifted a finger to implement any of the ideas contained within the report.

This report specifically recommended that the Parliamentary Legal Services Office be expanded to address the weak drafting capacity among members, and that this matter be prioritised. However, in 2012, the Cape High Court also found faults with the Sexual Offences Act, while the president returned to the house the Intellectual Property Laws Amendment Bill, citing constitutional concerns. Addressing the National Assembly during Parliament's 2012 budget vote, Max Sisulu also spoke out against the poor quality of legislation that sometimes comes out of Parliament. He argued that this has resulted in some bills being returned to the house on the grounds of constitutionality:

I am concerned that more and more legislation is returned to the National Assembly for correction, either section 75 legislation which the NCOP [National Council of Provinces] has recommended that the Assembly amends to make it constitutional, or legislation that was found to be un-

constitutional by the courts ... This speaks both to the constitutionality
of the legislation passed, as well as its quality ... As the subject matter of
legislation becomes more sophisticated and highly technical, our Parliament
and members must become more professional. This requires the necessary
capacity both in terms of technical support by the officials and capacity
building for members.[8]

Sisulu announced that the Constitutional and Legal Services Office was in the
process of establishing and capacitating a legal drafting unit.

A note on age (based on the 2009 designated list of MPs)

ANC MP Andrew Mlangeni is the oldest MP. Born on 6 May 1926, he was almost
83 when he returned to Parliament after the 2009 election. He is followed by Ben
Turok, who was born on 26 June 1927; Mangosuthu Buthelezi, born on 27 August
1928; and Makhosazana Njobe, born on 13 May 1930. The mean age person is
Edna Molewa, born on 23 March 1957. The youngest MP is the current deputy
minister of higher education, Mduduzi Manana, who joined Parliament in 2009
at the tender age of 25. Other young MPs include Luzelle Adams of COPE (born
on 19 December 1981), Masizole Mnqasela of the DA (born on 1 March 1981) and
Lindiwe Mazibuko of the DA (born on 9 April 1980).

The future of Parliament

Parliament will always be there, come hell or high water. The primary question
is whether MPs can, either by themselves or in sufficient numbers in committees,
overcome Parliament's innate structural flaws, which tend to give the ruling
party and its bosses an undue amount of power.

With fellow DA MP Dene Smuts, Maynier believes that in the case of the
secrecy bill, 'we played a significant role in strengthening the legislation, especially in terms of the definition of "national security" and the public interest
defence'. And on the defence committee, Maynier campaigned for the termination
of the Airbus A400M contract, on which he had worked for three years before
finally being handed a substantial body of documents after a PAIA request –
another important tool in the opposition MP's armoury.

In the case of another significant matter, 'using Parliament to crowbar more
information about the National Industrial Participation Programme [NIPP] in
respect of the arms deal, out of DTI [Department of Trade and Industry], showed
convincing evidence that the programme was voodoo economics and a mon-
strous political fraud,' says Maynier.

He had gained possession of a document produced by an American law firm,
essentially a report on an internal compliance investigation by one of the primary

contractors in the arms deal. The investigation found all manner of dubious activity. Maynier used it to refine a set of questions about the NIPP – which had been used by Alec Erwin when he was trade and industry minister in the early 2000s to justify the arms deal – including a detailed set of parliamentary questions to the minister and a detailed set of PAIA requests.

After pressure in Parliament, and with the arms-deal commission coming down the track, the DTI finally provided information and undertook to complete a policy review – a 'positive' development, concedes Maynier – and, again in anticipation of the arms-deal commission, a project-by-project analysis of the NIPP.

These are all 'small wins, but they add up,' says Maynier. 'One has to be unrelentingly determined and driven, year in year out, month in month out, week in week out.'

Can others emulate him? Maynier had a competitive advantage after all. He had spent time in the parliamentary research office earlier in his career and was Tony Leon's chief of staff, driving the issues on which Leon campaigned. He served a political apprenticeship in Parliament. 'So, the way Parliament functioned and the various methods that are available to one, to effectively drive an issue, were familiar to one,' he says now, somewhat demurely.

Another 'tool in the box' of the opposition MP is the parliamentary question. Chanza has noticed the increasing use of parliamentary questions as an oversight tool by the DA, which has enabled it to expose the undesirable actions of cabinet ministers.

Most of their questions in the past, and especially from 2009 onwards, have probed the spending habits of the executive in light of calls by the president and the finance minister for South Africans to tighten their belts.

There were challenges, though, as some ministers simply refused to respond to questions, citing security concerns. 'This,' Chanza notes, 'was when they were asked about the amounts they spent on luxury hotels. The minister of water and environmental affairs Edna Molewa was, for example, quoted as having responded by saying that "I am not able to answer this question as it deals with matters that may negatively impact on my personal security and operations of the department".

'It is unfortunate,' Chanza continues, 'that issues arising out of the responses from these questions were never really investigated further by Parliament or any of its committees.'

Despite this, Chanza has witnessed a willingness on the part of Parliament to have its performance of its duties scrutinised by outsiders. This could have been influenced by the processes of the African Peer Review Mechanism, she suggests, which recommended that Parliament have its performance assessed. As a result, a panel of experts was selected and tasked with the responsibility of providing a comprehensive review of Parliament's performance of its duties as outlined in the Constitution.

The aforementioned Independent Panel Assessment of Parliament was the first initiative of its kind, but many of its recommendations are still to be implemented and debated at length by the house.

Another important initiative was the establishment of a task team to produce a new oversight and accountability model for the institution in 2009. The task team produced its report, which proposed several structures to assist in enhancing Parliament's oversight abilities.[9] Many of these structures have not yet been established.

'Basically,' says Chanza, 'there are two documents out there with sound information on what needs to be fixed and how. While these documents are not entirely gathering dust, as they have been discussed even by the joint rules committee, there does not seem to be any rush in taking practical steps to implement the recommendations. Had this happened, maybe we would now be talking of some form of change in how Parliament goes about doing its work.'

In terms of providing resources for MPs, Chanza thinks there have been improvements. Parliament's research unit continues to be beefed up with the appointments of more researchers and content advisors to guide committees in their work.

'There is high turnover of researchers and this may impact on the work of committees. Besides committee secretaries, there are also committee assistants and committee chairs have their own PAs. There are also plans to strengthen Parliament's legal services to address the poor quality of some bills that come out of Parliament,' she adds.

Another question to ask when regarding the future of Parliament is whether or not outside bodies, especially campaigning civil-society organisations, such as R2K, can leverage some political space to advance their cases through Parliament. With the secrecy bill, given that it was a bill and there was a legislative process, Parliament could not be avoided.

How, in Maynier's eyes, did they do? 'They were successful in making the secrecy bill a national issue. How successful were they in influencing the legislative process? Very weak, I would say, for a combination of reasons: lack of drafting skills, legal capacity, and not appreciating the detail of the process.'

Maynier maintains that the most effective lobbyist is well-known Webber Wentzel attorney Dario Milo, who represents the *Mail & Guardian* and often takes on cause célèbre cases relating to free speech. Milo has the skills to scrutinise the secrecy bill from a legal point of view on behalf of his client – in this case Print Media SA – and to put forward alternative drafting, something that is absolutely crucial if one is to have an impact on the legislative process during the committee stage.

Maynier says that he does not want to be understood as writing off the R2K campaign, however: 'The art of lobbying is not really practised in the South African Parliament. Civil society has some power but does not effectively use it in the legislative process.'

Conclusion

Which brings us back to Zille's T-shirt. It was an awkward moment, to say the least. 'I said to her,' recalls Cedile, 'it is nice to have you here in an ordinary T-shirt, but not a DA one.' Cedile didn't want the campaign to be conflated with the opposition, which makes perfect sense. I remember how, when I was a regular lobbyist in Parliament in the 1990s and the early 2000s, we would be anxious not to attract 'too much' DA support. With DA MPs that we knew well enough, we'd say, 'Ease off a bit, pretty please'. We did not want the ANC position to harden because of our association with the main opposition. This lobbying principle remains as sound now as it was ten years ago – perhaps even sounder, as the DA presents more of a challenge to the ANC electorally. However, it also complicates things. The DA is also now in government – at least provincial and city government. And, as it mounts a more serious challenge to the ANC, so NGOs are going to have to think long and hard about their positioning in relation to both the ANC and the DA.

That, in turn, will likely expose any ideological or political differences within the civil-society organisation. R2K's strength was that it was a diverse campaign, with many different voices and organisations. But this was also, potentially, its greatest weakness. Indeed, there were at times vigorous differences of opinion about strategy and tactics within the R2K campaign's steering committee, which included hard-left organisations such as the Alternative Information Development Centre – who wanted to boycott the 'bourgeoisie parliamentary process' – and liberal organisations such as the Institute for Security Studies, then represented by Hennie van Vuuren. In the middle were progressive organisations such as ODAC and IDASA.

As Hunter says now, looking back: 'We had a strategic problem, but we resolved it by adopting the approach advocated by Dale McKinley, namely, "Comrades, we must occupy every space".' The R2K campaign proves the integrity – both intellectual and strategic – of such an approach: by occupying more than just the parliamentary space, the R2K campaign was able to make Parliament more powerful than otherwise it would have been, despite its many 'vulnerabilities' and other structural limitations and weaknesses.

Otherwise, you'd need an army of great parliamentarians like David Maynier.

7

The ANC

'The ANC is a fumbling, bumbling, chaotic organisation.'
~ ANC MP and minister's aside to the author, February 2013

A centenarian political cocktail

For cringe-worthiness, it took some beating. As the 100th birthday party of the ANC finally neared its end on 8 January 2012, the party's top brass poured each other glasses of champagne and ate cake in front of a stadium of supporters who, despite the unrelenting heat of a mid-summer Free State day, had not been given a single glass of water let alone a sausage.

Even the habitually thick-skinned Jacob Zuma appeared to wince as ANC chairperson Baleka Mbete raised her glass to him and the centenarian liberation organisation he now leads, while their more media-savvy colleagues in the national executive committee shuffled to get out of shot or hid behind colleagues.

They knew it looked bad. Earlier, the increasingly supplicant national broadcaster, the SABC, had obligingly declined to comment on the fact that as Zuma lapped the stadium perimeter, a section of the crowd had offered not applause but the wheeling hands that football managers use when they wish to signal a substitution. These were supporters of Julius Malema, the apparently militant, neo-fascist ANC Youth League leader whose populist rhetoric had won him notoriety internationally as well as in South Africa, but who was now facing disciplinary charges – charges that would soon after see his party membership suspended and ultimately terminated.

This was the very same hand signal that Malema and his followers had used in December 2007 at the ANC's last national elective conference in Polokwane to propel the crushing 'Zunami' that unseated Zuma's predecessor, Thabo Mbeki, from the ANC presidency and later led to his unceremonious removal from the presidency of the country in September 2008, just six months before his second and final five-year term of office was to end.

What goes around comes around.

You don't need many years to pass to recognise that this period, 2007 to 2009, was a pivotal time in the ANC's history, one in which old certainties were vanquished and new uncertainties cast long shadows into the future. Mbeki was present at the birthday party in Bloemfontein, showing signs that he was at last emerging from the long and perfectly understandable sulk that had followed his undignified ousting four years previously. He must have wondered whether to laugh or cry when he heard that at the first NEC meeting after the botched celebration, time had been taken to debate how best to deal with public cake-eating in the future. As a metaphor for the state of the nation they liberated, as well as that of the ANC, there may be no sharper image available.

Apparently, however, the ANC wants to have its cake and eat it too. An assessment compiled and presented by Mbete a month later concluded that in future celebrations 'the eating of cake should be made in private, as it does not augur well [sic] to be eating in front of our members and supporters while they are not eating'.

Bored and thirsty, thousands had actually already left the stadium by the time the ANC leadership made its clumsy faux pas. Many had departed during Zuma's hour-long, detailed recitation of the ANC's key historical accomplishments. Though it was a well-constructed speech – and to those with short memories, an ample reminder of the ANC's pivotal role in resisting apartheid – Zuma is not a riveting orator, at least not when speaking English.

In his mother tongue, isiZulu, he is charismatic and engaging, often slipping effortlessly into song and dance. It is one of the main reasons that he may still be an electoral asset for the ANC, despite his many personal flaws and indiscretions and the ongoing questions about his probity and fitness for high public office.

Though the circumstances are different, and the context is much changed, Zuma's job is fundamentally no different from that of any of his predecessors. The ANC has always been a broad political church. To many, its ideological diversity can be confusing, because it is tempting to think that, on the basis of its principled and courageous stand against apartheid, the ANC is an intrinsically progressive, left-of-centre organisation.

It is far more complicated than this. And you'd be forgiven for asking, what exactly is the ANC these days? Never mind the cake and champagne on the stage; a tour of the restaurants, bars and clubs of Bloemfontein on the nights either side of 8 January would have shocked those who nostalgically hang on to an outdated image of the ANC as a disciplined 'revolutionary' movement, self-sacrificing in character and disposition. As the Moët flowed, the ANC's nationalist elite – and its parasitic corporate hangers-on – flaunted its newfound wealth, presenting another side of the ANC: a bling culture of excess, which cannot easily be described as the embodiment of moderation.

Such has been the dominance of the ANC electorally since 1994 that to any opportunist seeking wealth, especially state resources, the ANC was the obvious route. In *Anatomy of South Africa*, I likened the ANC to the heart of the body politic, with every artery and vein running through it – a veritable marketplace of buyers and sellers.

These days it is more of a bazaar than a marketplace (pun intended), given the full extent of its eclectic and exotic inhabitants. Little is known about the origins of ANC rank and file, but if the parliamentary party is in any way indicative of the genealogy of the organisation as a whole, then its political roots are really showing.

As political scientist Susan Booysen's research on floor-crossing records, during the period when floor-crossing was permitted (enabling elected MPs and councillors to move from one party to another, during specific 'open-window periods', notwithstanding the overriding proportional representation dimension to South Africa's electoral system), 1 400 public representatives switched party affiliation and allegiance between 2002 and 2007, the great majority of them representing net acquisitions for the ANC.[1]

As a result, the ANC has within its ranks numerous members of the National Party, for example, as well as other smaller parties that – like the United Democratic Movement – exploded on the scene and then died away, welcomed into, and smothered by, the warm embrace of the ANC's commodious bosom. The impact on the way the ANC wields its power by virtue of having so many 'waifs and strays' within its ranks should not be underestimated; as I point out rather inelegantly in Chapter 6, with reference to former apartheid-era minister Luwellyn Landers and another floor-crosser, Cecil Burgess, in the case of the secrecy bill, a mongrel party is always likely to produce 'mongrel politics'.

Of course, the real motives for people joining the ANC are hard to discern; they may be good or they may be malign. But the inescapable fact is that someone who has not been brought up in the traditions of the ANC, and who has not been exposed to its value system and its basic ideological reference points through its political education programmes, is more likely to stray from it than someone who has.

Alternatively, like a Landers or a Burgess, they are so eager to please their new masters that they are excellent at following orders and doing the 'dirty work'.

Ronnie Kasrils, a former cabinet minister under both Nelson Mandela and Mbeki, once explained to me that the ANC has two great traditions: the one socialist, with a class-based analytical frame of reference; the other nationalist, with a primarily race-based analytical lens.

Kasrils used to wax lyrical about the ANC's hybrid ideological tradition. 'Put simply,' he once told me, 'it's about the relationship between class and race. As to the balance between the two, there are key divides and cleavages historically. On one side are the trade unions and the SACP, with their Marxist, socialist influence, as an agent for class change. On the other side, there is the instinct towards African nationalism. The ANC emerges from this as a broad-based movement.'

The socio-economic conditions of nineteenth-century South Africa, with its pronounced industrial revolution and growth in the mining sector, Kasrils now argues, meant that a class-consciousness arose, which was the primary ideological driver within the ANC during the early decades of its life. Offering a variation on this theme, long-time ANC member and activist Lawson Naidoo's view is that the early ANC leaders were quite focused on political rights for a black middle class rather than espousing the plight of black workers. The 'left tradition' only emerged with the formation of the Communist Party of South Africa in the 1920s and took a while to take hold in the ANC.

But, Kasrils then explains, the advent of an explicitly racist state in the mid-twentieth century meant that it was natural and inevitable that a black Africanist response would emerge and then compete for hegemony within the ANC. Since then, the two ideological traditions have jostled for primacy.

It is a complex subject that deserves and certainly requires a full treatise, for which there is no room here. But the key to understanding the ANC's finessing of the tension between the two great impulses is leadership. Mandela and Mbeki, Kasrils maintains, are both in their own ways classic examples of what is required.

'Look at Mbeki's speeches,' he urges, 'and there you will find the code-breaker for Mbeki is the class–race prism. His analysis always takes account of both and crosses the divide between them to a greater or lesser extent.' Whereas Mandela was more 'intuitive' in his resolution of the tension between the two, Mbeki was 'more analytical' – fond of asking his ultimate Socratic question: 'Will the centre hold?'

Arguably – and it is deeply contested within the ANC, not least by those who joined the Zuma bandwagon at Polokwane in order to oust Mbeki – Mbeki's greatest achievement was to have ensured, at least for a decade, that the ANC's fundamental division between its race-orientated African nationalist tradition and its class-based Marxist tendency was balanced sufficiently for the party to retain a sense of equilibrium.

At the risk of oversimplifying things, the socialist tradition – which is sometimes described as 'Charterist', in reference to the Freedom Charter that was launched in Kliptown in 1955 – is preoccupied with the fair distribution of wealth and power, while the nationalist tradition – sometimes described as 'Africanist' – is far more concerned with the acquisition of wealth and power by Africans.

Crossing the Sahara

Trying to clarify the ANC in one's own mind, let alone explain it to someone else, is like setting off across the Sahara. It is daunting and dangerous. Some routes are safer than others. Lots of things can go wrong. Even people who live there don't know enough about it to guarantee your safety.

As a starting point, it is certainly important to understand that the ANC is not ideologically monolithic or homogeneous; that there are these two broad traditions, continuously jostling for ascendancy.

But I would add two other dimensions to this ideological one: the first deals with the operational or institutional culture; the second is strategic. Within the first, there are also two competing traditions, loosely attached to the exile and non-exile ('incile') traditions of the ANC. The exile movement, represented most obviously by the characters of Mbeki and, in a different way, Zuma, was necessarily secretive, hierarchical, paranoid and neurotic in its organisational character and institutional temperament. It was also cosmopolitan and worldly, bringing complexity and sophistication to the ANC's strategy and tactics.

The 'inciles' were, and are, more approachable, straightforward and consultative, more naturally open and participatory, less hierarchical, and more down to earth in their approach – best characterised by the UDF's internal opposition to apartheid, although one must accept that there are obvious exceptions to this 'rule': the ANC's internal underground, with people like Mac Maharaj running Operation Vula for example, was necessarily highly secretive.

On the strategic dimension, there is also underlying tension: a sense of an unresolved issue that plays out in subtle ways, between the 'negotiate/dialogue' school on the one hand and the 'fight to win an incomplete revolution' school on the other. It is messier and more opaque than the other two, and stems, in my mind, from the early 1990s and the negotiations that led to the 1994 election and the Final Constitution. It is far too soon to offer any definitive or authentic historical view on whether the process was a 'sell-out' by the ANC or a 'great victory' or, most likely, somewhere in between. But the 'fight to win/no surrender' school, whether unrequited revolutionaries or zealot nationalists who want more wealth and power, increasingly want to blame the settlement, and the Constitution in particular, for any woes or 'lack of transformation' that catches their eye.

Those of the 'negotiate/dialogue' school, however, cling to the idea that South Africa's negotiated settlement was a wondrous process, with a beautiful outcome. I was not there, but I am certainly part of the school that admires the Constitution, whose creation I did have a modest hand in as an independent NGO lobbyist for IDASA, and believes that it continues to offer South Africa a sturdy, progressive, transformatory framework that is proving its value all the time, whether its transformational impact is fully understood or appreciated or not.

The tension between the progressive constitutionalists and the populist revolutionaries is rising all the time, and has yet to reach its boiling point. It mirrors the natural, longer-standing tensions and contradictions within the ANC over core ideology, though there is not a neat overlap between, say, the progressive constitutionalists and the democratic socialists, because some of the latter are suspicious of the law and/or do not understand the extent to which the Bill of Rights is continuing to provide protection to the most vulnerable workers and communities in the land.

These are all, in any case, caricatures, which I offer merely for some kind of guidance – a map for the Sahara – to anyone who is serious about trying to grapple with the giant creature that is the ANC.

Table 7.1: A rudimentary multidimensional prism for helping to understand the ANC

Analytical dimension	Tradition	Tradition
Ideological	Democratic socialist	African nationalist
Strategic	Negotiate/dialogue	Fight to win/no surrender
Organisational culture	Incile/UDF	Exile

(Note: The traditions are not aligned, in that not all the democratic socialists are negotiators and/or inciles, etc.)

Who is supposed to run the ANC?

The president

The primary task of any ANC leader, Kasrils maintains, is to pull together the predominant two traditions – nationalist and socialist. In order to do so, he says, 'every ANC president must have a foot in each camp but rule from the centre'.

Is this something Zuma is capable of? So far, his approach to coping with the ANC's broad church is not to pull the far reaches of the right and the left towards the centre, but simply to raise the sides of the tent to allow more space for everyone. It is not a strategy that is working or that is likely to succeed. Instead of pulling members towards the centre, he allows them to pull him outwards, in both directions.

He should never be underestimated. His ability to survive, to fight until the death, is extraordinary. In 2005/6 he had hit rock bottom, but he dragged himself out of the gutter, and built a remarkable if incohesive coalition. As an exile veteran, whose far-from-complimentary views on Zuma's relationship with money and women I cite in Chapter 2, says: 'Zuma has great quality as a leader. He is very brave; not a coward.'

The problem, she says, is that 'just like with Mbeki, no one stands up to him. The NEC is hopelessly weak and individuals who should have the guts to do so don't.'

Zuma's cabinet is effectively a coalition government – with representatives from the SACP and COSATU sitting alongside social conservatives from the nationalist right of the ANC, such as the deputy minister of correctional services, Ngoako Ramathlodi, who is one of a number of nationalist ANC politicians who have in recent times blamed the Constitution for the lack of progress in transforming South Africa, describing the adoption of the new Constitution as 'a grand and total strategy to entrench … white economic interests'.[2]

As one leading member of the SACP admits to me, 'we are now having to respond to the fact that while Zuma has given us the power that Mbeki denied us, he has also created space for the right of the ANC to exploit'.

Apart from Booysen, with her fascinating but intricate eight-sided framework for understanding ANC power and its capacity for regeneration,[3] there is no better analyst of the ANC than Mcebisi Ndletyana, a public intellectual who, having been wastefully spat out by the HSRC for not doing enough 'billable hours', is now working with the country's leading political thinker, Joel Netshitenzhe, at the think tank that Netshitenzhe set up after he himself was wastefully spat out by the Presidency once Zuma had settled in, the Mapungubwe Institute for Strategic Reflection (MISTRA).

Ndletyana's chapter in the HSRC's excellent 2013 State of the Nation book skilfully relates the ANC's own ideological heterogeneity, and class interests and tensions, to policy making in government.[4] Since it follows that the tighter the ANC's grasp on 'the ANC in government', the more likely government is to reflect the ANC, this is highly important. However, Ndletyana's conclusion is that 'ideological plurality ought not to lead to policy incoherence. That happens only if the leadership is unclear of its policy choice or lacks confidence to implement its policies because of a shaky power base. This is true of the Zuma presidency of the ANC. He is reluctant to lead policy direction either way, for fear of alienating critical constituencies within the Alliance. This has engendered policy contradictions within Cabinet, projecting the image of a government lacking in clarity over how it seeks to achieve its own objectives.'[5]

This is the core leadership responsibility of the ANC president. For all but the last of his twenty-four years as ANC president (from 1967 to 1991), the late great Oliver Tambo discharged this responsibility with elegant distinction, initially from his house in Muswell Hill, north London, where he was first exiled, and then from ANC HQ in Lusaka, Zambia. At least that is the mythology. Certainly 'OR', as he is affectionately referred to by all those who knew and served him, was a guileful tactician and an astute diplomat. But he was also ruthless, as he knew he had to be, in order to maintain the organisational discipline necessary to overcome the apartheid regime.

But 'OR' also had the singular advantages that came with that period of history: an exiled liberation movement had, by its very nature, to operate secretively and with a strict, essentially military, hierarchical structure. And there was one goal, with one enemy. Declared a 'crime against humanity' by the United Nations, apartheid was a cruel ideology, but its crudeness and its self-evident injustice had a unifying effect for its enemy. Differences in ideology and in political outlook within the ANC could be relatively easily contained by reference to the 'greater goal' of defeating Pretoria. All else was secondary. The nationalist and socialist traditions could thus be peaceably housed under the roof of this meta-objective.

Once victory over apartheid was secured, of course, a centripetal impulse was removed. And, with hindsight, it is relatively easy to see that the struggle served to paper over the inherent divisions and contradictions in the ANC's political genealogy. In the absence of the common enemy, leading the ANC has become a more complex task in many respects, requiring endless dexterity and ingenuity, but also an ability to command enough respect enough of the time to create the 'followship' necessary to hold such a large and unruly group of people together.

Judged solely on the decisiveness of his victory at the ANC's last national conference in Mangaung in December 2012, Zuma is doing just fine. But evidence suggests that his victory was a combination of a weak challenge from Kgalema Motlanthe – that never really got off the ground, due to Motlanthe's lack of ruthlessness and hunger for the top job – and Zuma and his lieutenants' ability to manipulate the membership system.

The ANC's electoral college is comprised mainly of the delegates who are nominated by branches, proportional to their volume of members, with extra votes cast by representatives of the ANCYL and the ANC Women's League (ANCWL). ANC secretary-general Gwede Mantashe announced in the run-up to Mangaung that KwaZulu-Natal – Zuma's stronghold – had gained 87 000 new members since the beginning of 2012, up from 244 900 members to 331 820 (out of a total membership of 1.2 million). Meanwhile, the Eastern Cape – potential fertile ground for a (non-Zulu) challenger to Zuma – had gone in the other direction: at the beginning of 2012, it was hot on KwaZulu-Natal's heels with 225 597 members, but by September, when the final tallies were done, Eastern Cape membership had mysteriously slid to just 187 585.

This meant that about 38 000 members had left the party in that province or had not paid the R12 annual membership fee. Mantashe attributed the Eastern Cape's decline to serious organisational problems, which is plausible. However, the weakening of a province hostile to Zuma's re-election raised eyebrows. Limpopo and the North West also grew, from 114 385 to 161 868 and 60 319 to 75 145 respectively – provinces that were both largely supportive of the incumbent, but no less dysfunctional than the Eastern Cape (if anything, more so). In fact, the North West is probably the ANC's most dysfunctional province. It has two distinct camps that are at war. Before that, the province was run by a task team led by people from other provinces, deployed by the ANC's NEC. With all the confusion, they still managed to attract 15 000 new members.

The membership trends would have been a big deal if the NEC had accepted the suggestion that branches be allocated voting seats at Mangaung as a proportion of their membership size. That would have seen KwaZulu-Natal being allowed to send more than 1 000 delegates. But that format was rejected at an NEC meeting, where it was decided that each branch must have at least one delegate, as per the ANC's constitution. So, in terms of the 4 500 delegates that were supposed to vote at Mangaung, Eastern Cape went down from 877 in 2007 to 676 in 2012; KwaZulu-Natal, however, went up from 606 to 974.

Zuma had won even before the buses bringing delegates to Mangaung had arrived.

The deputy president

If it were not for the fact that it is Cyril Ramaphosa who is now the ANC deputy president, I would not be taking up space with this position, since, much like the deputy president in government, it falls so much into the shadow of the president. Traditionally, the secretary-general, and even the national chairperson and treasurer-general, have been much more influential and powerful members of the ANC's NEC than the deputy president – because they respectively run the organisation, chair the NEC meetings, and hold the purse strings.

The deputy president of the ANC, in contrast, holds little. Indeed, as Motlanthe found out to his cost in the run-up to Mangaung, once it seemed likely that he would run against Zuma, he suddenly found himself being sent by either Zuma or Mantashe to all manner of weird and wonderful corners of the big and beautiful country, to prevent him from mustering a coherent campaign. Motlanthe, for his part, was powerless to refuse their orders.

Ramaphosa is a different kettle of fish. I remember well the first time I heard him speak. It was soon after I had arrived in South Africa in February 1994 to work for the ANC's election campaign in the Western Cape, and the country seemed to be as highly strung as a Stradivarius. Ramaphosa was speaking at the Baxter Theatre in the middle-class suburb of Rondebosch in Cape Town. The audience was middle-aged as well as middle class, and almost entirely white.

There was a buzz of nervous anticipation, which fell into a deathly hush as Ramaphosa walked in. Standing, he looked them in the eyes, paused, released his gentle smile and said – and I will never forget the words – 'In a few weeks, we are all going to make history together'.

He paused as the audience let out a sigh of relief. People looked around; did he say 'we'? *We* are going to make history together? Really? Not 'them' making it for us?

It was an opening line as simple as it was brilliant. It didn't really matter what else he had to say; he had already won them over. Ramaphosa is, naturally, by instinct, a one-nation leader. He is Mandela-ian in that sense. His CV is extraordinary: he bravely and skilfully led the National Union of Mineworkers during South Africa's most difficult days in the 1980s; he was secretary-general of the ANC; he was chairman of the Constitutional Assembly, the main negotiating channel for the final constitutional settlement; and, once Mbeki had deviously and unforgivably pushed him away, he became a successful captain of industry.

Of course, those last two items on his CV do not stand him well in the eyes of some – i.e. those who regard the constitutional settlement as a sell-out and those – not necessarily the same people – who regard serving on the boards of companies like Lonmin, or making shiploads of money, as another form of sell-out.

But his integrity, talent and competence meant that, at the end of an extremely bad 2012, there was a ray of light. However, too much emphasis was placed on Ramaphosa's ability to pull the ANC and the government back from the abyss of despair that loomed large during the course of the year. He is but one man. And the ANC is a big beast to control. Moreover, it is a very erratic one these days. In the past, election to deputy president meant that next time round you would be president. This no longer pertains, as Motlanthe's removal shows, although some would say he was the architect of his own fate. Perhaps a more apt reference is Zuma's own ascent to the top: Mbeki not only resisted it, seeking a third term as ANC president at Polokwane, but was not that far off from preventing it, thereby disregarding Zuma's status as the incumbent deputy president.

Indeed, on the night that Ramaphosa was elected, the usually cool-thinking political journalist Carol Paton of *Business Day* tweeted: 'Ramaphosa will never be president! The ANC is run by thugs!' I sent her a text asking if the heat of the big Mangaung tent was getting to her and whether she was going to develop her thought beyond 140 characters in the columns of her newspaper … which she duly did.

She might be right. In 2017, the mood in the ANC could be quite different. The 2016 municipal elections might knock the ANC onto a different course. Ramaphosa might be deemed as too centralist or moderate for the needs of that hour. We will see. I believe in him and his talents, as do many; and he has the calibre, experience and credibility to provide the leadership the ANC needs.

One question is simply whether his unpredictable and eccentric party recognises his quality. After all, it must be pointed out that Ramaphosa owes his election as ANC deputy president primarily to the fact that he was on the Zuma slate; he did not come in on his own steam and having laid out his vision for the

ANC. Accordingly, as one ANC traditionalist puts it to me, 'Cyril will find it very difficult to turn the ship around mid-course, especially after it has been steered into such choppy waters by Zuma and his henchmen.'

The secretary-general

There are certain junctions or roundabouts in certain cities – usually busy cities in developing countries in Latin America, Africa and Asia – where, buried amid the cacophony of cars arriving at all angles, there stands a traffic officer with pristine white gloves. While all around there is madness, those crisp white gloves stand out as a beacon of order.

In terms of the ANC, that traffic officer is Gwede Mantashe – a smart, streetwise, equable (mostly), approachable (often) and jocular (nearly always) character, a 'paid-up member of the human race', with a sense of humour and rhino-thick skin, who doesn't seem to take criticism personally, and who is impossible to dislike even when he is defending the indefensible with a contorted logic that defies any form of mental gymnastics.

The fundamental purpose of his position as secretary-general is to manage the traffic. And the ANC is a very busy, very messy and very noisy roundabout. Sometimes, the white gloves are obeyed, sometimes not. But without them, a greater chaos would ensue.

What sane person would want to be the secretary-general of the ANC? It is an impossible task. While comfort is derived from the traffic officer's presence, which suggests a level of order in an otherwise dog-eat-dog world, however sharply pressed his uniform – at this point, with all due respect, the analogy begins to break down in Mr Mantashe's case – no one really believes that he is fully in control.

Mantashe is, nonetheless, an enormously powerful individual and arguably even more so than his two predecessors: Ramaphosa (1991–7) and Motlanthe (1997–2007). This is certainly true in Motlanthe's case, where the ANC president at the time (Mbeki) was an exceptionally dominant figure, although it can be argued that in the end it was Mbeki's failure to take proper care of his organisation that cost him his presidency of the ANC. Mbeki was so all-consumed by the task of leading government that he lost track of the ANC – a mistake that Zuma will never make.

As Mbeki's 'ANC in government' dominated, so the role of the secretary-general as the organisational CEO of the 'other ANC' (out of government) diminished, both in policy and political terms. Part of the aim of the Polokwane revolt was to restore equilibrium and assert the ANC's control over government – a responsibility that now sits with the secretary-general, but which is complicated by the fact that Mantashe wears more than one hat: like his two predecessors, he is a former general secretary of NUM, but, unlike them, he is also a member of the SACP's politburo.

The ANC and the SACP

The relationship between the ANC and its Alliance partners is a complex one, and one of enduring fascination and understandable interest. Unlike most 'normal' political parties around the world, understanding the dominant ideological outlook and balance of forces within the organisation is not enough, because there are competing interests and lobbies from two external allies. To the nationalists within the ANC, this is generally a source of annoyance. Even moderates, whose loyalties are to the ANC and who are suspicious of socialist ideas, are prone to grumble: one such MP, a former minister, is forever complaining; whenever I see him, he moans ceaselessly about 'those fucking commies, fucking everything up'.

Certainly, the approach of the SACP, and COSATU for that matter, is unashamedly 'entryist' – encouraging members of the SACP and/or COSATU to join the ANC and to work their way up the structures, exerting as much influence as they can at every point. Students of the ANC – such as Stephen Ellis, whose *External Mission: The ANC in Exile, 1960–1990*[6] attempts to explain how the ANC operated in exile under apartheid and the impact that it had on its culture and its future – argue that the SACP's attempt to take over the ANC has been a perennial feature of the ANC's life (and, argues Ellis, one that had significant negative consequences on its strategy and tactics as a liberation movement), and is likely to continue to be the case indefinitely.

In this sense, the entryist strategy has prospered under Zuma's 'big-tent' politics, as well as from the fact that he was compelled to reward those who supported him against Mbeki at Polokwane. The SACP, with the vigorous voice of its own general secretary, Blade Nzimande, at the forefront, was a cheerleader for Zuma in his march to victory. The SACP now holds more positions in cabinet than it has at any other time since 1994.

Those who fear a *rooi gevaar* (red peril), however, should not be alarmed. Equally, those who would enthusiastically embrace a socialist, revolutionary party in government do not have cause for celebration. First of all, the SACP is no more leftist or radical now than a bog-standard social democratic party of the great northern European/Scandinavian tradition. Second, though their industry and volume of output when it comes to writing position papers outstrips any other faction within the broad ANC and enables them to punch above their weight, their power is severely curtailed by the forces on the right of the ANC. Thanks to WikiLeaks, we know that former ANC treasurer-general Mathews Phosa briefed the Americans in 2009, saying that Malema had attacked SACP deputy general secretary Jeremy Cronin over his opposition to Malema's call for nationalisation of the mines as a way of getting at Nzimande and Mantashe, whom Malema thinks are conflicted because of their roles as general secretary and chairperson of the SACP respectively.[7]

SACP politburo and central committee member Yunus Carrim was deputy minister of cooperative governance when I spoke to him. He has since been promoted to minister of communications. He is a man with a marvellous, and renowned, sense of humour, and a wonderfully irreverent perspective on life; he takes neither himself nor life too seriously, though he cares deeply about progressive politics. Carrim was appointed by Zuma, having had a distinguished career as a parliamentary committee chair for more than a decade, and offers a helpful perspective on his dual roles: 'The 2009 decision that senior SACP leaders, including the general and provincial secretaries, would serve in government executives has had its strengths and weaknesses. It's not so much that we serve in government that's the issue, but how we balance our government and SACP roles.

'The decision that our senior leaders would serve in government executives is not based on principle. We have a flexible approach to this based on considerations such as the political terrain, balance of forces, the nature of the ANC's and government's tasks, strategic concerns and organisational challenges at different times. So if we find at some time that, on balance, it doesn't serve the party's or Alliance's interests that our senior leaders serve in government, they will not. But this will not mean that we will opt out of the Alliance. It could, depending on the context, serve to strengthen the Alliance and be an outcome of discussions within it.'

The positive effect of the strategic, if pragmatic, approach of the SACP is, to the mind of one senior SACP leader, clear, even though for some reason he is rather coy about it (in that he declined to be quoted on the record): 'Under Mbeki, a version of the ANC was being frozen out. Definitely the party [SACP] has got more influence, not necessarily hotlines, but some warmish lines to the top.'

The SACP had to wait patiently during the Mbeki years. Cronin, as the SACP's deputy general secretary, was, like Carrim, a committee chairperson in Parliament, shadowing the executive for ten years before he was appointed as deputy minister of transport (although subsequently moved to public works) after the election in 2009. And so, while Cronin is quick to acknowledge that the 'balance of forces', to borrow the phrase that Cronin and anyone else schooled in Marxist theory tend to use, is fluid and not static, changing from one week to another, he is not sitting on any laurels: 'Power is polycentric and dynamic. It is contested. Second, the SACP is never going to be able to, and should not even want to, in technical terms outgun the government. It is more about the general trajectory. It's a huge asset [to be in government] and to seek to give it guidance and political direction.'

Zuma's leadership – and this is my view, not necessarily Cronin's – makes the balance of power even more fluid, a proposition that another SACP leader is willing to agree with, but, again, not on the record. Clearly, the SACP is not so confident of Zuma's loyalty to them.

Cronin also acknowledges that there are externalities at play: 'There are layers and layers of things that have contributed: one is the global economic crisis and our own national economic crisis, and the crisis of neoliberalism and privatisation here. There is space for a more "directive state" – call it what you like, a "developmental state". Reasons we were marginalised before have diminished.'

But Cronin also recognises the trade-offs, and refers to what he calls a 'neat capturing of it' by Adam Habib (whom I happen to think is one of the best, if not the best, political analysts in South Africa, and who was appointed as vice chancellor of the University of the Witwatersrand in 2013) – namely, that the left has won economic-policy space in exchange for social-conservative space (the judicial front and social values are the examples that Cronin gives).

Compared with COSATU, the SACP is much more comfortable with the path it has chosen. It is in power and glad of it. But has it worked, I ask? Was it – the support for Zuma – justified? I know it is too soon to say, but I am intrigued to hear what the erudite intellectual Cronin has to say and how he will rationalise it.

The SACP has begun to realise that it 'needs to form alliances with moderates, such as Trevor Manuel and Pravin Gordhan and Naledi Pandor,' he says, 'to realign, to form a block with them to fight corruption, because there is recognition that if we go soggy on that, then we will lose steerage on everything.'

Indeed.

My conversation with Cronin is in 2012, before the final publication of the National Development Plan, which he has subsequently criticised. He describes the diagnostic report of the National Planning Commission as a 'wonderful document'. He has a long-standing friendship with Manuel and recognises his strengths and commitments, and – unlike some people in COSATU who 'think they are still fighting him over GEAR [the Growth, Employment and Redistribution programme] – is willing to give him a second chance.

Cronin also refers back to a 2009 SACP conference, which Zuma addressed angrily and only after he had been told not to go with the planned ANC delegation comprising Tony Yengeni and Malema, two populist red rags to a bull. According to Cronin: 'We think we have disrupted the populist problem and created awareness about it; and that dealing with corruption is essential.' In other words, his view is that the SACP is a modifying influence in government – a bit like the Lib Dems in their coalition with the Tories in London.

'The SACP is more influential now than in 2006, in fact more than at any time since 1994, in shaping ANC and Alliance policies and politics,' Carrim insists in a typically effervescent and enjoyable conversation. 'There's a significant improvement in the quality, if not quantity, of consultation with the ANC. It's not just that there are now far more SACP leaders in national and provincial government executives, but the process by which they were appointed in 2009 involved the SACP having a say on the appointments, unlike previously when the ANC president would decide which communists were palatable for appointment.

'The ANC's greater openness to the SACP does not flow simply from the party's support for President Zuma or the president's generosity, as is often suggested, but reflects the party's more campaigning posture since the early 2000s, its greater profile and dramatic increase in membership, and, of course, increasing convergence between the ANC and the SACP, especially with the post-2008 global economic crisis, on the need for a more state-led growth path and other policies and strategies. But for all that, the ANC is still firmly in charge, and it's certainly not the case that the SACP is as influential on the ANC as is often made out, even if that influence has increased.'

Carrim agrees with Cronin that there is more corruption around now, but that 'the seeds were sown long before. It's not just corruption that we have to fight more effectively. There is also a more consumerist ethos, with a bling culture more internalised in our movement. But there are also countervailing tendencies, being a typically contradictory, broad movement. There is greater unease emerging about this, a feeling that we must fight this, that it's not con- sistent with the values of a progressive national democratic movement like ours, not with the huge inequalities that assail our society.'

Carrim acknowledges the greater role of money in ANC politics, concurrent with this other trend. 'The influence of business on politics is greater now than in 2006, as the ANC itself says in its own public documents. Business also funds the campaigns of ANC candidates seeking to be elected to leadership positions in the organisation, including through buying the votes of ANC delegates. Being in power is invariably contradictory. We are able to get things done, but we also draw people into our ranks with their own selfish agendas who serve to under- mine what we are about. Maybe we have become too broad, too open, and we let in people who do not belong to this movement. So we are less coherent now.'

The structure of the ANC

Where, though, does the real formal power lie in the ANC? The NEC is its formal seat of greatest authority, and the NEC election, which takes place every five years, is the most important election at the national conference. The ANC's decision to make the national conference a five-yearly event has in and of itself reduced the power of its wider membership. Although the national conference can influ- ence policy issues and is, therefore, important, its influence beyond and between the actual meetings is limited, even as it has tried to reassert itself since Polokwane. Its importance really lies in its rallying role.

As the primary constitutional structure within the ANC, the NEC matters a great deal. When it convenes, there is a sense of history; the full broad church of the ANC and its divergent ideological traditions are all represented. Doing well in the NEC elections is important – they are what allowed someone like Ramaphosa, essentially out of the political game since 1996, to sustain not just his connection, but his standing; both his locus (the right to be there and to speak) and his status. It is unlikely that he would have returned at Mangaung but for his continued role in the NEC and its subcommittees, most notably the disciplinary appeals committee, which upheld the long-term suspension of Malema from the ANC.

Examining the membership of the ANC NEC, therefore, provides all manner of clues as to the direction and orientation of the party. And what is interesting about the latest NEC is that, although Zuma won decisively at Mangaung, the conference delivered a rather balanced committee, which reflects the full heterogeneity of the organisation, with a mixture of Zumarite ethnic chauvinists, populist nationalists, sensible leftists, moderates and Mbekite centralists and 'returnees' (such as Tito Mboweni). The balance of power sits with the right-of-centre coalition of Zuma-loyalists and populist nationalists, but it is nowhere near as decisively dominant in the NEC as the ease with which the Zuma slate won the 'top six' positions would suggest.

NEC stalwarts

Another interesting thing to consider is the profile of survivors – that is, those who have been on all three NECs, including the present one, since 2002. What is

Table 7.2: Composition of the NEC, 2002–2012

NEC	Gender	Language	Race	Age
2002	Male = 45 (72%) Female = 17 (24%)	Xhosa = 20 Zulu = 9 Sotho = 6 Pedi = 6	Black = 49 White = 5 Indian = 6 Coloured = 2	50–59 years = 24 60–69 years = 20 70–80 years = 15
2007	Male = 46 (54%) Female = 38 (45%)	Xhosa = 25 Zulu = 20 Pedi = 11	Black = 72 Coloured = 7 White = 4 Indian = 2	50–59 years = 32 60–69 years = 20 70–80 years = 6
2012	Male = 44 (51%) Female = 42 (45%)	Xhosa = 29 Zulu = 19 Pedi = 12 Sotho = 4	Black = 78 White = 3 Coloured = 3 Indian = 2	40–49 years = 8 50–59 years = 27 60–69 years = 15 70–80 years = 5

Table 7.3: NEC stalwarts

Members on all three NECs: 2002, 2007 and 2012	Members on 2002–7 and 2007–12 lists
Jacob Zuma	Jacob Zuma
Sankie Mthembi-Mahanyele	Kgalema Motlanthe
Joel Netshitenzhe	Sankie Mthembi-Mahanyele
Malusi Gigaba	Manto Tshabalala-Msimang
Enoch Godongwana	Joel Netshitenzhe
Tony Yengeni	Malusi Gigaba
Lindiwe Sisulu	Lindiwe Sisulu
Jeff Radebe	Enoch Godongwana
Blade Nzimande	Tony Yengeni
Nkosazana Dlamini-Zuma	Jeff Radebe
Cyril Ramaphosa	Blade Nzimande
Ngoako Ramathlodi	Nkosazana Dlamini-Zuma
Naledi Pandor	Zweli Mkhize
Pallo Jordan	Naledi Pandor
Zweli Mkhize	Jessie Duarte
Ebrahim Ebrahim	Ebrahim Ebrahim
Thenjiwe Mtintso	Susan Shabangu
Jessie Duarte	Collins Chabane
Collins Chabane	Mathews Phosa
Max Sisulu	Thandi Modise
	Ngoako Ramathlodi
	Derek Hanekom
	Mohammed Valli Moosa
	Thenjiwe Mtintso
	Trevor Manuel
	Max Sisulu

it about these individuals that makes them such perennial figures? What would an individual optimised for political survival look like? And if we were able to describe one, could we make an obscene fortune with a pamphlet stand at the next ANC conference?

While it's impossible to draw a causal relationship between an individual's characteristics and the fact of their survival, we can, at the least, take a look at what the survivors look like.

For starters, none of them are white. Most are Xhosa (40 per cent), Zulu (30 per cent) or Pedi (10 per cent). A second observation is that a large portion of them (47 per cent) are generally affiliated to the ANC only, as opposed to any particular person or economic position.[8] Perhaps being a personality cultist is a poor choice not only in 2012, but generally as well – 21 per cent can be distinctly described as Mbekites (survivors or returnees from the Mbeki era), while 26 per cent are Zumarites (close associates of the current ANC president). A final point is that, overwhelmingly, they are male. Just 35 per cent of the stalwarts, if we can call them that, are female. This is, however, only slightly below the average of 41 per cent female representation in the NEC across all periods in question.

The NEC meets only four or five times a year, so, although it is the most important structure, its influence is constrained by the infrequency of its meetings, and by its size and political character. It is not well chaired; 'Mbete,' one NEC member tells me, 'is even worse than Terror [Lekota, 2002–7, who left to lead COPE after Polokwane].' An Mbekite describes to me how the NEC rambles, with one long pontificating speech after another. He tells me a story of how Motlanthe had told him that 'sometimes there will be forty people down to speak on a topic. I can go to the bathroom and come back, and they are still talking. I could fly to London and back, and they would still be talking.'

This may suit Zuma. A weak, vacillatory and inefficient NEC plays into the hands of the president and his staff at ANC HQ, Luthuli House. The problem for the ANC is that a weak NEC undermines the decision-making capacity of the organisation as a whole, as well as its ability to protect, nurture and develop its political principles and core character.

The NWC

The relationship of the NEC with its main subcommittee, the national working committee (NWC), is crucial to understanding how power operates in the ANC. The NWC generally meets every Monday at Luthuli House in Johannesburg. It comprises twenty members, plus the national office-bearers: president (Zuma), deputy president (Ramaphosa), national chairperson (Mbete – a political survivor of no fixed ideological abode, who pinned her colours to Zuma in the run-up to Polokwane, after having been sent to political Siberia by Mbeki), secretary-general (Mantashe), deputy secretary-general (Jessie Duarte – respected and liked within the ANC, but not much loved outside of it), treasurer-general (Zweli Mkhize – a rising star from KwaZulu-Natal, whose talent and self-assurance sets him apart from the 'KZN gang'), and the presidents of the ANCYL (Ronald Lamola), the ANCWL (Angie Motshekga – the controversial minister for education) and, a new addition brought in under a significant constitutional change in 2012, the ANC Veterans' League (Sandi Sejake). The ANC spin-doctor supreme, Jackson Mthembu, attends *ex officio*.

The three leagues are all potentially highly influential, the extent of their influence depending greatly on their leadership and its ambitions and willingness to speak out. If Malema was still the ANCYL's president, then a good deal more of this chapter would be devoted to it. But he is not. And the Youth League has been very much put in its place. The vigour of youth, and the importance of the league in terms of the ANC's electoral prowess and its ability to connect both with young voters – the so-called born frees – and with disaffected and angry young unemployed men, however, mean that it will continue to punch well above its weight in the ANC, once it has recovered its breath and rebuilt its own structures after a post-Malema purge.

The Veterans' League is potentially influential at the other end of the spectrum, as ANC activists from the apartheid era get older (you have to be over sixty and have served the ANC for forty years to be a member). Since many of its members are Umkhonto we Sizwe veterans specifically – the ANC's military wing in exile – inevitable comparisons with Zimbabwean president Robert Mugabe's militant war veterans will be made.

The current NWC has ten members from the previous body. The following were elected to the NWC on 17 January 2013 (the ten who were re-elected are indicated with a star):

Jeff Radebe*	Naledi Pandor
Lindiwe Zulu	Bathabile Dlamini*
Nomvula Mokonyane	Nosiviwe Mapisa-Nqakula
Jackson Mthembu (*ex officio*)	Nathi Mthethwa*
Lindiwe Sisulu*	Malusi Gigaba
Derek Hanekom	Susan Shabangu*
Maite Nkoana-Mashabane*	Collins Chabane*
Aaron Motsoaledi	Nomaindia Mfeketo*
Blade Nzimande*	Fikile Xhasa
Tina Joemat-Pettersson*	Sisi Mabe

While the NEC sets broad policy for the ANC – not so much in the 'pure' policy sense, as those decisions are taken in the national conference and the policy conference that takes place six months before and where the policy resolutions are debated and refined, but politically – the NWC must execute the political judgement of the NEC on a week-by-week basis. It's actually more like the 'exco' of a company with the NEC being the board and the national conference the AGM (albeit a five-yearly one).

The composition of the NWC tilts the balance of power expressed in the NEC in favour of Zuma and his nationalist and other loyalist allies (Radebe, Zulu, Mokonyane, Joemat-Pettersson, Dlamini, Mthethwa, Gigaba, Chabane, Mfeketo, Xhasa and Mabe), with the progressives and the 'left' (Hanekom and Nzimande) and moderates (Motsoaledi, Pandor and Mapisa-Nqakula) in the minority.

The contamination of the ANC

Speaking in April 2013 at a UCT seminar that asked the pertinent question, 'The ANC: Liberation movement or governing party?' Sipho Pityana asked a further question – 'Is the ANC captured?' – before launching a coruscating attack on the 'tenderpreneurs' who use their ANC connections to win lucrative government contracts. 'There is a lack of political will to deal with corruption. We have to ask, has the ANC lost moral high ground? And what does it mean to lose it?'

Pityana worked for the International Defence and Aid Fund (IDAF) in London and later served as director-general of the Department of Labour in the Mandela administration; if you cut him in half, you would undoubtedly find the letters A-N-C inscribed inside him, so no one can credibly accuse him of being a member of the opposition. Pityana is one of the few ANC moderates who is willing to publicly criticise his own party when he thinks it necessary. He is the founding chair of the Council for the Advancement of the South African Constitution that was launched in 2010 to mount a cross-class defence of progressive constitutionalism in the face of a new reactionary threat to constitutional rights posed by the Zuma era.

Pityana cites the evidence that has emerged of how dubious businessmen, such as Brett Kebble, who took his own life in a so-called assisted suicide in 2005, 'captured' the ANCYL with substantial donations – the same youth league that spawned the roguish Malema. In litigation that culminated in 2012, Kebble's estate sought to recover millions of rands that he donated to ANC leaders on the basis that no benefit was given in return. Rather than return the money, in their answering court papers the ANC stated that 'in return for the donation, Kebble obtained the benefit of access to political decision-makers and law-makers that would be beneficial to him both directly and indirectly by virtue of its benefits to companies in which he had interests … so as to promote conditions more favourable for the conduct of his business and those of the companies in which he had an interest'. The Kebble case is almost certainly just the tip of the iceberg.

In a curious attempt to clean up its act, the ANC has, in recent years, set up a company named Chancellor House, which it cheerfully admits is not only wholly owned by the ANC but invests in enterprises that do business with government, such as Hitachi's contract to supply boilers to the Medupi and Kusile power stations. 'Chancellor House,' says Pityana, 'is a blatant conflict of interest.' The ANC's main above-board fund-raising arm is called the Progressive Business

Forum (PBF). It is led by two pragmatic Afrikaners, Renier Schoeman and Daryl Swanepoel, both former NP MPs, who joined the ANC when the former party of the apartheid government merged into the ANC after the 2004 election. Who would ever have predicted such a turn of events back in 1985 at the height of the state of emergency, when the NP looked like it would brutally cling to power?

If you want to see Schoeman and Swanepoel at close quarters, you can visit them in their offices in Adderley Street, Cape Town. I go there myself and Swanepoel shows me around and tells me about how he got to be such an import-ant cog in the ANC's fund-raising wheel. He stumbled into politics, originally helping the NP to win the Progressive Federal Party (PFP)–held Hillbrow constit-uency in the 1986 election. He was then involved in Hillbrow politics 'extensively', as things were changing with an 'influx of non-whites into the constituency and standards were being affected and so forth and we had to try to take action'.

An interesting choice of words, though he then explains that he was a pro-ponent of removing the Group Areas Act. 'The move towards reform had already started. Multiracialism in Hillbrow per se was not the problem, it was the drop in standards,' he says, with emphasis. 'Landlords could not cope with the unnatural situation imposed by the Group Areas Act, which theoretically meant that they should not have had non-whites in their buildings at all, but could not take legal action against them.'

So, in a roundabout way, Swanepoel was a reformer and speaks with fondness about the campaign in support of continuing the reforms at the referendum in 1992. In the 1994 national election, he campaigned in Soweto and recalls not experiencing any animosity as the NP sought to convey that it was opening its door to all races, as its contribution to the 'dawn of a new era'.

He shows me a photo of the first Gauteng legislature, where he led the official opposition, though, as he admits, 'they had no understanding of the role of the opposition'. His account of the merger with the ANC is fascinating: get-ting his colleagues in the NP to agree to accept the Freedom Charter, which was a requirement of the ANC, was 'a bit difficult and took a bit of persuasion ... They thought it was a communist charter!' In due course, Swanepoel says, it was hard to find any real differences in policy; it was only when it came to 'morality ... We were for the death penalty, for example.'

'Now, we are not Nats in the ANC, we are ANC in the ANC,' says Swanepoel with great emphasis. 'We are doing more than just raise funds for the ANC, which we do pretty well. But Renier and I do two other things, reporting to the treasurer-general. The success of the ANC will depend on the success of our economic development. So, the PBF is also about ongoing dialogue.'

Six thousand corporates are involved, apparently, as donors to the PBF – the 'contact' programme that is one of the 'other two things' that they do. Swanepoel, however, wants to talk about the third programme, which is an 'inclusive' minority programme, concerned with demystifying the ANC to minorities. He reckons that he and Renier are the ones to do that, 'because of where we come from'.

He's proud of the fact that he has two business cards, one saying 'Office of the Secretary-general' (for the minorities programme) and another saying 'Office of the Treasurer-general' (for the fund-raising arm). 'So, you've got these two old Nats reporting to two of the most senior office-holders in the ANC.'

You're right at the centre of ANC power, I suggest. 'Absolutely,' says Swanepoel. 'I can't think of an occasion when I chuckled about this, but I have looked at it in amazement at how fortunate we are to be part of this.' Amazing indeed.

The PBF website promises members that 'you or your designated representative will be invited to opportunities for interaction with ANC policy makers at Ministerial, MEC and Metro Executive Levels'. On the home page, it asks corporates, somewhat menacingly, 'Can you afford not to belong to the PBF?' There are five levels of membership, ranging from Silver (R4 000 per annum) to Premium Platinum (R60 000 per annum), where there is a guarantee of at least four private meetings a year with no fewer than twenty members present.

Of course, this is selling access to government officials – public officials. No business leader is especially interested in meeting the ANC per se; it is the *relationship* with executive power that appeals. So, ANC government ministers and officials effectively sell their time to paid-up members. It's not illegal and it breaches no code.

Swanepoel says: 'It's standard fare internationally. These people are paying up to R60 000; if you are going to sell a government contract, you're going to sell it for a lot more than that. It's policy discussions. It's a party chamber of commerce … just like the breakfasts that a chamber of commerce may arrange, or IDASA, for that matter' (with whom Swanepoel had an axe to grind, because of their persistent complaints about the PBF and the conflicts of interest it encourages).

The difference is that none of these entities that Swanepoel cites, such as chambers of commerce or IDASA, are political parties who are in executive public office. The ANC is a big ship, and it needs plenty of fuel to keep it lubricated and moving. And, after years of lobbying and empty promises made to the high court, the ANC is no nearer to disclosing its donors than it ever has been.

The 2007–12 treasurer-general, Phosa, asked IDASA if it would count as transparency if he disclosed the donors to the ANC's NEC. We told him no, public disclosure is public disclosure. It's like being pregnant; you can't be half pregnant.

What this told us was how close to his chest Phosa's predecessor, Mendi Msimang, had held his cards; that only he, Mbeki and one or two others knew exactly where the money came from.

How it is now is anyone's guess. Phosa's successor has abandoned all pretence at reform. In an interview in Cape Town on 9 May 2013, Mkhize, the current treasurer-general, said simply: 'No party should be compelled to divulge the names of its funders. We do not want someone to be compromised simply for supporting a party he wishes to support or has approached him.'[9]

The new ANC

Many ANC traditionalists, especially from the community that grew up in exile, are exasperated by what the ANC has become, some complaining in private about the 'mongrels and scoundrels that have crossed the floor to contaminate us'. CASAC's director, Lawson Naidoo, who worked alongside Pityana in London, says that 'there are times when I look at the ANC now that I barely recognise the organisation. The ANC has lost not only its organisational discipline but also its principles. Its biggest mistake after 1994 was to abandon its long-held tradition of internal political education. As a result, we became exposed to opportunists who have exploited the ANC to enrich themselves at the expense of the public interest.'

It is difficult to listen to ANC traditionalists such as Pityana and Naidoo speak with such barely concealed pain about the state of the organisation to which they, along with many, many others, devoted so much of their lives. What exactly they must be feeling deep down one can only guess.

It must be deeply wounding. The ANC enjoys such a profound place in the history of liberation movements. It prompted and led the greatest-ever international solidarity movement – the anti-apartheid movement – winning it friends across the globe, many of whom are now confused by what, from afar, the ANC appears to have become. It was once regarded as a bastion of high-minded principles. For anyone who has ever been a member of the ANC, even for as short a period as I was, for example – I joined when I came to work for the ANC during the 1994 election (sent via the British Labour Party), but resigned from the Sea Point branch in 1995 after taking on a position at IDASA that required me to be patently non-partisan – it is saddening to see a once great movement descend into mediocrity.

It would be a profound mistake to blame all the present-day ills on the current leadership. Indeed, it was clear long before Polokwane that there were deep-seated problems, many of them explained by the ANC's contaminating relationship with its donors and with money in general. Mbeki, for so long a central figure in the organisation, seemed to wake up to the reality very late – too late. His final speech as ANC leader took place on the first day of the Polokwane conference. It was an extraordinary performance – perhaps the worst-judged political speech I have ever heard. Admittedly, Mbeki's responsibility was to deliver a 'political report' to the conference. But, whoever wrote the speech made a grave blunder in failing to read the mood of the conference and adjust the speech to align with Mbeki's political needs, which were in desperate straits.

It is unlikely that anything could have stopped the 'Zunami' that bowled into Limpopo that week. But, given that in the end the vote was relatively close between the two contestants, it is not entirely beyond plausible to think that Mbeki might have won over some of the delegates whose minds were not yet made up. For, although in theory they arrived in Polokwane with specific voting mandates from their branches, because the national conference ballot is a secret one they could have theoretically switched horses when the voting stations opened later that evening, after Mbeki had finished his long speech.

For two hours he droned on and on, reciting in unnecessary detail the achievements of his government. Although Mbeki attempted to link the performance of his administration to the resolutions of the Stellenbosch national conference of 2002, the effect was otherwise: it sounded like a very dull report from a senior public servant, rather than a rallying cry from the leader of a political party. If anything, it served to reinforce the impression of an aloof, out-of-touch technocrat, who was besotted by government and uninterested in the immediate concerns of the rank and file of his organisation.

But then, towards the end, Mbeki leapt into life. It was too little, too late. And moreover, the tone was wrong and tactically inept, even hostile, despite the aptness of the topic: the corrosion of the ANC's value system. Citing Mandela's speech at the 1997 Mafikeng conference, Mbeki told his by now desperately bored audience: 'One of these negative features is the emergence of careerism within our ranks. Many among our members see their membership of the ANC as a means to advance their personal ambitions to attain positions of power and access to resources for their own individual gratification. Accordingly, they work to manipulate the movement to create the conditions for their success.'[10]

Shortly before, as his anger – perhaps encouraged by the obvious lack of chemisty with the assembled delegations, and their apparent disregard for the detailed nature of his report – rose, almost shaking, he had said:

I have an obligation openly to convey the President's views to National Conference, especially on matters that are of vital importance to the defence of the character and historic tasks of our movement, and its reputation and esteem in the hearts and minds of the masses of our people …

Directly to confront the virus at the core of the disease that has produced and is producing this repulsive outcome, I would like to cite a vitally important observation our Secretary General made in his Organisational Report to our 51st National Conference, five years ago.

He said: 'We have also reported to the NGC (held in 2000), on the challenges being in power has on the structures of the movement. We found that the issues dividing the leadership of some of our provinces are not of a political nature, but have mainly revolved around access to resources, positioning themselves or others to access resources, dispensing patronage and in the process using organisational structures to further these goals.

'This often lies at the heart of conflicts between (ANC) constitutional and governance structures, especially at local level and is reflected in contestations around lists, deployment and the internal elections process of the movement. These practices tarnish the image and effectiveness of the movement.

'The limited political consciousness (among some of our members) has impacted negatively on our capacity to root out corrupt and divisive elements among ourselves. For the movement to renew itself as a revolutionary movement, we have to develop specific political, organisational and administrative measures to deal with such destructive elements.'[11]

This was hardly news. Two years earlier, in 2005, then ANC secretary-general Motlanthe had built on his 2002 report to conference when he said 'this rot is across the board ... almost every government project is conceived because it offers opportunities for certain people to make money. A great deal of the ANC's problems are occasioned by this.' As secretary-general, Motlanthe delivered a series of reports at national conferences and other occasions that set out in staggering detail the nature of the crisis facing the organisation – in terms of programmatic coherence, administrative competence, financial stability, membership discipline and capacity to mobilise.

But at Polokwane in 2007, Mbeki had barely begun his tirade. He continued, citing Mandela thus:

'During the last three years, this has created such problems as division within the movement, conflicts based on differences among individuals, the encouragement of rank indiscipline leading to the undermining of our organisational integrity, conflict within communities and the demoralization of some of the best cadres of our organisation ...

'In reality, during the last three years, we have found it difficult to deal with such careerists in a decisive manner. We, ourselves, have therefore allowed the space to emerge for these opportunists to pursue their counter-revolutionary goals, to the detriment of our movement and struggle.'

As the delegates know, the document 'Through the eye of a needle' also addresses some of the issues raised by the Secretary General. It says:

'Because leadership in structures of the ANC affords opportunities to assume positions of authority in government, some individuals then compete for ANC leadership positions in order to get into government. Many such members view positions in government as a source of material riches for themselves. Thus resources, prestige and authority of government positions become the driving force in competition for leadership positions in the ANC.

'Government positions also go hand-in-hand with the possibility to issue contracts to commercial companies. Some of these companies identify ANC members that they can promote in ANC structures and into government, so that they can get contracts by hook or by crook. This is done through media networks to discredit other leaders, or even by buying membership cards to set up branches that are ANC only in name.

'Positions in government also mean the possibility to appoint individuals in all kinds of capacities. As such, some members make promises to friends, that once elected and ensconced in government, they would return the favour. Cliques and factions then emerge within the movement, around personal loyalties driven by corrupt intentions. Members become voting fodder to serve individuals' self-interest.'

As a consequence of the disease to which our Secretary General drew our attention, all of us, cadres of our movement and the ANC itself, have been exposed to the shame and humiliation of people who are our members, who come to meetings of our structures carrying weapons, with the intention to terrorise members of the ANC to bow to their will.

We have been exposed to the pernicious practice of people buying others membership cards of the ANC to guarantee themselves a captive group of voting cattle, whose members had and have absolutely no desire to join the ANC.

All of us are aware of the poisonous phenomenon foreign to our movement, which many of us have characterised as the ownership of some members by other members. These are people who, while holding ANC membership cards, do not belong to the ANC but belong to those who paid their subscriptions.

This includes unqualified people who get appointed to such positions as Municipal Managers, placemen and women who serve as the pliable tools of their political masters, and who are used to advance the commercial and political interests of their handlers and patrons.

We are aware of members of the ANC whom our Secretary General characterised as destructive elements which tarnish the image and effectiveness of our movement. These are people who abuse their positions in government consciously, purposefully and systematically to engage in corrupt practices aimed at self-enrichment.

These engage in criminal and amoral activities driven by the hunger for personal gain, acquired at the expense of the poor of our country, who constitute the millions-strong constituency which regularly votes for the ANC, and which we proudly claim to represent.

We have been horrified to hear reports of ANC members who occupy positions in government, who have murdered one another as they competed about who would emerge as the victor in the process of awarding government tenders to private sector companies in return for financial and material kickbacks paid by the winning bidders.

All of us, delegates to the 52nd National Conference of the ANC, are perfectly conscious of the ferocious and unprincipled battles that took place last year as our structures selected our candidate local government councillors for the 2006 municipal elections.

All of know this very well [sic] that this was driven by the objective to remove sitting councillors on the basis that these had to move way to give other people, card-carrying members of the ANC, an opportunity also to serve as councillors, and thus to gain an opportunity for self-enrichment.

We know this too, that some of those who lost in this immoral battle promptly resurfaced as members of formations of the broad democratic movement, or as leaders of groups of so-called 'concerned citizens' to organise and lead public demonstrations intended to discredit members of our movement who had been legitimately nominated by our structures and elected democratically to serve in our system of governance for the prescribed periods.[12]

In its 100th year, the ANC began again to grapple with these issues, following a period when disunity and ill-discipline had been the organisation's most obvious public traits, thanks principally to Malema's efforts. Ahead of its five-yearly national conference in December 2012, it published a document entitled 'Organisational renewal: Building the ANC as a movement for transformation and a strategic centre of power'. Like previous internal discussion documents, it grapples with the role of the ANC at community level in the context of a still 'distressed' local government, cloaking the analysis in quasi-Marxist terms that will be mysterious to many: the 'motive forces', the 'balance of forces', and so on. In sixty-six pages, it essentially says, with commendable honesty, 'we're in a mess and we've got to sort it out'.[13]

The document points out: 'Cumulatively, the socio-economic conditions of the majority create a sense of grievance and social injustice, especially among the urban poor who live side by side with the rich. This also explains why people in urban areas quickly resort to protests, while the same or worse conditions in rural areas do not lead to protests.'[14]

Interestingly, on the subject of the growing number of violent protests, it notes:

'A key and recurring theme arising from our own research and independent surveys is that protests are not against the ANC but are often in its name. Contestation among ANC local leaders, between ANC leaders and their counterparts in the local Alliance structures often sparks the protests. The adverse socio-economic realities affecting communities are used by disgruntled or opportunistic elements within our ranks to outmanoeuvre sitting councillors.'[15]

All of which leads one to ask, is the ANC the problem or the solution, or both? Speaking at one of CASAC's first events in early 2011, Frene Ginwala, who was the Speaker of the first democratically elected Parliament after the 1994 election, lamented the decline in ANC traditional values and conceded that the organisation's leadership had been 'naive' in the 1990s 'to not realise that we needed to undertake a project to inculcate new values in our society. It was not enough to include these values in our Constitution, they need to be promoted throughout society.'[16]

This echoed Mbeki's words in his Polokwane speech: 'Repeatedly over the years, our leadership has drawn attention to the critical importance of political education and cadre development ... The reality is that we have not attended to this matter with the seriousness and consistency it demands. As a result of this failure we must therefore expect that we will have members who, among other things, will have very little familiarity with the history and traditions of the ANC, its policies, its value system and its organisational practices.'[17]

Another long-standing ANC traditionalist, who served the ANC in London alongside Pityana and Naidoo, is Patric Tariq Mellet, who is now a special advisor to the minister of home affairs. Mellet shares Ginwala and Mbeki's concern about political education, but provides a very significant additional angle. 'Freedom,' Mellet begins, 'saw a mad scramble for capital: I now want to get my leg into this. Guys rushed to buy off people who like me had nothing on day one, but by day six had capital. Where from? Such cadres went to white guys with money, or a foresighted, opportunistic white guy thought it would be a good idea to have this guy on my side.'

He continues: 'The ANC is a broad church. It contains businesspeople and aspirant people without capital. The consequences are not mysterious to me: you need money ... you can go to the people who always had it and they may or may not invest in you. Or you can go and find other, more primitive ways of accumulating capital, such as crime. The American immigrants did it, and it turned into the Mafia, who later laundered their money into respectability.'

Mellet ends with the obvious conclusion – the killer punchline: 'We didn't create a legitimate means for people to get capital. They were driven to patronage or the "birdy way" [criminal way], but didn't see it in these terms. Instead, people thought rather, let me duck and dive, I will see what I can get.'

Thus, these four strands come together: the breakdown of organisational capability and the sudden end of the tradition of political education; the weakness and ethical vulnerabilities of the leadership that create the wrong tone from the top; the failure to anticipate the need for capital; and the fact that comrades will be exploited as their needs are met.

This is where Malema and the gang of tenderpreneurs come from. This is the cause. They are the effect. The impact is all-consuming – on policy, on governance, on politics in general, corroding the principles of democratic accountability enshrined in the Constitution. A COSATU central executive committee resolution notes the 'growing tendency' to use money to secure positions and to ensure the adoption of certain policies. A 'new tendency' exists of people using political connections for their own 'accumulation interests', adopting an 'it's our turn to eat' stance. 'They rely on populist demagoguery politics to allow them enough political space and power to push for their accumulation agenda.'[18]

And from this grows a new populist class within the ANC, denuded of political principle or any ideology, driven only by the politics of voracious self-enrichment. As COSATU notes, this refers to some within the ANCYL: 'They seize and use popular working-class issues to stir emotions of unsuspecting and disgruntled sections of the working class in society when their actual agenda is to secure power and use such power against the very working class.' The resolution in turn suggested this group was backed by 'well-resourced and powerful business and politicians'.[19]

What is to be done?

The ANC is much changed, almost unrecognisable from what it once was. Not all the change is for the worse, as Carrim suggests: 'Polokwane for all its contradictions signaled the re-entry of ordinary members into ANC politics. The genie is out of the bottle! ANC members will not be restrained easily any more. The average ANC member is more assertive, and less obedient to the leadership, and even defiant.'

As such, the ANC is a less disciplined, less well-mannered and potentially more militant and unpredictable organisation. On the other hand, as Carrim implies, the leadership has more reason to remain on its toes: 'We have among the highest number of community protests in the world, and very often these are led by ANC members. These protests have become increasingly violent, with criminals sometimes becoming involved, but the message is clear – ordinary members are increasingly alienated and fast losing their patience with the leadership.

'While, overall, the increasing engagement of the rank and file is to be welcomed, some of this is quite destructive and does not serve progressive goals. The

ANC leadership has to engage with the membership far more actively in the interests of deepening the transformation.'

As Carrim says, 'since 2006, power has also shifted away from provincial structures to regional structures of the ANC. Given the switch of power to branch and regional structures, the PECs [provincial executive committees] are not as strong as they were and find it more difficult to develop coherent political approaches within the ANC.'

Thus, the political incoherence found at the top of government, in the 'coalition' cabinet, is replicated throughout the ANC, one reinforcing the other.

In *Anatomy of South Africa*, I suggested that the ANC represented the heart of South Africa's contemporary body politic. In that respect, nothing has changed. It is still the predominant political actor. But while some of the arteries have opened up, allowing a free flow of both good and bad guys into its midst, able to access and accumulate more power for themselves and their organisations, others have clogged up.

As with the human body, an unhealthy heart will disable and ultimately imperil the whole anatomy, the whole being. As Susan Booysen, one of the most eminent academic writers on the ANC, has put it: 'Nineteen years into formal state power, the ANC ... had reached the point where its political power remained formidable but, by all available indicators, beyond its peak.'[20]

The ANC appears to have reached imperial over-reach, in terms of its incoherent membership and its straining organisational capacity. Its leadership is constantly battling to cope. During the UN Framework Convention on Climate Change's COP17 in Durban towards the end of 2011, I ran into visiting former ANC activist Kumi Naidoo who served prison time for his efforts in the 1980s and who now heads the international organisation Greenpeace. Naidoo put it bluntly: 'Forget the ANC: in terms of what it once was, it's done for, finished. It will never recover what it has lost.'

Assume for the purposes of this argument that this assessment is right – and, to be clear, this was an observation about values and principles and organisational coherence rather than electoral prowess and the ability to continue to win power – how should one react to the news?

One reaction, to be found most obviously amid racist or otherwise reactionary circles, is: 'Good riddance.' Another, in traditional liberal households, is to think: 'Good, so weakened, the ANC will be vulnerable to a challenge for power by the opposition.' A third, more nuanced middle-class reaction is to pause for thought and say: 'Hang on, don't we need an effective ANC to absorb the self-evident social pressures that exist in South Africa? Without the ANC, won't the pressure cooker blow?'

Indeed, for the foreseeable future, the fortunes of South Africa seem still to be inextricably linked to the health of the ANC, or otherwise – an organisation that appears to be falling apart under the sheer weight of its eclectic ideological mix and the internal pressures of its political contradictions. The fundamental weakness of Zuma's leadership is that he appears to be failing to control, still less reconcile, the contradictory political impulses within his party, despite his use of the security apparatus to secure the moorings of his power.

I finished writing this chapter on 21 June 2013, the day a most extraordinary letter addressed to Zuma appeared in the Independent Newspapers, penned by infamous socialite and bling businessman Kenny Kunene:

Dear President Jacob Zuma …

I'm writing this because I've never been more disappointed with the ANC you lead. I was once your fervent supporter, I attended some of those night vigils during your trials, and, like many, I believed you would be the force for change the youth and the poor desperately need in our country. Like many others, I donated to your cause when I was called on, and allowed my facilities to be used for ANC and Youth League meetings, sometimes for unusual meetings where your political comeback was planned.

You may wonder what qualifies me to make any kind of political comment. As everyone knows, I'm just a socialite and a businessman, but it's also no secret I am a hobbyhorse for politicians to ride whenever they want to criticise 'crass materialism' and the decay of morals. It's true, I like to spend, and I'm not an angel, but unlike politicians I'm not spending taxpayers' money. My real point is that, as a socialite and a businessman, I meet many people, including politicians. When they speak to your face, Mr President, they tell you your imperial clothes are very stylish. When they talk to me, and feel they are safe from your army of spies, most of them admit that you, the emperor, have no clothes.

The Gupta issue alone should be the last straw for many South Africans. But the extent of how much the Gupta family controls you, and by implication this country, has not even begun to be understood. It's amazing how terrified most people in the ANC are to speak about this reality, because they truly fear you. Even if you're not in government, tenders are used to inspire fear among people of influence. Thank God my livelihood is not dependent on tenders. I'll save you the trouble of trying to find out if I have any tenders so you can cut me out of them. I don't have any.

You show no loyalty even to those who kept you out of prison. After the Shaiks and Julius Malema, the Guptas must know that you can drop them faster than they could drop your name. In your quest for self-preservation, you have become heartless.

The reason I supported you and your campaign is because you were marketed to us as someone who would unify us and get rid of the politics of fear, but today there's more fear and more division in the ANC than ever before. In public you smile and laugh, but in truth you behave like a monster, a tyrant who will target perceived enemies ruthlessly, and because of that fear few dare to speak openly. We'd have had yet another Cabinet reshuffle if your wings had not been clipped a little in Mangaung.

Of course, I am not so naive as to blame everything regrettable that happens in the ANC on you. But in my home province, the Free State, the premier, Ace Magushule, imitates your behaviour and even seems to be trying to outdo you in being entangled with the Guptas. He learnt it from you. He thinks it's okay to blow R40-million (or R140-million, others say) on a website. It's not a great website either, by the way. When even your Kenny Kunenes start thinking a guy is wasting money shamelessly, you should know how bad it is. Of course, we'd all like to know where that money really went.

This is not what the ANC is or should be. We thought it was bad enough with the Shaiks – but who could have predicted your, and therefore our, wholesale nationalisation by the Guptas?

Even your immediate community, your neighbours in Nkandla, have to walk past your ridiculously overpriced palace donated to you by a once-unsuspecting public, knowing how you have your own private clinic they cannot use and their children must play in the dusty streets among the stones, while your compound has an astroturf sports field that cost the taxpayer R3.5-million and costs R100 000 a month to maintain. How is fake grass a part of security upgrades?

Everyone knows the Public Protector's report will find damning evidence of what went on there – but something must be said now already, in case you find a way to shut her up too.

It's no wonder the ANC lost the vote in Nkandla. If the people who know you best, the place you are from and where you occupy tribal land, do not trust you enough to vote for you, why should the rest of us?

This ANC is no longer the ANC of John Langa Dube, Oliver Tambo and other illustrious names. I'm also getting tired of hearing about how the ANC is bigger than any individual.

There are those who are stubbornly loyal to the ANC, as if it's some kind of marriage, who keep the faith that some day the party will return to its roots. But even if they're my friends, I can't enthusiastically join in with the declarations of those who say they will die in coffins wrapped in ANC colours, no matter what, as my former business partner Gayton McKenzie once said to me.

Mr President, I don't want to be one of those who tell you in fear that you have clothes on, when it's obvious you are completely exposed. I know the dogs will be set on me for saying this, but you have been naked for longer than most of us were willing to admit. And you're now stripping the ANC of the last shred of its integrity. The world laughs at us.

I love the ANC, or what it's supposed to be, but I don't love your ANC. For those of us who care, the question now is, as Vladimir Lenin asked: 'What is to be done?'[21]

It is rather surprising to find oneself quoting Kunene, of all people, who is hardly a voice of progressive principles and reason. But although not exactly a credible expert on ANC politics, as a beneficiary of the business opportunities that the new democratic South Africa has provided, he is interesting because he has given surprisingly eloquent public expression to what many ANC people, and black businessmen, have been saying to me privately for the past few years, especially when it comes to their embarrassment with Zuma and his approach. They've spoken to me not just about the corruption in government and within the ANC, but also about the deliberate inverse snobbishness that now infuses much of the organisation. A successful professional, for example, working for a merchant bank, told me that after years of attending branch meetings of the ANC in her Johannesburg ward, she had stopped going because 'the Zuma boys tease me about my [model-C] accent and call me a "clever black"'.

It is this anti-intellectualism, this unprincipled dumbing-down, which is perhaps the most painful aspect of the ANC's current plight. A far more credible voice than Kunene's is that of ANC veteran intellectual Pallo Jordan, who, writing in *Business Day* in October 2012, concluded: 'For many in the ANC, Jacob Zuma's election promised relief from the managed internal democracy of Mbeki's incumbency. Instead, it has been marked by political problems, most notably a radical decline in the ANC's credibility. Zuma's own actions have also stripped the office he holds of dignity.'[22]

To arrest the ANC's decline will take great leadership. But where is this to come from? Ramaphosa is now in place, an alternative-leader-in-waiting. But is the ANC capable of another palace coup? In any case, what *is* to be done?

Despite the gains of the left, and its acquisition of executive power as its initial Polokwane dividend, and the tempering influence that it is exerting on government and the ANC's worst excesses, the most important part of the current narrative of the ANC is the rise of the right within it.

Malema was but one symptom of the proto-fascism that festers and threatens to grow. He has now been expelled from the party, but those who backed him are still around and still yearning for more access to power. Their time may yet come, and 2017 is the year when the ANC may face its own major fork in the road. Speaking at a UCT seminar, one of South Africa's most dynamic analysts, Eusebius McKaiser, remarked on the 'fascinating levels of paranoia' within the ANC leadership, adding that 'one wonders what the paranoia will be when it drags to beneath 60 per cent of the vote'.

Will that happen, or will the ANC rule until Jesus comes, as Zuma suggested during the 2011 local government election campaign? In 2016, there is a distinct possibility that the ANC could lose its majority in three, maybe four, more of the six biggest cities. How will it react? Perhaps it will raise its game in the face of greater competition; to last a century, the ANC has had to regenerate itself on many previous occasions. Or perhaps it will succumb to anti-democratic tendencies as it strives to hang on to power. Many people will have a great deal to lose if the ANC ceases to be the gateway to personal enrichment.

Hence, the ANC's choice of president to lead the party in the 2019 general election will be crucial, and so its 2017 national conference will be the pivotal moment. An even greater populist than Zuma could win then, in which case all bets will be off; South Africa could, as Mbeki's political-economist brother Moeletsi Mbeki has suggested, face its 'Arab Spring moment', as the ANC is compelled to make more and more reckless and implausible promises to an angry generation of unemployed, working-class young people, whose links with the ANC liberation movement are tenuous and whose loyalty can no longer be taken for granted.

This is not a prediction; it is but one possible future scenario. Quoting from his favourite Yeats poem, Mbeki was fond of asking, 'Will the centre hold?' At first I thought he was asking it of his country, but I later realised it was directed at his own party. The DA will contest this idea, but for now, the democratic future of South Africa is largely dependent on the commitment to constitutional democracy, or otherwise, of the ANC. At present, we need the ANC a lot more than it needs us.

Though South Africa's pampered, cloistered middle classes will not readily recognise or understand this point, the country's stability depends greatly on the ANC's ability to absorb the intense socio-economic pressures and inequalities that persist. If the ANC's own stability and capacity to play that role weakens much further, then, to deploy Yeats myself: 'Things fall apart; the centre cannot hold; Mere anarchy is loosed upon the world.'

Against this frame of reference, some people despair of the ANC, admits Carrim. Does he himself despair? 'Like everybody I have the odd moment of frustration, but, overall, definitely not,' he says with defiance. 'We are certainly not, as some who have drifted away say, beyond redemption. But we have to take a long-term, a twenty-year or so perspective. We have to incrementally rebuild the

ANC. Malema is out of our ranks, but Malema-ism, with its me-first-at-all-costs values and culture, remains in parts of our movement, mainly among the youth. Of course, we live in a new context and must adapt. Of course, these are not the times of Solomon Mahlangu. But we have to exorcise Malema-ism from our ranks. I think the ANC can certainly become what it's meant to be. In any case, it's too soon to give up. The stakes are too high. Too many people gave up too much for this transition.

'And it's not just about us in this country. It's also about what we represent to the global community,' Carrim adds, gaining momentum. 'Our struggle won the emotional, moral, political and material support of a huge chunk of the international community. Today, every time Mandela sneezes or wheezes the world seems to come to a standstill. Have you ever heard of anything like this before?

'Without seeking to be melodramatic,' Carrim continues, 'we have to succeed as a progressive, non-racial, non-sexist egalitarian democracy, not just for our own sakes but for progressives the world over. If we fail, it will be a setback not just for us, but for progressive people the world over who believe that people of different races can live together and that poverty and inequalities can be reduced.'

Carrim then riffs on the wonders both of the 2010 FIFA World Cup and the NDP – a 'marvelous document, for all its flaws'. Freed momentarily from the painful challenges of trying to deal with local government (at the time he was still deputy minister of cooperative governance and traditional affairs), Carrim's eyes light up and he launches into a jocular, sentimental soliloquy about 2010. He recalls with a big smile Siphiwe Tshabalala's stunning opening goal against Mexico and 'how we rose to the occasion and showed the potential we have'.

'You may say I am clutching at straws,' suggests Carrim. 'But this country produced a Nelson Mandela and a Desmond Tutu and a Nadine Gordimer and a Christiaan Barnard. They did not fall from the skies. And we negotiated an end to apartheid and held those magnificent 1994 elections and that splendid 2010 World Cup. What did we show if not our huge potential? We just have to fulfill that!'

If Carrim and the rest of the 'sensible left' can summon their resolve, and recover their voice, all may not be lost.

'You ask, is the ANC able to be rescued?' ends Carrim. 'Even if it is not, we cannot give up.'

Amen to that.

8

The unions

As they have become closer to government, less militant, less sure of their real destination, so their power has become harder to analyse. 'The trade unions,' one observer has written, 'have never been more powerful – and seldom used their power less.'[1]

If I didn't tell you that this quote comes from Anthony Sampson's 1965 *Anatomy of Britain Today*, you would be forgiven for thinking its originator is talking about contemporary South Africa. After all, South Africa's trade-union movement has been at the heart of the country's politics for decades. It is an important part of the country's power anatomy, however much its influence ebbs and flows. The past six years, since the watershed of the December 2007 ANC national conference at Polokwane, have been especially volatile and this period may well turn out to have been a turning point for the Congress of South African Trade Unions.

With the banishment of its chief antagonist Thabo Mbeki in 2007, COSATU's power at first appeared to increase, but quickly waned as its membership numbers have stagnated in terms of percentage of the working population, as breakaway rival unions emerged to threaten the political establishment of which COSATU is now a part, and as its leadership became increasingly divided and threatened by the duplicity and vandalism of Zuma's ANC.

And then Marikana happened.

COSATU may have been outside the old establishment, in the sense that Mbeki pushed it to the periphery of the policy-making circle, but it seems that being inside the new establishment – if that is what being a part of the Polokwane conglomeration of unlikely bedfellows that brought COSATU and the SACP into alliance with ANC nationalists amounted to – has not made much difference. It has not yielded the dividends that were presumably expected when COSATU chose to back Zuma over Mbeki at Polokwane. Moreover, it has enabled breakaway unions to challenge the hegemony of COSATU and its affiliates – such as the Association of Mineworkers and Construction Union (AMCU) and its challenge to the National Union of Mineworkers (NUM), for so long the blue-chip jewel at the centre of both the COSATU and the Alliance crowns – and to position them as part of an out-of-touch elite.

COSATU has traditionally derived its power and influence from four main sources: first, the sheer numbers of its membership; second, its credibility due to its ability to present itself as a worker-led organisation 'close to the people'; third, because of its broader non-syndicalist political outlook (meaning that COSATU has always defined its role beyond the narrow, 'mere' representation of workers in negotiations with their employers) and its close relationship to the ANC, it can exercise influence over government policy and law-making; and fourth, its organisational strength, including the calibre of its leadership, and unity, and thereby its ability to operate effectively in a labour market based fundamentally on a national regime of collective bargaining.

In order to understand their full implications, one must consider all four against the background of Polokwane and the Marikana massacre.

The strength and influence or otherwise of COSATU and its affiliate unions, and its ability or inability to maintain social cohesion and a stable economy, have enormous implications for South Africa and its future prosperity.

COSATU's membership numbers

COSATU is a federation of unions comprising twenty affiliates spread across South Africa. Formed in 1985, it has a long and proud history of militancy and defiance against apartheid rule. When there is a COSATU conference, representation is proportional to the size of the affiliated union. In addition to the formal structures, such as the central executive committee (where the general secretaries and the COSATU president meet on a monthly or biweekly basis), there are numerous forums, such as education, organisation and media. In the media forum, for example, the various unions' heads of media will meet twice a month to discuss issues of how to improve public media relations and communications within the federation.

A recent survey on COSATU affiliates, commissioned by COSATU and conducted by the labour-policy think tank NALEDI, found that 'COSATU affiliates represent a broad spectrum of industries ranging from the public sector to the private sector, including manufacturing, mining/engineering and the services industry. Most affiliates define their scope by the industry that they organise, since COSATU as a federation is based on industrial unionism. Of note is the fact that some unions like SADNU [South African Democratic Nurses Union], DENOSA [Democratic Nursing Organisation of South Africa], POPCRU [Police and Prisons Civil Rights Union], and SADTU [South African Democratic Teachers Union] are defined in terms of occupation, either in practice or by Constitution. In some instances, such as in the case of SAMWU [South African Municipal Workers Union] and NEHAWU [National Education, Health and Allied Workers Union], the nature of employer defines the union's scope.'[2]

The survey clearly demonstrates that the principle of one industry, one union is systematically undermined by public-sector affiliates. For instance, there are three health unions affiliated to COSATU, servicing the same members: NEHAWU, DENOSA and SADNU. This could be viewed as a case of duplicating (or triplicating) efforts rather than combining resources to fight rival non-COSATU unions. Another example is NEHAWU and PAWUSA (Public and Allied Workers Union of South Africa). The irony is that both these rival unions belong to COSATU, 'which automatically qualifies them as "sisters" who should at anytime unite and "funnel" ample resources towards servicing their membership. The reluctance of unions serving within the same industry to merge may be attributed to territorial and power struggles.'[3]

Interviewed for this book, national spokesperson of the South African Transport and Allied Workers Union (SATAWU) Mamokgethi Molopyane says, 'The benefits of affiliating with COSATU will always be the fact that through COSATU we can make presentations to NEDLAC [the National Economic Development and Labour Council] and have them heard, compared to if we were going to try and approach NEDLAC on our own. So there are benefits in terms of being a COSATU affiliate. Membership is a source of pride both for us in the organisation, as well as for the members at ground level. COSATU gets to make presentations to government, given that it is part of the Tripartite Alliance. When we talk, we get to be listened to through COSATU.'

Similar praise for the benefits of COSATU membership comes from Norman Mampane, the national spokesperson for POPCRU, who says that 'Unions have always emphasised through the motto of COSATU that an injury to one is an injury to all. In other words, our collective voices, when packaged together, will always crash through the barriers that are there in the workplace. We will attend meetings of the central executive committee and of the central committee. There, issues that affect workers in the country in general are discussed as well as issues that affect workers in particular sectors. Now, when we attend the central committee meetings we have reports in which COSATU will paint a picture of the status of the affiliates in terms of their membership, their campaigns, leadership – in terms of many areas of the state of the Alliance: the gains that we have made, collective bargaining, the question of recruitment, the question of women development, of campaigns relating to HIV/AIDS, labour broking – all those matters are tabled.'

But how influential are the affiliates within COSATU? As Sampson put it in his *Anatomy of Britain Today*, the 'general secretaries of the biggest unions ... are the sinews of the movement'. That applies to South Africa now. Relatedly, in the same paragraph, Sampson observes that: 'When you see the thirty-four people on the dais [at a Trade Union Council – the British equivalent of COSATU] you can easily imagine them as a miniature cabinet; but their power in fact is only the total of the powers of the individual unions, frequently at loggerheads: "Baronies in a kingless kingdom," as one general secretary said.'[4]

Dissimilarly, COSATU secretary-general Zwelinzima Vavi has been a powerful king over his fiefdom, deploying the collective power of the 'Baronies', because the individual unions have only rarely been at loggerheads. That has changed in recent times, infected by the division and factionalism of Zuma's ANC. Hence, the collective power has weakened, and the king's (Vavi) ability to hold it together and deploy it has diminished.

'Sometimes I think it [your involvement with COSATU] is also a matter of how close your secretary-general is to the secretary-general of COSATU,' says Molopyane. 'On a day-to-day level there is a lot of interaction as well. For instance, there will be a gender workshop and the union's gender coordinators will be invited to attend the workshop.'

Asanda Fongqo, the former communications manager of DENOSA, which represents 77 000 workers in the health sector, neatly puts the case for why COSATU is important in linking the shop floor with the policy world of government: 'COSATU is a giant workers federation that has influence in the policies of the country. We therefore view it as a strong and proper channel for us as a nursing organisation to drive our input as to how we want health care in this country to be run. So politically we have the muscle to influence the way that the country is run.'

Since 1994, COSATU's membership has risen, but not at the rate the federation would want. NUM membership has stayed relatively stable, which has significant political and economic consequences for the mining sector, partly as a result of splits, a phenomenon that has also plagued other sectors such as transport. There have also been battles between NUM and NUMSA (the National Union of Metalworkers of South Africa) for members in the same workspace, such as Eskom.

Overall, COSATU has approximately 2.2 million members. Membership grew by roughly 75 per cent between 1994 and 2012. The draft organisational report to COSATU's 11th congress in August 2012 describes this growth thus:

> Since the 10th Congress in 2009 there has been growth in every affiliate except CWU [Communication Workers Union], SADNU and SASAWU [South African State and Allied Workers Union]. The following affiliates grew by 15,000 or more members: - CEPPWAWU [Chemical, Energy, Paper, Printing, Wood and Allied Workers Union], NEHAWU, NUM, NUMSA, POPCRU, SADTU, SAMWU and SATAWU. None of the affiliates however met the 2015 Plan target of 10% annual growth.[5]

In 2012, there were 214 registered trade unions, from which COSATU identified 49 as rivals to its affiliates. These non-COSATU rivals together have an estimated membership of approximately 823 000.[6] This figure is likely to be an underestimate since membership data is not publicly available for all non-COSATU unions.

Table 8.1: COSATU membership by affiliate, 2012[7]

COSATU affiliate	2012 membership
NUM	310 382
NUMSA	291 025
NEHAWU	260 738
SADTU	251 276
SATAWU	159 626
SAMWU	153 487
POPCRU	149 339
FAWU*	126 930
SACCAWU**	120 352
SACTWU†	85 025
CEPPWAWU	80 658
DENOSA	74 883
SASBO††	67 402
CWU	18 666
PAWUSA	17 146
SADNU	8 655
SAMA‡	7 759
SASAWU	7 074
SAFPU‡‡	593
CWUSA^	unavailable
Total	2 191 016

* Food and Allied Workers Union
** South African Commercial, Catering and Allied Workers Union
† Southern African Clothing and Textile Workers Union
†† The Finance Union, formerly the South African Society of Bank Officials
‡ South African Medical Association
‡‡ South African Football Players Union
^ Creative Workers Union of South Africa

Figure 8.1: COSATU membership by affiliate, 1994–2012

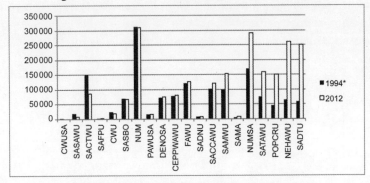

Figure 8.2: COSATU membership growth, 1994–2012

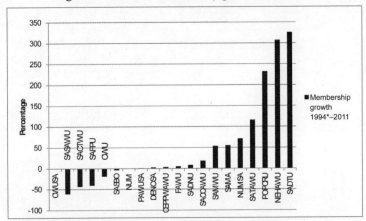

* Data for the following affiliates do not go as far back as 1994 (year of earliest
   available data in brackets): POPCRU (1997), SASBO (1997), SASAWU (2000),
   SADNU (2000), PAWUSA (2006), SAFPU (2009), SAMA (2009).

Figure 8.3: COSATU membership share of public- and private-sector affiliates, 1991–2012[8]

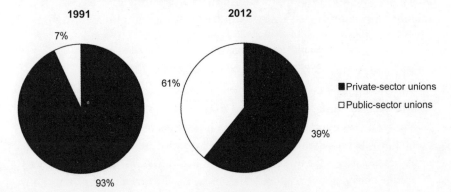

Table 8.2: Affiliate membership, 1991–2012[9]

	1991	1994	1997	2000	2003	2006	2009	2012	% shift
CWUSA	n/a	n/a	n/a	n/a	n/a	n/a	370	n/a	
SASAWU	n/a	n/a	n/a	18000	18000	9000	7804	7074	−61
SACTWU	186000	150000	150000	120000	105000	110000	85000	85025	−43
SAFPU	n/a	n/a	n/a	n/a	n/a	1000	472	593	−41
CWU	21000	23000	40000	35000	32000	25000	29699	18666	−19
SASBO	n/a	n/a	70000	63000	63000	61000	66093	67402	−4
NUM	270000	311000	311000	290000	279000	262000	272000	310382	0
PAWUSA	n/a	n/a	n/a	n/a	n/a	17000	16169	17146	+1
DENOSA	n/a	n/a	73000	70000	71000	64000	68450	74883	+3
CEPPWAWU	88000	78000	94000	74000	65000	62000	64182	80658	+3
FAWU	129000	121000	140000	119000	119000	115000	118974	126930	+5
SADNU	n/a	n/a	n/a	8000	8000	9000	9093	8655	+8
SACCAWU	97000	102000	102000	102000	102000	108000	115488	120352	+18
SAMWU	60000	100000	117000	120000	120000	118000	135906	153487	+53
SAMA	n/a	n/a	n/a	n/a	n/a	5000	7246	7759	+55
NUMSA	273000	170000	220000	200000	173000	217000	236909	291025	+71
SATAWU	70000	74000	91000	103000	74000	133000	140392	159626	+116
POPCRU	n/a	n/a	45000	71000	67000	96000	125732	149339	+232
NEHAWU	18000	64000	163000	235000	235000	204000	230445	260738	+307
SADTU	n/a	59000	146000	219000	215000	224000	236843	251276	+326
TOTAL	1212000	1252000	1791000	1869000	1768000	1841400	1974084	2191016	+75

Although the figures show both an aggregate increase and that most affiliate unions have either increased their memberships or held steady in recent years, the figures have fallen short of COSATU's own target to increase membership at a rate of 10 per cent per annum. Free-market analysts such as Adcorp's Leone Sharp are quick to present an alternative picture, one of crisis, when union membership is presented in the context of overall employment figures. The April 2013 Adcorp Employment Index stated:

> Currently only one in four workers (25.5% of the workforce) is unionized, and this figure is declining slowly but steadily. Less than half of the people who join the workforce for the first time (43%) are joining trade unions. In the five most populous sectors – trade, finance, manufacturing, construction and private households, which account for two-thirds of total employment in South Africa – the unionization rate is just 11.0% ... This is fertile ground for the emergence of rival trade unions, most of them splinter-groups from

the otherwise dominant trade union. Rival trade unions have now emerged in the mining, manufacturing, healthcare, teaching and transport sectors, and they are growing rapidly at the expense of the previously dominant trade unions ... strained consumer budgets are likely to make workers question the value of the R754 per annum paid to trade unions in the form of subscriptions and dues.[10]

Clearly, one of the fronts on which COSATU and the union movement in general are fighting is around membership and recruitment. Another, related front is around perceptions of what the figures actually mean – do they indicate crisis or resilience?

Credibility

Public trust in trade unions has plummeted in recent years, according to annual surveys carried out by the HSRC. The latest poll, which is based on a representative sample derived from census information, was conducted in the wake of labour turmoil in 2012, in which workers abandoned traditional trade unions and embarked on wildcat strike action. The survey found that among the public in general, trust in trade unions dropped from 43 per cent in 2011 to 29 per cent in 2012.[11]

Among black and working-class South Africans, who have traditionally formed the backbone of the labour movement, there was a significant growth in distrust: 35 per cent of black South Africans said they distrusted trade unions, compared to 21 per cent in 2011; 53 per cent of coloureds said they, too, distrusted them, compared to 37 per cent in the previous year. Among those who consider themselves to be part of the working class, distrust increased from 21 per cent in 2011 to 37 per cent in 2012.[12]

These findings indicate a deeper malaise within the unions themselves. The HSRC findings resonate with those of the NALEDI survey, which detected growing negativity among workers. NALEDI found, for instance, that one in three members believed there was corruption in their union and one in seven said they had actually experienced it.[13]

Research by a leading expert on South Africa's union movement, Sakhela Buhlungu, on COSATU's organisational modernisation, and specifically the changing social composition of the movement in terms of both its members and its officials, is particularly illuminating: regarding the latter, while ideological unionists still exist, the professionalisation of the union organisation has led to careerism. Union work can now be seen as a career, and those in careers seek to escalate their trajectories to the highest point, Buhlungu argues.[14]

In this regard, workers' perceptions of their leaders – including their shop stewards – have changed markedly. 'The core business of unionism is representing workers in their negotiations with their employers on issues that affect their daily lives at the workplace – pay, conditions, health and safety, and so on,' says Halton Cheadle, now a professor of law at UCT, but a long-time advisor to the labour movement and an architect of the Labour Relations Act of 1995.

COSATU's own August 2012 study of workers' attitudes revealed that when asked why they had joined a union, around two-thirds said either because they wanted protection at work from dismissal or discrimination (especially better-paid workers), or because they wanted the union to secure better pay and conditions (especially lower-paid workers). Only about 10 per cent said the reason was one of solidarity or wanting social change.[15]

Although NUM fared a little better in this respect compared to other unions, only around 50 per cent of its members expressed satisfaction with the union's performance in securing better pay – the key issue in the Lonmin dispute that led to the Marikana massacre.

The COSATU study found that across all unions 60 to 70 per cent of workers stressed that the shop steward was their first port of call.

'When workers begin to doubt the allegiance of their representatives, then trouble will quickly follow,' says Cheadle. 'Your core power dwindles. As we've seen with the AMCU breakaway, a union will start to bleed members and then the two main pillars of power – the ability to collectively bargain and the ability to call a strike – are shaken to their foundations.'

Buhlungu says a strike is a sign of power *and* a sign of weakness: 'You can bring everything to a halt. But it can also be a sign of weakness and desperation. When members become intimidating and violent, it indicates serious weakness. It means the members haven't been socialised properly into the ways of the organisation.'[16]

As to the causes of current confusion with union leadership and strategy, Buhlungu puts it this way: '[S]ince 1994 COSATU has been losing organisational power as hundreds of leaders left for politics and business and thousands of shop-floor activists were promoted out of the unions. The vibrancy of the movement has also been sapped by the effects of class formation and global economic restructuring.'[17]

The paradox of victory

Today COSATU is confronted with what Buhlungu calls the 'paradox of victory' – the long-term implications of its increasing political influence and diminishing organisational power. Speaking at the launch of his book *A Paradox of Victory: COSATU and the Democratic Transformation in South Africa* in September 2010, Buhlungu said that 'despite the visibility, influence and profile that the unions currently enjoy, a number of things happening behind the scenes indicated weaknesses in the system'.[18]

He suggested that these are invisible to all but specialist observers of the labour movement. COSATU was built on the tradition of worker control; however, that tradition has been eroded over time: 'The power of the union was supposed to be in the hands of members, people working in the factory, the mines, the shops, not full-time officials, like I once was. There was a time when that was strong, it was not perfect. It was messy, but strong. Now, there are those that sit in the background completely. Very seldom do you hear a union president, who is supposed to be a worker, speaking on these issues.'[19]

What, then, of the fundamental relationship between unions and employers? 'By definition there is a degree of adversarialism in the relationship – there are competing interests and there will be disputes and tough negotiations,' says Cheadle. 'But, intelligent business leaders will recognise the value of a well-run union and the stabilising impact of an orderly collective bargaining regime.'

And, speaking on a panel that I was moderating at the Franschhoek Literary Festival in May 2013, Moeletsi Mbeki, whom I find to be one of the most thoughtful as well as independent-minded public intellectuals in South Africa, rightly pointed out that business's relationship with the unions in South Africa is not what it seems.

'It is not correct to say that the business community is against unions,' he argued in Franschhoek. One of Mbeki's best characteristics is his ability to draw on history. 'The Wiehahn Commission in the 1970s was what compelled the National Party government; [it] was driven by big business. They wanted the legalisation of black trade unions ... they had no one to talk to. So business in SA is not against unions. What is coming out of the crisis within NUM is that a lot of the leaders of NUM are being paid their salaries by the big mining companies. One of them was getting over a million rand, to be a leader of NUM – business is quite friendly to trade unions.'

Perhaps, in this sense, too friendly. Certainly too friendly for their own good. As the economic and social distance between union leaders and members increases, so the perception is created that union leaders are feathering their own nests at best or working in the interests of employers at worst.

Historically, this has been a normal practice in the trade-union movement, in South Africa and elsewhere, where union officials retained their salaries from the employer when they were deployed to union functions full-time. In the past, these were relatively short-term deployments – you're elected as a shop steward for a year or two, then you return to your job. With the professionalisation of union officials, this practice has become anachronistic, as officials now serve the union for long periods of time.

Gavin Hartford, a long-time labour observer and commentator, is incisive in his analysis of how this professionalisation contributed to the causes of Marikana specifically:

> [T]he central point on union institutional failure is this: in the post democratic transition, the union office bearer representation process and the benefits associated with that representation, have lent themselves to the development of a union leadership aristocracy where senior employees (the most skilled and better off) dominate leadership and speak on behalf of all. When material benefit is derived from union representation, and where constituency based accountability of shop stewards and the branch office bearer is absent, the ability of the leadership to remove themselves from the life experience of the lowest ranked employees gets even stronger. Upon that basis a gap opens up between the life experiences of the membership versus that of the leadership. A gap between members and leaders that has been tragically exposed by the strike wave sweeping across the industry.[20]

On the ANC relationship, Mbeki responded to my question about the Alliance in this way: 'The single largest employer is now the state, not the private sector. One of the problems in COSATU, which started off as a union for blue-collar workers in the private sector, is that you now have white-collar workers – teachers, for example – so now, traditional blue-collar workers support [Zwelinzima] Vavi; however, they have joined hands with the white-collar workers who are very close to the state.'

As an aside, Mbeki added a quip about how 'amused' he had been, as someone who worked for COSATU in the early 1990s, to see a former unionist colleague from that era, former general secretary of SADTU Thulas Nxesi, now the minister for public works, defending the president's plundering of the government's coffers for his palace at Nkandla.

Amused? Mbeki has a nice line in wry humour.

COSATU's relationship with the ANC

Writing soon after Polokwane, two of South Africa's most seasoned observers of the labour scene, Roger Southall and Edward Webster, regarded Polokwane as an 'ambiguous' victory for COSATU.[21] In their view, the formation of COSATU was a strategic compromise between two of three long-standing political traditions in black unionism: on the one hand, the national democratic tradition (African nationalist, recognising the race/class intersection but emphasising the former, and represented by the ANC and the SACP), and, on the other, the shop-floor or workerist tradition (emphasising socialism and independent workplace-derived

union institutions), with the third tradition being the Black Consciousness tradition associated with the PAC.

While COSATU is a compromise between these positions, they nevertheless
remain in tension, with the workerist tradition subordinated to the national
democratic one. This state of affairs was well suited to opposing apartheid, but
was put to the test with the ANC's assumption of state power in 1994 because, in
the view of Southall and Webster, it is almost axiomatic that any party or grouping, when assuming state power, is both exposed to the corrupting influence of
the perks of power and also obliged to adapt to international capital, making it
inevitable that there will be a cleavage between itself and its extra-state constituent
organisations.

In other words, a centre and a margin will be formed. Deploying the metaphor
of Icarus flying too close to the sun, Southall and Webster argue that the consequence is that those on the margin will be attracted to the centre of power,
with equivocal results.

This is what happened in 1994, when COSATU deployees went to Parliament,
a move that seemed to institutionalise workers' representation in a key centre of
power, but which in fact yielded a loss to COSATU: it led to a brain drain, and
the deployees fell under ANC party discipline, and at the same time grew distant
from the workers' experience.

In 2010, Southall and Webster astutely predicted that this was likely to be
the case again, post-Polokwane. The tension between the national democratic
and shop-floor/workerist political traditions in the union movement still exists,
with the inherent limitations of the former putting the labour movement in a
relationship of subordinate dependency to the main party – the ANC.

As COSATU has drawn closer to the ANC in its attempt to influence the
government's use of democratic power, so it has sailed too close to the sun and
lost touch with its core source of power – that which comes from representing
workers. Some will disagree, arguing that significant victories in labour-market
regulation and substantial wage increases in the public sector have been secured
through COSATU's alliance with the ANC.

Southall and Webster also point out that a number of affiliate unions are in
the public sector, so, whatever their superficial grievances with the government
might be, they are direct beneficiaries of ANC governance. In other words,
the ANC has the capacity to dispense patronage, while COSATU internally has
the willing predisposition to receive it – a situation which the authors, with their
Icarus metaphor again in mind, regard as potentially deleterious for the union
movement.

COSATU enjoys political influence and visibility, but at the same time, in view of organisational modernisation and changes in social composition, loses organisational power, essentially through the growing distance between its top structures and its members, and between the unions and those who are not formally employed in the economy.

The difference between Buhlungu and Southall and Webster seems to be that Buhlungu treats the situation as an ironic paradox ('Funny how life is, huh?'), whereas the others see the negatives as a direct consequence or cost of this wholehearted embrace of the national democratic tradition.

While Southall and Webster use Icarus as their explanatory metaphor, the ANC–COSATU alliance is typically described in terms of matrimony – marriage, honeymoons, rows/spats, rumours of divorce, etc. – a set of metaphors that Vavi himself adopts in his secretarial reports and which I employed at the end of my chapter on COSATU in *Anatomy of South Africa*, where I said:

> It's a tricky position. Yet for the seasoned political gymnasts of the COSATU and SACP leadership, the alliance with the ANC represents more of an opportunity than a threat where, like a lengthy marriage, the dividends of inside influence outweigh the habitual frustration of reproach and resentment and the occasional ritual humiliation. Divorce is always an option. But staying together is the safer option. And it may even be the right thing to do.[22]

The metaphor could be extended in numerous ways to cover the various contingencies that beset a troubled marriage. For instance, Southall and Webster provide a detailed account of the strategies COSATU employed in setting the stage for Polokwane: essentially a massive incursion of its members in ANC branch structures, the aim being to capture the ANC from within after years of post-1996 exclusion following the neoliberal GEAR and BEE '1996 class project'. Crudely put, the Polokwane move could be styled as a kind of Viagra injection.

Writing in the *Mail & Guardian*, Verashni Pillay suggested that

> Cosatu is a bit like an abused wife who constantly wrings her hands at the disgrace she must suffer in her chosen alliance, but never leaves. The trade unions' poster boy Zwelinzima Vavi made that clearer than ever on Sunday, in his tortured reprisals of being invited to 'walk out' by the ANC in their last meeting. Poor Vavi. I may make some T-shirts saying just that: 'Poor Vavi.' Middle-class South Africans love that sort of thing. Slogan T-shirts, I mean, not endearing unionists, although they're pretty partial to those too of late, believe it or not. I love the fact that the firebrand leader of the revolutionary left has become the voice of reason that most middle-class South Africans

cling to. You know things are bad when the head of the trade unions is the only politician your average yuppie can listen to without flinching. So, Vavi made the front page of the Sunday papers for saying South Africa is becoming a banana republic. This made a lot of people angry – particularly resentful white 'refugees' in developed countries who had been saying this for years and never made so much as a Hayibo satirical article.[23]

Put another way, again more crudely, COSATU could be considered the kept woman to the ANC's sugar daddy, who provides access to key centres of social and economic policy formation, along with the baubles and trinkets of high palatial life. It is this distasteful thought that, whether he formulated it with quite the same metaphorical fervour or not, is likely to have driven Vavi towards a different sort of relationship with the ANC in recent times – one that Southall and Webster brand a 'multi-pronged' approach to power, and one that, if I stretch the marriage metaphor to the outer limit, might be described as an open relationship in which COSATU 'sees other people'.

The irony is that having chosen this very path, with a distinctive shift in strategy in 2010/11, Vavi's leadership has become imperilled. Despite the fact that the ANC has become a political and ideological mongrel, welcoming to its capacious political bosom all manner of waifs and strays from the right and the left, and, moreover, a leader who is both politically and personally promiscuous, Zuma's ANC has shown itself to be viciously intolerant and jealous of Vavi's 'multi-pronged' strategy of political engagement.

The key moment was a civil-society conference hosted in Ekurhuleni in October 2010 by COSATU, alongside fifty-six civil-society organisations, including Section 27, the Alternative Information Development Centre and the Treatment Action Campaign – some of the ANC government's fiercest and most robust civil-society critics.

The ANC's reaction betrayed extraordinary insecurity. ANC spokesperson Jackson Mthembu said at the time: 'If you have a friend and that friend goes out and finds a bloc that mobilises against you, how would you feel? We're speaking from the heart here. Our pain comes from this ganging-up against the ANC leadership.'[24] But those in the ANC weren't just heartbroken, they were angry. ANC secretary-general Gwede Mantashe was more direct. He called the conference 'oppositional' and said it threatened the ANC with an MDC-type breakaway party – referring to Zimbabwe's embattled Movement for Democratic Change opposition party, which started out as an alliance between workers and civil society.

COSATU's central executive committee (CEC) expressed concern at the tone of the ANC responses, which, it said, 'are adopting an increasingly antagonistic and paranoid posture, and questioning of bonafides, which is slowly, if not faster, taking us to the pre-52nd Polokwane conference era, where all were under scrutiny and suspected of being manipulated by the imperialists and or other forces hostile to the NDR [National Democratic Revolution]. A trend is developing where COSATU is subjected to ridicule, caricatured, dismissed and misrepresented, to advance an argument that the Federation is being oppositionist and generally problematic and not loyal to the Alliance. The CEC called for this to stop.'[25]

Polokwane: Dividend or mirage?

The most intriguing question, in terms of COSATU's current influence, is whether or not it has benefited from a Polokwane dividend, from its support for Zuma in his victorious power struggle against Thabo Mbeki. Remorse set in fairly quickly after Zuma took office in 2009. As early as 2010, NUM general secretary Frans Baleni said that both Zuma's State of the Nation address and finance minister Pravin Gordhan's budget speech showed that the union federation was not harvesting the fruits of its support for Zuma. 'We should have focused on policy rather than individuals,' he said, implying that COSATU should not have so publicly thrown its weight behind Zuma in the run-up to Polokwane. 'If we were more focused on policy we would have had better results.' According to Baleni, there was 'anger from our structures' over the ANC's treatment of COSATU once the elections were over. 'Before the elections we are taken seriously, but after the elections we are not taken seriously any more,' he complained.[26]

In his 2011 secretariat's report, Vavi complained about 'contradictory policy developments, zigzagging in government, and major resistance from old centres of economic power in the state ... The result has been that economic policy realignment, where it has taken place at all, has been partial, and has had to coexist within the old macroeconomic policy framework.'[27] Subsequently, complained Vavi, the government failed to provide direction during the economic crisis, when more than a million workers lost their jobs.

As a result, COSATU agreed to a 2015 plan, which, as the secretariat report to the 2012 national congress explains,

> proposes that COSATU assert the role of the Alliance as a Political Centre & table the proposal for an Alliance Pact. COSATU took both of these forward. Despite us tabling these proposals, & agreement in the 2008 Alliance Summit on the Political Centre, this was subsequently reversed. Lack of agreement on these 2 critical issues – the Alliance's modus operandi, & its policy platform – led the Alliance to constantly zigzag between functionality & dysfunctionality. Little progress has been made on these fronts, & it remains a key outstanding

task of the 2015 Plan. There is an agreed to 2011 Alliance programme on transformation, but this has not been implemented.[28]

Appealing 'across the aisle' of Alliance politics, in June 2011 Vavi told the ANC:
'Help us help you. We don't like the space we are in now. We don't like the
politics of this moment.' As 'selflessness' has been replaced by a 'me first' attitude,
a battle has begun to contain and maintain the Alliance as one which leads
society on moral issues, he said, noting that the ANC's elective conference was
eighteen months away and that 'everybody has a chance to change'.[29]

Again, the metaphor of the battered wife desperately hoping that her abusive
husband will mend his ways and reform springs to mind.

Vavi went on to add that COSATU had been instrumental in propelling Zuma
to power. Its task now was to ensure that the ANC leadership implemented
the five priorities outlined in the party's 2009 election manifesto. 'We want our
leaders to succeed, but when we are unable to show the results to COSATU
members, we get compromised politically,' he said.[30]

A year later, and the sense of dissatisfaction had not lessened. Vavi's report
to the 2012 COSATU national congress recorded the disappointments of the
post-Polokwane years. Among others were:

- Initial blocking of agreement on a New Growth Path proposal.
- The failure to clarify & legislate the mandate of the Economic Development Department, entrenching the de facto control of economic policy
  by Treasury.
- Attempts by the Minister for the National Planning Commission to usurp
  the function of economic planning, & to assert overall control of government policy, through the Planning Green Paper – both by COSATU's
  opposition, & opposition within the state. Nevertheless a conservative
  draft NDP is released in November 2011, & an even more problematic
  final NDP in August 2012.[31]

Yet, COSATU and its leadership continued to hope for the best, optimistically
positing the possibility of a high-road 'Lula moment' – a reference to the former
Brazilian president and trade-union leader. In 2012, Vavi suggested:

The ANC is proposing to launch a second, more radical, phase of the transition, which will coincide with the second term of the ANC post-Polokwane.
This raises interesting parallels with the Brazilian experience, where the
first term of the Workers Party (PT), led by President Lula from 2002–6,
was fraught with all sorts of difficulties. In President Lula's second term

(2006–10) he engineered a dramatic turnaround, which saw a series of amazing achievements in terms of improvements of the living standards of the working people of Brazil. These achievements continue to this day, under the leadership of his successor, President Dilma. We refer to this turnaround as the 'Lula moment' and pose the question as to whether we are able to drive our own Lula Moment, given the challenges, and possibilities we have outlined under the low road scenario.[32]

Nearly a year later, and Lula has still not arrived; it remains a figment of fevered imagination. The truth is, the only Lula in the Alliance is not in the ANC but in COSATU, and his name is Zwelinzima Vavi. The right of the ANC knows this; hence their apparent appetite for disposing of the troublesome unionist, notwithstanding the potential damage it would do to economic stability and to COSATU's ability to absorb socio-economic pressures and to act as a moderating force in society.

COSATU's leader: A beleaguered voice of reason and principle

One man has straddled the union movement over the past fifteen years: Zwelinzima Vavi. Like any human being, he is prone to error and misjudgement. But, given the pressures he is under and the delicate balancing act he must constantly perform in managing relations with the ANC and affiliate unions, and in his dealings with big business leaders, Vavi has one of the toughest jobs – if not the toughest job – in South Africa.

In May 2013 he faced a major challenge to his leadership with accusations of corruption – almost certainly cooked up by his enemies – even though less than a year had passed since his unopposed re-election as secretary-general at COSATU's September 2012 national conference. 'Unopposed' is perhaps misleading. Fact is, in the run-up to the conference, there were numerous rumours that Vavi would be challenged, presumably by the pro-Zuma COSATU president, Sidumo Dlamini. Fearing a divisive, scarring election, and the consequences that this would have for COSATU in the run-up to the ANC's national conference at Mangaung in December, an eleventh-hour deal was done behind closed doors and a temporary ceasefire was declared, allowing the two main protagonists to stand unopposed.

But as seasoned political journalist Ranjeni Munusamy wrote in her *Daily Maverick* column, the COSATU affiliates were deeply divided on Vavi's leadership just eight months after his 'unopposed' victory:

Cosatu is wobbly at the knees, going into a three-day central executive committee (CEC) meeting [27–29 May 2013] which will see the same warring factions face off over the future of the same two leaders. A loose alliance of the National Union of Mineworkers (NUM), the National Education, Health and Allied Workers Union (Nehawu), the Police and Prisons Civil Rights Union (Popcru), the SA Transport and Allied Workers Union (Satawu), Chemical, Energy, Paper, Printing, Wood and Allied Workers Union (Ceppwawu) and the SA Democratic Teachers Union (Sadtu) backs Dlamini and wants Vavi removed or, at the very least, sanctioned.

In Vavi's corner is metalworkers' union Numsa, the Food and Allied Workers Union (Fawu), the South African Municipal Workers Union (Samwu), the Democratic Nursing Association of SA and the South African State and Allied Workers' Union (Sasawu). Fawu, now publicly supported by Numsa, wants Cosatu to convene a special congress to deal with the leadership crisis. They know that Vavi's biggest asset is his popularity on the ground and that a congress with mass participation of ordinary workers would lean in his favour.[33]

Vavi appeared to have survived the late May 2013 challenge to his leadership, when COSATU's CEC announced that he was not to be suspended. However, the charges were not dismissed, as the CEC felt further investigation was required. The attempt to paper over the cracks of division was painfully superficial; Vavi may have won the battle, but the war is not yet over.

How did such a powerful union leader, who enjoys much widespread support among the rank-and-file members, come to be under such pressure? What has he done to deserve such torment, when he is clearly 'one of the good guys' – as Cheadle and several other seasoned union-watchers put it to me?

To understand Vavi's thinking and his overall approach to politics in recent years, one need only refer to the COSATU secretary-general's report to the June 2011 COSATU central committee meeting, in which Vavi dissects the immediate four years post-Polokwane with the precision of a brain surgeon and provides this incisive summary:

It has probably been the most dynamic and volatile 3½ years in South African politics since the democratic breakthrough nearly 17 years ago.

This period has seen a popular political revolt in the ANC in December 2007, followed by:

- The adoption of a new policy agenda, and the break away of the previous leadership;
- The removal of a President;
- The inauguration of a new administration;
- The emergence of a powerful, corrupt, predatory elite, combined with

a conservative populist agenda to harness the ANC to advance their
interests;

- A fight-back by conservatives in the State, and massive contestation over
  economic policy;
- Challenges by demagogues to the new leadership in the ANC;
- The development of political paralysis in the State and the Alliance;
- Deepening of social distress and mobilisation of communities;
- Massive international and domestic economic shocks as a result of the
  economic crisis;
- Resurgence of the progressive centre in the movement at the 2010 NGC
  and ANC NEC Lekgotla;
- A difficult but successful 2011 Alliance Summit;
- Attempts by progressive elements within government to assert a
  developmental agenda, and resistance by the old guard bureaucracy and
  conservatives in Cabinet; and
- Difficult national and provincial elections in 2009 and even more
  difficult local government elections in 2011 where we have witnessed a
  decline in the support of the democratic forces.[34]

Political science students looking for a neat framework to cover the key issues of
this period of history could not do better than to use this 231-word summary.
Each of the thirteen bulleted elements could constitute a class in a semester-long
course. The report as a whole, all 256 pages of it, replete with useful graphs and
data about the state of COSATU, its affiliates and the country, and embellished
with Zapiro cartoons, could be a set text for the course. When it comes to political
analysis, no one does it better than the left – even if not all of their conclusions
attract universal agreement.

For example, in its decisive, no-holds-barred critique of the ANC – which,
no doubt, would have won it few accolades in Luthuli House – Vavi's report
confronts the rise of the right within the ANC and the consequences for the left:

> Politically, therefore, the main task is to defend the ANC against attempts
> by these various interests to capture its soul; advance the resolutions that
> emerged in Polokwane; and support the leadership in taking this project
> forward. A failure to defend and advance this project, and the implosion of
> the ANC as a result of the machinations of the predatory elite, could be used
> by the liberal-right and capital in the country, not only to drive their agenda
> through the State, but also to mobilise more effectively for a change in the
> ruling party and change of the current largely pro-working class policies.

Such a disastrous scenario will not reflect so much as a failure of left policies but rather a failure of the left to politically deal with and defeat the contestation by these various class forces for the soul of the ANC and the State.[35]

In *Anatomy of South Africa*, I quoted from an SACP publication – *Bua Komanisi* – that had employed the concept of 'compradorism' to explain what it called the 'parasitism' of the new interlocking circles of political and corporate elites. Vavi's report develops this theme by referring to the '1996 class project', which is Vavi's shorthand for the political and socio-economic tendency that emerged during the Mbeki years:

[T]he 1996 class project was a long-term project which has rooted itself with concrete class interests in the State and society. It represented an alliance with big capital ... and the creation of a black capitalist class. It laid the basis for the politics of crass materialism as a replacement for the politics of service and solidarity, which has initiated its own dynamic. This new culture in turn laid the basis for corruption at all levels of society, including within the movement. This class project depended on low intensity democracy and brutal suppression of alternative views within the movement and in society. It represents the politics of labelling and closing down of the democratic space. The agenda of the 1996 class project still remains firmly entrenched within powerful State institutions, including the National Treasury ... [However,] the relative prominence of a predator class, which relies on access to state levers for accumulation, vis. a vis. big capital (which is arguably more prominent now), is growing by the day, in the most frightening way, with the Mittal deal and ICT consortium being the most prominent example of this. This could foreshadow a form of accommodation between these two centres of capital. However, this accommodation comes at a big price to established capital, which would pursue a different path, if this were open to them. There are pro-capital elements and institutions in the State who would see this comprador elite as being a threat to the stability of the accumulation project of big capital, and therefore would be hostile to their attempt to colonise the State for their own parasitic agenda.

We must not confuse the 96 class project with the new tendency. The former were clear about their class agenda and followed this agenda with military precision. The difference is that with the current clique such ideological clarity is absent. The new tendency largely depends on demagogue zig zag political rhetoric in the most spectacular and unprincipled fashion and is hell bent on material gain, corruption and looting.[36]

It's a barely concealed reference to Julius Malema, who was still at large in 2011. Now he has gone, at least for the time being, banished from the political scene and probably on his way to jail. But the 'tendency' remains. According to COSATU, Malema was, in any case, a symptom and not a cause. The threat remains.

In late 2011, Vavi spoke of the need to 'fumigate' the ANC in the run-up to the ruling party's elective conference in Mangaung in 2012:

> In a reference to the ANC's unbanning in 1990, Vavi implied that while 'fresh air' was let in when the 'window was opened', other undesirable elements infiltrated the party.
>
> 'There a number of blue flies and mosquitoes inside the house who are making life unbearable. We need a good Doom to fumigate our house of these undesirables,' Vavi said.
>
> Delivering Cosatu's end of year statement in Johannesburg, Vavi maintained those needing to be removed from the ruling party 'have no business in the ANC'.
>
> 'They are the ones who could not care less about the problems of the masses. They are only interested in government positions and tenders,' he said.
>
> Vavi added that while the ANC was 'entrenched' in the hearts of many South Africans, it must deal with the problems associated with being an 'incumbent'.[37]

He repeated the point in September 2012 in the run-up to Mangaung: 'An emerging organisational crisis, in which the ANC, in particular, is increasingly wracked by factionalism, patronage and corruption, and is unable to reassert the mission and strategic vision of the organisation. Struggles are increasingly over control of the levers of accumulation. Those challenging these abuses find their lives in danger. There is growing social distance between the leadership and the rank and file.'[38]

Vavi has taken a principled stand against corruption, one that has created enemies from the right wing of the ANC that may yet bring him down. Speaking at the National Anti-Corruption Forum in 2011, he said:

> COSATU, alongside other organisations, has taken a keen interest in this battle against graft. We have done so for the simple reason that corruption is a programme of the elite in society to steal from the poor. Corruption has become endemic in South Africa. It has become a matter of life and death, literally and metaphorically. In parts of South Africa today, people are being intimidated or even killed for exposing and preventing corruption. Corruption is a threat to a better life for all. The flood of corruption scandals and the

spread of the culture of greed and self-enrichment are threatening to unravel the fabric of society and to undermine all the great progress we have made.[39]

Then, with great perspicacity, as if predicting the Guptagate scandal that engulfed South Africa in May 2013, Vavi went on to say:

> We face the nightmare future of a South Africa up for auction to the highest bidder, a society where no-one will be able to do business with the state without going through corrupt gatekeepers, who demand bribes and who unless are stopped may systematically use their power to control large areas of the economy.[40]

COSATU's commitment to the fight against corruption led it to set up Corruption Watch – directed by David Lewis, the widely admired former Competition Commission head – which Vavi's enemies accuse him of using to target his own adversaries, and to engage in sustained opposition to the so-called secrecy bill. As Right2Know campaign leader Nkwame Cedile tells me: 'Zwelinzima Vavi is very outspoken on corruption, and we agree with him 100 per cent as far as corruption is concerned. We also agree with him on many other things. The secrecy bill, the Protection of State Information Bill, is another one. His arguments are very trenchant, he has taken very similar positions to what we have taken, and if we go to the Constitutional Court on the matter, we will be on the same side.'

COSATU's unity
Far from delivering a dividend, Polokwane has sown the seeds of division within COSATU, thereby threatening it, as different union leaders have positioned themselves either as loyal to Zuma or in opposition to him. This became clear during the NUM and NUMSA conferences in 2012, both of which were dominated not by issues of strategy or their sectoral, workplace concerns, but by their relationship with the ANC president.

In late 2011, Vavi decided that COSATU needed to seize the nettle. 'We felt it was time to address emerging divisions. We are becoming increasingly incoherent. This has been a major concern,' he told journalists, adding that the problems stemmed from the ANC's succession battle. 'Matters of succession are affecting us. We warned before that the issue of succession was likely to take our eyes from the ball. We felt it was time to confront this.'[41] The leadership contests within the ANC have infected COSATU, deflecting the focus of union leadership from shop-floor organisation and collective bargaining, and undermining the founding principles of COSATU – namely, worker democracy and control.

In the run-up to Mangaung, Vavi looked like he might go either way. Zuma's challenger, Kgalema Motlanthe, was a former unionist after all and, like both his predecessor (Cyril Ramaphosa) and successor (Gwede Mantashe) as ANC secretary-general, a former secretary-general of NUM.

Zuma held numerous private meetings with Vavi, who in the end hedged his bets. Perhaps he had to: there are clear signs that Vavi had lost faith in Zuma but that many of his core supporters in the rank and file of the affiliates still believed in Zuma. Switching horses at this point, especially to back a horse as unconvincing and potentially lame as Motlanthe, would have been highly risky for Vavi.

Accordingly, he offered qualified support for Zuma, a 'yes, but' support, hoping, no doubt, that this would serve to moderate Zuma and his nationalist/populist lackeys. In the event, it has failed to do so. Zuma won decisively and the knives have been out for Vavi ever since.

I put the issue to Carol Paton, one of the country's best political journalists and now writer at large for *Business Day*, who was with Moeletsi Mbeki on the May 2013 Franschhoek Literary Festival panel I moderated. She argued that the 'very close relationship between Zuma and the SACP solidified after Polokwane, which has split COSATU between those that go with it, partly because they themselves are SACP leaders [like Mantashe] and recognise that that is their power base and their career path, and those that say it is not good for workers and the interests of workers'.

As already noted, Vavi has been prepared to speak out and, in Paton's words, 'shoot holes in the rhetoric that is used to justify all that is going on, and that makes him vulnerable'.

At the time (a week or so before the crucial CEC meeting at which the complaints against Vavi would be considered), I asked Paton whether she thought he would survive. She predicted that he would, for two reasons: firstly, 'there are allegations that he has done this, done that, and politically deviated from what we understand to be the line of the union federation, and that he needs to be brought back into line, but there is no dirt on Vavi', and secondly, 'the CEC will have to think about the likely fallout if the CEC was to remove him when he is still so popular amongst the wider membership'.

Which brings us to Marikana.

Marikana

It represented a turning point for everyone, for the country as a whole, and a massive institutional failure on the part of government, employers and unions. As Hartford says in his insightful opinion piece about the root causes of the mining industry strikes: 'The hard reality is that the pattern of migrant labour super-exploitation – characterized by 12 long months with only a Christmas and Easter break – has remained unaltered in the 18 years of democracy.'[42]

For him, it is the 'heart of the economic and social crisis ... that the specific migratory and housing conditions of migrants have led to a double economic burden; that the collective bargaining processes and institutions failed dismally to hear the signs of discontent and address its causes; that the company leadership in HR and the line management functions is complicit in this failure'.[43]

For the unions, it brought into very sharp relief how they had taken their eyes off the ball. The 1995 social consensus had disintegrated. One key part of it was the system of collective bargaining, dependent to a large extent on union unity and, specifically, on the cogency and coherence – strategic and ideological, as well as organisational – of COSATU and its affiliate members.

AMCU burst the bubble. Outwitted tactically, apparently sleeping on the job, NUM's leadership was nowhere to be seen. Lonmin's management were confused: should they recognise AMCU or not? They didn't especially want to, because they had got used to the relatively genteel cosiness of their relationship with NUM. This was the new establishment at work.

But workers were suffering. Pay was terrible and the socio-economic conditions in the Marikana area were awful. Despite eighteen years of power, neither the government nor the unions had addressed what Hartford argues is the fundamental cause of the misery – the migrant labour system, which links to the hostel system and the informal settlements that sprawl around the mines. Hartford points out that it was in response to NUM demands that mining houses introduced measures to address the worst features of the pre-1994 migrancy legacy. One was the introduction of family accommodation for employees near mine areas of residence:

This initiative took the form of a home ownership bond subsidy offered to employees to purchase a family unit. To ensure equity in the distribution of employee benefits amongst all strata of employees, the mining houses sought to address the needs of the migrants from afar (Mozambique, Lesotho and Eastern Cape primarily) by offering an equivalent benefit in the form of a living out allowance – a cash allowance to 'live out', that is to exit the migrant hostel system. Migrants took this allowance, preferring the cash reward to supplement their pay packets, and headed for the shacklands to create their homes.

The unintended consequence of the living out allowance was that migrants headed into the shacklands of the platinum and (to a lesser degree) gold belt, so that today the bulk of migrant platinum employees live in newly constructed, zinc shacks in areas adjacent to the platinum mining operations. With this migration, the migrants took on not only the shack, but also all that a human being needs for their material comfort to support their work. In a word, the migrants took on a secondary home which was typically characterised by the acquisition of a dinyatsi (the second or third wives who live and care for migrants in the shacklands), the bed, the stove, the fridge, the ablutions and the new transport costs associated with 'living out'.

This new socio-economic condition added significantly to the wage pressure on the migrant. Notwithstanding annualised real wage adjustments, the migrant became significantly worse off in respect of the actual amount of remittances to their rural homes post apartheid. For the first time in the history of migrancy, the migrant worker of today now supports two families and households: the first in the shacklands with their dinyatsis and the second in their traditional homesteads in the Pondoland villages of Lusikisiki and Flagstaff. It is not surprising therefore that we have witnessed the proletarianised urban community of the shacklands declaring the miners' strike action 'a service delivery protest', since these communities have a primary and direct beneficiary interest in the wage settlement outcome.[44]

It was against this bleak and inherently unsustainable socio-economic backdrop that a fight was brewing, with an inevitability that now seems obvious. And AMCU was stoking it. The result was the deaths of thirty-four striking miners at the hands of the South African Police Service.

The contest for power between NUM and AMCU continues. COSATU's power is being attacked not at its periphery, but at its very heart: NUM is its blue-chip union, the stallion in the stable ... or, at least, it was.

Nowadays, it looks more like a donkey. As one newspaper crisply put it: 'The Association of Mineworkers and Construction Union is clearly the National Union of Mineworkers's worst nightmare.'[45] But NUM's leaders are fighting back:

Leaders of the NUM feel under attack from Amcu, not only physically, but also in terms of representation in mining structures.

Their response is to warn their members against abaxhoki (those who mislead) and to encourage their shop stewards to do a better job of providing a service to their workers.

[NUM president Senzeni] Zokwana, who delivered his entire address in isiXhosa, was particularly pronounced on the dangers of Amcu, accusing it of lacking its own programmes.

'What they do, instead of raising problems with employers, is just run to workers and instruct them not to go to work,' he said. 'And when members are fired, they are nowhere to be found. Miners are then left on their own.'

Zokwana also accused Amcu of 'business unionism', saying Amcu president Joseph Mathunjwa owned five companies, a statement greeted with expressions of shock and disbelief in the crowd.[46]

As the Marikana commission of inquiry slowly chugs along, with seemingly every week bringing news of the assassination of a key witness from the frontline, and as the battle between AMCU and NUM intensifies and becomes more murderous, there are some signs that a degree of stability is returning:

> [I]t is heartening that in a week in which there was seemingly carefully targeted violence in Marikana and the death of Amcu regional heavyweight Mawethu Steven, Amcu founder Joseph Mathunjwa at least temporarily halted the tide of violence with a masterful performance.
>
> The Amcu president took to the stage at the Wonderkop stadium on Wednesday, faced the crowd and the famous Marikana koppie in the background, shared and sympathised with their anger over Steven's death, promised them swift action, then eloquently sent them on their way – and back to their jobs at the various nearby Lonmin platinum shafts – with not so much as a grumble. All without seeming to back down, or give an inch of ground to what he and his members perceive as the aggressors of the NUM.
>
> In so doing, he put on display an Amcu very different from that seen immediately before and in the aftermath of the Marikana massacre. Then, the union had seemed not at all in control of its members, unable to connect with them, and unpredictable to the point of caprice. On Wednesday, however, Amcu listened and commanded, and most likely boosted Lonmin management's confidence in its abilities. Hours before, the company had said it expected workers to return to their jobs that evening, clearly with foreknowledge of Mathunjwa's intent.
>
> But the union, though nearly a decade and a half old, is still caught in the throes of its birth pangs as a real force and faces significant problems it has little time to overcome: a slumbering giant of an opponent in the NUM; a deep, mutual distrust of Lonmin; and a severe lack of capacity to rule what it has conquered.[47]

Even with AMCU facing its own challenges, NUM and COSATU are in a tricky spot. Inevitably, to reclaim lost ground and to recover lost membership and lost credibility, they will have to talk to 'the left' in a more militant fashion, at a very delicate time in industrial relations and when investor perceptions of South Africa's economic future are febrile to say the least. Right on cue, as I conclude this chapter, NUM has tabled a demand for a 60 per cent pay hike.

Numerous questions circle AMCU: Is it a coherent force or an opportunist organisation that has emerged due to frustrations with NUM? Is it not akin to the 'coalition of the disenchanted' that grouped together to get rid of Mbeki and then found they had little to bind them afterwards? Is it likely to be any different from NUM? On the evidence so far, perhaps not.

AMCU's leadership does not seem to be embracing a need for realignment of labour relations in the mining sector – a move away, in other words, from the 'winner takes all' approach that saw NUM dominate the sector. Instead, they want the same perks as NUM enjoyed in the past in terms of the recognition agreement, whereas Lonmin is seeking an inclusive approach that would see NUM remain a player, as indeed are Solidarity and UASA (formerly the United Association of South Africa).

If AMCU simply slips into the dominant position once occupied by NUM, how long before workers get frustrated with the new set-up? The lack of a political culture (and, therefore, organisational discipline) within AMCU may lead to more wildcat strikes and instability, putting yet further pressure on the beleaguered industrial relations of a key economic sector.

In turn, as COSATU wrestles with how to handle the impact of the crisis on NUM's and its own position and stature in the mining sector, there will be consequences for COSATU's relationship with the ANC and government.

Vavi's job just got a whole lot tougher and the balancing act even more delicate.

Caught perpetually in the horns of a dilemma that it cannot escape, the last few years have seen COSATU's power and influence rise and then fall. What the future holds is anybody's guess. But as membership declines further, and as division among its leadership continues to be encouraged by nefarious factions within the ANC for their own short-term interests, COSATU's ability to be a powerful, progressive and stabilising influence in South Africa's economy looks to be very much in doubt.

9

The opposition

The official opposition

I usually don't mind being kept waiting, but by the *Daily Telegraph* – the British-establishment conservative newspaper? No, thank you. But there I was, sitting patiently on the ground floor of the Marks Building of the national Parliament, on the left as you walk up Government Avenue towards Table Mountain, opposite the grand old Senate Chamber.

Most of the opposition members of Parliament are holed up in the Marks Building; the further up the building you go, the more eclectic the mix – like an aviary.

On the fourth floor, for example, you now find the Azanian People's Organisation (AZAPO) and the Freedom Front Plus (FFP) in offices cheek by jowl, and apparently cohabiting perfectly contentedly, like an old couple who have been together for too long and have forgotten how to quarrel.

In the upper reaches of the Marks Building, at least, the Rainbow Nation is alive and well.

Down nearer the ground are the big birds of the Democratic Alliance (DA), who now occupy the better part of two floors where their seventy-seven MPs are housed (sixty-seven members of the National Assembly and ten permanent members of the National Council of Provinces). The official opposition.

How things have changed. It seems like yesterday that their meagre-numbered but determinedly effective group of just seven MPs was running rings around the ANC in the first democratically elected Parliament in 1994.

Then, they had the upper hand in parliamentary procedure – old lags, if they will pardon the expression, like Ken Andrews, Douglas Gibson and 'father of the house' Colin Eglin. Dene Smuts was the one woman, though she punches like a man and can certainly hold her own in all-male company.

Now, the parliamentary party has a dynamic young woman as its leader, who is keeping me waiting. Or, rather, her interview with the *Telegraph* is.

As I sit, I ponder. First, the DA's increase in numbers. How big a shift is it? Have they reached a new, final glass ceiling, or will they carry on pushing, ever upward?

Second, as the clock ticks and my mind wanders, where did the FFP get the 'Plus' from? Why can't I remember? Does it matter and does anyone care? It makes them sound like a packet of condoms. I brainstorm a possible strapline: 'Safe Sex for Big Boers'.

Now I'm really in trouble: I'm thinking about Terre'Blanche's last stand, so to speak. Thankfully, the door swings open and the woman from the *Telegraph* swans past me, with a swish of long red hair and a casually tossed 'Sorry 'bout that' in a posh Sloaney drawl, and she's on her way, click click click down the wood-panelled corridor.

They say that first impressions matter greatly. Lindiwe Mazibuko is young, very young. But she's got something. My first impression is a strong one. When I meet her, she's just days into the job as DA parliamentary leader and the ANC are treating her like an errant little schoolgirl.

It will be interesting to see how she handles this. She will have to be tough, very tough. I think about the election campaign in 2009 and the afternoon I spent in Khayelitsha on an election analysis panel. The DA's leader, Helen Zille, was also on the panel. The afternoon took forever because, although it was being recorded as 'live', in the great sports hall just off the N2 highway, 'live' turned out to be a stop-start affair that in all took over three hours.

I had ample opportunity to see what Zille has to put up with. It's not pleasant at all. Politics in South Africa is really not for the faint-hearted, especially when opposing the ANC.

As expected, and as the programme producers wanted, there was a boisterous township crowd assembled inside the hall. Both during the recording itself and during the many breaks, even when she was milling around chatting informally with her staff or supporters, Zille was subjected to a constant stream of abuse.

'White madam' was one of the politer refrains.

I watched her carefully. She bristles, sometimes winces, but she takes it. She absorbs it. Though she 'fights back' – a phrase I use cautiously, given that it was the unfortunate, misconceived slogan for the 1999 election campaign – she is smart enough and, more importantly, empathetic enough to understand where this hostility comes from: decades of discrimination; eons of pent-up anger and justified rage against the systematic attack upon a people – apartheid's betrothal.

So Zille takes it. She has an immensely thick skin. Far thicker than her predecessor, Tony Leon. He was brittle, as well as shallow. He talked tough, but he did not walk it like Zille does.

There is a qualitative difference between them. Leon did not empathise; he did not think he had to. To him, his was a righteous cause: to defend liberalism against the majoritarian onslaught (oh, and protect white-owned business and other minority interests in the process).

Zille's is far more strategic: to build a plausible argument against ANC rule.

Her argument is built on a number of key pillars. Mazibuko is one of them. Not in and of herself necessarily, but because she is black and presents an entirely different image.

There is no point in beating around the bush or succumbing to political correctness: Mazibuko is in her early thirties; politically, she is a babe-in-arms. She is leader of the DA's parliamentary party because she is black (as well as talented).

Wilmot James, the DA caucus chair, whom I interviewed a few days before he and she won the internal parliamentary party elections to secure their new, significant positions of influence and leadership, put it simply: 'In Lindiwe's case she is externally facing … she is looking at the voters, okay? She is an externally facing parliamentary leader, which is different from the existing structure that we have.'

'Externally facing': a new term in the art of political strategy? Is Mazibuko just branding?

What is impressive about her is that she acknowledges this, even before I can put the question to her (maybe Miss Telegraph was, in this respect, my fluffer).

'We've always said we need to be more diverse in our political make-up and in our leadership,' she tells me. 'And of course, diversity is not just about race, it's about age and gender, but race is the one that the ANC continues to whip us with.'

The DA does more polling than any other party, which sets it apart in terms of capacity and tactical wherewithal. As Mazibuko then admits: 'Our polling showed that this [the ANC whipping] had an effect on our potential black support.'

She then performs some interesting mental gymnastics: 'It's not the basis on which I ran [for leader of the parliamentary party]. I didn't say vote for me because I am black. I did say vote for me because I add to the diversity of the DA's leadership.'

This is a bit like Lionel Messi saying that as an Argentinean he's in the Barcelona team to make it appear more cosmopolitan. But never mind. One can see the necessity of the mental somersaults that are being performed, presumably for her sanity and sense of self-respect. Mazibuko is clearly a capable person, so why should she not be leader of the opposition in Parliament, notwithstanding her age and lack of experience?

And I mean that. It may read like a discourteous deployment of irony, but it is not actually meant that way. I am sitting there trying to assess Mazibuko from a purely technical point of view: Does she appear to have the requisite skill-set necessary to succeed in the higher echelons of politics?

Articulate: check.

Telegenic: check.

Thick-skinned: apparently so, but probably too soon to say; let's see.

Is she a political animal? Does she have politics in her blood? Well, that's an interesting question, and far harder to answer.

Mazibuko, as her accent suggests, was educated in private schools, having moved back to South Africa in 1986 from Swaziland. Her grandfather, who was an Anglican cleric, had moved the family there from South Africa a generation before.

'We lived in Umlazi township, and so weren't allowed to go to model-C schools, so rather than go to Bantu education, our parents sent us to a Jewish primary school in Durban North' – her parliamentary constituency now – 'and then to St Mary's, an English, Anglican private school.' Her mother was a nurse; her father a banker, who became an entrepreneur when he returned to South Africa.

Unusually for someone who has ascended the 'somewhat greasy ladder' at such a tender age, she was not involved in student politics at all, which is one of the things that makes one wonder whether she has it in her blood: even though she is now a 'huge advocate' of the DA Students Organisation (DASO), 'my interest in politics did not extend to student politics ... I did not really understand the link between the two. I didn't see how ANC policy fitted in with university parking.'

It is comments like this that underscore the perception that she is a johnny-come-lately to politics, and one with a slightly naive understanding of the subject. It similarly betrays an entirely upper-middle-class orientation – one concerned with student parking rather than the enduring challenges of access to higher education in South Africa. Furthermore, it is not a stretch to understand that 'parking' – that predicament concerning those wealthy enough to own a car, fill it with petrol each week and pay the premium required to access parking facilities at UCT – is fundamentally linked to politics. The structural conditions that dictate which students at UCT own or have access to cars, and can afford to park on campus, are entirely tied to politics in South Africa.

For Mazibuko, it all changed one Sunday in 2007, when she opened the *Sunday Times* and saw an advertisement for the position of DA researcher. Was it a hard decision, because she was black? 'It was hard for Sizwe Mchunu, my provincial leader; he was shot three times because he was in the original DP [the Democratic Party become the DA in 2000]. It was hard for him but not for me.'

Times were changing in 2007; it was pre-COPE, but, says Mazibuko, 'disillusionment with the ANC was setting in. I did not face any uphill from friends or family. And because I did not live in a place where joining the DA would have life-threatening consequences, it was not a hard decision to take, no.'

In the end, politics requires a whole lot of commitment. And it can be life-threatening, as numerous political assassinations in the months before and after the ANC's national conference in Mangaung show. Half measures will not do.

A new ideology?

Which brings me back to Wilmot James. I've known him for quite a while now. With Mamphela Ramphele, he employed me at IDASA in 1995. It changed my life, and I owe him and Ramphele a great deal for their leap of faith.

James has rapidly become one of the most influential people in the DA. Along with stalwart James Selfe, James is likely one of the most powerful behind-the-scenes people inside the DA, both as chair of the federal council and as advisor to the inexperienced Mazibuko.

He's an intellectual, a real one, with a real thirst for ideas and knowledge and discovery. And intellectuals generally don't prosper in politics. Not real ones anyway.

Look at Pallo Jordan in the ANC. A thoroughbred intellectual, but a totally hopeless minister. Twice. Appointed to Mandela's first 1994 cabinet, he was reshuffled sideways in 1996 and then not reappointed by Mbeki after the 1999 election (he did, however, return for Mbeki's second term in 2004). Because he thought and cogitated too much and did too little. Good, effective politicians understand that nuance is a nuisance, and that the endless pursuit of perfection is an impediment to progress.

It is not yet clear whether James will succeed in politics. He could, because although he is an intellectual he has what many intellectuals lack – a driving ambition. After a few years at IDASA, he returned to his old stamping ground at UCT to be head of the Faculty of Humanities. Ramphele, whom he had persuaded to join him at IDASA for a year to establish the raft of public-policy programmes, one of which – the Political Information and Monitoring Service – I was hired to set up and lead, was by then vice chancellor. James expected to succeed her.

But by all accounts he made a mess of the deanship, underestimating the tenacity of varsity politics, and made too many enemies in too short a time. But it was not for want of ambition.

Having been overlooked for the vice chancellorship when Ramphele went to the World Bank in 2000, James retreated licking his wounds and sought new pastures. He liked the sound of being the editor of a newspaper and Tony O'Reilly, the then owner of the Independent Group, duly obliged, taking him on as de facto editor-in-waiting of the *Argus*.

The scheme failed because James, so it proved, had no nose for news or no sense of what the public wanted to read. Given a whole page to edit, he published long earnest treatises on science or culture that went over the heads of most readers.

I admire James's unrelenting curiosity in ideas. Politics needs people with ideas. And in the context of the deeply disturbing dumbing-down of South African politics, they are needed more than ever before.

After his time at the *Argus*, and encouraged by his own brush with mortality from a rare genetic blood disorder, James set out to explore the origins of the human species: human genome science. It was a suitably epic pursuit and it no doubt satisfied his desire to make a difference, as did his role as a board member of one of the leading global philanthropic organisations, the Ford Foundation.

In late 2008, it was announced without warning that James was going to be on the DA list for the April 2009 election.

That very day, we were holding a consultation in Johannesburg as part of the process of building support for the idea of the Council for the Advancement of the South African Constitution. James had been involved in some of the preliminary discussions, which included a range of people such as Kader Asmal, Geoff Budlender, Tseliso Thipanyane (then CEO of the South African Human Rights Commission) and Ramphele.

Ramphele was the main speaker at the Johannesburg event and James was due to chair the evening's discussion. Shortly before we started, I mentioned James's new political affiliation to her and, quick as a flash, she said, 'Then he can't chair tonight, no way.'

I was not as surprised as others by James's decision. It seemed to me entirely in keeping with his sense of ambition, his desire to serve his nation and his political instincts, which are part liberal. I say 'part liberal' because James is very much the embodiment of the new DA, which is now only part liberal. It is also part social democrat – the other half of James's ideological make-up, to my mind – and part conservative. Remember, it subsumed the remnants of the National Party in 2005 and, moreover, the part of the NP that did not want to be taken into the all-enveloping ANC – in other words, its more right-wing members.

This is the new DA: a much broader political church than it has ever been, including, as I say, some pretty unpleasant conservative and probably racist elements from the old NP – especially from that contingent that had run the vicious Western Cape NP's campaigns against the ANC at successive elections in the 1990s – as well as 'natural' social democrats such as Patricia de Lille.

If you want evidence of James's social democracy, you need look no further than his fine speech to the National Assembly marking the occasion of the death of Frederik Van Zyl Slabbert, the leader of the Progressive Federal Party and one of the forefathers of the DA.

There was a time when, as executive director of IDASA, James wanted to change the organisation's name to the Institute for Social Democracy in South Africa. Interestingly, and relevantly in terms of his new preoccupations and responsibilities in the DA, he wanted to shift IDASA's brand from that of a liberal organisation (because some in the ANC perceived it as such, they were being unnecessarily adversarial) to something more to the left.

I remember contesting the idea, on the basis that IDASA was by then an established brand name and that to change it would be risky; we would shift opinion and attitudes towards us rather by our work and by who represented the organisation in the public space, and by what we said and how we said it. My view held sway and James changed his own mind. Although we fell out later, and barely spoke during the last part of his tenure as head of IDASA, one of the things I continued to respect was his willingness to listen to others' views and to change his own when presented with better arguments.

At the centre of the DA's new ideological spectrum lies its traditional liberal heartland. Just as at the centre of the ANC there is a centrist, moderate heartbeat, so, a little to the right, lies the DA's traditional ideological pivot. The question is whether this will remain. Will the DA's own centre hold? It is a much more complex political creature now. It has, like the ANC, an awful lot of – even more, in fact – former Nats. The divide in the DA between liberal-minded, modern, tolerant people and conservative nationalists with traditionalist views is reflected in the wider country.

On the Civil Union Bill – to introduce civil wedding ceremonies for gay people – there were black and white members of the DA on both sides of the divide.

The DA is also in government now – in the Western Cape provincial government and the City of Cape Town, having won decisive victories to acquire both – which means that it can no longer afford to luxuriate in opposition, making wild promises and unreasonable criticisms of those parties in government. *It is in government.*

If he stays the course, James is likely to be a central figure in what unfolds. He is not only the parliamentary caucus chair but also the federal chairman of the party, and a natural policy wonk. He was, for example, the main architect of the party's major policy document to emerge in recent years – the DA's Plan for Growth and Jobs, which is long on ideas about how to grow the economy, but rather short on how to reduce inequality, which James conceded when I bumped into him at a cocktail party at the British High Commission shortly after its release.

He was also, therefore, the one who put in the phrase 'Enough, for all, forever' – a slogan first coined by the British sustainability thinker Jonathon Porritt. It is an essentially progressive notion. 'Enough, for all' has egalitarian overtones. It is certainly a qualitatively different idea to the Karl Popperian 'opportunity society' that Zille has espoused over the past few years, to distinguish her own brand of liberalism from that of her essentially neoliberal, conservative predecessor, Leon.

The Popper form of liberalism is essentially one that emphasises the creation of equal opportunities over socio-economic outcomes. This distinguishes it, deliberately and powerfully in Zille's view, from the mainstream thinking of the ANC – from left and right of the ruling party – which is concerned with manufacturing a set of socio-economic outcomes designed to transfer power.

This is not uncontested territory within the ruling party. Its nationalist right wing is concerned with transferring power to it and its members – the new elite – and is largely unconcerned with equality and the genuine upliftment of the poor, whereas the 'sensible left' of the ANC, and its moderate middle ground, has a more socialist, class-based analysis of power and the need to shift its structure to extend access to wealth and resources, to a materially enhanced life, to as many people as possible (what human rights lawyers would call 'substantive equality' rather than 'procedural equality').

So, small to the point of being pedantic though it may seem, the difference in ideological outlook between, say, Zille and James on the nature and purpose of the form of equality that they each espouse, is indicative of the emerging new ideological contours of the DA. 'Enough for all,' says James; 'Enough *opportunity* for all,' Zille/Popper would say.

For a former outsider's perspective, I chat to Lance Greyling, MP and chief whip of the Independent Democrats. 'The DA is now a broad liberal tradition and they do try to stay away from branding themselves as such. There is a lot that is in common between social democracy and liberalism ... especially in terms of moral issues,' he tells me, which is one of 'three ideological planks' – the role of the state in the economy and racial transformation being the other two – that are the key elements of the ideological terrain in South Africa.

I ask him about equality and recount my conversation with James about this subject and the DA's big growth-strategy document, which Greyling contributed to, as well as the 'alternative budget' process. (Greyling says Tim Harris, the dynamic young DA MP, has made the 'shadow ministry of finance quite sexy'.) He gives a Zumaesque chuckle; James was easy to work with, he says, and 'I deliberately put social democracy on the table and Wilmot made a point of saying "you're welcome"'. Cue another chuckle.

'On the economic stuff, clearly the DA is very much market-economy driven, and to a large extent I am too. The real question is the role of the state.' Greyling points to the growth document: 'There is an acceptance of a certain amount of industrial policy. The sense I get is that it is a wide church ... some are free marketeers and some are more social democratic and the growth document is a compromise between the two.'

Greyling, who cut his political teeth on environmental policy and now focuses on the important issue of energy policy, has a neat sound bite: 'The DA works for less government, the ANC for more, the ID argues for better government. So, the first order of business is to get government working.'

This is what De Lille is grappling with in Cape Town – trying to get the officials in the municipal government to serve their citizens with efficiency and without unnecessary bureaucratic fuss, something that she cares passionately about, while having to watch her back, as conservatives from the 'old' DA seek to stab her in it.

The new guard

But back to Mazibuko; what of her? Despite doubts about Mazibuko's political genealogy, it is clear that she is talented. Her lack of political pedigree may even be to her advantage. She is an example of a new breed of South African politician: one that chooses it as a profession rather than grows up with it as an inevitable vocation.

The ANC has its own equivalents, of course; young tyros (by which I mean young whippersnappers with a lot still to learn) who see the party as the pathway out of unemployment and into riches, but whose commitment to, let alone knowledge of, its political lineage, traditions and practices is limited – something that is hurting the ANC badly.

In the absence of a political 'upbringing', where does the politics come from? How deep are its roots? I ask Mazibuko what she would put if the immigration declaration form had a space for 'ideology'. She sees the question a mile away, even though I doubt the *Telegraph* asked it.

'Liberal,' she says, very quickly.

My follow-up – What does 'liberal' mean in this day and time? – induces a rather revealing answer that deserves a full and unadulterated transcription despite the meandering path to its destination:

> There was a time when I was sitting on Jammie Steps [at UCT] debating things with my friends when I would have described myself as socialist. And it had to do with race more than it had to do with economic policy or even social socialism, which is to say the role of the state in your private life. Socialists are much more comfortable with government regulation of the press or with ideas. They are much more comfortable with, what is it called when you must all develop at the same pace, with not too many outliers – the ANC advocates it in its education policy? Don't let the model-C schools do too well, they must at least come down to the level of the former Bantustan schools.

At this point I am beginning to wonder where this will all lead, and try to interject to bring things to a halt. But Mazibuko presses on, unabashed: 'There's an actual name for it. Something equal development. It's got the word development in there.'

Not, I presume, separate development, which rings a bell. Actually, I think she's reaching for the notion of 'equal opportunity', which is one of those rare occasions where the left steals a word – in this case 'opportunity' – from the right, or the liberal centre at least. Undeterred, Mazibuko proceeds:

These are very socialist ways of viewing the world. But for me it was more about race. It was to say, um, that these things should happen, er, as a response to the disadvantage levered against black people by apartheid. We referred to it as scar tissue: black rage and white guilt. Even though we had grown up with great privilege compared to most black South Africans, there was an emotional sense of injustice that, you know, you felt it had to be rectified. What struck me about the DA was this idea of individualism, coupled with social responsibility. Not individualism but individual freedom. Socially, and by socially I mean in relation to issues like whether you are gay or straight or religious or not, I have always been borderline libertarian, rather than just a liberal.

So there you have it. The new, young leader of the DA parliamentary party. Black, polished, ideologically confusing. A former 'socialist' – sort of – and a part-time 'libertarian'. Oh, but yes, undoubtedly a liberal. All at the age of thirty-one.

Her statement that she would have identified herself as a 'socialist' and her linking this more to racial solidarity over principle is very interesting. But it is clear that racial solidarity and the black experience are concepts that sit uncomfortably with her. One reading of the latter part of the quote could suggest that the DA has allowed her to transcend race in a way, and escape the discomfort of being a black woman with the privileges that accrue to an Anglo private-school accent at sea in a world where others still attend the equivalent of 'former Bantustan schools'.

If I had to nail it down, I would describe Mazibuko as a social liberal, rather than a neoliberal or a classical liberal. I'll spare you the transcript, but I say this because Mazibuko goes on to speak about ramping up the state, the importance of social responsibility within liberalism, and the need to recognise constraints on access to opportunities in developing countries.

She ends by talking about the need for a clear social compact, where the state knows where its role and responsibility ends and where the compact is about reaching consensus about the regulatory framework for maximising job creation and galvanising private-sector investment to do so.

Though they would undoubtedly quarrel about where precisely the role of the state starts and finishes, and would no doubt seek a more interventionist, assertive contribution from the state in the market, as a general proposition I doubt whether Trevor Manuel or even Rob Davies or Ebrahim Patel would differ greatly in this, though they would find the comparison disagreeable.

Unfortunately, Mazibuko then spoils it by wandering off to talk about the freedom to start up a government newspaper, 'but please can you stick to the limits of your mandate and make sure the public broadcaster is free and is public and isn't a government mouthpiece before you start going onto these other things … and stop monopolising electricity distribution'. And, within two minutes of having spoken of the need to 'ramp up the role of the state', she embarks on a riff about how 'the state actually hampers the market and should get out of the way'.

At the risk of patronising her, which I am about to do, her grasp of political theory and practice betrays her age. Frankly, at times Mazibuko sounds as if she is still on the steps of Jammie Hall with her mates, arguing the toss about the future of the country.

Despite this, Mazibuko is astute enough to realise that she will have to watch her back in her party. At this point in our conversation she slows down, and picks her words very carefully, one at a time: 'We have an openness for new blood, but of course that is going to cause some resentment' – and this is where she really slows down – 'amongst those for whom politics has been a slow climb up a slightly greasy ladder, you know what I mean?'

I do. And they will indeed be resentful of how this, at the time, thirty-one-year-old, with less than five years' experience in the DA, became their parliamentary leader. She cites, however, the case of someone like KwaZulu-Natal MP Alf Lees, whom she describes as 'one of the hardest-working members of the party … although I don't want to put scale of hard work on things' – but you just did – and who, instead of feeling aggrieved that she leapfrogged him in the DA KwaZulu-Natal list, welcomes the new diversity in the party's leadership 'because he knows that he adds less to the diversity of the party's list than I do'.

I put it to her that, like policemen, politicians are getting younger – just days before, the Swedish Social Democratic Party had elected as leader a woman even younger than Mazibuko – and that this will be an asset to the DA in its strategy of trying to win young votes, but, even if this is the case, isn't she simply too posh to win working-class votes?

She rejects this on the grounds that 'it has no basis other than the mistaken analysis that has prevailed since 1994 that it's a battle between race groups and it's a battle between socio-economic groups …'

Reflecting now on her precise words, and how her easy communicative style slipped at this point, I realise that it's because the point is flawed: it can't have been about both race and class; the point is that until now it has been seen as either one or the other, not the overlap between the two. In other words, her 'mistaken analysis' analysis is, well, mistaken.

She picks up her flow quickly enough, however, with a clearer point: '… that it's the same faulty analysis that says that you can only appeal to people who look and sound like you, or come from the same background as you'. In aid of her argument she praises Leon's ability 'to speak in his Houghton Afrikaans to a whole constituency to whom he should have absolutely no appeal to, and was more appealing to them than Van Zyl Slabbert was, and had absolutely nothing in common with them other than an interest in where they came from and what their concerns were'.

Indeed, he was very good at preying on their fears and exploiting their racism and *swart gevaar*.

Of her current leader, Mazibuko says this: 'Zille koekie-loekies her way across the Cape flats, and speaks Xhosa and Afrikaans. Even though she's German, she still communicates with them better than the ID and so we were able to take a huge chunk of votes from them in 2009.'

Interestingly, Mazibuko majored in Latin at university, a fact few people know. Yet she says in her very precise, crystal-clear English, 'I don't think I am too posh, no, not at all. Any more than I think Zille was too white for the Cape Flats. Or Tony too English – and Jewish – for the Afrikaans community. The only limit on your ability to communicate with anyone is your ability to engage with them.'

This is why the DA is so much stronger and more powerful than six or seven years ago. The diversity of leadership does not just make for good billboards. It broadens the language – the political language – with which they can talk to and engage the electorate.

A party for all?

A long-time astute observer of DA politics, analyst Jonathan Faull, challenges my assertion: 'This is true, but to some extent it does not change the DA's other enduring challenge – one that reared itself again in the recent past with the party's statements during "toiletgate" and the farm workers' strike – the party still finds it very difficult to speak with empathy to the poor black experience, and it returns to abrogate their gains in other areas.'

In other words, the DA may have acquired more melanin, but it continues to speak – with some exceptions, most notably regarding the working-class coloured experience – from the perspective of the old establishment.

Faull penned an op-ed in 2004, the core sentiment of which still rings true:

It should thus come as no surprise that, at the core of the DA's re-visioning process, are the twin objectives of building more effective party infrastruc-ture (to capture and get out the vote), and to increase black representation, presence in black communities, and to 'demonstrate ... concern for, and commitment to poor and marginalised people'. Ryan Coetzee recently, and less euphemistically, put it: '[the party] needs to be empathetic to black experi-ence and circumstances ... to communicate empathy [towards] black people specifically' (to increase their African vote). What are the DA's prospects in this regard? Is the future fabulous or will the funk of stagnation and piece-meal growth continue? Is it possible to talk about a 'government in waiting' or is their long-term role to be the perpetual 'lib dems' of South African politics: a principled, effective, liberal opposition of conscience, but not of ambition? Is it possible to be both? It appears that the DA has identified the key impediments to their growth. To inverse Coetzee's soliloquy, the party remains too 'empathetic to the experience and circumstances' of minority groups, specifically white people. As a consequence the DA leadership retains a melanin deficiency, its structures are too concentrated in established constituencies inherited from the DP and, to a lesser extent, the NNP [New National Party], and its messages, by and large, do not reach the ANC-dominated African electorate and when they do so, they fail to resonate sufficiently to swing any votes.[1]

In any case, the pluralism of the DA's new leadership (Zille, Mazibuko, De Lille and James, with remnants of the old guard: James Selfe, and formerly Ryan Coetzee and Gareth Morgan) presents threats as well as opportunities. As Mazibuko herself says: 'That's the trouble with a more pluralist leadership, that you risk things getting out of control. As we get bigger, message unity will become ever more important.'

Spoken like a real politico. But who will make the decisions and hold the line? First, says Mazibuko, it must be the federal executive, and second, the national leader: 'And she must take advice and, like all good leaders, she does. So the people she has around her will be absolutely important and it's a question of who she decides to keep around her, which fluctuates.'

Mazibuko is then surprisingly frank in saying that Zille and Ryan Coetzee, the long-time confidant and strategy advisor to Leon, have 'only recently forged a relationship' (this was speaking in spring 2011).

This makes sense. When Zille won the DA leadership in May 2007, one of her biggest internal tactical issues was how to deal with the old boys' club and, specifically, the supremely talented but cocksure Coetzee.

Well, that is one perception of the man who is now living in London, having been recruited by a beleaguered Nick Clegg, the British deputy prime minister, to help save his Liberal Democrats ahead of the next general election. As Coetzee himself says: 'There is one narrative about how I seek to try to control everything in the southern hemisphere.'

Coetzee also refers me to other narratives, of greater importance, that have emerged since 2006. The first is about diversity, about the DA being – in the words of the title of the internal party strategy document that Coetzee penned in 2006 – 'a party for all the people'. The other narrative is about becoming a party of government. Coetzee again: 'the first time since 1994 that voters had an alternative governing party to the ANC'.

A crucial milestone in the first narrative took place in spring 2011 at the internal DA election – arguably, an event that was almost as significant as Polokwane was to the ANC.

I met with Wilmot James to interview him for this book just a few days before the crucial election, held on 27 October 2011, at which he and Mazibuko were elected as part of a 'change' slate (my phrase, not theirs).

Speaking before James and Mazibuko won, Coetzee told me he viewed it as a litmus test. It was far from a foregone conclusion; Coetzee at that point thought that it 'was going to be tough. But that, win or lose, it would advance the process of change within the party.'

It's a process of change that Coetzee attaches maximum strategic importance to: 'If you get the inside right, the outside takes care of itself ... if you externalise in the right way. You still have to market, but that's a technical exercise – you can't spin fundamentally what you are not.'

Is this a new Coetzee, or has he always thought this? If he's always thought it, he hid it well during the long years as Leon's strategic *handlanger*.

Coetzee and Zille's approach has been to try to populate the party with the 'right' people, painfully aware of the fact that as you grow you become vulnerable to dodgy opportunists. Since 2006, the DA has started to succeed in doing this. The 2007 Young Leaders' Programme – Coetzee's great legacy (he laughs and says, 'Well, greatest legacy in the balance sheet of my legacy', and one of the more appealing aspects of Coetzee's personality is that although he is supremely arrogant – perhaps deservedly so – he also has the self-deprecating ability to laugh genuinely at himself) – is a major plank in the DA's current and long-term political strategy.

Coetzee has been such a pivotal figure in DA strategy for so long – since becoming Leon's right-hand man in 1997 at the tender age of twenty-four – that it will be interesting to see how they manage without him. It is rumoured that he and Zille were struggling to get along before his departure to London. Perhaps they did not entirely see eye to eye and perhaps she was not entirely sad to lose him given her determination to shake up the old boys' club that dominated the DA for so long under Leon.

But she recognises Coetzee's talents, and there is a high degree of mutual respect between them. He will be back, I am sure of that, probably after the 2015 UK general election, and in time for what I see as a potentially watershed 2016 municipal election in South Africa. The reason he is with British liberals now is not because he sought out an escape. In fact, like so many things in life, it was an accident. Coetzee and a group of other DA people were on a trip to the US to attend an international convention of liberals, Liberal International. They broke their journey in London and, on hearing this, Jonny Oates, Clegg's chief of staff who spent two years in South Africa working for the Inkatha Freedom Party at the turn of the century and who had got to know Coetzee, invited the latter to speak with some leading Lib Dem leaders. Coetzee made a good impression.

Suffering badly in the polls as a result of their coalition with the Tories, the Lib Dems were eager for fresh thinking. Coetzee is providing them with just that. In November 2012, I visited Oates at 10 Downing Street and was shown the large committee room where that very morning Coetzee, after just a few weeks in his position, had made his first formal presentation to party leaders and advisors, based on the results of his first opinion poll.

According to a clearly impressed Oates, he 'had them in the palm of his hand', taking them through a ninety-minute PowerPoint presentation and 'keeping them with him every step of the way'. His central message was a straightforward, classic exposition of good political communication – and none the worse for that – that what they needed was a clearer message about what distinguishes them from David Cameron's Tories, to be delivered consistently, in volume, over time.

No doubt about it, Coetzee will be back, resuming his influential position within opposition ranks in his homeland.

Managing the leadership

As for Zille, she has definitely taken the DA forward, and will continue to do so in the medium term. Her track record in the anti-apartheid movement, especially her unearthing of the truth surrounding the death of Steve Biko, makes her a less-easy target (although it has not protected her) for the ANC than Leon.

As Faull tells me: 'The most pervasive change under Zille has been a recognition of politics as a long haul. Leon, following the 1999 "fight back" breakthrough, fell too easily for the trappings of short-circuiting election cycles – evidenced by the initially disastrous formation of the DA to contest the 2000 local government elections.'

The DP–NNP marriage quickly fell apart and, instead of saving resources, led to a long internecine opposition battle that came to a close only when the straggling remnants of the NNP collapsed into the ANC in 2005. Says Faull: 'This could have been avoided by contesting an independent and terminally declining NP/NNP in the 2000 and 2004 elections.'

How is Zille different from Leon? Significantly, I would argue, in terms of character. Zille may be as steely in her resolve as Leon, even more so in fact, but there is something qualitatively different about her personality. Zille has compassion and a genuine concern for people less fortunate in life, something that was beyond Leon's human compass.

I suspect a lot of people can't – or can no longer or don't want to – see past the tough exterior within which she has necessarily had to encase herself in the face of the harsh brickbats that the ANC throws at her. I would add that she is partly to blame – she is so driven that her schedule is absurdly punishing, which, from my vantage point, tends to limit her ability to shift gear. She is always 'on'; always on the attack or counter-attack.

But, in fact, the blame lies with her own organisation, which has not yet figured out that leaders – all leaders, but especially those like Zille who push themselves so hard – need to be 'managed'. Here are two examples to illustrate the point, and the problem.

In early 2013, Zille was to close an afternoon meeting that brought together a group of thinkers from Western Cape provincial government, City of Cape Town, UCT and the business community to deliberate on issues of resilience to climate change and green economic development (Zille's government, with the help of former ANC intelligence operative and BEE analyst Jenny Cargill, who is now Zille's special advisor for the purpose, is developing a green economy strategy). The meeting was proceeding well when Zille arrived halfway through, looking like death warmed up. Urban expert and UCT academic Edgar Pieterse, who was once an economics advisor to ANC premier Ebrahim Rasool, turned to me and mouthed what I think was 'she looks absolutely fucked'. It turned out that Zille had bad toothache and was in an exceedingly bad mood, which she displayed as she started to heckle the speakers with sharp rejoinders such as 'that can't be so', 'nonsense' and 'check your facts, we'd never have allowed that'.

The facilitator for the afternoon was Peter Willis from the University of Cambridge Programme for Sustainability Leadership. He had shepherded us along with his customary skill and tact, and duly asked 'Madam Premier if she would care to close the proceedings'. The intention was for her to give a gentle little five-minute speech, thanking people for giving their time and making such a thoughtful contribution to helping her government think through some difficult issues. But, clearly, she had not been properly briefed and/or was in no mood to obey instructions. Whichever it was, she launched into a long diatribe, attacking virtually everyone in the room and complaining about 'academic twaddle' and the need for action not talk. When Willis interrupted to excuse himself because he had to take the guest speaker, Norwegian climate expert Jørgen Randers, to his next speaking engagement, Zille responded abruptly: 'You go, go, it's fine, I've barely started.' It was Maggie Thatcher incarnate.

Her desire for concrete steps rather than endless consultative process is perfectly understandable. What was unforgivable was her tone, which was completely inappropriate and counterproductive. Pieterse and I chuckled, but some people were seriously offended, including the woman from a Cape Town–based oil company who told me afterwards, 'I came here to help, not to be lectured and given a party political broadcast.' Foolishly, I quietly mentioned this to Zille as we filed out to take refreshments at the end, whereupon she said, 'Right, point her out to me, who accused me of that', before steaming off to confront the unfortunate oil executive (who, for the record, happened to be a black woman).

The second example is from 2012, when Zille arrived at the offices of a major South African corporate with the intention of persuading them to donate money to the DA. The company has a clear 'no donations' policy (wisely, in my view). She was late because the traffic was bad; she had a junior aide with her. She was tired and irascible. So when the company's representatives informed her of their policy and their determination to stick to it, they were given a 'right royal hand-bagging', in the words of someone who was present. In fact, the company had been minded to discuss how they might contribute to democratic politics in general, in a way that would help all parties, and they were interested in learning about the DA's policies in those parts of the country where it is in power and overlaps with the company's business operations. But they were completely put off by Zille's tone and attitude.

In both cases, there are common features: Zille was exhausted and bad-tempered, and there was no one of sufficient seniority to guide her. She needs a serious chief of staff. Not one who has other responsibilities in the party, but who is solely responsible for managing Zille – in all aspects of her political life – with the clout necessary not only to brief her properly about what lies ahead, but to intervene strongly to prevent her from making unnecessary mistakes. In the first case, Zille's schedule was beyond ridiculous: she had cycled the Cape Argus Pick n Pay Cycle Tour the previous day, in seven hours something. She had then caught the 5:45 a.m. flight up to Johannesburg for a DA meeting. And she had toothache. Who on earth permitted such a schedule? Of course, she's a hard person to say no to. But great leaders have great chiefs of staff, who are able to do just that. And Zille plainly doesn't have one – something that will cost her and her party in due course, because the DA needs her, and her current relentless pace is entirely unsustainable.

The difference between Zille and Leon is also, in part, one of inheritance: Zille inherited a largely consolidated opposition vote from Leon's stewardship, but, apart from easily and without too much complexity consuming the ID, she has not spent much time beating back the rest of the opposition, but rather has forthrightly focused on the ANC and its record.

Demonstrating the comparative governance record of the DA in the Western Cape and Cape Town is her calling card to win black votes over to the opposition, less so to cannibalise the opposition by gobbling it up, which was Leon's objective with the NP.

Faull continues: 'To put it somewhat simplistically, Leon's arrogance was conditioned by the long-standing liberal South African belief that they are on the right side of history, and that as everyone became more educated, they would fall into line and vote liberal. Zille is far more attuned to the fact that this is not the case, and that South African liberalism must demonstrate its utility to new voters if it is to remain relevant, and grow.'

But there is a difficult thing going on in the DA now: seeking to 'promote diversity without it degenerating into ethnic contestation', as one of their strategists puts it. 'The trouble with diversity is that every nationalist and ethno-type can advance their cause under its banner. We are trying also to avoid head counting. That requires a lot of judgement and dextrous management and leadership. And it takes a bit of time. It's much harder than legislating quotas.'

Holding the party together as it grows will become more and more difficult. There is a point at which you become sufficiently big that the scope for disunity becomes much wider. More importantly, you can no longer know all of the people you have and so the danger of weaker or dishonest people becoming involved surreptitiously is also far greater.

Leadership and organisational power will be crucial in the years ahead if the DA is to cope with this challenge. Recognising this, the new leadership has begun to reform the party. As James noted two years ago when the process of change began: 'The existing structure is confused ... Athol [Trollip] interviews people to be secretary and he doesn't lead. He's just another MP. There's a slight adjustment in the division of labour and what we need to do is raise the quality of what we do.'

As to the future, James talks of doing two things at once: 'We need to realign the opposition on the one hand, and increase our voter base on the other.' He expresses the strategic goal in very straightforward terms: 'to see if we can by 2014 attract 30 per cent of the national vote'.

To do so would represent a sea change in political power in South Africa. Can the DA do it?

As can be seen from Figure 9.1, the DA vote has been steadily rising, while the ANC vote has been steadily declining. From just under 70 per cent at the 2004 election, the ANC is now closer to 60 per cent, as evidenced in the 2011 local government elections. The DA has gone from around 12 per cent in 2004 to around 24 per cent in 2011. It has doubled its share of the vote in just seven years – an undeniably strong performance. Meanwhile, the other parties have been squeezed, as can be seen from Figure 9.2.

Now, there are two ways of looking at this. Either the DA has simply mopped up all the other parties or it is a new age of electoral competition. In the one case, the DA has simply reached its new 'natural limit to growth', having collected most of the available non-ANC votes; in the other, having done so, it continues to grow, competing with the ANC on an ever-widening front.

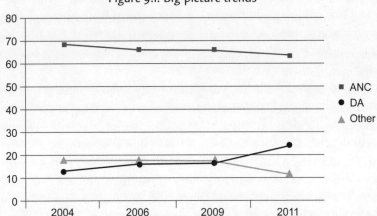

Figure 9.1: Big-picture trends

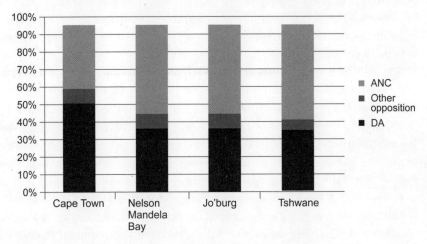

Figure 9.2: A new age of competition? Or DA mopping up the opposition?

I give further evidence that points in both directions later on. But first, a word or two about the other opposition parties.

The others

Actually, there is not a lot to say. As *Anatomy of South Africa* described in some detail, with the exception of the DA, the opposition has struggled since 1994 to operate in an effective manner, due to a combination of factors: poor leadership, lack of resources – financial and skills – and, in most cases, a serious legitimacy deficit, especially in comparison with the ANC.

The story of small opposition parties that I told in *Anatomy* is a story of misery and failure, usually preceded by a brief, shining moment of promise. The

United Democratic Movement led by Bantu Holomisa and the ID led by De Lille were the prime examples of this. Both attracted a lot of attention when they were launched in 1997 and 2003 respectively, but neither was able to build on their initial spurt of energy, despite having credible leaders with integrity and genuine commitment.

Holomisa has soldiered on, but with flagging levels of intensity. At the 2009 national election, the UDM managed just short of 1 per cent of the vote and so emerged with only four MPs. Many of their better people had proved to be opportunists, men and women like Cedric Frolick and Annelize van Wyk, who jumped ship to the ANC at the first sign of trouble, where they have built not inconsiderable careers as parliamentary apparatchiks for their new political masters – Frolick as house chairperson of the National Assembly and Van Wyk as the acting chair of its parliamentary police committee.

It would probably have suffered a slow death in any case, but the rotten and short-lived system of floor-crossing that existed from 2001 to 2009 was sufficiently long-lived to kill off the body of the UDM. It did precisely what the ANC's political managers expected of it when it was introduced: it enticed weak-principled individuals from smaller parties who were worried about losing their parliamentary positions (and salaries).

De Lille did not lose heart entirely. Rather than suffer the slow road to oblivion that Holomisa has chosen for the UDM, De Lille took an even harder road, submitting to what in effect amounted to a merger and acquisition by the DA.

It started immediately after the 2006 local government elections in Cape Town. It was a hung council, with the DA as the biggest party (with 90 of the 210 council seats). The ID had emerged as the potential kingmaker, and was courted by both the ANC and the DA. Ideologically, there is no doubt that De Lille has more in common with the ANC. She is, as I have said, by instinct if not label – which she eschews – a genuine social democrat. Some of her closest and most able MPs, such as Lance Greyling, are even more assertively social democrat in their outlook, and for Greyling and some of the others, De Lille's decision, made quickly and with moderate levels of consultation, to go with the DA was hard to take. Greyling, for the record, now seems remarkably at ease with the decision, despite his earlier discomfiture.

De Lille has not yet had a chance to regret the decision to join the DA. Indeed, it is not altogether clear that she has come to terms with it herself. In conversation she hangs on to the technical fact that the ID still exists, and will do so until the 2014 national election, at which point it will simply vanish, subsumed into the DA.

Now, she is a DA mayor. She is in power, something every politician rightfully aspires to, but far from comfortable with some of her new political bedfellows, diehard liberals from the DP, like Belinda Walker, the sharp, no-holds-barred former deputy mayor. Holding the City of Cape Town, as well as the Western Cape provincial government, gives the DA a significant political base – a launch pad for electoral growth and a chance to prove itself in government.

And you hear people, ANC people, saying, sometimes with gritted teeth or a wry shake of the head: 'I have to admit, when I come to Cape Town I see a well-run city' ... or words to that effect.

COPE looked like it might break the mould when it was hurriedly formed in 2008, post-Polokwane. It looked like it might have some important attributes that previous new parties did not have or did not have enough of: cash; ANC genetics and, therefore, legitimacy; decent leadership; and mobilising capacity on the ground.

The UDM had had the decent leadership and the ANC genetics, but neither the cash nor, really, the mobilising capacity. The ID had the decent leadership and some mobilising capacity (at least in the Cape), but neither the cash nor the ANC genetics.

COPE came, it saw, it briefly conquered (sort of) and then it went. Blink and you missed it.

Mazibuko's view is that despite this, COPE was good for the opposition and good for competitive democracy in South Africa because it was 'a milestone in the sense that it legitimised black South Africans to vote not for the ANC ... at the time that was the preserve of IFP voters in KZN, no one else could do it. It was a stepping stone in that it made it much easier for people to understand why a black person would join the DA.'

This is an interesting observation. It was tempting to think, at least at the time, that COPE was a threat to the DA, that it would be fighting for those voters who had abandoned the ANC, not creating a new, bigger market of such voters.

Coetzee sees it slightly differently: 'COPE threatened our existing support, and we had to beat them off. Our 2009 campaign was changed on a tickey, literally, one afternoon, when it occurred to me that we couldn't run the campaign we were going to run ... we had to adjust.'

He adds that they succeeded because, unlike some opposition parties he'd 'care not to mention', the DA 'actually knows how to run a campaign and win', which, he observes drily, is 'terribly attractive to voters'.

Says Coetzee: 'We squeezed COPE, then the ANC squeezed COPE and then COPE squeezed itself.' Which is a very neat way of putting it; a phrase turned like the true spin-meister he is.

I have always harboured my own suspicions about COPE – that it was some kind of 'ANC project'. That is not to say that the ANC leadership sat around one day and thought, 'Now, how can we best ensure that we stay united and no one ever dares leave the organisation?' But to my mind there is little doubt who the real winners of the swift rise and fall of a party like COPE are: the ANC, despite what Mazibuko says.

COPE built a bridgehead at the 2009 election. Winning over 7 per cent of the popular vote (7.42 per cent to be exact) was a very good result for a new party, especially as its support came from a diverse range of sources in geographical, class and racial terms. It was certainly the first opposition party to win both black African working-class votes and middle-class white votes: 1.3 million in total.

But it failed to kick on; and the leadership fight between its two main leaders, Mosiuoa 'Terror' Lekota and Mbhazima 'Sam' Shilowa, was disastrous. Another of its leading lights, former SACP treasurer Phillip Dexter, described in detail to me how COPE's politics and psychology mirrored the ANC's: instead of offering a credible alternative, 'all we were doing was carrying on a fight that started in the ANC and organisationally we quickly degenerated into how the ANC behaved'.

When I meet with Dexter at one of his favourite lunchtime hang-outs, the Maharaj in Kloof Street, he is on the verge of returning to the ANC, as many COPE people have. The ANC welcomes them back, one by one, like errant children who have disobeyed a curfew on a school trip. There will be some admonishment, but the error of judgement will be quickly forgiven even if not entirely forgotten.

When I ask Dexter about infiltration, he concedes that it was very possible. A COPE councillor I bumped into once went further, intimating that he thought state intelligence operatives were rampant within COPE, stirring up the divisions and feeding information to the ANC. Now, not only would it be hard to prove, but there is also perhaps little point: COPE is on its last legs. It will win 1 per cent of the vote in 2014, whereupon Lekota will repent and be given a nice ambassadorship somewhere and that will be that – another failed opposition breakaway.

Start-up parties in the post-1994 dispensation have followed a general formula: high-profile person X becomes disaffected with his or her mother party and leaves to become leader, or co-leader, of a new entity. This is true of the UDM (Holomisa and Roelf Meyer from the ANC and NP respectively), the ID (De Lille from the Pan Africanist Congress), and COPE (Lekota, Shilowa et al. from the ANC).

The media, ever hungry for a black-led alternative to the ANC, create an initial storm over the new party; seed funding and core staffers follow. But the critical missing ingredient is a grass-roots infrastructure and functional, committed membership. Members of new parties have proved remarkably fickle, not altogether unsurprising given that they either abandoned a party ship with their leader or were mobilised out of apathy by a naive vision of a 'new' kind of politics.

The recurring problem for parties that follow this formula is that they lack the ballast that membership, branches and party infrastructure give to leadership. Internal squabbles – inevitable in party politics – very easily escalate into existential crises as a consequence, with competing leaders mobilising personality cults and patronage networks to undermine their competitors. Fratricide ensues – most vividly in the example of COPE's serial lawsuits and petty internal factions – to the detriment of the political project as a whole.

A contingent challenge is that many of these parties have been established by political mavericks. This is especially true of De Lille and Holomisa, and also, to a lesser degree, Lekota. Mavericks, in the South African milieu, attract attention and support within larger parties because they are skilful in driving personal political projects distinct from, but complementary to, the mother party.

But mavericks, almost by definition, act with the zeitgeist and, crucially, tend to do so without consultation. They are generally tolerated by larger entities because they attract more support than they drive off, and when push comes to shove, they toe the party line. But mavericks generally make poor political managers, and are generally poorer still at managing the nuanced messaging and branding that a successful political movement requires to transcend an individual's quick-fire positions.

Holomisa, Lekota and De Lille are fine people as well as politicians, but they are not good managers. For De Lille, this is an ongoing challenge in light of her stewardship of the City of Cape Town, where she herself is carefully managed politically by DA party apparatchiks (Paul Boughey, her chief of staff, most prominent among them) dispatched to her office to curb what they would regard as her maverick instincts, but which I would regard as her naturally very good social-democratic instincts.

The UDM's enduring Eastern Cape support, as well as the remnants of what passes for the IFP in KwaZulu-Natal, has more to do with the vestiges of homeland patronage politics than political management. The IFP's decline underscores a party that – like the NNP – never adjusted to what it means to act politically in a democratic country. The personality cult that surrounds Mangosuthu Buthelezi, and his egregious need for unquestioned power, has stunted the development of a new cadre of leadership in that party, and it will die with its increasingly elderly supporters.

All that will be left, then, at the next election will be a couple of tiny regional or narrow-interest parties: in KwaZulu-Natal, the IFP – whose own health is declining as fast as Buthelezi ages, as well as being squeezed by Zuma's popularity in his home province; the FFP for Afrikaner diehards; and, for fanatical Christians, the African Christian Democratic Party. As I said in my column on 1 February 2013: 'If those three parties get over double figures between them at the 2014 National Election I will eat my hat (an Arsenal baseball cap or a straw panama, as it happens). It is now entirely possible that the two big parties will share more or less 90 per cent of the popular vote (cut, roughly, 60–30).'[2]

Which brings me to Dr Ramphele. She is very hard to say no to. She is a force of nature. A compelling and utterly persuasive character. When she sets her mind on something, she is all but irresistible. As I was working on this book, Ramphele announced that she had now set her mind on leading a new political party – a news story that has caused not inconsiderable excitement and interest – but when the actual announcement came on 18 February 2013, it was not a political party as such that she was launching, but a 'platform' (whatever the distinction may be), with the name 'Agang'.

Speaking at the launch event at the Old Fort on Constitution Hill, Johannesburg, the former apartheid-era Black Consciousness activist, UCT vice chancellor, World Bank managing director and businesswoman said: 'I am consulting widely with fellow South Africans on forming a party political platform with a view to contesting the 2014 elections. The initiative is called Agang, or in the Nguni languages of our country, Akhani, which can be interpreted in English as "Build South Africa".'

My initial reaction, expressed in the *Mail & Guardian* before the launch, was this: '[T]his is not easy to say, because I can hear her voice in my ear, berating me for my lack of imagination, perhaps even my lack of loyalty, I think she is making a very big mistake if she thinks that she can break the mould of South African politics by striking out on her own.'[3]

When I first heard that she had spent the last part of 2012 working her contacts in the US and elsewhere, and had even hired a professional fund-raiser to continue the effort in 2013, my first reaction was to scratch my head in puzzlement. I am still scratching. I just don't get it, for all the available evidence suggests that South Africa is heading towards a two-party system, a tussle between the ANC and the DA, and that there is no room for any new entrant to the electoral marketplace, even one as well endowed as Ramphele in terms of resources and resolve.

Where does Ramphele see her slice of the action? She usually gets what she wants, so why the scepticism? As noted above, to be successful in a tough electoral environment like South Africa requires, on an organisational level, money and people, good people. Because she is so hard to say no to, and because she has such an extraordinary network of people around the world – many of them rich and influential – raising the bucks will not be Ramphele's problem.

Finding the right people will be. No doubt there are plenty of individuals with talent and time on their hands, or salaries to make, who would be all too happy to work close to such a dynamic woman. Surprising characters immediately surfaced at or after the launch. For example, Zohra Dawood, the ornery former head of George Soros's Open Society Foundations in South Africa, who had been fired in late 2012 after a former employee's exit interview exposed her managerial shortcomings (her turnover of staff was unremittingly high; and she bullied her board into submission, according to a former member who had the audacity to challenge the secrecy with which she veiled her own pay and conditions of service) and was conveyed to the foundations' new global chief executive, Chris Stone, in New York, who acted decisively. Dawood presented herself initially as Ramphele's spokesperson – a less ill-suited appointment would be hard to imagine – and then as her chief of staff. Her natural belligerence may, however, provide Ramphele with precisely what I earlier said Zille lacked.

Archbishop Emeritus Desmond Tutu's long-serving spokesman, John Allen, stepped in to handle the media during the interregnum before they could identify and then appoint the former editor-in-chief of the *Sowetan* newspaper, the tall and admirably laconic and lugubrious Thabo Leshilo, as Agang's director of communications. Ramphele's appointment of Nkosinathi Solomon as director of campaigns raised more eyebrows, however, since his background is very much in the corporate rather than the political world.

Even if Ramphele were able to assemble a skilled group of political organisers, they will need something to organise, which, in turn, means boots on the ground. A political party, especially one that is taking on a large, diverse, complex electoral market crowded with two big players, needs organisational heft – which is not something that can be built overnight.

And it cannot be built on the back of one strong, charismatic personality alone – ask De Lille. So, where will Ramphele get her votes? At the time of the launch, there was great excitement among the chattering classes – especially among those who are chronically ill-disposed towards both the DA and Zuma and his ANC. But the numbers are small. What of the born frees? Might they not like the look of a dynamic black woman who is courageous enough to speak out against the ANC, but who has all the authority and credibility that comes from her near half-century of political activism?

Some of them might. But, just as the ANC's own history means less to them than to their elders, so, too, will Ramphele's own track record and CV. A couple of years earlier, Zille not only courted Ramphele to be the next leader of the DA – as if one could actually parachute someone into such a position in a real political organisation – but told me that was the plan. Not realising that she had not yet told her colleagues in the DA federal council, I inadvertently shocked them when I mentioned it in passing in my *Mail & Guardian* column.

The plan almost came to fruition in February 2013. The idea had been crystallised in conversation between the two leaders: Ramphele would be slotted in as leader of the DA and the party would be renamed 'the Democrats'. I am still amazed that the two women honestly believed this would be acceptable to any political organisation, one that has processes and decision-making bodies. Did they really believe that the national structures of the DA would have simply accepted the will of Zille and their new leader, Ramphele?

I rather doubt it. I think it would have been messy and damaging.

The idea was shelved for a number of possible reasons: perhaps because Zille, and Ramphele, came to realise that there would be opposition from within the more conservative parts of the DA to the idea of parachuting her in as successor; or because Zille's colleagues persuaded her that it would be a terrible mistake to vacate the leadership too early; or because Ramphele herself could not quite bring herself to join the DA and do what any normal political animal would do – namely, work her way up through the ranks, building loyal support along the way.

But Ramphele is not a normal political animal (indeed, I am not even sure she is a political animal at all, in the party political sense; frankly, I doubt whether she has the self-discipline necessary to lead a political party; she is too independent a mind – that is her greatest strength). Since she cannot be risking so much merely to be a new 5 per cent voice in Parliament, the only way that Ramphele's move makes any sense is if the game plan is to build a new bridgehead in 2014, having perhaps garnered a decent number of young black independent first-time voters (even though that is a key part of the DA's own political strategy), and then to merge with the DA in a deal in which Ramphele can bring something to the table and thus can take on the leadership of a new political conglomerate.

Otherwise, I am left still scratching my head.

Electoral power: The numbers

The turnout figure for the municipal elections in 2011 was higher than usual, and especially high in the cities where the DA was competing the most vigorously, as Figures 9.3 and 9.4 show.

After the 2011 local government elections, analysts were split between those who said it was 'business as usual', with high levels of ANC support largely undisturbed, and those who called it hyperbolically a 'watershed'. It was neither. There was evidence of significant shifts, but it did not yet represent a watershed, because there was not enough evidence of change in the underlying, fundamental allegiances to suggest the swing in voting patterns required for the ANC hold on national power to be seriously threatened.

As we saw, the DA not only won a decisive majority in Cape Town, but also surprised many commentators, and the ANC, with their strong showing in three other cities, with, at or around 40 per cent of the vote in Johannesburg, Pretoria (Tshwane) and Port Elizabeth (Nelson Mandela Bay).

Did the DA win anything more than just a 'majority of the minorities' (i.e. most of the coloured, white and Indian votes)? Here one does have to be careful

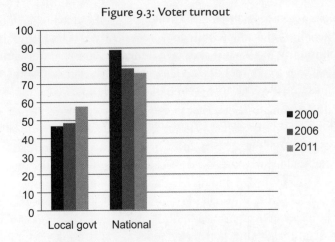

Figure 9.3: Voter turnout

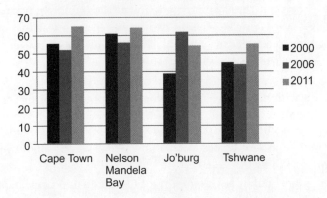

Figure 9.4: Competition and voter turnout

and build turnout into the analysis, as changes in turnout can account entirely for perceived 'swings' in party support. Electoral outcomes under proportional representation are significantly influenced by turnout: every vote counts; the totality of the vote comprises 100 per cent of the pie. Hence, if supporters of party X turn out in lower numbers than supporters of party Y compared to a previous election, the effect on eventual outcomes will be to inflate (potentially disproportionately) gains for party Y.

Even allowing for this, an examination of specific wards provides some fascinating evidence of significant, structural changes in voting patterns. Ward 79800032 in the famous Johannesburg 'township' of Alexandra, or Alex as it is colloquially known, is an especially interesting place. Drive around there and you begin to see a different South Africa, certainly different from the spatial development of apartheid and the strict demarcation of class in Cape Town. There is evidence of upward mobility in this area of Alex, of lower-middle-class, aspirant black people, as well as white people. In the absence of exit polling, it is impossible to know how the votes might have cut across the different strata and segments of this community, but what is clear is that the DA did well in this 'mixed' ward, winning just over 50 per cent of the votes, up from 37.5 per cent at the 2006 election, and pushing the ANC into second place (Table 9.1).

Table 9.1: Electoral support in Johannesburg Ward 79800032 by party

Party name	2011		2006	
	Per cent	Votes	Per cent	Votes
DA	50.18	4 234	37.5	1 602
ANC	46.41	3 946	56.02	2 393
COPE	1.47	125		
ID			1.5	64
ACDP			1.29	55
UDM			1.08	46
Total		8 305		4 160

Source: SABC News Research and IEC.

These sorts of mixed-class wards are very difficult to analyse, because they can include working-class voters in Alex and middle-class (and highly wealthy) voters in Sandton – as some wards span the two places. They may also include some upwardly mobile, aspirant black lower-middle-class voters – about whom there is a growing mythology.

As Faull points out, it is also important to note that local elections have, to some extent, different dynamics from those of national elections. As he tells me:

> Whites consistently vote in higher numbers relative to the overall populace in local elections, in part as a consequence of long-standing engagement with local politics through ratepayers associations, etc. African voters are far more critical of local government than they are of national institutions, and engage against a different set of indicators. Moreover, many black communities are emerging from a history of conscious rejection of formal local institutions through the apartheid years.

My own instinct in 2011 was that, for the first time, a group of middle-class black voters were voting DA. I have no direct evidence of it, only anecdotal. Coetzee claims the DA has both the anecdotal stuff about how, as he puts it, some voters walked 'halfway across the bridge but could not make it to the other side', and the polling data; about how some black lower-middle-class families had met and discussed it as a family and agreed to vote DA, but when they came out of the booth the parents had to admit that they were unable to abandon the ANC, to the horror of their children, who thought that they had made a family pact.

I know of precisely such a family; the parents and three daughters met at breakfast on election day, discussed the options and agreed to make 'the big switch' to the DA, more out of a sense of frustration with Zuma's ANC, and, as such, a protest vote, than anything else. But when they emerged from the voting station an hour or so later, one of the parents and one of the daughters had not been able to do it, and had stayed loyal to the ANC.

Part of the DA's strength is that they have increased their own polling capacity, now doing it all themselves, which is more cost-effective, with a unit devoted to telephone polling, headed up by Johan van der Berg. Coetzee says that the DA's own polling confirms the presence for the first time of 'swing voters', people who will move from one party to another, and back again, between elections – these voters are crucial for a vibrant, competitive electoral democracy.

And the academic literature is broadly supportive, too. In a piece in the *Journal of Public Administration*, Ebrahim Fakir and Waseem Holland assert that the evidence from 2011 suggests that 'new class solidarities are emergent, reflected in part within voting patterns and support for the DA from a small percentage of socially upwardly mobile black South Africans'.[4]

Fakir and Waseem conclude: 'The DA was perhaps able to increase support from an embryonic black professional class as well as seemingly increase its support of the upper and middle class stratums across racial cleavages.'[5]

Further east, in a different part of Alex, is Ward 32, an essentially entirely working-class or poor community. At first glance, the picture here is very different. The ANC is totally dominant, with over 90 per cent of the vote (Table 9.2). But, look carefully, and you will see that the DA has doubled its vote between the two elections, from, admittedly, a very low base of 2.43 per cent.

Table 9.2: Electoral support in Alexandra voting district Ward 32 by party

Party name	2011		2006	
	Per cent	Votes	Per cent	Votes
ANC	90.99	1 282	90.35	1 002
DA	4.76	67	2.43	27
COPE	1.7	24		
PAC			1.35	15
UDM			2.61	29
Total		1 373		1 073

Source: SABC News Research and IEC.

Now, depending on whether you are a glass-half-full or glass-half-empty kind of person, this may represent some kind of progress for the DA. In Khayelitsha in Cape Town, a similar picture emerges. Table 9.3 shows the voting in one ward in the middle of the poor working-class township.

Table 9.3: Sea change? Electoral support in Khayelitsha by party

Party name	2011		2006	
	Per cent	Votes	Per cent	Votes
ANC	93.91	9955	91.94	6557
DA	1.64	174		
COPE	1.55	164		
UDM	1.43	152	2.8	200
PAC			1.91	136
ID			1.36	97
Total		10445		6990

Source: SABC News Research and IEC.

The DA's vote has gone up exponentially, but from the lowest of bases: 0 per cent in 2006. The fact that, for the first time ever, 174 people in this ward made the choice to abandon the ANC, and in doing so go not to COPE, which might have been seen as an 'intermediate step', as 164 of their neighbours did, but to the DA, will surely provide the DA with a source of encouragement.

Fakir and Waseem's analysis is consistent with my findings. They conclude, looking only at wards that fall entirely within traditionally black working-class township areas – that is, Khayelitsha, Soweto and Alexandra – DA support went up on average 5.82 per cent, 5.64 per cent and 3.7 per cent respectively.[6]

So what next? There are a number of different scenarios for the years leading up to 2020. In one – and this is a scenario, not a prediction necessarily – the DA continues to do well, building on its governmental track record and base in the Cape, looking good while the ANC struggles for unity against the pressure of an increasing number of service-delivery protests around the country, and removes the ANC's majority in Pretoria, Port Elizabeth and Johannesburg at the 2016 elections.

Having lost power, or at least a majority, in four of the five metros, the ANC then faces a big strategic and political moment. How it reacts will determine the next generation of politics. In one sub-scenario, the ANC reacts like Manchester United when a new rival arrives on the scene, such as Manchester City in recent years, and ups its game. The alternative sub-scenario is that it does not react well and, crossly, sets about hanging onto power by whatever means possible (the political equivalent of 'bribing the referees').

This, obviously, is the bleak scenario in which democracy becomes threatened by a ruling party that is disinclined to give up power.

Pause here for a moment to look at how the country's demographics correspond with the current share of the vote nationally (Figure 9.5).

Figure 9.5: South African demography and current electoral split

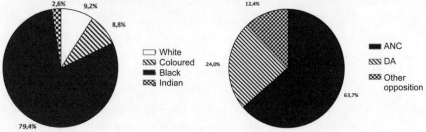

It can be seen how on one rather simplistic reading, the opposition, non-ANC share of the vote corresponds roughly with the non-black-African segment of South African society. As the evidence suggests, lower-middle-class black people have already begun to vote DA, so the exact overlap is already questionable.

However, as things stand, it is hard to see the DA making substantial inroads into black working-class areas in the next few elections, given their very modest base of 2–5 per cent. Although the DA has reasonably high hopes of winning on the basis of the longer-term strategy mentioned earlier, a significant portion of the voters will be the born frees, two to three million youngsters who will be voting for the first time in 2014. If the DA were to win, say, 20–25 per cent of the black born frees, that could add 500 000 votes onto its 2009 tally of just short of three million voters. Assuming similar registration and turnout figures to last time, half a million is likely to correspond to around 3 per cent of the vote, which, if one thinks of these young black voters as 'substitutes' for older black ANC voters who have died in the intervening five years, amounts to a 6 per cent swing, which in South Africa's proportional representation system takes the DA into at least the mid-twenties in terms of overall percentage share of the vote.

A senior DA source revealed their private thinking: 'To get 25 per cent on even turnout we need 10 per cent among black voters and are currently [June 2013] tracking above that (at around 15 per cent). The problem is that the DA gets squeezed in the last two weeks of a campaign as up to two-thirds of its black support gets cold feet and so declines to vote or goes back to the ANC. So the question for the DA is how to drive up the trust/confidence levels of the black voters who actually want to vote for it. That is what the "Know Your DA" campaign is about. Polling suggests it is working. But the true test is the election.

It is not an exaggeration to say that the DA could get anywhere between 2 and 15 per cent of black voters (depending on how strong its pull is, how forcefully the ANC's push and other contextual issues) … the party is very, very focused on that 15 per cent of voters and will focus 80 per cent of the campaign on that audience. So, overall, anything from 22 to 30 per cent is possible.'

So, for the foreseeable future, the ANC's core vote is likely to be black working-class voters, with the DA increasingly dominating middle-class voters, including a fair proportion of black middle-class voters who have abandoned the ANC because of either their disgust with Zuma and/or corruption and/or what they might regard as either extreme left- or right-wing entryism (infiltration).

Thus, the bleakest scenario of all is the one where the ANC elects as leader at its 2017 national conference, a year after having lost power in the three metros, not a moderate centrist – like Cyril Ramaphosa, who as deputy president of the ANC should be next in line – but someone whom they believe is best placed to 'speak' to their core constituency. This is not a prediction, but a scenario. It is bleak because it would not only serve to further entrench class and race divides, but would also entrench the sort of emergent populist, anti-democratic tendencies that the ANC has begun to show under Zuma's leadership, such as the retreat towards secrecy, the 'tenderpreneurial' looting of the state, the incursions on free speech best represented by the controversy over the satirical *Spear* painting, and so on.

The scope for an even more populist leader to emerge in these circumstances, even one who talks 'to the people' but governs for the elite, would be there – with all the democratic dangers that might well accompany it. In other words, faced by increased competition from the DA, and with its hold on power seriously threatened for the first time, perhaps as early as 2019, the ANC could lurch in a panicked state to the right and elect a populist leader – if not Malema, then someone of his ilk – which would be very bad for South Africa. As the ANC weakens and the opposition becomes more powerful in a more competitive electoral landscape, the consequences for South Africa and democracy should not be taken for granted.

10

The traditional leaders

Pathekile Holomisa is one of the most intriguing politicians in South Africa, and certainly one of my favourites. I cannot but admire his languid style. I have only once seen him in anything other than a totally composed and comfortable state – and I'll get to that shortly – usually, he seems totally at ease with himself and his surrounds.

This cannot be said of many South African politicians, who, in the main, and with the eccentric exception of veteran IFP MP Koos van der Merwe, appear to be far too tightly strung. Both Holomisa and Van der Merwe appear comfortable in their own skin, unconcerned by the issues of race and class that bedevil most political relationships in South Africa. Both are the sort you wouldn't mind finding yourself next to on a long plane journey or in a country pub, even if, at least in my case, you hold a seriously different world view.

Perhaps it is Holomisa's aristocratic heritage. He is Xhosa royalty, a traditional leader, the inkosi or chief of the amaHegebe. The goings-on around him are like water off a duck's back – from the reprimands of his own chief whip in Parliament, admonishing him for his apparently reactionary views on gay rights, to the curious looks from the largely white patrons of Blues Restaurant & Bar in Camps Bay, Cape Town, as he enjoys sundowners with a sleek female companion.

An MP since 1994, and therefore one of the few remaining members of the first democratic parliamentary cohort, he is at once both very modern and very old-fashioned. He is also now the president of the Congress of Traditional Leaders of South Africa (CONTRALESA).

CONTRALESA 'styles itself as "the sole and authentic representative of the progressive traditional leadership of South Africa" because it is aligned to the ANC,' notes my colleague, law professor Pierre de Vos.[1] 'The organisation aims to promote and protect traditional leadership, traditional customs and practices and the heritage of the 18 million South Africans who live under the authority of traditional leaders.'

Looking at their website, De Vos remarks, 'one cannot help but wonder whether Contralesa is not also spurred on by the far less noble goal of self-enrichment. Contralesa thus complains that traditional leaders are being discriminated against:

> Traditional leaders of all ranks, i.e. kings, inkosi (chiefs) and inkosana (head-men), are, like politicians in government, public office bearers. They are entitled

to be remunerated in a manner commensurate with their responsibilities and status. The truth, however, is that in this regard traditional leaders are discriminated against. The best that they receive is a basic salary without the concomitant allowances such as medical aid, motor vehicle allowances, pension benefits, etc. Due to lack of uniformity in the manner in which provincial governments treat the institution, some traditional leaders have been provided with motor vehicles, while others have not. Needless to say, this gives rise to resentment and annoyance on the part of those who do not get this form of support.

'Kings and Queens currently earn over R900 000 a year, while other traditional leaders earn between R180 000 and R650 000 a year. Not being provided with a free vehicle at taxpayers' expense must therefore cause serious financial hardship for traditional leaders, but not to the extent that they are not prepared to engage in robust engagement about important issues of the day (other than the salaries and benefits paid to them by the taxpayer).'[2]

To say that traditional leaders in contemporary South Africa are a part of the 'new' establishment is not, therefore, a contradiction in terms. The root of their authority is traditional and hereditary, by definition, but they have been accommodated within the new dispensation, notwithstanding the tensions they inevitably evoke and the angst that they cause to modernisers, especially those understandably concerned with gender equality.

In a sense, Holomisa embodies the complexities and confusions of South Africa's constitutional transition, with its competing cultural and legal customs. He is an ANC MP living in Cape Town part-time *and* a traditional leader living in the Transkei part-time. It is what he calls the 'two hats' phenomenon. But, having been brought before the ANC's disciplinary committee on at least one occasion, it is clear that his primary responsibility is to his community, as a tribal chief.

I am not sure if it is fair or accurate to describe him as a chameleon, not least because that is precisely the word that has been used on plenty of occasions to describe Jacob Zuma, given the president's own traditional, and reactionary, views on many social issues, including gay rights, and his apparent ability to flip-flop in and out of his traditional 'persona' when the occasion demands (such as when meeting with tribal chiefs).

Whereas Zuma does it because he has to, as a perceived political requirement and part of his innate survivalist skills, Holomisa appears to slip in and out of the leopard skin, so to speak, because he wants to. Though he often favours high-necked, neo-Nehru-style, African-cloth-cut jackets and shirts, he has his fair share of Armani suits and Boss ties among the traditional clothes of an inkosi in his wardrobe.

Despite his princely lineage, he is always friendly and willing to meet; time and venue can be arranged without fuss or protocol, via SMS. We arrange to meet for the purposes of this chapter at IDASA's old offices in Spin Street, around the corner from Parliament.

But when the time comes, there is no sign of Holomisa, which is unlike him. However, it had started raining earlier, and so when I call him at his office in Parliament he explains simply: 'I was about to come, but then I saw that it was raining.'

My researcher, Babongile Mandela, who for his own self-evident reasons is not unacquainted with powerful families, is with me. He chuckles when I relay this news to him. 'Will he melt in the rain?' he asks, with a twinkle in his eye. But by the time we have wandered up Government Avenue into the new block of the National Assembly and located Holomisa's office, Mandela's impish humour is carefully hidden under the prudent cloak of deference to an elder.

I have to take the lead in the conversation. Even when my young researcher is finally coaxed into posing the questions that he has prepared with the scholarly diligence befitting a UCT postgraduate, Holomisa continues to look at me, the 'elder on the other side', when he languorously responds.

We are interested in a number of questions: How does traditional leadership impact on formal political processes? Out of sight and way beyond the experience of most middle-class people, traditional structures exert an informal pressure on the allocation of resources. But, unelected, are traditional leaders totally unaccountable? Has there been any significant shift in their influence over the past two decades since the first democratic election in 1994?

There are two established perspectives on traditional leadership: one normative and commonly referred to as the Africanist view; the other 'rights based', which is the practical manifestation of traditional leadership in a democratic society with its inherent tension between the values of customary law and those of a modern, liberal constitution such as South Africa's.

'Since leadership in its elementary form is about power, traditional leadership is no different,' says Mandela. It is this power that we are interested in. Who holds it, for what purpose and why? The main idea informing this exploration was advanced by Peter Ekeh in 1975, when he argued that Africans exist in two realms, one private, which is informed by their traditional beliefs, and the other public, which is concerned with processes outside the private realm.[3]

The distinction Ekeh makes is that in Western society generally the characteristics of the private and public are separate, and yet they share a common morality. However, Mandela's view is that experiences of colonialism in Africa have led to the emergence of a unique historical configuration in modern postcolonial Africa: the existence of two publics instead of one public, as in the West. You have the world of the traditional leader, on the one hand, and the world of the urban citizen, represented by democratically elected local councillors, on the other.

In order to be successful, governance systems have to find ways of coping with the two. Governance, on one simple definitional reading, is simply how particular actors and institutions affect/direct the flow of events. As a major player, the state has different actors and institutions that influence the direction the government takes when responding to particular events. Traditional leadership is but one of these, actively seeking to direct the flow of events at a local level.

In some of the academic literature, traditional leadership is referred to as the 'fourth tier of government' – alongside the national, provincial and local 'spheres' (to use the precise word of the Constitution). Traditional leaders are, therefore, directly engaged in the process of governance and should not be ignored.

Traditional leadership in numbers

At the conclusion of the Nhlapo Commission established by Thabo Mbeki in his quest for African regeneration, it was established that South Africa had 11 recognised kings (including two court interdicts in Limpopo) and 829 senior traditional leaders. The kings and senior traditional leaders lead more than 830 traditional councils. According to the Department of Traditional Affairs (DTA), traditional councils are legally established structures of traditional leaders that administer the affairs of a traditional community in accordance with customs and tradition. Nationally, there are 5311 headmen/women who form the pillars of these traditional councils, responsible for their day-to-day running. When ward councils were established in the late 1990s, traditional leaders were given a role as non-voting members of municipal councils to support municipalities in identifying community needs.

The DTA is currently profiling the traditional councils to determine, among other things, the number of people under each. An estimated 22 million people live under the system of traditional leadership; that is to say, approximately one in three people in South Africa are governed by traditional authority.

The influence of traditional leadership must, therefore, be extremely significant.

On a provincial level, the statistics show the following:
- The **Eastern Cape** has 4 kings, 260 senior traditional leaders, 1193 headmen/women and 239 traditional councils.
- The **Free State** has 2 kings, 13 senior traditional leaders, 96 headmen/women and 12 traditional councils.
- **Gauteng** has only 2 recognised traditional leaders and 2 traditional councils. The traditional councils used to be in Mpumalanga and the North West respectively. This changed recently after a re-demarcation process.

- **KwaZulu-Natal** has 1 king, 257 senior traditional leaders, 1284 headmen/ women and 296 traditional councils.
- **Limpopo** has 2 recognised kingships; however, they are both still subject to litigation. There are 183 traditional leaders and traditional councils in the province, and 2118 recognised headmen/women.
- **Mpumalanga** has 2 kings, 589 senior traditional leaders, 522 headmen/women and 59 traditional councils.
- The **Northern Cape** has 8 senior traditional leaders, 25 headmen/women and 9 traditional councils.
- The **North West** has 54 recognised senior traditional leaders and traditional councils, and 59 headmen/women.
- The **Western Cape** is the only province that currently has no recognised traditional leaders and communities.

It should also be noted that there are traditional leaders and communities who do not have a traditional council and area of jurisdiction. A case in point is the Free State. Kgosi Tsotetsi of the Batlokwa ba Mokgalong does not have a traditional council, and the Batlokwa ba Mokgalong traditional community does not have an area of jurisdiction, as it is one of the landless communities.

The wide-ranging presence of traditional leadership in South Africa is important to note. When examining the influence that traditional leaders have, the local sphere of government best reflects their level of power. Traditional leaders in most provinces participate in municipal councils; in some provinces, such as KwaZulu-Natal and the North West, the provincial governments in conjunction with traditional leaders have developed a systematic way in which traditional structures participate in municipal structures and processes such as integrated development planning and the provision of services to communities.

On an individual level, a person living within a traditional local authority has to get a letter from the traditional leader in order to open a bank account, to acquire a loan and to get the most basic of documentation, such as an ID. On a municipal level, the municipalities that fall under a traditional local authority have to consult with the traditional leader if they want to build infrastructure such as schools, hospitals or clinics on land belonging to the chief. On a societal level, take as an example the North West, where almost every mining company has to pay royalties to traditional leaders. Foreign investors, in addition to paying business taxes, have to pay taxes to traditional leaders. In this context, it is clear to see that traditional leaders are very important actors in local development, as well as important stakeholders in the general operation of South Africa's economy.

The highest-level influence of traditional leaders can be seen when legislation is passed, as each bill that comes before Parliament that affects local communities has to be sent to the National House of Traditional Leaders for consideration.

Which begs the question, where does this leave local councillors?

The democratic problem with traditional leaders

The debate around traditional authority as a governance model usually focuses on the apparently undemocratic nature of traditional leadership and how it impacts on 'modern' constitutional democracy. Indeed, one of the most controversial bills introduced into Parliament since Zuma took office in 2009 is the Traditional Courts Bill, which threatens to give chiefs 'more autocratic power than they had under apartheid', in the words of long-time land-rights activist and UCT academic Aninka Claassens.[4]

Parliamentary hearings on the bill in September 2012 were, Claassens stated, 'dominated by the testimonies of rural people describing various forms of abuse by traditional leaders and traditional courts. These included the extortion of tribal taxes and excessive fines, women being treated with derision, the banning of community meetings, the sale of community land and high-handed chiefs engaged in corrupt mining deals ... and that the Bill would exacerbate these abuses.'[5]

Which brings me to the one occasion that I saw Holomisa flustered. Well, almost flustered.

My research unit at UCT hosted a debate in partnership with Claassens's Law, Race & Gender Unit. My then colleague in the UCT law faculty, Sindiso Mnisi Weeks, opened the proceedings with an impressive piece of forensic surgery, setting out the background, provisions and legal effect of the Traditional Courts Bill with clinical efficiency and persuasive authority. At times, you could hear the audience's sharp intakes of breath, as the egregious, true nature of the bill's likely impact became clear.

One provision attracted my particular attention. The bill would give the traditional court – which would be constituted by a 'king, queen, senior traditional leader, headman, headwoman or a member of a royal family who has been designated as a presiding officer of a traditional court by the Minister'[6] – the power to order that 'one of the parties to the dispute, both parties or any other person performs some form of service without remuneration for the benefit of the community under the supervision or control of a specified person or group of persons identified by the traditional court'.[7]

I found myself thinking, and then expressing to my neighbour, that it sounded 'positively medieval' – the sort of cosmopolitan response that traditional leaders would no doubt expect from someone of my social background and professional history.

When Holomisa rose to speak after Mnisi Weeks, the audience was already against him, and he knew it. He offered a half-baked defence, but his heart was not really in it. With a plaintive shrug, as if to say, 'You know, I have to say this, but I'd like to suggest that I don't really fully believe in it myself' – although I think he does – he explained politely how the bill would simply give legal effect to the authority that traditional leaders already enjoy and then, with greater animation, suggested that the real choice was between respecting or obliterating traditional values and systems.

Have a look for youself; see whether, in fact, they do or do not invoke justice, was how Holomisa ended his presentation. He was charmingly self-effacing, having thanked the audience for its applause at the beginning, 'even if you don't do so at the end, at least I will I have enjoyed some applause now'.

He knew that he was very much alone, sandwiched between two defiant and, in their different ways, powerful women: the one exercising her power through her legal analysis; the other – Mamphela Ramphele – through the power of her passion and her rhetoric.

To Ramphele, who followed Holomisa, the Traditional Courts Bill amounts to 'goodbye Apartheid 1994, hello Apartheid 2012', as she put it at the UCT debate. There was a quiet but poignant whistle from the audience; an exclamation mark to her peroration.

Ramphele, who was on good form, had begun by saying that having been born in the rural areas, she had no need to visit to see for herself. Showing her versatility, Ramphele spoke of her own 'direct experiences', which, she said, did not accord with the anodyne account of traditional power presented by Holomisa.

Within the context of modern democracy, traditional leadership is often viewed from two different, and polarising, perspectives, with most scholars usually arguing for/from one or the other. In the dominant discourse, traditional leadership is associated with despotism and feudalism. The institution itself is seen and understood as 'despotic', creating a kind of democratic despotism. The other perspective sees traditional leadership fulfilling the different needs of people who understand more than one type of democracy, and is referred to by scholars as 'organic democracy'.[8]

With democratic despotism, the relationship that democracy, traditional leadership and human rights have with one another is seen as frail. As a system that allows for inheritance of leadership, traditional leadership is seen as incompatible with a modern, constitutional democracy, as is any paternalistic, inheritance-based system of governance that excludes women and children and makes them subjects instead of citizens. Traditional leadership is a constant reminder of how domination is so entrenched in South Africa that the Constitution remains a meaningless document for millions of rural 'subjects' under traditional authorities. The amount of power vested in these authorities conjures up memories of apartheid and colonial legacies.

Some proponents of this perspective, like Professor Peter Delius, even go so far as to argue that apartheid created a combination of racism and social Darwinism that led to a caricatured representation of African systems of land tenure, which exaggerated the role of chiefs and diminished the rights of lower-level political authorities and households. Due to their exaggerated role, argues Delius, chiefs have become less responsive to the interests of their subjects, a trend that has created opportunities for coercion and corruption.[9]

Democratic despotism is based on the assumption that traditional leadership is under threat of becoming extinct, but continues to survive and even flourish both because the local governance institutional reform process in rural areas is lagging and because government is mistakenly supporting this system despite the fact that it may contradict the fundamental precepts of the new constitutional dispensation.

At the end of the day, despite the cultural relativism of those who support traditional leadership, the objective and rational principles of democracy demand that the state ensures access to democracy as a commodity to which all humans are entitled.[10]

Organic democracy explores the political relationships between traditional leadership and citizen participation in decision-making at the local level.

'The relationships between traditional leadership are here construed as constituting a field of local power politics,' says Mandela, 'in which the state and traditional actors all have stakes. Political processes that take place within this field of local power politics are referred to as constituting local governance in South Africa.'

Mandela explains it in these terms: Public authority does not always fall within the exclusive realm of government institutions; in some contexts, institutional competition is intense and a range of seemingly apolitical situations become actively politicised. Africa has no shortage of institutions that attempt to exercise public authority: not only are multiple layers and branches of government institutions present and active to various degrees, but so-called traditional institutions bolstered by government recognition also vie for public authority, and new emerging institutions and organisations also enter the field.

What Mandela is describing is the institutional mix that one often finds in Africa – part modern, part traditional.

The practices of these institutions make concepts such as public authority, legitimacy, belonging, citizenship and territory highly relevant.[11] Scholars of organic democracy propose an analytical strategy for understanding public authority in such contexts. They argue that despite the abuse of power and the

THE TRADITIONAL LEADERS | 261

manipulation of traditional leaders by the apartheid regime, traditional leadership as a form of governance pre-dates this and has persisted over the governance practice based on state democracy in Africa.

Traditional leadership should perhaps be seen as an alternative form of democracy that places less emphasis on how governance comes into being, but more emphasis on the rationalisation of justice based on cultural-moral principles and expressed human feeling, all of which will be under vigorous negotiation on a case-by-case social-issue basis.

The logical conclusion of this view is that traditional leadership requires a 'facilitatory' democracy more focused on issues than on rigid governance processes.[12]

Traditional leadership has been a tricky issue for most post-colonial African countries. The institution is the bedrock of African custom, history, knowledge and well-being. To deny it would be to deny the source of ethics and morality of most African communities. As Holomisa tells us, 'traditional leaders are the custodians of these values'.

Traditional leadership and formal politics

Since the birth of South Africa's non-racial democracy, traditional leadership has fallen under scrutiny. What role should it play and how will it affect formal political processes? The problem with such questions is that they turn traditional leadership into something informal, a piece to be placed somewhere on the puzzle board. Illustrating the conundrum, De Vos frames the constitutional position of traditional leadership thus:

> When the Constitutional Assembly drafted the final Constitution in 1994 and 1995, it dragged its feet in finalising the provisions dealing with traditional leadership because it was not clear how such a system could be accommodated – except in a purely symbolic way – within the democratic system of government established by the Constitution. In the end, chapter 12 of the Constitution, which contains provisions regarding traditional leaders, provided for such leaders in rather wishy-washy language, stating (in section 211(1)) that 'the institution, status and role of traditional leadership, according to customary law, are recognised *subject to the Constitution*' … But despite the incompatibility of undemocratic traditional leadership with a constitutional democracy, some elements of traditional leadership and customary law were retained. This attempt to accommodate the chieftaincy – despite its tainted past as enforcers of apartheid – was animated by both emotional as well as practical considerations.[13]

Mandela points out that the functional position of traditional leaders is viewed largely from the emergence and dominance of liberal theory or liberalism – primarily, a commitment to individual liberty, in the sense that each individual has the right to pursue his/her own good. In South Africa, these assumptions are misplaced given the collective disposition of Africans and their general under-standing of the world in terms of collectivism. This is reflected in how African communities are structured on the assumption that *umntu ngumtu ngabantu* ('a person is a person because of other people').

In reality, the majority of South Africans have a patrilineal association to some form of traditional authority and/or leader. As a point of departure, one should evaluate how this currency influences the decision-making of the new political elite.

As Mandela points out, 'interesting enough, the first democratically elected South African president, Nkosi Nelson Rolihlahla Mandela (Dalibunga), *ngumtana wegazi*, is born of royal blood. It is necessary for us to therefore take a step back and look at the politicised nature of traditional leaders and how this came about and how this has been understood in post-apartheid South Africa.'

Historically, traditional leadership has been involved in wars of resistance against colonial pillage. For the longest time, this resistance was constituted due to an immediate threat posed by colonial soldiers and was highly localised and tribally aligned in nature. At no time was a united effort mounted by the various African kingdoms for purposes beyond frontier wars.

This changed on 8 January 1912, in Bloemfontein, when traditional leaders, alongside the educated elite of the African community, gathered to participate in the formation of the South African Native National Congress. This symbolised the entry of traditional leadership, as an institution spreading across the terri-torial land of South Africa, into formal political structures.

Under Mandela: The ambiguous role of traditional leadership

Since the birth of democracy in South Africa, the ANC-led government has shown indecision as to how to extend democracy to rural areas. Leading up to the Convention for a Democratic South Africa (CODESA), CONTRALESA lobbied for representation as an independent entity, as Holomisa (then first vice president) felt that the mass democratic movement as led by the ANC had not adequately addressed the needs of traditional institutions.

'President Mandela would often speak of traditional leadership in public forums, but this was, however, not translated into policy,' Holomisa tells us. 'Just like Zuma now,' he adds, intriguingly.

Some might argue that traditional authorities gained public attention only in so far as they revealed how the ANC would relate to people such as Chief Mangosuthu Buthelezi, another traditional leader of royal descent.

Buthelezi, who had been accused of working within the apartheid structures, posed a destabilising force in the run-up to CODESA. The CODESA negotiations and the Interim Constitution both depended on the cooperation of the IFP, led by Buthelezi, who had taken a hostile stance towards the ANC and CONTRALESA. The IFP, along with the Conservative Party, Lucas Mangope's Bophuthatswana, Oupa Gqozo's Ciskei and various traditional leaders, formed the Concerned South African Group (COSAG) in the run-up to the 1994 elections.

COSAG subsequently rejected the Interim Constitution in 1993. The IFP's main concern was the need for more powers delegated to the provinces and the recognition of King Goodwill Zwelithini and the Kingdom of KwaZulu. The rejection of the Interim Constitution sent out fears that the Government of National Unity would be compromised. In response to this, the ANC and the National Party conceded to devolve more powers to the provinces and incorporate the institution of traditional authority in the Final Constitution of 1996.

Traditional leadership under President Mandela's administration thus managed to secure guarantees in the Constitution, albeit of a subordinate position to those of elected bodies. Moreover, the Constitution failed to outline clearly defined roles and functions for traditional authorities. Traditional leadership was dealt a further blow when elected councillors were introduced in 1995 and 1996.

The relationship soured when Holomisa was summoned to appear in front of the ANC disciplinary committee. He had argued that the introduction of ward councils in rural areas would confuse people, and in his crusade he had called on some rural communities in the Eastern Cape to boycott local government elections. The boiling point for the ANC was when Holomisa met with IFP-aligned traditional leaders to canvass for his cause. In 1999, CONTRALESA sent a memorandum to President Mandela outlining its grievances, which ranged from remuneration to authority to oversee relevant criminal and civil cases.

CONTRALESA rightfully points out that the Constitution, which is based on liberal principles, recognises the hereditary institutions of traditional leadership without clarifying the most important elements of any operating institution: its role, function and power.

Under Mbeki: The re-emergence of traditional leadership

Was the dilapidated state of affairs between government and the institution of traditional leadership irreparable, and would this provide the answer to the question of compatibility of traditional leadership with liberal democracy? The response of the Mbeki administration was to seek to revive the traditional structures rather than to oversee their demise. 'He was more practical,' says Holomisa. 'Though he was too late in coming to the view, he decided that traditional leadership could be used to galvanise his idea of the "African renaissance", as the pan-African home of traditional leadership.'

Ten years of contact with formal political structures coupled with former president Mbeki's vision of an African renaissance and, hey presto, enter centre stage: traditional leadership.

'The South African political elite saw the opportunity as ripe to assert their identity and dream of an African renaissance,' agrees Mandela. In the years following Mbeki's 'I am an African' speech in Parliament, the ANC shifted from a position of ambiguity and suspicion towards traditional authorities to one of acceptance and accommodation.

Traditional leadership under Mbeki represented 'a lost sense of African pride and it was an institution that once so easily defined who they are as a people [the African elite],' says Mandela. 'This nostalgia is often translated into a romanticised notion of traditional life and leadership in general – one where remembrance only allows one to recall the most distinguished and often few practices that set Africans apart from the rest of the world and in a positive light.'

Under Mbeki, the Traditional Leadership and Governance Framework Act (TLGFA, Act 41 of 2003) and the Communal Land Rights Act (CLARA, Act 11 of 2004) were passed. Section 28 of the TLGFA did not discontinue the traditional authorities established by the Black Authorities Act (BAA, Act 68 of 1951), but instead provided for their continuation as traditional councils. The BAA once stood as a pillar of imperial rule against the efforts towards black liberation in South Africa. Many African leaders, including former ANC presidents Oliver Tambo, Nelson Mandela and Albert Luthuli, denounced the BAA and traditional leaders who cooperated with the apartheid government, accusing them of maintaining the subjugation of Africans as second-class citizens.

The TLGFA and CLARA symbolised a return of power to chiefs and to segmenting millions of Africans in rural areas, women being the worst-affected segment of this particular grouping. Broadly favourable to the role of traditional leadership, this trio of laws represented a significant step towards cementing traditional leaders' roles in a liberal democratic South Africa.[14]

In essence, the Mbeki administration was addressing the vacuum that had occurred during the ANC's transition from a liberation movement to a governing party. This power vacuum, embodied in symbolic notions of identity and governance, has now seemingly been occupied by traditional leaders. In the context of Mbeki's project of an African renaissance, Mandela believes that traditional leadership 'offered political elites a fundamental pillar to which [they] could tie some absolute truths. For even though Mbeki was seen as somewhat detached from the common man, his actions in offering traditional leadership space in which to operate remains an interesting anomaly.'

An example of this can be found in the small Eastern Cape town of Qamata. The Thembu chieftaincy, based in Qamata, had been pleading with the government to recognise the gravesite of Tiyo Soga as a national heritage site. Soga is considered by many to be the first major modern South African intellectual. Among the first to assert the right of black Africans to freedom and equality, he wrote poems about great African chiefs and translated John Bunyan's *Pilgrim's Progress* into isiXhosa (*U-Hambo lom-Hambi*).

Eventually, CONTRALESA called a forum to which Mbeki was invited as a guest. The issue of Soga's gravesite was raised by one of the speakers and, as the chiefs were outlining his contribution to African communities and the institution of traditional leadership through his literary work, Mbeki got up, went to the podium, excused his interruption, and there and then declared the site a national heritage site. The gesture symbolised the importance of the relationship between government and institutions of traditional leadership under Mbeki.

Under Zuma: The resubjugation of traditional leadership

Zuma often uses culture as a defence mechanism against probing questions that interrogate his motives or integrity. The immediate guardians and custodians of 'African culture' in South Africa are traditional leaders. One would therefore assume that, in political terms, traditional leadership would constitute a natural part of Zuma's political arsenal.

Yet, surprisingly, this has not translated into any noticeable devolution of powers to traditional authorities, with the exception of the formation of a new ministry of traditional affairs – though, interestingly, CONTRALESA did not request the government to establish such a ministry and was not consulted before the decision was taken; and Holomisa, for his part, is quietly dismissive if not contemptuous: 'The department talks about the interests of traditional leadership, something like a department of native affairs from the old days.'

'The production of culture in this sense has not been created in the context of everyday life, but is seen by the government of the day as a fundamental tool to legitimise its power,' argues Mandela. The question of culture and traditional leadership generally has a blind spot in that it is not understood by most middle-class South Africans. Zuma and other African political elites in turn have to yield or leverage power to traditional leaders in order to use the institution as a defence against liberal critics.

Under the Zuma administration, traditional leaders have managed to influence decisions in their favour on matters that affect them directly. This is done through lobbying structures such as CONTRALESA and through involvement in various political parties – most obviously, Holomisa's in the ANC. Their influence under the Zuma administration is not one of mutual cooperation, but of constant negotiation and capitalising on the ambiguous role/policy of the ANC towards traditional leadership.

At the opening of the National House of Traditional Leaders in the National Assembly on 3 June 2011, the familiar issues concerning financial needs and poor relations with locally elected ward councillors were raised.[15] While under Mbeki the institutions of traditional authority had their foundations laid, it was assumed that under Zuma active pronouncement of their roles and their visibility in official state functions would become more apparent. This, however, has not been the case. Instead, Zuma's stance and approach towards traditional leadership resembles that of President Mandela's government.

Traditional leaders under the Zuma administration say that they are not properly recognised and that government favours urban areas over rural ones. In response, Zuma advises: 'As traditional leaders you must also take some initiatives. After finding out what the needs of the people are, you must take them to government. If they are not addressed you can come to me then we will be able to deal with them.'[16]

His response is reminiscent of similar statements made by the Mandela administration, when traditional leaders were accorded a role subordinate to their elected representatives. In the 1990s, such statements led to CONTRALESA calling for election boycotts, and while it remains to be seen what reaction, if any, will follow under the Zuma administration, trouble in 2014 could be damaging for the ANC, unless Zuma is able to come back to CONTRALESA with an alluring inducement.

'Traditional power' in South Africa

Traditional leaders enjoy power as gatekeepers to the electorate, which means that the ANC treads carefully when it comes to traditional leaders. The existence of chiefs, coupled with their good relationship with the government of the day, gives the ANC leverage with voters who come from rural areas with strong traditional leadership structures.

But equally, Holomisa cautions, 'with local government imposed on communities, I warned about the confusion it would cause about whether this was doing away with traditional leaders. The danger is that people will be told not to vote. This could jeopardise ANC rule.' In support of his contention, he cites the way in which some traditional leaders were successfully courted by his namesake Bantu Holomisa's United Democratic Movement after its launch in 1999. After his expulsion from the ANC, Bantu Holomisa went to the former homelands in order to galvanise traditional leaders who now found themselves displaced from power after the introduction of local government systems in 1996.

Clearly, traditional leadership will continue to be a site of contestation and, therefore, like others around the country – such as university campuses – more and more fraught as and when electoral competition increases. In her presentation at the UCT debate, Mnisi Weeks made the important point that the Traditional Courts Bill was not a Zuma invention. On the contrary, the idea was first hatched under Mbeki, tabled as a bill in Parliament in 2008 and then shelved after complaints about the consultation process.

However, the relationship is more complicated and the access-to-voters argument is but one of several variables at play. The influence that traditional leadership enjoys, as history suggests, depends on the leadership style of the incumbent state president and his disposition towards traditional leaders.

President Mandela, a reconciler, was influenced more by fear and the need to avoid violence than by his patrimonial association with the institution of traditional leadership. Mbeki, however, had no association with the institution, but his vision of an African revival informed his sympathetic relationship with traditional leadership.

Under Zuma, the institution looked set to become fully established, as his 2009 campaign was largely based on the fact that he is a man of the people who, unlike his predecessor, is more traditional and understanding of South Africa's marginalised communities, especially rural communities. However, his actions have not reflected the same enthusiasm, and previous concerns such as remuneration and the allocation of power have been put back on the table.

The existence of a traditional leadership in a liberal democracy creates obvious and unavoidable tensions that have to be managed as well as recognised, as it leads to the creation of two spheres of existence – both for citizens who live in rural areas where tribal chiefs have power, and for leaders who participate in both sorts of institutions, such as Holomisa. This creates obvious challenges and ambiguities. As Mandela puts it:

Take, for example, as a metaphor, the social space in which townships exist. They constitute a midway point between two realities. In essence, South African townships constitute a physical embodiment of the African psyche. At any given time most township dwellers will readily admit that they are from some particular rural area and that is where their ancestors are. Dinner-table talks often go something like this: 'The day I retire, I will return home.' At another level, however, the same person would usually speak of how he/she wants to earn enough money to live in 'town' or in the suburbs. The appeal of modernity is a constant drum beat that rolls alongside a parallel desire to

268 | THE ZUMA YEARS

return to the old ways of tradition. The township itself is left in a state of transition, which is often manifested in neglect and hostility. A sense of 'non-responsiveness' to the environment and its destruction is reinforced by a sense of imminent mobility to an alternative sphere. This duality is in fact a representation of African political elites who have dual identities and see their present state as transitional at best.

The changing face of power in South Africa is a complex story. To reduce it to a binary between 'progress' towards a 'cosmopolitan modernity' on the one hand, and a 'reactionary backwardness' reflected in the values and customs of traditional leaders on the other, is neither helpful nor illuminating, however much of a no-brainer it is to assert that the values of the Constitution and its liberal Bill of Rights are supreme.

Understanding the competing instincts and the impact on the psyche of an emerging African middle class is, as Mandela suggests, essential to appreciating the undulations of the new anatomy of power. Which is why someone like Holomisa is so interesting, sitting as he does astride the two worlds, no doubt appreciating them both, and having to manage the impulses that pull him, and others, in both directions.

11

The judges

The gents' bathroom in the Cape Town International Convention Centre (CTICC) is elegantly appointed, but there is a design flaw that no architect could have foreseen. The passageway between the basins on one side and the urinals on the other narrows substantially, creating a curious funnel effect.

What *no one* could have easily anticipated was the sort of occurrence that took place there around teatime on Saturday 3 September 2011, the first day of Justice Mogoeng Mogoeng's momentous two-day public interview for the position of chief justice of South Africa by the Judicial Service Commission (JSC).

Having sat transfixed all morning and into the early afternoon, I had dashed to the Sea Point municipal hall to watch my daughter, India Jane, dance in the annual ballet eisteddfod examinations and then rushed back to town hoping not to have missed too much of the drama unfolding inside the CTICC. As I raced up the stairs, I noticed people beginning to leave the hall and, realising that it was the tea break, I changed direction and entered the gents' lavatories.

First in, I quickly relieved myself and headed towards the basins, but found myself face to face with deputy chief justice Dikgang Moseneke. It was my second conversation with him that day and, curiously, the second in the vicinity of the bathroom. The thought crossed my mind: people would begin to talk …

'Ah, Richard, we meet again. How do you think it's going?' he asked with a twinkle in his eye.

'I think you know the answer to that question,' I replied.

With a chuckle, Moseneke began to say something else, but at that moment, the interviewee himself arrived on the scene.

Since, as I say, the aperture was narrow, and since Moseneke and I were pretty much blocking it, Mogoeng had little choice but to stop and say something.

About an hour earlier he had lost his temper in an exchange with Moseneke, who was chairing the JSC hearing, and had been compelled to apologise there and then. Now, in the confines of the marbled bathroom, Mogoeng found himself stutteringly trying to repeat his apology.

'Deputy CJ,' he began, 'er, um, I really wish to apologise for what happened in there …'

With an imperious wave of his hand that wafted over the head of the much shorter Mogoeng, Moseneke dismissed the shuffling attempt at contrition: 'This is not the time or place for such a thing.'

Indeed not. Mogoeng tried to turn away from Moseneke, only to find me impeding his escape route, whereupon, out of some kind of misplaced English-politeness-in-an-awkward-moment, I sought to introduce myself to the soon-to-be-appointed, controversial chief justice.

By now, Lex Mpati, the president of the Supreme Court of Appeal (SCA), had entered the scrum. In demeanour and manners as 'English' as I, Mpati paused momentarily, presumably to contemplate the strange sight of Moseneke, Mogoeng and Calland in the bottleneck. Then, whether pushed by the growing numbers behind him or in frustration at the blockage in front, I do not know, he abandoned his usual courtesies and, dropping his shoulder, deployed skills he could have only learnt from his favourite game, rugby.

A loose maul immediately ensued and our curious little ménage à trois was broken up.

Moseneke was completely unruffled. (In fact, it is hard to imagine what event could penetrate his debonair composure.) Twice now overlooked for chief justice, disappointment must surely have tested his suave sangfroid. The first time was fair enough: President Zuma chose Justice Sandile Ngcobo ahead of Moseneke when Chief Justice Pius Langa's term of office came to an end in mid-2009, even though Moseneke was the sitting deputy chief justice. Ngcobo had been on the Constitutional Court longer than Moseneke and so could properly be described as his senior. Ngcobo also happens to be a very fine jurist and had been an outstanding member of the court, penning many of the most significant and progressive judgments. No one could reasonably criticise Ngcobo's appointment in terms of competence and experience, just as they could have found no fault with Moseneke.

Moseneke knows full well why they – the Zuma establishment – did not want him as chief justice. At his birthday party in January 2008, shortly after Polokwane, Moseneke was quoted as having told his guests that he had another ten to twelve years left on the bench, and that he wanted to use his energy to help create an equal society. 'It's not what the ANC wants or what the [Polokwane] delegates want; it is about what is good for the people,' he said.

Moseneke was referring to judicial independence – that delicate, yet vital, part of any constitutional democracy, and the subject of much power play in recent years. This can be considered a 'natural tension', for in any such democratic system where the judicial branch of government has powers of review over the executive and legislative branches – the 'political branches', as they refer to them in United States discourse – there is likely to be a certain amount of frustration or irritation when the unelected judiciary exercises its powers of review and overturns executive action or legislative law-making.

But there is a line, a thin line, over which the political branches may easily step if they express too much frustration or too much irritation and start, by deed or omission, to exert undue pressure or downright intimidation on the judicial branch.

It can easily get personal, too.

Moseneke was – and is – too much of an Mbekite. This might seem a curious thing to say, given that Moseneke is well known, and well regarded, for his political independence and non-partisanship. He was, after all, not a member of the ANC during his distinguished career as a lawyer prior to 1994, which was preceded by ten years on Robben Island, but a member of the PAC.

Mbeki, who appointed Moseneke to the Constitutional Court in 2002, had more than a soft spot for compatriots from the Black Consciousness Movement. Their approach fitted neatly with his own Africanist tendencies and lifelong commitment to the acquisition of rightful power by black people. As *Anatomy of South Africa* revealed, Mbeki's most influential advisor came to be Mojanku Gumbi, who was also not ANC, but rather AZAPO-aligned.

Just as Moseneke shared many things with Mbeki – his cosmopolitan urbanity, his enjoyment of the cerebral, as well as finely cut suits – so, as with Mbeki, did this clash starkly with the rustic character of the Zumarites.

Mogoeng Mogoeng is in many respects the judicial equivalent of Zuma. Like chalk and cheese, he is to Moseneke what Zuma is to Mbeki.

And, sadly, South Africa is the worse off for it.

Back at the CTICC in September 2011, for the better part of two days, Moseneke tried ever so hard to conceal his contempt for Mogoeng. But he failed.

All day on the Saturday he tried, as he knew he had to, to hide his disdain for the jurisprudential inferior that had been brought before him. And all day, and most of the next, he failed.

And who can blame him for that? Mogoeng's rise had been meteoric, to the point of implausibility. Born in 1961 in Zeerust, Mogoeng began his legal career as a Supreme Court prosecutor in Mafikeng in 1986. He was first appointed to the bench, as a judge of the North West High Court, in 1997. In 2002 he was appointed as judge president of the North West High Court – a court that, as Moseneke elicited from him at one point in his forensic dismembering, had just four judges – a rather less onerous managerial responsibility than that of chief justice as head of the whole judicial branch of government. It is interesting that in his 2009 Constitutional Court interview, Mogoeng acknowledged this and actually used it as a reason why he should be appointed to the Constitutional Court – he described the North West High Court as a small court, in 'a corner of a corner … I've gone as far as I can, I need to move up in the world'. In 2011, it seems the small size of the North West court was not an obstacle to him ascending to chief justice.

His nomination by President Zuma had elicited howls of protest from the human-rights sector, primarily on the grounds of his attitude towards rape, and gender issues more generally, in a number of cases over which he had presided in the North West High Court. In one 2005 case, Mogoeng reduced the sentence of a man convicted of the attempted rape of a seven-year-old on the basis that, even though he accepted the evidence that the girl's vagina had been penetrated, 'the injury she sustained is not serious'.

As the Southern Africa Litigation Centre (SALC) pointed out in its research, submitted to the JSC, 'it is hard to see how an injury to a seven-year-old which results from sexual abuse can ever be classified as "not serious"'. Even allowing for the fact that, although abhorrent, 'grading' the severity of rape is not uncommon – it happens in the SCA – there were legitimate concerns about Mogoeng's approach, for, in another case a year earlier, he had found reason to reduce the sentence of another convicted child rapist from life to the minimum permitted sentence of eighteen months on grounds that the SALC denounced as creating 'the impression of arbitrariness ... at worst, that child rape is not among the most egregious crimes in our country deserving the law's full effect'.

In yet another case involving child rape, in 2007, Mogoeng dismissed the convicted man's appeal but made a number of remarkably troubling comments, including: 'One can safely assume that [the accused] must have been mindful of [the victim's] tender age and was thus so careful as not to injure her private parts, except accidentally, when he penetrated her. That would explain why the child was neither sad nor crying when she returned from the shop, notwithstanding the rape ... there is no mention of limping or crying or anything of the kind, notwithstanding the complainant's assertions that she was heartbroken and limping as a result of the sexual intercourse.'

It is difficult to know where to begin in responding to the inherent prejudices that underpin these words. It is even harder to explain how someone with such a hopeless – and dangerous – level of understanding of rape and the harm it causes, and the different ways in which this harm manifests itself, in a society such as South Africa's in which violence against women and children is so prevalent, could become the country's leading judge, other than as a representative of a patriarchal class that finds political representation in the form of President Zuma himself.

There were also concerns about Mogoeng's religious beliefs – he is a member of the Winners' Chapel International Church, an international congregation of which he is a lay preacher.[1] Not long after his appointment had been confirmed, in a moment of extraordinary ill judgement in March 2012, Mogoeng circulated a flyer to an event in Johannesburg that was being addressed by the American evangelist and motivational speaker John Maxwell, in which the chief justice 'requested' the presence of the heads of court.

Apart from the obvious inappropriateness of such a 'request', given that the email was sent just days before the event that was to be held on a normal working Monday, it begs the question what exactly the chief justice thinks his heads of court and senior judiciary are doing with their time. Are they twiddling their thumbs, with blank diaries, and no cases to hear or judgments to write?

Mogoeng's evangelical character was on vivid display during his late-2009 interview for a place on the Constitutional Court. These were important interviews – in terms of the powers of the Constitution and the balance of power in the body politic, the most important appointments to be made since the publication of *Anatomy of South Africa*. Overall, 2009 was a big year for the court: four of its most senior judges were reaching the end of their terms: justices Pius Langa, Albie Sachs, Yvonne Mokgoro and Kate O'Regan. All four had been members of the court since it was first established in 1994. All four were not only stalwarts of that court, but had been among its most industrious, as well as progressive, members.

One of the many shifts in the anatomy of power since 2006 has been the shift in power on the bench and in the Constitutional Court generally. Prior to recent times, any attempt to speak of the 'progressive' or 'conservative' wings of the court – as commentators and legal academics will speak of the US Supreme Court, for example – seemed not so much inappropriate as unnecessary. The court, even when it differed, and even though there were different points of jurisprudential emphasis, was generally pulling in the same direction.

With its first two chief justices, Langa and his predecessor Arthur Chaskalson, the court had found leadership that was anxious to broker compromise and to do a great deal to preserve the intellectual integrity and collegial unity of the court. Chief Justice Ngcobo was no less committed to this unity and to providing such leadership, though his leadership style was regarded by some members as being somewhat imperious.

Indeed, Ngcobo had a bold ambition, which to some was considered 'imperial': to build a far stronger judicial branch of government. Ngcobo unfortunately came and went in the blink of an eye – appointed by Zuma in 2009, his term was over just two years later, in 2011. Yet, in those two years, Ngcobo provided as much leadership, with clarity of vision, as any other chief justice in this country has ever done.

Indeed, had he stayed in office, I predict he would have become the greatest reforming chief justice in South Africa's history. This, I appreciate, is a bold statement. And I am not entirely impartial. My own unit at the University of Cape Town – the Democratic Governance and Rights Unit (DGRU) – benefited from the very good relationship that I enjoyed and continue to enjoy with Ngcobo. But, my assertion is premised on this reasoning: he had the vision of an independent courts' administration – independent of the Department of Justice and the executive arm of government – and the wisdom to understand its importance for the long-term democratic sustainability of the country. Moreover, he had the guts and the political clout to push it through.

Since Ngcobo's departure, his successor, Mogoeng, has found to his increasing frustration that the executive has turned away from the idea, unsurprisingly, and has starved the Office of the Chief Justice (OCJ) of funding, placing one of its own staff (a senior justice department official) into the crucial position of secretary-general of the OCJ. This has strengthened Mogoeng's determination to stand up to the executive, and he finally lost his cool and expressed his anger at a meeting with the president and the minister of justice in early 2013. So, perhaps one should not write him off just yet; indeed, former Constitutional Court judge Kate O'Regan has suggested that we should not do so and should respect his office and his attempts to promote access to justice. Yvonne Mokgoro, brought in by Ngcobo, continued to serve Mogoeng for a while, but I was reliably informed as this book went to press that she had decided to give up the good fight and leave in frustration.

Perhaps Mogoeng will yet emerge as a strong and reforming chief justice. Though, if he does, it will be a remarkable turnaround from his early days in the position, when one of the officials managing the transition from one chief justice to the next, and who has subsequently gone on to greater things, told me Mogoeng was 'hopelessly out of his depth, embarrassingly so'.

During the difficult days leading up to the unnecessarily premature end to Ngcobo's term of office in August 2011, I found myself on a number of occasions, and in very different settings, having to defend Ngcobo's record but also, far trickier, advocate for the retention of his position in the face of the legal challenge that had been mounted against President Zuma's decision to extend his term.

Although there was considerable media interest in the fate of the chief justice and in the legal challenge to the extension of his term, and much chatter in the legal community, few legal commentators apart from my loquacious UCT colleague Pierre de Vos were willing to speak on the record. Having sought to diminish my media appearances in recent years, on the basis that others needed to take and share the responsibility, I decided to respond to the high demand for comment and analysis in the Ngcobo case because I felt strongly that a very bad turn of events was about to occur. In fact, I put the case for his retention so strongly that at one point I could not help but feel as though I had become his spin doctor. So when the *Mail & Guardian*'s 'Serjeant at the Bar' column accused me of being Ngcobo's praise singer, it was a fair, if somewhat cowardly (masked behind the anonymity of the column), comment.

Before returning to the current incumbent of the OCJ, it is necessary to dwell on the demise of former chief justice Ngcobo and necessary also to explain its relevance to the changing anatomy of power.

Ngcobo's first goal as chief justice was to create space for the independent leadership that he believed was essential if the judicial branch of government was to flourish and to operate in the way that the Constitution envisages. Hence, his first objective was to establish the OCJ, from which he would be able to lead the reform of the administration of the judiciary and the building of a strong judicial branch of government.

To say that this was an important, nay historic, undertaking is a great understatement. What was so intriguing, and so revealing, were the reactions of people I thought would know better. Slyly, in corridor conversations and at dinner parties, the legal establishment – especially the liberal legal establishment – cast aspersions on his intentions, at times implying that it was a self-aggrandising plan.

These were the same people who had expressed concern about the 'imperial presidency' of Mbeki. So there was consistency, at least. It is a core part of the liberal political disposition to be against the acquisition of power by any one body or institution or person. Fine, fair enough, not least in the context of a Constitution that is very clear in wanting to distribute public power across the system of governance.

But what is intriguing is this: when Mbeki built his 'imperial presidency' in the late 1990s and the early part of this century, it was in order to seek to provide stronger leadership from the top, based on a greater capacity to manage and coordinate government – the very weakness that was so lamented by the very same complainants. So, too, now with the judiciary: there were well-justified concerns that the judiciary was 'too weak' in relation to the executive branch of government which had designs to weaken it further.

But when Ngcobo took steps, necessary in my view, to build the power and authority to counterbalance the executive, it was viewed with great caution. This was partly because Ngcobo is very much his own man.

Although he has a very good sense of humour, enjoys a glass of good red wine and provides very good company over supper, he can come across as somewhat shy or aloof, and even awkward. In these respects, Ngcobo is different from the gentlemen's club-able, easy-going Moseneke, who fraternises with the northern-suburbs Johannesburg legal community.

Needless to say, Ngcobo is not a part of the liberal legal establishment, who view him with some suspicion, even though when pressed they are more than willing to accept the strength of his intellect and his progressive track record as a jurist.

So when President Zuma announced his decision to extend Ngcobo's term of office in March 2011, the liberal legal establishment did not feel the pinch of the dilemma that I felt. On the one hand, the law was plainly bad. In 2001, Parliament had purported to give the president the power to extend the term of office of a chief justice. This was an unhealthy, thoroughly rotten idea constitutionally, for when assessing the wisdom of a provision it is always worth pausing for a moment and considering how it might be used in the wrong hands.

In 2001, the purpose of the change in the law had been to extend the terms of office of Constitutional Court judges in order to specifically sustain for a little longer the term of Chief Justice Chaskalson. At the time, legal commentators such as my UCT colleague Professor Hugh Corder wisely expressed their concern that, much though they admired Chaskalson, it was bad practice to change the law for any one individual. In any case, Chaskalson's term was not, in the event, extended by the power that the president had reason to think Parliament had given him in section 8 of the Judges' Remuneration and Conditions of Employment Act 47 of 2001 ('the Judges' Act'), which read:

> A Chief Justice who becomes eligible for discharge from active service in terms of section 3(1)(a) or 4(1) or (2), may, at the request of the President, from the date on which he or she becomes so eligible for discharge from active service, continue to perform active service as Chief Justice of South Africa for a period determined by the President, which shall not extend beyond the date on which such Chief Justice attains the age of 75 years.

President Zuma wrote to Ngcobo on 11 April 2011 to request pursuant to section 8 of the Judges' Act that he continue as chief justice. Accepting on the basis that he still had work to do in reforming the judicial branch of government – a project that was by then very much under way, as we'll see below – Ngcobo wrote back accepting the request on 2 June.

Why Ngcobo waited so long to reply is known only to him. I have reason to believe that he was engaging the Presidency during this period, because Ngcobo knew that section 8 was very probably unconstitutional and he was, therefore, exploring whether his (re)appointment could be placed on a sturdier legal basis.

Ngcobo is a proud man, and he did not want to retain office – or appear to be trying to retain office – on the back of a faulty legal provision that could then be challenged. Understandably for someone whose respect for the rule of law is profound, he did not want to hold office in an unconstitutional manner.

Once Zuma announced that Ngcobo had accepted his request, a legal challenge was soon mounted to the effect that to give a sitting president apparently unfettered power to extend the term of a chief justice was a recipe for bad governance. A chief justice wanting to stay in office could curry favour by steering judgments in favour of the executive. Or, no less harmful, the perception could be created that he or she is doing so.

As a member of the executive committee of the Council for the Advancement of the South African Constitution, the organisation that I had helped found the year before, in 2010, I was involved in a discussion about whether to join the application to challenge the constitutionality of the appointment. I agreed wholeheartedly with the principle at stake – that it was entirely wrong and unconstitutional for such a power to be in the hands of the president – but I was deeply concerned about what the consequences of the challenge would be. At one point, I recall saying that we should be careful, otherwise we could end up with Mogoeng Mogoeng as chief justice.

While some members of the legal community pursued the case solely because of the principle, I have little doubt that some did so in the vain and foolhardy belief that if Ngcobo went, their charming cocktail-party companion, Dikgang Moseneke, would replace him.

To reiterate, Moseneke would have made a very fine chief justice; he still could and should be chief justice. He, not Mogoeng, *should* have succeeded Ngcobo if the latter could not remain in office. But there was more likelihood of Zuma appointing Thabo Mbeki or Julius Malema than Moseneke – a fact borne out by what actually transpired in the days following the end of Ngcobo's term at midnight on 14 August 2012.

I urged my colleagues on the CASAC exco not only to challenge the constitutionality of the appointment, but also to help the government find a constitutionally principled and enduring way of ensuring that Ngcobo could remain in office. Looking back, I don't think they listened or took my major point seriously – that while the short-term issue of presidential power was of substantial constitutional importance, there was a longer-term, macro issue of even greater significance: the independence of the judiciary. As one member of the JSC subsequently put it, the problem with the challenge to the extension of the term was that it was 'constitutionally correct but administratively disastrous'.

Ngcobo, as I tried to explain to them and to anyone else who would listen, was engaged in a project of monumental reform: to build a truly independent judicial arm of government. In the current political climate, this was like trying to ascend Everest. He had achieved base camp with the creation of the OCJ, which was established as a separate department of state by a three-line presidential proclamation (No. 44 of 2010) dated 23 August 2010.

From small acorns grow large oaks. Few, if any, paid attention to the Notice when it appeared in the Government Gazette. I doubt if it received any column inches, despite widespread reporting about 'threats to the independence of the judiciary'. Ngcobo was executing his revolution quietly, beneath the radar.

That he had got this far (and would get even further in the following year) was testimony not only to his vision and leadership, but to his political guile as well. Remarkably, he had built a viable relationship with the minister of justice, Jeff Radebe.

I say 'remarkably' because Radebe is no pushover. On the contrary, he is a tough and wily old fox, and a political bruiser – a natural survivor who was well aware of what the Polokwane Resolutions had said about the judiciary: they had called for more, not less, control by the executive. Yet here was Radebe being persuaded by the chief justice to relinquish some of the administrative power that the Department of Justice had over the judiciary.

We will never know if Ngcobo would have made the summit, though he was just days away from securing an independent bank account for the OCJ, which would have meant that the executive was acceding to his demand for budgetary independence. Now the Department of Justice is back in control: no separate bank account or budgetary independence, and a departmental apparatchik placed as secretary-general within the OCJ to keep an eye on Mogoeng.

I saw Ngcobo a few weeks after his term came to an end. He was staying at the Mount Nelson Hotel in Cape Town and we met mid-morning, him looking relaxed as well as suitably and immaculately attired in a neatly pressed blue polo shirt.

'Tea or coffee?' the waitress asked.

'Tea, Earl Grey, please,' I replied.

'Excellent,' Ngcobo said with a nod of approval. 'I will have the same.'

I asked him how he had got as far as he had without attracting opposition from Radebe and despite the inclement political attitude towards the judiciary from the top of government. He told me how important it had been to meet with the minister of justice to explain his plans and his reasons, and how the minister had been willing to listen and grant him licence to proceed.

Indeed, Radebe had permitted the secondment to the OCJ of one of the ANC's most experienced constitutional bureaucrats – Hassen Ebrahim, chief executive of the Constitutional Assembly back in the mid-1990s and author of *Soul of the Nation*, the excellent account of those historic days – to work on a report on the future institutional modality of the judicial branch of government.

My unit at UCT, the DGRU, had been contracted to conduct some of the necessary research for that report, which was then presented to a committee that Ngcobo had wisely set up under the chairmanship of his two predecessors, justices Chaskalson and Langa, and which included a number of legal academics, as well as former Constitutional Court justice Yvonne Mokgoro.

When I visited Ebrahim to discuss the last phase of our work with the OCJ in April 2011, I discovered that he and a small group of energetic researchers ably led by the talented Advocate Kevin Malunga (who was later appointed Deputy Public Protector – an encouraging appointment if ever there was one, I thought at the time, although, as I was finalising this book, Malungu seemed bent on undermining his boss, the Public Protector Thuli Madonsela, by criticising her to the justice committee in Parliament for reasons that only he can know but which appeared to be extremely suspect) were holed up in a rather dilapidated office block in downtown Johannesburg.

This made no difference to the unfussy Ebrahim, whose first words to me were, 'Richard, this is the last frontier. And we have to act fast. The window will not remain open very long.'

Whether he had the prescience to know that Ngcobo's term would not be able to be extended, or the political wit to think that Mangaung would slam shut any thoughts of progressive reform of judicial institutional independence, I cannot say. But I certainly think he was right.

And, in light of other changes to the anatomy of power, protecting the power of the courts, and the rule of law, was – and is – the last frontier.

With Ebrahim driving the project, the committee was able to panel-beat the report, which contained extensive recommendations about the future administration of justice in South Africa. The proposed new institutional modality would have created a separate court administration, such as the Norwegian Courts' Administration in Trondheim that I had visited along with Chief Justice Ngcobo, SCA president Lex Mpati and several other senior members of the judiciary in June 2011, at the invitation of the Norwegian chief justice.

The report now lies gathering dust. Back in the Mount Nelson tea room that day, I asked Ngcobo about the future of the report. His already doleful outlook gave way to a graver look of disappointment that even his natural reserve could not conceal. Such a reform project, he said, requires the building of both trust and respect between the executive and the judiciary.

I asked, bluntly, if he thought the new chief justice could do the same and if he would be able to sustain the reform project. I cannot recall precisely what Ngcobo said, because on this occasion I was not taking notes, but what I do recall is that he indicated that it had required great strength and a certain level of experience, as well as a certain seniority and gravitas, to engage with Radebe and to persuade him – a typically thoughtful and diplomatic answer.

I then asked a leading question, suggesting that the new chief justice, being relatively junior, would find it difficult. Ngcobo did not respond; he simply tilted his head to one side, raised his eyebrows a tad and took another sip of Earl Grey.

When asked about his youthfulness during his JSC interview, Mogoeng had rather curiously chosen to compare himself with US chief justice John Roberts, adding that 'there is nothing wrong with being fifty; I am six months older than President Obama' – which hardly served to diminish the sense of hubris that he was conveying to the packed conference hall.

Mogoeng was certainly bristling with pent-up anger over what Radebe, who as minister of justice is a member of the JSC, had called the 'vicious mobilisation against the president's nomination'. Many in the human-rights community and other interested members of the legal community had turned up that Saturday.

Finally, I thought, the JSC is attracting appropriate levels of interest. Established under section 178 of the Constitution, its primary function is the appointment of judges. It therefore clearly has a very important formal power, for in the new South African system of government, considerable power is reposed in the courts, reflecting the desire of the drafters to make a clean break from the country's apartheid past.

Prior to 1994, Parliament was the supreme authority, and the laws it passed could not be overruled by the courts. The Interim (1993) and Final (1996) Constitutions changed this. The Constitution not just empowers, but requires, the courts to declare any law or conduct that is inconsistent with the Constitution to be invalid (section 172).

The Constitutional Court is the highest court in the country on constitutional issues. It has the last word on whether a national Act of Parliament, a provincial Act or the conduct of the president is constitutional, and any decision of unconstitutionality on these matters by a lower court must be confirmed by the Constitutional Court (section 167(3)(a) and (5)).

It is perhaps unsurprising, given the extent of the power vested in the courts, including the power to overturn legislation passed by a democratically mandated Parliament (the so-called counter-majoritarian dilemma, in that in such a case unelected members of the judiciary overrule the choice of a Parliament and a government democratically elected by a majority of the people), that the role of the courts has been the subject of increasing contestation.

Tensions regarding the appropriate role of the judiciary in its relationship with other branches of government have been highlighted in comments made by President Zuma and ANC secretary-general Gwede Mantashe, among others, which have raised concerns about the courts overriding policy choices made by the elected branches of government.

These tensions have been exacerbated by the tendency for what might ordinarily be considered 'political' disputes to be resolved in the courts. Given the powerful role of the courts and the electoral dominance of the ANC, this trend is perhaps not surprising. But it does make the courts a crucial site of political, as well as legal, contestation.

This leads to scrutiny of the judges who occupy the bench, and how and by whom they are appointed. The JSC is the most important body in this respect, but the question remains, how influential is it in practice and, within it, which members have the most influence?

At its best, the JSC is a fine example of modern democracy at work. Unlike in many other countries, judges are interviewed for positions in all of the high courts, as well as the SCA and the Constitutional Court.

In the case of the Constitutional Court, the power of the JSC is circumscribed to some extent in that it must provide the president with a list of possible candidates for appointment, of three more than the number of vacancies to be filled, from which the *president* must choose.

In late 2009, there were four places to be filled and so the JSC needed to prepare a list of seven for the president. Over twenty people were interviewed at the JSC hearings in Kliptown: a long list, which contained legal heavyweights like the characterful polymath Dennis Davis, controversial Western Cape judge president John Hlophe, Labour Court judge president Raymond Zondo, who was to be appointed to the Constitutional Court three years later, and experienced SCA justices Azhar Cachalia, Mandisa Maya and Dunstan Mlambo (the latter was subsequently appointed to head the Labour Court and the Gauteng high courts). Then there were the rank outsiders, including unheralded high court judges such as Frans Legodi and James Yekiso, as well as Ntsikelelo Poswa, who withdrew his application at an abortive interview when it transpired that he would have to retire in less than a month due to his age. And then there was Mogoeng Mogoeng, who gave what can best and most politely be described as an eccentric performance that illustrated his skills as an evangelical pastor, but shed little light on his jurisprudential philosophy.

One observer described it as a 'bizarre performance that induced great amusement amongst the onlookers'. Another, an MP who was sitting as a member of the JSC at the time, could hardly believe what was happening when, within twenty minutes of the interviews ending, the JSC had decided on the list of seven. 'It was clear the ANC had already long decided who was going to be put forward to the president,' she says now, looking back. 'The rest of us went along with it because there were some quite decent names on the list – not the best maybe, but certainly not the worst … as to Mogoeng, well, I honestly thought he was there just to make up the numbers; I did not imagine for a minute that the president would actually appoint him.'

But the president did appoint Mogoeng: the process of neutering the Constitutional Court was under way. Zuma's revenge, anti-intellectualism, dumbing-down, call it what you like: the last frontier was being breached.

Mogoeng was appointed along with justices Sisi Khampepe, Chris Jafta and Johan Froneman, while justices Leona Theron, Maya and Zondo were overlooked. Khampepe was regarded as solid, even though few judgments could be attributed to her name. That she was a woman was welcomed, given that two women judges had finished their terms, leaving only one on the bench: Justice Bess Nkabinde.

There are still just the two of them, four years later.

The position in the Constitutional Court created by Ngcobo's departure in 2011 took almost exactly a year to fill, which was notable in and of itself; it took the JSC three attempts, with two sets of re-advertising and plenty of behind-the-scenes cajoling, to get the requisite number of four (the one vacancy plus three) for the interviews that were finally held in June 2012.

With others, I worked to encourage women lawyers to agree to be nominated for the shortlist. It was hard work. Directly and indirectly, I approached eight women, some already judges and some prominent legal academics. To save their own embarrassment, I will not name them, other than the one who did agree to be nominated by a number of progressive women's groups, who were eager to do so, given Mandisa Maya's progressive jurisprudential philosophy and fine track record and reputation as a member of the SCA.

One other woman judge agreed to be nominated, after considerable arm-twisting by an intermediary, but then after a few days of reflection changed her mind. Her reasons were much the same as the other six: she no longer trusted the JSC process as it had become too politicised; she thought that it was a foregone conclusion that Justice Zondo would be appointed regardless of the interview process; besides, she did not really want to serve a court led by Mogoeng.

In November, Zuma duly overlooked Maya and appointed Zondo from the list of four names submitted to him by the JSC.

The Constitutional Court used to be the jewel in South Africa's new demo-cratic firmament. Being on the court was regarded as one of the best legal jobs *in the world*. Now it is hard to get good people even to apply to be on it. How very sad.

As Mogoeng entered the conference hall that spring Saturday morning in 2011, accompanied by his wife and daughter, Moseneke looked up and greeted him with the words 'Justice Mogoeng, you are the president's nominee for chief justice'. He tried, at least I think he tried, to conceal the note of incredulity in his voice. But he failed.

'Our task,' the silver-tied deputy chief justice continued, 'is to determine whether you are a suitable candidate to be appointed.' Tembeka Ngcukaitobi, the eminent young constitutional law advocate from Joburg, leant over and whispered in my ear, 'This is South Africa's Clarence Thomas moment' – a reference to the excoriating US congressional hearings into the conservative Justice Thomas's nomination to the US Supreme Court by President George H.W. Bush in July 1991, hearings that centred on an accusation that Thomas had made unwelcome sexual comments to a subordinate female attorney.

One of the differences in South Africa is that whereas Congress can block a presidential nomination for chief justice, it is far from clear whether the JSC can do the same. According to section 174(3) of the Constitution, the president appoints the chief justice *after consulting* the JSC and the leaders of the political parties represented in the National Assembly. 'After consulting' is the weaker of the two versions of consultation that generally appear in legal tracts, including the Constitution; 'in consultation' being the other, stronger version.

'In consultation' means deciding together. In effect, this gives each of the consulting parties a veto power. In contrast, 'after consulting' means simply having to inform the other party of your intentions; you can still proceed with your appointment even if they are against you.

This raises the interesting legal question of what exactly is the role of the JSC in the process of appointing a chief justice? What has emerged is the following practice: the president will nominate a candidate, and the JSC will conduct an interview with the nominee, in public, after which it will communicate its views to the president.

In Mogoeng's case, because of the controversy that his nomination had generated, some organisations and members of the JSC suggested that the JSC should be entitled to entertain other nominations. What if the JSC has views of its own and wishes to advance the candidature of another person? This point was raised both before and at the start of the JSC hearing on 3 September 2011. Dumisa Ntsebeza, the independent-minded advocate who acts as one of two spokespersons for the JSC (as well as being one of its members), was overheard saying that the DA was going to propose Moseneke for chief justice.

As one would have expected, the ANC members of the JSC – notably Radebe, Fatima Chohan and Ngoako Ramathlodi – closed ranks behind their president's nominee and quickly called for a vote, which went against those opposition members of the JSC who were calling for a debate on whether the JSC could accept other nominations.

On 3 September, Mogoeng began to read from a prepared written statement. After three-quarters of an hour, he was still going strong, his voice booming out as he responded item by item to the criticisms that had been levelled against him in the preceding weeks. Moseneke brought him to a halt and asked him how long the statement was and how far he had got. Provoking a horrified gasp from the assembled audience, the answer came: page 9 out of 49.

'Then give us the highlights,' said Moseneke, sardonically.

Radebe interjected: 'We must give him a full opportunity to express himself in response to the vicious mobilisation.' Judge President Bernard Ngoepe of the Gauteng High Court also spoke up in favour of a full rendition: 'There appears to have been an onslaught on you through the media. You have kept a dignified silence, knowing that the day would come when you would speak fully.'

Ngoepe was at that point one of the most senior members of the JSC, sitting just two seats away from Moseneke at the top of the horseshoe arrangement that the JSC favours. He went on: 'I took the trouble to brush my teeth this morning and I am not going to mention some of the contemptuous and offensive remarks that have been made against you.'

But Moseneke had had enough. The statement could be handed in, but it was not to be read out.

The ANC members then served up some gentle patsy questions. The first was about access to justice, Mogoeng's favourite subject and one upon which he can wax lyrical but without saying anything that a reasonably well-informed and intelligent observer of the creaking lower court system might say.

Then, from Radebe, with reference to the role as head of the Constitutional Court: 'Can you carry your colleagues with you?'

'Absolutely,' the candidate replied.

'But how can you assess that?' came the rejoinder from the insider, Moseneke.

Things were heating up. Mogoeng spoke at length about the confidence that Chief Justice Ngcobo had shown in him in asking him to organise a conference on access to justice in July 2011. 'It's one thing to run a conference, another to be chief justice,' observed Moseneke, aridly.

There was no answer to that question, though Mogoeng hit back a few minutes later when he suggested, in an answer to a similar question about holding the confidence of his colleagues, that 'any of the Constitutional Court judges would have some reasonable disappointment, to varying degrees, but I don't believe they would be so disappointed that they would prevent the court from operating'.

This was throwing the gauntlet back at Moseneke. And by most accounts, the glove remains firmly on the ground. Moseneke was on sabbatical leave for six months of Mogoeng's first year in office, but has since returned and leads the progressive faction of the court that still holds the majority – at least for the time being.

The question of how Moseneke handles himself in the court remains a very live issue. Few would have judged him harshly had he resigned; equally, few would hope that he would do so. Most progressive-minded constitutionalists hope earnestly that he will continue to stay on, however awkward for him and for Mogoeng. Many of the most recently retired members of the court have expressed this wish, in the hopes that the good practices of collegiality, intellectual rigour and consensual problem-solving built up over the first fifteen years of the court's life will continue.

But the news from behind the scenes is not promising. Instead, the Constitutional Court is now largely divided – the chief justice separated from the former philosophical hub of the court, but now joined by the relatively conservative justices Jafta and Zondo. Khampepe keeps to herself, a moderate in the middle by all accounts. The 'left' of the court – Nkabinde, Froneman, Thembile Skweyiya and Johann van der Westhuizen – have rallied around Moseneke and Justice Edwin Cameron, the self-appointed defender of progressive values on the court and an arch-ally of Moseneke.

Justice Zak Yacoob retired in March 2013 and has been replaced by yet another man, the well-regarded senior counsel Mbuyiseli Madlanga. A fine lawyer and jurist, and a progressive, Yacoob was very mindful of the democratic legitimacy of the government and careful when overturning its decisions. While the balance of the court is still decidedly in favour of the progressive world view espoused during the first fifteen years, it could rapidly tip the other way.

Justice Skweyiya will be the next to go, in 2014, followed by Moseneke and Van der Westhuizen in 2016. Justice Nkabinde will serve until 2018.

Moseneke and Cameron are jurists of the highest order; they provide leadership to the younger, less experienced members of the progressive wing of the court: Nkabinde, Van der Westhuizen and Froneman. By 2016, both of them will be gone – replaced by whom, one wonders.

Thus, the battle for control of the Constitutional Court continues, requiring the full attention of the media and progressive civil-society organisations. As the gatekeeper to the bench, the JSC also demands our full attention.

In September 2011, the ANC closed ranks behind its president's chosen man. Nothing less would have been expected of Ramathlodi, a conservative nationalist par excellence. He would take great pleasure in excising the progressive intellectual horsepower of the court. But Radebe and Chohan will have to reflect in later years over their role in Mogoeng's appointment. Just before lunch on 3 September 2011, Moseneke put the point succinctly in adjourning the hearing: 'The CJ is an intellectual leader, she or he is the flag-bearer, and to provide leadership, must have a deep intellect … after lunch I'd be grateful if you could provide some answers that help us assess that.'

It was said without hope or expectation. As I stood and filed out, a leading member of a black lawyers' association turned to me and said: 'The real chief justice has just spoken.'

How, then, did this come to pass? The ANC must take the most responsibility. They do not necessarily fully control the JSC as some have argued, but they certainly have a major say in it.

The ANC, on current numbers, falls just short of a majority on the JSC, if you add their members in the National Assembly and the National Council of Provinces (NCOP) to the minister of justice (a total of eight). But, if you add the presidential nominees, who one can safely assume will be well disposed towards the ANC, then you get to twelve (out of twenty-three), which is a majority when the JSC is deciding on a position for the Constitutional Court or the SCA, but either just short or just enough of a majority for high court appointments, depending on the party alignment of the premier of the particular province where the high court is situated.

Thus, more often than not, the ANC will enjoy a majority on the JSC. And why should it be otherwise? The Constitution-makers sought to strike a balance with the JSC. The Constitution does not give complete power to the politicians in the judicial appointments process, but nor does it remove their voice.

Figure II.I: JSC composition

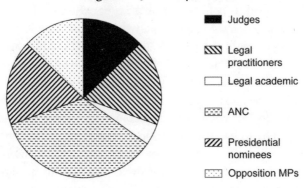

Chief Justice	1 – Mogoeng Mogoeng
President of SCA	1 – Lex Mpati
Judge President	1 – Bernard Ngoepe
Minister of Justice	1 – Jeff Radebe
The Bar	2 – Mbuyiseli Madlanga SC, Izak Smuts SC
Side Bar	2 – CP Fourie, Krish Govender (state attorney)
Legal Academy	1 – Engela Schlemmer
MPs	6 – Fatima Chohan (ANC); Ngoako Ramathlodi (ANC); Jonas Sibanyoni (ANC); Koos van der Merwe (IFP); Hendrik Schmidt (DA); Nick Koornhof (COPE)
Members of NCOP	4 – Tjheta Mofokeng, Johannes Mahlangu, Bertha Mabe, Grace Boroto (all ANC)
Presidential Nominees	4 – Dumisa Ntsebeza SC, Ishmael Semenya SC, Vas Soni SC, Andiswa Ndoni
Judge President & Premier of particular province when relevant	2 – varies

The constitutional inference to be drawn is that the people should have a say in the appointment of judges; not directly, but indirectly through their elected representatives. Concurrently, the legal profession, which has a large stake in the judiciary for obvious reasons, has a significant representation on the JSC.

In recent years, some of the main players in JSC hearings have been advocates Ntsebeza and Semenya, and commissioners Ramathlodi and Chohan. Ntsebeza is probably the most vocal member of the commission in consistently raising transformation issues. Ramathlodi has increasingly put candidates on the spot with questions of judicial deference and the separation of powers. Chohan is not far behind and indeed is sometimes the more vocal of the two in asserting the need for the courts to steer clear of policy-making areas. Semenya is wont to raise both issues, often through the lens of governance and politics of the legal profession. Until his term on the JSC expired at the end of 2012, Krish Govender, representing the attorneys' profession, also used to highlight the challenges government faces in a developmental state, but showed a greater willingness than most to acknowledge the need for judges to push at boundaries in order to achieve the society envisaged by the Constitution. His distinctive approach will be missed.

Radebe is quieter than some of his colleagues, but when he speaks he is a forceful presence. This was evident in his defence of Mogoeng and in his April 2012 grilling of South Gauteng deputy judge president Phineas Mojapelo, about an article in which Mojapelo was perceived to be critical of the consultation process followed by the JSC in the build-up to the appointment of Ngcobo as chief justice (the article had been written prior to Mogoeng's appointment).

Ngcobo, in chairing the JSC, would take some time at the outset of an interview not just to establish the biographical details of a candidate, but also to canvass issues such as their jurisprudential outlook and philosophy of adjudication. Mogoeng, thus far, has been briefer, tending to focus more on the candidates' backgrounds before opening the floor to other commissioners, though he will often ask questions later in the interviews. Case management is a favourite theme of his, and he has increasingly begun to canvass transformation issues, too.

Of the opposition MPs, the most active is the IFP's venerable Koos van der Merwe, the longest-serving member of the current JSC. He can be relied upon to ask questions about languages used in the courts, whether candidates have written academic articles, and delays in writing judgments. Appropriate to their designations, the Bar council representatives, advocates Madlanga and Smuts, tend to ask questions more closely related to specific judgments candidates have written, and candidates' theories of adjudication and judicial philosophy, as did the late Professor Schlemmer.

Viewed as a whole, the JSC's performance is a hard one to analyse. Doubtless there have been candidates who should have been appointed who have not, but accusations that it wilfully fails to appoint suitably qualified white male candidates are wide of the mark. What is apparent is that the JSC is representative of a diverse range of interests, which can result in interviews straying far from the terrain that would traditionally be considered core judicial functions.

Under Mogoeng's chairmanship, interviews initially seemed to become more focused – indeed, in April 2012 many of the interviews seemed to swing too far the other way, with several perfunctory interviews lasting only a few minutes. Even allowing for the fact that some candidates had been interviewed before, this practice was concerning. But the biggest concern, and where the greatest need for future vigilance lies, is whether the increasingly forceful assertion of separation-of-powers issues will stymie the appointment of potentially excellent judges who may be perceived as too 'radical', in that they are seen as too likely to make decisions that infringe on the competencies of other branches of government.

In this regard, the JSC surpassed itself at its April 2013 hearings. In contrast to the gentle warmth of a delightful Cape autumn and the sparkling sunlit blue sea outside the Sea Point hotel where interviews were being held for high court and SCA vacancies, the JSC loped towards its darkest hour, with procedural impropriety so egregious and unfair that it took my breath away and left me shaking with anger.

The start of the hearings had been mired in rancour following the leaking of Advocate Izak Smuts's memo to the JSC in which he essentially said to his colleagues: 'If the JSC is no longer going to appoint white men, we better just be done with it and say so.' This followed the overlooking of, among others, the enormously pompous and arrogant Jeremy Gauntlett, a fine lawyer but one who many believe lacks the temperament necessary for the bench.

Smuts was factually wrong because, in fact, the JSC *does* often appoint white men (by my count, twenty-two were appointed to the superior courts between 2010 and 2012 inclusive). He was also tactically wrong, because he diverted attention away from the bigger question about what sort of people were being appointed from the perspective of ideology and jurisprudential philosophy.[2]

Rather than a preoccupation with race – with its bleak binary logic that white male candidates are the best and that anyone else is appointed simply because the JSC 'must take into consideration the need for the bench to broadly reflect the racial and gender composition of South Africa' (section 174(2)) – the JSC should be focusing on who will deliver a transformative approach to dispensing justice and give full effect to the values and principles of the Constitution.

Clearly, and rightly, the JSC's job is to drive the transformation of the bench, and in this respect it has made reasonable progress on the race front, but not on the gender front.[3]

And I do not mean to be disrespectful to the JSC. On the contrary, it is an institution that is a vital cog in our constitutional wheel. And it has a very difficult assignment because, in their wisdom, the Constitution-makers enjoined the JSC to appoint people who are 'appropriately qualified' and 'fit and proper' (section 174(1)), while at the same time taking into consideration the country's demography.

The relationship between the two provisions is far from clear. And the JSC has clearly not yet figured it out, because it spends so much time arguing about it.

Indeed, having spent the whole of its first day, Monday 8 April, in a closed and apparently dissonant session debating Smuts's memo and related matters, the JSC played out its internal divisions and anguish in the first three candidate interviews for two SCA vacancies, which took place on the Tuesday morning.

Clive Plasket, an attorney who conducted a fearless human rights and labour law practice with the Legal Resources Centre in the 1980s, but who is now an equally fearless member of the Eastern Cape High Court, was the first up.

For two hours he faced a barrage of angry questions about the transformation issue and the related spring 2012 SCA ruling that the JSC's decision not to appoint a 'fit and proper' and 'appropriately qualified' white male candidate to fill a vacancy on the Western Cape High Court bench in 2011 was unlawful for the JSC's failure to give reasons as to why it left the vacancy empty.[4]

Despite the unrelenting pressure, which was so uncomfortable that Plasket's wife was twice compelled to leave the room because she could take it no longer, the bluff-spoken administrative lawyer from Grahamstown maintained his composure and stuck to his line: that the SCA was right in law; that the JSC is a public body subject to the principle of legality like all other public bodies; that, when invited to accept that section 174(2) was peremptory, it meant what it said: namely, that the JSC must take into consideration the racial and gender demography of the country.

Only at the very end, when asked by Mogoeng whether he had anything else he would like to say, did Plasket finally – and understandably, one might think – crack and show his frustration: 'I was hoping,' he said, 'to have been asked about my competence and my long track record as a judge.'

There had been not one question of substance about his human rights record, his judgments or his judicial philosophy. Nada.

After a relatively short and bland interview with Justice Halima Saldulker, who was later recommended for appointment to one of the vacancies, in swans Justice Nigel Willis of the South Gauteng High Court.

Mogoeng begins by asking him about his recently acquired MPhil and PhD qualifications, and it emerges that Willis's extracurricular studies span the Pentecostal Church and the relationship between religion and science.

'Are you a sangoma, Judge?' Radebe asks. There is hilarity all round.

'Well, I am halfway to being one … a sort of preacher,' replies Willis.

Mogoeng, whose own religious zeal is well known and who is a lay preacher himself, appears mighty delighted.

IFP MP Van der Merwe is especially interested and expresses the hope that the good judge will send him copies of his theses. There is some equally lighthearted banter about Willis's tendency to get annoyed with the Constitutional Court – the General Council of the Bar of South Africa has sent a submission noting that in one case the judge lashed the Constitutional Court for having the temerity to overturn one of his judgments.

'I would have preferred to see such an argument in an academic piece or a newspaper article, but not in a judgment,' Mpati points out.

Oh, I know, naughty me, replies Willis. I suppose I shouldn't have got so annoyed, but, well, you know, those Constitutional Court judges – 'before your time, Chief Justice' – can be mighty infuriating, can't they?

There is much nodding among some members of the JSC for whom, indeed, the Constitutional Court can be mighty infuriating, what with its irritating tendency to overturn government policy and legislation. Rather like Plasket tends to do now, with the persistently incompetent and unlawful Eastern Cape provincial government.

Never mind. Willis is avuncular and charming and eccentric, and obviously a good egg. It's as if a rather errant but delightfully charming relative has popped in for a pre-lunch aperitif. And, indeed, lunch is approaching. So pass the sherry, old chap, and let's 'keep the show on the road', as Chohan puts it in her last question to Willis.

If Alice had walked in then through a looking glass and the Mad Hatter had asked her to solve the riddle 'Why is a raven like a writing desk?', no one who was watching would have been surprised at this point. (Alice, as you will recall, soon gives up and the Hatter admits: 'I haven't the slightest idea.')

Willis did not get one single question about transformation; his interview lasted barely forty-five minutes. Instead, a recent letter he wrote to the *Mail & Guardian* in support of the National Development Plan's economics was read back to him approvingly by Mogoeng.

The Constitution should not be 'interpreted as if judicial fiat can succeed where every socialist revolution has failed', Willis had written.

A human rights lawyer who works on cases of eviction and the right to housing told me after the hearing that 'Willis is a disastrous judge who sees the Constitution through the lens of private property. His judgments have caused massive harm to poor people and their eviction rights.' By the end of the next day, by which time Willis's appointment had been made public, copies of some of his more bizarre judgments had been circulated, including one on a BEE deal in which he observed that the cast of actors 'included the usual suspects' as well as various albinos with a pink hue – by which he meant 'white people' – an example, presumably, of a misplaced attempt at judicial humour.

A high court judge who knows both Willis and Plasket explained it this way: 'Plasket is one of Arthur's boys' – a reference to Arthur Chaskalson, the first president of the Constitutional Court and the founding director of the Legal Resources Centre – 'and the ANC's backlash against the Constitution is directed at Arthur and his boys, who they blame for forcing them to have the Constitution in the first place.'

Of course, the idea that the ANC had the Bill of Rights forced upon it is errant revisionist nonsense. As Justice Albie Sachs reminded his audience at the launch of the Kader Asmal Human Rights Awards at the University of the Western Cape

in May 2013, it was Oliver Tambo who insisted that the ANC convert its commitment to the Freedom Charter into an operational bill of rights.

These days, however, the ANC wants obedient judges who 'know the limits
of judicial power'. It's not being a white man that's a disqualifier for judicial
office, it's being a white man with a commitment to the progressive values of the
Constitution and the protection of human rights that will destroy your prospects.

So that week in April 2013 was not only the JSC's lowest moment so far, it
was also the week in which it appointed a judge who is, to my mind, a libertarian,
neo-Thatcherite maverick, instead of a progressive lawyer with a proud human
rights record. It was the week in which the ANC and its members of the JSC,
including its unprincipled minister of justice, betrayed the legacy of Tambo,
something it may care to think on if Justice Willis starts handing down eccentric
judgments from Bloemfontein, because that is one appointment that might well
come back to bite them on the butt.

The last few years have been a rocky ride for the JSC and, unless it can fix
itself and find consensus about its role and about the criteria to be applied when
interviewing candidates for judicial office, it will lose even more credibility, to the
point where its processes will lack legitimacy, thereby dangerously diminishing
the rule of law and the strength of the judiciary.

In addition to the controversies that inevitably swirl around the appointments
process, it has also been placed at centre stage in the controversies surrounding
Western Cape judge president John Hlophe. The JSC is charged with dealing
with allegations of misconduct against judges, and in the most serious cases may
recommend a judge's impeachment to Parliament. The JSC's attempt to dismiss
complaints against Hlophe, relating to his alleged attempt to influence members
of the Constitutional Court in deciding a case against President Zuma, has been
overturned by the SCA, and the ongoing saga is likely to prove a damaging one
for the JSC, the judiciary and the legal system in general.

Indeed, the JSC's record when challenged in court has been abysmal. Whether
on issues relating to the appointments process or the Hlophe saga, the JSC has
consistently been overturned by the courts when its decisions have been challenged. In litigation brought by the Western Cape Bar council challenging the
JSC's failure to fill certain vacancies on the Western Cape High Court, the JSC
was not even able to explain its own voting procedures consistently.

At lunch, on the first day of the JSC Mogoeng hearing, a last-minute submission from COSATU, presumably prepared on its behalf by Neil Coleman, its
erstwhile veteran parliamentary lobbyist, was passed around. It was a devastating
critique of Mogoeng's appointment. That it came so late and that it held so little
sway is telling: the formal left – the SACP and COSATU – deploy little of their
political capital on institutional governance and on the rule of law, though they

are quick to carp about state corruption and infringements of people's human dignity.

Their analytical faculties are unable, it seems, to join the dots between the pursuit of a substantively equal society and the structural inequities of the economy on the one hand, and the importance of having a progressive-minded judiciary on the other.

That, presumably, is why they failed to intercede to help save a man whose mission was to provide the country with the strong, independent legal system that it needs if it is to resist the populist, right-wing assault that is now being occasioned upon it.

As the clock ticked towards the end of Ngcobo's term in mid-2011, Parliament could have moved to pass a law to extend the term of all Constitutional Court judges. At one point, it looked like it was going to consider doing so. But it paused, first to wait for the judgment in the Ngcobo case, and then to decide what to do in the light of its consequences.

As already noted, Ngcobo accepted the president's request on 2 June. The president then acted fast, announcing his decision to extend Ngcobo's term by three years on 3 June. The application to challenge the constitutionality of the decision by the Centre for Applied Legal Studies (CALS) and CASAC was launched on 20 June, and the Constitutional Court heard the case on 18 July and handed down judgment on 29 July, conscious of the fact that the 14 August deadline was looming.

The court decided that Parliament had no constitutional authority to delegate power to the president to extend the term of the chief justice since the latter is also a member of the Constitutional Court and the term of the Constitutional Court judges is set by the Constitution: section 176(1) sets the term as twelve years non-renewable or until he or she is seventy, whichever comes first.

However, by virtue of the 2001 amendment referred to earlier in this chapter, section 176 also says that an Act of Parliament may extend the term of a Constitutional Court judge.

The court in the Ngcobo case then went on to say that when the Constitution refers to 'a' Constitutional Court judge, it is not permitting differentiation in terms of office. Although the court recognised that the chief justice and his or her deputy are appointed by a different process to 'ordinary' Constitutional Court judges, and although it acknowledged that they have significant special responsibilities beyond their membership of the court, it concluded that 'once appointed, however, the Chief Justice and Deputy Chief Justice take their place alongside nine other judges in constituting membership of this Court'.

My unit's submission to the court, accompanying its rather belated application to join the proceedings as *amicus curiae*, contended ('novelly', the court observed) that Parliament does not have the power to extend the terms of office of all Constitutional Court judges generally, or those of all present and future chief justices. It has, we argued, only the power to extend the term of a specific judge or judges.

In other words, we were pushing for a 'Ngcobo law' that would have extended his term by name – a law to specifically extend the term of Chief Justice Ngcobo himself, and no other – with the view that the Constitution anticipated a situation where, such as then, an exceptional need arose. The exceptional circumstance we identified was the need to maintain continuity in the epic institutional reform project that Ngcobo had embarked upon.

Few agreed with this approach, and the court was not persuaded either. I am far from sure we were right; I think the court was. But it need not have closed the door entirely. Now, it was clear to Parliament that it could not pass a 'Ngcobo law' extending the term of this one member of the court, even though he was the chief justice, but it could, according to the court, pass a law to extend the terms of all Constitutional Court judges.

This is where the ANC lost its bottle or, rather, its support for Ngcobo evaporated into thin air. Until the judgment was handed down on Friday 29 July, the Justice and Constitutional Affairs Portfolio Committee was willing and ready to process a law that would extend Ngcobo's term and had even made provisional arrangements for the National Assembly to be recalled on Tuesday 9 August to pass the law, since Parliament was in its winter recess.

Although he would likely contest this version of events, I believe John Jeffery, the veteran member of the justice committee and a long-time ally of Jacob Zuma, decided in consultation with justice minister Jeff Radebe, his political principal, that they would not proceed to 'save' Ngcobo.

Why not? Procedurally, it amounted to the same thing: an Act of Parliament, albeit one that would extend the term of not just one member of the court – which the court had now declared was constitutionally impermissible – but of all eleven. The president had wanted to extend Ngcobo's term from twelve years to fifteen, so why not all of them?

Only Jeffery and Radebe know the answer to this question. My conjecture, which, as I say, they will no doubt contest, is that they did not want to extend the terms of justices like Moseneke and Cameron, whose end of terms they were – and are – looking forward to.

Ngcobo had convinced them of the need to strengthen the judicial arm of government or, at least, he had managed to persuade them. They were willing to go along with it. It was a long game, in any case. The bigger political project, however, was to diminish the power of the Constitutional Court and so, now that the chips were down and the choice had to be made, the ANC chose the latter over the former.

Ngcobo, it turned out, was expendable.

In Cape Town four weeks later, thanks to a transparent process that we should be glad of, we all got to see what we were getting as Ngcobo's replacement. I don't know what Moseneke had for lunch, or what he drank, but the afternoon was his, by a mile.

Drawing on his considerable forensic expertise, he applied the scalpel. Professor Schlemmer, representing the legal academy, had asked Mogoeng about his dissent in the Dey case. In the two years since his appointment to the Constitutional Court, Mogoeng had written only five judgments (including a pugnacious dissent in the *Citizen v McBride* case). In the Dey case, which concerned the constitutionality of a defamation claim where mischievous schoolchildren had photoshopped the head of their principal, Mr Dey, onto some rather lurid if obviously fake pictures that presented him as gay, Mogoeng had taken the rather bizarre option of offering a dissent on a point without giving reasons.

The point he was dissenting was the judgment written by justices Froneman and Cameron that on one reading can be summarised simply, if rather crudely, as saying it cannot be defamatory to depict someone as gay, in the light of constitutional norms and values that guard against discrimination based on sexual orientation. Thus, they found 'it cannot be actionable simply to call or to depict someone as gay even if the subject chooses not to be gay and dislikes being gay'.[5]

In response to Schlemmer's question, Mogoeng replied: 'On reflection, I should have provided some reasons ... I did not have time to reflect on the point.'

Moseneke pressed him: 'If it is not actionable to refer to someone as gay, you dissented from this, what is your jurisprudential take?' He was asking him, clearly enough, what his view as a jurist was on the proposition of law.

Mogoeng floundered: 'I did not have enough time to reflect properly. I don't have an answer to your question.'

Moseneke, calmly and slowly, to complete silence from the huge auditorium, retaliated: 'If you listen to the question, you might be able to answer.' Mogoeng was trying to jump back in to reply immediately and Moseneke was trying to get him to pause and actually understand what was being asked.

Mogoeng snapped back, bitterly: 'You don't have to be sarcastic, sir.'

This was class warfare; a cultural clash between the epitome of the modern, progressive Constitution – Moseneke – and the reactionary, socially conservative world view of another place, Mogoeng's – and Zuma's for that matter.

There was a palpable gasp in the auditorium at the friction of the exchange, followed by a long pause. Silence. As if everyone present was holding his or her breath.

Moseneke, with a tiny sigh: 'I'll try again. What is your answer?'

Mogeong: 'I believe it now.' From which we are to infer that he could not accept it then, because of his religious beliefs, but he is forced to accept it now, in public, because needs must.

Moseneke: 'Why did you dissent?'

The best questions in cross-examination are the simplest.

No answer.

Moseneke: 'You should not have dissented.'

Mogoeng: 'Yes, I should not have dissented.'

Shortly afterwards, Koos van der Merwe asked Mogoeng if he had a short temper and suggested that in all his long years on the JSC he had never encountered an applicant with such an arrogant attitude, that it 'points to your suitability negatively'.

Mogoeng was forced to apologise: 'I did a wrong to the DCJ [deputy chief justice] and I apologise.'

Game, set and match to the DCJ.

Hence the sparkle in Moseneke's eye when we encountered each other in the gents'. And hence my reply to his question.

This particular battle had gone to the old new establishment, but the war will be prolonged and the new new establishment could yet prevail. After all, Mogoeng was appointed chief justice, not Moseneke.

Though, as an epilogue, it ought to be stated that Mogoeng was neither the ANC's nor the president's first choice. After they abandoned Ngcobo, they tried at least two, maybe three, others. Mpati and Khampepe were asked, but they declined. Mpati likes his life in the Free State, not far from his Eastern Cape farm, and is close to retirement. Unlike Mogoeng, Khampepe modestly thought that she was too new on the Constitutional Court to lead it.

The government initially requested research on the judicial records of five people: Mpati, Khampepe, Ngoepe, Khayelihle Mthiyane (SCA judge) and Mlambo. And then, a day or two later, of Mogoeng. It wasn't a long research assignment, as he has written few significant judgments and no academic articles; as he told the JSC, 'I don't have a passion for writing articles'.

I told you so, I thought to myself when we got the request to do the report on Mogoeng. I knew that it meant that my worst-case scenario premonition was looming large.

And so it came to pass: a president who doesn't read appoints a chief justice who doesn't write.[6] It makes perfect sense.

12

Money and politics

Maybe because it was the first time all morning that I had managed to hit my drive into the centre of the fairway, but I finally found myself strolling down the lush green grass of the ninth hole of the Clovelly golf course alongside one of my playing companions, Sipho Pityana. As usual, he seemed at ease with himself and the world. And why not? It was the Christmas holiday; after an initial early morning shower, the air was clear and warm; the surrounding mountains looked glorious; and the sea glistened beyond the end of the valley cradling the charming little course.

I made an idle comment about the erratic condition of my game. But Pityana stopped suddenly in his tracks, turned to me and hissed fiercely: 'It makes me so very angry! It has got to be stopped!'

I was astounded. Rarely has my tendency to slice my drives so ludicrously far and wide of the fairway provoked such passion. I began to form an apology or an excuse when Pityana again cut me dead: 'The greed, the greed!'

He walked on, shaking his head. Now I was truly flummoxed. I caught up with him just as we reached our balls, which, for the first time, were just a few yards apart in the middle of the fairway, but still a fair distance from the lengthy but narrow raised green on the left, nestled dangerously close to the thorn-covered mountainside.

Pityana began to elaborate as I wrestled with the dilemma of whether to aim ambitiously for the green with a fairway wood, risking everything, or to lay up with a prudent little six iron.

'There is this obsession with money. It's greed, pure and simple. It's driving corruption. Too many comrades are involved and they should know better. It's time to take a stand, Richard.'

This was fast turning into one of those conversations you never, ever forget. Like the one I was to have six months later on the way to a meeting in Ghana. The SAA plane was stopping at Lagos, the destination, it turned out, of the man sitting beside me. When I first took my seat next to him, I was too tired to bother to assess if he was South African or Ghanaian or Nigerian, and he was napping. We sat in silence as the plane took off and through most of our meals. It was only once the wine and food had begun to revive us that we struck up a conversation.

After some preliminaries, in which I established that he was a South African businessman on his way to Nigeria to close a deal to set up a new call centre there, I asked him about his history. With our tray tables cleared and a full glass of dark cabernet in front of each of us, my companion was forthcoming. He had begun life as a teacher in the apartheid era, in a Johannesburg township; it was hard, but then he moved into human resources at a large mining company and things began to improve for him and his family. He worked his way up, but then, a few years into democracy, he was retrenched. Bravely, extraordinarily, with a recklessness that made him shake his head as he recounted his story, he threw all his money into setting up a call-centre business. There were precarious moments, but he got through them; and now, he is a millionaire with an enormously successful business.

I was strangely moved by his story. So simple, and yet so full of resonance for the old and the new South Africa. I asked what he thought about modern entrepreneurs. This was the 'Pityana-on-the-ninth-at-Clovelly' moment. The glass, luckily drained of wine, went flying, as my companion threw up his arms in disgust and, in animated fashion, proclaimed his deep-seated disgust: 'They're not entrepreneurs! They're not businessmen! What have they done to earn their wealth? Nothing!'

We discussed the 'tenderpreneur' class for a while. I could easily understand his frustration. He had worked hard; had worked his way up. And then had to watch as these young whippersnappers, with little or no education, thrust their way into 'business' simply by gaming the system.

This is just one of many similar conversations I have had on planes in recent years, in which hard-working black South Africans, who have earned their places in business or government, express their anger about the current situation. Many hark back, longingly, to the Mbeki era.

Obviously, that was an era in which they made good, and advanced. Although Pityana's route to wealth was different to my travel companion's, it was no less decent. A former exile, he was made the director-general of labour during the crucial reform period of the mid-1990s, but then, after a rather trickier period as DG of foreign affairs in which he did not see eye to eye with the then minister, Nkosazana Dlamini-Zuma, he moved into business.

There was a period of 'apprenticeship' – what Pityana calls an 'incubation period', when I ask him about it during an interview, which we conduct, rather incongruously, after a misunderstanding between our PAs, amidst the noisy chatter of the 'ladies who lunch' at Melissa's in Newlands, Cape Town – at Nedbank, under the watchful eye of Chris Liebenberg, who urged him to 'learn business first' before embarking on the big BEE deal that would make him very wealthy, very quickly, as the founding executive chairman of Izingwe Capital, a BEE company that in 2004 was given a 30 per cent shareholding of Aberdare Cables, one of the world's leading cable companies.

Sitting among the chattering classes of Cape Town's southern suburbs, where, incidentally, he is more than comfortable (he has a house in Bishopscourt and a penchant for meetings at the Mugg & Bean in Constantia Village), Pityana tells me in no uncertain terms that 'the credibility of BEE schemes' depends 'on the way in which we conduct ourselves and that we should not be greedy vultures'. Unfortunately, 'some people let the side down'.

While in government, he says, 'I had numerous opportunities for "funny business". But the respectability one has sets the tone. A black person has an extra burden – to dispel the stereotype and to show competence at all times. I would rather make money slowly and do it right, than sacrifice my values and principles.'

The full history of BEE, and that extraordinary period in which BEE capitalists emerged seemingly overnight during the late 1990s and early 2000s, has yet to be written. Clearly, it had a significant impact on the landscape of corporate South Africa. But it was also an era that, according to people like Pityana, set the right tone – one of education and intellectualism, in which, as Pityana recalls now, Mbeki liked to engage with the 'business intelligentsia', such as Saki Macozoma at Standard Bank. It was not the bling, get-rich-quick culture of accumulation and conspicuous consumption that seems to be the hallmark of more recent years.

Which brings me back to the cloistered course at Clovelly in late 2009. When our mutual friend, AngloGold Ashanti's shrewd, seasoned public-affairs man, Alan Fine, had invited me to join the two of them for a round, I had been delighted, not only because of the charm of the Cape seaside course's layout and its old-world charisma, but also because of the potential to put forth an idea for a new organisation that I had been incubating – what is now CASAC, the Council for the Advancement of the South African Constitution.

The idea had originated with the first signs of attacks on the Constitution in the run-up to the ANC's national conference in Polokwane in 2007. During its development phase, a number of conversations took place among constitutionalists that essentially homed in on the question: If the constitution is under threat, who will defend it?

The late, great human rights activist and ANC cabinet minister Kader Asmal had launched an ill-thought-out 'constitutional charter' initiative, in which citizens could sign up to a charter, but he had not mobilised the resources to administer the 'charterists', and so it quickly fizzled out. Undeterred, he, with Mamphela Ramphele, convened a conversation in 2008 in the middle of the Cape winter: I remember attending a dinner in a chilly downtown restaurant, at which Geoff Budlender and others called for a new organisation that could mobilise support at different levels of society to defend the progressive values and principles of the Constitution.

I ran with the idea, reporting loosely to Budlender and Ramphele, consulting with a range of interested, progressive constitutionalists, and raising a US$1 million grant from Atlantic Philanthropies, eventually launching CASAC from its greenhouse – my research unit at the Department of Public Law at UCT. I had also drawn my old friend Lawson Naidoo into the project and, nearing the end of 2009, we were poised to move towards the official launch phase.

But we needed to find a leader. Naidoo had suggested we talk to Pityana, with whom he had worked closely for the ANC in exile in London in the eighties and early nineties. We wanted someone who could not be easily dismissed as a 'counter-revolutionary' or as DA-aligned and anti-ANC. I had met Pityana when he was still the widely respected labour DG in Mandela's government and had liked him greatly then.

He certainly fitted the bill in many ways; and there was no doubting his ANC credentials – as I've said before, if you were to cut Pityana in half, you would find the letters A-N-C inscribed.

Which made his outburst on the ninth hole at Clovelly all the more captivating. Perhaps he *would* be the ideal person to lead CASAC? I had planned on *maybe* broaching the topic at the nineteenth, when the game was over. I really did not want to interrupt a summer holiday unless it was clear that a work conversation was not inappropriate. Now I found myself talking about it as we approached the ninth green, and we continued talking about it at the halfway house and, sporadically, depending on the accuracy of my drives, through much of the rest of the round.

When CASAC was launched at Liliesleaf Farm in Johannesburg in September 2010, Pityana was at the helm, the new organisation's first chairman. And he has led CASAC with distinction ever since. Pityana's anguish in December 2009 reflects a viewpoint held by many ANC 'traditionalists' – that is to say, ANC comrades who grew up in the cradle of the struggle and were fully immersed in, and schooled by, the ANC's approach to politics.

One of the most distinctive aspects of the last few years has been the way in which such traditionalists have responded to the current challenges and the plight of the ANC. The ANC is a pale shadow of what it once was – a 'mongrel' party, with all manner of strange bedfellows and opportunists who have inveigled their way into the organisation for nefarious purposes.

Some have reacted by leaving the ANC to join other parties – most notable was the formation of COPE in 2008. Although his older brother, Barney, was closely associated with COPE, Sipho has never entertained the idea of leaving the ANC. He prefers to fight from within, to wrestle for control of the ANC with the charlatans who have driven its reputation ever downwards.

Of course, it would be idle to ignore the class considerations involved in this and any other authentic attempt to understand the current trajectory of the ANC. The overlap between the worlds of business and government – of money and politics – is a crucial part of the modern South African story, just as it is a pivotal part of the old South Africa's history, including the apartheid era.

Conflicts of interest: The root of the corruption problem?

Speaking at a debate on party political funding hosted by IDASA in February 2012, Pityana asked: 'Democracy has been good for business, but has business been good for democracy?'

This is a profound question and speaks directly to the issue of conflicts of interest. Political parties, government officials, the media, trade unions and institutions like the Public Protector have all weighed in on conflict of interest and the need to manage it better.

ANC secretary-general Gwede Mantashe was a fellow panellist at the IDASA debate, and defended the ANC's interest in its investment arm Chancellor House without any apparent shame or embarrassment, accepting in response to a question from me that it has a controlling share in the company.

'Chancellor House is an example of a transparent source of funding,' Mantashe said. He further defended its existence by saying it was created to close the gap when donor funding – which had supported the ANC during the struggle – retreated after democracy had been obtained. The ANC had taken the initiative to create an alternative funding arm, he said. 'That we should not take initiative is saying we should starve ourselves to death and collapse.'[1]

He called antagonism towards Chancellor House by opposition parties 'sour grapes', as they had not been as resourceful as the ANC. The ANC needed money, he said. 'We have constituencies to service.'

Yet the ANC leadership knows there is a serious problem caused by dodgy secret donations. The only question is whether they will choose to act to stem the tide. The answer lies in Mantashe's attitude to Chancellor House: the ANC will act only if its own interests are not harmed by any reforms. And since Chancellor House serves its interests, it will do nothing about what Pityana bravely calls 'a blatant conflict of interest'.

At one of its first events, on 21 January 2011, CASAC council member Frene Ginwala, an ANC stalwart and the first Speaker of the democratic Parliament (1994–2004), made the point, with contrition and even shame I thought, that the ANC leadership had underestimated the impact power would have on its membership in terms of the ability to withstand temptation and not enter into corrupt practices.

A year earlier, the ANC had said it wanted to manage potential conflicts of interest due to leaders' private business interests, admitting that it was battling to contain corruption, but only in July 2011 did Mantashe announce plans to create an integrity committee to advise and counsel its members on their business interests and possible conflicts of interest. The committee would be proactive and look into the behaviour of its members. 'The approach is that political discipline is not like a school principal disciplining kids, but about people themselves internalising the need for that discipline,' Mantashe told *Business Day*.[2]

Dr Collette Schulz-Herzenberg, senior researcher in the Conflicts of Interest project, Institute for Security Studies (ISS) Corruption & Governance Programme in Cape Town, wrote in a Public Service Commission (PSC) magazine that the reason for the lack of regulation regarding cooling-off periods between leaving the public sector and working in a private-sector entity with whom the official may have dealt when in public office – and, in so doing, may have laid a nice little feathered nest to land in – is that fundamentally there is 'uncertainty about what constitutes conflicts of interest in public life in the first place'.[3]

According to Schulz-Herzenberg, conflicts of interest range from taking bribes, kickbacks and extortion to abuse of influence, favouritism and the misuse of state information.

A key concern when dealing with conflicts of interest is preventing the misuse of knowledge by civil servants and elected officials. Their actions may take on two forms:

- 'insider trading', whereby government knowledge is shared with a company, business partner, friend or family member; or
- 'revolving door', whereby people flow in and out of business into government and back.

A PSC report of the 2008/09 financial year shows the possible extent of conflicts of interest among senior managers in government by looking at 30 per cent, or 2 628, of the 9 128 financial disclosures filed.[4]

Analysis of the sampled group revealed that 20 per cent (497) of the managers from national and provincial departments may have had conflicts of interest. Gauteng had 207, while, at national level, Treasury had the most managers with possible conflicts of interest.

What constituted these potential conflicts? Of the sample, 351 managers had a link to companies doing business with their department, and 259 cases were noted of managers where colleagues had a shared interest in companies doing business with other departments. The report also identified 41 department heads who were too involved in private business.

The PSC further identified three situations that may exacerbate the longevity and scope of conflicts of interest, namely: department heads don't always address these conflicts with their guilty managers; some managers are complacent when it comes to declaring their interests (the PSC found that 210 and 26 managers didn't fully declare their gifts and property respectively); and no clear register is kept and managed for gifts received.

On 15 March 2011, PSC commissioner Sellinah Nkosi said in a presentation that 'it is an open secret in some departments that service providers offer gifts before and after tenders are being awarded'.[5] She affirmed that the prevention of conflicts of interest and possible corruption could be strengthened with lifestyle audits by the PSC.

Nkosi was actually quoting a PSC press statement dating all the way back to December 2008. In August that year, the Auditor-General brought out a report stating that provinces had spent around R540.2 million between 2005 and 2007 on contracts with companies linked to employees or their spouses. In Limpopo alone, the provincial government spent R269 million on such companies. Altogether, 929 Limpopo government employees were company directors.[6]

In December 2010, the Western Cape government passed a law effectively banning civil servants and their immediate family from doing business with the province. According to the law, a civil servant's direct or indirect family cannot own more than a 5 per cent share in a company doing business with the provincial government.

But civil servants are not the only ones with business interests outside their primary occupation. In the Western Cape in 2011, 30 per cent of MPLs held directorships; in the Northern Cape 45 per cent; in the Free State 58 per cent; in the Eastern Cape 26 per cent; in KwaZulu-Natal 27 per cent; in Gauteng 30 per cent; in Limpopo 39 per cent; and in North West 26 per cent.[7]

For what it's worth, the average number of MPLs holding directorships in all provinces except KwaZulu-Natal declined between 2008 and 2012. On 17 March 2010, the *Mercury* reported how MPLs in KwaZulu-Natal only rushed to complete their paperwork to declare their interests when legislature officials warned them about the newspaper sniffing around.

In Parliament and the national executive, however, more members held directorships in 2010 than in 2008: 47 per cent of ministers and their deputies and 59 per cent of MPs. (The number in the executive increases to 76 per cent when you consider directorships, shares, and shares and directorships.)

As we can see, the problem of conflicts of interest did not arise overnight. It has been there for years, growing like a cancer in the heart of the public service. In late 2012, PSC director-general Professor Richard Levin told Parliament that more than 30 per cent of senior managers had potential conflicts of interest in their private businesses. In February 2013, he reported to Parliament that in the latest round of disclosures of outside interests, there had been an improvement, with 74 per cent of public servants complying with disclosure requirements.

However, there were some departments where the disclosure rate was zero and 37 per cent of directors-general had failed to disclose.

A whole new class has stealthily emerged, one that is distinct from but, like a first cousin, related to the more common and easily spotted 'tenderpreneur'.

While the tenderpreneur operates ostensibly outside of government, using ANC contracts to chisel out large segments of state business for BEE front companies, the new class – which Lindiwe Sisulu had set her sights on in early 2013 – cuts out the middleman and simply does business with itself. Nice work if you can get it. The sums involved may not match the juicy slices that the tenderpreneur procures, but they are sufficiently significant to have elicited an interesting reaction: one senior manager in the public service reportedly said, 'Most of the 1.5 million public servants are at the lower level and they don't earn enough to sustain their lives. They have no choice but to explore other opportunities.'[8]

As I said at the time, 'Thus doth a new class speak to defend its interests.'[9]

It's a powerful interest group, too. Many of the most active members of ANC branches overlap with this class. A typical delegate to the ANC national conference in Mangaung in December 2012 would have come from this class.

This may explain why the government has been so leisurely in its various attempts to clamp down on such corrupt practices in recent years. That, and the weakness of the ministers of public service who have held office since Geraldine Fraser-Moleketi was banished after Polokwane to the wilderness – in her case to the bureaucratic quagmire of the UN family – along with a multitude of other Mbekites.

Her successors do not even merit naming, so pathetic has their impact on their portfolio been. While Fraser-Moleketi was prone to Mbekitis – that is to say, a tendency to over-elaborate and to set so many targets that her staff were running constantly from pillar to post – she was tough, hard-working and dedicated to reform.

The current incumbent, Lindiwe Sisulu, is the same, keeping her core staff busy most weekends. The press reported that Zuma's decision to move her from defence to public service in mid-2012 was a demotion designed to clip her wings.

Indeed, defence is a seminal portfolio, traditionally in the 'Class A' category of cabinet positions. And it is also true that Sisulu was fond – perhaps a little too fond – of some of the trappings of the military (she should never, for example, have worn a naval uniform on occasions during her three-year tenure in defence).

While she may not be an instinctively progressive person on some social issues – more of a Christian democrat than a social democrat, perhaps – Sisulu is nonetheless a democrat, and one who understands the importance of accountable governance to economic development – a relationship that, deploying the

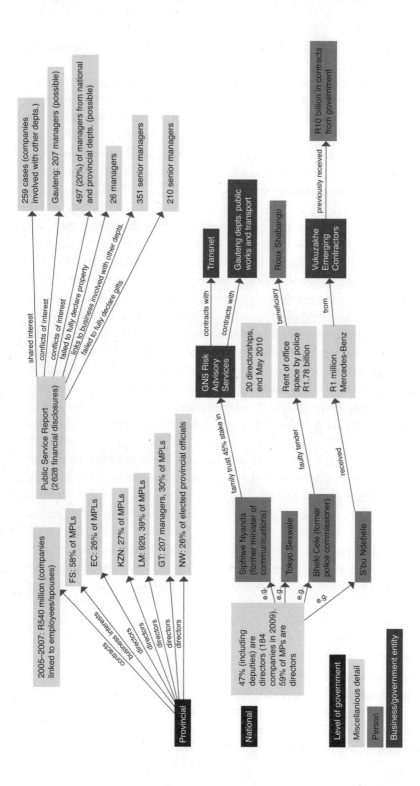

Figure 12.1: Illustrative graphic showing conflicts of interest and the interplay between business and politics in South Africa

language of the 'capable state', the National Development Plan asserts is a pivotal precondition to progress.

Beyond some platitudinous statements of the bleeding obvious, the ANC's Mangaung resolutions offered nothing new on the governance and corruption front. Not surprising, one might think, given the composition of the conference delegation.

Instead, it is government that is pressing ahead. The proposal to outlaw public servants from entering into contracts with companies they own or control has safely made it from Levin and the PSC, through cabinet (in December 2012) and into Sisulu's in-tray.

To succeed in the broader effort of containing corruption within the public service, Sisulu is going to have to find allies in other sectors, namely civil society and the private sector, organisations such as COSATU's Corruption Watch, and international initiatives such the Construction Sector Transparency Initiative, which, given the scale of public investment in infrastructure and the justified concerns about graft, South Africa should join without much further ado.

There is a grotesque Bermuda triangle entrenched at the heart of South Africa's body politic: public servants, in all three spheres of government; their companies and the donations that are made to the ANC; and the competing factions within the ANC and the patronage proclivities that they tend to provoke.

Another tough, uncompromising ANC woman leader journeyed into these murky, choppy and dangerous waters not so long ago: although Nkosazana Dlamini-Zuma's report is focused on ANC election-list irregularities in the 2011 municipal elections, it is likely to form the basis for a fresh effort to understand the overlapping interests involved, in order to then try to rebuild integrity in the public service by untangling them.[10]

For the overlapping individuals it is all win, win, win. For the rest of us, especially those who need an efficient, honest public service to deliver much-needed welfare services and infrastructural development, it is all lose, lose, lose.

Sisulu is walking into the Bermuda triangle now. To avoid disappearing without a trace, she will likely need more than her ANC aristocracy and her robust political shell, but if anyone can do it, she can.

Zuma Inc.

The pivot: Jacob Zuma

What of the leadership? What, specifically, of the president?

Jacob Zuma surely must be the first to disclose his own and his dependants' financial interests, assets and liabilities. After all, he was acting president in July 2000 and proclaimed the Executive Ethics Code himself.[11]

That's wishful thinking. After he became president in 2009, Zuma failed to declare his interests within the appointed sixty days. DA MP Athol Trollip took the new president to the Public Protector for his non-compliance. In April 2010, the Public Protector, Advocate Thuli Madonsela, found Zuma had breached section 5.2 of the Executive Ethics Code, but that his delay in declaring suggested 'tardiness on his part ... rather than any improper motives'.[12]

However, Madonsela also noted 'a systemic pattern of non-compliance with the time-lines and some of the requirements stipulated in the Code by a substantial number of Members of the Executive, which should be attended to by the Cabinet urgently'.[13]

In the year that she reviewed, 'only 40 out of 64 Members of the National Executive, which amounts to 62.5 per cent, complied with the stipulated 60 day period of grace [to declare their interests]. At least one of the declaration forms was not even dated.'[14]

In December 2010, Zuma refused to release to the opposition the names of the twenty-four who failed to comply, as he did 'not believe that any purpose would be served in releasing the names now as the mistake was bona fide'.[15] However, a month later, he did an about-turn and released the names, saying that the 'executive has nothing to hide on this matter'.[16]

Zuma was not the first president since 1994 to submit his declarations late. Madonsela noted in her report that 'at least one of the previous Presidents consistently disclosed after six months of assumption of office'.[17] She also pointed out that Parliament or cabinet had not acted on recommendations in several reports by her predecessors relating to the declaration of interests: 'It further emerged that officials charged with the management of the Register, were not aware of previous recommendations of the Public Protector and that neither Cabinet nor Parliament appeared to have acted on those recommendations.'[18]

Among them was Deputy President Zuma in 2003. Other non-compliers included:

- Zola Skweyiya, then minister of social development and now ambassador in London, for not properly disclosing an interest-free loan granted to his wife in December 2003;
- Phumzile Mlambo-Ngcuka, then deputy president, who took an unofficial visit to the United Arab Emirates in December 2005;
- several ministers and deputy ministers who didn't comply with the Executive Ethics Code in and around 2006; and
- Geraldine Fraser-Moleketi, who accepted a gift.

Madonsela also highlighted certain 'anomalies and uncertainties' in the Executive Members' Ethics Act and Code that needed to be amended. These included:

- who should the president approach regarding the acceptance of gifts with a value of more than R1 000, and should the cabinet secretary give permission or just advise the president;
- to whom should the Public Protector report when he or she investigates the ethical conduct of the president; and
- how can the administrative functions of the interest register be strengthened?

Madonsela also pointed to the fact that neither the Act nor the Code makes provision for the consequences of violating the Code. She suggested applying the same sanctions that are currently brought against MPs found guilty of violating the Parliamentary Code of Conduct. Zuma, as president, is not an MP. Regarding Zuma's own 'guilt', Madonsela asked cabinet to 'deal with the matter appropriately'.

Cabinet did nothing. On 6 May 2010, then cabinet spokesperson Themba Maseko said he was 'not aware of any plan or intention [from the president] to apologise' for his transgression.[19]

Trollip reacted: 'In contravening the Executive Ethics Code, and refusing to account for this behaviour, President Zuma acted as if he was above the law. Cabinet's decision has confirmed that, in the eyes of the Executive, he is.'[20]

Just two months later, on 27 July 2010, cabinet adopted interim sanctions as a measure against members who breached the Ethics Code: a fine not exceeding the value of thirty days' salary and a reduction of salary or allowances for a period not exceeding fifteen days.[21]

Neither Zuma nor any of the previous offenders were sanctioned retrospectively.

In reply to a parliamentary question about whether the cabinet's decision to apply interim sanctions on those found guilty of violating the Executive Ethics Code would apply retrospectively, Jeff Radebe, the minister of justice and constitutional development, said: 'Cabinet has been advised that there is no basis in law for the application of sanctions, which are not prescribed (or authorised) under the said Act or the Code, to members who are subject to the Act and the Code.'[22]

The Presidency *has* since set out to strengthen the administration and an amendment bill to the Act was published for comment in the Government Gazette in May 2011. The new amendments give the Speaker in Parliament the power to receive a report by the Public Protector if an investigation is done into the president's ethical conduct.

But the dust around Zuma and especially his family's business interests has not settled.

On 16 August 2011, Speaker Max Sisulu denied Trollip's request to debate the Zuma family's business dealings in Parliament, saying such a debate doesn't 'deal with a matter for which the government can be held responsible'.[23]

The DA then promised to submit a private members' bill to amend the Act 'to reduce the scope for presidential power abuse'.[24] One such amendment would be to have the Public Protector adjudicate whether the president has complied with the Ethics Code. Another would make the president's interests register more accessible to the public.

The Presidency accused Trollip and the DA of 'political grandstanding', implying 'malicious intent' in calling for a debate on the issue.[25] Zuma's office repeated its stance that the president 'does not hold any personal or financial interest in any business or corporate entity. He makes his annual declaration of interests to the Secretary of Cabinet ... The financial interest that the President must disclose relates directly to the President as well as to spouses and dependents. He does not declare assets or interests that belong to persons other than spouses and dependants ... The properties and assets of adult children are likewise not declared and are not the President's responsibility or liability.'[26]

Regardless, several members of Zuma's extended family are involved in some kind of business. And certain members have been increasingly active in business since he was elected ANC president in Polokwane. Eighty-three and counting of the 134 companies some fifteen Zuma family members are involved with were created after December 2007. It is worth looking at some of the most prominent cases of benefits accruing to those closely associated with our president.

The sugar mom: Sizani Dlamini-Dubazana

From 2005 until he became president, Zuma stayed at a house in Forest Town, Johannesburg, owned by Sizani Dlamini-Dubazana. Dlamini-Dubazana has shot up the ranks of the ANC, from being the PA to Zuma's former wife Nkosazana Dlamini-Zuma in the 1990s to ANC regional secretary in Johannesburg in 2007. After Polokwane, she was elected to the ANC KwaZulu-Natal provincial executive committee.

In 2010, it was reported that state institutions had 'bent over backwards' to help Dlamini-Dubazana secure financial stability.[27] 'When creditors closed in on her, government bought her KwaZulu-Natal game farm for land restitution. She stands to receive R6 million – more than double what she paid for it – though neighbours were told there was no budget to buy their farms. Dlamini-Dubazana denies preferential treatment.'[28]

In 2008, the IFP had been angered when Dlamini-Dubazana was appointed to the board of Ithala Bank, a provincial government lending entity and the same bank from which she secured more than R8 million in loans. According to a statement by the IFP's Lionel Mtshali, 'Dlamini-Dubazana was appointed to the board of Ithala last year after she had taken out two loans from this taxpayer-funded institution in 2005 and 2006 and subsequently defaulted on repayments.'[29]

The nephew: Khulubuse Zuma

Zuma's nephew, Khulubuse Zuma, hails from KwaMashu, just north of Durban. A former taxi operator, he has shot to business prominence since his uncle took power, with the help of close Zuma confidants like the Gupta family and Zuma's personal lawyer, Michael Hulley.

Companies and Intellectual Property Commission (CIPC) records show Khulubuse has held thirty-two directorships, four of which he has resigned.[30] Twenty of these have been subsequent to Zuma taking power at the ANC conference in December 2007. He took up his most recent directorship at Meziblox on 10 February 2011. Hulley serves on the same board.

To date, Khulubuse's most prominent business dealing has been as a director for Aurora Empowerment Systems, which he joined on 18 June 2009, together with Nelson Mandela's grandson Zondwa Zoyisile Gadaffi Mandela.[31]

In October 2009, Aurora took over the management of bankrupt Pamodzi Gold's Grootvlei mine on the East Rand and Orkney mine in the North West. Pamodzi's liquidators also named Aurora as the preferred bidder to buy the mines for R605 million, this despite the fact that Aurora had never owned a mine before. If all went according to plan, Aurora would take over ownership in early 2010.

The prospects looked good; it seemed the two sons of prominent political families had struck gold, literally. Aurora had a Malaysian investor, AM Equity, lined up to invest around R1 billion and Hulley was at hand to assist.

But only a few months after Aurora took over, the mines had run up incredible debts to Eskom, Rand Water and a security company. Even worse, Aurora had failed to pay workers, who then held a strike in April 2010. Police had to be called in to calm tempers.

AM Equity then pulled out of the deal. Aurora told long-running investigative journalism programme *Carte Blanche* they lost the Malaysian investor because the mine wasn't making any profits. *Carte Blanche*, however, learnt that AM Equity pulled out over concern about Aurora's lack of transparency and financial management.[32]

Thulani Ngubane, another director at Aurora, told *Carte Blanche* Grootvlei mine wasn't making a profit and Aurora was losing R30 million a month. But the South African trade union Solidarity questioned this, saying the mine was producing gold in the first few months of Aurora taking over. Workers and managers at Grootvlei told *Carte Blanche* and various newspapers how trucks loaded with gold ore were being sent to 'mystery destinations' on the East Rand.

What occurred between October 2009, when Aurora took over the mines, and 26 May 2011, when the company was finally dropped as a preferred bidder, can only be described as gross financial and operational mismanagement, which included the issuing of unauthorised cheques, the channelling of funds intended for JSE-listed company Labat Africa Ltd into Aurora's bank account and the illegal dumping of acid water, and which ultimately led to the opening of a high court inquiry in 2011.

Inevitably, during Aurora's tumultuous tenure at Grootvlei and Orkney, Khulubuse's lavish lifestyle came under scrutiny. It was revealed that he owns nineteen cars, one of which, a R2.5 million Mercedes-Benz, he drove to then national police commissioner Bheki Cele's wedding, in 2010. As reports trickled in about his expensive taste in whisky and French champagne, Khulubuse held a cocktail party at a Durban hotel in 2010 for a whopping R70 000. He later infamously told *Business Times*: 'I don't drink at all. I only have one kidney. I've donated the other kidney ... I'm a very generous person.'[33]

In the same period, about 5 300 workers were left unpaid. An estimated 42 000 dependants suddenly faced poverty, as workers sold off all their possessions to stay afloat. There were suicide attempts; successes too.

The Department of Labour intervened in August 2010 when it found Aurora had contravened section 32 of the Basic Conditions of Employment Act of 1997, and ordered the company to pay the wages and bonuses of 1 278 workers at Grootvlei mine. Aurora paid R2 million to the department when the compliance order was made an order of the court.

The department paid 987 workers with R1 986 237.55 for their work from December 2010 to the end of March 2011, while 291 workers failed to report to the department's offices. About 493 new claims from workers also surfaced, totalling about R1 730 741 of unpaid wages.

The department followed the same process at the Orkney mine, ordering Aurora to pay R3.95 million in outstanding wages.

The Commercial Crime Unit: Klerksdorp Directorate for Priority Crime also launched an investigation into Aurora's alleged misconduct when it became apparent the company had made monthly deductions from employees' pay in respect of personal income tax, union membership fees and pension fund contributions, which were not paid over to the relevant parties (i.e. SARS, the unions and the pension fund). Both SARS and the Financial Services Board were involved in the investigation.[34]

Aurora also faced serious opposition from within the ruling alliance, despite its directors' political connections. COSATU and the National Union of Mineworkers were especially critical. In April 2011, COSATU general secretary Zwelinzima Vavi said: 'Bosses still have a life of luxury ... selling the mining equipment and searching for companies to sell the mine to, while workers of Aurora in both Grootvlei and Orkney struggle.'[35]

NUM was further angered by Khulubuse's generous donation of R1 million to the ANC in KwaZulu-Natal: 'Over two thousand workers remain unpaid at Aurora's Orkney mine for a period of over two years whilst the fat cat itself moves around with expensive luxurious vehicles and has a nerve to donate some of his excesses whilst poor workers starve at his mines.'[36] NUM demanded that the ANC give the money back or to the workers, but the ANC refused.

Somewhat outrageously, in June 2011 Susan Shabangu, the minister of mineral resources, expressed sympathy in Parliament for Aurora's directors, describing the Grootvlei-Orkney mine deal as painful, 'in the sense that not only workers have gone for years without income but also that our aspirant black entrepreneurs are misled into buying DARK HOLES so that they must fail.'[37]

Aurora was liquidated in late 2011 and the Grootvlei and Orkney mines have subsequently been sold.

The Africa expansion

Khulubuse's ambition is not limited to South Africa. He has told newspapers in the past that his taxi business helps fund his trips around Africa in search of new business opportunities, one of which is an oil deal. His business partner? None other than Michael Hulley, Jacob Zuma's lawyer.

In June 2010, President Joseph Kabila of the Democratic Republic of the Congo awarded oil rights in exploration blocks 1 and 2 of Lake Albert in the east of the country to Foxwhelp and Caprikat, two companies with no known track record in the oil industry and both publicly owned (fronted) by Khulubuse. In fact, both were only registered in March 2010. According to a media investigation conducted at the time, 'ownership of the two companies is shrouded in mystery. Mossack Fonseca, a law firm with headquarters in Panama, registered both in the British Virgin Islands, a haven of corporate anonymity, and acts as their letterbox. Marc Bonnant, a Swiss advocate specialising in "business crime defence", fronts as the two companies' sole director.'[38]

Khulubuse, with no prior experience in the oil business, signed on behalf of Caprikat and Hulley on behalf of Foxwhelp in the agreement with the DRC government.

Tokyo Sexwale and Mark Willcox, the chief executive of their investment vehicle, Mvelaphanda Holdings, denied having any stake in Khulubuse's companies, but Willcox admitted that he and Mvelaphanda were giving Khulubuse 'strategic advice'.[39] Interestingly, in 2008, Sexwale's New African Global Energy tried to get a stake in oil exploration along the same lake. Although he resigned from all his directorships when he took up a cabinet post in 2009, his family still benefited from Mvelaphanda through two trusts that were set up.

Platform, a London-based watchdog, described in a May 2010 report how

South African companies had increased their interest in oil exploration along Lake Albert in eastern DRC.[40] The South African state-owned PetroSA had looked for opportunities in the area, and the South Africa Congo Oil Company, linked to the Maponya and Moseneke families, has oil interest along the lake in neighbouring Uganda. In addition, Kabila's government had previously allocated the oil rights to blocks 1 and 2 to Irish oil major Tullow Oil and South Africa's Divine Inspiration Group (which has links to Tiego Moseneke's Encha Group and other Mbekites), but reneged, saying the deals were not favourable to the DRC.

However, Platform's report read: 'President Kabila is said to be reluctant to go through with the second deal [with Divine Inspiration] if it risks alienating new President Jacob Zuma.'[41] Scarcely a month later the rights were awarded to Khulubuse's Caprikat and Foxwhelp.

'President Zuma's ethical conundrum is that his relative looks set to benefit from the kind of commercial smash-and-grab that is swayed as much by diplomatic consideration as financial sense,' the *Mail & Guardian* wrote in July 2010.[42]

According to the 2008 *Africa Yearbook*, South Africa has offered patrol boats in the past to help protect South African oil companies' interests.[43] Zuma himself has been intensely involved as a peacemaker in the Great Lakes region since the 1990s, and in 2001 he appointed his national security advisor, Welile Nhlapo, as South Africa's Special Representative to the Great Lakes Region.

Less than two months after Khulubuse secured the DRC oil rights, his Impinda Group sealed a major deal with South Korean multinational Daewoo Shipbuilding and Marine Engineering. The day before the deal was signed, President Zuma met with Nam Sang-Tae, Daewoo's chief executive, in Pretoria.[44]

The deal entailed Daewoo acquiring 49 per cent of Impinda's transport arm, which could be expanded to a commodities, oil and gas shipper. Quite rightly, the media concluded: 'The latest meeting suggests that as president he is lending himself to advance the business interests of a relative.'[45]

The son and the Guptas

Jacob Zuma's son Duduzane is set to become one of the country's youngest black billionaires. From computer programmer to soon-to-be billionaire businessman: not bad for a man who has described himself in the past as a 'circumstantial businessperson', because business wasn't something he had 'looked to get involved in'.[46]

Regardless of his intent or lack thereof, Duduzane's career change is undeniably the result of his widely talked-about relationship with the Gupta family.

The Guptas came to South Africa from India in 1993 and started Sahara Computers in 1994. Besides Sahara, the family has interests in mining (one of which is a stake in Tokyo Sexwale's Mvelaphanda Resources Ltd), publishing, real estate and tourism. The three brothers, Atul, Rajesh and Ajay, run the show.

Duduzane serves on the board of Sahara Holdings and has stayed at the Gupta compound in upmarket Saxonwold, Johannesburg. His sister Duduzile has also been linked to the Sahara board.[47] Tellingly, in a March 2011 interview with Talk Radio 702 presenter John Robbie, Duduzane said of his relationship with the Guptas: 'I look at them as my family members and I'm their family member.'[48]

Duduzane has none other than his 'old man' to thank for his lucrative relationship with the Gupta family. Zuma introduced the Guptas to his son, who soon after joined Sahara Computers, in 2001.[49]

'Yeah, I've been introduced to so many people. It happens. I'm still being introduced to people, so I don't see what's wrong with that,' Duduzane defensively told Robbie of that introduction.[50] But it is what followed that introduction – myriad business dealings with Gupta family members – that has raised eyebrows.

The Guptas' power had tongues wagging in the Alliance all the way back in 2010, with some party members questioning the relationship between the Gupta and Zuma families. Reports appeared in newspapers of ministers being summoned to the Gupta family's Houghton compound if they had to discuss an issue with a certain department.

In June 2011, then cabinet spokesperson Jimmy Manyi scolded reporters, saying they were on 'an irresponsible fishing expedition' when they dared to ask ministers if they had visited the Gupta compound.[51]

It seems Duduzane's business involvement has only increased since his father became president of the ANC in 2007: CIPC records show Duduzane has taken up directorship of sixteen companies since his old man was elected. Before 2007, he was director of only three. Currently, he is an active director on eleven of the nineteen companies created since 2005.

Duduzane describes reports about his sudden rise in business as 'ridiculous … It makes it seem like I just jumped straight out of a taxi into a sports car. I've been working my butt off for years. I get up every morning and I put in the work.'[52] He alleges that he has been flooded with people offering him business deals, but has turned a lot of them down. 'At some point I don't want to prostitute myself to the market,' he told Robbie.[53]

Mabengela Investments is likely to be Duduzane's most noteworthy and lucrative business deal so far. He and Rajesh Gupta are the two sole directors of the company, owning less than 50 per cent and between 20 and 26 per cent of the company respectively.[54] It's Mabengela's involvement with the Ayigobi Consortium that may make Duduzane a billion rand richer.

The consortium is set to gain 26 per cent of ArcelorMittal South Africa's operating assets, along with an employee stock ownership plan, in an empowerment deal to the value of more than R9 billion. Mabengela has a 12.5 per cent stake in Ayigobi. Oakbay Investments, the company that handles all of the Guptas' non-IT investments, and Zico, a private investment company chaired by business-man Sandile Zungu, each own a 6.25 per cent stake in Ayigobi. Meanwhile, Gugu Mtshali, Kgalema Motlanthe's long-time girlfriend, owns about 4.2 per cent; and Jagdish Parekh, who runs Oakbay Investments on behalf of the Guptas, owns 25 per cent. A 25 per cent stake is still to be allocated to a broad-based youth and women component.[55]

The Gupta family and their associates seem to be the brains behind the ArcelorMittal deal; it came about when the Guptas, doing initial consulting work for ArcelorMittal, suggested such an empowerment deal, one that Nonkululeko 'Nku' Nyembezi-Heita, ArcelorMittal's chief executive, described as 'strategic' as opposed to broad-based. This type of deal, she said, is useful 'where a company needs assistance in a particular area'.[56]

Whatever 'strategic' may mean, Ayigobi is packed with deal-makers with high-ranking political connections who can surely be of 'assistance' to ArcelorMittal in the future.

The Guptas brought in Duduzane and Zungu. Zungu serves on the president's Broad-Based Black Economic Empowerment Advisory Council and is a non-executive director of the Jacob G Zuma RDP Education Trust. When Mbeki sacked Zuma as deputy president, Zungu stuck by him, rallying behind business-people to support Zuma. Now Zungu leads the Ayigobi Consortium.

Duduzane's considerably larger stake than Zungu's and the Guptas' Oakbay in Ayigobi has raised questions about what Duduzane could possibly have contrib-uted to the consortium aside from being the president's son.

Zungu has defended Duduzane's participation in Ayigobi, telling *Moneyweb* not to crucify Duduzane for being the son of the president, 'as if he must be condemned to being poor … From what I understand, Duduzane wants to be a seasoned businessperson and he wants to ply his trade, creating wealth for the country, for himself in the mining sector and beyond. This may well be just the start – let's look at him in 20 years' time and let's see whether this transac-tion called Ayigobi will have been the fillip that catapulted him to better growth trajectory – I would like to hope so.'[57]

Duduzane himself told Robbie: 'If we have done anything wrong, grab us by the collars to a court of law or whatever the case may be, but if we've done nothing wrong, leave us the hell alone. We want to carry on doing our business.'[58]

The uranium deal
Another deal involving Duduzane that grabbed attention was the acquisition of Canadian-listed Uranium One's South African subsidiary. The company's main asset is the Dominion mine in North West outside Klerksdorp. It is worth R280 million but has been under care and maintenance since 2008.

Oakbay Resources and Energy took over the funding, care and maintenance of the mine in December 2009, and took operational control of the project in January 2010. Negotiations with Uranium One had started in December 2008, with a sale agreement being reached in May 2009. The transaction was closed, including payment of the full purchase price, on 14 April 2010.[59]

On the same day, Duduzane and Atul Gupta took over directorship of the company, which was renamed from Uranium One to Shiva Uranium. A third directorship is held by iThemba Governance and Statutory Solutions, a company run by a group of white women from Monument Park in Pretoria.[60]

Shiva is owned by Oakbay Resources and Energy, which is 85 per cent owned by Oakbay Investments and 15 per cent owned by Mr Agarwal of Action Group, based in India.

According to a Shiva statement, Oakbay Resources and Energy secured part of the funding for the project from the state-owned Industrial Development Corporation. The balance came from shareholders.[61]

At the time of the deal, journalists noted: 'Duduzane's participation [in Shiva] leaves the president exposed to the accusation that his reported intervention last month [April] to extend the tenure of controversial Public Investment Corporation (PIC) boss Brian Molefe was designed to smooth negotiations towards a large PIC investment in the project.'[62]

The Presidency denied this, calling Duduzane 'a businessman in his own right', who did not need his father's help.[63] But it did confirm that President Zuma met with Nhlanhla Nene, deputy minister of finance and chair of PIC, around the same time.

Around 26 per cent of Shiva Uranium is owned by a black consortium that includes Duduzane's Mabengela Investments, 'MK war veterans' and its women's group (an apparent reference to the ANC's MK Military Veterans' Association),[64] a local community trust and an employee trust.

In March 2011, the MK Military Veterans' Association chairperson, Kebby Maphatsoe, accused the media and some ANC leaders of peddling lies about the Gupta family. Denying that he was in the Guptas' pocket, he said: 'I have never received a single cent from them [the Guptas]. What I know is that they gave us [the veterans' association] shares worth R250-million through the Shiva Uranium Mine, for the benefit of our members.'[65]

The son-in-law: Lonwabo Sambudla

As I noted in *Anatomy of South Africa*, the 1 000-strong attendance list from Brett Kebble's funeral paints 'a vivid sample of the eclectic mix that constitutes South Africa's contemporary establishment'.

The guest list from Zuma's daughter Duduzile's wedding to businessman

Lonwabo Sambudla in April 2011 paints a similar picture, but this time in post-Polokwane hues. The only thing that sparkled more than the bride's Swarovski crystal-encrusted dress and R1.5 million diamond necklace (on loan from Browns Jewellers) was the 'star'-studded audience.

Among the 650 guests were Durban businessman Vivian Reddy, 'sushi king' Kenny Kunene, Duduzile's cousin Khulubuse Zuma and the bride's twin brother Duduzane.

Few would have noticed the presence of two civil servants linked to the groom. Even fewer would have known that they both worked for government departments where a decision was pending to award a R1 billion government contract.

The contract, for the building of new office space, eventually went to the Billion Group, a company with close ties to Zuma's new son-in-law.[66]

The two officials, who had been entertained by Kunene in East London the day before the wedding, were Eugene Motati, then special advisor to minister of public works Gwen Mahlangu-Nkabinde, and Thuli Manzini, chief director of strategic management at the Department of Public Service and Administration.

The Department of Public Service and Administration had advertised in February 2011 for developers with available land in the Pretoria area to submit bids for its new home. According to reports, the Billion Group had been listed in fourth place during the evaluation of the bids and Motati was said to have been the driving force behind the Billion Group. Motati admitted that he knew Sisa Ngebulana, chief executive of Billion, and was quickly suspended in August 2011.[67]

Sources said that Sambudla had been personally involved in lobbying for the contract, and Ngebulana confirmed to the newspaper that Sambudla had done consulting work on property brokering for him. In April, the two had also attended a meeting with then acting director-general of public works, Sam Vukela. Ngebulana denied, however, that Sambudla was part of the tender.[68]

In addition, in August 2011 it emerged that Public Works had been paying the Billion Group in a separate rent agreement R3.6 million a month for the rental of a building standing empty in Pretoria's CBD. The R612 million property deal to upgrade the justice department's offices was awarded to Phomella Property Investments, a subsidiary of the Billion Group, but renovations to the Salu Building dragged on, preventing the department from taking occupation. From January 2010 until the projected occupation date in November 2011, it is estimated that government paid up to R84 million rental for the empty building.[69]

'In addition to the dodgy lease,' reported the Mail & Guardian, 'we now have evidence suggesting that the Billion Group channelled a payment of R1-million to the ANC or its senior office bearers.'[70] The newspaper had apparently obtained cellphone and bank records, and had been informed that Ngebulana had told colleagues he had made a donation to the ANC. The payment was simply recorded as 'fees' in a Billion Group bank statement. Mathews Phosa, ANC treasurer-general, denied that the party had received any payment from Ngebulana.[71]

However, Ngebulana himself told the newspaper: 'As a successful black business person, you are under pressure when asked for donations and things. You need to give or there is a lot of jealousy.'[72]

In April 2010, contemplating the Zuma offspring's dodgy deals, Ferial Haffajee, editor-in-chief at the *City Press*, wrote: '[D]eals like these give BEE a terrible name and squeeze black businesses out of the economy because increasingly you have to be politically connected to gain any empowerment traction ... Young business-people are the icons of the global economy today, but Zondwa, Duduzane and Duduzile, all twenty-somethings, are not entrepreneurs in their own right ... these politically connected young businesspeople are rented by foreigners and local businesspeople who know how cronyist systems work.'[73]

Even back then she warned: 'We have chosen the path of elite accumulation that is a cul-de-sac of everything the ANC says it stands for.'[74]

Business and government

As we filed out of the media box at the end of the 2013 State of the Nation address in February, my wiry-in-mind-and-body *Mail & Guardian* editor, Nic Dawes, and I chatted casually, swapping notes on our respective impressions of the president's latest offering. As we turned the corner at the back of the upper deck of the National Assembly, we were joined first by the ambassadors and high commissioners who were exiting from their box, which is high above the Speaker's podium to the left, and then by those exiting the section of the public gallery with the best view: the president's box.

The first genie out of that particular box was Atul Gupta. To my slight surprise, Gupta, probably twice Dawes's weight, warmly clasped the diminutive though dogged editor around his shoulders. I say slightly surprised, because the *Mail & Guardian* has regularly turned its steadfast investigative journalistic attention to the Guptas. Even more surprising was the editor's cheery greeting back: 'Hello, Atul! Nice to see you.'

As we moved along, I turned to Dawes with a no-doubt quizzical look. With a wry smile and an apologetic shrug he said, 'I have a love–hate relationship with those Guptas.'

One senses that for both men, it's a game. For Dawes, a deadly serious one, but one, nonetheless, in which there is room for humour as well as earnest intent. For people like the Guptas, one might say it's just a game, that everyone is a potential pawn in their pursuit of wealth and power.

What an impact the Indian moguls Atul, Rajesh and Ajay Gupta have had: their relationship with Zuma and his family, first and foremost; the funding of the

New Age newspaper; and, as I finalised this chapter, Guptagate – the controversy over their use of Air Force Base Waterkloof for the arrival from India of a private jet full of guests for the wedding of their niece Vega Gupta. Guptagate looked like a sort of tipping point – not necessarily in the overall fight against corruption and cronyism, but against the specific intrusion of the Gupta family into South African political life.

Clearly, Zuma was sufficiently annoyed by it to unleash his favoured hound dog, Gwede Mantashe, who on May Day heavily criticised the use of Waterkloof for private use. Others rapidly jumped onto the bandwagon, the muzzle apparently now removed from the mouths of people like Blade Nzimande and Jeremy Cronin, who for so long had remained silent – publicly, at least – about the rich and powerful friends of the man they helped put into the Union Buildings.

When Jeff Radebe – the minister for justice and constitutional development and Zuma's 'cleaner' (think Harvey Keitel in his cameo role as the cleaner, or fixer, in Tarantino's *Pulp Fiction*) – announced the results of the inter-ministerial committee inquiry into Guptagate on 19 May 2013, it provoked widespread amusement in the media and in the commentariat. The problem, said Radebe, was the phenomenon of 'name-dropping', which ought to become a criminal offence.

The report scapegoated two or three poor officials, to protect Zuma and his ministers, despite the fact that one of the officials – the government's head of protocol at the Department of International Relations and Cooperation, Ambassador Bruce Koloane – had given evidence that he was under pressure 'from Number One' (i.e. Zuma himself).

The implication – which seems to have escaped Radebe – is that even without such an overt instruction, officials felt compelled to grant a substantial favour to a private family of foreigners, which is actually worse than if an individual minister or head of state had given a specific instruction. Clearly, the Guptas have bought themselves a huge dose of influence within the Zuma administration: the rebuttable presumption is that in addition to funding the government-aligned *New Age* newspaper and its cosy sponsorships of government media events, the wealthy Indian family and its businesses have also donated substantial sums both to Zuma and to the ANC.

The Guptas' presence in the president's box at the State of the Nation address should not be underestimated. The box itself only seats around fifty people. So it's a prize ticket. Cyril Ramaphosa was in the front row, just over the rail from the diplomats, who queued patiently to chat with him before Zuma arrived to deliver his typically long and poorly delivered address. Patrice Motsepe was nearby.

The toxic – intoxicating – mix of political power and wealth has troubled many democracies. That it should exist in South Africa is no great surprise. Zuma's own troubles with money – someone who knew him in exile told me money was 'always Jacob's number one problem … not women, money. His finances were always chaotic' – are emblematic. The Shaik trial revealed the grimy details of Zuma's relationship with one wealthy individual who was only too happy to exploit JZ's vulnerabilities and extensive financial needs.

It is not yet known whether the Guptas have enriched Zuma directly or whether they have focused their funding on the ANC and ANC pet projects. All of it will, in due course, come out in the wash.

But before plunging into the abyss of despair, it's important to try to segment the money and politics game. It's not all one and the same. And, while there are plenty of charlatans around who are all too ready to take advantage of the congealing embrace of money and politics, so too are there plenty of good guys, on both sides, who, like Pityana and my friend on the flight to Lagos, are deeply angry by what is happening and are struggling for the necessary footholds to stem the tide.

Consider that terribly interesting and influential businessman Iqbal Survé, for example. I first met him several years ago on a University of Cambridge Sustainability Leadership programme. He was a fellow contributor. He told a spellbinding story about his foray into the fishing industry on the West Coast of South Africa.

Corruption was pivotal to the industry: there was a tidy little win-win-win, whereby the fishing companies would bribe the government inspectors so that they could overfish their quotas. The fishermen got more work as a result, and more pay, so they were happy. The fishing companies got more fish to sell. The inspectors topped up their modest public salaries. Only the fish suffered. And, of course, the sustainability of the fishing industry; such long-term notions of business resilience are the first casualties of corruption.

Survé turned up for his first meeting of the company's management committee. The car park was lined with Ferraris, Lamborghinis and Audi 4×4s. He told them that they had to stop, that the corruption had to stop. The managers smiled wryly and nodded. But nothing changed. So Survé sacked them all. When he turned up for the next manco, the car park was empty. Suddenly, he had no managers and, therefore, no business. He nearly went under, but he managed to rebuild.

It's a story that captures the essence of what Malini Naidoo, an advocate who works for the National Prosecuting Authority, suggests to me. Her view is that corruption is now endemic. And she's not alone. The evidence, some of it alluded to in this chapter, points to a political establishment whose conflicts of interest are now so ingrained that graft is inevitable.

But Naidoo's analysis is different from others in that she insists it is a chronic national condition, as opposed to one that came with and was promoted by a small group of devious hustlers in and around the ruling party. 'It's across the board, at every single level, in every place where we – as a society – transact. It's become *the way in which we work*. As a society.'

This is a terribly sobering point, coming from someone who is well acquainted with the grit of corruption and its various contours. She speaks of the stop at the roadblock and the backhander to the cop; of the shyster amateur landlord, who rents out a slice of his backyard so that someone can put up a shack; of the respectable Cape Town attorney who is actually, to all intents and purposes, an international money launderer.

A different source tells me a story about a city attorney, one highly regarded in his field, who fronts the operations of the gangsters who run the city's strip joints and exploit the Russian and Asian women lured to our shores. Many of these women end up in arranged marriages with wealthy farmers, who pay fat fees to the club owners, who then pay the immigration attorney his slice to make it all pass legal muster.

Naidoo has plenty to say about the legal system and its strengths and weaknesses, but her core point is that 'we need to change the culture and mindset … which must start with school programmes and needs the buy-in of a wide range of social stakeholders, such as the unions, so that, for example, whistleblowers are protected and not intimidated or assassinated'. And she does not shy away from accepting that the state prosecutorial authorities have been far from perfect.

Naidoo's thesis coheres with that of Ginwala's – that the business–politics interface that the ANC inherited in 1994 was also rotten to the core. Business's relationship with government, and especially the ruling party, was likely to follow the well-trodden road of the apartheid era, unless something significant and powerful was done to knock it onto a different course.

Ginwala acknowledged that the ANC were naive in failing to take adequate protective measures to secure their own cadres from the temptations presented by unscrupulous businessmen.

So, where does this leave us? In a book about the changing face of power in South Africa, what influence does money have over politics? How great a hold does corruption have on political power and what does it mean for the future as well as the present?

These are demanding questions. I will return to them in my Conclusion, which bleakly outlines the nature of the crisis that South Africa faces. Corruption is clearly a major part of it. It is undeniably one of the ways in which you 'get on' in modern South Africa. One of the ways – perhaps one of the most efficient ways – up the ladder is with political connections. Cronyism, with the opportunities for business that it presents, is without a doubt a key feature of 'transformation', as is the respectable, but no less controversial, BEE route that was Mbeki's preferred stimulant for the rapid development of a black middle class.

If hard-working entrepreneurs, like my friend on the flight to Lagos, are to be outflanked by the tenderpreneurs – who uplift themselves not through hard work but by graft of a very different sort, using their contacts in government or doing business with themselves from positions of influence within government – then there are grave dangers ahead. What is the incentive to work hard at school, to get to university or learn a trade, if you can 'get rich quick' through other faster, yet nefarious, means?

The fact that the roots of this culture of corruption are deep and historical lets no one off the hook, even if it helps to explain the genealogy of the problem. Rather, everyone needs to acknowledge their own role and responsibility, especially in the corporate sector. Corporate leaders need to take a stand against corruption, doing everything within their power at every level of their businesses, to banish corrupt practices. They must also engage constructively with public servants, from a position of knowledge and empathy about the trials and tribulations of government and the profound and complex challenges of transforming the country.

But primary leadership and standard-setting has to come from the political leadership – in government and in the ANC. If the ANC, and the DA for that matter, continue to refuse to declare transparently where they get their major donations from, then the culture of corruption will never be defeated. Dodgy donors will always assume, rightly, that they can peddle influence by secretly buying influence with their secret donations. And if the government does not get serious about public servants who use their positions in government to feather their own nests, then the idea of the 'capable state' that is so pivotal to the National Development Plan can be quickly cast aside as unattainable.

From the arms deal onwards, the sad reality is that South Africa has got itself into a terrible quagmire. That deal set the wrong standard; we failed the litmus test for our country's new democracy. It meant that when Zuma's case came up, it could be elided and a 'political solution' found. And once you do that, once you permit someone who should be facing corruption charges to make their way into the highest public office, then you are bound to face inescapable negative consequences. Those responsible should hold their heads in shame, because more than anything they have ensured that the congealing, toxic embrace between money and politics will only get worse, not better, with untold, disastrous consequences for the future of South Africa.

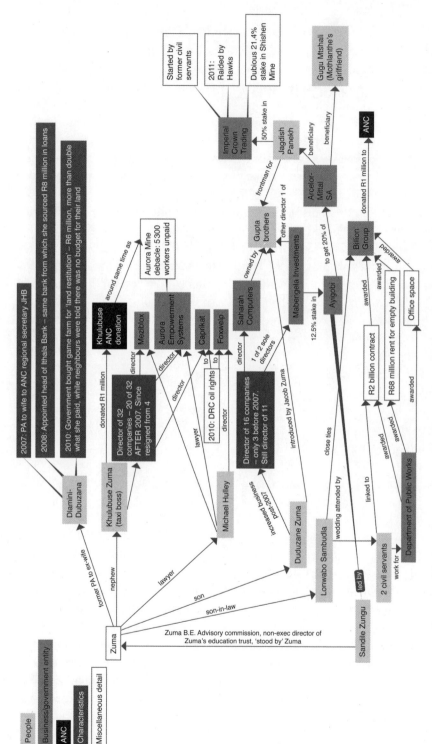

Figure 12.2: Who is Zuma Inc? Illustrative graphic depicting Zuma family and associates' business interests

13

The corporate boardrooms

South Africa's wealthy elite and the stewards of capital

Some time ago now, Nedbank released a series of television advertisements featuring strange South Africans cavorting in foreign climes, frolicking in steaming natural baths and generally enjoying some kind of fabulous wealthy living. Through the course of the ads, a cosmopolitan-accented man voices over pastoral scenes: 'Who are these people? They seem so content. They have business interests in Helsinki. You see them driving with the top down on Tuesday afternoons. Where do they go? They look so well rested. Even while jogging in their deep green suburbs ... Nedbank. Approach life differently.'

For the overwhelming majority of South Africans, Finland will forever be out of reach, as will 'driving with the top down' and 'deep green' suburban life. However, if there was some truth to the representation, it was, and is, that there is a significantly wealthy, globalised elite in the country, as well as many South Africans who spend far too much money on cars and polo shirts in an attempt to project proximity to 'these people'.

While banking with Nedbank and/or having 'business interests in Helsinki' may not correlate with who constitutes this very wealthy class, the questions posed in the adverts – Who are these people? Where do they go? And, perhaps more pertinent, where do they come from? – do demand answers.

A society's 'establishment' is largely defined by its members' access to, and ability to use, power. Money is one proxy for power, and no discussion of the modern South African establishment would be complete without an analysis of big business and its representatives in the boardroom.

Lest we forget, South Africa is not a poor country. In 2012, the IMF estimated the GDP of the country to be US$391 billion; or, to put it another way, the South African economy was the 29th largest in the world. Taking into account purchasing power parity (PPP), a measure that mitigates disparities in exchange rates to equalise the value of a basket of goods across global economies, the IMF's estimate of South Africa's GDP rises to US$579 billion, coinciding with the 25th-largest economy in the world.[1] South Africa's GDP per capita (PPP) at US$11 302 came in 80th among the 182 countries for which the IMF had credible data in 2012, on the whole comparing generally well with its BRICS colleagues Russia (53rd – US$17 617), Brazil (77th – US$12 038), China (90th – US$9 146) and India (127th – US$3 851).

But, as any South African citizen knows and as any interloper in our midst will attest, the country's wealth is extremely unequally distributed. South Africa's Gini coefficient[2] – a statistical tool that measures the distribution of income or wealth in any given country – is among the worst in the world. The most recently available World Bank measure of inequality in South Africa (2009) gives us a whopping Gini score of 63.1, ranking us the most unequal society in the world for which the bank had measurable data (Honduras at 57 and Colombia at 55.9 complete the dubious medals table).[3]

What this means in practice is that, in South Africa, the wealthiest 20 per cent of income earners together account for over two-thirds, or 68 per cent, of the national wage, while the poorest 20 per cent earn only 2.7 per cent. The unequal social distribution of income is further underscored by the fact that the highest 10 per cent of earners accrue 51.69 per cent, over half, of the national income.[4] If one assumes that South Africa is not a strange international outlier, and that human capability is distributed evenly across the entirety of society, the accrual of over half the national wage to a tenth of the population is a national scandal.

Haroon Bhorat and Charlene van der Westhuizen of UCT's Development Policy Research Unit (DPRU) estimate that distribution of income within the South African economy has worsened during the post-apartheid period. Analysis by the DPRU demonstrates that the Gini coefficient worsened by approximately 5 per cent through the years 1995–2005, despite a concurrent 5 per cent fall in absolute poverty. These figures would be catastrophically worse were it not for the rolling out of social grants and other forms of transfers to the poor (housing, electricity and water subsidies; public health facilities; etc.), which Bhorat and Van der Westhuizen estimate contribute in the region of 55 per cent of income for the poorest 20 per cent of South African households.[5]

When one overlays the distribution of income with GDP and GDP per capita data, one begins to realise just how wealthy the wealthy in South Africa are: South Africa's GDP per capita, at PPP, was estimated by the IMF to be US\$11 302 in 2012. However, we already know that this is a blunt measurement in light of the unequal distribution of income in the economy. By isolating 51.69 per cent of the total South African GDP (PPP) in 2012 at US\$299 099, we have a proxy for the earnings of the top 10 per cent of income earners. In turn, if we divide this value by the number of people corresponding with 10 per cent of the national population (10 per cent of the census estimate for 2012 is 5 177 056) we can roughly approximate the income for the highest-earning South Africans at US\$57 773 per annum (around R500 000).

This puts the wealthiest 10 per cent of South Africans into the ballpark of the oil-rich Scandinavian welfare state of Norway (2012 GDP per capita US\$55 264) and the opulent city state of Singapore (US\$60 883). One can only assume that

– pace the 99 per cent rallying call of the Occupy movement – the distribution of income among the wealthiest 10 per cent of income earners in South Africa is also uneven, with an even smaller moneyed elite accruing a significant share of the pie.

What remains clear is that, while South Africa might be relatively rich in global terms, our wealthy are über-rich and rival the wealthiest people in the world.

But the mid-Atlantic-accented voice still calls: 'Who are these people?' Unfortunately, publicly available data in this regard is a little patchy, but we are able to piece together some semblance of the broad swathe of wealth in South African society. Unsurprisingly, given the entrenched legacies of apartheid, there is a strong correlation between relative wealth, race and class.

In introducing a debate on national reconciliation in 1998, Thabo Mbeki stated in a speech to Parliament that

> the material conditions in our society ... have divided our country into two nations, the one black and the other white ... One of these nations is white, relatively prosperous, regardless of gender or geographic dispersal. It has ready access to a developed economic, physical, educational, communication and other infrastructure. This enables it to argue that, except for the persistence of gender discrimination against women, all members of this nation have the possibility to exercise their right to equal opportunity, the development opportunities to which the Constitution of '93 committed our country. The second and larger nation of South Africa is black and poor, with the worst affected being women in the rural areas, the black rural population in general and the disabled. This nation lives under conditions of a grossly underdeveloped economic, physical, educational, communication and other infrastructure. It has virtually no possibility to exercise what in reality amounts to a theoretical right to equal opportunity, with that right being equal within this black nation only to the extent that it is equally incapable of realisation. This reality of two nations, underwritten by the perpetuation of the racial, gender and spatial disparities born of a very long period of colonial and apartheid white minority domination, constitutes the material base which reinforces the notion that, indeed, we are not one nation, but two nations.[6]

Mbeki's commentary lacked nuance both then and as an applicable critique on contemporary South Africa. We are, no doubt, a country broadly divided into two economic clusters – a critique Mbeki later extended into his 'two nations' thesis – one premised on formal economic activities and the other mired in the challenges of the informal economy. While the poor and informal economic agents remain overwhelmingly black, with a significant bias towards the African demographic (as well as female-headed households, and spatially rural), the upper echelons of the formal economy are increasingly de-racialised.

This latter observation is not inconsistent with disproportionate wealth accruing to white South Africans – a persistent characteristic of formal economic activity in the country – but a meander through the business-class lounges of South Africa's airports, the gleaming malls of Sandton and the classrooms of our most prestigious schools will demonstrate a significant change in the composition of our economic elite.

The National Planning Commission's Diagnostic Overview states: 'The majority of low income households are black. In 1995, median per capita expenditure amongst Africans was R333 a month compared to whites at R3 443 a month. In 2008, median expenditure per capita for Africans was R454 a month compared to whites at R5 668 a month.'[7] The database maintained by the South African Institute of Race Relations (SAIRR) demonstrates that between 1996 and 2011, average annual household income for Africans increased by 210 per cent, 277 per cent for coloureds and 212 per cent for Indians, while white households enjoyed a 235 per cent increase over the same period. In 2011, average white household income was more than five times that of Africans, almost three times that of coloureds and approximately one and a half times that of Indians, underscoring the legacy of apartheid and a racialised hierarchy of class interests.[8] Moreover, net private ownership of assets per capita – that is, assets owned minus private debt – for whites was more than ten times that of African individuals, almost seven times that of coloureds and approximately two and a half times that of Indian South Africans.[9]

However, there has been some significant change among the ranks of wealthier South Africans, with the proportion of Africans in the top 20 per cent of income earners increasing from 39 per cent in 1995 to 48 per cent in 2009, corresponding to a 23 per cent real increase in the number of Africans represented in the top quintile of earners across the fourteen years surveyed.[10]

Black ownership of the Johannesburg Stock Exchange has also risen, predominantly among Africans. If one considers individual South African ownership – that is, ownership of shares excluding state and foreign bodies – between 2000 and 2010, one sees that African holdings increased from 16 to 25.8 per cent and Indian holdings from 2.5 to 3.7 per cent, while coloured holdings decreased from 5 to 4.5 per cent. Interestingly, white ownership of the JSE declined from 76.5 to 66 per cent over the same period, perhaps as a consequence of successful BEE interventions to diversify ownership of capital.[11] Black ownership of shares in JSE retirement funds also increased from 23 per cent in 1995 to 37 per cent in 2010, while white ownership declined from 77 to 63 per cent.[12]

The JSE and the boardroom

The transformation of South Africa from a sleepy backwater populated largely by an agrarian peasantry (white and black) into a globalised, industrialised economy was powered by the development of a significant extractive industry driven by the discovery of diamonds in Kimberley in 1867 and gold on the Witwatersrand in 1886. A stock exchange was developed in the nascent city of Johannesburg in 1887 to raise investment and distribute share capital associated with the mining sector; the JSE has functioned in one form or another ever since.

As of January 2013, the market capitalisation of the JSE was estimated by the World Federation of Exchanges (WFE) to be US$896 billion, making it the 19th most valued exchange in the world. The value of capital traded on the JSE is disproportionately important in the context of the South African economy: in 2011, the WFE valued the JSE at 187 per cent of South African GDP, compared to 104 per cent in the US (NASDAQ + NYSE relative to US GDP), 69.1 per cent for the London Stock Exchange and, with respect to developing economies, 48.8 per cent in Brazil, 82.5 per cent in Russia (RTS + MICEX) and 108 per cent in India (NSEI + BombaySE).[13]

The composition of the JSE has tracked the ebb and flow of formal economic activity. From its inception, the bourse was dominated by companies representing the mining and minerals sector, characterised by the left as the 'Mining and Energy Complex' (MEC).

The increasing costs of gold mining, accruing as a consequence of the exploitation of lower-grade ore and deeply embedded ore, forced increasing consolidation and the creation of leviathan-like conglomerated mining houses through the course of the twentieth century. By the 1930s, the overwhelming majority of mining interests in the country were exploited by six mining conglomerates. As Roger Southall has documented, the consequences of apartheid – isolation from global capital markets, foreign capital flight and the state's intervention in the economy through parastatals – forced further consolidation of interests on the JSE and, by 1990, 'just three conglomerates – Anglo-American, Sanlam and Old Mutual – controlled a massive 75 per cent of the total capitalisation on the JSE'.[14] However, the advent of democracy and the subsequent reintegration of the South African economy into the global capitalist system saw a number of large corporations seize the opportunity to list abroad – ostensibly to access international capital flows – and the systemic unbundling of non-core assets at home.

As Southall has observed, these concurrent effects radically realigned the composition of the JSE:

> The non-core assets of the conglomerates were largely taken up by institutional investors, both public (for instance, the Public Investment Corporation)

and private (pension funds etc), as well as by new BEE players who were, in turn, backed by the banks and institutional investors themselves. Unbundling had a major effect upon the big three and the other major conglomerates. Most notably, whereas in 1992, Anglo controlled some eighty-six JSE-listed companies, by 2008 it had become a more focused miner with holdings of more than 25 per cent in only four: AngloGold Ashanti, Anglo Platinum, Kumba and Tongaat Hulett. A proportion of the unbundled assets were taken up by the renewed inflow of international capital. Against this, from 1997, amidst a general relaxation of exchange controls, the government granted permission for some of the largest South African companies – notably, Billiton, South African Breweries, Anglo-American, Old Mutual and Liberty Life – to move their primary listings from the JSE to London, thereby facilitating their evolution into major multinationals. In short, the transition provided the conditions under which significant domestic funds could exit South Africa and foreign capital could come in, this facilitated by Johannesburg's moving to become the continent's primary financial centre for global capital.[15]

Table 13.1: Percentage of total JSE market capitalisation by industry[16]

	2002	Jan 2013	Real growth (%)
Minerals and energy			
General and other mining	21.2	17.8	152.8
Platinum and precious metals	9.3	3.6	16.0
Gold mining	11.2	2.7	−28.5
Integrated oil and gas	4.8	3.1	93.2
Subtotal	*46.5*	*27.1*	*75.6*
Finance			
Banks	9.2	8.5	176.8
Life insurance	6.2	4.3	107.9
Investment services	4.3	3.7	161.8
Other finance	1.8	0.8	35.9
Subtotal	*21.4*	*17.3*	*142.3*
Industry and construction	2.9	3.3	243.8
Tobacco		11.7	
Brewers	4.1	9.4	587.4
Telecoms and IT	3.2	9.8	811.9
Retail	8.8	10.6	259.1
Real estate	2.7	2.4	175.1
Other	10.2	8.3	144.4
Total market capitalisation (2012 R billions)	2 680.5	8 069.2	201.0

An analysis of the composition of the JSE through 2002–13 (see Table 13.1) demonstrates further changes to the bourse: through the course of the decade, the JSE has seen a marked decline in the share of minerals and energy (from 46.5 per cent in 2002 to 27.1 per cent in 2013), coinciding with a general downturn in the South African mining and minerals sector. Platinum and gold mining, in particular, have seen their shares plunge quite dramatically – from 9.3 to 3.6 per cent and from 11.2 to 2.7 per cent respectively.

Data released by the Chamber of Mines of South Africa in 2011 underscores a sector with mounting challenges. The data is particularly worrying: the number of miners working in the gold sector more than halved from around 490 000 in 1990 to 145 000 in 2011 as a consequence of increasing mechanisation and the mothballing of marginal mines. Across the mining industry as a whole, the sector shed a third of its workforce over the same period, with employment falling from 780 000 to 513 000. An important area of growth for the sector has been in platinum, which added about 100 000 jobs in the two decades to reach approximately 195 000.[17]

South Africa contains 80 per cent of the world's known platinum reserves, but the economic downturn, poor demand for vehicles (catalytic converters are a major end product for platinum) and spiralling production costs linked to electricity and wage agreements are eroding the viability of much of the industry. According to data made available by the South African Department of Mineral Resources, the platinum industry closed nine mines and shed 3 332 jobs in the second half of 2012. The Chamber of Mines claimed that 50 per cent of South African platinum mines and 37 per cent of gold mines were loss-making in 2012,[18] and it is likely that Anglo American Platinum (Amplats) and Gold Fields' stated intentions to restructure their South African assets represent the beginning of a new realignment in the South African mining and minerals sector.

While the share of the MEC on the JSE has shrunk demonstrably, one should not confuse this with a sector in free fall. On the contrary, the value of companies listed under the minerals and energy sector of the JSE grew by approximately 76 per cent in real terms across the decade under review. The average was dragged down by the disappointing performance of platinum and precious metals, which showed real growth of only 16 per cent, and gold mining, which actually shrunk in real terms by an alarming 28 per cent.[19]

Over the same period, the share of finance has also declined, from 21.4 per cent in 2002 to 17.3 per cent in 2013. Again, the smaller share of companies associated with the finance sector is somewhat misleading and, in real terms, financial services on the JSE have flourished over the past decade, with overall real growth of approximately 140 per cent. Interestingly, Remgro, which was subject to restructuring in 2008 and 2009, was classified as an investment service in the 2002 JSE data, but under 'diversified industrials' (which falls under the industry and construction category) in 2013. Remgro continues to hold significant interests in investment services, in tandem with a range of other investments. If the company is added back to 'investment services' in 2013, we see the share of that sector increase by 0.4 percentage points (from 4.3 to 4.7 per cent) instead of decrease by 0.6 (to 3.7 per cent). Correspondingly, this reclassification sees a decline of 0.6 percentage points in the share of industry and construction (from 2.9 to 2.3 per cent) rather than a rise of 0.4 (to 3.3 per cent).

So it is not declining absolute performance that bedevils the mining and energy and finance sectors, but rather astounding growth in other sectors – indeed, the JSE as a whole grew by approximately 200 per cent between 2002 and 2013.

But who are these winners, and why have they exploded this past decade?

The most obvious contender is tobacco. British American Tobacco (BAT), the sole occupant of this category, listed on the JSE in 2008.[20] With a market capitalisation of approximately R950 billion, it is the largest listed company on the JSE and commands an impressive 11.7 per cent of it. What the fact that a tobacco company leads our corporate big leagues says about the world is interesting in and of itself, but the importance of this listing in the here and now of our analysis is that it, perhaps more than any other individual change, places the shifting-sector shares in context. After all, there were no tobacco companies listed in 2002.

Another sector demonstrating significant growth is telecommunications and IT, which grew from 3.2 per cent of the bourse in 2002 to 9.8 per cent in 2013. The sector accrued growth of approximately 800 per cent in real terms, driven largely by the 850 per cent growth of the MTN Group, the sector's largest company, and Naspers' phenomenal leap ahead of 1900 per cent. The period also saw the listing of Vodacom, the third-largest telecommunications company (market capitalisation of R181 billion), and Telkom, the fifth largest in the sector (market capitalisation of R8.5 billion). MTN and Vodacom have become significant players in the African telecommunications market, with MTN going further abroad as an operator in Afghanistan, Iran and Montenegro. Similarly, Naspers has driven an expansionary agenda during the past decade, establishing operations across Africa and throughout eastern Europe, Russia, Brazil, China and Thailand.

The share of brewers has also more than doubled, from 4.1 per cent in 2002 to 9.4 per cent in 2013, with the two largest companies, SABMiller and Distell, realising real growth of 600 and 350 per cent respectively. The retail sector grew from 8.8 to 10.6 per cent through the decade under review, with Shoprite, Mr Price and Truworths growing in real terms by 1400, 1300 and 800 per cent respectively. Concurrently, the share of real estate shrunk slightly, from 2.7 to 2.4 per cent.

Despite these changes, an analysis of the top twenty firms listed on the JSE continues to illustrate a high concentration of economic clout among a small number of firms (see Table 13.2).

Table 13.2: Market capitalisation of top 20 firms listed on the JSE[21]

Company	Market capitalisation (R billions)	Percentage of total JSE market capitalisation
British American Tobacco PLC	943.3	11.7
SABMiller PLC	737.8	9.1
BHP Billiton PLC	656.5	8.1
Compagnie Financière Richemont SA	388.4	4.8
Anglo American PLC	380.0	4.7
Total % market capitalisation top 5	*3 105.9*	*38.4*
MTN Group Ltd	326.8	4.0
Sasol Ltd	246.2	3.1
Naspers Ltd	233.9	2.9
Kumba Iron Ore Ltd	192.7	2.4
Standard Bank Group Ltd	192.0	2.4
Total % market capitalisation top 10	*4 297.6*	*53.2*
FirstRand Ltd	190.2	2.4
Vodacom Group Ltd	181.1	2.2
Old Mutual PLC	131.8	1.6
Absa Group Ltd	123.0	1.5
Anglo American Platinum Ltd	119.5	1.5
Impala Platinum Holdings Ltd	103.6	1.3
Sanlam Ltd	97.5	1.2
Shoprite Holdings Ltd	96.7	1.2
AngloGold Ashanti Ltd	96.6	1.2
Nedbank Group Ltd	96.4	1.2
Total % market capitalisation top 20	*5 534.0*	*68.5*
Others (385)	2 546.0	31.5
Total	8 080.0	100.0

Taken together, the top twenty firms on the bourse accounted for over two-thirds, or 68.5 per cent, of the JSE. A closer examination of the data reveals an even greater accumulation of capital at the top of the market, with the top ten companies accounting for 53.2 per cent of total capitalisation, and the top five – British American Tobacco, SABMiller, BHP Billiton, Richemont and Anglo American – alone representing over a third of the market's value, at 38.4 per cent of total capitalisation.

Growth in new sectors and the relative decline of the MEC have diluted the dominating effect of mining houses on the bourse. However, of the top twenty firms listed, seven – a plurality – are the children of the mega-mining conglomerates that dominated the JSE through the course of the twentieth century, with financial-services firms constituting the second-largest group of six companies.

The boardroom

Overseeing the orchestration of South African capital are the boards of companies. In the post-apartheid period, corporate governance has been radically overhauled, most significantly through the three King Committee reports on corporate governance that outline the duties and responsibilities of companies and of the directors and managers that oversee them, and the rights of shareholders with regards to the companies in which they hold interests.

The first King report, published in 1994, constituted the first institutionalised code of practice for corporate governance in South Africa. The report recommended standards of practice and disclosure for boards, the appointment of executive and non-executive directors and their duties, and auditing standards. The code was binding for all companies listed on the JSE and parastatals.

King II, published in 2002, introduced sustainability measures and clarified internal and external auditing processes and accounting standards. It broadened the application of the code to encompass anybody performing a function or exercising power under the Constitution or any national legislation. Importantly, this included provincial and municipal governments, but excluded the courts.

The third and final King report, King III of 2009, is applicable to all entities: public, private and not-for-profit, but provisions are not equally binding on the latter.[22] King III clarifies aspects of reporting mechanisms for sustainability and financial management, and includes provisions to ensure shareholder approval of directors' remuneration and evaluation of board members.

Although none of the King reports constitute legislation, companies listed on the JSE are required to adhere to the code in its entirety, and extensive provisions have been integrated into *inter alia* the Companies Act, the Public Access to Information Act, the Municipal Financial Management Act and the Public Financial Management Act.

King III requires that the board of any given company should comprise a balance of executive and non-executive directors, while maintaining a majority of non-executive directors. Further, the code requires that the majority of non-executive directors should preferably be independent to ensure freedom from conflicts of interest. The code moreover stipulates that at least one-third of non-executive directors should be rotated on an annual basis. King II defined the critical components of any given board against the following conditions, for which only minor changes were introduced through King III:

Executive director – an individual that is involved in the day-to-day management and/or is in full-time salaried employment of the company and/or any of its subsidiaries.

Non-executive director – an individual not involved in the day-to-day management and not a full-time salaried employee of the company or of its subsidiaries. An individual in the full-time employment of the holding company or its subsidiaries, other than the company concerned, would also be considered to be a non-executive director unless such individual by his/her conduct or executive authority could be construed to be directing the day-to-day management of the company and its subsidiaries.

Independent non-executive director – a non-executive director who:

i. is not a representative of a shareowner who has the ability to control or significantly influence management;

ii. has not been employed by the company or the group of which it currently forms part, in any executive capacity for the preceding three financial years;

iii. is not a member of the immediate family of an individual who is, or has been in any of the past three financial years, employed by the company or the group in an executive capacity;

iv. is not a professional advisor to the company or the group, other than in a director capacity;

v. is not a significant supplier to, or customer of, the company or group;

vi. does not have a direct or indirect interest in the company (including any parent or subsidiary in a consolidated group with the company), which is either material to the director or to the company. A holding of 5 per cent or more is considered material; and

vii. does not receive remuneration contingent upon the performance of the company.[23]

King III also requires the annual election of an independent, non-executive director as chairperson of the board, although the CEO can assume this role after three years of employment. If the chairman is not independent or is executive, a 'lead' independent non-executive director should be appointed. The role of the chairperson and lead independent director was primarily envisaged to provide leadership and advice to the board in situations in which the CEO or chairperson could have a conflict of interest. In this scenario, the independent non-executive director is mandated to lead the board to ensure the integrity of the process with a strong emphasis on upholding standards of corporate governance and rigour.

The code further specifies that in appointing a board the company should ensure that all directors have relevant skills, knowledge, experience and access to resources to conduct the business of the board. Concurrently, when appointing board members the code requires that the board consider whether its size, diversity and demographics make it effective. Diversity is considered holistically and includes maintaining an appropriate mix of academic qualifications, technical expertise, experience, nationality, age, race and gender.[24]

In practice, the board of directors is further disaggregated into standing committees that oversee the operational aspects of company business. Typically, standing committees include audit, a critical and mandated component of any listed company; remuneration, which oversees salary, bonus and incentive schemes, and communicates these to shareholders; and a nominations committee, which is tasked with identifying and recruiting suitable candidates for the role of non-executive director and, when necessary, overseeing the recruitment of senior operational directors and facilitating succession planning. Companies are not limited to this list and in practice many other committees may be constituted, including investment committees to oversee the management of asset portfolios and weigh the risks and feasibility of potential investments (typical of the financial-services industry), sustainability, health and safety, and social or ethics committees.

Board members do not come cheaply. Each year, PricewaterhouseCoopers (PWC) undertakes a thorough survey of companies listed on the JSE through an analysis of company annual reports. This survey includes an analysis of fees and the composition of company boards. Their analyses demonstrate that in 2011 the median total guaranteed package – the amount at which half of the sample is above, and half below – paid to executive directors of firms in the top forty of the JSE was R3.75 million, with further incentivised compensation (bonuses) of R3 million. For executive directors of the top forty companies in the 75th percentile – at which three-quarters of the sample is below – pay rises to an astronomical R6.4 million as a guaranteed package, with additional bonus pay of R6.7 million.[25]

At the comparatively poorer end of the boardroom, the median fee for chairpersons in 2012 was R394 000, while at the 75th percentile fees received were R941 000. Deputy chairpersons, somewhat counter-intuitively, receive more, as this position is often filled by an executive director or an individual undertaking a similar role to that of a lead independent non-executive director. In 2012, the median fee for a deputy chairperson for a company listed on the JSE was R748 000, with those at the 75th percentile raking in R1.2 million for their time. Lead independent directors at the median received fees of R811 000 in 2012 and R1.275 million at the 75th percentile. The median fee for a non-executive director was R276 000 and R511 000 at the 75th percentile.[26] While some of these numbers may not appear too ridiculously large (although relative to a wage earner, they would dwarf a blue-collar worker's annual pay), it is worth remembering that many non-executive directors maintain primary employment elsewhere and sit on more than one board, and as a consequence receive fees from more than one company.

So who are these people?

Table 13.3 breaks down data from a desktop study undertaken for this book regarding the composition of the South African boardroom as it applies to the top twenty publicly traded South African companies with primary listings on the JSE by market capitalisation[27] as at close of business on 29 January 2013.[28] The list excludes five of the largest companies on the JSE, as they maintain their primary

Table 13.3: Composition of the South African boardroom

Director demographic	Total	% of total	% of South African
African female	36	13.1	15.5
African male	49	17.9	21.0
African subtotal	*85*	*31.0*	*36.5*
Coloured female	3	1.1	1.3
Coloured male	10	3.6	4.3
Coloured subtotal	*13*	*4.7*	*5.6*
Indian female	4	1.5	1.7
Indian male	9	3.3	3.9
Indian subtotal	*13*	*4.8*	*5.6*
Black female	43	15.7	18.5
Black male	68	24.8	29.1
Black subtotal	*111*	*40.5*	*47.6*
White female	9	3.3	3.9
White male	113	41.2	48.5
White subtotal	*122*	*44.5*	*52.4*
Female subtotal	52	19.0	22.3
Male subtotal	181	66.0	77.7
South African subtotal	*233*	*85.0*	*100.0*
Foreign female	3	1.1	
Foreign male	38	13.9	
Foreign subtotal	*41*	*15.0*	
Total female	55	20.1	
Total male	219	79.9	
Total	274	100.0	

listings abroad (four in London – BHP Billiton PLC, SABMiller PLC, Anglo American PLC and Old Mutual PLC – and one in Switzerland – Compagnie Financière Richemont). To include these five in an analysis of boardroom composition would skew the analysis significantly: while they account for over 40 per cent of market capitalisation on the bourse, their more cosmopolitan orientation means that a full 80 per cent (68) of their directors are foreign nationals, with the balance made up of South Africans (17).

The top twenty companies with primary listings on the JSE represent approximately 34 per cent of total JSE market capitalisation. This analysis also draws on data for the bourse as a whole compiled by PWC in the course of their annual surveys of directors of publicly listed companies. On the whole, the smaller sample of larger companies (top twenty) performs significantly better with regard to demographic representivity than a wider survey of all 373 companies listed on the exchange. This is likely a consequence of their attractiveness to employees in general (a nice embellishment on the résumé), as well as their buying power. Due to the comparatively large size of the companies in the sample, and the scrutiny accruing to them as a consequence, it may be that they feel a greater need to promote inclusivity in the boardroom and comply with government targets.

Scratching the surface of the data, we can see a marked bias towards men in the boardroom. Of the entire sample of 274 directors, only 55, or 20 per cent, are female. If one removes the three foreign female directors, the female share of South African domiciled directors rises slightly to 22 per cent. PWC's analysis of the bourse as a whole paints a more egregiously patriarchal picture, with only 16.6 per cent of directorships having accrued to women by January 2013, although this was a significant improvement compared to 2012, when only 12.5 per cent of boardroom positions were held by female directors.[29]

While this is not great news for a country that prides itself on promoting gender equity, with 16.6 per cent female representation in the boardroom the JSE outperforms the London-based FTSE, where just 12.5 per cent of board members are women.[30] The high-water mark for gender representation on corporate boards is in Scandinavia, where Finland (24.5 per cent), Sweden (27.3 per cent) and Norway (40.1 per cent) have blazed the way for gender equity.[31]

Unsurprising given the legacy of apartheid, white South African directors outnumber their black compatriots 122 (52 per cent) to 111 (48 per cent), with white men occupying 48.5 per cent of all positions held by South Africans. This is consistent with the data collected by PWC, who observed black representation on the bourse as a whole at 42.5 per cent, with a year-on-year increase of 6.9 per cent.

As Table 13.4 shows, of the total pool of black South African directors, 77 per cent are African, with the balance shared between coloured and Indian directors (roughly 12 per cent each). At 39 per cent, the proportion of black female directors to all black directors compares favourably to the 22 per cent of South African female directors.

Table 13.4: Black South African directors by demographic

Directors	Total	% of total black directors
African female	36	32.4
African male	49	44.1
African subtotal	*85*	*76.5*
Coloured female	3	2.7
Coloured male	10	9.0
Coloured subtotal	*13*	*11.7*
Indian female	4	3.6
Indian male	9	8.1
Indian subtotal	*13*	*11.7*
Black female	43	38.7
Black male	68	61.3
Black subtotal	*111*	*100.0*

With direct black ownership of shares on the JSE standing at just 34.5 per cent in 2010,[32] and given the legislated barriers to corporate entry accruing to black South Africans under apartheid, at first glance the 48 per cent of positions on the top twenty boards of South African–based firms accruing to black South Africans sounds pretty good compared to many other indicators as we approach the third decade of democracy. Unfortunately, a closer look at the data paints a more disheartening picture from a representivity perspective.

Table 13.5: South African directors by designation (*n* = 233)

	Executive	% Exec	Non-exec	% Non-exec
Black	12	24	99	54
White	37	76	85	46
Male	42	86	139	76
Female	7	14	45	24
Total	49	100	184	100

Table 13.5 disaggregates directorships held by South African directors for the top twenty South African companies on the JSE by race and gender against the type of directorship held. As one can immediately grasp, the majority of black and female directors are appointed to non-executive positions, which underscores the broader continuity of disproportionate white male control and influence in

corporate South Africa. Of the total number of executive positions held by South Africans in the sample, only 24 per cent are held by black South Africans, while the majority – 76 per cent – are held by whites. Concurrently, the 12 black executive directors in the sample constitute only 11 per cent of total directorships held by black South Africans on the bourse.[33] It follows that the overwhelming majority – 89 per cent – of black South African directors hold non-executive positions, to such an extent that they slightly outnumber their white compatriots in our study, with 54 and 46 per cent of non-executive appointments respectively.

Executive directors – those that occupy roles such as CEO or CFO – enjoy considerably more decision-making power within any given business than do non-executive directors. They are employed by the company to occupy a specific operational role and are invested in the day-to-day decision-making processes. Non-executives, on the other hand, often have other 'day jobs' (non-executive board members may spend most of their time in executive positions at other companies, for example) and may only sit in on a handful of board meetings each year. This is not to suggest that non-executives are minor figures; indeed, they are integral to the strategic direction of the company and it is no small commitment to accept an invitation onto a public company's board. However, the data suggests that barriers remain for black entry into executive positions, and that black directors are less influential in corporate South Africa than a superficial analysis suggests.

This view is further buttressed by research undertaken by Mandhlaenkosi Nyirenda in fulfilment of his MBA at the University of Pretoria, in which he analysed the composition of audit committees by race for a random selection of companies listed on the JSE. The audit committee is arguably the most important component of any given boardroom, with legally prescribed duties and responsibilities. Service on the audit committee is prestigious and critical from an operational perspective. Nyirenda's analysis of 287 directors serving on audit committees demonstrated that in 2006 the average company surveyed had less than one black director on the committee, and an average of more than two white directors.[34]

Matthew Andrews, a South African professor at Harvard's John F. Kennedy School of Government, explored BEE in South Africa in a 2008 working paper. He makes the observation that board members in contemporary South Africa are overwhelmingly sourced from what one might call the 'tried and tested' fields of accountancy, law and business administration. Chartered accountants (CAs), in particular, make a strong showing in the upper economic echelons, typically occupying upwards of 30 per cent of directorship positions among the JSE's top 300 companies.[35] The top twenty companies I looked at are no exception:

Table 13.6: Directors (top 20 SA-listed companies) by qualification

Qualification	Number of directors	Percentage of directors ($n = 274$)
CA	90	32.8
MBA	43	15.7
Law	31	11.3
Engineering	30	10.9
Executive management programmes	23	8.4
Accounting	10	3.6

As Table 13.6 shows, CAs dominate, occupying around one-third of directorship positions, broadly in line with the data collated by Andrews in 2008. Chapter 14 interrogates some of the reasons for the attractiveness of CAs in the corporate job market, as well as demographic trends for the profession. Lawyers, engineers and MBA graduates also make a strong showing, as do those who have completed executive management programmes at business schools. Taken together, those with a qualification of some kind in the field of accountancy comprise roughly 36 per cent of directorships.

The legacy of Bantu education continues to influence the composition of the pipeline of the commercial professions. As of December 2012, for example, 80 per cent of CAs were white.[36] Andrews argues that the small number of black professionals and the pressures on firms to meet BEE targets have created a disproportionate demand for black professionals (especially CAs). High demand translates into higher salaries and, importantly, greater opportunities for job hopping, as firms compete with one another to attract black talent. But if this is the case, then why are so few of them in executive positions?

The answer, perhaps, lies in the way in which companies source directors. Consider the fact that firms generally prefer to promote executive directors from within their own ranks – indeed, Andrews states that 'internal promotion is an understandable and established approach to finding new managers', as it is easier both to screen potential candidates once they are involved with the company and to ensure that they are able to function within a specific business environment and organisational culture.[37]

In contrast, non-executive directors may be sourced for their broader business or industry expertise rather than operational acumen, and are valued for their exposure to environments beyond the company walls. A poor pipeline of graduates, and incentives for black professionals to remain mobile in the directorship market, could be contributing to the bias towards non-executive retention.

Is the ANC the main hunting ground for finding black directors? The perception in the suburban popular imagination that the ANC is the breeding ground for black corporate South Africa is not entirely supported by the data. The majority of black directors at the top twenty South African–listed firms cut their teeth in the business world, with many accruing the accounting and legal academic accoutrements beloved of the corporate world. That said, a significant number of directors do emerge from the state (24 per cent) and state-owned companies (14 per cent). Given the legislated and social barriers to black upward mobility imposed by apartheid, and the historically few entry points for black business-people into corporate life, one area where black managers could thrive and demonstrate competence through the early years of the transition was in the state.

White business, initially slow to transform but now under pressure from BEE codes to alter the composition of boardrooms, has not been able to lean – as it has historically – on the pipelines of legal and accountancy professionals to source black talent, and consequently, in many instances, it has had to recruit from state apparatuses.

If these recruits bring with them political connections, information and access to decision-makers in addition to managerial and technical competence, then all the better. Conflicts of interest can arise, and have emerged, when former state employees move seamlessly from their field of practice in the public sector to the private sector and utilise information and/or relationships to the unfair advantage of their new employers – a perennial problem that is canvassed in passing in Chapter 12.

Table 13.7: Black directors by previous affiliation

Previous affiliation	Number of directors	Percentage of directors
ANC	4	3.6
Government	27	24.3
Parastatals	15	13.5
Business	61	55.0
Chapter 9*	2	1.8
Academia	2	1.8
Total	111	100.0

* Chapter 9 institutions refer to a group of organisations established in terms of Chapter 9 of the South African Constitution to guard democracy. The institutions are: the Public Protector; the South African Human Rights Commission; the Commission for the Promotion and Protection of the Rights of Cultural, Religious and Linguistic Communities (CRL Rights Commission); the Commission for Gender Equality; the Auditor-General; the Independent Electoral Commission; and an Independent Authority to Regulate Broadcasting.

Things get even more interesting when one takes a look at the business interests
of ANC national executive committee and cabinet members. The Institute for
Security Studies maintains a database that they refer to as 'Who owns what?'[38] Its
goal is to promote transparency and minimise the opportunities for corruption
within government by tracking officials' possible conflicts of interest. It gathers
publicly available financial disclosure information submitted by officials, such
as details regarding directorships and shareholdings. At the time of writing, data
for the ANC NEC and national cabinet members was mostly from 2011, though
for some only older information was available (primarily from 2009 and 2010).
Of the 80 official members of the ANC NEC, the database contained records for
only 60. However, all 36 cabinet members were present and accounted for. An
analysis of the information reveals the following:

Table 13.8: Directorships and shares held by
members of the ANC NEC, various years

	Number	Percentage ($n = 60$)
Directors	29	48
More than 1 directorship*	20	33
3 or more directorships	16	27
5 or more directorships	7	12
Members with shares	43	72
Shares in more than 1 company	30	50
Shares in 3 or more companies	20	33
Shares in 5 or more companies	11	18

* Directorships include family and arts/cultural trusts.

Table 13.9: Directorships and shares held by
members of the national cabinet, 2011

	Number	Percentage ($n = 36$)
Directors	17	47
More than 1 directorship*	11	31
3 or more directorships	7	19
5 or more directorships	3	8
Cabinet members with shares	23	64
Shares in more than 1 company	17	47
Shares in 3 or more companies	10	28
Shares in 5 or more companies	5	14

* Directorships include family and arts/cultural trusts.

As can be seen, almost half of the members of both the NEC and the cabinet are directors. Furthermore, roughly a third of each group holds more than one directorship, while a small number of individuals from each group (12 per cent for the NEC and 8 per cent for the cabinet) hold more than five. Owning shares is a far more prevalent form of business activity than holding a directorship. A whopping 72 per cent of NEC members hold shares, while 50 per cent own shares from more than one company and 18 per cent from more than five. Cabinet exhibits a weaker, though still significant, trend of share ownership, with 64 per cent of its members owning shares and approximately half (47 per cent) owning shares from more than one company. Only 14 per cent, however, own shares from more than five companies.

Having crunched the numbers and considered the origins of modern-day South Africa's corporate boardrooms, one question remains, one that defies quantitative elaboration: how much power do the new, black directors wield in their respective boardrooms?

According to Sekunjalo founder and chairman Iqbal Survé, not a lot: 'Black directors? They are powerless. Black people may be on boards, but it is visibility without power. You only have power if you have shares. The significant shareholding is what makes the difference.'

'There are always exceptions,' he adds, as I offer the name of Cyril Ramaphosa. Survé breaks stride ever so slightly before carefully telling me that he has 'enormous respect for [Ramaphosa] personally, but I don't know what he says in the board meetings since I am not on the same boards as Cyril' – an issue that, of course, arose in relation to Ramaphosa's role on the Lonmin board at the time of Marikana.

'You are only in the inner circle if you have shareholder support,' Survé adds. 'People will say things privately to me. I will sit in a board and five or six black directors will agree with me in private conversation – let's say on a sustainability issue, about using new cleaner technologies – but when I go back in, I am the only one … I look like a left-wing socialist greenie!'

So there you have it. Survé is different, he says, because he is the majority shareholder in his group of companies. Secondly, he says, 'I don't owe anyone anything. I can say what I like.'

Corporate-government relations

Finally, what differences have changes in the corporate boardrooms made to corporate-government relations – to the 'public affairs' business, as lobbying is so delicately labelled these days – and to the ability of business South Africa to understand the society in which it operates and respond appropriately and strategically?

My own experience with corporates suggests that the answer is 'not a lot'. But I need another perspective. Survé and I are meeting at the UCT Graduate School of Business, of which he is council chair, located in a splendid conversion of the old prison near the V&A Waterfront in Cape Town. He is an establishment man nowadays; a very wealthy one, with extensive interests across the continent.

I am interested to get his views on the subject, as he is regarded as someone who is close to Zuma. He appears to have anticipated this – not hard perhaps – and before I have even asked the question, he says: 'I get the impression that people overestimate the impact of business on politicians and, to an extent, the opposite way. I think business has very little influence, and rightly so.'

How do businesses engage then? 'Access to power is about conveying to people the need to talk to each other. You must not compromise yourself. I have survived many administrations in South Africa through the presidencies of Mandela, Mbeki, Motlanthe and Zuma … I am the only businessman to do so. It was possible to make this seamless transition since I did not get factionalised.' (He adds a brief aside about how, as evidence of his ability to build new relationships with anyone, he and his partner went to the Baxter Theatre for the UCT vice chancellor's concert in Cape Town in 2012, and 'the whole DA leadership that was attending the concert and were seated in the row behind me got up to greet me and my partner said to me, "I didn't know you knew these people, and they know you so well."')

This is a substantial claim. If it's justifiable, and I suspect it is, then Survé is in a very unique position. I remember when I once saw him interact with Zuma, apparently for the first time. It was at the jazz festival at the Cape Town International Convention Centre in about 2008. Zuma was in the no-man's-land of having won at Polokwane but still unsure if he would make it to the Union Buildings, because of the corruption charges hanging over him. Businesses – traditional corporates, that is – didn't really know how to handle him or the situation. They were worried about getting too close; and they didn't know what the entry point should be. British American Tobacco was a little less timid and had invited Zuma to join them in their corporate area at the festival. But it proved a nightmare for BAT. Zuma missed his flight, arrived late and, despite the fact that the company had paid for his trip down, decided that he was a little too tired to join the festivities and would rather head for his bed at the adjacent luxury hotel, the Westin Grand, also, needless to say, paid for by BAT.

The BAT hierarchy didn't know whether to laugh or cry. An anxious huddle formed around the tall Australian CEO, David Crow. What to do? BAT obviously wanted some value for their investment, but as Crowie, as he is known, put it with his customary panache: 'We can't very well go over there and fucking drag him out of his bed.'

But that is exactly what happened. Zuma was 'encouraged' to honour his commitment. The problem was that by the time he had changed his mind and wandered sleepily across the road to the CTICC, Crow and his senior execs had gone home, so there was hardly anyone for him to talk to. A brief panic swept the remaining BAT ranks before Fay Kajee, the company's then public-affairs manager, thinking quickly on her feet, ran around the corner to the Sekunjalo company suite. At that time, her husband, Mo, was Survé's CEO.

In short order, Survé and Mo Kajee went over to the BAT section to save the day. They chatted earnestly to Zuma and occasionally drew others into the conversation, although it did seem that Survé and Zuma were not at all well acquainted. The latter appeared sullen and taciturn, with none of the genial, hail-fellow-well-met reputation that precedes him. Perhaps he was just tired. Perhaps he couldn't be bothered.

This modest observational anecdote invites consideration of a wider point about corporate-government relations, which have gone through a number of different phases since 1994, but have yet to find an even keel. What prompts BAT to invite Zuma to their festival suite in the first place? What do they think they will get out of it? Clearly, they want to encourage a positive relationship with the individual politician concerned. Presumably they think that if he accepts the invitation it will generate some goodwill that they will be able to draw on in due course.

Indeed, there can be no doubt that building relationships is a key part of any corporate/public-affairs strategy. The questions are how best to do it and, assuming good faith and a reasonable level of honest intention – i.e. not wishing to build a relationship based on undue influence and corruption inducement, such as payments – how best to do it effectively in a decent way.

Perhaps the starting point is the prevailing mindset of the corporate leader. As Survé puts it to me: 'Corporates don't understand the broader dynamics of society … we miss the opportunity to engage with government to find solutions. Sometimes this will benefit us as a business, sometimes it won't.'

It has certainly become clear to me in my various dealings with business leaders that there is this common dread of politics, which is partly born out of fear that if you enter the game it will be too risky and too much can go wrong, or that you will say the wrong thing and pay for it. Reuel Khoza's comments on political leadership, with their thinly disguised criticism of Zuma, for example, got him into great trouble in April 2012, prompting a stinging rebuke from the ANC.

Alan Fine, AngloGold Ashanti's public-affairs man, put it to me neatly: 'There [are] three types of CEO in South Africa. One type – the majority – doesn't understand politics and doesn't dare say anything, so he keeps his head beneath the parapet. The second tries, but gets it horribly wrong, usually through tone as much as anything, like a bull in a china shop. The third, a small minority, is not afraid to engage, sometimes robustly, but because they understand and because of their tone, can do so and be listened to.'

Fine cited his then boss, Mark Cutifani, now CEO of Anglo American PLC, as an example of the third, an opinion that was backed up by the government ministers I spoke with. In fact, many of those ministers would long for more and better engagement from, and dialogue with, business leadership, which makes one wonder why it does not happen.

As Sipho Pityana pointed out to me when I interviewed him in November 2011, 'If you are in government, you want to hear the views of labour, and you get that through the [Tripartite] Alliance usually, but you don't have the same thing with business.'

In the Mbeki era, things were more organised; now they are more organic. Mbeki created a number of business-government councils and other formal channels for engagement, although Pityana concedes that 'Thabo's main council was focused on international business, with only a tenuous relationship with local business'. It was undoubtedly one of his ways of using process to control things. Zuma's world is more chaotic.

Pityana is critical of Zuma: 'Now, JZ has to play with smaller fishes – which is unstrategic, and relates to business at the wrong level. There is a big disconnect as a result between business and government.'

Pityana's 2011 analysis pointed the finger at Jimmy Manyi and his gate-keeping tendencies as chief government spokesperson and head of the Black Management Forum (BMF), an organisation whose mandate is partly about lobbying the interests of black businesses to government.

Zuma's appointment of Manyi was strange. He was initially appointed director-general of labour in 2009 (a reward, apparently, for his role in Zuma's Polokwane campaign), despite remaining in his role at the helm of the BMF. It was mind-boggling that anyone should tolerate such a blatant conflict of interest, and is further evidence of just how badly off track the country's moral radar has gone. It took the usually discreet and demure Norwegians to make the complaint that ultimately led to Manyi's removal from his director-general position in 2010. By chance, I was on a panel with the Norwegian ambassador the day after they had had a meeting with Manyi that had shocked them to the point where they had taken the very exceptional step of leaking the information to *Business Day*. Manyi, purporting to represent government at the meeting with visiting Norwegian businessmen, had begun to lobby blatantly for the interests of some black-owned businesses.

But instead of being removed from government completely, Manyi was made head of the Government Communication and Information System (GCIS), a disastrous appointment: he managed to upset the media and ministers such as Trevor Manuel in equal measure, and his contract was not renewed in late 2012, by which time much damage had, as Pityana says, already been done.

Bonang Mohale of Shell has now replaced Manyi and will be a far blander figure, but hopefully a more measured presence in the conversations between the BMF and government. Manyi's appointment revealed Zuma's short-sightedness: rewarding someone to whom you owe a favour, even at the cost of your relations with the media and the international reputation of your government.

In Survé's opinion, 'Zuma is a very different leader and gives lots of authority to his ministers. He is the perfect example of a decentralised CEO – a CEO who delegates, whereas Mbeki was completely involved in the portfolios. So a crucial thing for Zuma is to make sure he appoints the right ministers.'

Indeed. But for business, this means you have to be well equipped to be able to play the game. You have to understand it and be well advised about it, if you are to play it safely. Enter it properly prepared, and my experience is that your business will do well.

At times it is devilishly difficult to deal with, but you are not dealing with devils.

My main corporate client in recent years has been Massmart, the large retailer that was bought by US multinational Walmart in 2011. I took them on because they are a 'thinking' company; modest in their public attitudes and rarely boastful; with a desire, back in 2009 when I started to work with them, to acquire a better grasp of South African domestic politics and what makes it tick.

Brian Leroni, Massmart's group corporate affairs executive, is supremely good at his job and a pleasure to work with. He sets the tone, which is about calm, dispassionate digestion of the issues of the day; taking the long view; not getting sucked into short-term controversies; recognising the ebbs and flows of domestic politics; and, with my help, learning to read the tea leaves and to distinguish between the public rhetoric and the quieter signalling about policy and its future trajectory.

During the transaction itself, when Walmart's takeover was challenged by the government and by the unions in the competition commission and the competition appeal court, it was not so easy for Massmart to maintain their sangfroid. As I record in Chapter 3, the minister for economic development, Ebrahim Patel, deliberately tried to rattle them. But the tough unionist came up against an equally tough and no less abrasive man in the Massmart CEO, Grant Pattison. Each probably thought he could and would outwit, or out-negotiate, the other.

In the end, after a long and costly legal battle, peace broke out. Now Massmart works cosily with the Department of Agriculture, Forestry and Fisheries to roll out the Ezemvelo emerging farmers' development programme. Both the agriculture minister, Tina Joemat-Pettersson, and Patel are happy to claim it as a victory; Massmart were going to do it anyway, because it's the right thing to do and it makes business sense. So all's well that ends well; and pragmatism is a powerful force in politics.

Survé mentions Walmart in passing: 'I warned the Walmart people at Davos [the Swiss ski resort where the World Economic Forum – an annual gathering of global leaders from business and government – meets], but I don't think they were listening. I met the CEO. They were very American. I think people misunderstand government.' This was very early on in the transaction process, before Walmart realised that they needed to leave the government-relations stuff to Massmart, that South Africa was not Washington DC and did not conform to the usual lobbying rules of the game, an unsettling prospect for them.

The Walmart-Massmart case proved the point that doing business – above-board, honest business – in South Africa requires a degree of intelligence, in both senses of the word: intelligence in terms of being thoughtful and being seen to be thoughtful by thoughtful ministers; and in terms of gathering intelligence about how the system operates and the anatomy of political power and its character and trends.

What is so intriguing is how prejudiced many big South African corporates are. Not so much about race as about ideology, although, as Survé points out, 'top management in the top corporates are largely white – and this is not a race issue – but for whatever reason, the white individuals tend to be introspective and tend to focus just on their business. I see that within my own group. It's very difficult to get people to embrace the complexity of society.'

So, many top business leaders are fearful of 'the left'. But their understanding of what constitutes 'the left' in contemporary South African politics is scarily feeble. While Massmart, for example, have inevitable regular disputes with their unions, they fully understand the role that unions play in South Africa, not just in the workplace but also in broader society. They understand that a weaker union movement is not necessarily good for South Africa or good for their business trajectory. They understand that a complex society, such as we have in South Africa, needs the unions as a social filter or sponge, and that a divided union – or a divided ANC – may lead to the sort of disintegration of social cohesion that led to Marikana.

But put a few asset managers in a room and, generally, the ideological preju-dices will surface very quickly. Trust me, I've been there. On one such occasion, with a bit of wine-fuelled Dutch courage, I brought the dinner-table conversation to a halt and challenged, 'List the problems you have with the government and with politics, and then let's see what COSATU and the SACP have to say about them.' To cut the story very short, their concerns – about corruption and cronyism; about the education system; about nationalistic, populist language, such as that employed by Julius Malema – all corresponded with those of COSATU and the SACP.

You should really be fearful of 'the right' – the populist, nationalist wing of the ANC – not 'the left', I argued vigorously, as I have on many occasions and in similar company since.

One of the chief problems is that many corporate leaders are unaccustomed to dealing with politics and are ill-equipped to do so, whether for reasons of history and birth, upbringing, class and/or race, and get scanty, if any, assistance in understanding what is really going on from the press or from any other source.

As a result, business has yet to crack the post-1994 public-affairs code, though it has toyed with various different models in response to the challenge. This is how I see it: in the first phase, from 1994 to, say, 1997, corporate leaders were so relieved by the 'peaceful transition' and so comforted by the reconciliatory rhetoric of President Mandela that they did little else other than take the odd Robben Islander onto the board, assuming that such an individual would be able to provide sufficient political intelligence as well as political 'cover' and credibility.

But when Mbeki assumed more power after 1997, and his complex mode of communicating, with intricate layers of messaging, became more prominent in the public discourse, corporate leaders began to panic. What did Mbeki stand for? Was he a threat to them? Was he dangerous? He was enigmatic and the Robben Island board member was apparently no better able to decode his mixed signals than they were.

Disenchanted, they ran for the hills and put their heads down. When one of their number, such as then CEO of Anglo American Tony Trahar, criticised Mbeki or the ANC or the government, the president would launch a vicious counter-attack, generally using his famous/notorious 'Letter from the ANC President' weekly column to swoosh the sabre.

Soon enough, however, and partly because the economy was doing okay, and big business was making money and expanding into new markets across Africa, and Mbeki had learnt how easy it was to 'manage' expectations and calm frayed nerves with his various business councils and other processes for dialogue and negotiation, corporate South Africa shrugged and concluded, 'Well, we don't really understand this oke; he's terribly complicated, and seems rather difficult to get close to, but he also seems business-friendly enough, and, well, also seems to know how to keep most things under control – including those confounding unions and unreconstructed commies on the left – so let's not fret any longer or worry that we don't really understand the politics of our own country or what makes the government really tick.'

Alongside this, the odd black, ANC-connected, public-affairs guy was hired to look good and to offer platitudinous or erroneous advice about government policy making, and life went on. Until Polokwane. Then the comfort zone was really rattled; and frayed nerves became the new order of the day. Who the hell was this Zuma chap? And what was this Zunami all about?

Some of corporate South Africa woke up to the need for a better, more sophisticated grasp of domestic politics. And they realised that having one guy – an ANC guy, a former Robben Islander – was not the answer, not least because such a person, for all his struggle credentials and cellphone contacts, could not offer anything other than a partial – in both senses of the word – view of political life.

Some corporates responded by appointing a new type of CEO, one who was politically savvy and had direct experience of government: ABSA's appointment of Maria Ramos, the former director-general of Treasury and CEO of Transnet, as their new CEO in March 2009 is one example.

Others chose to appoint full-time public-affairs officers with seasoned expertise in South African politics – Alan Fine at AngloGold Ashanti is one good example – or retain people like myself or Lawson Naidoo, or, I imagine, analysts or public intellectuals such as Prince Mashele or Songezo Zibi of the Midrand Group, who can offer a detached, dispassionate view of politics based on years of experience rather than on who I last happened to speak to or the particular contact I can reach on the issue at hand.

The key is knowing how to approach government. 'You have to convince them [government] on the basis of three things,' advises Survé. 'You need friendly access – access based on what is the common interests of people. Second, you need a value proposition that is a win-win for both government and business. Third, it must be done in a way that is transparent so that there is no suspicion … because the private sector is inherently suspicious that government is not sincere about what it wants to do; and government is inherently suspicious that the private sector is only interested in its own kingdom, if you like.'

While companies, or even sectors, can develop their own channels of communication – the Energy Intensive User Group is one example of a very effective form of lobbying by a group of companies that desperately need the government's ear on issues of electricity pricing, for example, and are ruthless at dominating the policy-lobbying space in pursuit of their own interests – the absence of more formal communication channels, such as those that existed under Mbeki, is unfortunate.

Yet, having admitted that under Zuma the relationship between corporate South Africa and government (the Presidency specifically) is less ordered and more unruly, Survé then introduces a line of defence: 'In fairness to Zuma, we go to Davos, every South African president has a luncheon, this year [2013] it was a tea. There is something about being in a foreign land, you come together better. We talked and people said, "Why can't we do this in South Africa?"'

And Zuma apparently acted fast, calling a meeting a week after everyone got back from Davos. Says Survé: 'We had to go to Pretoria and spend the whole bloody Sunday with the cabinet. I was there representing myself; there were one or two others; thirty business leaders in total there. Zuma did not want to go to his cabinet lekgotla without first engaging with business. Tells you something about the president, does it not?'

Well, yes and no. It tells me that he acted fast on *this* occasion. But it also begs the question: Why only then? Why did it take him so long, when much of the previous year (2012) had been mired in economic woe and socio-political trouble, most obviously the labour disputes in the mining sector that came to a tragic and disastrous head at Marikana?

The Pretoria meeting itself could not escape the limitations that exist, to be even-handed in this analysis, on the side of business. As Survé says, 'My own view was that this is a great opportunity, and the business groupings sit there on a Sunday, not really presenting. I don't think you need a list of twenty things ... but they were caught by surprise by the speed at which the president organised the meeting. Jabu [Mabuza] from BUSA [Business Unity South Africa] said, "We want to meet with government" ... and [Zuma] took it seriously. If you call me to a meeting, I will think about it and present one or two main ideas. If you sat there like I did observing these machinations – [it was] the business side and government side, sitting on two different planets.'

And here lies the rub. Two different planets. The organisational and structural disorder on the government/president's side is matched by that on business's side. To the Pretoria meeting, business brought not one single delegation and voice, but two: the Black Business Council (BBC) – 'looking,' says Survé, 'at the interests of smaller black business; some define it as pro-Zuma, but I say bullshit, it's just something to look after taxi industries and businesses like that' – and BUSA.

The BBC was revived after the BMF broke away from BUSA in late 2011, the result of an acrimonious battle over transformation. Having been persuaded by Mbeki's call for a more united voice from business in 2003, the BBC had joined with Business South Africa to form BUSA. Now, ten years later, the country is back to square one – with a divided business community, unable to speak with one voice, even when the president does get his act together and calls for a proper engagement.

The changing face of South Africa's boardrooms is significant, and yet it is impossible to conclude whether these changes have either translated into a major shift in real corporate power or altered the way in which traditional corporate South Africa conducts itself in relation to government and politics generally.

There are some hugely influential, as well as wealthy, individuals such as Survé, Pityana, Ramaphosa, Patrice Motsepe and all the other beneficiaries of the BEE boom. But structurally, institutionally, the corporate establishment's fundamental anatomy of power is proving stubbornly resilient to change, while failures on both sides mean that the space for government to influence big business and vice versa, through strategic engagement, is far more limited than it could or should be.

14

The professions

Institutions frame the societies in which we live, and South Africa is no exception. Institutions regulate to a greater or lesser extent the relationships, interactions, transactions and agreements we engage in as both public and private citizens. In turn, institutions police the contours of what is acceptable behaviour on the part of groups of people – governments, civil entities and firms – and sanction those who stray beyond the pale.

Governments determine the institutional mechanisms that affect the ways in which firms and individuals relate and do business together. Regulative mechanisms, in turn, shape behaviour through the threat of sanction for those who do not abide by the rules of the environment. The assertion and maintenance of norms define what kinds of behaviour and practice are socially acceptable and appropriate.

Critically, in the South African context, it is useful to remember that apartheid itself is often referred to as a 'systemic' or 'institutionalised' set of discriminatory practices that structured the lives of all citizens. Apartheid would have remained the dark fantasy of a minority of the population had it not found an institutional framework and an army of civil servants and professionals to give it life, and reproduce its perverse effects on a day-to-day basis.

In the same way that institutions are implicated in our past, so, too, are they front and centre in the struggle for what a post-apartheid South Africa should look and feel like, tracing the contours of what is acceptable, what is good and what lies beyond the pale.

Central to both the foundation of apartheid and the new democratic dispensation is the law, most dramatically evident in the now not-so-new South African Constitution of 1996, and institutions relating to law – Parliament and the provincial legislatures, the courts, the prosecuting authorities and the police.

But these institutions are static, meaningless constructs without the people that make them function and the societies that bend to their authority. In many instances, the professions are critical to the effective functioning of institutions. There are two professions that concurrently enable and hold to account much of contemporary public and private life: lawyers and accountants – the professional princes who make the world go round.

Suburban South Africa is wont to bemoan the erosion of standards and the watering down of enforcement. Rarely does a day go by without newspaper letters pages and talk-show hosts mediating the clarion calls of retired denizens of the professions, sketching in hyperbolic terms the precipitous slippery slope of societal decline.

In the 2012/13 edition of the World Economic Forum's *Global Competitiveness Report*, South Africa is assessed as the 52nd most competitive country for business out of a total of 144; down one position from 2011/12. The designation puts us in not entirely edifying company: third of the four BRICS, with India (59) bringing up the rear (Brazil at 48 and China at 29), and keeping touch with the likes of Portugal, Indonesia, Kazakhstan and Mauritius.

On many of the indicators, the country's performance would probably not come as too much of a surprise to many South Africans. Perhaps predictably, the country performs woefully on measures such as the cost of crime and violence to business (134 of 144) and tensions in labour–employer relations (144 of 144).

Yet the same global survey of the perceptions of business towards accounting and legal standards demonstrates a South African community more than pleased with the efficacy and fairness of the standards to which they are held, and the work of the professionals who negotiate the interface of business and these standards.

In response to the question 'In your country, how would you assess financial auditing and reporting standards regarding company financial performance?' the sample of South African businesspeople surveyed were more effusive of the institutional environment framing accounting and auditing, and the work of their colleagues in the accounting and auditing profession, than any equivalent business sample used for the study.

Indeed, a self-assessment of the strength of South Africa's auditing and reporting standards puts the country as the best in the world, higher than oft-cited paragons of business virtue and competitiveness Finland and New Zealand, beaten into second and third places respectively.

Moreover, in response to the questions 'How efficient is the legal framework in your country for private businesses in settling disputes?' and 'How efficient is the legal framework in your country for private businesses in challenging the legality of government actions and/or regulations?' South Africa's business community was almost as favourably disposed, with the country placing 17th and 16th respectively among the 144 countries surveyed.

Of course, the World Economic Forum report is a rather blunt instrument, lacking in nuance and, in many respects, context. However, it does underline the high regard in which South Africans – or, more accurately, the South African business establishment – hold the financial and legal standards to which they are held, and the work of the members of the South African accounting and legal professions.

Princely profession I: The bean counters

'Accountants are the witch doctors of the modern world and willing to turn their hands to any kind of magic.'

~ Lord Justice Harmer, February 1964[1]

For tax and debt liabilities to mean anything they must be embedded in a system of law and practice that is generally accepted to be legitimate, and to be recognised as such by the people and firms who enter into exchange, trade and other social contracts – the daily grist of the modern economic mill, and, as such, crucial to the power relations that help to organise any complex modern society.

Accountants enable these mechanisms through the maintenance and policing of auditing and financial reporting standards that frame the norms of commercial life and mediate the obligations of the citizen as taxpayer. By virtue of their core function, then, they wield significant power.

The South African chartered accountant (CA) is a curious phenomenon: reified in business and society, CAs adorn the boardrooms of South Africa's largest companies and festoon the wood-panelled smoking rooms of private clubs in numbers disproportionate to the utility of their profession.

This is a profession proud of its achievements; a vigorously defensive fraternity. If you're in, you are likely to do quite well for yourself, get your kids into leafy suburban schools and retire with a respectable sum in the bank. If you're out, it can seem inconceivable that these bean counters and ledger balancers should command such social prestige and bank as much buck.

So who are they? What do they do? And what do they look like?

Historically, the South African CA is white, male and – to add insult to injury – very likely English-speaking. He (and 'he' he is likely to be) most probably attended one of the better university feeder schools in Cape Town's southern suburbs, Johannesburg's north or the leafy rugger nurseries of KwaZulu-Natal and the Eastern Cape. Matriculating with above-average marks in mathematics – already a significant achievement in a country with woeful maths scores – our intrepid future CA still faces significant hurdles en route to his prestigious charter.

Typically, the odyssey of a CA in training entails four years of study and a further three years of apprenticeship. Seven years represents a very real sacrifice, one that is possibly accessible only to those who don't have to support parents or an extended family. Concurrently, as we will see, seven years of 'sacrifice' could equally be considered a very good example of deferred gratification with a significant pay-off.

Each year, thousands of South African teenagers and young adults enrol for a Bachelor of Commerce (BCom) degree. The BCom itself probably deserves a chapter of its own, falsely endowing its graduates as it does with a presumed ticket for the private-sector gravy train and the keys to the establishment. The degree is so ridiculously overburdened with expectation that it attracts many students who would be far better off pursuing qualifications in the humanities and social sciences, and who merely enrol on the basis that they will probably get in (due to high maths scores).

As such, the first year of the BCom represents a deeply troubling churning of young minds; many students fail to progress, some dropping out entirely, while others are politely ushered towards other faculties. At the University of Cape Town, of the students who enrol for the Commerce and Business Science (BSc) degree programmes in their first year, a full 25 per cent will drop out entirely. For the BCom and BSc degrees taken together, for the years 2009–11, 13 per cent of students repeated their first year (4 per cent white, 20 per cent African, 19 per cent coloured, 20 per cent Indian and 13 per cent international) and 6 per cent dropped out at the end of first year (7 per cent white, 5 per cent African, 5 per cent coloured, 4 per cent Indian and 10 per cent international).[2]

A subset of those students who graduate with a BCom – typically a three-year qualification – will go on to pursue a specialised one-year honours degree in commerce that will culminate in sitting the formidable Certificate of the Theory of Accounting (CTA) exam. In 2011, of the 5 179 students in the country as a whole that sat the CTA, only 41 per cent passed, underscoring the difficulty of the qualification.

The results are somewhat misleading due to the fact that approximately two-thirds of those who sit the CTA are enrolled as distance learners through UNISA. Those who sit the CTA having completed a full programme of study at a traditional landed university enjoy much higher pass rates.[3]

At the end of their fourth year, brandishing their CTAs, our accounting heroes are actually only halfway towards full professional immersion. Three more years of an articled apprenticeship and a final qualification exam administered by the South African Institute of Chartered Accountants (SAICA) await those who stumble towards the finishing line to earn the coveted mantle and certification of CA.

For those who choose to practise in the profession, the landscape is dominated by four multinational accounting firms: PricewaterhouseCoopers, KPMG, Ernst & Young and Deloitte. There are also significant numbers of CAs employed at mid-tier accountancy practices such as Mazars and Grant Thornton. All of these firms are globally integrated and offer their employees the opportunity to specialise in the different branches of accounting practice and to build their careers internationally.

Given the significant pressure on the profession to transform, and the incentives built into BEE codes of practice to retain black-owned audit and accounting firms, there are a number of important new small and medium players emerging in the South African context – such as SizweNtsalubaGobodo, which has grown exponentially in the past decade in large part through rents accrued catering to parastatals and other public-sector contracting – once again highlighting the role the state plays in shifting traditional power structures in the economy.

The work of a professional CA at a medium-to-large firm can be generalised across four areas of practice: assurance; specialist tax consultancy; transaction advisory services; and management consultancy. Historically, the overwhelming majority of the work of the profession, and its *raison d'être*, was to provide assurance to capital markets by attesting to the quality and viability of a firm's finances. The Companies Act of 2008 requires all limited-liability companies to open their books for audit each year to forestall fraud and promote trust in the financial system. Financial information that accurately attests to the underlying value of firms and transactions is critical to the effective functioning of capital markets, and the work of the profession in this regard is central to oiling the wheels of exchange and capitalism at large.

Providing assurance still constitutes about 50 per cent of the work of large accountancy firms, but it has become more complex, with higher risks due to new regulations implemented in the aftermath of the bursting of the dot.com bubble, the Enron crisis and, most recently, due to the ongoing overhaul of the capital and financial-market regulations following the global financial crisis of 2008.

Significant areas of growth for the South African accounting profession, with lower risk and larger paydays, have arisen as a consequence of the weighty technical skills implicit in the profession. Tax, transaction and general financial advisory services that help companies improve systems and more effectively manage risks are growing areas of practice.

The growth of advisory services is not entirely without controversy, as advice and audit can contribute to conflicts of interest – most egregiously underscored by the central role played by the now defunct Arthur Andersen audit and advisory firm in the Enron scandal of 2001, wherein Andersen was implicated in manipulating Enron's audit results so as not to jeopardise the enormous sums Andersen's management-consultancy practice earned by contracting to the same company.

After Enron, the major accounting firms, bar Deloitte, sold off or scaled back their management-consulting practices. But practices have re-established themselves, and all of the Big Four now offer boutique suites of actuarial and IT consulting, as well as services designed to assist companies in the effective execution of strategy, and to provide guidance and assurance in the implementation of process management. Given the increasingly complex regulatory environment, these specialist or boutique skills are once again in high demand, and management consulting is again a growing and important area of practice for the accounting profession.

However, the majority of those who qualify as CAs do not practise formally in the profession. The rigorous academic and practical training that underscores the CA qualification is the source of immensely practical business knowledge applicable in the economy at large, and serves as a significant indicator of value in the employment market, contributing to the aggressive recruitment of CAs to positions in asset management, financial control, management consulting and a plethora of other business practices.

Data collected by SAICA gives some indication of the value of the broader profession in the South African economy, demonstrating that the overwhelming majority of the country's 4 000 registered auditors are registered CAs and that 32 per cent of firms listed on the Johannesburg Stock Exchange are headed by certified CAs.[4] As Chapter 13 on the corporate boardrooms of South Africa illustrates, membership of the profession can serve as an important ticket to the upper echelons of the South African business establishment.

That the profession is representative of privilege is underscored by the utterly woeful demographic data associated with the accounting profession. Wiseman Nkuhlu, former economic advisor to Thabo Mbeki and former chief executive of the NEPAD secretariat, was the first black African to be chartered as an accountant in South Africa when he completed his articles in 1976.

As can be seen in Table 14.1, in 2002, eight years after the first democratic election – coincidentally, one more year than the minimum time required to obtain certification as a CA – and thirty-six years after his pioneering qualification, Professor Nkuhlu could count himself among only 322 African CAs registered with SAICA, representing just 1.5 per cent of a profession of 20 903.[5] African, coloured and Indian accountants taken together accounted for only 7.4 per cent, or 1 555, of all South African CAs in 2002.

In 2003, whites claimed 91.4 per cent of the ranks of the profession, down nearly a percentage point from 92.3 per cent in 2002. Of those, white men accounted for 81.9 per cent, or 16 361 – just short of three-quarters of the entire profession. White women, the next largest demographic, trailed white men in a distant second at 18.1 per cent, or 3 610. (2003 is the first year for which a gendered breakdown of SAICA data is available.)

Needless to say, these figures are representative of an entirely unsustainable status quo from the perspective of an inclusive and democratic South Africa. As a consequence, the accountancy profession has come under significant pressure to enhance the representation of black South Africans and women.

Table 14.1: Demographic breakdown of registered CAs, 2002–2012[6]

	2002	% of total	2003	% of total	2012	% of total	Real growth 2002–12	Real growth 2003–12
Total CAs	20 903		21 856		34 293		64.1%	56.9%
Male			17 721	81.1%	23 560	68.7%		32.9%
Female			4 135	18.9%	10 733	31.3%		159.6%
African	322	1.5%	403	1.8%	2 416	7.0%	650.3%	499.5%
Male			281	69.7%	1 321	54.7%		370.1%
Female			122	30.3%	1 095	45.3%		797.5%
Coloured	202	1.0%	257	1.2%	944	2.8%	367.3%	267.3%
Male			167	65.0%	473	50.1%		183.2%
Female			90	35.0%	471	49.9%		423.3%
Indian	1 031	4.9%	1 179	5.4%	3 291	9.6%	219.2%	179.1%
Male			884	75.0%	1 938	58.9%		119.2%
Female			295	25.0%	1 353	41.1%		358.6%
White	19 285	92.3%	19 971	91.4%	27 513	80.2%	42.7%	37.8%
Male			16 361	81.9%	19 747	71.8%		20.7%
Female			3 610	18.1%	7 766	28.2%		115.1%

SAICA and the government are intimately aware of these challenges. In light of the significant structural barriers to entry (unequal secondary education, seven years' tertiary and practical training, opportunity cost, etc.) and an entrenched and persistent poverty profile that remains highly correlative with race, the profession's primary stakeholders (government, business and SAICA) agreed to a substantive programme of intervention to alter the supply of candidates entering the profession.

The Thuthuka Bursary Fund, established in 2002 under the indomitable stewardship of Chantyl Mulder at SAICA, systematically targets students from the coloured and African communities for training towards the CA qualification, and is largely responsible for the mushrooming supply of African and coloured candidates. Initially piloted in the Eastern Cape with an intake of 50 students, the programme now supports over 1 000 students at undergraduate level and a further 350 at honours level.

The bursary programme is funded through a public-private partnership, with statutory funds dispersed on a matching-grant basis (each rand raised by SAICA and its partners in business is matched by government). Each student within the programme secures a loan through the National Student Financial Aid Scheme (NSFAS) that covers approximately half of tuition costs, with the shortfall in overall funds covered by SAICA and its partners. At the end of each year, conditional on passing final exams, 40 per cent of each student's NSFAS loan is written off as a bursary – a significant incentive towards passing end-of-year exams. During and following qualification, Thuthuka recipients benefit from work experience and workplace training with the stakeholders to the bursary consortium.

The programme has significantly altered the profile of the pipeline of candidates entering the profession and demonstrates the utility of its innovative funding structure. Thuthuka candidates perform, on average, well above the general pool of aspiring accountants, with 72 per cent of supported students passing their third-year examinations and a full 66 per cent passing the CTA. In 2011, 81 per cent of Thuthuka candidates writing the first component of their final qualification exams (QE1) passed, 17 per cent above the national average of 64 per cent.

The latest available data (from 2012) demonstrates a profession at pains to wrest itself from history with some impressive results. The number of African CAs, for example, has risen 650 per cent since the inception of the Thuthuka initiative, while the number of coloured CAs has increased 367 per cent. The number of female CAs increased by 160 per cent between 2003 and 2012.

However, when one takes into account the catastrophically low base for previously disadvantaged members of the profession, and when one considers that white accountants still outnumber their black[7] colleagues by four to one and continue to make up 80 per cent of the profession, one begins to realise the scale of the representivity challenge. A further conundrum is the 'over-representation' of Indian CAs, who in 2012 constituted almost 10 per cent of the profession, against a national demographic profile of 2.5 per cent.

A closer inspection of the data shows a thoroughly transformative programme in play. Data collected by SAICA by cohort (see Table 14.2) demonstrates both the legacy of privilege as well as the dividends of democratisation: CAs registered with SAICA over the age of 60 are both overwhelmingly white (98.4 per cent) and extremely male (98.5 per cent). This general pattern holds for CAs who received their high-school education under apartheid (35 and older), although there is some progress towards gender inclusivity and the beginning of an erosion of the white stranglehold on the profession.

However, when one looks at those cohorts who were educated and/or born in the democratic dispensation, the generational change is encouraging.

Female CAs under the age of 36 have achieved near parity with their male counterparts and comprise almost exactly half (49.9 per cent) of the profession

Table 14.2: CA demographics by cohort

COHORT	20-30		31-35		36-40		41-45		46-50		51-55		56-60		>61	
Female	3 167	49.9%	2 965	43.6%	2 140	35.8%	1 021	25.8%	446	16.9%	183	9.7%	77	5.2%	61	1.5%
Male	3 183	50.1%	3 832	56.4%	3 840	64.2%	2 930	74.2%	2 190	83.1%	1 709	90.3%	1 404	94.8%	3 979	98.5%
TOTAL	6 350	100.0%	6 797	100.0%	5 980	100.0%	3 951	100.0%	2 636	100.0%	1 892	100.0%	1 481	100.0%	4 040	100.0%

COHORT	20-30		31-35		36-40		41-45		46-50		51-55		56-60		>61	
White	4 206	66.2%	4 969	73.1%	4 802	80.3%	3 484	88.2%	2 385	90.5%	1 708	90.3%	1 359	91.8%	3 976	98.4%
Other	16	0.3%	21	0.3%	23	0.4%	6	0.2%	7	0.3%	5	0.3%	7	0.5%	7	0.2%
Coloured	272	4.3%	240	3.5%	189	3.2%	81	2.1%	39	1.5%	34	1.8%	6	0.4%	12	0.3%
Indian	991	15.6%	860	12.7%	617	10.3%	233	5.9%	135	5.1%	112	5.9%	94	6.3%	42	1.0%
African	865	13.6%	704	10.4%	349	5.8%	147	3.7%	69	2.6%	33	1.7%	14	0.9%	3	0.1%
Chinese	0	0.0%	3	0.0%	0	0.0%	0	0.0%	1	0.0%	0	0.0%	1	0.1%	0	0.0%
TOTAL	6 350	100.0%	6 797	100.0%	5 980	100.0%	3 951	100.0%	2 636	100.0%	1 892	100.0%	1 481	100.0%	4 040	100.0%

under the age of 31. While white accountants comprise two-thirds of the profession under the age of 31, growth within the Indian (15.6 per cent) and African (13.6 per cent) CA demographic in the same cohort is happening. However, even with repeated increases in the numbers of incoming cohorts of African and coloured CAs, 2021 will still see whites dominating 75 per cent of the profession.[8]

A critical intervention that will boost the changing composition of the CA pipeline is the expansion of undergraduate programmes accredited by SAICA. Until recently, UCT, Stellenbosch, the University of KwaZulu-Natal, the University of Johannesburg, Wits University, Nelson Mandela Metropolitan University and the universities of Pretoria and the Free State – all inheritors to varying degrees of apartheid privilege in the tertiary-education sector – were the only universities in which graduates could move seamlessly from undergrad to CTA qualification without the additional burden of having to register in a bridging programme.[9]

In October 2011, the historically black University of Limpopo's (previously Turfloop) Bachelor of Accountancy Science was accredited by SAICA, allowing graduates to transfer to an accredited CTA honours programme without having to navigate the further barrier to entry of a bridging programme.[10] SAICA is also working with the universities of the Western Cape and Zululand, and the Walter Sisulu University (formerly the University of Transkei), to bring their programmes up to speed for full SAICA accreditation.

In addition to efforts to transform the pipeline of candidates entering the CA track, the accounting profession and the government have entered into an extremely ambitious charter to accelerate transformation of the profession by 2016. The agreement, gazetted by the Department of Trade and Industry in May 2011, aims to concurrently alter the composition of the profession and influence the ownership of accounting firms.

The charter sets a high bar for transformation, aiming, *inter alia*, for 32.5 per cent black ownership and voting control of accountancy firms, 50.1 per cent black senior management (of which half should be female), a target of 60 per cent black management generally, and a full 70 per cent of all staff being black. All this by 2016! However, as the data above suggests, the supply of candidates entering the profession remains extremely melanin deficient, and subsequently the profession is unlikely to meet these targets. A midterm review of achievements towards fulfilling the charter is due in 2014, and it is likely that the targets will be revised.

The path to transformation is made steeper by the fact that black candidates who pass their QE exams are more likely than their white colleagues to exit the profession for business.[11] This is in part a consequence of demand factors stemming from the success of the CA qualification itself, which makes qualified CAs generally attractive to a broad range of employers, as well as the plethora of BEE charters and incentives offered to business at large to increase the representivity of their workforces, making black CAs extremely competitive for work placement. The premium these broader economic forces generate for black talent means that the staid and secure professional practices of auditing and assurance lose their most promising black candidates to sectors in the economy that can pay more.

Princely profession II: The legal eagles

Thabani Masuku looks fit and happy with life. He ushers me into his large ninth-floor office at Huguenot Chambers in Cape Town. Since I last visited him, he has moved along the corridor and, more significantly, across it. Masuku now has an unbeatable view of the front of Table Mountain and, below, a rare aspect to the verdant Company Gardens unfolds. From the wall, a specially mounted set of photos of him and his wife and two children, professionally taken, smile at you. They, too, look abundantly well. Mrs Masuku, a doctor, is, I am told, pregnant with their third.

Along the walls next to the photos are the massive bulging files that speak volumes – of a busy, successful practice. I note the files marked 'Hlophe', for Masuku is the controversial Western Cape judge president's counsel, and has become close to him based on their professional relationship, though Masuku has yet to join Hlophe in his favourite pastime of hunting. By the time this book is printed, Hlophe will have gone through another round in his seemingly perpetual legal troubles, this time in front of a newly constituted subcommittee of the Judicial Service Commission, required by the Supreme Court of Appeal to hear evidence and properly determine a complaint against Hlophe for allegedly inappropriately approaching two members of the Constitutional Court back in 2008.

But I have not come to admire the view or to talk about Justice John Hlophe, interesting though that might be. I want to hear Masuku's views on the Bar. He is now the head of the Western Cape section of Advocates For Transformation (AFT), an increasingly influential body that monitors progress in transforming the profession. He came to the Bar some ten years ago. In 2003, there were just four Africans at the Cape Bar. Masuku got good support; he was lucky with his pupil masters. He has prospered.

In the South African system of government, considerable power is reposed in the courts. This reflects the desire of those who drafted the Constitution to make a clean break from the country's apartheid past. Prior to 1994, Parliament was the supreme authority; the courts could not overrule the laws it passed.

THE PROFESSIONS | 363

The rise of the courts is moreover reflected in the rise of lawyers as an even more powerful class of professional in the post-apartheid period. High-profile members of the legal establishment such as Michael Hulley – President Zuma's legal advisor – and Wim Trengove – savant advocate in chief at the Constitutional Court – have become minor celebrities and household names as a consequence of their legal shenanigans (in Hulley's case) and excellence (in Trengove's).

Moreover, and again unsurprising given the power of court decisions, there is considerable attention given to, and invective levelled at, the composition of the legal profession at large, which, despite significant progress in injecting melanin into its ranks since the fall of apartheid, remains correlated with the broad swathe of privilege in the country.

Yet the South African legal profession is internationally renowned. Silks and retired judges from the higher courts are routinely courted by some of the most prestigious international ivory towers for fellowships and visiting professorships. Post-apartheid jurisprudence – a major output of the legal system – is increasingly influential, often cited and sourced by legal practitioners across the world as best practice and a high-water mark for progressive legal practice.

Justice Albie Sachs's devastating and utterly humane dismantling of the argument against gay marriage, for example, was cited in significant detail in a relatively recent Delhi High Court decision to strike down laws criminalising sodomy in that jurisdiction. The United Nations Human Rights Committee, in another instance, drew in detail from the argument framing the right to human dignity in the Constitutional Court's judgment against the death penalty in a recent report on the conditions of death-row prisoners.

More recently, in offering advice to the nascent democratic movement in Egypt, Justice Ruth Bader Ginsburg of the US Supreme Court controversially stated that 'I would not look to the US Constitution, if I were drafting a Constitution in the year 2012. I might look at the Constitution of South Africa ... [The South African Constitution was] a deliberate attempt to have a fundamental instrument of government that embraced basic human rights, had an independent judiciary ... It really is, I think, a great piece of work that was done.'

Elsewhere, Cass Sunstein, a Harvard scholar and, until recently, a key policy czar in the Obama administration, stated that the South African Constitution is 'the most admirable constitution in the history of the world'.[12]

While the South African Constitution and legal fraternity may be at the top of its game – at least in a reputational sense – it is a considerably more complex and dysfunctional enterprise than these international accolades suggest. The profession, lest we forget, worked at the coalface of crafting, interpreting and struggling over the laws that breathed life into the edifice of apartheid, and continues to battle to find a coherent 'transformational' voice in the post-apartheid period. The profession, too, is spread over a range of institutions and incarnations far less edifying than the nguni-hide halls of the Constitutional Court.

Beyond the high courts, the profession continues to preside over and populate a grubby, dysfunctional and overburdened system of magistrates' courts, the primary interface for ordinary citizens in the legal system. Access to justice, for the ordinary man and woman, is very uneven, to say the least.

The profession, too, is far more complex and varied than the popular cliché of the penny-pinching lawyer suggests. As a consequence of its history and the shifting structural forces shaping the institutional landscape, the profession itself includes a range of actors relatively far more diverse in practice than the straitjacket enveloping the fraternity of CAs.

But who exactly populates the ranks of the legal profession in South Africa, and how did they get there?

There are broad and narrow definitions of the 'legal profession'.[13] A narrow interpretation of the South African legal profession comprises attorneys, advocates, state prosecutors, state attorneys, state advocates, regional magistrates and the bench. A broader definition would include the thousands of legal advisors retained by government and the private sector to dispense advice away from the cut and thrust of the courts. For the purpose of this analysis, I will limit myself to those who represent a client in court and those who are qualified to preside in court, and exclude the panoply of legal advisors who are retained in various capacities to advise clients and institutions.

To act in the lower or magistrates' courts, a person must hold, at a minimum, a three-year legal degree: a BProc or BJuris. However, since the passing of the Qualifications of Legal Practitioners Amendment Act in 1997, the four-year LLB, or the five-year combination of a BCom (Law) and BA (Law) with the LLB, now constitute the only qualifications offered at universities towards practising as an attorney or advocate, with the result that the BProc and BJuris will, in time, fall by the wayside.

Following their academic qualification, aspiring legal professionals can choose from a range of paths into the profession. Typically, an aspirant private-sector attorney must obtain an LLB and serve two years as an apprentice in an articled clerkship, and thereafter sit the attorney's admission exam administered by the Law Society of South Africa (LSSA). In general, those who want to become advocates must, following qualification as an attorney, become members of their regional Bar association by serving an additional one-year apprenticeship, or pupillage, and pass the Bar admission exam administered by the regional Bar under whose auspices they wish to serve.

Members of the profession who choose to work in the public sector are

THE PROFESSIONS | 365

not required to serve an apprenticeship and do not need to sit any admission exams, although six months of training has been introduced by the Department of Justice for aspirant prosecutors. Magistrates are required to undergo training at the Justice College, administered by the justice department, and thereafter are mentored by experienced magistrates for the first six months of their service.

The distinction between attorneys and advocates hinges on the rights they have with respect to the type of court in which they appear. Historically, South African attorneys were only permitted to act in the lower – magistrates' – courts, while the higher courts were the preserve of advocates. This changed with the passing of the Rights of Appearance in Courts Act of 1995, which allows attorneys to act in the higher courts provided they have practised as attorneys for at least three years and have applied for and received permission to do so from the registrar of the high court in question. In practice, however, the historic division of labour generally remains, with the overwhelming majority of cases heard in the high courts being represented by advocates.

Advocates, on the other hand, enjoy the privilege of acting in any South African court – high or low – but, somewhat circuitously, can only act in the high court on the instruction of an attorney. In practice, this means that a client requiring representation in the high court will retain a law firm or attorney to represent the client's case and dispense advice; in turn, the firm or attorney will contract and brief an advocate from the regional Bar associated with the court in question, who will speak on behalf of the client in court. Technically, an advocate acting in a high court is not permitted to take instruction directly from a member of the public, and the relationship between the client and the advocate is mediated by the attorney.

Thus, the attorney is the key to developing a successful practice as a young advocate. Either you get briefed or you don't. And it is briefing patterns that most enervate Thabani Masuku. Sitting at his large table that juts out from his actual desk – the table where he holds his 'conferences' with clients and where he can spread the voluminous papers of various briefs – in his beautiful office high in Huguenot Chambers, Masuku's voice imbues a new tone.

There is no sign of bitterness or rancour, but there is certainly a different energy and sense of focus to what he has to say: 'Private law firms don't brief Africans – black people.'

That's quite a statement, of course. Masuku says that 80 per cent of his 'bigger instructions' – the bigger cases – have come from the state and that fortunately the state attorney is a 'big litigator'. There are five big law firms in South Africa: Edward Nathan Sonnenberg, Webber Wentzel, Bowman Gilfillan, Norton Rose and Cliffe Dekker Hofmeyr.

Table 14.3: The 'big five' law firms in South Africa[14]

	Founded	Offices	Attorneys (2012)	Employees (2012)
Bowman Gilfillan	1885	2	307+	554+
Cliffe Dekker Hofmeyr, allied with DLA Piper	1853	3	250+	600+
Edward Nathan Sonnenberg	1905	9	550+	1 000+
Norton Rose	1922	3	200+	500+
Webber Wentzel, allied with Linklaters	1868	2	400+	750+

They dominate the market, especially in commercial law, and they are 'conservative', says Masuku. 'They want certainty. They've built a reputation based on trust. They could come and brief x or y. But they don't consciously go out and brief a Thabani Masuku.' The implication is that they have the power to shift briefing patterns, but they don't. As a result, black advocates don't get exposed to commercial work. And there is a very serious knock-on effect that is no less serious and worrying than the fact that commercial law at the Bar continues to be dominated by white advocates.

And that is, because judges are traditionally drawn from the profession and the Bar especially, it is very hard for black lawyers to come to the judiciary with experience in commercial law. In addition, admits Masuku, some black judges will take up appointment because they are struggling as advocates. 'It's an easy way out,' he says, 'if you can't make it at the Bar ... thus, some people who come into the system are timid.'

Now, when 'you have judges who do not understand, or have to learn on the job, in commercial matters, you risk stunting the development of the law and consumers will not trust the bench'. This is why there has been such growth in private arbitration in recent years. Commercial litigants no longer trust the bench, fearing that they will come up in front of an inexperienced or incompetent black judge. So they opt for private arbitration in front of – usually – a retired white judge.

This denudes the jurisprudence of the country and the development of the law, because private arbitrations have no precedential value – that is to say, because they are outside of the formal court system, unlike the decision, say, of the high court or the Supreme Court of Appeal, cases that come up in the future do not have to follow the precedent that is set by the reasoning of the judgment, which means that the formal jurisprudence does not 'grow' as it usually would.

Hence, arbitrations represent a 'privatisation of the law'; alongside the formal, public face of the legal system, a private parallel system of law grows. It is, argues Masuku, institutional racism. 'You stick with what you know, who you know and what you are familiar with. There is a constitutional requirement to transform society, every part of it, but there is no sense of urgency.'

And not enough is being done to help young black advocates, laments Masuku, who knows of three African advocates who came to the Bar, 'were absolutely good guys, would definitely have made it, but [for] their financially depressed backgrounds. They went to work for government because they said "How will I fund it [the early years at the Bar]?"' Once you start getting briefed, it's fine, but there's a time lag. Masuku was in a different, better position. He had worked elsewhere first, built up some savings, was married to a doctor and had parents who were willing and able to look after their young children during Masuku's pupillage.

'Who could and should be doing what?' I ask him.

'The more senior advocates could speak up on behalf of more junior, vulnerable advocates,' he answers. The white silks could also persuade the private law firms. After all, as Masuku points out, 'personal relationships are the real drivers of briefs. They went to the same schools, grew up together, play golf together.'

As we part company, Masuku, with a chuckle, tells me that he has been invited to play in the Presidential Golf Day later that week (early February 2013). He is joining the establishment; in fact, he is already a part of it. Comfortably so, but with a burning desire to push transformation further and faster – for others; he is already set fair. Masuku has broken through the class and race barriers. Whether as a judge or a silk, he will go far, I have no doubt of that.

In practice, advocates and attorneys structure their work in very different ways. Attorneys often become highly specialised in the arcane aspects of the law (tax, labour, divorce, estate conveyance, etc.) and limit their practices to their specialisations, or join firms that offer a boutique or wide range of personal and/or commercial legal services. Much of an attorney's time is spent outside the courtroom, offering advice directly to clients, mediating disagreements and dispensing correspondence in accordance with the law; only a small proportion of attorneys engage with the court and even then they do so indirectly, through advocates.

Advocates, on the other hand, are the veritable kings of the courtroom, a fraternity of savants with photographic memories who nimbly argue and pivot the intricacies of established practice, crossing rhetorical swords with the advocates in the opposite corner, as well as witnesses and presiding justices – 'with respect', of course.

The skilled South African advocate is a spectacle to behold: measured, not prone to emotion him- or herself, but adept at exploiting emotion with argument, and the possessor of a keen scent for the kill.

Unsurprisingly, the broad division running through the profession is reflected in the professional bodies overseeing the legal profession as a whole. Attorneys are required to register with one of four regional law societies (anachronistically coinciding with South Africa's colonial inheritance – namely the Cape, KwaZulu-Natal, Free State and Northern Provinces law societies) that, together with the Black Lawyers Association (BLA) and the National Association of Democratic Lawyers (NADEL), constitute the LSSA.

Eleven Bar councils, corresponding to the regional high courts, fall under the overarching auspices of the General Council of the Bar of South Africa (GCBSA), and professionally coordinate the working lives of the majority of advocates. While advocates must pass a Bar exam administered by a regional Bar, they do not need to maintain membership in order to practice, although the over-whelming majority do.

The LSSA plays an important role in overseeing the curricula of university programmes and the in-service training of aspirant lawyers. Ultimately, the body has the power to decide who becomes an attorney and joins the profession through the administration of the attorney's admission exam.

Legal professionals play a critical role in the public sector, representing the interests of the state and the public at large as state attorneys, state prosecutors, state advocates, magistrates, regional magistrates and judges. Like their counter-parts in the private sector, state attorneys are required to hold a four-year LLB, undergo two years of articles (although they have the option of pursuing this with the State Law Advisor, in addition to the option of a private law firm) and pass the LSSA-administered attorney's admission exam. State attorneys represent the state primarily in civil matters, such as when the government is the subject of judicial review proceedings brought, for example, by disgruntled ratepayers or by interest groups resisting the introduction of e-tolling.

State prosecutors and state advocates are retained by the National Prosecuting Authority to represent the interests of the state in criminal matters before the magistrates' and high courts respectively. State advocates do not have to pursue a pupillage or seek membership of a Bar, but can appear in the high court by seek-ing permission from the relevant registrar. State prosecutors and magistrates are required to possess a three-year law degree, but are not required to sit articles or an admission exam, although magistrates are required to have at least five years' legal experience and undergo training at the Justice College. To serve as a regional magistrate, however, one must hold the four-year LLB and have a minimum of seven years' experience of the law.

How has the legal profession transformed?

Table 14.4: Practising attorneys registered with the LSSA, 2011

	Cape Law Society		Free State Law Society		KwaZulu-Natal Law Society		Law Society of the Northern Provinces		Law Society of South Africa	
African	670	12.4%	148	16.6%	463	17.0%	2725	24.6%	4006	19.9%
Coloured	167	3.1%	6	0.7%	31	1.1%	66	0.6%	270	1.3%
Indian	799	14.8%	0	0.0%	1108	40.7%	517	4.7%	2424	12.1%
White	3719	69.0%	736	82.7%	1122	41.2%	7642	69.0%	13219	65.8%
Unknown	32	0.6%	0	0.0%	0	0.0%	131	1.2%	163	0.8%
Total	5387	26.8%	890	4.4%	2724	13.6%	11081	55.2%	20082	100.0%

An analysis of all practising attorneys registered with the LSSA in 2011 demonstrates a profession broadly in line with an apartheid inheritance. Almost two-thirds of attorneys, or 65.8 per cent, are white; and whites constitute 69 per cent of practising professionals in the two largest law societies in the Cape and Northern Provinces. Africans constitute just under a fifth of the total pool of practising attorneys, at 19.9 per cent, and 68 per cent of all registered African lawyers practise in the Northern Provinces (although 55 per cent of all attorneys are registered there). Coloured attorneys are severely under-represented nationwide, making up only 1.3 per cent of those registered with the LSSA. Indian lawyers, like their counterparts in the accounting profession, punch well above their demographic weight, at 12.1 per cent, with the majority aligned with the KwaZulu-Natal Law Society, where, with 40.7 per cent, they are near parity with the whites, who constitute 41.2 per cent of registered attorneys in the province.[15]

The legacy of patriarchy is similarly evident in registration data:

Table 14.5: Gender composition of practising attorneys registered with the LSSA, 2011

	Cape Law Society		Free State Law Society		KwaZulu-Natal Law Society		Law Society of the Northern Provinces		Law Society of South Africa	
Female	1686	31.3%	255	28.8%	974	35.8%	3729	33.7%	6644	33.1%
Male	3701	68.7%	630	71.2%	1750	64.2%	7352	66.3%	13433	66.9%
TOTAL	5387	26.8%	885	4.4%	2724	13.6%	11081	55.2%	20077	100.0%

Of the total number of practising attorneys registered with the LSSA in 2011, just over two-thirds, or 66.9 per cent, were male. KwaZulu-Natal not very impressively led the pack in terms of gender equality, with only 35.8 per cent women.

This static snapshot of the demographics of the profession is, however, somewhat misleading. Information from the LSSA demonstrates that the pipeline of candidates for the profession is very different from the status quo. In 2006, the year for which data by race was most recently available for graduates from the LLB, Africans constituted the plurality of positions with 42.9 per cent of the national graduating class, with whites (31.8 per cent), Indians (17.7 per cent) and coloureds (7.6 per cent) bringing up the rear. Impressively, female graduates constituted almost three-fifths of the LLB class, with 59.1 per cent representation.

Table 14.6: Demographic breakdown of LLB graduates, 2006

	African	Coloured	Indian	White	Total	Male	Female	Total
LLB graduates	1 611	285	666	1 192	3 754	1 533	2 218	3 751
Percentage	42.9%	7.6%	17.7%	31.8%	100%	40.9%	59.1%	100%

But structural barriers to entry continue to persist for success in certain fields within the profession, diluting these impressive gains. For aspirant private-sector attorneys, serving time doing articles and passing qualification exams must follow graduation from an LLB programme. While data from the LSSA for 2011, tracking the number of aspirant attorneys registered for articles, signals progress in diluting the pipeline, like the 2006 LLB graduate data it demonstrates the utility of social networks and privilege in accessing and being able to afford the further delayed gratification required to serve articles. Of the total pool of candidate attorneys, a plurality is white (43.6 per cent). Africans comprise the second-largest demographic group at 31.8 per cent, while aspirant Indian attorneys at 21.5 per cent punch high above the national demographic profile of 1.5 per cent. Coloured representation among the ranks of those pursuing articles remains woeful at only 3.1 per cent.

Table 14.7: Demographic breakdown of aspirant attorneys registered for articles, 2011

	Cape Law Society		Free State Law Society		Law Society of the Northern Provinces		KwaZulu-Natal Law Society		Law Society of South Africa	
African	194	27.4%	28	26.9%	257	36.6%	91	32.5%	570	31.8%
Coloured	32	4.5%	1	1.0%	19	2.7%	4	1.4%	56	3.1%
Indian	222	31.4%	1	1.0%	53	7.5%	110	39.3%	386	21.5%
White	259	36.6%	74	71.2%	373	53.1%	75	26.8%	781	43.6%
Total	707	39.4%	104	5.8%	702	39.2%	280	15.6%	1 793	100.0%
Male	402	56.9%	53	51.0%	177	63.2%	372	53.0%	1 004	56.0%
Female	305	43.1%	51	49.0%	103	36.8%	330	47.0%	789	44.0%
Total	707	39.4%	104	5.8%	280	39.2%	702	15.6%	1 793	100.0%

Moreover, the gendered breakdown of graduates pursuing articles demonstrates further regression to the mean, with male candidates comprising 56 per cent of attorneys in training and women only 44 per cent.

Taking into account new attorneys admitted to the LSSA's constitutive Bars for the period 2000 to 2010 – a general proxy for those who have found employment in the private sector – the picture of demographic change is even less rosy, underscoring the enduring legacy of privilege and social connections in the profession:

Table 14.8: Demographic breakdown of new attorneys admitted to the Bar, 2000–2010

	2000	2001	2002	2003	2004	2005	2006	2007	2008	2009	2010	% in 2010	Total 2000–10	Ave % 2000–10
African	396	459	389	405	390	476	408	432	510	613	491	32.2%	4 969	30.8%
Coloured	72	62	65	72	92	84	151	58	84	96	33	2.2%	869	5.4%
Indian	91	85	83	133	85	77	101	82	213	279	228	14.9%	1 457	9.0%
White	945	869	830	759	632	705	627	854	744	1081	775	50.8%	8 821	54.7%
Total	1504	1475	1367	1369	1199	1342	1287	1426	1551	2069	1527	100.0%	16 116	100.0%

For the decade under review, whites constituted 54.7 per cent of the cohort of attorneys admitted to the regional law societies, 14 percentage points above those currently pursuing articles. In 2010, the most recent year for which data is available, white domination of the incoming cohort of attorneys fell slightly to 50.8 per cent. African representation at 30.8 per cent across the decade is largely in line with those currently pursuing articles, and coloured representation at 5.4 per cent is higher (although very poor in 2010 compared to previous years). The proportion of Indian attorneys admitted to the regional societies is lower than the number pursuing articles in 2011, although still significantly higher than the national demographic footprint of 1.5 per cent.

In terms of gender transformation, the data demonstrates significant progress: through the decade under review, newly admitted female attorneys achieved near parity with their male counterparts at 48.6 per cent, while in the most recent year for which data is available, 2010, female candidates formed the majority of the incoming cohort at 55.1 per cent:

Table 14.9: Gender breakdown of new attorneys admitted to the Bar, 2000–2010

	2000	2001	2002	2003	2004	2005	2006	2007	2008	2009	2010	% in 2010	Total 2000–10	Ave % 2000–10
Male	950	892	840	784	789	814	761	688	697	1039	693	44.9%	8 947	51.4%
Female	680	705	639	621	736	783	810	747	854	1031	849	55.1%	8 455	48.6%
Total	1630	1597	1479	1405	1525	1597	1571	1435	1551	2070	1542	100.0%	17 402	100.0%

However, as the results of a survey reported on as this book was close to completion suggest, there is still a major problem at leadership level in the profession. South Africa's major corporate law firms are still dominated by white men, especially in the upper echelons where the power – and will – to transform institutions lies:

> The survey, conducted by Plus 94 Research, found that 'senior positions [at law firms] seem to be dominated by white males': 100% of the chief executives of the 12 firms canvassed in the survey were white men. According to the survey, 45% of all salary partners, 53% of all equity partners and 68% of all managing partners – the upper reaches of law firms – were also white and male. Bonnie Meyersfeld, director of the Centre for Applied Legal Studies at the University of the Witwatersrand, said this scenario further entrenched racism, patriarchy and misogynistic behaviour and thinking at law firms from the top down, as these positions were 'where the power plays happen'. National Association of Democratic Lawyers spokesperson Nokukhanya Jele concurred, telling the *Mail & Guardian* that the 'old boys club' within law firms and at the Bar still clung to unreconstructed notions of race, gender and ability: 'I've been told on more than one occasion: "Don't bother reading the Public Finance Management Act, my girlie, you wouldn't understand it." It's these sorts of mind-sets that become institutionalised by those at the top and require changing,' said Jele.[16]

The legacy of privilege is more evident, and significantly more controversial, in the upper echelons of the profession, specifically with regard to membership of the regional Bar councils and the bench. The bench is covered in Chapter 11, so this section will deal specifically with the composition of those members of the legal profession who practise as advocates and maintain their membership of a regional Bar council.

Table 14.10 shows that there were 2 268 advocates registered across the eleven regional Bar councils in 2011, compared to the 20 082 attorneys registered with the LSSA.[17] Advocates represent the pinnacle of trial litigation in South Africa and a privileged class in the profession. Importantly, trial advocates are generally required to undergo further training in addition to that of attorneys, which requires further delayed gratification and personal sacrifice for aspirant advocates.

Given this and other barriers to entry – historical and structural – as well as the fact that advocates are usually more senior and experienced members of the profession, it should not be altogether surprising that this subsector of the profession is especially challenged when it comes to racial representivity. As Table 14.11 shows, over three-quarters of advocates (77.3 per cent) associated

Table 14.10: Regional Bar council membership

Bars	WHITE		AFRICAN		COLOURED		INDIAN		TOTAL		
	Male	Female	Male	Female	Male	Female	Male	Female	Male	Female	Total
Cape	299	67	5	5	32	21	5	3	341	96	437
Port Elizabeth	39	8	7	3	0	1	3	3	49	15	64
Grahamstown	17	4	1	0	3	0	1	0	22	4	26
Free State	49	10	4	0	0	0	0	0	53	10	63
Northern Cape	8	1	2	0	0	0	0	0	10	1	11
Johannesburg	453	139	126	35	4	7	38	21	621	202	823
Pretoria	341	86	56	21	0	0	2	7	399	114	513
KwaZulu-Natal	121	25	21	7	5	4	66	30	213	66	279
North West	8	1	2	2	0	0	0	0	10	3	13
Transkei	1	0	21	1	0	0	0	0	22	1	23
Bisho	6	1	7	1	1	0	0	0	14	2	16
Total	1342	342	252	75	45	33	115	64	1754	514	2268

with the GCBSA are male and almost three-quarters (74.3 per cent) are white. Only 14.4 per cent of advocates in South Africa are African, with pitifully low representation in the Cape (2.3 per cent, or 10 of 437 advocates) and Free State (6.3 per cent, or 4 of 63) Bars.[18] The painful under-representation of African advocates deepens when one considers that only 3.3 per cent of the total South African advocate pool is African *and* female. Coloured advocates are similarly under-represented, at only 3.4 per cent of the total Bar; female coloured advocates constitute a pitiful 1.5 per cent, with only 33 practising nationwide. Indian advocates again punch above their weight demographically, just short of 8 per cent nationally and 34.4 per cent of the KwaZulu-Natal Bar.

The GCBSA is at pains to change the demographics of this subset of the profession, but progress is slow. In the period 2007–11 (2007 being the earliest year for which we can disaggregate data by race), the number of black advocates as a whole increased by 88, off a base of 136, representing solid growth of 39.7 per cent. As can be seen from Table 14.13, over the same period, African, coloured and Indian candidates admitted to the Bar represented 36.8 per cent, 32.2 per cent and 19.3 per cent of the incoming cohort respectively. However, when one considers that the number of white advocates grew by 10.4 per cent against an overall growth of 15 per cent over the same period, the picture pales somewhat, although black candidates as a whole constituted 46 per cent of all advocates admitted to the GCBSA for the period under review (136 of 295). Impressively, the number of female advocates grew by 40.1 per cent, with women constituting 49.8 per cent of the incoming cohort – near parity with their male colleagues.

Table 14.11: Demographics of regional Bar council membership

Bars	WHITE			AFRICAN			COLOURED			INDIAN			TOTAL		
	Male	Female	Total White	Male	Female	Total African	Male	Female	Total Coloured	Male	Female	Total Indian	Male	Female	Total
Cape	68.4%	15.3%	83.8%	1.1%	1.1%	2.3%	7.3%	4.8%	12.1%	1.1%	0.7%	1.8%	78.0%	22.0%	19.3%
Port Elizabeth	60.9%	12.5%	73.4%	10.9%	4.7%	15.6%	0.0%	1.6%	1.6%	4.7%	4.7%	9.4%	76.6%	23.4%	2.8%
Grahamstown	65.4%	15.4%	80.8%	3.8%	0.0%	3.8%	11.5%	0.0%	11.5%	3.8%	0.0%	3.8%	84.6%	15.4%	1.1%
Free State	77.8%	15.9%	93.7%	6.3%	0.0%	6.3%	0.0%	0.0%	0.0%	0.0%	0.0%	0.0%	84.1%	15.9%	2.8%
Northern Cape	72.7%	9.1%	81.8%	18.2%	0.0%	18.2%	0.0%	0.0%	0.0%	0.0%	0.0%	0.0%	90.9%	9.1%	0.5%
Johannesburg	55.0%	16.9%	71.9%	15.3%	4.3%	19.6%	0.5%	0.9%	1.3%	4.6%	2.6%	7.2%	75.5%	24.5%	36.3%
Pretoria	66.5%	16.8%	83.2%	10.9%	4.1%	15.0%	0.0%	0.0%	0.0%	0.4%	1.4%	1.8%	77.8%	22.2%	22.6%
KwaZulu-Natal	43.4%	9.0%	52.3%	7.5%	2.5%	10.0%	1.8%	1.4%	3.2%	23.7%	10.8%	34.4%	76.3%	23.7%	12.3%
North West	61.5%	7.7%	69.2%	15.4%	15.4%	30.8%	0.0%	0.0%	0.0%	0.0%	0.0%	0.0%	76.9%	23.1%	0.6%
Transkei	4.3%	0.0%	4.3%	91.3%	4.3%	95.7%	0.0%	0.0%	0.0%	0.0%	0.0%	0.0%	95.7%	4.3%	1.0%
Bisho	37.5%	6.3%	43.8%	43.8%	6.3%	50.0%	6.3%	0.0%	6.3%	0.0%	0.0%	0.0%	87.5%	12.5%	0.7%
Total	59.2%	15.1%	74.3%	11.1%	3.3%	14.4%	2.0%	1.5%	3.4%	5.1%	2.8%	7.9%	77.3%	22.7%	100.0%

Table 14.12: Real percentage change in demographic representation by the Bar, 2007–2011

Bars	WHITE		AFRICAN		COLOURED		INDIAN		TOTAL		
	Male	Female	Male	Female	Male	Female	Male	Female	Male	Female	Total
Cape	9.1%	39.6%	25.0%	66.7%	23.1%	61.5%	150.0%	0.0%	0.1143791	0.4328358	0.17158
Port Elizabeth	18.2%	14.3%	0.0%	~	~	~	0.0%	50.0%	0.1395349	0.6666667	0.23077
Grahamstown	−15.0%	0.0%	0.0%	~	50.0%	~	0.0%	~	−0.083333	0	−0.07143
Free State	28.9%	100.0%	33.3%	~	~	~	~	~	0.2926829	1	0.36957
Northern Cape	100.0%	~	~	~	~	~	~	−100.0%	1.5	0	1.2
Johannesburg	0.0%	37.6%	34.0%	29.6%	100.0%	40.0%	58.3%	23.5%	0.0837696	0.3466667	0.13831
Pretoria	3.0%	38.7%	36.6%	250.0%	−100.0%	~	−33.3%	40.0%	0.0611702	0.5616438	0.14254
KwaZulu-Natal	−0.8%	78.6%	61.5%	16.7%	66.7%	0.0%	8.2%	11.1%	0.0703518	0.2941176	0.116
North West	100.0%	−50.0%	100.0%	~	~	~	~	~	1	0	0.625
Transkei	0.0%	~	−4.5%	~	~	−100.0%	~	~	−0.043478	0	−0.04167
Bisho	200.0%	~	−12.5%	−66.7%	−50.0%	~	~	~	0.1666667	−0.333333	0.06667
TOTAL	4.68%	40.74%	29.90%	66.67%	25.00%	43.48%	22.34%	14.29%	9.22%	40.05%	14.95%

Table 14.13: Newly admitted advocates by race and gender 2007–2011

Bar	White	African	Coloured	Indian	Total Male	Total Female	Total
Cape	44	3	14	3	35	29	64
Port Elizabeth	7	3	1	1	6	6	12
Grahamstown	−3	0	1	0	−2	0	−2
Free State	16	1	0	0	12	5	17
Northern Cape	5	2	0	−1	6	0	6
Johannesburg	38	40	4	18	48	52	100
Pretoria	34	30	−1	1	23	41	64
KwaZulu-Natal	10	9	2	8	14	15	29
North West	3	3	0	−1	5	0	5
Transkei	0	0	−1	0	−1	0	−1
Bisho	5	−3	−1	0	2	−1	1
TOTAL	159	88	19	29	148	147	295
Real % change 07–11	10.4%	36.8%	32.2%	19.3%	9.2%	40.1%	14.95%
Proportion of new advocates by subtotal 07–11	53.9%	29.8%	6.4%	9.8%	50.2%	49.8%	

Aside from issues of race and gender, a little side issue about status and hierarchy has blown up in recent times, concerning 'senior counsel', or 'silks' as they are colloquially known – an expression inherited from the English Bar, and a reference to the fabric of the gowns worn by senior advocates in the past. South Africa's system of senior counsel was inherited from British law, where royalty had the power to appoint a queen or king's counsel. In South Africa, an advocate has the title of senior counsel conferred upon him or her by the president after successfully applying to the Bar association to which they belong. The Bar association is responsible for considering applications and a list of approved names is submitted to the judge president of the high court in which that advocate appears. The relevant judge president then makes recommendations via the justice minister to the president, who decides whether to confer the 'honour' pursuant to authority given to the president under section 84(2)(k) of the Constitution.[19]

The tradition of conferring 'silk status' is not without controversy and has been the subject of recent debate within the profession, and even litigation – in February 2012, a group of advocates led by Urmilla Mansingh, believing the status of senior counsel to be part of a colonial legal tradition that has no place in modern South Africa, took the matter to the high court, challenging the president's authority to confer silk status.

One member of the group, Advocate Nazeer Cassim, wrote on the Abolish Silk website: 'The institution of silk must go. It does not facilitate access to justice and has come to represent some of the pernicious evil features of our society, greed and elitism. It is divisive in its nature, particularly in the manner it is applied and this divides the Bars.'[20]

Mansingh and her associates succeeded in the high court (a decision which effectively scrapped the institution of senior counsel), but in March 2013, the Supreme Court of Appeal overturned the decision, deciding that the president *did* have the power to award such 'honours'. And so, for now, silks are here to stay.

The best of the best?
A survey of advocates appearing before the Constitutional Court

The debate about the transformation of the legal profession in South Africa usually focuses on the role of the bench, and specifically the decisions of judges serving on the Constitutional Court. This is unsurprising given the court's critical role as the final arbiter of what is acceptable and just, and its role in shaping jurisprudence and precedent in the post-apartheid landscape. Yet, relatively little attention is paid to the lawyers who argue cases in the court.

This is surprising, as those who argue the cases play a potentially crucial role in shaping the jurisprudence of the courts. This is particularly so in the case of the lawyers who argue cases in the Constitutional Court. As we have seen, the Constitutional Court potentially has the last word over the legality of legislation or other government conduct. Therefore, those who seek to persuade the Constitutional Court judges of the correctness of a particular position are themselves in a position to exercise considerable power in the South African political and legal landscape.

I surveyed the decisions handed down by the Constitutional Court from the beginning of 2006 until the end of 2011. I focused on the lawyers who argue the cases in court. My survey, therefore, concentrates overwhelmingly on advocates who finalise and sign off on written pleadings, rather than the attorneys who brief them. I use the generic term 'counsel' to refer to the lawyers covered.

The cases were surveyed by referring to all the judgments listed on the Constitutional Court's website. These are not necessarily limited to cases where counsel argues a matter in court, but include cases where decisions were made based on written arguments. Whenever a decision handed down by the court lists the counsel who appeared for a party to the case, those counsel were taken into account in this survey.

A couple of further remarks on methodology should be made at this stage. Advocates will usually work in teams of two or three (plus a team of attorneys) and even more in especially large and complex cases. It seemed necessary to distinguish between 'lead' counsel and other counsel. I identify lead counsel as those listed first in the judgments (as a matter of practice, the most senior advocates are listed first). I refer to the other counsel as 'supporting' counsel.

I also distinguish between cases where counsel argued for a party to the litigation and those where they appeared as an *amicus curiae*, or 'friend of the court'. An *amicus* is not a party with a direct interest in the case, but applies to be involved in proceedings in order to assist the court in coming to its decisions. An *amicus* will attempt to assist the court by putting forward 'information or argument regarding questions of law or fact'.[21] *Amici* are usually NGOs or other special-interest groups who have a particular interest in the subject matter of a case.

During the period 2006–11, the Constitutional Court handed down 148 judgments (excluding summary dismissals of applications for leave to appeal, which do not list the counsel involved). A total of 381 counsel appeared in these cases.[22] To the extent that this suggests that a wide range of advocates argue cases before the Constitutional Court, however, the statistics are misleading. If one eliminates those counsel who have only argued one or two cases during the survey period, a remarkable 304 counsel are removed from the analysis. In other words, out of the 148 cases argued before the Constitutional Court between 2006 and 2011, only 77 advocates appeared before the court three times or more:

Table 14.14: Cases argued before the Constitutional Court

Number of cases argued	Number of advocates appearing	Number of counsel appearing in three cases or more
148	381	77

Which counsel appeared most often before the Constitutional Court?

The survey revealed that Advocate Steven Budlender appeared in the Constitutional Court more often than any other advocate during the survey period, with 28 appearances – 10 as lead counsel, 12 as supporting counsel and six as *amicus curiae*. Advocate Gilbert Marcus SC followed closely behind as the senior counsel who appeared most often, having appeared 27 times – 24 times as lead counsel, once as supporting counsel and twice as *amicus*. He is followed by Wim Trengove SC, who has appeared 22 times – 21 times as lead counsel and once as an *amicus*. Geoff Budlender SC has appeared 17 times – 11 as lead counsel, three as supporting counsel and two as *amicus*. Jeremy Gauntlett SC has appeared 14 times – 13 times as lead counsel and once as *amicus*. Among junior counsel, Advocate Karrisha Pillay has appeared 21 times, and Advocate Max du Plessis 13 times.

Table 14.15: Leading appearances by counsel before the Constitutional Court

Counsel	As lead counsel	As supporting counsel	As *amicus curiae*	Total
S. Budlender	10	12	6	28
G.J. Marcus SC	24	1	2	27
W. Trengove SC	21	0	1	22
K. Pillay	0	15	6	21
G. Budlender SC	11	3	2	17
J.J. Gauntlett SC	13	0	1	14
M. du Plessis	0	12	1	13
A. Katz SC	4	8	0	12

There does seem to be a notable imbalance between the large proportion of the advocates who only appeared once or twice before the court, and the relatively small number whose appearance numbered between 10 and 20 or beyond. Indeed, as shown in Table 14.15, only four have broken the '20' barrier for appearances. Indeed, the counsel listed above are the only ones to have appeared 10 times or more (although another four counsel have each made nine appearances). It is also notable that the group of leading appearances is not a very diverse one – with the exception of Advocate Pillay, all are white men.

Total appearances before the court are all very well, but they do not give the full picture. The inevitable question that springs to mind is, how successful were these counsel? This is more difficult to quantify. Law is not football or cricket – while in some cases it is clear that one party has 'won' and another 'lost', this is not always so. Sometimes a party will obtain a favourable outcome, but on a different basis to what they argued for. At other times, they will only obtain some of what they asked for from the court.

Notwithstanding these challenges, I have attempted to quantify the success of counsel as follows: The number of cases argued is divided up into those where counsel was successful or substantially successful; cases where counsel was partly successful; and cases where they were unsuccessful. Distinguishing between 'substantially' and 'partially' successful may seem semantic, but it was noticeable that while in some cases a party obtained most of the relief wanted, there were others where only one aspect of the case was successful (the other claims being rejected). It seemed important to draw this distinction.

A further distinction has been made between cases where the court was unanimous, and those where the court was divided or found for a party on a different basis to the lower courts. No 'won/lost' quantification has been made in cases where counsel appeared as *amici curiae*. While *amici* may often be extremely influential on a court's judgment, it is not always easy to ascertain this from simply reading the judgment. While in some cases the court might identify a specific view that an *amicus* put forward which was accepted or rejected, this is not always so. I am also mindful of the court's comment that 'an *amicus*, regardless of the side it joins, is neither a loser nor a winner'.[23]

It should also be noted that, while I have made the best effort possible to demonstrate the success rates of counsel, this survey should not necessarily be seen as the last word on the quality or otherwise of a particular lawyer. For example, it has not been possible, in cases involving multiple parties taking broadly similar positions, to differentiate the impact of different counsel arguing a broadly similar position but for different parties. Similarly, neither is it possible to distinguish which of multiple advocates representing the same party in a case was most influential, nor do I attempt to quantify the role of the briefing attorneys. The survey also does not identify cases that might have been badly argued, but the court nonetheless found for that party – cases, in other words, that might have been won in spite of the lawyers, not because of them.

With these caveats in mind, I proceed to examine the success rates of the leading counsel in the Constitutional Court.

Table 14.16: Success rates of counsel appearing before the Constitutional Court

Counsel	As lead counsel							As supporting counsel						
	A	S	S/D	PS	PS/D	U	U/D	A	S	S/D	PS	PS/D	U	U/D
S. Budlender	10	4	3	0	0	3		12	2	1			6	3
Marcus	24	9	3	2	0	5	5	1	1	0	0	0	0	0
Trengove	21	8	1	1	2	6	3	0	0	0	0	0	0	0
Pillay	0	0	0	0	0	0	0	15	3	0	2	0	3	3
G. Budlender	11	5	2	3	0	0	1	3	3	0	0	0	0	0
Gauntlett	13	4	1	2	0	2	4	0	0	0	0	0	0	0
Du Plessis	0	0	0	0	0	0	0	12	3	0	3	0	4	1
Katz	4	3	0	0	0	1	0	8	0	0	2	1	3	0

Key
A   – number of appearances
S   – cases where successful or substantially successful
S/D   – cases where (substantially) successful, but with dissenting judgments or where the court followed significantly different approach to lower court(s)
PS   – cases where partly successful
PS/D – cases where partly successful, but with dissenting judgments or where the court followed significantly different approach to lower court(s)
U   – cases where unsuccessful
U/D   – cases where unsuccessful, but with dissenting judgments or where the court followed significantly different approach to lower court(s)

These figures suggest that even the country's top advocates can usually expect to be successful not much more than half of the time they appear (in the Constitutional Court, at least). The exception, and statistically the most successful counsel to appear before the court in the survey period, was Geoff Budlender, whose ratio of cases successfully argued was over 90 per cent (although three of these were classified as only partly successful). Steven Budlender has a significant success ratio as leading counsel, being substantially successful in seven of the ten cases in which he has led. However, only three of the twelve cases in which he has appeared as supporting counsel were classified as successful, giving him an overall success ratio of 45 per cent. Of the others, advocates Marcus (58 per cent), Trengove (57 per cent) and Gauntlett (54 per cent) are all successful in slightly more than half of their appearances in the Constitutional Court.

It is noticeable that, while his percentage of success is extremely high, Geoff Budlender has appeared in fewer cases than many of the other counsel listed above – seven fewer than Trengove, eleven fewer than Marcus and eight fewer than Steven Budlender. Indeed, one conclusion that might tentatively be advanced is that the more cases one appears in, the more 'wins' and 'losses' tend to be averaged out.

There are other counsel who do not feature among those who appear most frequently before the court, but who have relatively higher ratios of success, although the differences in the numbers of cases argued indicate that caution may be required in interpreting these results:

Table 14.17: Counsel with high rates of success but under 10 total appearances

Counsel	As lead counsel							As supporting counsel							Amicus
	A	S	S/D	PS	PS/D	U	U/D	A	S	S/D	PS	PS/D	U	U/D	
H. Barnes	0	0	0	0	0	0		6	5	1			0	0	3
V. Soni SC	9	3	0	1	0	2	2	0	0	0	0	0	0	0	0
I.V. Maleka SC	5	3	0	0	0	2	0	3	1	1	0	0	0	1	0
A.M. Breitenbach SC	4	1	1	0	0	2	0	3	3	0	0	0	0	0	0
P. Kennedy SC	6	4	0	1	0	0	1	0	0	0	0	0	0	0	0

Other significant figures in the South African legal community may be mentioned briefly. Advocate Soni SC, whose statistics appear in Table 14.17, is a member of the Judicial Service Commission (JSC), the body effectively tasked with appointing judges to South Africa's superior courts. Other members of the JSC have appeared before the Constitutional Court.

With some degree of success (either substantial or partial) in five of his six appearances before the court, Advocate Ish Semenya SC has a notably successful track record, as does Advocate Mbuyiseli Madlanga SC in his four appearances before the court. It is slightly surprising to note that of the other advocates on

Table 14.18: Counsel who are members of the JSC

Counsel	As lead counsel							As supporting counsel							Amicus
	A	S	S/D	PS	PS/D	U	U/D	A	S	S/D	PS	PS/D	U	U/D	
I. Semenya SC	6	1	2	2	0	0	1	0	0	0	0	0	0	0	0
M.R. Madlanga SC	3	2	0	0	0	0	0	1	1	0	0	0	0	0	0
M.T.K. Moerane SC[24]	9	4	1	0	0	3	1	0	0	0	0	0	0	0	0

the JSC, Dumisa Ntsebeza SC appeared before the court only once during the survey period and Izaak Smuts SC not at all.

Finally, the presence of two Budlenders among the country's leading Constitutional Court advocates invites brief consideration of the importance of family connections in a field that is often characterised as insular and hard to break into. In addition to Geoff and Steven Budlender, the latter's wife, Nasreen Rajab-Budlender, has appeared in seven cases before the court, five as supporting counsel and twice as *amicus*. (She has a high rate of success in these cases, with two classified as successful, one substantially successful but with dissenting judgments, and two partly successful.) Advocate Seena Yacoob, the daughter of retired Constitutional Court justice Zak Yacoob, has appeared before the court four times; and Advocate Matthew Chaskalson SC, son of former chief justice Arthur Chaskalson, has appeared eight times.

Within an already elite profession, there are grounds for asserting that a 'super-elite' – an elite within an elite – wields great, oligarchical power, by virtue of their consummate skills and their command of the marketplace, thereby exerting considerable influence over not just the trajectory of constitutional and public law jurisprudence, but over the use and restraint of public power generally.

15

The universities

'Some twenty years on, the landscape has changed substantially. I am now firmly a UCT person. Institutionally there is a growing recognition of the place and importance of UCT in the City of Cape Town and in the country. There is a growing recognition, not a full recognition yet, that the university is not the University of Rondebosch, Claremont and Bishopscourt, but the University of Cape Town. It is not simply that UCT now is a very much more mixed institution that has won me over to its side. That is important. Much more important for me, is the growing recognition of UCT's responsibility to Langa, Hanover Park and Mitchell's Plain.'
~ **Anonymous interviewee sound bite, UCT alumni study, 2002**[1]

'It's terribly difficult for anyone to get out of the Oxford-Cambridge feeling: it's like class itself in Britain, it's the last thing we let go after our clothes, I think.'
~ **Richard Hoggart, 1960**[2]

Sometimes, though not often, I fall back on my own roots to help me understand what is happening in South Africa. While the societies are so different, the colonial heritage of South Africa means that there are often inescapable cultural and other attitudinal similarities that do bear comparison. Anthony Sampson's *Anatomy of Britain* and *Anatomy of Britain Today* were written in 1962 and 1965 respectively, when Britain was going through a massive social transformation, prompted partly by the welfare state and the radical post-war period of reform that shook up established class patterns, and partly by what Labour prime minister Harold Wilson described as the 'white heat' of the technological revolution.

My father had been the first of his family to go to university. He became a teacher and later a school inspector in London, whereas his father was a farm worker who, after serving in the army in the First World War, became a policeman in the Lancashire Constabulary in Liverpool for the remainder of his working life. I grew up in a comfortable, middle-class world, attended an interesting 'direct grant' school (Alleyn's) that at the time was part public and part private (rather like model Cs here), and went on to one of the top three universities aside from Oxbridge (Durham). With a law degree tucked under one arm and a second, informal degree in 'British class and society' (acquired from the port and debating societies of varsity and the picket line of the collieries where I stood shoulder to shoulder with mine workers against Thatcher's decimation of local industry in the mid-1980s and learnt my progressive politics) under the other, I went to the Bar. Such is upward mobility in a so-called normal society.

During the same period, South Africa was entering its own even worse hell of the mid-1980s' state of emergency, only to emerge, remarkably, ten years later as Mandela's rainbow 'democratic miracle'.

When assessing where power lies in a society, it is crucial to analyse the impact of education on the transformation of power. In most modern societies, the general assumption can be made that a university degree is the gateway to numerous professions; that, as in Britain in the 1960s, a society in transition will be reflected in its universities, with any ripples of real change being felt in the corridors of its institutions of higher learning.

As Sampson put it in *Anatomy of Britain Today*:

> Whatever happens to the schools, the most important question among ambitious men is no longer, 'What school did you go to?' but 'What university, or which college? Or did you go to university at all?' And the most important function of a successful school is to send a boy to the right university.[3]

These are appropriate questions to ask in contemporary South Africa. While attention, inevitably and appropriately, focuses on the dismal state of the school system – which, no doubt, has great consequences for learners hoping to attend university – in the meantime, it is also important to assess the extent to which universities are or are not contributing to transformation, whether by serving a new, aspirant black middle class or otherwise.

Although I am now based at a university (University of Cape Town, or UCT), I do not claim to be in any way an expert on education. So I seek guidance from someone who has devoted his life to education, Crain Soudien, a deputy vice chancellor and much-respected member of UCT's senior executive, and a long-time professor of education. Arriving at the Bremner Building, the seat of the university's administration, one notices the tranquillity. The large block is surrounded by space and lush trees. Table Mountain forms its backdrop. There is hardly any traffic, pedestrian or motor vehicle. The atmosphere is serene, genteel almost. Mamphela Ramphele's curt sound bite upon her appointment as vice chancellor here in 1995 pings into my mind: UCT, she said, needed to stop churning out 'good little Englishmen'.

Soudien is one of a small group of people playing a major leadership role in transforming South Africa's higher-education landscape. In March 2008 he was appointed by then minister of education Naledi Pandor to chair the Ministerial

Committee on Transformation and Social Cohesion and the Elimination of Discrimination in Public Higher Education Institutions, the aim of which was to 'investigate discrimination in public higher education institutions, with a particular focus on racism and to make appropriate recommendations to combat discrimination and to promote social cohesion'.[4]

The committee came about at least partly in response to the appalling Reitz incident that took place on the University of the Free State (UFS) campus in 2007, when Afrikaans students forced black workers to consume food and drinks laced with urine. The students were fined in court and the university, under the leadership of Jonathan Jansen since mid-2009, began a period of intense navel-gazing and reform.

The committee's report, delivered in November 2008, contained far-reaching findings about the state of transformation in South Africa's institutions of higher learning.[5] One finding was that while 'all institutions have a comprehensive range of policies in place to deal with issues of transformation and discrimination ... it was evident that there is a disjunction between policy development and implementation'.[6] Another notable finding was that submissions received from both historically white and black universities were very inconsistent in their degree of attention to issues of transformation. Furthermore, the committee found that 'although all institutions raised issues of gender in relation to access, few institutions raised the impact of gender in the context of patriarchy and unequal relations of power. The challenges of ethnicity, social class, sexual orientation and disability were also, by and large, given less attention'.[7]

Soudien is a UCT man through and through – he graduated from the university in the mid-1970s and has been employed by UCT since 1988, with the odd sojourn to the US (he was a Fulbright Scholar in 1991). However, unlike many academics, Soudien has also done his time at the coalface as a practitioner; as his online CV reveals, he taught for nine years at schools in Johannesburg and Cape Town before joining the School of Education at UCT.[8]

Soudien's style is famously understated; he is not prone to verbosity or exaggeration. So when he says now that during the period leading up to that report 'there was a real crisis of leadership in higher education', it is a substantial statement. It was the calmly expressed findings of his 2008 report that prompted a new period of introspection for the sector and, arguably, the new wave of innovative and largely progressive leadership that has appeared in recent years.

I have exactly one hour with Soudien, and not a minute is wasted. He gives such an incisive and fascinating rendition of the current phase of university transformation, which looks like it may be a watershed one, that I intend him to be our guide through this complex world. I have the occasional interjection, as does another rather interesting character, Patric Tariq Mellet, with whom I have been acquainted for a long time through my great friend Lawson Naidoo (both former ANC comrades-in-arms from their days in exile in London).

Power with a purpose

The story that unfolds in Soudien's office is one of great promise – of a new, powerful and progressive leadership taking root in many of South Africa's universities – but also one of continued division and inequality and, therefore, dare one say it, 'separate development', albeit more along class than race lines.

'It was not clear ten years ago,' begins Soudien, 'where this new cadre of vice chancellors and, even more problematic, deputy vice chancellors [who tend to be the engine room of university management] were going to come from to provide the intellectual and, even more critically, organisational leadership necessary.'

Luckily, what Soudien calls an 'astonishing group of intellectuals' has taken the reins and has, in his view, 'come to provide the sector with very innovative and, in some ways on a global scale, path-breaking interventions'. I deliberately use the word 'powerful' to describe this new leadership because, although they may be countervailed by other parts of the university governance structure, the vice chancellor is akin to the CEO of a major corporate. His or her character and sense of purpose is likely to have a major impact on the institution.

Soudien quickly adds that it 'needs to be said, however, that the system is effectively a two-tier system' – at this point, we exchange a reference to Mbeki's 'two nations' – 'so, while you've had these extraordinary leaders taking up positions at the top of important universities – well, the most historically important ones – at the same time there has been a crisis of leadership in those parts of the system which most need it'.

So who are the members of this new cadre of vice-chancellor leaders? Soudien lists current incumbents Jonathan Jansen (UFS, appointed in 2009), Saleem Badat (Rhodes University, 2005), Cheryl de la Rey (University of Pretoria, 2009), Russel Botman (University of Stellenbosch, 2007), Ihron Rensburg (University of Johannesburg, 2006), Peter Mbati (University of Venda, 2009), Derrick Swartz (Nelson Mandela Metropolitan University, 2008) and his own boss at UCT, Max Price (2008).

'All of those people are very capable in their own right,' says Soudien, before hastily adding a few other names of people who have played transformative roles – namely, Njabulo Ndbele (UCT, 2000–08), Brian O'Connell (University of the Western Cape, or UWC, 2001), Loyiso Nongxa (University of the Witwatersrand, or Wits, 2003) and Barney Pityana (University of South Africa, or UNISA, 2001–10).

Almost as an afterthought, but with a spring in his verbal step, Soudien then adds a final name to his list: Malegapuru William Makgoba (University of KwaZulu-Natal, 2002). 'Controversial, but astonishingly provocative.'

It is clear indeed that this is a charismatic as well as dynamic group of individuals; they are men and women of substance. But while they have considerable power within their universities, it varies from place to place, depending on tradition and culture. By way of example, 'JJ [Jansen] is larger than life,' says Soudien. 'He walks in and pronounces on these sorts of issues … and for the time being, as VC [vice chancellor] he is able to lead. He has a huge amount of power.' Similarly, at the Afrikaans universities, there is much deference to authority. The vice chancellor is able to shape policy in a more authoritarian way. There is 'The Leader' – it is part of Afrikaans culture. 'You can't do that here [at UCT],' says Soudien, who has worked at the institution for most of the past twenty-five years. 'It is rule by negotiation! Govern – *sorry* – by negotiation … which is necessarily slower.'

Mamphela Ramphele's tenure as UCT vice chancellor is a perfect example. She was extremely forceful, but it didn't always work and UCT is now back, in institutional cultural terms, to where it was before, where, as one Bremner insider puts it crisply, 'the Senate rules'.

One is reminded of one of Ramphele's detractors, English professor John Cartwright, who was quoted on her departure as saying: 'In this process of "transformation", dissenting voices were either ignored or dismissed as reactionary. The undergraduate offerings in the humanities would have benefited from an intelligent and informed re-assessment [but instead had undergone] an arrogant and authoritarian bulldozing, thinly camouflaged in traditional rhetoric.'[9]

Blade vs the 'VC club'

The vice chancellors meet regularly in a vice chancellors' forum and, while they may not agree on everything, there can be little doubt that they now constitute a much more formidable grouping – Soudien refers to it several times as a 'community' – to defend the interests of the sector and keep a watchful eye on what they perceive as 'threats' to academic freedom.

Which is a good thing, given that they face probably the most robust minister in the history of the sector and one, moreover, who can focus solely on higher education – Dr Blade Nzimande. As one of several structural changes introduced by the Zuma administration in 2009, the education department was split into two separate departments and ministries, the two line functions related to basic (school) education on the one hand and higher education (and training) on the other. Nzimande got the latter, while Angie Motshekga was appointed to head the former.

Has the split ministry been helpful? According to Soudien, the officials say it's the 'best thing we ever did' and it has 'focused attention on the two sectors thereby putting ourselves in a position where we can look at the sector in more searching kinds of ways'.

However, the split has meant a loss in terms of what Soudien calls 'an articulated vision'. What does this mean, in practice, I ask? 'Blade hates it when we say we are at the mercy of the school system. But it is almost determinative.' Why? 'Because he is tired of hearing people make excuses for the poor work that is being done at universities.'

Nzimande is one of the most interesting and colourful characters in South African politics. He tends to attract affection and disdain in equal measure. 'In some respects, the most intellectual minister we've had in a long time,' says Soudien, who concedes that on the question of Nzimande, opinion amidst the 'VC club' is far from unanimous. I'm reminded of being told by a source that one of Nzimande's deputy directors-general, Di Parker, once said approvingly of her new minister that 'he reads'. (Unlike, I would add, the president.)

Soudien's view is that the minister has been too far-reaching in his appointments and that his idea of establishing an institute for the humanities is controversial: 'We [UCT] are anxious about it, but it is motivated by a good sense of the importance of humanities.'

Not even Kader Asmal talked about the humanities, apparently. Nzimande's interest in the humanities is worrying to institutions such as UCT, because they may be inclined to think it's about taking resources away from where they should be – i.e. at their 'traditional homes', the great liberal institutions like UCT.

Furthermore, with the creation of new institutions of higher learning – the proposed two new universities in Mpumalanga and the Northern Cape – there is a concern that resources will be spread too thinly and that more will be less. This takes me back to Sampson's account of 1960s Britain and the expansion of higher education during that period of social reform:

> This stretching is causing strains and groans. For the old British universities have been preoccupied with their own values, and detest the idea that universities should be an expanding national investment producing practical results. The anti-expansionist attitude has been summed up simply and surprisingly by Kingsley Amis: 'More Means Worse': or by John Wain: 'There's a natural ceiling in the population who are able to profit by academic education, and I think we've reached that ceiling.'[10]

Swap Wain's classist 'natural ceiling' for the racist undertones of those who use the language of 'standards' to conceal their own opposition to educational emancipation, and one can see the resonance of social change between societies.

Nzimande's intention to establish a National Institute of Humanities and

Social Sciences has been bubbling since 2012. In April 2013, at the funeral of Professor Ben Magubane, he announced plans for its establishment. On the face of it, the purpose of the institute is a noble one. It is intended to provide a much-needed focus on the often marginalised and underfunded humanities and social sciences. The humanities are, after all, critical to understanding the human condition and the underlying social conditions that ought to be informing government policy.

The establishment of such an institute would see amendments to the Higher Education Act of 1997. According to Nzimande in a speech in March 2012, the proposed institute would 'advise the government – particularly the Department of Higher Education and Training – and other stakeholders on issues affecting HSS [humanities and social sciences] in the country'.[11] He spoke then of securing funding to 'pilot' the institute by way of an 'interim structure', which would map out areas of work and make recommendations regarding the structure of such an institute in the long term. The concern seems to be not only that funding will be withdrawn from universities and pumped into this new idea, but also that academic freedom and independence of thought will be compromised via such a directly government-funded institute. Nzimande, however, is clear that while the institute must not be 'market driven', government cannot fund it from the fiscus alone.

Given the minister's ideological bent, the VC club may well be right to have cause for concern – though perhaps the glass is half full in this instance. Soudien himself seems, on balance, to prefer to be glad that Nzimande is taking the stance that he is on humanities, restoring a balance. 'The dominant thrust previously is not unproblematic.' He repeats the phrase, with emphasis: '*not* unproblematic', which one senses means in Soudienese that it is very problematic indeed.

His concern was that the previous, pre-Nzimande approach was in line with neoliberal thinking elsewhere in the world, of taking money away from what Soudien calls the 'formative faculties' and giving it to universities that are concerned primarily with 'creating professionals to serve the economy' and the employment market. This is the 'education as a commodity in a marketplace' paradigm that is so contentious and so irritating to education traditionalists.

In line with his long-held opposition to neoliberal thinking and market economics, Nzimande, however, takes a different approach and understands the case for humanities better than most people.

Soudien suggests that the 'idea of being able to determine the substance and trajectory of a discipline is very unsatisfactory. You can't tell people what kind of economics they must study and support; they must go their own way.' It doesn't mean you must be inert or passive, but 'if you wish to push economics in a different direction, then put money on the table'.

The point about Blade is that he is a mixed bag; a curate's egg of a politician. He is a natural contrarian, a 'difficult character' and an ideologue – though his detractors would accuse him of being erratic and hypocritical. Given this, it would be surprising if the relationship between him and the VC club was not somewhat fraught. He is not always easy to manage, even by this group of talented leaders.

'There's a confusion about Blade,' admits Soudien. 'There are deeply contradictory things in what he is saying, and as a result the VCs have not known how to respond to him … and have tended to fixate on one or other aspect of what the guy is all about, rather than trying to understand the core things that drive him.'

Vice chancellors Rensburg and Badat are apparently deeply turned off by Nzimande and see him as attacking academic freedom. Soudien remains positive: 'I think it's more complicated than that and there are possibilities.'

And, most importantly, in the institutions themselves, there are massive shifts and changes, asserts Soudien.

Winds of change

What do the hard figures look like?

Table 15.1: Headcount enrolment in universities and universities of technology by race, 1995 and 2010

Year	African	Coloured	Indian	White	Total
1995	286 000	33 000	37 000	214 000	570 000
2010	595 777	58 175	54 492	178 189	886 633
1995–2010	108.3%	76.3%	47.3%	-16.7%	55.5%

Figure 15.1: Headcount enrolment in universities and universities of technology by race, 1995 and 2010[12]

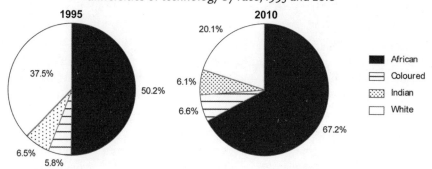

As Table 15.1 and Figure 15.1 show, the demographics of higher education have changed substantially since 1995, mostly due to an increased number of African students. In 2010, black (that is, non-white) students accounted for 79.9 per cent

Table 15.2: Demographic profile of enrolled UCT law students, 2009–2013

2013	INTERNATIONAL	SOUTH AFRICAN				TOTAL
		B	C	I	W	
Undergraduate LLB (1st year)	9	41	20	8	11	89
Undergraduate LLB (all years)	20	51	29	13	52	165
Undergraduate LLB (ADP)*		34	15	4		53
Graduate LLB	18	44	33	17	205	317
Graduate LLB (ADP)		5	7	1		13
TOTAL	38	134	84	35	257	548
2012	INTERNATIONAL	SOUTH AFRICAN				TOTAL
		B	C	I	W	
Undergraduate LLB (1st year)	7	23	11	7	14	62
Undergraduate LLB (all years)	21	38	25	11	53	148
Undergraduate LLB (ADP)		24	9	2		35
Graduate LLB	15	24	22	19	193	273
Graduate LLB (ADP)	1	8	7	2		18
TOTAL	37	94	63	34	246	474
2011	INTERNATIONAL	SOUTH AFRICAN				TOTAL
		B	C	I	W	
Undergraduate LLB (1st year)	5	11	10	3	13	42
Undergraduate LLB (all years)	18	36	28	7	53	142
Undergraduate LLB (ADP)		21	7	1		29
Graduate LLB	20	19	29	24	173	265
Graduate LLB (ADP)	1	6	4	1		12
TOTAL	39	82	68	33	226	448
2010	INTERNATIONAL	SOUTH AFRICAN				TOTAL
		B	C	I	W	
Undergraduate LLB (1st year)	5	27	11	4	10	57
Undergraduate LLB (all years)	26	40	27	7	48	148
Undergraduate LLB (ADP)		20	6			26
Graduate LLB	28	21	33	18	165	265
Graduate LLB (ADP)		4	1			5
TOTAL	54	85	67	25	213	444
2009	INTERNATIONAL	SOUTH AFRICAN				TOTAL
		B	C	I	W	
Undergraduate LLB (1st year)	5	23	8	3	17	56
Undergraduate LLB (all years)	27	27	26	7	57	144
Undergraduate LLB (ADP)		20	4			24
Graduate LLB	23	28	27	18	149	245
Graduate LLB (ADP)						0
TOTAL	50	75	57	25	206	413

(Source: Academic administration, Faculty of Law, UCT)
* Academic Development Programme.

of total headcount enrolments. In the same year, 51.3 per cent of degrees were awarded to African graduates (as opposed to 20.9 per cent in 1991), 7.1 per cent to coloured graduates (as opposed to 5.8 per cent in 1991), 7.7 per cent to Indian graduates (as opposed to 5.7 per cent in 1991) and 33.7 per cent to white graduates (as opposed to 67.7 per cent in 1991).[13]

As can be seen from Table 15.2, in my own faculty at UCT there is a certain amount of racial diversity, though as a percentage of the total, the number of black students studying law is still modest – hovering stubbornly just below the 25 per cent mark for black Africans, but just under 50 per cent if black is broadly defined to include coloured and Indian students.

However, headcount enrolments and the racial split of graduates do not tell nearly the whole story. Participation levels – that is, the proportion of all 20- to 24-year-olds enrolled in higher education – vary widely between races, going from lows of 14.1 and 14.9 per cent for Africans and coloureds respectively to 45.4 and 59.1 per cent for Indians and whites respectively.[14] In addition, throughput rates (proportion of those graduating within a specific time frame) and success rates (proportion of total enrolments passing their courses in a given year) vary widely between races.

Figure 15.2: Throughput rates by race for three-year degrees with first year of enrolment in 2005 (excluding UNISA), accumulative[15]

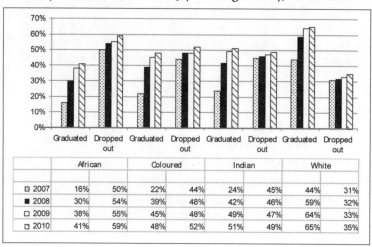

	African		Coloured		Indian		White	
	Graduated	Dropped out	Graduated	Dropped out	Graduated	Dropped out	Graduated	Dropped out
2007	16%	50%	22%	44%	24%	45%	44%	31%
2008	30%	54%	39%	48%	42%	46%	59%	32%
2009	38%	55%	45%	48%	49%	47%	64%	33%
2010	41%	59%	48%	52%	51%	49%	65%	35%

Figure 15.2 shows the throughput rates by race for students that first enrolled in a three-year course in 2005. In other words, it tracks what percentage of those students graduated, in total, in 2007, 2008, 2009 and 2010. This graph and its accompanying table clearly show that African students lag behind the other groups, particularly whites, in their rates of undergraduate completion. In par-

ticular, remarkably few (16 per cent) African students manage to complete their degrees in the minimum allotted time of three years. Furthermore, less than a third of these students have completed their degrees after four years, while more than half of white students have.

Figure 15.3: Success rates of students enrolled in higher education institutions by race, 2005–2010[16]

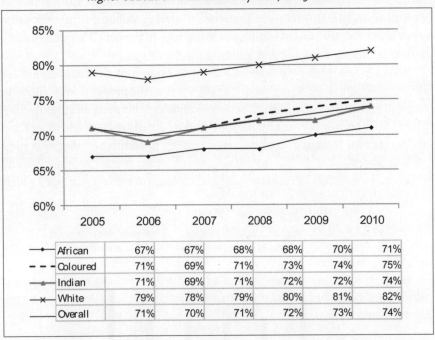

	2005	2006	2007	2008	2009	2010
African	67%	67%	68%	68%	70%	71%
Coloured	71%	69%	71%	73%	74%	75%
Indian	71%	69%	71%	72%	72%	74%
White	79%	78%	79%	80%	81%	82%
Overall	71%	70%	71%	72%	73%	74%

And, as Figure 15.3 and its accompanying table show, Africans also lag behind in terms of success rate (the proportion of full-time equivalent enrolled students that pass their courses). A similar trend was in evidence from 2001 to 2004.[17]

So what we're seeing is that, even though more black students are being admitted, a greater proportion of them fail to complete their degrees. This doesn't help anyone, least of all the students themselves, and perhaps indicates an over-emphasis on admissions that blinds crippling obstacles to performance.

It's very tricky. When I took up my current position at UCT in 2007, I was disturbed to discover the prejudices of some of my colleagues. One, who shall remain nameless as she is still a colleague, had horrified my Constitutional Law class by telling them when she set an assignment that had to be conducted in small groups that they 'mustn't just group with their own race'. The students were horrified for the rather obvious reason that should have been apparent to my colleague: that undergrads don't work like that any more. Just wander through the UCT campus and the evidence is right there. There is a new generational attitude and, while it would be silly and premature to pretend that there are not still some serious issues of race relations and discriminatory behaviour to contend with, the idea that black students only work with other black students, and whites with whites, is really outdated thinking.

Moreover, the supposition, also still commonplace among some of my colleagues in the law faculty, that black students are automatically weaker is bizarre (as well as racist). It is obvious that class is already making a big difference. I remember Ramphele's successor as vice chancellor at UCT, Professor Njabulo Ndbele, telling me once that the financial aid was barely used because the black students UCT was attracting weren't poor enough. These days, UCT spends almost R100 million of its own money on financial aid, supporting 3 000 students.

Many of the black students in my undergrad class are from more privileged homes than their white counterparts. Some of them grew up in exile in the US or the UK, and benefited from the educational systems there before their families returned to South Africa. Others are children of diplomats, or went to model-C schools and got a decent educational start in life as members of the new, transforming South African middle class.

I discuss this with Soudien, which prompts another very interesting discussion, initially about the role of elite schools; that despite what he refers to as the 'morphology of society' there are still issues around race and racism that one should not underplay.

As a brief interlude, it is worth quoting what one of my favourite black liberal commentators has had to say about transformation at UCT since he joined the university recently:

> The idea that disadvantage can be measured in terms of parents who went to university or the quality of caregivers is simply preposterous. I come from an educationally privileged background with lots of university graduates in my family. I did not lack for good caregivers. That, however, did not prevent the apartheid government from shutting the door in my face when I wanted to register at Wits University. I spent the whole year loitering on the university campus and being abused by racist Afrikaner officials whenever I went to beg them to give me the much sought after ministerial permit. That kind of racist traumatisation has very little, if anything, to do with economic disadvantage. It has something to do with what Steve Biko called 'the totality of the white power structure – the fact that though whites are our problem it is still other whites who tell us how to deal with that problem'. In this case it is whites, by dint of their numbers, who are going to decide how blacks will be admitted to UCT. Irony of ironies, indeed. Suffice to say if majoritarianism is wrong in the broader political culture, it would surely be wrong at UCT as well, wouldn't

it? Biko further described the experience of racism as an institutional and cultural experience – not a mere matter of economic disadvantage: 'The racism we meet is not only on an individual basis; it is also institutionalised to make it look like the South African way of life'.[18]

For the record, says Soudien, again with emphasis, the 'real issue about the black middle class is that it is still pretty immature ... people have all the *accoutrements*, but it is form and not substance. This is what Max [Price] has been going on about [in his very nuanced argument about why even African applicants from private schools should get some advantage in the application process to UCT]', and what Soudien now calls a 'Bourdieuian thing about "cultural capital" ... We're in the midst of that here. The kids of many of the new leaders who are running the country – and thank heavens that has shifted – are here, but there are still residual kinds of effects and we have difficulty working with that.'

Some argue that race is not a relevant criterion with regards to UCT admissions, because when you look at the composition of the Africans being admitted, you find that it's the 'new emerging black elite'. At UCT, you have a situation where financial aid funds are not being used because most of the students come from good schools, and their parents can afford the fees. This is not the case with other tertiary institutions, says Soudien.

'We are meeting complicated young people. They have been to fancy schools, many of which are pretty integrated now. St John's [College, a private boys' school in Johannesburg] – I was there yesterday – they are astonishing places ... equal to the world's leading private schools like Eton and Harrow.'

Foolishly, I suggest that Westerford High School, a former model-C school where my own two children go, and where I now learn one of Soudien's two also went, is also very privileged. 'No, no,' he says firmly, 'as comfortable as it looks, it is a class away from what these elite privates are all about.'

'I don't want to throw complexity at it,' Soudien says, as he prepares to do just that, 'but the aunt might be a sangoma, but dad owns a private jet ... disparate things to work out. They come to a school and are expected to be coherent and completely together. Some kids thrive on this kind of stuff, but others buckle underneath it.'

And this, as Soudien was quick to point out earlier, is the supply chain that the universities must work with, which in turn calls for a new kind of leadership – in a sense, a new paradigm. 'Some people understand this complexity very well ... Derrick Swartz at NMMU [Nelson Mandela Metropolitan University], where he is pushing the university to respond to it in different ways, recognising the wonderful world these young students come from, developing programmes that are innovative.'

But we have to recognise, argues Soudien, that 'this is a tiny, tiny hyper-elite that this country has … We're aware of it, trying to develop programmatic interventions – such as global citizenship here at UCT – that help them understand their responsibilities as future leaders to the environment out of which they come.'

Campus politics

Enter Patric Tariq Mellet, a special advisor to the minister of home affairs.

At Lawson Naidoo's quirky fiftieth birthday party in April 2013, I found myself clinging, literally, to the mast with the bearded Mellet, as the *Jolly Roger* pirate ship that Naidoo had hired for the occasion embarked for the open sea from the V&A Waterfront on the first night of winter, the seas far too choppy for the little tub of a boat.

While most of the guests huddled for safety in the bow where the bar was located, I risked the waves and the wet for fresh air and a stiff breeze, as did Mellet. We ended up having the most extraordinary and, for the purposes of this book, apt conversation. The rather curious venue for our discussion was not entirely absurd, given one aspect of Mellet's work for Home Affairs: namely, modernising the Port Authority's customs capacity – a project that, it is clear from his description, is clipping along at a rate of knots … much like the *Jolly Roger*.

Mellet told me of a report that he researched and wrote with veteran fundraiser Shelagh Gastrow in 2002, when both were working for the new UCT Development Office that Ramphele had established during her tenure.[19] The office was led by an American, Andy Sillen, who is now again working for Ramphele as part-time fund-raiser in the US for her new party, Agang. The report, which examined UCT alumni, was embargoed by the university's new leadership at the time because it was 'too explosive'. Reading the report now, one can understand why. As the sound bites from UCT alumni interviewed for the report reveal, there was some very pointed commentary that did not reflect well on either the alumni and their apparent prejudices or, thereby, on UCT itself.

> 'If our tertiary bodies are not world class, competitive, arrogant – all of which makes a great university – then this country is finished. We will lose our brains if we don't have top universities.'
> ~ **Anonymous interviewee sound bite, UCT alumni study, 2002**

'Campus politics was quite fraught at the time,' explains Mellet.[20] Sillen was pitted against a very single-minded deputy vice chancellor, Martin Hall (who subsequently left for a UK university leadership position after being overlooked when

Price was appointed UCT's new vice chancellor). Mellet's analysis of UCT is intriguing. 'There were five main factions. The dominant one – the WASPs – was split into a liberal and conservative grouping. Then there is a very strong divide with the Jews on the other side, with conservative-Zionist and liberal strands … wielding their own power, often fighting their own battles with the WASPs. Then there are the black alumni who have fitted in neatly with the WASPs and then the black alumni who are disaffected. The fifth faction is non-affiliate and small, but one can't discount them.'

This may or may not have resonance nowadays. But Mellet's argument is that it 'filters down into the alumni' and 'that the factionalism plays out in different ways, including fund-raising and the ability to get funds in certain ways'. The bottom line for potential givers is who does the asking. If the person asking is not from the group they are aligned with, they will not give.

> 'I believe that the character of the university has changed (though this could be hearsay) and I therefore have no real interest in re-engagement. However, I remain connected to my school which I feel has remained the same.'
> ~ **Anonymous interviewee sound bite, UCT alumni study, 2002**

In turn, it plays out in all levels of civil society. 'UCT matrics are everywhere … legal, political, commercial,' says Mellet. 'There are feeder schools: Bishops and SACS to WASPs … Herzlia to the Jewish community.'

Having spent an awful lot of time recently in the chambers of various advocates, Mellet cites the legal profession as an example of how these ethnic and class fissures impact on the UCT–society relationship: 'It would surprise me, how top advocates and silks … wouldn't mind their words … "flipping Jews" and "flipping WASPs". It compromises the rule of law. People on the bench, people in prosecution, in the defence line, are all working with double agendas, given their interconnectedness; they go off to church or shul and meet counterparts, and you would see deals done and favours exchanged … Inner DA politics … [you] find it also on those lines … WASPs and Jews in mortal combat with each other.'

But this is how the establishment operates in any society. Isn't it as natural as it is inevitable, I suggest? 'What I see is a thread,' argues Mellet, 'where at UCT you have this breeding ground for people who will go off with not just an education but a socialisation that will accompany you through your professional life … this "natural" thing becomes larger than life.'

He gives another example to bolster his point that has particular resonance for me: 'If you look at the DA-ANC division … youngsters don't have huge choices of universities of excellence. If a university is captured by a single political entity, then it can have a dramatic influence on what is a relatively small middle class. So your university becomes a battleground of partisan political ideas.'

'You might as well go to a party school,' Mellet suggests emphatically but, I think, more than a little hyperbolically. The resonance for me is that, in the weeks leading up to completing this chapter, I was asked to serve on an ad hoc committee appointed by Vice Chancellor Price to reform the rules for student representative council (SRC) elections at UCT, following a massive controversy in 2012 in which the DA Students Organisation (DASO) candidates were expelled from the electoral process after seriously breaching the rules.

DASO had appealed the decision of the SRC (which, curiously, has jurisdiction to rule on breaches of the electoral process for its own institution, rather like Parliament making rulings about whether X or Y has been duly elected to be an MP) and Price had appointed my colleague Professor Hugh Corder, who then suspended the expulsion, reinstating the DASO candidates and permitting them to take office as a majority on the SRC, but ordering a comprehensive review of the rules, which were, he found, largely outdated and confusing.

Besides the numerous technical issues that would be of interest only to an electoral-law fundi, the ad hoc committee had to deal with one major issue of principle: whether or not to prohibit candidates from standing as representatives of political parties. The effect of such a prohibition would be to ban national political parties, such as the DA and the ANC, from being active forces in student politics. As such, it would amount to a limitation of the right to freedom of association enshrined in the Constitution.

Jansen took this significant step at UFS when he became vice chancellor, primarily as part of his response to the Reitz incident. The view taken was that party politics was serving to increase division and racial tensions on the Free State campus and that, therefore, the constitutional infringement was justified.

Although in the ad hoc committee the case for such a prohibition was put very ably by a smart young man called Geoffrey Kilpin, who in effect was representing the non-aligned independents, it did not persuade the majority. Of course, DASO and ANC-aligned South African Students Congress (SASCO) representatives on the committee were against it. For both of them, the fight for political influence on campus has entered a new and crucial phase, more important now than at any time since 1994, with the emergence into the electoral market of the so-called born frees (those born after 1994, who will be voting for the first time at the 2014 national election).

The DA sees university campuses as very important sites for its party-building project, especially in terms of developing a strong cadre of young black leaders for the next phase in the contestation for power with the ANC.

So Mellet's thesis deserves attention, both for what it says about the impact of universities on society, through the professions and other institutions that they supply, and in terms of how the cultures of the universities may impact on national politics and the electoral trajectory in the longer term.

As Mellet puts it: 'UCT has very strong links with its graduates, in law and in commerce. They are the receiving organisations of these young people … so you can get a UCT hegemony in society, which, if you take disaffection and dis-illusionment among young people and it bolstered the middle-class vote … could have a silent political coup, intelligentsia getting a disproportionate share.

'As UCT transforms and a majority of black middle-class kids attend it, if the faculties have not really transformed and it is married to an ideological outlook and unashamedly bats for that outlook, they will be trying to create clones.'

This sounds suspiciously to me like the 'Oxbridge phenomenon' that my father brought me up to recognise as an elitist golden thread running through Britain, one to be resisted and countermanded wherever possible. But is it fair to point such a finger only at UCT? Mellet's response is this: 'UCT has a distinctive thing; there may be something like it at Wits. I travelled around the other univer-sities when I set up Inyathelo [the South African Institute for Advancement] after leaving UCT and I never came across it so strongly elsewhere. Maybe Stellenbosch from a different paradigm, more so than UP [University of Pretoria] or Potch [Potchefstroom – now University of the North West], in terms of the old-boy network for Afrikaners. If UCT is the English-speaking home for this kind of thing, then Stellenbosch is the Afrikaans one.'

Speaking about Stellenbosch, Soudien says: 'There is a deep, deep fight around Afrikaans, which brings out the best and worst in a place.' He thinks that Stellen-bosch has 'not quite managed, in terms of transformation; we've done better than they have – and I'm not just saying that because I'm here – they are in deep contestation about their mission, which is not a bad thing.'

One has to recognise the 'tribal' perspective from whence Mellet's analysis comes. His is an unashamedly ANC perspective; as he says, 'trusting our future intelligentsia from a UCT perspective into the enemy camp … it's about mould-ing an old and deep-rooted liberal approach, in a political sense'. What Mellet is suggesting is that the traditional – and what he regards as innate – liberalism of UCT, which is deeply suspicious of accumulated power whether it is that of the nationalists before 1994 or the ANC after, is not likely to be friendly to the ANC and is more likely to be a fertile breeding ground for opposition.

And for Mellet, who grew up on the other side of the Cape Town tracks, in the tough working-class streets, 'Cape liberalism was very exclusive; there is a snob-bishness still, with all the old stuff as when I grew up, but with the edge taken off.

'It worries me. They don't say kaffirs any more, but they are saying it.'

'Shambles. On the medical side this has been torpedoed. The phrase "African University" sounds like Marxist Economics or Democratic Republic.'
~ **Anonymous interviewee sound bite, UCT alumni study, 2002**

As in Britain with Oxbridge, the political consciousness in respect of elite South African universities runs deep. Unsurprisingly. Mellet – and here's another important rub – sees the potential 'counter-reaction' to it as 'very worrying, and leading to violence'. Seeking clarification, I ask him to explain. What concerns him is that if other powerful elites see universities such as UCT harbouring an ideological outlook that is intellectually condescending and politically oppositional, and nurturing students who are loyal to that world view, 'there will be a knee-jerk anti-intellectualism pushback', one that will end 'in tragedy if we don't deal with it'.

Moreover, he says, 'if it is perceived that your opponent is an enemy because of intellectualism, then it is going to have a negative impact on the organisation's own intellectual base' (by which he means the ANC) and 'anyone who speaks out will be tarred with the same brush and they will be played off with the masses, as with the Malema phenomenon'.

When one puts this concern in the context of, for example, the infamous 'clever blacks' comment made by Jacob Zuma when he departed from a prepared speech to the National House of Traditional Leaders in Parliament in 2012, suggesting that black people 'who become too clever … become the most eloquent in criticising themselves about their own traditions and everything', then one can easily make the link between Mellet's thesis and the anti-intellectualist populism of the Zuma era and the threat that it poses to the progressive vision of the Constitution.

Progressing beyond

Which brings one back fairly neatly to the new VC club and what I would suggest is one of its defining features: that, ideologically, it is a fairly progressive as well as strong-minded group of people. I had the pleasure of serving on the board of the Harold Wolpe Memorial Trust with Saleem Badat a few years ago. I have rarely come across such an impressive person, both intellectually and in his strategic thinking and grasp of the bigger picture, and decent and progressive to boot.

'You've got a drift towards a much stronger sense of accountability on the part of the VCs towards what they consider their constituencies,' says Soudien. 'There is a much sturdier defence of intellectual freedom than before. There is a different mood … a different *gestalt* [shape and wholeness].'

Can this cadre of leaders cope, I ask, with the extraordinary demands they face?

'They are activists,' Soudien replies. 'They are out there not necessarily writing blogs, but through op-eds taking on public issues, which has been extraordinary. The relationship between universities and their hinterlands is much more profound. Each of the three universities in Cape Town has attempted to define themselves much more clearly with their communities.'

I am intrigued, because my own direct experience with my immediate university superiors has not been entirely consistent with this. When I was employed by Corder, who was generally regarded as a wise and reforming visionary as dean of the law faculty and who introduced significant progressive reforms such as students getting credits for community-based service, he made it abundantly clear that one of my chief tasks would be to help the university engage more effectively with various legal stakeholder communities – in government, in the profession, on the bench and in the NGO world.

Yet I now face a very different dean and head of department, who have told me to concentrate on behaving 'like a normal academic' (in the latter's words), whatever that may be, and that 'the external world comes second; look after the internal [UCT] world first'. As one UCT law graduate who is still in reasonably close touch with the law faculty, Judith February, put it to me: 'It seems as if the law is being seen as a more "technocratic" matter and churning law graduates out for the market, especially the commercial law firms.'

This plays into the hands of the established law firms in Cape Town, and arguably around the country, who see the law as being about purely commercial interests, she says. 'So, the law firm I joined in the late nineties and early 2000, quite unashamedly did not subscribe to the constitutional law reports simply because, as the senior partner said, "We would never need them, really". So for law schools to fall into the same trap by being insular and marginalising questions of social justice in favour of "law as commodity" would be fundamentally undermining the crucial role lawyers ought to be playing in broader society, specifically in these days where our Constitution is under attack from ideological forces all around us. Law schools must be at the heart of pushing for change and asking the difficult questions about the nature of constitutional design and the society in which we live. Those arguments must be made by design and not by accident – but above all, it requires risk – in putting law schools at the heart of the debate about the future,' February says.

February seems to be advocating that faculties, such as law, should develop their own broader perspective on transformation. Inside the faculties themselves, however, the subject of transformation rarely escapes the vexed grip of the issue of 'standards'. In the week in which I was finalising this chapter, the quarterly meeting of the Faculty Board – a body comprising all the academic members of the faculty, and one that the student law council's president, Jonathan Singh, described as an 'extreme sport' when attending, on this occasion, for the very first time – took place and had to consider, among other things, a proposal to relax the rules relating to supplementary exams, or 'supps' as they are referred to in-house.

When a student narrowly fails an end-of-year exam (getting between 47 and 49 per cent), he or she may be permitted to retake the exam in the following January, after the long vac, if he or she has not failed more than three half-year courses. In other words, you can't fail all your exams narrowly and then get another set of bites at the cherry.

The proposal was to increase the number of failed half-year courses to six. This was vigorously opposed by Associate Professor Anne Pope of the private law department, who submitted a written memorandum that was as eloquent as it was persuasive, and which no doubt helped defeat the proposal.

I certainly agreed with her argument that the purpose of the supp rule 'is to maintain the desired standard and hence the integrity of the degree. That standard is that students are expected to pass the usual load of courses in one sitting. This is a matter of academic rigor and measures academic capacity.' In life, and especially in the legal profession, my experience has been that you rarely if ever get more than one bite of the cherry. So, while the proposal was advanced on the rather vague, and to Pope's mind un-evidenced, basis that it would 'empower' students, my instinct is that such 'reform' would likely do the opposite, since it would serve to ill-prepare them for real life in the legal profession.

Pope ended her memorandum by stating: 'Students and staff members are attracted to this faculty at least in part because it is the premier law faculty in the premier university, as current rankings show. Yet it seems that considerable energy and effort are being directed towards making this faculty more like the others in SA.' This apparently upset some members of the faculty who had joined UCT from 'other' universities, and she felt compelled to circulate an apology. I wonder if she really had anything to apologise for. If UCT's law faculty has good reason to consider itself the strongest in the country, then I am not sure why it should be shy about saying so and doing everything to maintain its superiority.

At a time when there is a good deal of intellectual dumbing-down in South Africa, the very last thing we need is for our strongest academic institutions to fall into the trap of doing so. The challenge is to justify 'elite' attitudes to educational standards and attainment while preparing students not just for 'professional life', as defined by the needs of the commercial law firms, but for a society that is in transformation and which has many complex and interdependent social, economic, environmental and political imperatives.

For the latter, we need graduates to have a heightened sense of their own delicate surroundings, to be aware of the enormous privileges they have in comparison to most of their compatriots, and to be attuned to the consequences of the inequality of power and opportunity that bedevil South Africa.

Preparing students for the 'real world' in this sense is clearly a complex undertaking. Most lawyers are not good at interdisciplinary, complex-systems thinking. They tend to be linear thinkers, fixated on 'problem solving' in a one-dimensional sense. This is an argument for even higher standards of teaching and research in law faculties – in *all* faculties for that matter, whether engineering or medicine or economics – as the complex demands of South Africa are going to require a new form of leadership from its professional classes.

We are probably falling short in this respect, which has implications for future power relations in the country as a whole. If the professions are ill-equipped to cope with, let alone lead the response to, the intense socio-economic challenges that threaten South Africa's future stability and prosperity, then the likelihood of populist politics and populist leaders prevailing sadly increases. It is up to the great universities to shoulder this responsibility. So when a law student of mine, who happens to be the child of a progressive, independent-minded judge, bemoans the lack of critical thinking in the faculty and tells me that she feels she has 'got stupider' during her time at UCT, I despair; and even more so when she informs me that one esteemed law professor lectures by simply reading out sections of his textbook 'because I can't put it better now than I did in the book'.

I also have to acknowledge that the attitude of the law faculty management is essentially conservative and managerialist, and provides little support to the research units that exist for the purpose of applied research and that have great potential for the sort of social outreach that Soudien argues is essential, though he accepts when I put this to him that the question of how universities should interact in a socially responsive way is 'not cleared up. You have got this very distinct sense of engagement with these publics,' he says, 'but you need a real discussion amongst the leadership and the public intellectuals with an interest in higher education ... about the role of the university, in the specifics of the context in which we find ourselves.'

An example of a vice chancellor who has come close is Ahmed Bawa (Durban University of Technology, 2010). After the publication of the 2008 Ministerial Committee on Transformation and Social Cohesion report, he was involved with Soudien in a number of public forums to discuss the role of universities in South Africa and the question he put was, 'How will we begin to define a South African university?'

Says Soudien: 'I think that in terms of things such as the vision and mission we have deferred too much to a sort of globalised-speak about what a university is about. Universities across the country, very few of them articulate a view of the university beyond very traditional language such as "excellence" and "relevance" ... very popular key words in the repertoire of thinking about the institutions ... It is the question of specificity that is most challenging ... What distinguishes us from Zimbabwe or UK? What is that mark of distinctive specificity? ... Historical issues would need to be considered ... Where the university has been in the past. Not thinking about TRC, but it is undoubtedly true that this whole colonial history has been actually formative ... Law, for example, the character of the discipline, and the ideal outcome and product and how this discipline sits in wider context.'

For my part, the discussion about the social responsiveness of universities bears an uncanny resemblance to the debate I have been exposed to, through my work with the University of Cambridge Programme for Sustainability Leadership, about 'corporate social responsiveness'. In that world, issues about social, economic and environmental sustainability are all too often relegated, however sincerely or well intended, into silos separate from the company's core business operations.

There is a collective failure of imagination and strategic thinking and, therefore, of leadership, in failing to appreciate that the business's long-term sustainability is ineluctably tied to the overall sustainability of the world in which it operates.

'Social responsiveness' is not, therefore, an add-on, an act of philanthropy, but enlightened self-interest. Transposed to the law faculty, this means that, for example, the university should be engaging strongly with issues of constitutional democracy, judicial appointment and ethics, and the independence of the rule of law, because there is little point in producing a long line of well-qualified law graduates if the legal system into which they are moving has broken down. That is why it should be seen as core business and not simply as 'social responsiveness'. That is why the 'external world' is, in fact, more important than the 'internal world'.

Where is transformation happening?

You can speak of a South African ivy league: UCT (the only South African university in *The Times*'s top 200 world universities), Wits, Stellenbosch, Pretoria and Rhodes. Soudien acknowledges this, but adds one that has moved up in recent times: UWC, which 'may not quite have cracked the top five, but is quite close'. Soudien knows of some white students who have opted to go to UWC, recognising that there are leaders in their field at UWC, and that in some instances it's head of the class. One example is nursing.

There are twenty-one designated universities plus two in the process of being established. Four or five are under administration at the moment, Soudien tells me. We are, he says, 'in deep apartheid legacy territory, with institutions that belong in very narrow terms to particular communities and so these institutions are conduits of patronage, nepotism and consequent corruption that was endemic in Bantustan culture. It is immensely difficult to shift out of these cultural tendencies.

'There are clearly not enough places of learning and knowledge production. By and large, and there are exceptional scholars and teachers in all of these institutions, we find ourselves in the classic situation where the country and bureaucracy as a whole finds itself: that the institution becomes a pathway to upward mobility, as the easiest ways of thinking about rapid social mobility. They've stopped being universities in the more traditional sense, and so these opportunities for thinking of them as spaces of knowledge gathering and acquiring have been cruelly compromised.'

Soudien says all this with pain in his voice, adding by way of example that the 'history department at a university I know reasonably well does not have the capacity to produce a single honours' degree. Not even the minimum characteristics of what a reasonable historian should be all about.'

Nonetheless, those who graduate from there are 'better off than the kids who don't have degrees, compared with poor matrics, but relative to the elite universities they are distinctly second class'.

I want now to turn to the individual universities. It is of interest to us, after all, to see where the increased numbers of black students are headed. Are they focusing on specific institutions, as was the case pre-democracy, or have racial demographics shifted relatively evenly across the country? In particular, have we seen meaningful change in those universities that lead the higher-education pack, or are black students being funnelled to lesser-known universities with poorer reputations?

Unfortunately, data on the racial composition of individual South African universities does not stretch as far back as 1994. And, while we can look at how the scenario has changed over the past decade or so, the comparison is not a straightforward one. Following plans to reform higher education, in 2004 several universities merged with one another to create larger, more encompassing institutions. This was a good move for the country, mostly because we now have sexy names like Nelson Mandela Metropolitan University and the Tshwane University of Technology. It created a data problem, however, in that the racial composition numbers from 2001 don't match up with those from 2009. To solve this, I placed the 2001 universities into the 2009 categories – that is, if 2001 university A and 2001 university B are now 2009 university A, I just added the numbers for 2001-A and 2001-B and called it 2009-A for both 2001 and 2009. This does the trick all right, but for the fact that certain universities weren't absorbed into a single institution (the University of Vista, for example). Figure 15.4

thus presents an imperfect, but broadly accurate, representation of the changing picture between 2001 and 2009.

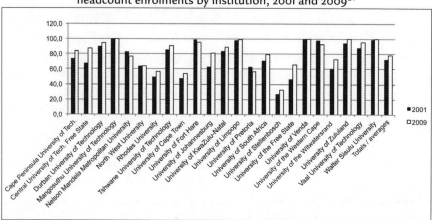

Figure 15.4: Percentage of black students in total
headcount enrolments by institution, 2001 and 2009[21]

The first thing to notice is that, generally, the proportion of total headcount enrolments accounted for by black students has increased by around 5 percentage points. This is good news. However, consider that in 2009, 79.5 per cent of enrolments were black students, while this group accounts for 91.9 per cent of South Africa's population.[22] Now we cannot take it for granted that national demography is the appropriate measure to use when considering higher education, but it does provide for an easily calculable and easily understandable benchmark. So, using national demography as a crude but quick-and-easy precedent, how have individual institutions been measuring up? How would we know? One way is to consider 91.9 per cent as a kind of 'target proportion' for black students and to see how much closer or further away from that target universities have moved. Table 15.3 does just that, indicating whether, how much and in what direction the proportion of black students must increase/decrease to mirror national racial demographics.

We see that the Central University of Technology, Free State, UFS, Johannesburg, Wits and the Cape Peninsula University of Technology (CPUT) have most impressively increased their proportions of black enrolments.

UFS and Wits, however, are still quite out of sync with the national split. On the other side of the spectrum, we have those such as the University of Zululand, the Durban University of Technology and the Vaal University of Technology. These have actually moved further away from the national split since 2001, and host a disproportionately large number of black students.

Table 15.3: Changing proportion of black students
in total headcount enrolments, 2001–2009

Institution	% points closer (+) or further (−) from national split	Need to increase/ decrease black representation	% point increase/ decrease
Central University of Technology, Free State	19.2	increase	3.9
University of the Free State	18.3	increase	25.7
University of Johannesburg	18.2	increase	10.1
University of the Witwatersrand	13.0	increase	18.1
Cape Peninsula University of Technology	10.2	increase	7.2
University of South Africa	8.0	increase	12.1
Rhodes University	7.4	increase	34.1
University of Cape Town	6.0	increase	37.1
Tshwane University of Technology	5.5	increase	0.1
University of KwaZulu-Natal	5.4	increase	1.5
University of the Western Cape	5.0	decrease	1.9
University of Stellenbosch	4.9	increase	59.1
University of Fort Hare	3.3	decrease	4.9
Mangosuthu University of Technology	0.0	decrease	8.9
University of Venda	0.0	decrease	8.9
University of Limpopo	−0.3	decrease	7.9
Walter Sisulu University	−0.3	decrease	8.9
North West University	−0.5	increase	27.2
Vaal University of Technology	−1.8	decrease	4.9
Durban University of Technology	−2.8	decrease	3.9
University of Zululand	−5.0	decrease	8.9
University of Pretoria	−5.9	increase	33.9
Nelson Mandela Metropolitan University	−6.8	increase	14.6

Academic heavyweights such as UCT, Stellenbosch, Rhodes, Wits and Pretoria are quite heavily dominated by white students (Stellenbosch especially, though this will come as quite a shock to absolutely no one). Pretoria has actually seen a decrease in its proportion of black students (by 5.9 percentage points). The University of KwaZulu-Natal, another leading university, is practically aligned with national demographics, as are the Tshwane University of Technology and

UWC. Lastly, it is noteworthy that universities have a relatively lower proportion of black students than do universities of technology. The proportion of black students in total headcount enrolments for the former is roughly 76 per cent, while this figure is 91 per cent for the latter.

Overall, then, we see that 'transformation' in higher education has progressed over the last decade, but unequally and in different directions. This is to be expected – again, it is by no means the case that national racial demography should act as a proxy for all institutions and, indeed, it would be absurd to suggest that each university conform to it. Furthermore, it is important not to fixate too much on headcount enrolments. After all, universities that have 'transformed' by a smaller degree in terms of these enrolments may bring a much higher proportion of their black students to graduation, perhaps because of more holistic policies and better management.

What are black students studying?
Another interesting trend to look at is whether black students are being admitted to certain types of programmes and not others. Does transformation speak in the language of numbers, equations, medieval history, rands and cents, or the idiosyncratic religious rituals of that strange Amazonian tribe you've never heard of and probably never will?

Figure 15.5: Headcount enrolments by race and field of study, 2005 and 2010[23]

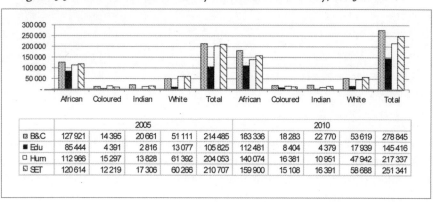

	2005					2010				
	African	Coloured	Indian	White	Total	African	Coloured	Indian	White	Total
B&C	127 921	14 395	20 661	51 111	214 485	183 336	18 283	22 770	53 619	278 845
Edu	85 444	4 391	2 816	13 077	105 825	112 481	8 404	4 379	17 939	145 416
Hum	112 966	15 297	13 828	61 392	204 053	140 074	16 381	10 951	47 942	217 337
SET	120 614	12 219	17 306	60 266	210 707	159 900	15 108	16 391	58 688	251 341

Figure 15.5 and its accompanying table show the numbers of students enrolled in the fields of business and commerce (B&C), education (Edu), humanities (Hum) and science, engineering and technology (SET). There is nothing particularly striking – all racial groups seem to show a preference for B&C and SET over humanities and education. African students seem to show a stronger preference for B&C over SET, while the opposite is true for white students. Education is most

popular among African students, drawing roughly 19 per cent in 2010 as opposed to 14 per cent for coloured students and 10 per cent or below for the other groups. Overall, in 2010, non-white students demonstrated a slightly greater preference for B&C (31.7 per cent share versus 30.1 per cent), a considerably greater preference for education (17.7 versus 10.7 per cent) and weaker preferences for SET and humanities (23.6 versus 26.9 per cent and 27 versus 32.9 per cent respectively) than white students. Between 2005 and 2010, it seems that African students were increasingly drawn to both B&C and education at the expense of other fields, particularly humanities (its share dropped by 2.3 percentage points). White students, meanwhile, have been drawn increasingly to education and B&C (these shares increased by 3 and 2.6 percentage points respectively), wholly at the expense of humanities. The share of this field was the only one that declined for white students, by a significant 6.1 percentage points. Why? Perhaps the recession triggered a wave of youthful anxiety about learning the ins and outs of those rapidly dwindling rands and cents.

Figure 15.6: Headcount graduates by race and field of study, 2005 and 2010[24]

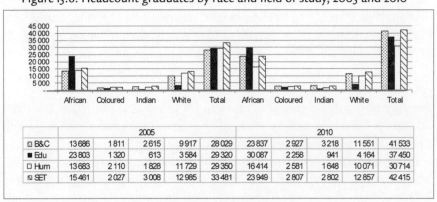

		2005					2010			
	African	Coloured	Indian	White	Total	African	Coloured	Indian	White	Total
▨ B&C	13 686	1 811	2 615	9 917	28 029	23 837	2 927	3 218	11 551	41 533
■ Edu	23 803	1 320	613	3 584	29 320	30 087	2 258	941	4 164	37 450
▯ Hum	13 683	2 110	1 828	11 729	29 350	16 414	2 581	1 648	10 071	30 714
▨ SET	15 461	2 027	3 008	12 985	33 481	23 949	2 807	2 802	12 857	42 415

Figure 15.6 and its accompanying table show a slightly different picture. While this doesn't show how many of the students previously discussed are passing (the graduates in 2005, after all, probably started in 2002 or 2003), it may indicate where the most disappointing throughput rates are concentrated.[25] Accordingly, we may be seeing a situation where African students, to a greater degree than their white counterparts, drop out or fail B&C courses, leaving a significant share of those that remain in the generally lower-paid field of education.

Additional analytical texture can be gleaned from a major study conducted by the HSRC in 2005[26] and the subsequent dissection of the results by Bhorat, Mayet and Visser.[27] The study collected data from a sample of 5 491 individuals from a 2002/3 cohort of students who attended seven universities that included both historically black institutions (HBIs), such as the University of Fort Hare, and historically white institutions (HWIs), such as Stellenbosch University.

Analysis showed that certain household variables are to an extent important in determining how likely an individual is to graduate, especially household income, whether the home language is English, and if the student's schooling was urban rather than rural.[28] In addition, students who did well in mathematics in matric were more likely to graduate.

Students who attended HBIs had a lower probability of graduating than those from HWIs. In terms of employability, Africans at both HBIs and HWIs had a lower probability of securing employment relative to whites at HWIs. In additon: 'Being African lowers the probability of finding a job relative to being white, and being female lowers the probability of finding employment relative to being male.'[29]

A recent study by the Cape Higher Education Consortium, which assessed the post-graduation experiences of graduates of institutions of higher education in the Western Cape – Stellenbosch, UCT, UWC and CPUT – also showed that '[e]mployment by race continues to reflect Apartheid-era patterns of discrimination. Data from the survey shows that, whereas 61% of Whites and 58% of Indians are employed in the private sector (as at 1st September 2012), only 35% of Africans and 44% of Coloureds are employed in the same sector.'[30]

The study commented that, but for the public sector, which employs 42 per cent of African and 45 per cent of coloured graduates, unemployment in the province would be far greater than it is: with 19 per cent of African graduates unemployed and looking for work (and 7 per cent of coloureds), compared with 5 per cent of whites and 3.2 per cent of Indians.

HBIs, the HSRC study found, 'are much poorer in ensuring success in the labour market for their client base than HWIs ... African graduates are finding it distinctly harder to secure employment than their white counterparts.'[31] While employer discrimination 'must feature as a key factor', the unemployment rates for white non-completers, which were significantly less than those of African non-completers, 'suggest the existence of informal networks that improve both search behaviour and the probability of finding employment'.[32]

Interestingly, the household characteristics that were significant in determining graduation were not significant in influencing employment. However, using matric mathematics as a proxy for grades at varsity suggested to the researchers that mathematics grades were a factor that influenced employers. Moreover, there was no evidence to suggest that those who drop out of university are significantly worse off in finding employment than those who complete their studies and graduate, prompting the researchers to conclude: 'This may be attributed to the fact that the non-completers in our sample have completed some years of tertiary education and perhaps also acquired some soft skills while at the higher education institution, which may give them some employability advantage over those without any tertiary education.'[33]

Finally, the study found no evidence that race had any significant impact on the earnings (salary) of graduates: '[I]ndividuals are selected into employment on the basis of a number of characteristics but, once over the entry-into-employment hurdle, the race-based differences are eroded.'[34]

In other words, coming from a well-off, urban home, being good at mathematics in matric and attending a historically white university will likely secure you a good, well-paid job, especially if you are white and male, even if you study social sciences or the humanities.

With this in mind, it is clear that the powerful and dynamic new leadership group that is now running South Africa's universities has a lot to do if the new face of power in South Africa is to be anything other than a superficial veneer.

CONCLUSION

Anatomy of a crisis

SAM: Don't forget the comic books. [Hally returns to the counter and puts them in his case. He starts to leave again.] [To the retreating back of the boy.] Stop … Hally … [Hally stops, but doesn't turn to face him.] Hally … I've got no right to tell you what being a man means if I don't behave like one myself, and I'm not doing so well at that this afternoon. Should we try again, Hally?

HALLY: Try what?

SAM: Fly another kite, I suppose. It worked once, and this time I need it as much as you do.

HALLY: It's still raining, Sam. You can't fly kites on rainy days, remember.

SAM: So what do we do? Hope for better weather tomorrow?

HALLY: [Helpless gesture.] I don't know. I don't know anything anymore.

SAM: You sure of that, Hally? Because it would be pretty hopeless if that was true. It would mean nothing has been learnt in here this afternoon, and there was a hell of a lot of teaching going on … one way or the other. But anyway, I don't believe you. I reckon there's one thing you know. You don't have to sit up there by yourself. You know what that bench means now, and you can leave it any time you choose. All you've got to do is stand up and walk away from it. [Hally leaves. Willie goes up quietly to Sam.]

~ **From *Master Harold and the Boys* by Athol Fugard**

As my writing of this book finally gathered pace in early 2013, I happened to see a production of Athol Fugard's play *Master Harold and the Boys* at the splendid Fugard Theatre in Cape Town. It was an excellent production, superbly acted. For those who don't know the play, it is a three-way conversation between two black men (Sam and Willie), who work in the shop owned and managed by the mother of the third character, a white teenage boy called Hally. The two men have known the boy all his life. The three are friends. But apartheid places limits on the relationship between the black men and the white boy, which are exposed in the painful final scene, when an argument breaks out and culminates in Hally spitting in Sam's face.

What is extraordinarily moving is how – in the brief excerpt above – it is Sam, and not Hally, who ends up both apologising and seeking reconciliation.

He, the man who has been spat at, *he* is the one who is *apologising and seeking reconciliation*, not the perpetrator.

It struck me then that this still rings true in modern South Africa. Perhaps it is wisdom, as well as strength of character, that enables Sam to behave with such dignity, despite the indignity of what has just happened to him. Perhaps it is his way of recovering his dignity, knowing, as he says, that it is Hally who has hurt himself. Perhaps it is 'learned behaviour': the onus always falling on the less powerful to make the move towards the more powerful, even when the more powerful has perpetrated the injury.

South Africa's balance of power

This book reaches, to my mind, an inevitable conclusion: that the state of play, the balance of power, the plight as well as the aptitude and attitudes of the establishment, points towards crisis. I am not alone in this finding. '[W]e are a country in crisis; a country that, by virtue of a leadership void and a state apparatus that has badly lost sight of the principles of ethics, integrity and honesty, is losing traction – and fast,' writes Udesh Pillay in the conclusion to the HSRC's most recent *State of the Nation* book.[1]

While I would be the last person to use the past to permit any powerful actor or institution to escape censure or responsibility for acts of culpable negligence, dishonesty or corruption now, it would be equally wrong to ignore the past and not to recognise where South Africa has come from. After all, much has changed for the better. The socio-economic data, summarised in Chapter 1, shows that the material conditions of all South Africans have improved, alongside the complete dismantling of the legislative basis of apartheid during the golden period of constitutional and legal reform in the 1990s. A black middle class has formed, to ensure that black people are able to take up opportunities that were denied them before 1994, not just in the political sphere but in the corporate sector as well. Visit the bars and restaurants of Melrose Arch, Rosebank and Sandton in Johannesburg on any day or night and you will see for yourself the changing face of suburban, middle-class South Africa.

But, while some of the harder edges of poverty have been knocked off, for the great majority of South Africans life remains substantially unchanged from before 1994. For millions, the vote has not yet delivered a decent education system or the dignity of a decent job and the chances to improve oneself and one's family that come with it.

The terrible murderous events of Marikana in August 2012 revealed the extent to which inequalities of power still dominate the traditional industrial base of South Africa. Eighteen years of democratic government has not yet managed to change that. Moreover, a supposedly democratic government chose to go back in time, using its raw power to suppress the understandably angry protests of workers and unemployed for whom life is miserable and unsustainable.

In the larney shopping malls of Cape Town and other wealthy urban suburbs around the country, the white middle class seem inexplicably unable to understand their own country – the one that surrounds their islands of wealth and privilege. All too often, the way that they conduct themselves towards their black compatriots demonstrates not only a lack of empathy but also a thoughtlessness about their society, classically illustrated by their refusal to understand the links between poverty and inequality, and crime or violent protest.

The undercurrent of racism, of hate and contempt, continues to bubble away, not far beneath the surface. Many white people continue to spit in the faces of black people, while expecting 'Sam' to apologise and seek reconciliation.

There is great and understandable concern about socio-economic pressures and the future stability of the country, but little if any willingness to sacrifice or share power or wealth so as to create a more equal and just society. Indeed, displays of wealth by new, black entrants to the middle class are viewed slyly and often with contempt, even though to a large extent they are mimicking established patterns of consumerism in South Africa.

The middle class want their privileged lifestyle to remain intact; they want a stable democracy and a vibrant economy. Yet they are blind to the sacrifices and changes they may need to make to ensure there is social cohesion and to generate new forms of social capital sufficient to prevent this complex, wounded and precarious society from falling apart completely. The point is this: if we want things to stay as they are, things will have to change – as Tancredi said in The Leopard.[2] Or, to apply and then adapt an Mbekism, if we want the centre to hold, then the centre has to give as well as take. In other words, if the wealthy, privileged middle class wants to retain its comforts and lifestyle, it will have to make sacrifices.

The political establishment in crisis

The centre is not holding. Shortly before Polokwane, I visited a friend who used to be one of the government's leading spin doctors. He had moved into the private sector, seeking a break from the pressures of high-level government communications. As I left the plush corporate surrounds of his new offices, I mentioned that I was going straight to the airport to fly to London on a work trip. 'If they win, keep a seat for me, won't you?' he said with only the barest twinkle in his eye. 'They' meaning Zuma and his crowd. They did win. And they are still in power and doing their utmost to build it for the long term.

My friend did not emigrate, I am pleased to say, as he is far too talented to not be missed. He thought about leaving instead for COPE. But, he tells me now, a friendly ANC leader advised him that 'you must be like a frog and stay in the mud'. He is still in the mud, having returned, in fact, to serve government, while being paid by a large company – an intriguing little arrangement.

It would be an enormous mistake to think that the roots of the crisis can be traced solely to Polokwane. Far from it; Mbeki and his approach to government had many shortcomings, not least his own tendency to abuse state institutions to fight factional wars aimed at keeping his enemies at bay. The roots of the corruption that now defaces the government's ability to serve the public can be traced much further back, not least to the arms deal that was entered into at the end of the last century right under Mbeki's nose.

The Zuma administration, despite, rather than because of, Zuma's leadership, is in some important respects more progressive in intent and more focused in its implementation of strategy – for example, in terms of the public infrastructure programme and, overall, the prioritisation of governmental interventions that are job-creating.

And yet Mbeki is much missed. Certainly, the loss of some of the most influential people that were at the centre of Mbeki's power – such as the leading intellectual Joel Netshitenzhe, Mbeki's head of policy – has weakened government. Under Zuma, the social compact that was forged in the 1990s has unravelled. Marikana was the ultimate expression of this. Weakened by internal division and rancour, neither the ANC nor COSATU were able, or remain able, to absorb the socio-economic pressures in the way that they did for so long, inviting pessimistic assessments of the capacity of government to navigate South Africa out of the choppy waters it now finds itself in.

The need to build a capable state is identified by the NDP as a key strategic goal, not least because the social contract between taxpayers and their government is an important one for democratic legitimacy and the consent to govern that accompanies it. This book has not found space to dwell on the public service, focusing instead on the Presidency – and its two new institutional innovations, the National Planning Commission and the Department of Performance Monitoring and Evaluation – and one area of government, namely, foreign policy making. But it is clear that the efforts of the powerful new minister of public service and administration, Lindiwe Sisulu, to combat corruption in the private sector and to get a higher return from the large public-sector wage bill are a necessary thought not necessarily sufficient part of improving public service delivery.

Government spending, performance and protest action

The public sector is a safe haven for many; and it is getting bigger. But is it more powerful? It is a driver of social transformation, and for the changing face of South Africa, because it is the area where the government has the most direct control, especially in state-owned enterprises – another site of great power and influence that this book has not been able to dwell upon. South Africa is now spending more on government salaries and benefits for those employed by national, provincial and local government than at any time since 1994. This increased spending can be explained by a combination of increased hiring and higher salaries.

Figure 16.1: Actual and inflation-indexed wage bill per employee, 1998–2011

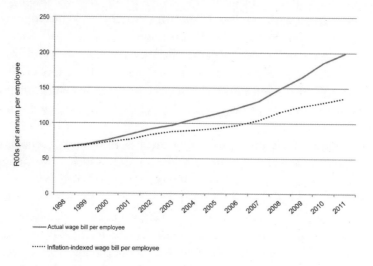

Source: Statistics South Africa, 2012

Firstly, the number of staff employed by the national, provincial and local governments has increased by approximately 20 per cent between 1998 and 2011.[3] Secondly, as Figure 16.1 illustrates, the wage bill *per employee* has increased. The graph also shows that these increases cannot be justified by appeals to inflation, as salaries are well above what they would be if they had increased along with inflation. So we are hiring more public-sector employees *and* we are paying them more.

The pressing question, then, is, are we getting value for our money? The fact that we have been experiencing unprecedented social unrest and a marked increase in service-delivery protests over the last several years does not seem to suggest so.[4] In other words, the public does not seem especially satisfied with the return that they are getting. Further, as the 2012 budget review damningly noted, large increases in compensation for employees have 'resulted in fewer resources available for social and economic infrastructure, and other priorities'.[5]

It appears, then, that an unproductive ballooning of public-sector employment has occurred, especially since Zuma took office in 2009. The next question to ask is, who are the recipients of these windfalls? After all, there are various levels of government.

Figure 16.2: Employee compensation by level of government, 1998–2011

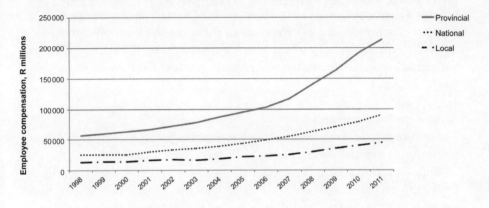

Figure 16.3: Employee compensation per employee,
actual and inflation-indexed, 1998–2011

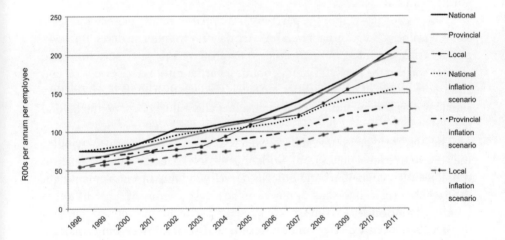

Figure 16.2 illustrates that, although the wage bill has increased across all levels of government, the most marked increase has been for the provinces – indeed, one can see a distinctive upward spike beginning from around 2007. Figure 16.3, meanwhile, shows that provincial employee compensation per employee has

sharply increased, well above inflation, from around the same period. Per employee compensation for national government has also increased steadily, though the current growth trajectory seems to have been in evidence since around 2005. The number of provincial employees, meanwhile, has also been increasing by a relatively larger amount than other levels of government – the provinces have experienced a 32 per cent increase in staff since 2004, as opposed to 23 per cent for national government and 25 per cent for local government.

So it seems that, while we have seen a general increase in both the numbers and remuneration levels of government posts, much of this is owing to the provincial wage bill.

A note on local politics

The relationship between the ANC, with its internal problems, and government performance, especially at municipal level, needs to be understood.

Yunus Carrim, a leading member of the SACP and then deputy minister for local government, tells me: 'In a sense, local government is a concentrated expression of the country's problems as a whole. While there are some problems with the local government model, and changes are going to be made, the core principles, values and features of the model are, I think, sound. But until we have a more stable, strong and cohesive ANC, it's going to be difficult to sort local government out.

'Power struggles within the party are translated to municipalities and serve to undermine good governance and service delivery in municipalities. But, also, power struggles within municipalities get transferred to party structures and serve to weaken the party. Of course, political parties must exercise political and strategic oversight of municipalities, especially through their councillors. But they should not seek to micromanage municipalities and influence appointments and tenders.'

The ANC recognised this and passed a resolution at Mangaung to mandate the NEC to develop a policy framework on how ANC structures should relate to municipalities, councillors and officials. Developing this and implementing it soon will be crucial if the face of power in the local government sphere is not to be scarred for decades to come.

Since 2006, a new class of 'tenderpreneurs' and their followers have emerged. As my interlocutor on the aeroplane to Lagos whom I speak of in Chapter 12 relates, the tenderpreneurs are not real businesspeople or entrepreneurs; they are not capable of making it in the private sector.

But, as Carrim says, 'they can't retreat somewhere else if they don't get elected or [if they fail] to find a niche in the local government; [it] is about life and death. There is desperation and [with] the dependencies that there are in local communities, this is understandable. There is a structural underpinning.'

This structural underpinning undermines the sound socio-economic transformation of South Africa. It threatens the legitimacy of the democratic project,
rendering it more, not less, vulnerable to populist opportunists like Malema.

Increases in employee compensation do not seem to be contingent upon better performance by government. Although not the only measure of government
performance by any means, service delivery is a useful way with which to observe
the outcomes of the complex intergovernmental process of governance.

According to the Multi-Level Government Initiative, an organisation that
tracks service-delivery protests across South Africa, protests increased from an
already worrying annual count of 95 to an astounding 226 in the first eight
months of 2012 – an average annual growth rate of approximately 28 per cent.[6]
That is a startling increase in protest action that follows a marked *increase* in the
government wage bill.

But this is a very general figure and is, one might say, suggestive rather than
conclusive. A more precise investigation can be conducted using recent National
Treasury data on local government expenditure. For 2010, Treasury has provided
detailed information on salaries for senior managers and executives in the various
municipalities, differentiated by province. This data includes the value of performance bonuses paid to senior managers at these municipalities. When compared
to the Multi-Level Government Initiative's service-delivery data differentiated
by province, an interesting picture emerges.

Figure 16.4: Share of service delivery protests by province[7] versus
share of unemployment[8] and relative size of performance bonuses,[9] 2010

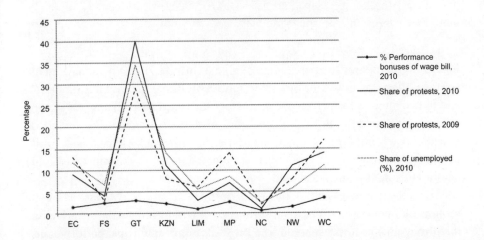

If you look at Figure 16.4, you can see that those provinces with (a) the greatest share of performance bonuses and (b) the greatest numbers of unemployed people are the ones that host the most service-delivery protests. I reason that the number, rather than the rate, is relevant here, because a certain critical mass of people is required to incite protest action. This is interesting, if not unexpected, in that the data suggests a compelling, and alarming, story of the confluence of disillusionment, anger at mismanagement and desperation that gives rise to increasingly violent protest.

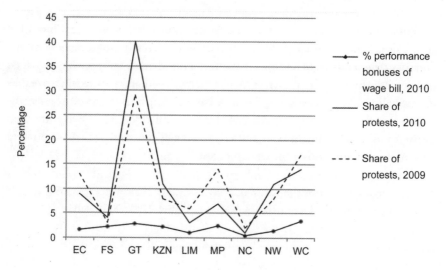

Figure 16.5: Percentage of total executive and senior management compensation accounted for by performance bonuses versus share of service-delivery protests; all provinces, 2010

Figure 16.5 compares the percentage of all executive and senior management compensation accounted for by performance bonuses at the municipality level and by province, to the percentage of service-delivery protests that took place in each province in 2010. Both 2009 and 2010 protest shares have been included in order to account for possible delays in the performance review process – it is possible, for example, that incidents that occurred in 2009 were only taken into account during the 2010 fiscal year.

Arguably, municipalities are at the frontlines of service delivery. Though protests may be owing to failures at various levels of government, it seems logical that the avoidance thereof should be a key indicator of municipal performance. On the performance scorecard, one could say, being able to tick the 'did not have any violent protests that destabilised our area and placed our citizens' lives in danger' box would be a good thing. It is thus surprising that, in Figure 16.5, the relative share of performance bonuses seems to *track* the relative share of protests in each province. This is, to put it mildly, not the desired result. An ideal situation would see the share of performance bonuses decline as protests increase, though perhaps not vice versa – absence of protest may not be as notable as its presence. The logic is not outlandish: if your province is one in which people are most likely to take to the streets and proclaim the failure of government, perhaps it is not prudent to pat yourself on the back.

Interpretations: Back to power

Various explanations may be offered for the above results. One possibility has to do with the way in which the current administration conceives of the state. Firstly, let us consider the broad movements of the wage bill. Here we have an expanded public service, its activities not credibly tied to increases in public-sector productivity, which has grown markedly since the ascendancy of Zuma and his camp. This could be a result of alternative ideas on the appropriate levels of government staffing, but it could also be evidence of an increasing trend of giving political patronage in return for loyalty and support. Such patronage as a means of securing power is particularly important in a time when the ruling party is increasingly unable to justify its sustained rule on the basis of poverty alleviation, job creation or mitigated income inequality.

The apparent divorce of reward from actual performance at the local level – which, quite apart from the limited analysis undertaken here, has been widely noted in the media[10] – seems consistent with this. If, increasingly, the state is being used as a resource for elite accumulation, then it would make sense that those areas in which performance bonuses are highest would be those areas in which service-delivery protests are most prevalent. This is so because, given resource constraints, the drawing of resources for state employees comes at the expense of spending on goods and services. High performance bonuses, rather than high performance, may be suggestive of pernicious conceptions of the state not as a vessel for service but as an elite resource pool.

New faces of power: Anatomy of a crisis

This book attempts not only to describe the changes in the face of power since my 'first' *Anatomy of South Africa*, in 2006, but to cast those changes against a longer-term perspective of change since 1994, as the twenty-year mark for South Africa's new democracy approaches. This second volume seeks to emulate Anthony Sampson's series on the changing face of power in Britain in the 1960s. Sampson found his second book 'a more interesting, and certainly more agreeable task than writing the first book'.[11] I wish I could say the same. Though I, too, have 'found it easier to pick up information and moods, against the background of the earlier *Anatomy*, and I have been able to look at the shifts and movements within institutions', the outlook is altogether less cheerful than in 2006 and I have found it harder to reach positive conclusions.

It is important to recognise the impact of external factors. Adapting Marx, DTI minister Rob Davies noted in his 2012 budget speech that men make history but not necessarily under circumstances of their choosing. And the 2008 global economic crisis has certainly hurt South Africa and limited the options, to some extent at least, for economic policy making, which, for all the ideological contradictions of the ANC and Zuma's cabinet, arguably has greater strategic focus than previously.

Like Sampson's Britain of the mid-1960s, 'much of the solid substructure ... – the aristocracy [read the captains of industry and traditional leaders], the City, industrial corporations – has hardly changed; but in a large part of Whitehall and politics, in management, education and communications, there have been considerable and exciting upheavals'.[12] Sampson was intent on describing the 'special impact of Harold Wilson'. I am intent on trying to assess the impact of Jacob Zuma, which has been largely negative for the country: he lacks credibility as a leader of modern government; he sends out confusing and contradictory messages on, for example, the rule of law and the Constitution; his own social values appear at loggerheads not only with the Constitution but with the progressive values of the ANC; his ability to lead on the fight against corruption is fatally undermined by his own conflicts of interest and the cloud about his own integrity that continues to hang over him, unresolved because of the political deal that enabled him to escape the opportunity to have his day in court and to clear his name.

There are also new faces in the Presidency itself, largely because the Polokwane victors came with demands in terms of both institutional change and the individuals that would hold positions in government. The cabinet is a 'coalition' cabinet, but without an agreed programme, although the elevation of the NDP to ANC policy now provides the government with a longer-term vision to work towards and to gear the new performance and monitoring system that the Presidency is rolling out to potentially very useful effect.

There are new faces in the leadership of the ANC compared with 2006, and its NEC now contains more populists and ethnic chauvinists than before, but also some returning Mbekites. The game is not over by any means, though the sensible left's ability to find its voice and hold its own remains very much in doubt.

There are new faces in the opposition parties, too. Three powerful women, and some new men, lead the DA, bringing new challenges of complexity and diversity, as well as opportunities. The DA's prospects are far greater now than before – partly because they have changed; partly because the face of the electoral market-place is changing, with two to three million new 'born free' voters voting for the first time in 2014; and partly because the ANC makes so many mistakes. The DA's excursion into the black vote may gather momentum in the 2014 national election, where they could get close to 30 per cent of the vote, notwithstanding the fact that Mamphela Ramphele's Agang may steal some of their votes from the middle-class electorate.

Zuma may still be an electoral asset in KwaZulu-Natal, but elsewhere, as Moeletsi Mbeki suggested in a public discussion that I chaired at the Franschhoek Literary Festival in May 2013, 'Zuma doesn't care about the sophistication of\South Africa; he has targeted the poor, to whose gallery he plays, presenting himself as a messiah. However, the poor are beginning to suss out his game.'

Despite his decisive (if gerrymandered) victory at Mangaung in December 2012, Zuma is not invulnerable. There is a large body of ANC people, many of them traditionalists ashamed of Zuma's conduct and attitudes, who are eager for him to go. Many of Zuma's allies are no more loyal to him than he is to them. In so many sad and disillusioning ways, the politics of opportunism and expediency, as well as social conservatism and kleptomaniac accumulation, have replaced the politics of progressive principle that the ANC once stood for – though there are good men and women, some of whom are introduced or cited in this book, both in the ruling party and in government, who remain steadfast, some-how battling on despite what is going on around them.

As champions of decent governance, these individuals can yet create the 'islands of effectiveness' that UCT and World Bank economist Brian Levy has argued are possible, notwithstanding the inclemency of the political economy and the difficulty of current governance settings.[13] Small gains, with greater trans-parency and the inspiration of courageous, independent oversight, such as that being displayed by the Public Protector, Advocate Thuli Madonsela, can correct the course and right the ship.

Beyond government and the ANC, the rule of law remains strong, though its independence is being subtly and not so subtly undermined by government's decision to squeeze the Office of the Chief Justice, limiting the power of the new chief justice, Mogoeng Mogoeng, and bringing to a halt the grand reform process that his predecessor, Sandile Ngcobo, had begun before the ANC abandoned him, and by virtue of the mediocre and/or conservative appointments that the troubled JSC are making to the bench. The face of the Constitutional Court has also changed markedly in recent years, and it is now possible to discern different ideological wings of the court and a substantial tipping of the balance of power away from a progressive world view.

The face of the universities is much changed, both in terms of their leadership and also their student population. And, while there are different faces in the boardrooms, their real influence is, apparently, questionable. There are new faces in the professions, too, but far fewer than one would expect after twenty years. The old establishment is not relinquishing private power in the way that it has had to give up public power.

So, to bring the analysis back to the central question that this book grapples with, let us ask again how one becomes powerful in South Africa. The above may indicate a pathway to power that, increasingly, is mediated by the centre – the centre being the ruling party and its use of public (government) power and patronage. To advance is not necessarily to perform according to benchmarks of service delivery or accountable governance; but, rather, it may be to give support when it is required and, when the time is right, receive compensation in the form of cadre deployment.

The loyalty-reward link hardly constitutes a novel thesis, but the data above may indicate that its current dynamics are threatening, on an unprecedented level, the country's fiscal and social harmony. This is particularly so because, in these extremely trying times, the increasing distance between the means of political progress and the dictates of effective governance could provoke a higher incidence of violent protest, domestic instability and international apprehension.

As Moeletsi Mbeki and others have suggested, South Africa may be approaching its 'Arab Spring' moment. This, more than the individual actors, is the changing face of power in South Africa – one that is dangerous and fragile, precarious and unpredictable, giving rise to greater uncertainty and political risk, and genuine concerns about future prospects. Significant steps must be taken without further delay. The need for clear, unambiguous, visionary leadership, not beholden to an endless list of interests, is urgently required. As ANC stalwart and Reserve Bank governor Gill Marcus said in an unusual and therefore significant display of public candour in early June 2013: 'Much more important than the precise elements of a strategy is for the government to be decisive, act coherently and exhibit strong and focused leadership from the top.'[14]

South Africa must reclaim its capacity for processing conflict and organising dialogue. A new social compact must be built – one that recognises that redistribution of wealth and power, as well as job creation, is in the national strategic interest of us all, because it is inequality more than anything that drives anger and despair.

The private sector must do all it can to contribute constructively to such an effort, engaging more effectively and meaningfully with those in government and politics, developing the antennae to understand the socio-economic milieu and the public-policy environment. Innovative leadership is required from corporate South Africa as well as from the political leadership.

More than anything, the toxic nexus between money and politics must be delinked.

Otherwise, greater trouble lies ahead. The new establishment that emerged between 1994 and 2005 was challenged and partly displaced by a new, new establishment in Polokwane in 2007 – for good and bad.

The face of power in South Africa has changed dramatically, but if it cares to look at itself in the mirror, what it will see is the anatomy of a crisis.

APPENDIX 1

Cabinet ministers

Agriculture, Forestry and Fisheries: Tina Joemat-Pettersson

Tina Joemat-Pettersson was born on 18 December 1963 in Kimberley, Northern Cape. She is the widow of Thorwald Pettersson, whom she married in May 1998. She was at the time the MEC for education, arts and culture in the Northern Cape legislature – a post she held for ten years.

She matriculated from the William Pescodia High School, and has a higher diploma in education, as well as a BA degree from UWC. She completed the Executive Management Programme at UCT Graduate School of Business in 2002.

Joemat-Pettersson served on the NEC of the ANCWL from 1998 to 2003, and has been a member of the SACP CEC since 1998. She has also served in, or been a member of, several NGOs, such as the Northern Cape Provincial HIV and AIDS Council, and is the acting president of the Association of University English Teachers in South Africa.

She was appointed to the cabinet in 2009, to the newly created Department of Agriculture, Forestry and Fisheries.

In 2010, her stated concerns were food security, enabling farmers to access finance, skills development and research. To develop the requisite skills, she said, government had to speed up the reopening of agricultural colleges.

In November 2012, the Public Protector, Thuli Madonsela, reported that Joemat-Pettersson had violated the executive ethics code, and recommended that President Jacob Zuma consider reprimanding her and that the department's acting director-general recover about R150 000 from the minister for unlawfully incurred return flights for her two children and their au pair from Sweden to South Africa in January 2010. Joemat-Pettersson agreed to repay the money, but gave an account of the extensive problems she had experienced as a single mother following her cabinet appointment.

She recently came under attack in Parliament over her department's plans. Issues that arose included the management of a fleet of ships meant to police the country's fishing zone, the lack of skills within her department, irregular appointments and non-compliance with the NDP.

Not one to shy away from public drama, Joemat-Pettersson claimed that a fishing company had threatened her life and the lives of her children after having failed in an attempt to bribe her.

Arts and Culture: Paul Shipokosa Mashatile

Paul Mashatile was born in Geraldsville, Pretoria, on 21 October 1961. He attended Alexandra High School in Gauteng and has a postgraduate diploma in economic principles from the University of London.

As a student, he was an anti-apartheid activist in COSAS, and was the co-founder and first president of the Alexandra Youth Congress. He was detained without trial from 1985 to 1989, and participated in a nationwide protest by engaging in an eighteen-day hunger strike. When the ANC and the SACP were unbanned in 1990, he helped to re-establish them and continued to organise on their behalf.

Mashatile served in the Gauteng Provincial Legislature and Government as leader of the House. He has held the position of MEC for various departments, including transport and public works (1996–98), Safety (1998–99), housing (1999–2004) and finance and economic affairs (2004–08). When Mbhazima 'Sam' Shilowa resigned in protest against the decision to recall President Thabo Mbeki, Mashatile replaced him as premier of Gauteng on 7 October 2008, and held the post until 2009, when he was appointed to the cabinet as deputy minister of arts and culture. In October 2010 he was made minister.

Within the ANC, Mashatile was a member of the NEC from 1992 to 1998. He served as a political education officer under the chair of the ANC deputy president, Kgalema Motlanthe. He was also the Gauteng provincial secretary under the chair of the ANC's former Gauteng premier, Tokyo Sexwale. And when another former Gauteng premier, Mathole Motshekga, was the provincial ANC chairperson, Mashatile was his deputy.

Although Mashatile campaigned for Motlanthe in his bid to replace Zuma at the ANC's 53rd elective conference in December 2012, when Zuma was re-elected, Mashatile nonetheless congratulated him.

When delivering the 'political overview' at the ANC's Special Provincial General Council in February 2013, Mashatile observed: 'There have been many ANC conferences before and there will be many more to come and all of us must learn to live with the fact that from time to time we will have different views on any matter. Once a conference pronounces on a matter there is only one view: the view of the ANC.'

As he is a leading member of the so-called Alex Mafia – a group of youngish ANC men who grew up in the Johannesburg township of Alexandra, and who now occupy positions of influence within the Gauteng ANC and government – Mashatile's political base is undoubtedly in Gauteng, which has both advantages and limitations.

Basic Education: Angelina Motshekga

Angie Motshekga was born in June 1959. She obtained a BA from the University of the North and thereafter an MA in education from Wits.

Prior to her appointment to a cabinet portfolio, she was a teacher at Orlando High

School in Soweto (1981–83); a lecturer at the Soweto College of Education (1983–85); a lecturer at Wits (1985–94); a director in the Presidency in Pretoria (1994–97); and the MEC for social services and population development in the Gauteng government (2000–04). In addition, she served as deputy secretary of the ANCWL from 1997 until 2007, when she became its president.

Motshekga was appointed to the cabinet in 2009. Her work as minister of basic education has been highly controversial and provoked a great deal of hostility, to the extent that SADTU engaged in industrial action in 2013, demanding her resignation and threatening to continue striking until she did so. The union claimed that her department had gone back on a 2011 collective-bargaining agreement covering the remuneration of examination markers. Her reply was that the agreement could not be implemented because of a technical problem that would have added R700 million to the bill.

There was also a strong reaction to a proposal in Zuma's 2013 State of the Nation address to Parliament to the effect that teaching should be declared an essential service, thus preventing teachers from striking. The ANC eventually backed down; it appears that they were persuaded that such a step would have been unconstitutional.

However, it was in the context of a crisis relating to the non-delivery of school textbooks in Limpopo for the first seven months of 2012 that there was a major uproar. Motshekga denied that she was responsible for the provincial department's failure, saying, 'I'm not responsible for delivering textbooks in Limpopo; I can't be blamed for that.' She claimed that textbook delivery 'is an administrative function and it has nothing to do with me as a minister', adding that as she is responsible only for policy crafting: 'I don't even know what is happening in classes.' Zuma defended her, saying, 'You don't know who's responsible for that. You can't say the minister, who is sitting in Pretoria in the office, is responsible.'

A group of NGOs, including Section 27 (which draws its name from section 27 of the South African Constitution, which is central to the commitment to socio-economic rights), took the matter to court and obtained a deadline for the textbooks to be delivered to the schools. This deadline and a series of others were not met. The matter was further complicated when it was discovered that much-needed textbooks were being dumped and shredded. In one case, a newspaper reported, an education official dumped textbooks meant to be delivered to schools so that he could use a state vehicle for joyrides and had to return an empty vehicle to the warehouse. In another report, a contractor who was paid by the weight of books he shredded and burned was said to have continued to do so despite the illegality of destroying state property.

The Department of Basic Education claimed that in 2013 the problem would not be repeated. Motshekga said that all deliveries were expected to be completed by 30 November, but in February 2013 admitted that there was a shortage of 42 000 textbooks, despite having earlier in the month issued a statement to the effect that the department strongly rejected 'reports that some schools in Limpopo had not received textbooks'. In April 2013, SADTU claimed that 25 per cent of schools in Limpopo had still not obtained teaching materials. At the time, the union was engaged in industrial action to bring pressure on Motshekga to resign.

She has also faced strong criticism over her department's long-protracted efforts to redraft regulations for minimum norms and standards for public school infrastructure. Overall, she has attracted far more brickbats than compliments over the management of her portfolio.

Communications: Yunus Carrim

Yunus Carrim replaced Dina Pule as minister of communications when Zuma reshuffled his cabinet on 9 July 2013.

Carrim holds an MA in sociology from the University of Warwick and an international diploma in journalism from Darlington College of Technology.

In 1971, while in high school, he organised demonstrations against the Republic Day festivities. He was chairperson of National Youth Action in Pietermaritzburg between 1972 and 1973. While studying at the University of Durban-Westville in 1976, he was detained without trial from August to December after organising demonstrations in the wake of the Soweto massacre. When released, he received a UN scholarship to study in England.

Carrim was a member of the executive committee of the Natal Indian Congress, and of the executive council of the UDF in Pietermaritzburg. He was secretary of the Pietermaritzburg Combined Ratepayers and Residents Association from 1986 to 1990. He became a senior lecturer in sociology at the University of Natal.

He has served as a member of both branch and regional structures of the ANC and the SACP, and was re-elected for the 2012–15 term as a member of the central committee and politburo of the SACP.

He has been an MP since 1994. He was a member of the Select Committee on Private Members' Legislative Proposals and Special Petitions, and was chairperson of the legislature's ad hoc committee. He served as chairperson of the Provincial and Local Government Portfolio Committee from 1998 to 2004, then of the Public Enterprises Portfolio Committee from 2004 to 2007, and thereafter of the Justice and Constitutional Development Portfolio Committee from 2007 to 2009. He served as deputy minister of cooperative governance and traditional affairs from 2009 to July 2013.

Carrim contributes articles on current affairs to various journals. Commenting on his appointment in the reshuffle, he was described as 'hardworking, quiet and loyal' by one opposition MP though, privately at least, he is well known for his apparently irrepressible cheerfulness and his irreverent sense of humour. Though he is thought by some politicians to have a reputation for supporting nationalisation and opposing privatisation, in a paper in the *African Communist* in 1999 he was cautious, distinguishing between privatisation and public–private partnerships.

As he lacks direct experience relative to his new portfolio, so his appointment as minister of communications was viewed sceptically by some in the industry and, indeed, he himself may be forgiven for regarding it as something of a poisoned chalice given the current disarray in the department. It will be interesting to see how he does in the short time available before the election.

Cooperative Governance and Traditional Affairs: Solomon Lechesa Tsenoli

Lechesa Tsenoli was born on 10 February 1955 in Bultfontein in the Free State. He was appointed in Zuma's cabinet reshuffle in July 2013.

Tsenoli studied in a 'programme of instruction for lawyers' at Harvard University, and obtained a certificate in public policy management at UWC. He also has a certificate in adult education from UKZN and a certificate in development planning for community leaders from Wits.

In 1981, he was a member of the Joint Rent Action Committee and a founder-member of the Masibonesane Lamontville Youth Organisation. He was publicity secretary of the UDF during 1983 and a coordinator of the Durban Civic Forum. He served as both deputy and national president of the South African National Civic Organisation. He is a member of the Institute of Local Government, the National Housing Corporation and the Transitional National Development Trust.

Tsenoli has worked variously as a clerk at the Pelonomi Hospital (from 1975 to 1976), a reporter and translator for *Bona* magazine and a freelance reporter on *The Friend* newspaper (1979).

He was a member of the Free State Provincial Legislature from 1999 to 2004. An MP from 2004, he served on the portfolio committees of Arts and Culture (as chairperson), Justice and Constitutional Development, and Housing. He sat on various ad hoc committees, including the Special Ministerial Committee on Removing Obstacles to Housing Delivery and the Special Ministerial Political Committee on the White Paper on Local Government. From 2011 to 2013, Tsenoli was deputy minister for rural development and land reform.

Correctional Services: Sibusiso 'S'bu' Joel Ndebele

S'bu Ndebele was born on 17 October 1948 at Rorke's Drift, KwaZulu-Natal. He attended primary school at Makhaseneni, near Melmoth, and matriculated from Eshowe Teachers' Training College in Eshowe. He studied library science at the University of Zululand (1972), and holds a BA in international and African politics from UNISA (1983) and an honours degree in development administration and politics (1985).

While a student, he was publicity secretary of the South African Students' Organisation (SASO) at the University of Zululand. He joined the ANC in 1974 and went into exile in Swaziland. In May 1976, he was arrested for ANC activities and served ten years on Robben Island from June 1977.

Ndebele has been on the ANC NEC since 1997, and was ANC provincial chair from 1998 to 2008. He served in the KwaZulu-Natal government as MEC for transport (1994–2004) and thereafter as premier (2004–09). Zuma appointed him first as minister of transport (2009–12) and then as minister of correctional services in June 2012.

In March 2013, Parliament's Correctional Services Portfolio Committee learnt of serious problems in the department's affairs, including management failures and improperly awarded and monitored contracts.

Defence and Military Veterans: Nosiviwe Mapisa-Nqakula

Nosiviwe Mapisa-Nqakula was born on 13 November 1956. She is married to Charles Nqakula, who served as minister of defence from September 2008 to 2009.

Mapisa-Nqakula matriculated from Mount Arthur High School. She holds a primary school teacher's diploma from the Bensonvale Teacher Training College, and studied project management with the Canadian University Service Overseas. She has done courses in basic human relations, community development, communications, youth leadership and psychology.

In 1984, she left South Africa to undergo military training in Angola and the Soviet Union. During this time, she served as the head of a commission that was set up to report to the United Nations High Commissioner for Refugees (UNHCR) on an investigation into desertions by MK members in Angola.

In 1993, Mapisa-Nqakula was elected secretary-general of the ANCWL. She lost the position but remained in the ANCWL NEC at their 1997 conference, and was eventually elected president of the league in 2003. In 2002, she was elected to the ANC NEC and since 2007 she has also served on the NWC.

She has been an MP since 2004, and was first minister of home affairs (2004–09) and then minister of correctional services (2009–12).

Following the events at Marikana in August 2012, when thirty-four striking miners were shot by the SAPS, Mapisa-Nqakula was the first government representative to apologise and to seek forgiveness. She said: 'We agree, as you see us standing in front of you here, that blood was shed at this place. We agree that it was not something to our liking and, as a representative of the government, I apologise … I am begging, I beg and I apologise, may you find forgiveness in your hearts.'

This was in sharp contrast to the views expressed by the national police commissioner, Riah Phiyega, who addressed the police shortly after the shooting, saying: 'You did what you did because you were being responsible by ensuring South Africans are safe. I want to thank you once more for doing what you did … All we did was our job, and to do it in the manner in which we were trained … Don't feel you are being persecuted as police – you were doing your work.'

Economic Development: Ebrahim Patel

Ebrahim Patel was born in 1962 in District Six, Cape Town, and grew up in Lansdowne and Grassy Park – areas designated for coloured occupation under the notorious Group Areas Act. He has three children.

Patel distinguished himself simultaneously as a student and as a trade-union activist: while at school, he won bursaries and scholarships which took him to university, and led the student boycott of Fatti's & Moni's (a long-established South African manufacturer of pasta products) during a strike by the workers for higher wages and better working conditions. While at university, he helped to organise staff at UCT, UWC and the University of Stellenbosch, who are now part of NEHAWU. In 1980, his first year at UWC, he was detained under Section 10 of the Internal Security Act as one of the leaders of a nationwide student uprising that started in Cape Town. In 1981 and 1982, he was detained twice more under the Terrorism Act. No charges were brought against him and he was released.

He campaigned against the celebration of the old republic, the Coloured Representative Council and the Tricameral Parliament. He became involved in struggles over access to housing and electricity, supporting and organising community organisations in the Lotus River–Grassy Park–Parkwood area.

Patel left university to work full-time at the Southern Africa Labour and Development Research Unit (the research division of the UCT School of Economics) in the first half of 1982 and completed his degree part-time at UCT shortly thereafter.

He was one of the founding activists and organisers of the UDF and thereafter COSATU.

Patel joined the National Union of Textile Workers (NUTW) as a full-time organiser in 1986, having worked on a voluntary basis with the auto, food and textile unions during his period at the School of Economics. NUTW merged with other unions to form SACTWU in 1989. He was made deputy general-secretary in the early 1990s, and became general secretary in 1999, a position he held until 2009, when he became a cabinet minister.

In 1993, Patel led the negotiations in the National Economic Forum (NEF) that drew up interim plans on jobs, combated customs fraud and promoted a new framework for small enterprise development.

He has also been heavily involved in international trade-union activities. He served as the global spokesperson on employment and social policy for the Workers Group on the International Labour Organization's (ILO) governing body; subsequently, he led negotiations that resulted in the adoption of the ILO's Global Employment Agenda, which contributed to international efforts to promote decent work and to tackle unemployment and the employment-growth challenge. He was a member of the South African delegation on trade policy at the WTO ministerial meeting in Singapore in 1996.

434 | THE ZUMA YEARS

Domestically, Patel has been involved in numerous roles and activities in the con-text of economic development and labour. Among other things, he was the overall labour convenor at NEDLAC; he served on the board of the Commission for Concili-ation, Mediation and Arbitration (CCMA) and on the NEF (NEDLAC's predecessor); the Presidential Working Group; the UCT Council; the Millennium Labour Coun-cil; the Proudly South African Board; the CEC of COSATU; the Council for Higher Education; the Clothing Industry Training Board; the Textile Industry Training Board; the Chris Hani Institute; the National Bargaining Council for the Clothing Indus-try; the National Textile Bargaining Council; the Financial and Fiscal Commission; and the JSC.

In 1994, he was awarded the Global Leaders of Tomorrow Award by the Davos-based Global Economic Forum; and in 2000, UCT presented him with the Special Medal for Public Services.

Patel's specific role is to coordinate and plan government economic policies, focusing on the elimination of poverty. He has had to battle hard to develop both a niche and the institutional strength to exert a meaningful influence in government. Through his hard work and bloody-mindedness, he has in this respect probably made far greater progress than most would have expected. Not least, Patel persuaded Zuma to allow him to lead the secretariat of the PICC, which is responsible for overseeing South Africa's huge SIPs programme – a major play in terms of both job creation and economic growth.

Energy: Dikobe wa Mogale Ben Martins

Dikobe Ben Martins was born on 2 September 1956, in Alexandra township, Johan-nesburg. He attended St Joseph's School in Aliwal North, Bechet College in Durban and Coronationville High School in Johannesburg. He has a BA (UNISA), an LLM in international law (UCT), an LLB (UKZN) and a postgraduate diploma in manage-ment practice (UCT).

Before his arrest and imprisonment, Martins contributed poetry, graphics and essays on art and culture to *Staffrider* magazine. He worked for the Community Care Centre and the Edenvale Ecumenical Centre in Pietermaritzburg from 1977 to 1983.

In 1984, while in detention and on trial, his book of poetry, *Baptism of Fire*, was published. A second anthology, *Prison Poems*, was published in 1992. He is a patron of the Congress of South African Writers. His work can be found in the Killie Campbell Collection at UKZN, in Pretoria and Johannesburg art galleries, and in private col-lections nationally and internationally.

During the 1970s, Martins was an activist in the Black Consciousness Movement. In 1978 he was charged and acquitted for producing banned Steve Biko T-shirts, and he produced the poster distributed at Steve Biko's funeral. In 1979, he joined the ANC and MK. In November 1983 he was arrested under the Terrorism Act, held for seven months in solitary confinement and imprisoned for eight years. He is a member of the politburo and of the central committee of the SACP. Martins has also served as deputy chairperson of the Robben Island Museum Council.

He became an MP in 1994. He was chairperson of the Portfolio Committee on Home Affairs and then deputy minister for public enterprises (2010–12). He became minister of transport in June 2012 and then minister of energy in July 2013.

Finance: Pravin Jamnadas Gordhan

Pravin Gordhan was born on 12 April 1949 in Durban. He is married and has two children.

He was drawn into political activity in the 1960s, and while a university student was involved in organising student and civic structures during the 1970s and 1980s. He graduated with a BPharm from the University of Durban-Westville in 1973 and worked as a pharmacist at the King Edward VII hospital in Durban from 1974 to 1981, when he lost his post after he was detained by the police. In fact, he was detained three times by the apartheid government. In 1984, he was active in supporting the Natal Indian Congress's call to boycott the election under the Tricameral Constitution following the whites-only referendum of the previous year. He was also active in the SACP and the ANC.

Gordhan was a participant at the multiparty talks at CODESA in 1990, and from 1991 to 1994 he was a co-chairperson of the Transitional Executive Council, which prepared the country for the 1994 elections. Subsequently, while an MP between 1994 and 1998, he was chairperson of the Constitutional Committee in Parliament. In March 1998, he was appointed a deputy commissioner for SARS, and then a commissioner from November 1999.

He served as chairperson of the World Customs Organization and, from 2008, as chairperson of the Forum on Tax Administration within the Organisation for Economic Co-operation and Development.

Gordhan was awarded honorary doctorates by UCT and UNISA in 2007, and an honorary diploma by the Free State Central University of Technology in 2009.

He was appointed minister of finance on 11 May 2009 and quickly gained the confidence of the markets and much of 'Team Treasury', despite their hankering after their former, long-serving boss, Trevor Manuel. Part of Gordhan's achievement in office has been to keep much of Team Treasury together. He is now regarded as a principled centralist in government, winning sufficient respect from both wings of the ANC to be elected onto the party's NEC at the December 2012 national conference in Mangaung – something that should strengthen his hand in government.

Health: Pakishe Aaron Motsoaledi

Aaron Motsoaledi was born on 7 August 1958 in the village of Phokwane in the Hartswater region of the northern Transvaal – what is now Limpopo province. His father was a school principal and he was part of a large family of seven boys and two girls. He is married and has three daughters and two sons.

Motsoaledi went to Setotolwane High School and, thereafter, for premedical studies to the University of the North at Turfloop. He completed his medical studies at the University of KwaZulu-Natal (UKZN), where he graduated with an MBBCh in 1983. Medicine appears to be something of a family tradition, for his brother and his oldest daughter have also chosen it as a career. Dr Motsoaledi maintained a surgery in the town of Jane Furse prior to his appointment in government.

Throughout his university career and thereafter, he was politically active. He was a member of the SRC while at medical school, and in 1982 became president. He was one of the founding members of the Azanian Students Organisation (AZASO) and became the national correspondence secretary. In 1983, he was involved in mobilising students in Natal for the formation of the UDF. In the course of his work as a practitioner, he continued his political involvement and joined MK.

Motsoaledi served the ANC as deputy chairperson of the northern Transvaal (now Limpopo) region when it was launched in 1990, and then, for nineteen years, on the Limpopo PEC before being elected to the ANC NEC.

From 1994 to 2009, he was a member of the Limpopo Provincial Legislature, and became a member of the Limpopo PEC in various capacities: for education (1994–97; transport (1998–99); and agriculture, land and environment (1999).

Other roles he filled included chairperson of the Sekhukhune Advice Office (1986–94) and chairperson of the Hlahlolanang Health and Nutrition Education Project (1999).

Motsoaledi is piloting the proposed NHI scheme, and in August 2012 promoted legislation to establish a public entity called the Office of Health Standards Compliance to address the deteriorating quality of healthcare in public hospitals – a matter which he explicitly noted during the debate.

A measure of his success as a minister is that Treasury is now taking the idea of the NHI scheme far more seriously. Motsoaledi has been effective at 'righting' a rickety ship and rebuilding administrative and management capacity throughout the public health sector with a careful, painstaking approach, thereby slowly rebuilding confidence in its reputation after a decade-long battering at the hands of Manto Tshabalala-Msimang.

Motsoaledi administered to the first South African state patient a fixed-dose combination antiretroviral tablet of emtricitabine/tenofovir/efavirenz on 9 April 2013 in Ga-Rankuwa.

He is well regarded and popular, and is seen as a most successful appointment. In December 2012, Motsoaledi was described by the DA as the best cabinet minister. A ministerial colleague in government described him to me as 'someone who makes you laugh, he's just such a funny guy ... But also, such a good guy, hard-working and honest.'

Higher Education and Training: Bonginkosi Emmanuel 'Blade' Nzimande

Blade Nzimande was born on 14 April 1958 in Edendale near Pietermaritzburg, in what is now KwaZulu-Natal. He was one of three children. He attended the Roman Catholic school Henryville, then the Plessiers Lower Primary School, and thereafter the Mthethomusha School in Edendale – the first school in the area established under the new Bantu Education system. He matriculated in 1975 at Georgetown High, Edendale. He is married.

Nzimande registered at the University of Zululand in 1976 for a BA in public administration and psychology. Following the Soweto uprising and political disturbances during 1976, the university closed; when it reopened in 1977, Nzimande returned and completed his BA in 1979. He went on to complete an honours degree in psychology at the University of Natal (Pietermaritzburg) in 1980, a master's degree in industrial psychology in 1981 and a PhD in sociology.

In 1985, he joined the University of Zululand as a lecturer in industrial psychology. During this period he became increasingly involved with the trade unions and served on the editorial board of the *South African Labour Bulletin* in 1986. He also assisted with trade-union seminars, teaching the history of trade unionism.

Nzimande was politically active throughout his student career in AZASO, and ultimately identified with the ANC, becoming a member of the National Deployment Committee. He is currently the general secretary of the SACP.

His major interest has been in the field of education. He was a council member at UNISA; the chairperson of the board of trustees at the Centre for Educational Policy Development; a council member at the University of the Transkei and UKZN; and the chairperson of the ANC Parliamentary Study Group on Education and of the Parliamentary Select Committee on Education. In addition, he has authored monographs and papers on education policy.

As deputy chair of the SACP CEC in 2007, Nzimande was involved in a sharp dispute with Malawian businessman Charles Modise, who claimed to have made a R500 000 donation to the SACP in 2002. The money was said to have been packed in black plastic bags and handed to Willy Madisha, who claimed that he carried it in the boot of his car to Nzimande. Nzimande denied that the money had reached him.

Nzimande was prominent in the decision to remove Mbeki from office in 2009. He has described a free press as the greatest threat to democracy, and has spoken of court challenges to government decisions as part of a counter-revolutionary threat.

Zuma appointed Nzimande as minister of higher education and training in 2009. Some of the proposed policies and comments he has made have caused unease regarding the development of university policy and academic freedom, but his commitment to the humanities has won him an equal measure of respect from the high-powered group of progressive-minded university vice-chancellors with whom he deals.

Home Affairs: Naledi Grace Pandor

Naledi Pandor was born in Durban in December 1953. She converted to Islam when she married, and has three children.

She was raised in one of the ANC's most famous families. Her grandfather was Professor Zachariah Keodirelang 'ZK' Matthews, who became head of Fort Hare's Department of African Studies. He was also the president of the ANC in the former Cape Province, and was one of the key figures who organised the Congress of the People and drew up the Freedom Charter. Pandor's father, Joe Matthews, was an activist in the IFP since 1994, and a former deputy minister of safety and security.

Due to her family's political activities, Pandor grew up predominantly in exile in Lesotho, Botswana and Britain. She matriculated from Gaborone Secondary School in Botswana in 1972. Her qualifications include a BSc and a certificate in civil engineering from the University of Botswana and Swaziland (1973–77); a DipEd (1978) and an MEd (1979) from the University of London; a diploma in higher education, administration and leadership from Bryn Mawr Summer Programme (1992); an MA in general linguistics from the University of Stellenbosch (1997); and a diploma in leadership development from the Kennedy School of Government, Harvard University (1997).

She returned to South Africa in 1989 to take up a lectureship position at UCT. She later moved into the university's administration, before being elected to Parliament in 1994.

Pandor served as a whip, and later as deputy chief whip, in the ANC caucus. During this time she also convened the Education Committee's subcommittee on higher education. In 1998, she was deployed to the NCOP as deputy chairperson, and in 1999 was elected chairperson. She was elected to the ANC NEC in 2002.

Pandor's hands-on experience of higher education in South Africa, both as a lecturer and senior administrator, and her understanding of the broader sector brought her into cabinet as the minister of education under Mbeki from 2004 to 2009. She then served as minister of science and technology from September 2009 to October 2012, when she took up her current portfolio to replace Nkosazana Dlamini-Zuma following the latter's election to the post of chairperson of the African Union Commission on 15 July 2012.

This has not been an easy portfolio for Pandor, as the Department of Home Affairs has been involved in serious refugee crises and has its own internal organisational problems. But she has inherited a good start from Dlamini-Zuma, and has a record of tough-minded competence to bring to the task.

Human settlements: Cornelia 'Connie' Carol September

Connie September was born on the 26 June 1959. She holds an MA in economics from Warwick University. She became a minister in Zuma's July 2013 cabinet reshuffle.

September has a history of dedicated trade-union and political activism. In 1982, she became involved in *Grassroots*, a community newspaper in Cape Town. She was working at the Rex Truform garment factory in Salt River (Cape Town) at the time, and in 1983 started organising at the factory. In 1985, she became involved in demonstrations against the tri-cameral parliament. While employed at Rex Truform, where she worked for twenty years, she became a shop steward in SACTWU (in 1988) and was one of the leaders of a successful strike there. She served as national treasurer of SACTWU from 1991 to 1999 and as deputy president of COSATU from 1993 to 1999, when she became an MP.

Though an ANC member, September is primarily a trade unionist. Addressing the COSATU inaugural central committee meeting in June 1998, she made it clear that as a member of COSATU she was totally opposed to the GEAR programme advanced by the ANC. In her speech, she drew attention to the harm caused by GEAR to workers' concerns for jobs, education, housing and social services.

In the National Assembly, from 2004 till her appointment to the cabinet, September served as chief whip, chairperson of the Portfolio Committee on Water Affairs and Forestry, and as a member of the Portfolio Committee on Trade and Industry.

She has involved herself significantly in community affairs. One of her most interesting accomplishments is the Franschhoek Valley Transformation Charter, drawn up in 2012, which articulated the need to overcome deep divisions characterised by 'relationships ... scarred by suspicion, arising from a long history of conflict and abuse'.

International Relations and Cooperation: Maite Emily Nkoana-Mashabane

Maite Nkoana-Mashabane was born on 30 September 1963 in Ga-Makanye, Limpopo. She is the widow of Norman Mashabane, who was a former South African high commissioner to India and Malaysia, and who died in a car accident in 2007. Her immediate predecessor was Dlamini-Zuma, who left the post in 2009 to become the minister of home affairs.

Zuma's appointment of Nkoana-Mashabane was controversial, as it was noted that she lacked experience in foreign policy matters. The president responded, effectively saying that 'the ANC knows the strengths of this comrade' and noting that she was a member of the ANC NEC. In fact, she had served in the South African high commission to Malaysia from 1995 to 1999 and India from 1999 to 2005.

She also has experience within the ANC's structures. From 1992 to 1995, Nkoana-Mashabane was chairperson of the ANCWL in Limpopo, and also served as a member of its NWC. From 2004 to 2008, she served as the provincial deputy secretary of the ANC in Limpopo, and over the same period was a member of the ANCWL NEC and NWC. Since 2007 she has been a member of the ANC NEC and NWC, as well as provincial convenor of the Limpopo chapter of the Progressive Women's Movement.

She served as an MP from 1994 to 1995 and as MEC for local government and housing in Limpopo from 2004 to 2005.

Dlamini-Zuma has been a hard act to follow, but Nkoana-Mashabane is generally well regarded, even though there is an ongoing lack of clarity about South Africa's foreign policy vision and a failure to articulate its national interest.

Justice and Constitutional Development: Jeffrey Thamsanqa Radebe

Jeff Radebe was born on 18 February 1953 in Cato Manor, Durban. He qualified as a lawyer at the University of Zululand and completed his articles in 1976. In the same year, he joined the ANC after the student uprisings in Soweto. He left South Africa for exile the following year and underwent military training. While abroad, he obtained an LLM in international law at the Karl Marx University, Leipzig, in 1981.

He was infiltrated back into the country to establish underground structures for the ANC and the SACP, but was arrested in 1985 and sentenced to six years' imprisonment, which he served on Robben Island.

On the island he was active in the ANC's political department, heading its committee by the time political prisoners were released in 1990. During the transition he served as deputy chairman and later chairman of the ANC's southern Natal structures. In 1991 he was appointed secretary of the SACP.

Radebe has served on both the NEC of the ANC and the CEC of the SACP. He currently serves on the NWC of the ANC. In 2002, he was not re-elected to the SACP CEC after his relationship with the party soured with his implementation of centre-right policies in ministerial appointments. He now heads the ANC's policy subcommittee.

In 1994, Radebe was elected to Parliament and appointed minister of public works in the first cabinet. In 1999, he was appointed minister of public enterprises by Mbeki. After Dullah Omar fell ill in 2000, Radebe became acting transport minister until Mbeki appointed him to the position in 2004. In 2007, when then minister of health Tshabalala-Msimang was ill, Radebe was appointed acting minister of health. Finally, in 2009, he was appointed to his current position as minister of justice and constitutional development.

Both as a member of the NEC and in his current position as minister, Radebe has not always shown good judgement. During the clash between Mosiuoa 'Terror' Lekota and the ANC, which ultimately led to Lekota's resignation from the ANC and the formation of a new political party (COPE), Radebe wrote a fiercely critical letter to Lekota on behalf of the ANC on 2 October 2008. In it, he pointed out that the high court had, on 12 September 2008, ruled that a prosecution of Zuma for corruption had violated the constitutional rights of the president of the ANC, as the decision to prosecute had allegedly been influenced by then president Mbeki. In fact, Radebe already knew that an appeal against the high court's judgment had been lodged by the national director of public prosecutions. In January 2009, the SCA upheld the appeal and set aside the lower court's ruling, criticising Zuma's case in blistering terms. It would have been wiser for Radebe to have awaited the SCA's decision before relying on what the court below had said to support his attack on Lekota. At the very least, one would expect that he would issue an acknowledgement that the political situation had been turned around by 180 degrees by the implications of the SCA's decision, however much he might have regretted it.

Moreover, while minister of transport, Radebe claimed on 12 April 2009 that the institution by the DA of proceedings to review the subsequent decision by the NPA to discontinue Zuma's prosecution was politically motivated and unsound in law. It appears that, in his anxiety to support Zuma, he did not distinguish between his political party and the state; as a cabinet minister bound by the usual conventions, he should abide by the outcome of legal proceedings instituted by a party with a constitutional right to do so, and not object to the exercise of that right, however politically distasteful it might be to him in his role as a party member. One wonders whether his studies in Leipzig have influenced him into a jurisprudence inconsistent with South Africa's constitutional democracy.

As a member of the JSC, and as one of Zuma's trusted lieutenants, Radebe is highly influential on a number of fronts, not least because he is often brought in as 'the cleaner' (think of Harvey Keitel's cameo in Tarantino's *Pulp Fiction*) to sort out political problems – such as Guptagate, when he chaired the inter-ministerial committee inquiry that whitewashed ministerial and presidential responsibility for the scandalous landing of a private jet full of Gupta wedding guests at Waterkloof Air Force Base.

Labour: Nelisiwe Mildred Oliphant

Mildred Oliphant has been an MP since 1994. She proceeded as far as Form 3 at school, and holds certificates in macroeconomics and project management.

Within the ANC, she has been a member of the KwaZulu-Natal Provincial Working Committee, as well as secretary, convenor and chairperson of the ANCWL north coast region, and provincial treasurer.

Oliphant has done service as an active trade unionist, having been a COSATU local secretary and chairperson of the COSATU Women's Forum. She also served in the KwaZulu-Natal local treasury of SACCAWU.

She was appointed minister of labour in November 2010, when she succeeded Membathisi Mdladlana, who had been appointed by Nelson Mandela and who had continued to serve under both Mbeki and Zuma until being made ambassador to Burundi and, thereafter, high commissioner to Canada. Oliphant took her portfolio as a newcomer to the cabinet in a reshuffle of ministers.

In Parliament, she was the NCOP provincial whip and NCOP chairperson from 1994 to 1999, and from 2004 to 2009. She has been the chairperson of the Portfolio

Committee on Public Services; and a member of the Portfolio Committee on Land and Environmental Affairs, the Joint Rules Committee, the Programme Committee, and the Joint Ethics and Members' Interests Committee. She has also been a member of the KwaZulu-Natal Provincial Legislature, where she was the convenor of the ANC's Health Study Group.

Oliphant has had to face a series of severe tests in the work of her portfolio in industries that are historically at the heart of South Africa's economy – mining and agriculture.

Mineral Resources: Susan Shabangu

Susan Shabangu was born on 28 February 1956. She completed her studies at the Madibane High School, Soweto, in 1977. She is a widow.

She became involved politically from 1980, when she became the assistant secretary of the Federation of South African Women, a position she held until 1985. During the 1980s, she was an active member of the Anti-Republic Campaign Committee and the Release Mandela Campaign Committee, and from 1984 to 1985 she was an organiser and administrator for the Amalgamated Black Workers' Project. Shabangu has represented the Transport and General Workers Union (TGWU) at the Industrial Council as the union's national women's coordinator, was a member of COSATU's National Women's Subcommittee, and has been involved in the voter education programme with COSATU's National Election Task Team. She has also been national treasurer of the South African National Civic Organisation and, from 1995 to 1996, was a member of the management committee of the ANC's East Rand Parliamentary Constituency Office.

Shabangu became an MP in 1994. From 1996 until 2004 she was deputy minister for minerals and energy, and from 2004 to 2009 she was deputy minister for safety and security. In 2009, when the Department of Minerals and Energy was split into two separate departments, Shabangu was appointed to her current position as the minister of mineral resources.

Some of her conduct has led to unease about her judgement. In April 2008, as deputy minister for safety and security, she told an audience of police officers to 'kill the bastards if they threaten you or the community ... I want to assure the police station commissioners and policemen and women that they have permission to kill these criminals ... You must not worry about the regulations. That is my responsibility. Your responsibility is to serve and protect.' There was widespread condemnation but no reaction from Mbeki, who had appointed her.

People who have worked for Shabangu and on the opposite side of the negotiating table in the mining sector tell me that she is well respected because she has her own mind and is brave enough to say what needs to be said, even though her grasp of the detail of policy is sometimes lacking and she does not have a distinct ideological outlook. She has been a largely stabilising force in her portfolio, given the tumult caused by Malema's repeated calls for nationalisation between 2009 and 2011. On more than one occasion, she has said, simply and clearly: 'There will be no nationalisation in my lifetime.'

Police: Emmanuel Nkosinathi Mthethwa

Nathi Mthethwa was born on 23 January 1967 in KwaMbonambi, KwaZulu-Natal. He holds a diploma in community development from the University of Natal, a certificate in mining engineering from the University of Johannesburg (UJ) and a certificate in communications and leadership from Rhodes University.

He became a member of the Klaarwater Youth Organisation from the age of fifteen and served as its chairperson from 1987 to 1989.

While serving as a shop steward of FAWU, Mthethwa was recruited into the underground work of the ANC as part of Operation Vula in 1988, and was arrested during the 1989 state of emergency. He was secretary of SAYCO in southern Natal, and also chairperson of the Southern Natal Unemployed Workers Union, a COSATU initiative, from 1989 to 1990.

He served as regional secretary of the southern Natal ANCYL from 1990 to 1992, and was elected to the ANCYL NEC and served in its NWC as secretary for organisation from 1994 to 2001, when he was deployed into the ANC's National Organising Team.

Mthethwa became an MP in 2002. He served as chairperson of the minerals and energy portfolio committee from 2004 to 2008, and as the ANC chief whip in 2008. After Mbeki's resignation, Mthethwa was made minister of safety and security on 25 September 2008, as a member of Motlanthe's cabinet. In 2009, Zuma appointed him to his current portfolio, police.

Perhaps his severest problem has been dealing with police misconduct against a background of bad publicity and mistrust for the SAPS. He faced criticism for not interrupting his honeymoon to deal with the public outrage following the death of Emidio Macia, a Mozambican taxi driver who was filmed being dragged behind a police van. Macia died shortly afterwards in police custody, and the officers who were allegedly involved were charged with murder.

Public Enterprises: Knowledge Malusi Nkanyezi Gigaba

Malusi Gigaba was born on 30 August 1971 in Eshowe, KwaZulu-Natal. He attended Mathonsi Primary School in Mandeni, and matriculated from Vryheid State High School in 1988. He graduated from the University of Durban-Westville with a BEd in 1990 and completed an MA in social policy in 1994. During 1993, he worked as an assistant in the public affairs department of the University of Durban-Westville and served as chairperson of SASCO. In 1994, he was regional chairperson of the southern KwaZulu-Natal ANCYL, and eventually became president of the whole organisation.

From 1994 to 1996, Gigaba was ANC provincial secretary for KwaZulu-Natal, a member of the PEC and convenor of the Provincial Education Forum. In 1997, he worked as a consultant for Macsteel Service Centres.

He became an MP in 1999, resigned in 2001 and was re-elected in 2004, when he was appointed by Mbeki as deputy minister of home affairs. Zuma appointed him minister of public enterprises in 2010 – a very significant ministry for a rising star.

A member of the ANC NEC, Gigaba is popular within the party. In fact, during all the manoeuvring before the ANC's elective conference in Mangaung in 2012, there were suggestions that he should be the ANC's deputy president if Motlanthe challenged Zuma for the party's presidency.

As deputy minister of home affairs, Gigaba spoke openly and vigorously against xenophobia in 2008 and 2009, actively advocating for the inclusion of all Africans. One of the major issues he has had to address in his current portfolio is the financial problems of SAA.

Gigaba has come a long way from his somewhat 'wild' days as president of the ANCYL, maturing rapidly under Mbeki's guidance – in contrast, perhaps, to Zuma's handling of Malema – and rising quickly in the intervening years. He came in the top three in the ANC's election for its NEC at Mangaung in December 2012, giving him an additional boost to his growing political power.

Public Service and Administration: Lindiwe Nonceba Sisulu

Lindiwe Sisulu was born in Johannesburg on 10 May 1954. As the daughter of Albertina and Walter Sisulu, both distinguished ANC leaders, she is, therefore, part of the ANC's political aristocracy.

Sisulu attended high school at Waterford Kamhlaba United World College of Southern Africa in Mbabane, Swaziland. She returned to South Africa in the 1970s and participated in student politics while working within MK, where she underwent military training, specialising in intelligence. She was arrested and detained in 1975, and left the country after her release.

Sisulu has a diploma in education (1980), a BA (1981), an MA in history from the University of Swaziland and an MPhil from the Centre for Southern African Studies at the University of York (1989). She worked throughout the 1980s variously as a teacher, lecturer and journalist.

On returning to South Africa in 1990, she re-entered formal Alliance politics, working as a PA to Zuma, who was then the head of ANC intelligence. During the transition years, she continued to work for ANC intelligence structures, as well as participating in the ANC's team at CODESA I.

In 1994, Sisulu was elected to Parliament, where she initially served as a backbencher. In 1995 she became the first chairperson of the Intelligence Committee. She left the post after the break-up of the GNU to take up an appointment as deputy minister of home affairs in Mandela's cabinet. She was retained in the post by Mbeki in 1999, but later appointed minister of intelligence after the death of Joe Nhlanhla in 2001. In the interim, in 1997, Sisulu was elected to the ANC NEC. She was later returned to the NEC at the 2002 Stellenbosch conference. She currently serves on the ANC NWC.

Sisulu is widely held to have performed dynamically in her housing portfolio, implementing a valuable 'mapping exercise' of what was needed on the housing front and a change of approach underpinned by the concept of 'human settlement'. But she was moved by Zuma in 2009, taking up the position of minister of defence and military veterans, where she served until 2012, when she was appointed to her current portfolio in the course of a cabinet reshuffle.

As minister of public service and administration, Sisulu is grappling with the question of the politicisation of directors-general in the public service. Drawing attention to the high turnover of directors-general, she has expressed the view that this is largely to blame on a breakdown in the relationship between the incumbent and the relevant minister. This is to be addressed by rotating directors-general, rather than losing their expertise to the private sector when there is a breakdown.

One of her controversial appointments, in April 2013, has been that of Menzi Simelane as an advisor. Simelane's appointment to the post of national director of public prosecutions had been set aside by the Constitutional Court in October 2012, in the light of the Ginwala Commission's strongly critical findings against him.

Despite her disappointment at being moved away from defence, which she loved (not least for its pomp and circumstance), Sisulu quickly knuckled down in her new portfolio, winning admiring glances with her apparent determination to take on vested interests in the public service and by introducing proposals to prohibit public servants from 'doing business with themselves or their companies' – a growing cancer in the public administration.

She works immensely hard, keeping her advisors and officials busy most weekends.

Public Works: Thembelani Thulas Waltermade Nxesi

Thulas Nxesi was born in the Eastern Cape on 1 January 1959. He was expelled from school several times for involvement in political activities, but went on to tertiary education. He has a BEd (Wits, 1997), a BA (Fort Hare, 1983) and a higher diploma in education (UNISA, 1986). He taught at Ikusasa Senior Secondary School from 1985 to 1990, heading the social sciences department.

He was assistant secretary-general and then secretary-general of SADTU from 1990 to 2010. He was also president of Education International and secretary of the National Education Union of South Africa (NEUSA). He is currently the deputy national chairperson of the SACP and a member of the ANC NEC.

Previously the deputy minister of rural development and land reform (2010–11), Nxesi was appointed minister of public works by Zuma. Perhaps his most challenging problem has been the question of the use of public funds on Nkandla, Zuma's home in KwaZulu-Natal. Claiming that the premises are a national key point, as defined under apartheid-era legislation, Nxesi withheld details on the grounds of national security, occasioning considerable criticism, which he has had to face in and outside Parliament.

Rural Development and Land Reform: Gugile Ernest Nkwinti

Gugile Nkwinti was born on 18 December 1948. He holds a diploma in nursing (psychiatry); a BA in political science, public administration and applied economics (UNISA); and an MSc in public policy and management (University of London).

Nkwinti was a member of the UDF REC in the Eastern Cape from 1986 to 1988, during which period he was also the UDF coordinator in the Albany zone. He was the Eastern Cape regional treasurer from 1989 to 1990, the regional secretary from 1990 to 1991, and a national convenor from 1991 to 1992. He was also the ANC's regional secretary at the time.

From 1972 to 1984, Nkwinti worked as a professional nurse, and from 1989 to 1991 as a research assistant in the Department of Psychology at Rhodes University.

In 1994 he became the Speaker of the Eastern Cape Provincial Legislature and from 1999 served as MEC for housing, local government and traditional affairs in the Eastern Cape.

In 2009 he was appointed as minister of rural development and land reform.

Science and Technology: Derek André Hanekom

Derek Hanekom was born on 13 January 1953 in Cape Town. He attended the German Primary School, and matriculated from Jan van Riebeeck High School in Cape Town in 1970.

After completing his compulsory national military service from 1971 to 1973, Hanekom went abroad, working on farms, factories and building sites. He returned to South Africa when he was in his early twenties and continued farming for six years. He was imprisoned from 1983 to 1986 for providing the ANC with information about the involvement of the South African Defence Force (SADF) in attempts to overthrow the Mozambican government through the rebel movement RENAMO (Mozambican National Resistance). When his wife, who was also imprisoned, was released in 1987, he went into exile in Zimbabwe and worked as coordinator for the Popular History Trust in Harare from 1988 to 1990.

Hanekom returned to South Africa when the ANC was unbanned, and was the coordinator at the Land and Agricultural Desk of the ANC from 1990 to 1994. He is a member of the ANC NEC and chairperson of its NDC. The disciplinary proceedings against former ANCYL president Malema were highly publicised and followed with keen attention by the South African public.

Hanekom entered Parliament in 1994 and was appointed by Mandela as minister for agriculture and land affairs, serving until 1999. From 1999 to 2004 he sat on the backbenches. He was then appointed deputy minister for science and technology in 2004 and, thereafter, minister in October 2012.

The South African scientific community has responded warmly to his support for the advancement of research and technology, and he has established himself as a popular minister in this context.

Social Development: Bathabile Olive Dlamini

Bathabile Dlamini was born on 10 September 1968 in the rural area of Amanzimtoti, KwaZulu-Natal. She graduated with a BA in social studies from the University of Zululand in 1989.

As a student, she was active among the youth at St Mark's Anglican Church in Imbali, and in SASCO. She was elected to the first REC of the ANCWL as part of the interim leadership formed to rebuild the league's structures in KwaZulu-Natal in 1991. She was secretary-general of the ANCWL from 1998 to 2008 and is a member of the ANC NEC.

In addition, Dlamini worked for the Pietermaritzburg Cripples' Care Association from 1991 to 1993.

She served as deputy minister for social development from 2009 to 2010 under interim president Motlanthe. Zuma appointed her to her present position in 2010.

Sport and Recreation: Fikile Mbalula

Fikile Mbalula was born on 8 April 1971 in the Free State. He was trained in leadership skills by the Careers Research and Information Centre, and as a counsellor in psychotherapy by the Organisation of Appropriate Social Services in South Africa.

Mbalula served as president of the Botshabelo Youth Congress from 1986 to 1987, and as its publicity secretary and vice president in 1987. He became a member of the UDF in 1989. In 1990, he was made secretary of the ANC's Provisional Youth Committee. He served as regional secretary of the ANCYL from 1991 to 1994, provincial secretary from 1994 to 1996, secretary of its political education programme from 1996 to 1998, and secretary-general from 1998 to 2004, when he was elected ANCYL president. He retired from this post in 2008 at the age of thirty-six, when he ceased to be eligible for membership of the Youth League. In the 2009 general election, he managed the ANC's election campaign.

Mbalula was a member of the local Branch Executive Committee of SAYCO in 1998, an affiliate member of Socialist International and president of the International Union of Socialist Youth in 2004.

Mbalula has not hesitated to speak his mind. He is reported to have said that transformation of higher learning institutions had turned UKZN, for example, 'into nothing but Bombay' and that black African students 'suffer on the periphery of transformation ... When you get into that institution you can think it's an exclusive university of Indians only.' In a letter to Manuel, then minister of finance, Mbalula called him arrogant and an 'attention-seeking drama queen'.

Mbalula was originally a fierce Zuma loyalist, claiming, in 2005, that the prosecution of Zuma was a political plot orchestrated by Mbeki. Mbalula did not, however, explain how the 'plot' was thought to operate in view of the many people and resources that a prosecution would have entailed. Neither Mbalula nor Radebe, who made similar statements, have publicly addressed the constitutional implications of such a 'plot', which would include that, *prima facie*, Mbeki is guilty of treason.

Subsequently, however, when campaigning began for the ANC's elective conference in Mangaung in 2012, Mbalula described Zuma as a 'politically bankrupt' leader who thrived on corruption, saying, 'I have no time for Zuma. He has caused his own problems. He marries every week. He is building a mansion in Nkandla.'

Zuma appointed Mbalula deputy minister of police in 2009, and then minister of sport and recreation in 2010.

State Security: Siyabonga Cyprian Cwele

Siyabonga Cwele has an MBChB from UKZN (1984) and an MPhil in economic policy from the University of Stellenbosch. He married his wife Sheryl in 1985. They were divorced in August 2011 after she was convicted and sentenced to twelve years' imprisonment on drugs charges.

Cwele was in the ANC's underground structures from 1984 to 1990.

In Parliament, he was a member of the NCOP from 1994 to 1999 and was the chairperson of the Standing Committee on Social Services. He was appointed minister of intelligence by Mbeki in September 2008; when Zuma appointed his first cabinet, he retained Cwele in the portfolio but renamed it state security.

Cwele had the task of piloting the Protection of State Information Bill through Parliament. This was bitterly contested at all stages and its constitutionality challenged.

The Presidency: National Planning Commission: Trevor Andrew Manuel

Trevor Manuel was born on 31 January 1956 in Kensington, Cape Town. He is married to Maria Ramos, former director-general of National Treasury, CEO of Transnet, Group CEO of Barclays' subsidiary ABSA and, thereafter, CEO of Barclays itself.

Manuel entered South African resistance politics in 1983, when he was elected at the age of twenty-five to the national executive of the UDF, also serving as the regional coordinator of the UDF in the Western Cape. During the 1980s, he was repeatedly held in detention by security forces, accruing thirty-five months of detention with-

APPENDIX 1: CABINET MINISTERS | 449

out trial before 1990. After the unbanning of the ANC, Manuel worked full-time for the party and was elected to the NEC at the 1991 national conference. In 1997, he was elected to the NEC in seventh place, and in 2002 he topped the list of NEC members nominated from the floor.

During the transition years, he headed the ANC's Department of Economic Planning. In 1994, Mandela appointed him minister of trade and industry; he held this position until 1996, when he was redeployed to the finance ministry. He became minister of finance in 1996, following the NP's withdrawal from the GNU.

Manuel was extremely popular with business for his policies and implementation, but not with the ANC's Alliance partners and progressive civil-society organisations, because he implemented the GEAR economic stabilisation policy in the early years of his tenure. Despite growing unemployment and misgivings among key constituencies regarding his performance, Manuel remained extremely popular with the party's grass roots, especially in the Western Cape.

Manuel was one of the longest-serving finance ministers in the world. There was speculation that he would depart government to assume a position in a multilateral body such as the WTO, but he was instead appointed to his present position in 2009 by Zuma.

Together with several other ministers, he resigned on 23 September 2008, when Mbeki was forced to resign. He subsequently made it known that he was willing to serve under the next president, and accepted the renewal of his appointment when asked by Motlanthe later that month.

In his current post, Manuel has not hesitated to speak his mind and has indeed clashed with Zuma. He criticised ANC members employed in government for showing loyalty to the party at the expense of South Africans. Addressing civil servants in April 2013, he said: 'Many of you are members of the ruling party and many have risen through the activist ranks of the political party I also represent ... No matter how you were appointed, no matter who appointed you, you are not accountable to the ruling party. You are civil servants who are meant to serve all citizens irrespective of political persuasion.'

He said that South Africans cannot continue to blame apartheid for our failings as a state: 'We cannot plead ignorance or inexperience. For almost two decades, the public has been patient in the face of mediocre services. The time for change, for ruthless focus on implementation has come.' In reply, Zuma stated that government would not stop blaming the legacy of apartheid for South Africa's problems.

Manuel is well known and respected on the international stage, playing a role, for example, in the establishment of the new Green Climate Fund (as chair of the transitional committee set up by the UN Framework Convention on Climate Change's 15th Conference of the Parties in Copenhagen in December 2009). He was recently appointed co-chair, with British former Labour politician David Miliband, of the Global Ocean Commission.

Despite the obvious lure of many alternative positions, either in the private sector or in international governmental organisations, Manuel's commitment to public service remains strong and enduring, something that even his greatest critics are forced to acknowledge.

The Presidency: Performance Monitoring and Evaluation and Administration: Ohm Collins Chabane

Collins Chabane was born on 15 May 1960 in the village of Xikundu in Limpopo. He attended Shingwedzi High School. In 1979 he registered for a BSc at Turfloop University, but his studies were interrupted when he went into exile in 1980. Subsequently, he was awarded a management diploma from the Eastern and Southern African Management Institute in Arusha, Tanzania, and later, while a prisoner on Robben Island, a diploma in aircraft maintenance and a higher national diploma in electrical engineering from UNISA. He developed an interest in music while on Robben Island and formed a marimba band. He has released several albums.

He joined the ANC while a student at Turfloop in 1979 and was a founding member of AZASO. He joined MK in 1980. On his return to South Africa, he was arrested and imprisoned on Robben Island from 1984 to 1990. In 1990, he was the ANC's administrator in the northern Transvaal region and, thereafter, provincial secretary in the Northern province (1990–98). He has been a member of the ANC NEC since December 2007, as well as a member of the NWC. Chabane was granted amnesty by the Truth and Reconciliation Commission (TRC) in 1999.

He became an MP and served from 1994 to 1997. In 1994, he was a member of the Joint Committee on Defence and Intelligence, and of the Standing Committee on Finance, Minerals and Energy Affairs. He was also a member of the constitutional and management committees in the Constitutional Assembly.

In 1997, Chabane became a member of the NCOP and the Limpopo Provincial Legislature, and served as MEC for economic development, environment and tourism in Limpopo. In 1998, he was made MEC for public works and from 1997 to 1998 he served as MEC in the Limpopo premier's office.

He once again became an MP on 6 May 2009, and was appointed minister in the Presidency responsible for performance monitoring and evaluation and administration on 11 May 2009.

Tourism: Marthinus Christoffel Johannes van Schalkwyk

Marthinus van Schalkwyk was born on 10 November 1959. He is married and has two children. He matriculated from Pietersburg High School in 1977, and then served in the SADF from 1978 to 1979. He holds an MA in political science and a BProc, both from the Rand Afrikaans University (now UJ).

He was chairperson of the SRC, the Afrikaanse Studentebond and, later, the Ruiterwag (the youth wing of the Afrikaner Broederbond). In the 1980s, he was a founding member and chairperson of Jeugkrag (Youth Power), an organisation purportedly opposed to the Afrikaner establishment, but which was secretly funded by military intelligence.

Van Schalkwyk was elected to the last apartheid Parliament in 1990, and returned to Parliament in 1994, having coordinated the NP's media election campaign. He became leader of the NNP from its inception on 8 September 1997. In June 2002, he left the National Assembly to take up the post of premier of the Western Cape until April 2004, when the NNP walked out of the DA. Van Schalkwyk subsequently joined the ANC after the demise of the NNP in 2005.

Van Schalkwyk was nominated by Mandela to the position of minister of environmental affairs and tourism after the ANC made good on its electoral agreement with the NNP regarding the 2004 general election. He inherited a well-run and coordinated ministry from his predecessor, Mohammed Valli Moosa, who declined to run for re-election on the ANC lists.

Van Schalkwyk has done well to maintain the profile and reputation of his ministry, and in a wider political context he has identified wholly and explicitly with the aspirations of the new democratic South Africa. This has been recognised internationally. It is significant that he became president of the African Ministerial Conference on the Environment in June 2008, when South Africa assumed the presidency of the forum at its twelfth session; and in March 2010 he was nominated by Zuma to succeed Yvo de Boer as executive secretary of the UN Framework Convention on Climate Change.

Trade and Industry: Rob Haydn Davies

Rob Davies was born on 12 May 1948. He holds an honours degree in economics (Rhodes University), an MA in international relations (University of Southampton) and a PhD in political studies (University of Sussex). He has published more than eighty articles and research publications.

He lived in exile in Britain and Mozambique between 1979 and 1990, and was attached to the Centre for African Studies at the Eduardo Mondlane University in Mozambique. On his return from exile he conducted economic research for the ANC and the SADC. In 1990, he became co-director of the Centre for Southern African Studies at UWC. He is a member of the CEC of the SACP.

Davies became an MP in 1994. He was chairperson of the Portfolio Committee on Trade and Industry from 1996 to 2004, and thereafter, the Portfolio Committee on Finance. Mbeki then appointed him deputy minister of the DTI in 2005, a position he held until 2009, when Zuma appointed him minister.

One of the most important challenges Davies has to address is how best to exploit South Africa's membership of BRICS. Ultimately, the extent to which South Africa benefits will certainly be the standard by which his work will be judged.

Transport: Elizabeth Dipuo Peters

Dipuo Peters was born in Kimberley, in the Northern Cape, on 13 May 1960. She attended Tidimalo Junior Secondary and Tshireleco Senior Secondary schools. She graduated in 1987 with a BA from the University of the North. She completed her studies at UWC, receiving a certificate in development and public policy in 1996. In 2002, she obtained a certificate in executive management from the UCT Graduate School of Business and a certificate in international policy management from the University of Havana, Cuba.

Prior to her appointment as minister for transport in July 2013, she was an ANC MP (1994–97); then the ANC's chief whip in the Northern Cape provincial legislature (1997–99); and thereafter MEC for health in the Northern Cape provincial government (1999–2004). In 2009 she was appointed minister for energy by Zuma.

Within the ANC, Peters was head of the Women's Department in the South African Youth Congress (SAYCO) from 1987 to 1990, and then secretary for Women's Affairs in the ANCYL in 1990. She was also a member of the Northern Cape Provincial National Youth Committee from 1990 to 1991. She served as treasurer for the Northern Cape province from 1997 to 2003, and held the position of provincial deputy chairperson from May to December 2003 and then acting provincial chairperson in 2004.

As part of her other activities, during 1987 she was a volunteer regional organiser for the South African Domestic Workers Union. Her duties were to recruit, organise, educate and counsel domestic workers in the Northern Cape. She also worked with the UNHCR, dealing with the repatriation of political exiles and the reintegration of political prisoners who were released after South African political organisations were unbanned.

As minister for energy, Peters was regarded as an active and successful appointment. South Africa's serious energy shortage was a problem that she had to address. In her view, there is the political will to use nuclear energy for peaceful purposes to provide baseload energy. South Africa's reliance on coal must be reduced, she said, but solar and wind power are not alternatives on which to rely. She also pointed out that the development of nuclear power would create decent and sustainable employment, pointing especially to the Eastern Cape.

She supported the development of nuclear power stations in South Africa and the development of a programme to explain that nuclear technology is not only about power stations and bombs, but also about medicine and agriculture, for example. Under her watch, a nuclear education centre was set up by the South African Nuclear Energy Corporation (NECSA). How she will fair in her new portfolio, transport, remains to be seen.

Water and Environmental Affairs: Bomo Edna Molewa

Edna Molewa was born on 23 March 1957. She is married. She completed a course in economic leadership and administration management at the Wharton School, and a course in leadership at Kennedy School of Government, in the US. She also holds a certificate in negotiating skills issued by the Independent Mediation Services of South Africa.

Molewa taught at Moloto and Makaunyane secondary schools from 1976 to 1981 and was a buyer for Shoprite Checkers from 1987 to 1994.

She became active in the underground structures of the liberation movement in 1976. She was a member of the Federation of Transvaal Women from 1984 to 1990. In 1986, she served as secretary of the Warmbaths branch of SACCAWU and became deputy president of the union in 1987 (until 1993). She was a member of the REC of COSATU in the northern Transvaal from 1987 to 1989 and served on the National Labour Economic Institute from 1992 to 1994. Within the ANCWL, Molewa served as deputy chair in the Ga-Rankuwa region from 1992 to 1994 and then as chair in the North West province. She became a member of the PEC in 1996 and of the NEC in 2003.

Molewa became an MP in 1994 and was the chairperson of the Portfolio Committee on Trade and Industry until 1996. After that, she served as first MEC for economic development and tourism in the North West province (1998–2000), and then MEC for agriculture, conservation and environmental affairs. In 2004, she was made premier of the North West province.

In 2009, she returned to the National Assembly and became minister for social development. In 2010, she was made minister for water and environmental affairs.

Women, Youth, Children and People with Disabilities:
Lulama 'Lulu' Marytheresa Xingwana

Lulu Xingwana was born on 23 September 1955. She holds a BSc (Wits, 1985) and postgraduate diplomas in rural development and development and leadership studies (both University of Zimbabwe, 1998) and economic principles (University of Limpopo, 2002).

She gave classes for domestic workers from 1985 to 1986 and was a tutor with the NGO Learn and Teach from 1985 to 1987.

Xingwana joined the UDF in 1983 and has been a member of the ANCWL since 1993, serving as its head of development from 1991 to 1994. She served on the Gauteng ANC PEC from 1998 to 2001, and was chairperson of the Malibongwe Rural Development Project for Women from 1998 to 2000.

She became an MP in 1994 and was chairperson of the Portfolio Committee on Sports and Recreation until 1999. She also served on the portfolio committees for environmental affairs and tourism (1996–2004) and defence (1999–2004). In addition, she was chairperson of the Parliamentary Women's Caucus from 1999 to 2004.

Xingwana was appointed by Mbeki as deputy minister of minerals and energy in 2004. In 2006, she was made minister of agriculture and land affairs. She was then appointed by Zuma first as minister of arts and culture in 2009, and then as minister of women, children and people with disabilities in 2010.

She is a controversial and even unpopular minister. As minister for arts and culture, she antagonised many with her negative reaction to a highly praised exhibition at the Constitutional Court of same-sex couples embracing each other. The subsequent claim by her spokesperson that the minister objected to the stereotyping of black women and was actually protecting women's rights was desperate and imaginative, and unconvincing.

In her current position, Xingwana has thoroughly antagonised the portfolio committee her department reports to. She has made extraordinarily unpleasant public comments (and has had to apologise for some of them), and has been reported as having engaged in self-indulgent and unreasonable expenditure and undignified conduct. For example, Xingwana told Parliament in November 2011 that she couldn't fly 'la-la class' for health reasons after she was questioned why she flew business class on overseas trips. Unsurprisingly, there have been calls for her to be replaced.

The following sources were used to compile these profiles: the ANC website (www.anc.org.za); *Business Day* (www.bdlive.co.za); *Daily Maverick* (www.dailymaverick.co.za); various departmental, local and national government websites; Independent Online (www.iol.co.za); *Mail & Guardian* (http://mg.co.za); SAPA (www.sapa.org.za); the Small Enterprise Development Agency website (www.seda.org.za); the SACP website (www.sacp.org.za); South African History Online (www.sahistory.org.za); Who's Who Southern Africa (http://whoswho.co.za); and Wikipedia (http://en.wikipedia.org).

APPENDIX 2

Constitutional Court judges

Chief Justice Mogoeng Mogoeng

Born in 1961, Mogoeng Mogoeng obtained a BJuris degree from the University of Zululand, an LLB from the University of Natal (Durban) and an LLM from UNISA.

He began his professional career as a Supreme Court prosecutor in Mafikeng in 1986, but resigned in 1990 to complete his pupillage at the Johannesburg Bar. He then practised as an advocate in Johannesburg in 1991, and left to join the Mafikeng Bar Association in the North West province, where he stayed until 1997. He was deputy chairperson of the Mafikeng Bar Council, and chairperson of the Bophuthatswana chapter of Lawyers for Human Rights. From 1992 to 1993, he was a part-time senior lecturer at North-West University. In 1994, he served in the legal section of the Independent Electoral Commission (IEC) in the North West province.

Mogoeng served as a member of the Industrial Court from 1989 until the court's dissolution. In 1997, he was appointed as a judge of the North West High Court, and later as its judge president in 2002. As Chris Oxtoby[1] of the DGRU at UCT notes, while Mogoeng was a judge of the High Court, he delivered the judgment in *Lesapo v North West Agricultural Bank*, declaring a section of the North West Agricultural Bank Act, which allowed the bank to seize and sell the property of a defaulting debtor without any judicial recourse, to be unconstitutional. In *DVB Behuising v North West Provincial Government and Another*, Mogoeng found the power of the provincial government to repeal regulations relating to the registration of property rights in former TBVC states (Transkei, Bophuthatswana, Venda and Ciskei) to be invalid.

In 2000, Mogoeng was appointed as a judge of the Labour Appeal Court. He was also a member of a committee headed by Chief Justice Pius Langa, which was set up to investigate racism and gender discrimination within the judiciary. In 2009, he was nominated as the judge presidents' representative on the Council of the South African Judicial Education Institute.

Besides being a member of the BLA, Mogoeng has also served on numerous committees, including serving as chairperson for the North West Parks Board and the Agricultural Services Cooperation of the North West province.

He was appointed to the Constitutional Court in 2009, and became chief justice in 2011. Mogoeng's appointment as chief justice proved to be extremely controversial, which he attributed to his Christian beliefs. However, a major cause for concern was that more experienced judges were passed over for the position. Mogoeng himself had served only two years on the bench. In addition, his judicial track record elicited much debate. Because of his judgments, Constitutional Court reviewer Pierre de Vos[2] labelled Mogoeng the most conservative judge on the bench. The JSC's role in appointing Mogoeng as chief justice was also criticised.

Examples of his conservative stance include his views on gay rights, such as were demonstrated in *Le Roux v Dey*, where Mogoeng was the only judge not to concur in a portion of the majority judgment, where it was held that it was not injurious to refer to someone on a ground protected by the Constitution – in the Dey case, the injury in question was being mislabelled as 'gay'. Yet, despite his objection to the majority opinion, Mogoeng did not write a separate opinion to explain the grounds for his disagreement. His 'silent dissent' was criticised by the Women's Legal Centre as a failure of a judge's duty to account for their findings by giving reasoned decisions, thereby undermining judicial accountability and transparency.

As Oxtoby notes, exacerbating this issue is the fact that Mogoeng is an ordained pastor and has served in several church structures. The concern is that his religious views might conflict with his oath of office to uphold the Constitution. During his interview for the position of chief justice, Mogoeng denied any anti-gay sentiment. However, controversy over his religious views re-emerged in March 2012, when an email in which he requested heads of court to be available to attend a leadership conference headed by the evangelist John C. Maxwell was leaked to the media. According to Niren Tolsi of the *Mail & Guardian*, the email ignited criticism because it appeared that the chief justice was using his judicial office to promote the private interests of a third party.[3] Mogoeng was accused of blurring the separation between church and state.

Mogoeng's views on rape are also cause for concern, as evidenced by his high court judgments in rape cases. These decisions tend to demonstrate a pattern of reducing sentences in cases of domestic violence and sexual assault against women. Mogoeng was criticised for overlooking the SCA decision in *S v Abrahams*, which had been penned by fellow justice Edwin Cameron when he had previously sat on the SCA. Abrahams rejected the belief that rape within a family is less reprehensible than a rape outside the family. Mogoeng found that the fact that the parties knew each other was a mitigating factor for sentencing purposes. He was accused of relying on myths about rape, gender stereotypes and patriarchal attitudes in his approach. He was further criticised over his handling of cases prior to his appointment to the Constitutional Court. Specifically, in *S v Dube and Others*, Mogoeng's decision to hear the case himself, though his wife was appearing before him as the state prosecutor, was a decision that many thought unsound, including the SCA, which overturned his judgment in that case.

Other decisions that have garnered criticism from progressives include Mogoeng's judgment in *The Citizen v McBride*. Mogoeng dissented from the majority and, according to De Vos in his blog *Constitutionally Speaking*, his reasoning suggests that he has a 'curious understanding of the way in which freedom of expression operates in a constitutional democracy'. Concern was also raised regarding Mogoeng's views on traditional leadership due to his dissenting opinion in *Pilane and Another v Pilane and Another*. The issue in that case was the right to freedom of speech and assembly, where residents of Motlhabe Village sought to conduct a meeting to discuss the possibility of secession from the traditional community and were discouraged from doing so by the SAPS. Mogoeng, in a co-written opinion with Justice Bess Nkabinde, found that the plaintiffs, by previously declaring their intent to secede and stating that they did not recognise the legitimacy of the tribal community, in effect sought to undermine and threaten the senior traditional leader, in disregard of the relevant customary law and statutes. Therefore, the applicants had no authority under custom-ary law or any relevant statute to convene a meeting as they had planned. Additionally, the villagers' right to free speech and assembly had not been compromised, though they did not hold the meeting.

Deputy Chief Justice Dikgang Moseneke

Dikgang Moseneke was born in 1947. At the age of fifteen, he was arrested, detained and convicted for participating in political activity that was opposed to the apart-heid regime. He was sentenced to ten years' imprisonment, all of which he served on Robben Island.

While in prison, Moseneke obtained a BA degree (in English and political science) and a BJuris degree. Subsequently, he completed his LLB. All three degrees were conferred by UNISA. He started his professional career in 1976 as an attorney's clerk. In 1978, he was admitted as an attorney.

He was called to the Bar in 1983, where he practised as an advocate at the Johan-nesburg and Pretoria Bars. Ten years later, in 1993, he was elevated to the status of senior counsel (silk). He served on the technical committee that drafted the 1993 Interim Constitution, and in 1994 was appointed deputy chairman of the IEC, which conducted the first democratic elections in South Africa. In September 1994, he was appointed to the Supreme Court as an acting judge.

From 1995 to 2001, Moseneke left the Bar to pursue a full-time corporate career in various capacities, most notably as chairman of Telkom and chief executive of New Africa Investments Ltd. Before his appointment to the Constitutional Court, Moseneke was a judge of the High Court in Pretoria in 2001. He is a founder mem-ber of the BLA and of NADEL. From 1986, he was appointed visiting law professor at Columbia Law School, Columbia University, New York.

Moseneke was appointed to the Constitutional Court in 2002 by then president Mbeki. He subsequently became deputy chief justice in 2005. Mosneke has been dubbed the 'great chief justice that South Africa never had'. Though he currently serves as deputy chief justice, he has been passed over twice for the top spot. Moseneke and the current ANC administration under Zuma have a difficult relationship. This strained relationship was brought to the fore during an incident that transpired around Moseneke's sixtieth birthday. According to the *Mail & Guardian*, Moseneke reportedly told guests that he had dedicated his life to working for an egalitarian society. 'I chose this job very carefully. I have another 10 to 12 years on the Bench and I want to use my energy to help create an equal society. It's not what the ANC wants or what the delegates [to the Polokwane conference] want; it is about what is good for our people.'[4] The NWC of the ANC questioned Moseneke's integrity, and stated that these remarks showed 'disdain' for the ANC delegates who attended the party's conference in Polokwane in December 2007. The ANC subsequently compared Moseneke to opposition political parties and 'untransformed' apartheid-era judges. Following these events, Moseneke issued a statement reaffirming his commitment to strive for 'what is good for all our people', and the ANC retracted their statement.

The ANC continues to demonstrate its dislike of the deputy chief justice. They have expressed their displeasure at rulings that they believe infringe upon their authority. For example, the ANC issued criticism for Moseneke's opinion (co-written with Justice Cameron) in the seminal case of *Glenister v President of the Republic of South Africa and Others*. Glenister was involved in the formation of the Hawks, a new crime-fighting unit created after the dissolution of the Scorpions. The Hawks were designated by government officials to investigate only 'priority crimes'. According to De Vos, a majority of Constitutional Court judges found that the Hawks were not sufficiently independent and that the state had therefore failed to fulfil its obligations to respect, protect, promote and uphold the Bill of Rights as required by section 7(2) of the Constitution. This decision was extremely unpopular with the ANC, and the decision deepened the division between Moseneke and the party.

As a judge, Moseneke is known to be extremely progressive in his views and has often labelled the court as 'pro-poor'. *Abahlali baseMjondolo Movement of South Africa and Another v Premier of the Province of KwaZulu-Natal and Others* is a case that illustrates his progressive stance. In that case, Abahlali baseMjondolo, an organisation representing several thousand people who lived in informal settlements, alleged that section 16 of the KwaZulu-Natal Elimination and Prevention of Re-emergence of Slums Act was unconstitutional. Section 16 allowed provincial government officials to issue a notice directing that eviction proceedings be instituted by owners and local municipalities against informal settlements. Moseneke found that section 16 would make residents of informal settlements more vulnerable to evictions should an MEC decide to issue a notice under that section. He also noted that the power given to the MEC to issue a notice was over-broad and irrational, because it applied to any unlawful occupier on any land or in any building even if not a slum. The majority judgment granted an order declaring that section

16 of the Act was inconsistent with section 26 of the Constitution and therefore invalid.

In another judgment, *Barkhuizen v Napier*, Moseneke dissented from the majority, arguing that the appropriate test for determining the constitutionality of a clause within a contract is to assess whether the contractual term is so unreasonable as to offend against public policy. A court should not look at the individual circumstances and characteristics of a party to the contract, but more broadly ask whether a clause in a contract clashes with public norms. This opinion runs counter to more traditional and conservative views on contract law.

Though Moseneke is widely respected in the legal world, his term has not endured without its share of controversy. For example, in *De Lacy and Another v South African Post Office*, the plaintiffs filed a complaint with the JSC after losing their case in the Constitutional Court. According to the *Mail & Guardian*, the complainants alleged that Moseneke should not have presided over the matter, since his brother was a director of the company that was awarded the disputed tender.[5]

Despite the disappointment of being overlooked for a second time for the position of chief justice in 2011, Moseneke did not resign from the court, as some thought he might, but is now regarded as the intellectual leader of the progressive wing of the court, along with Justice Cameron.

Justice Bess Nkabinde

Bess Nkabinde was born in 1959 and obtained a BProc degree from the University of Zululand, and an LLB from North-West University. She also attended Damelin College, where she was awarded a diploma in industrial relations.

Her professional career began in 1984, when she worked as a state law advisor, doing legislative drafting in Bophuthatswana. She did this until 1988, when she was admitted as an advocate. In 1989, she did her pupillage at the Johannesburg Bar. From 1990 until 1999 she practised as an advocate at the North West Bar in civil, commercial, matrimonial and criminal matters. In 1993, she attended a judicial training programme in Canada, and from 1994 to 1995 was involved in investigating and leading evidence in the commission of inquiry into the mutiny of warders at Mogwase Prison.

Between February and October 1999, Nkabinde served as acting judge of the High Court of the Bophuthatswana provincial division. In November of the same year, she was officially appointed judge of this court. In 2000, she served one term as acting judge of the Labour Court in Johannesburg, and then another term in the same position in 2003. She was also appointed to serve on the Special Tribunal on Civil Matters Likely to Emanate from Investigations by the Special Investigative Units (established in terms of Act 74 of 1996) in that same year. From October 2004 to May 2005, she served as acting judge of the Labour Appeal Court, and from June to November 2005, she was acting judge of the SCA. She has served in numerous organisations, including the North West Bar Association, the AIDS committee in Bophuthatswana and the BLA.

Nkabinde was appointed to the Constitutional Court in 2006.

Though Nkabinde has traditionally demonstrated a progressive outlook in terms of interpreting the Constitution, some of her judgments indicate otherwise. For example, she and Chief Justice Mogoeng were harshly criticised by progressives for their dissenting opinion in *Pilane and Another v Pilane and Another* (for a more in-depth discussion of the case, refer to the profile on Mogoeng Mogoeng).

Other notable opinions that Nkabinde has authored include the majority opinion in *Prophet v Director of Public Prosecutions*, where provisions of the Prevention of Organised Crime Act were upheld. She also authored the majority opinion in *The Association of Regional Magistrates of Southern Africa v The President of the Republic of South Africa and Others*, where the Constitutional Court dismissed an application for confirmation of part of an order of the North Gauteng High Court, Pretoria, that set aside the president's decision to increase the annual remuneration of regional magistrates and regional court presidents.

Justice Johan Froneman

Johan Froneman was born in 1953. He obtained a BA degree from the University of Stellenbosch and an LLB from UNISA.

After completing his pupillage at the Pretoria Bar, he began practising as an advocate at the Eastern Cape Bar in Grahamstown in 1980. He obtained silk status in 1990 and was appointed as a judge to the Eastern Cape High Court in 1994. In 1996, he was appointed deputy judge president of the Labour and Labour Appeal courts, a post he held until 1999. In 2002, he acted for two terms in the SCA. His notable judgments include *Nguza and others v Secretary* and *Department of Welfare, Eastern Cape Provincial Government, Kate v MEC, Department of Welfare, Eastern Cape.* These cases dealt with non-payment by the provincial government of social grants, and failure to comply with court orders.

Between 2003 and 2008, Froneman was a professor in public law at the University of Stellenbosch. In 2009, he was appointed to the Constitutional Court by Zuma. Though Froneman is relatively new to the Constitutional Court, in terms of total years spent as a judge he is the most experienced among the current judges on the Constitutional Court. As noted by Adrienne Carlisle in *Grocott's Mail*, Froneman is known to be a judicial activist and has been quoted as describing the Constitution as the country's 'never again' document, designed to ensure the atrocities of apartheid are never repeated.[6]

He is one of the more progressive justices on the bench, as evidenced by his opinions in *Gundwana v Steko Development and Others* and *Bengwenyama Minerals (Pty) Ltd and Others v Genorah Resources (Pty) Ltd and Others*. In the Gundwana case, he found it unconstitutional for a registrar of the high court, when granting default judgment, to declare immovable property specially executable, to the extent that this would permit the sale in execution of a person's home. In the *Bengwenyama Minerals* case, he set aside a decision by the Department of Mineral Resources to grant prospecting rights on land reclaimed by a community that had been dispossessed during apartheid.

As observed by Oxtoby, Froneman wrote a separate concurring judgment in *F v Minister of Safety and Security*. Whereas the majority found the minister vicariously liable for a rape committed by a policeman while on standby duty, Froneman would have found the minister directly liable. In *Road Accident Fund and Another v Mdeyide*, he dissented from the majority decision that provisions of the Prescription Act 68 of 1969 did not apply to claims under the Road Accident Fund Act 56 of 1996. He further found the limitation to be unconstitutional.

Recently, Froneman co-wrote the opinion in *Modjadji v Ngwenyama and Another*, where the court held that Tsonga customary law required that the first wife in the case be informed of her husband's subsequent customary marriage. Thus, the first respondent's marriage was found to be invalid because the applicant had not been informed.

Justice Sisi Khampepe

Born in 1957, Sisi Khampepe obtained a BProc from the University of Zululand and an LLM from Harvard Law School in the US.

She began her legal career as a legal advisor in the Industrial Aid Society. In 1981, she worked as a fellow at the Legal Resources Centre, and in 1983, she joined Bowman Gilfillan Attorneys as a candidate attorney. After being admitted as an attorney in 1985, she founded her own law firm, SV Khampepe Attorneys, and specialised in defending workers' rights.

In 1995, Khampepe was appointed as commissioner of the TRC, and the following year she was appointed to the commission's Amnesty Committee. Following this appointment, Khampepe served as a deputy national director of public prosecutions between 1998 and 1999. In December 2000, she was appointed to the Transvaal provincial division of the High Court and, in November 2007, to the Labour Appeal Court.

As Oxtoby notes, in 2002 Khampepe and Moseneke were appointed by Mbeki to evaluate the constitutional and legal issues relating to the Zimbabwean presidential elections. The report produced by the two judges was never released, which elicited complaints from the media and various campaign groups. In order to have the report made available to the public, litigation ensued, most notably the case of *President of the Republic of South Africa and Others v Mail & Guardian Media Ltd* and *Mail & Guardian Media Ltd v President of the Republic of South Africa and Others* (for a more in-depth discussion of the case, refer to the profile on Edwin Cameron).

In 2005, Khampepe was appointed by Mbeki to chair the commission of inquiry into the mandate and location of the Directorate of Special Operations, also known as the Scorpions. The commission's finding that the Scorpions should remain part of the NPA ran counter to the government's ultimate decision to disband the directorate. This decision did not create any rift between the government and Khampepe, as she informed the JSC during her Constitutional Court appointment interview. In 2006, she was appointed as a member of the Commonwealth Observer Group to the presidential and parliamentary elections in Uganda to be held in February that year.

Outside the judiciary, Khampepe has held a wide array of positions, including vice chairperson of the Mediation and Conciliation Centre; trustee of the SACCAWU Investment Trust; member of the Helen Joseph Hospital Board of Governors; member of the selection committee of the Public Service Commission; member of the BLA; and vice chairperson of the National Council of Correctional Services.

Khampepe was appointed to the Constitutional Court in 2009 by Zuma. During the search for a new chief justice in 2011, reports circulated that Khampepe, along with Moseneke, was a top contender for the position.

Though she is known to be a progressive on the court, she has a relatively sparse judicial track record. As noted by Oxtoby, since joining the Constitutional Court, she has issued judgments in *Mankayi v Anglogold Ashanti Ltd*, finding that the right of an employee entitled to compensation under the Occupational Diseases in Mines and Works Act to claim damages from an employer at common law was not expunged by the Compensation for Occupational Injuries and Diseases Act; and in *MS v S*, where she wrote the dissenting opinion. In that case, the court had to decide what impact the fact that a convicted person was the primary caregiver to minor children should have on sentencing. Khampepe found that the sentencing court had given insufficient attention to the quality of the alternative care the children would receive, and the impact of a custodial sentence on the children. She would have placed the appellant under correctional supervision.

In *Children's Institute v Presiding Officer of the Children's Court, District of Krugersdorp and Others*, Khampepe wrote on behalf of the unanimous court that Rule 16A of the Uniform Rules of Court allowed for an *amicus curiae* to adduce evidence if the interests of justice required. Recently, Khampepe co-wrote the opinion in *Modjadji v Ngwenyama and Another* with justices Froneman and Thembile Skweyiya (for a more in-depth discussion of the case, refer to the profile on Johan Froneman).

Justice Edwin Cameron

Edwin Cameron was born in 1953. He attended the University of Stellenbosch on the Anglo-American Open Scholarship, where he obtained a BA in law and an honours degree in Latin. He lectured in Latin and classical studies before studying at Oxford on a Rhodes scholarship. While at Oxford, he obtained a BA in jurisprudence and the BCL. He received his LLB from UNISA.

Cameron practised at the Johannesburg Bar from 1983 to 1994. From 1986, he was a human rights lawyer based at Wits's CALS, where he was awarded a personal professorship in law. His practice included labour and employment law; defence of ANC fighters charged with treason; conscientious and religious objection to compulsory military service; land tenure and forced removals; and gay and lesbian equality. From 1988, he advised NUM on HIV/AIDS, and helped draft and negotiate the industry's first comprehensive AIDS agreement with the Chamber of Mines. While at CALS, he drafted the Charter of Rights on AIDS and HIV, co-founded the AIDS Consortium (a national affiliation of NGOs working in AIDS), which he chaired for its first three years, and founded the AIDS Law Project.

He oversaw the gay and lesbian movement's submissions to the Kempton Park negotiating process. This, with other work, helped secure the express inclusion of sexual orientation in the Constitution. He was awarded silk status in September 1994 and Mandela appointed him an acting judge and later a judge of the High Court. In 1999, Cameron served as an acting justice in the Constitutional Court and, in 2000, was appointed a judge of appeal in the SCA. He served as chairperson of the governing council of Wits from 1998 to 2008.

Cameron was appointed to the Constitutional Court in 2008 by Motlanthe. He is the first openly gay judge to be practising on the Constitutional Court, as well as South Africa's first senior official to publicly state that he is HIV-positive. Cameron's decision to inform the public of his AIDS status was influenced by the stoning and stabbing of Gugu Dlamini after she disclosed that she was HIV-positive.

Cameron is notably progressive in his views, and he is known to craft creative opinions that tie the law to the spirit of the Constitution and his interpretation of its underlying values. During his interview with the JSC upon his application to the Constitutional Court, Cameron informed the JSC that a woman's right to choose to terminate an unwanted pregnancy and the death penalty were two issues that he as a judge would seek to protect against the will of the majority.

Examples of his progressive inclinations can be evidenced in such decisions as *Maphango and Others v Aengus Lifestyle Properties (Pty) Ltd.* According to De Vos, the judgment in this case was significant due to the fact that it wrestled with the transformative effects of the Constitution and the Rental Housing Act. The decision empowered Rental Housing Tribunals, which were created to protect the rental housing market while also addressing the unequal power relations between landlords and tenants.

Cameron also penned the minority decision in *President of the Republic of South Africa and Others v Mail & Guardian Media Ltd.* The issue in that case was the public dissemination of a report prepared by two judges sent to Zimbabwe by then president Mbeki to look into that country's elections. Cameron stated that the Presidency had to hand over the report immediately and that the Presidency had failed to justify its refusal to release the report under PAIA.

Most recently, Cameron wrote the opinion for *KwaZulu-Natal Joint Liaison Committee v Member of the Executive Council Department of Education, KwaZulu-Natal and Others*, where he found that once a public official had made a public statement of a promise to pay specified amounts, that amount could not be unilaterally reduced after the due date for payment.

Justice Chris Jafta

Chris Jafta was born in 1959. He was a student at the University of Transkei, where he obtained his BJuris and LLB.

He began his legal career as a court interpreter in 1983, before being appointed as a district court prosecutor in 1984. Jafta's authority to prosecute was withdrawn by the Attorney-General at the insistence of the security police after he had rejected instructions from the security police on how he should conduct prosecutions in some cases. However, he was subsequently appointed as a magistrate in 1986. In 1988, he resigned in order to join the firm of Mbuqe & Mbuqe as a candidate attorney. After six months, he left this post in order to lecture at the University of Transkei, where he taught commercial law and constitutional law.

Jafta took pupillage at the Johannesburg Bar in 1992, and began practising in Mthatha in 1993. He served as an acting judge of the Transkei division of the High Court in 1997 and 1999, before being appointed to the High Court in 1999. While a High Court judge, Jafta authored the opinion in the case of *Mjeni v Minister of Health and Welfare, Eastern Cape*. He held that ministers and other public officials could be held in contempt of court in a finding which was disapproved by the SCA in *Jayiya v Member of the Executive Council for Welfare, Eastern Cape, and Another*. Between 2001 and 2003, Jafta served as acting judge president of the Transkei division of the High Court, before moving to the Labour Appeal Court. In 2004, he served as an acting justice of appeal on the SCA, until he was officially appointed that November.

Jafta served as an acting judge of the Constitutional Court from December 2007 until May 2008. He was permanently appointed in 2009 by Zuma.

Jafta is the most frequent dissenter among the judges on the court. According to De Vos, Jafta, Mogoeng and Justice Raymond Zondo are among the most conservative judges on the bench. Oxtoby highlights several notable judgments authored by Jafta since his appointment to the Constitutional Court. These include *Competition Commission of South Africa v Senwes Limited*, which dealt with the nature and scope of the powers of the Competition Tribunal; *Mvumvu and Others v Minister of Transport and Another*, which found the provision of the Road Accident Fund Act that capped certain damages claims to be unconstitutional; and a separate concurring judgment in *SATAWU and Another v Garvas and Others*, which dealt with the liability of the organiser of a gathering for ensuing riot damage, under the Regulation of

Gatherings Act 205 of 1993. While the majority found the section to be a justifiable limitation of the right to freedom of assembly, Jafta found no such limitation.

In *C and Others v Department of Health and Social Development, Gauteng, and Others*, a majority of the court confirmed that sections of the Children's Act 38 of 2005 were unconstitutional. These sections allowed state officials to remove children from their families and place them in temporary safe care, without providing for automatic review of removal by the Children's Court. Jafta dissented, stating that he would have found the sections to be constitutional.

In 2008, while serving as an acting judge of the Constitutional Court, Jafta wrote the majority decision in *Walele v City of Cape Town and Others*, which dealt with the approval of building plans by local authorities. More recently, he wrote the unanimous opinion in *eThekwini Municipality v Ingonyama Trust*. According to the South African Legal Information Institute, eThekwini Municipality sought leave to appeal against the judgment of the SCA. However, the municipality's application was two months late and the court rejected the explanation given for the delay. The court further held that there were no prospects of success, because the land in question constituted state property exempt from rates in terms of the Property Rates Act.

Justice Thembile Skweyiya

Thembile Skweyiya matriculated in 1959 from the Healdtown Institution in the Eastern Cape. He was awarded a BSocSc and an LLB by the University of Natal. From 1968 to 1970, Skweyiya served his articles of clerkship in an attorney's office. In 1970, he was admitted as an advocate of the Supreme Court, and became a member of the Society of Advocates in Natal.

From 1971 to 1996 he practised as an advocate in Durban, dealing almost exclusively in commercial and civil matters. From about the end of 1979, however, his work became more varied and he began handling human-rights and civil liberties cases not only in Durban, but in all Supreme Court divisions in southern Africa. Skweyiya was admitted as an advocate of the High Court of Lesotho in 1974.

From 1980 to 1982 he was a member of the Bar Council of Natal, and in 1989 became a silk. In 1992, the High Court of Namibia also admitted him as a silk.

During his interview with the JSC for appointment to the Constitutional Court, Skweyiya stated that he then left the Bar, believing that he would be appointed to a judicial position. However, five months later, no date for such an appointment arose, and he decided to pursue employment in the business world.

Skweyiya has held many positions in business, including chairperson of Worldwide African Investment Holdings (Pty) Ltd, KFM Radio (Pty) Ltd and Zenex Oil Ltd; deputy chairperson of Fortune Beverages Ltd and the SA Tourism Board; director and vice chairperson of Fasic Investment Ltd; director of Fedics Group Ltd, Lion Match (Pty) Ltd, Gold Circle Racing and Gaming, Premier Group Ltd and Southern

Bank of Africa Ltd; and member of the regional advisory board of Nedcor Bank, KwaZulu-Natal.

Between October 1995 and January 2001, Skweyiya served as an acting judge in the KwaZulu-Natal and Eastern Cape divisions of the High Court. He took up a permanent appointment on 1 February 2001.

He was appointed to the Constitutional Court in 2003 by Mbeki. There was some initial rankling about the appointment, with some commentators asserting that Skweyiya was appointed only because he had powerful ANC connections. His brother, Zola Skweyiya, is the former minister of public service and administration and of social development.

Skweyiya had garnered similar criticism when he headed a commission of inquiry in 1991 into allegations made by political prisoners and detainees concerning poor conditions, maltreatment and the loss or destruction of property in ANC detention camps. The commission reported to the ANC president, and, although it found that human-rights abuses *had* occurred, such as unlawful detention for periods of three to seven years without trial and overcrowding in cells, the commission was criticised for not assigning responsibility to individual ANC members.

The commission was further rocked by scandal when it was brought to the public's attention that the secretariat of the commission was in the hands of Dali Mpofu, a young lawyer who was the reputed lover of Winnie Mandela, head of the ANC's Department of Social Welfare. Because of the threat posed by Mpofu's affair to the independence of the commission, he resigned his post.

Notwithstanding his connections in the ANC, Skweyiya has written several opinions that are viewed as checking the government's authority. For instance, in a case relating to press leaks regarding the ANC's budget and its mismanagement (*Print Media SA and Another v Minister of Home Affairs and Another*), he emphasised the importance of freedom of expression and freedom of the media.

Skweyiya also wrote the majority opinion in *Pilane and Another v Pilane and Another*, an opinion that held significant implications for traditional authorities and customary law.[7] The case concerned members of a traditional community in North West province who sought to hold a meeting to discuss seceding from the established authority. The leaders of the established authority opposed this secession and sought to prevent the meeting by obtaining several interdicts from the North West High Court.

Skweyiya reasoned that no right of the established leaders had been infringed. The members of the community had not tried to use the titles of the authority. 'It is … difficult to see how in these circumstances one might consider the applicants to be attempting to appropriate the identity, authority or powers of the respondents when the terms and tenor of their attempted meeting … speak to the very dissociation from the respondents,' Skweyiya wrote. The majority held that core constitutional rights of expression, assembly and association apply to all law, including customary law. The case highlighted a divisive issue in the court, as the dissent and the majority expressed extremely different views on the role of traditional leadership in a constitutional state (for a more in-depth discussion of the case, refer to the profile on Mogoeng Mogoeng).

Justice Johann van der Westhuizen

Johann van der Westhuizen received his BA Law, LLB and LLD degrees from the University of Pretoria in 1973, 1975 and 1980 respectively. In 1975, he received the Grotius Medal, which is awarded by the Pretoria Bar Council to the University of Pretoria's best final-year law student.

Van der Westhuizen was admitted as an advocate in 1976. In addition, he served as both professor and head of the Department of Legal History, Comparative Law and Legal Philosophy in the University of Pretoria's law faculty. He was the founding director of the university's Centre for Human Rights from 1986 to 1998, before joining the Transvaal provincial division of the High Court in 1999. He was an associate member of the Pretoria Bar from 1989 to 1998.

Prior to embarking on his judicial career, Van der Westhuizen acted as counsel in human-rights litigation and argued many appeals against the censorship of socially and politically significant films and books such as *Roots*, *Cry Freedom* and *A Dry White Season*. He acted as a consultant and in-house advocate for the Legal Resources Centre and Lawyers for Human Rights, and also served on the national council and board of trustees of the latter from 1990 to 2001.

Van der Westhuizen was intimately involved in the drafting of South Africa's Constitution in 1995 and 1996. He was a member of the Independent Panel of Recognised Constitutional Experts, which advised the Constitutional Assembly, and was part of the technical refinement team responsible for the final drafting and editing of the Constitution.

Before that, he convened task groups at the multiparty negotiations in 1993, which resulted in the adoption of the Interim Constitution, and at the Transitional Executive Council in 1994. In 1998, he coordinated the equality legislation project of the justice ministry and the SAHRC.

Van der Westhuizen was appointed to the Constitutional Court in 2004 by Mbeki. His appointment was not without controversy. As Tony Leon notes in his autobiography, *On the Contrary*, candidates for the vacant judicial position were very weak because choices were 'flavoured by the nominees' close connection to the ANC in terms of the Constitution'.[8] The Van der Westhuizen appointment was criticised because he was considered the lesser qualified of two Afrikaner candidates, the other being Ben du Plessis.

Van der Westhuizen has written opinions dealing with matters from constitutional amendments, provincial boundaries and powers, fair trial issues and equality, to the development of African customary law, asset forfeiture, search-and-seizure procedures and the right to privacy.

He wrote the majority opinion in *Phumla Ruth Patricia Ngewu and Another v Post Office Retirement Fund and Others*, in which all parties agreed that the Post Office Act was unconstitutional to the extent that it did not provide for the payment of pension interest at the time of divorce. Thus, this provision was held to be unconstitutional.

Justice Raymond Zondo

Raymond Zondo obtained a BJuris from the University of Zululand in 1983, followed by an LLB from the University of Natal and three LLMs from UNISA.

He began his legal career as a fellow at the Legal Resources Centre, where he worked between 1984 and 1985. After becoming an attorney, Zondo became a partner in Durban-based Mathe and Zondo Inc. where he practised until his appointment to the bench. He also served as a mediator and arbiter in a part-time capacity.

In 1991 and 1992, Zondo served in two committees of the Commission of Inquiry Regarding the Prevention of Public Violence and Intimidation, also known as the Goldstone Commission, which investigated violence in South Africa during the early 1990s. In 1994, he assisted in drafting the labour relations bill and, in 1996, he was appointed as the first chairperson of the governing body of the CCMA.

In 1997, Zondo was appointed to the Labour Court. During his service there, the Johannesburg Bar Council noted that his 'contribution to developing our labour law jurisprudence is probably unsurpassed by any other judge'. In 1999, he was appointed to the North Gauteng division of the High Court.

In 2000, he was elevated to judge president of the Labour Court, a position he served until 2010, when he returned to the High Court. Upon his return, he wrote the judgment in *Sishen Iron Ore Company (Pty) Ltd and Another v Minister of Mineral Affairs and Others*, which dealt with the issue of mining rights. The case was later described by Judge President Bernard Ngoepe as the biggest commercial matter in South Africa's history. From November 2011 to May 2012, Zondo served as acting judge of the Constitutional Court until his permanent appointment by Zuma in September 2012.

He is known as one of the more conservative justices on the bench, who holds onto the notion of legal formalism. An example of his conservatism can be seen in his opinion in the case *Maphango and Others v Aengus Lifestyle Properties (Pty) Ltd*, which displays what progressives such as De Vos term 'a surprisingly formalistic and pre-constitutional attitude to the law that applies between landlords and tenants'.

Zondo also wrote the majority decision in *Minister of Home Affairs and Others v Tsebe and Others*, holding that the respondents could not be extradited or deported to face murder charges in Botswana in the absence of a written assurance that the death penalty would not be imposed on conviction.

Zondo has written several academic publications, including *The New Labour Courts and Labour Law: The First Seven Months of the New LRA* and *Redundancy and Retrenchment.*

Justice Mbuyiseli Madlanga

Mbuyiseli Madlanga obtained a BJuris from the University of Transkei in 1984, followed by an LLB from Rhodes University and an LLM from the University of Notre Dame in the US.

Madlanga worked as a prosecutor in the Department of Justice in 1984. He lectured at the University of Transkei from 1987 until 1989, and then practised as an advocate in Mthatha from 1991. In 1996, he was appointed to the Eastern Cape High Court in Mthatha. He served as acting judge of the SCA from 1998 to 1999. From 1999 to 2000, he served as acting judge president of the Transkei division of the High Court. In 1999, he was also appointed to the newly established Competition Appeal Court. From 2000 to 2001, he served as acting judge of the Constitutional Court.

In 2001, Madlanga resigned from his judicial post to practise as a silk. He held chambers in Mthatha and later in Johannesburg. Leaving a judicial position is highly uncommon and looked upon with disapproval. He was questioned about his decision during his interview for the Constitutional Court. He told the JSC that it was well known at the time that he had resigned because he could not afford to stay on as a judge. He said he went to the bench very young and had a wife, a bond and six children. Since then, his circumstances had changed, enabling him to re-enter the judicial profession.

In 2003, Madlanga served as chairperson of the Exchange Control and Income Tax Amnesty Unit and was appointed by the president as a part-time member of the Competition Tribunal. In 2009, he became deputy chairperson of the Competition Tribunal and, in 2010, was appointed by the president as a member of the JSC, where he would eventually also serve as a representative of the advocate's profession.

Madlanga served as chief evidence leader for the Marikana commission of inquiry, which was established to look into what led to the deaths of thirty-four miners during an unprotected strike at Lonmin's Marikana mine in August 2012. He was also evidence leader in the inquiry into the fitness for office of former national police commissioner Bheki Cele.

Madlanga has been a member of various associations, including the Lawyers Association, the BLA and NADEL. He also represented South Africa before the International Court of Justice at The Hague, in the matter of the 'Separation Wall Constructed by Israel on Occupied Palestinian Territory'.

Madlanga was appointed to the Constitutional Court in 2013 by Zuma and is the newest justice on the bench. His appointment was criticised, as one of his chief rivals for the position, Advocate Jeremy Gauntlett, was eliminated from the list of potential candidates. Gauntlett has earned a reputation as being one of South Africa's best advocates, yet has been passed over by the JSC five times.[9]

As Madlanga has only just been appointed, it remains to be seen where he will fall in the spectrum of judicial philosophy on the court. De Vos has criticised him for having a lack of legal imagination and a lack of enthusiasm for the transformation of the legal system.

Madlanga's noteworthy cases include *Zair v Minister of Home Affairs and Another* and *Matiwos v Minister of Home Affairs and Another*, in which the applicants were seeking their release from detention, having been detained pending deportation to their countries of origin. Madlanga found that they were entitled to release. He also wrote the opinions in *Bangindawo and Others v Head of the Nyanda Regional Authority* and *Hlantlalala v Head of the Western Tembuland Regional Authority and Others*, in which he held that section 7(1) of the Regional Courts Authority Act, which denied parties the right to legal representation in regional authority courts, was invalid. As a result, the convictions of the applicants in the first application were set aside.

Besides those references specifically cited, the rest of the information in this appendix comes primarily from the Constitutional Court of South Africa website (http://www.constitutionalcourt.org.za) and ConCourtBlog.com (http://concourtblog.com).

Notes

CHAPTER 1: FROM MBEKI TO ZUMA

1 Frank Chikane, *Eight Days in September*, Johannesburg: Pan Macmillan, 2012.

2 Section 89 of the Constitution provides for what in other systems would be called the 'impeachment' of the president: he or she may be removed in the case of serious misconduct, a serious violation of the law or the Constitution, or incapacity, by a vote of two-thirds majority. Section 102(2) of the Constitution states that the president must resign if there is a vote of no confidence in him or her (by a simple majority).

3 Henry Fairlie, 'Political commentary', *The Spectator*, 23 September 1955.

4 Anthony Sampson, *Who Runs This Place? The Anatomy of Britain in the 21st Century*, London: John Murray Publishers, 2004.

5 Data from World Bank Group, World Development Indicators, 2013. Available at http://data.worldbank.org/data-catalog/world-development-indicators [last accessed 18 June 2013].

6 Data from SAIRR, *South Africa Survey 2012*, Johannesburg: SAIRR, 2012.

7 Ibid., p. 242.

8 Ibid., p. 293.

9 Ibid., p. 295.

10 Ibid., p. 308.

11 Ibid., p. 288.

12 Adapted from SAIRR, *South Africa Survey 2012*, p. 307.

13 Adapted from SAIRR, *South Africa Survey 2012*, p. 299.

14 There could be several reasons for this. For example, it is possible that many forgo schooling in favour of employment. In any case, this is not the place for a detailed analysis of this particular anomaly.

15 Adapted from SAIRR, *South Africa Survey 2012*, pp. 258 and 260.

16 SAIRR, *South Africa Survey 2012*, p. 216.

17 Adapted from SAIRR, *South Africa Survey 2012*, pp. 586–587.

18 Ibid., pp. 258 and 269.

19 Roger Southall, 'The power elite in democratic South Africa: Race and class in a fractured society', in J. Daniel, P. Naidoo, D. Pillay & R. Southall, *New South African Review* (3), Johannesburg: Wits University Press, 2013.

20 C.W. Mills cited in Southall, 'The power elite in democratic South Africa: Race and class in a fractured society', p. 35.

21 Southall, 'The power elite in democratic South Africa: Race and class in a fractured society', p. 35.

22 Richard Calland, *Anatomy of South Africa: Who Holds the Power?* Cape Town: Zebra Press, 2006, p. 279.

CHAPTER 2: THE PRESIDENCY

1 David Smith, 'Jacob Zuma risks removal over handling of Marikana mine killings', *The Guardian*, 26 August 2012, http://www.guardian.co.uk/world/2012/aug/26/jacob-zuma-marikana-mine-killings [last accessed 22 June 2013].

2 Kenny Kunene, 'Kenny Kunene's letter to Zuma', *The Star*, 21 June 2013, www.iol.co.za/the-star/kenny-kunene-s-letter-to-zuma-1.1535280#.UcafgYwaySM [last accessed 23 June 2013].

3 Ibid.

4 Michael Barber, *Instruction to Deliver: Fighting to Transform Britain's Public Services*, York: Methuen Publishing, 2008.

5 The Presidency: Department of Performance Monitoring and Evaluation, 'Outcomes approach', available at www.poa.gov.za/pages/overview.aspx [last accessed 23 June 2013].

6 Jonathan Powell, *The New Machiavelli: How to Wield Power in the Modern World*, London: Vintage Publishing, 2010, p. 59.

7 Ibid.

CHAPTER 3: THE CABINET

1 Walter Bagehot, *The English Constitution*, London: Chapman and Hall, 1867.

2 Anthony Sampson, *Anatomy of Britain Today*, London: Hodder & Stoughton, 1965, p. 130.

3 Extract from *The Devil in the Detail: How the Arms Deal Changed Everything* by Paul Holden and Hennie van Vuuren, published in the *Sunday Times*, 'The rise of the Shadow State', 16 October 2011, http://www.timeslive.co.za/Feeds/2011/10/16/the-rise-of-the-shadow-state [last accessed 7 June 2013].

4 The Presidency, press statement, 'Ministerial clusters reconfigured to improve coordination and delivery', 19 November 2009, http://www.thepresidency.gov.za/pebble.asp?relid=858. Cabinet members obtained from Western Cape Government, 'The government of South Africa: Overview', http://www.westerncape.gov.za/your_gov/595 [last accessed 7 June 2013].

5 Anthony Butler, 'Zuma's appointments and the mills of rumour and distrust', *Business Day*, 3 August 2009, http://www.bdlive.co.za/articles/2009/08/03/zuma-s-appointments-and-the-mills-of-rumour-and-distrust [last accessed 7 June 2013].

6 Haroon Bhorat & Charlene van der Westhuizen, 'Economic growth, poverty and inequality in South Africa: The first decade of democracy', paper commissioned by the Presidency, 2009, http://dev.absol.co.za/presidency/docs/reports/15year_review/social/economic_growth.pdf [last accessed 18 June 2013].

7 Amanda Visser, 'Broadside for Patel's "competition meddling"', *Business Day*, 5 April 2012.

8 See Mcebisi Ndletyana, 'Policy incoherence: A function of ideological contestations?' In U. Pillay, G. Hagg and F. Nyamnjoy, *State of the Nation: South Africa 2012–2013*, Cape Town: HSRC Press, 2013.

9 Paul Trewhela, 'Pravin Gordhan: A political profile', *Politicsweb*, 18 May 2009, http://www.politicsweb.co.za/politicsweb/view/politicsweb/en/page71619?oid=129489&sn=Detail [last accessed 18 June 2013].

CHAPTER 4: FOREIGN POLICY

1 See, for example, one critical summary of South Africa's record on the UN Security Council: Olivier Serrão, 'South Africa in the UN Security Council 2011–2012', Berlin: Friedrich Ebert Stiftung, 2011, http://library.fes.de/pdf-files/iez/08166.pdf [last accessed 11 April 2013].

2 Hoffmann's report can be found at http://www.mtn.com/Investors/Circulars/Circulars/hoffmann_report.PDF [last accessed 11 April 2013].

3 My appendix to the report can be found at http://www.safpi.org/sites/default/files/publications/Appendix_6_calland.pdf [last accessed 11 April 2013].

4 'Pahad comments on Tehran-Pretoria relations', Iran News Agency, 7 May 2006.

5 WikiLeaks cable 05PRETORIA4297, 'SAG makes no progress on stalemate with Iran', 24 October 2005, http://wikileaks.org/cable/2005/10/05PRETORIA4297.html [last accessed 11 April 2013].

6 Eduard Jordaan, 'Barking at the big dogs: South Africa's foreign policy towards the Middle East', *The Round Table* 97(397), 2008, pp. 547–559 at 547.

7 Jacob Zuma, 'Statement of the National Executive Committee on the occasion of the 96th anniversary of the ANC', 8 January 2008, http://anc.org.za/show.php?id=52 [last accessed 11 April 2013].

8 Department of International Relations and Cooperation, http://www.dirco.gov.za/foreign/index.html [last accessed 11 April 2013].

9 Sections 84 and 85 of the Constitution set out the powers and authority of the president as head of state and as head of the national executive. Although the language is not entirely clear, the most reasonable interpretation is that the express authority enumerated in section 84(2) – a list of specific responsibilities that the president has, including 'appointing ambassadors, plenipotentiaries, and diplomatic and consular representatives' – is in relation to the president's role as head of state.

10 Charles Molele, 'Yet another dodgy diplomat', *Mail & Guardian*, 9 September 2011, http://bit.ly/zpYF79 [last accessed 11 April 2013].

11 Andisiwe Makinana & Glynnis Underhill, 'Rasool could be forced to fly back to face music', *Mail & Guardian*, 13 January 2012, http://bit.ly/AbKxDs [last accessed 11 April 2013].

12 Mandy Rossouw, 'Past could cost Rasool US posting', *Mail & Guardian*, 2 July 2010, http://bit.ly/wVYQoX [last accessed 11 April 2013].

13 Sabelo Ndlangisa, 'Zuma posts away problems', *City Press*, 26 September 2011, http://bit.ly/z9lVuw [last accessed 11 April 2013].

14 Siyabonga Mkhwanazi, 'Ngconde Balfour resigns from diplomatic post', *Independent Online*, 4 July 2010, http://www.iol.co.za/news/politics/ngconde-balfour-resigns-from-diplomatic-post-1.488774 [last accessed 11 April 2013].

15 Mandy Rossouw, 'Another surprising diplomatic choice', *Mail & Guardian*, 16 July 2010, http://mg.co.za/article/2010-07-16-another-surprising-diplomatic-choice [last accessed 11 April 2013].

16 Mandy Rossouw, 'New envoy in plagiarism scandal', *Mail & Guardian*, 30 July 2010, http://mg.co.za/article/2010-07-30-new-envoy-in-plagiarism-scandal [last accessed 11 April 2013].

17 Theresa Mallinson, 'Jon Qwelane still representing SA in Uganda – And Dirco doesn't understand what all the fuss is about', *Daily Maverick*, 11 November 2011, http://dailymaverick.co.za/article/2011-11-11-jon-qwelane-still-representing-sa-in-uganda-and-dirco-doesnt-understand-what-all-the-fuss-is-about [last accessed 11 April 2013].

18 Richard Calland, Contretemps: 'Tony, I want your job in Buenos Aires', *Mail & Guardian*, 23 August 2009, http://mg.co.za/article/2009-08-23-tony-i-want-your-job-in-buenos-aires [last accessed 11 April 2013].

19 ANC press statement, 'Zimbabwe must honour SADC guidelines on free elections', 6 June 2008, http://anc.org.za/show.php?id=5967 [last accessed 11 April 2013].

20 ANCWL press statement, 'Sisisi Tolashe's statement of the ANC Women's League on Zimbabwe crisis', 10 December 2008, http://www.anc.org.za/wl/show.php?id=5787 [last accessed 11 April 2013].

21 Fiona Forde, 'ANC questions Mbeki's role in Zim', *Sunday Independent*, 25 January 2009, http://bit.ly/mWpx4L [last accessed 11 April 2013].

22 Maureen Isaacson, 'The man with the president's ear and the African agenda: Ebrahim Ebrahim believes it's time for South Africa to take a strong stand on human rights', *Sunday Independent*, 7 June 2009.

23 Tonderai Kwenda, 'Zuma threatens Mugabe', *Daily News*, Zimbabwe, 20 July 2011, http://www.zimbabwesituation.com/jul21_2011.html [last accessed 11 April 2013].

24 Mandy Rossouw, 'Mugabe and Mantashe at Zanu-PF conference', *City Press*, 9 December 2011, http://bit.ly/rCvX57 [last accessed 11 April 2013].

25 Ibid.

26 White paper on South Africa's foreign policy, 'Building a better world: The diplomacy of ubuntu', final draft, 13 May 2011.

27 Mzukisi Qobo is also a member of the Mbeki-aligned Midrand Group of black intellectuals who see themselves as non-aligned intellectuals who want to provide a non-partisan critique of government regardless of who is in power – and who do so eloquently, often on the op-ed pages of *Business Day*.

28 Mzukisi Qobo, 'South Africa's foreign policy stuck in the doldrums', *Mail & Guardian*, 29 August 2011, http://bit.ly/mXhHlD [last accessed 11 April 2013].

29 Jacob Zuma's inaugural address, 9 May 2009, http://anc.org.za/show.php?id=3031 [last accessed 11 April 2013].

30 Chris Landsberg, *The Diplomacy of Transformation: South African Foreign Policy and Statecraft*, Johannesburg: Pan Macmillan, 2010.

31 'Minister Maite Nkoane-Mashabane on name change to Department of International Relations & Co-Operation (DIRCO)', 14 May 2009, http://bit.ly/yQrk1e [last accessed 11 April 2013].

32 AFP, 'Dalai Lama applies for SA visa', 31 August 2011, http://bit.ly/zQ9luN [last accessed 11 April 2013].

33 SAPA, 'Dalai Lama issue "dead in the water"', 6 December 2011, http://bit.ly/wYEOSP [last accessed 11 April 2013].

34 IBSA, http://www.ibsa-trilateral.org/ [last accessed 11 April 2013].
35 Ayanda Ntsaluba, DIRCO media briefing, 31 August 2009, http://bit.ly/z3u3f1 [last accessed 11 April 2013].
36 Jim O'Neill, 'Building better global economic BRICs', Goldman Sachs, 30 November 2011, http://www.goldmansachs.com/our-thinking/archive/archive-pdfs/build-better-brics.pdf [last accessed 11 April 2013].
37 *Business Report*, 'SA mulls membership of BRIC league – Ntsaluba', *Independent Online*, 16 October 2009, http://bit.ly/sowzoh [last accessed 11 April 2013].
38 Ibid.
39 Mzukizi Qobo, 'SA's foreign policy lacks confidence', *Mail & Guardian*, 14 October 2011, http://bit.ly/mUfToB [last accessed 11 April 2013].
40 Sean Christie, 'An armchair guide to SA's foreign policy challenges', *Mail & Guardian*, 25 March 2011, http://mg.co.za/article/2011-03-25-an-armchair-guide-to-sas-foreign-policy-challenges [last accessed 11 April 2013].

CHAPTER 5: THE FOREIGN POLICY MAKERS

1 Russel Brueton, 'Zuma is proving to be more than just a "domestic president"', South African Institute of International Affairs, 10 June 2010, http://www.saiia.org.za/diplomatic-pouch/zuma-is-proving-to-be-more-than-just-a-domestic-president.html [last accessed 12 April 2013].
2 Hajra Omarjee & Karima Brown, 'Reassuring faces mingle with some unusual choices', *Business Day*, 11 May 2009, http://bit.ly/soZytP [last accessed 12 April 2013].
3 Carien du Plessis & Gaye Davis, 'Who's who in Zuma cabinet', *Independent Online*, 11 May 2009, http://bit.ly/skce6j [last accessed 12 April 2013].
4 SAPA, 'Presidency announces Zuma advisers', *Mail & Guardian*, 26 May 2009, http://mg.co.za/article/2009-05-25-presidency-announces-zuma-advisers [last accessed 12 April 2013].
5 Presidency press statement, 'Ambassador Welile Nhlapo to boost Great Lakes relations', 29 June 2011, http://bit.ly/o69uyf [last accessed 12 April 2013].
6 Presidency press statement, 'President Zuma to send envoys to Libya and Zimbabwe', 18 March 2011, http://www.info.gov.za/speech/DynamicAction?pageid=461&sid=17127&tid=30330 [last accessed 12 April 2013].
7 Presidency press statement, 'Staff changes in the Presidency', 5 July 2010, http://www.info.gov.za/speech/DynamicAction?pageid=461&sid=11276&tid=11464 [last accessed 12 April 2013].
8 Ibid.
9 Karima Brown, 'Economic adviser Mpahlwa tipped as envoy in Presidency shake-up', *Business Day*, 6 July 2010, http://www.businessday.co.za/articles/content.aspx?id=113825 [last accessed 12 April 2013].
10 Simon Allison, 'Madagascar peace deal: At last, a South African diplomatic victory', *Daily Maverick*, 19 September 2011, http://bit.ly/rVFRzS [last accessed 12 April 2013].
11 Mandy Rossouw, 'SA envoy embarrassed by new Zambian president', *City Press*, 6 November 2011.
12 'Zulu has earned her stripes as a cadre', *Sowetan*, 23 February 2009, http://bit.ly/t2iAwz [last accessed 12 April 2013].
13 Ibid.
14 Munyaradzi Huni, 'South Africa's Lindiwe Zulu in trouble', *The Sunday Mail*, 21 May 2011, http://bit.ly/qpaXKQ [last accessed 12 April 2013].
15 Charles Molele, 'Lindiwe Zulu: Talking tough for Zuma', *Mail & Guardian*, 25 November 2011, http://bit.ly/tdkwth [last accessed 12 April 2013].
16 SAPA, 'ANC to be "tough" on Malema', 8 August 2011, http://bit.ly/oXO6j8 [last accessed 12 April 2013].
17 Carien du Plessis, 'Youth League lives to die another day, maybe', *Daily Maverick*, 8 August 2011, http://bit.ly/oAwpuv [last accessed 12 April 2013].
18 Sibusiso Ngalwa, 'Malema ready to rumble', *Sunday Times*, 20 November 2011.
19 Ibid.
20 Charles Molele, 'Lindiwe Zulu: Talking tough for Zuma'.
21 A highly critical report of the SADC's

security organ troika in Livingstone, Zambia, on 31 March 2011, the Livingstone communiqué severely rebuked ZANU-PF (though not by name) for being slow in implementing its commitments to the Global Political Agreement that underpins the unity government, and for violence, arrests and intimidation of the MDC.

22 Judy Smith-Hoehn, 'SADC still hesitant to take a tougher stance on Zimbabwe?' Institute for Security Studies, 17 June 2011, http://bit.ly/okifnH [last accessed 12 April 2013].

23 Tererai Karimakwenda, 'Zuma's SADC report talks tough on ZPF and security reform', SW Radio Africa, 26 August 2011, http://bit.ly/qIMo5X [last accessed 12 April 2013].

24 Ibid.

25 Tererai Karimakwenda, 'SADC Luanda summit ends with no Zim solutions', SW Radio Africa, 18 August 2011, http://allafrica.com/stories/201108181242.html [last accessed 12 April 2013].

26 Raymond L. Brown, 'Zuma's cabinet is brilliant politically, but will it be effective?' US diplomatic cable, 4 June 2009, http://bit.ly/sm4y6q [last accessed 15 April 2013].

27 Sibongakonke Shoba & Sam Mkokeli, 'Intense lobbying ahead of Limpopo ANC elections', Business Day, 18 November 2011, http://bit.ly/twZRPO [last accessed 15 April 2013].

28 Pearlie Joubert, 'Plan to embarrass Moloto at funeral', Mail & Guardian, 26 October 2007, http://mg.co.za/article/2007-10-26-plan-to-embarrass-moloto-at-funeral [last accessed 15 April 2013].

29 SAPA, 'Zuma intervenes after Limpopo premier booed', 20 October 2007, http://www.e-tools.co.za/newsbrief/2007/news1022.txt [last accessed 15 April 2013].

30 Yolanda Spies, 'Trends and developments in South African foreign policy: 2009', South African Yearbook of International Law (34), 2009, pp. 268–288, http://bit.ly/yEo7m6 [last accessed 15 April 2013].

31 Maite Nkoana Mashabane, written reply to question 1909 (NW2147E), 29 July 2011, http://bit.ly/qhykcN [last accessed 15 April 2013].

32 Maite Nkoana-Mashabane, 'Debate on budget vote 5: International Relations and Cooperation', 22 April 2010, http://bit.ly/y9X4FY [last accessed 15 April 2013].

33 Marius Fransman, 'Budget vote speech by deputy minister of international relations and cooperation, Mr Marius Fransman to the National Assembly', 31 May 2011, http://bit.ly/AewlfN [last accessed 15 April 2013].

34 Scoop, 'Cablegate: Part 2 of 3: A look at Jacob Zuma's cabinet', US diplomatic cables, 19 May 2009, http://bit.ly/nzVzF4 [last accessed 15 April 2013].

35 Lionel Faull & Trond Sundnes, 'Don't touch me on my handbag', Mail & Guardian, 16 September 2011, http://bit.ly/oZfVIo [last accessed 15 April 2013].

36 Maite Nkoana-Mashabane, written reply to question 1943 (NW2181E), http://bit.ly/zmJJRQ [last accessed 15 April 2013].

37 National Treasury, 'Joint statement by Minister Pravin Gordhan and Deputy Prime Minister and Treasurer of Australia Wayne Swan, on the selection process of the managing director of the International Monetary Fund (IMF)', 22 May 2011, http://bit.ly/oAW6EK [last accessed 15 April 2013].

38 GCIS, 'Manuel not vying for IMF head', BuaNews, 10 June 2011, http://bit.ly/qTKesK [last accessed 15 April 2013].

39 On 6 May 2011, a cabinet statement said it had 'the policy on the nomination, election and appointment of candidates to international organisations. The policy seeks to strengthen coordination among the various departments regarding appointments to international bodies. A committee on candidatures will be established in the Department of International Relations and Cooperation to consolidate all vacancies in international bodies and to make recommendations to Cabinet on proposed names for consideration.'

40 Yolandi Groenewald & Mmanaledi Mataboge, 'Cloud over preparations for COP17', Mail & Guardian, 29 July 2011, http://bit.ly/oENRZa [last accessed 15 April 2013].

41 Sipho Hlongwane, 'Environmental Affairs,

Dirco: We're on track for COP17. And we're not fighting', *Daily Maverick*, 3 August 2011, http://bit.ly/pfQ7TP [last accessed 15 April 2013].

42 Russel Brueton, 'Zuma is proving to be more than just a "domestic president"'.

43 John Vidal & Fiona Harvey, 'Durban climate deal struck after tense all-night session', *Guardian*, 11 December 2011, http://www.guardian.co.uk/environment/2011/dec/11/durban-climate-deal-struck [last accessed 15 April 2013].

44 Profile of Mr Ebrahim Ismail Ebrahim on the DIRCO website, http://bit.ly/xhT5VS [last accessed 15 April 2013].

45 Ebrahim Ebrahim, 'Lecture by deputy minister of international relations and cooperation, Ebrahim I Ebrahim, on the occasion of the Speakers Meeting at the South African Institute of International Affairs (SAIIA)', 22 July 2011, http://bit.ly/AmwrMn [last accessed 15 April 2013].

46 Ebrahim Ebrahim, 'Keynote address by the deputy minister of international relations and cooperation, H. E. Mr. Ebrahim I Ebrahim at the BRICS round-table discussion hosted by the IMC and the *Financial Times*', 11 May 2011, http://bit.ly/y3KIhK [last accessed 15 April 2013].

47 Ebrahim Ebrahim, 'South Africa's position vis-à-vis recent UNSC resolutions on Libya and the Libyan crisis as a test of South Africa's leadership role on "African solutions to African problems"', 2 August 2011, http://bit.ly/xBoRHo [last accessed 15 April 2013].

48 Ebrahim Ebrahim, 'Libya, the United Nations, the African Union and South Africa: Wrong moves?' 15 September 2011, http://bit.ly/yuXREI [last accessed 15 April 2013].

49 Steven Gruzd, 'Foreign policy under Zuma: Change of style or substance?' *Growth Magazine*, 21 December 2009, http://bit.ly/wBgCQe [last accessed 15 April 2013].

50 Ebrahim Ebrahim, media statement following bilateral engagements with Dr Mohammad-Javad Larijani, head of the Supreme Council for Human Rights of the Islamic Republic of Iran, 12 May 2011, http://bit.ly/yA9Pj6 [last accessed 15 April 2013].

51 Jacques Dommisse, 'Cape coloureds tackle youth league', *City Press*, 3 October 2011, http://bit.ly/whGjsw [last accessed 15 April 2013].

52 Steve Kretzmann, 'Mother of all battles for Cape Town', *City Press*, 16 May 2011, http://bit.ly/xpUHCr [last accessed 15 April 2013].

53 Sabelo Ndlangisa, 'Remaking the Cape', *City Press*, 21 February 2011, http://bit.ly/AtnY7S [last accessed 15 April 2013].

54 Mandy Rossouw, 'Maestro of Malagasy diplomacy', *City Press*, 24 October 2011, http://bit.ly/zkc2H4 [last accessed 15 April 2013].

55 Ibid.

56 Ed Stoddard & Alain Iloniaina, 'Madagascar's Ravalomanana back in South Africa', Reuters, 21 January 2012, http://reut.rs/wosjnM [last accessed 15 April 2013].

57 Ivor Powell, 'WikiLeaks document suggests SA violated arms rules', *Sunday Independent*, 12 February 2012.

58 SAPA, 'Ntsaluba must go', *Independent Online*, 17 July 2009, http://bit.ly/zqsb4Y [last accessed 15 April 2013].

59 GCIS, 'Ambassador Jerry Matthews Matjila appointed acting DG', *BuaNews*, 3 April 2011, http://bit.ly/wVFpVS [last accessed 15 April 2013].

60 Maite Nkoana-Mashabane, press statement on the chairperson of the AU Commission, 18 January 2012, http://www.dirco.gov.za/docs/2012/auo118.html [last accessed 16 April 2013].

61 Mandy Rossouw, 'Polokwane moment ahead of AU summit', *City Press*, 21 January 2012, http://bit.ly/xLTPse [last accessed 16 April 2013].

62 Sean Christie, 'SA and the AU: It's complicated', *Mail & Guardian*, 3 February 2012, http://bit.ly/wL6DSA [last accessed 16 April 2013].

63 Aaron Maasho, 'Dlamini-Zuma elected to head AU Commission', *Mail & Guardian*, 16 July 2012, http://mg.co.za/article/2012-07-16-dlamini-zuma-elected-to-head-au-commission [last accessed 16 April 2013].

64 Tanja Hichert, Peter Draper & Talitha Bertelsmann-Scott, 'What does the future hold for SACU? From own goal to laduma!

Scenarios for the future of the Southern African Customs Union', SAIIA Occasional Paper No. 63, July 2010, http://bit.ly/yXCnRa [last accessed 16 April 2013].

65 Ibid.

66 Interview with Catherine Grant, programme head of economic diplomacy at the South African Institute of International Affairs, September 2011.

67 Ibid.

68 Sam Sole & Lungile Dube, 'Swaziland loan a "handout from a sugar daddy"', *Mail & Guardian*, 5 August 2011, http://bit.ly/ycCyAH [last accessed 16 April 2013].

69 SAPA, 'Conditions attached to Swazi loan: Gordhan', 3 August 2011, *Timeslive*, http://bit.ly/ww7EYj [last accessed 16 April 2013].

70 Moyagabo Maake, 'Swaziland's R2bn loan left dangling', *Business Day*, 13 February 2012, http://www.trademarksa.org/news/swazilands-r2bn-loan-left-dangling [last accessed 16 April 2013].

71 DIRCO, white paper on South Africa's foreign policy, 'Building a better world: The diplomacy of ubuntu', 13 May 2011, http://bit.ly/wAerO9 [last accessed 16 April 2013].

72 Maud Dlomo, 'The role of economic diplomacy in a new world', *Sunday Independent*, 22 August 2011, http://bit.ly/wK282b [last accessed 16 April 2013].

73 Interview with Catherine Grant, programme head of economic diplomacy at the South African Institute of International Affairs, September 2011.

74 Maud Dlomo, 'The role of economic diplomacy in a new world'.

75 Lyal White & Nomfundo Xenia Ngwenya, 'SA risks being left behind in fertile Angola', *Business Day*, 9 April 2010, http://bit.ly/xMb1TS [last accessed 16 April 2013].

76 DTI, 'Trade and Investment South Africa', http://www.dti.gov.za/about_dti/tisa.jsp [last accessed 16 April 2013].

77 Mduduzi Tshabangu, 'Moving up', *Public Sector Manager* magazine, July 2011, http://www.gcis.gov.za/sites/www.gcis.gov.za/files/docs/resourcecentre/newsletters/regulars_psm_july%202011.pdf [last accessed 16 April 2013].

78 SAPA, 'BRICS nations moot trade in own currencies', *Mail & Guardian*, 18 April 2011, http://bit.ly/wKZdat [last accessed 16 April 2013].

79 Rob Davies, 'Customs union gives added economic clout', *Mail & Guardian*, 15 August 2011, http://mg.co.za/article/2011-08-15-customs-union-gives-added-economic-clout [last accessed 17 April 2013].

80 AFP, 'SA defends Chinese expansion in Africa', *Mail & Guardian*, 25 August 2010, http://bit.ly/ySCI6J [last accessed 16 April 2013].

81 Miriam Mannak, 'EU "afraid of losing foothold in Africa"', *Mail & Guardian*, 26 February 2008, http://bit.ly/wstAMc [last accessed 16 April 2013].

82 Ibid.

83 SAPA, 'Davies: EPA must not undermine customs union', *Mail & Guardian*, 16 June 2009, http://bit.ly/yuwmf6 [last accessed 16 April 2013].

84 Ibid.

85 Rob Davies, 'Customs union gives added economic clout'.

86 Roman Grynberg, 'New knife to cut Sacu pie', *Mail & Guardian*, 29 July 2011, http://bit.ly/xkEW2K [last accessed 16 April 2013].

87 SAPA, 'African mega-treaty "to funnel free-trade fortunes to SA"', *Mail & Guardian*, 13 June 2011, http://bit.ly/zJUsTe [last accessed 16 April 2013].

88 SAPA, 'Ministers say Walmart-Massmart merger poses a risk', *Mail & Guardian*, 2 August 2011, http://bit.ly/wXwFIL [last accessed 16 April 2013].

89 Ministry of Public Enterprises, 'Board changes at Eskom and Denel', 10 June 2011, http://www.dpe.gov.za/news-1081 [last accessed 16 April 2013].

90 Carol Paton, 'The new guard: More questions than answers', *Financial Mail*, 1 July 2011, http://www.accessmylibrary.com/article-1G1-260388401/new-guard-more-questions.html [last accessed 16 April 2013].

91 Carol Paton, 'State-owned enterprises: State capitalist act', *Financial Mail*, 1 July 2011, http://www.accessmylibrary.com/article-1G1-260388400/state-owned-enterprises-state.html [last accessed 16 April 2013].

92 Ibid.
93 Ibid.
94 Ibid.
95 Chris Baron, 'So many questions: Minister of public enterprises, Malusi Gigaba', *Sunday Times*, 7 August 2011, http://www .timeslive.co.za/opinion/ commentary/2011/08/07/so-many- questions-minister-of-public-enterprises -malusi-gigaba [last accessed 16 April 2013].
96 Malusi Gigaba, 'How state-owned companies can better serve SA's needs', *Business Day*, 7 February 2012, http://bit.ly/ waaEEb [last accessed 16 April 2013].
97 Sibongakonke Shoba & Sibusiso Ngalwa, 'Malusi wants control of all state entities', *Sunday Times*, 29 January 2012, http://times -e-editions.newspaperdirect.com/epaper/ viewer.aspx [last accessed 16 April 2013].
98 MDC1: the original Movement for Democratic Change led by Morgan Tsvangirai. MDCM: Movement for Democratic Change-Mutambara, a faction led by Arthur Mutambara that broke away from MDC1.
99 Baleka Mbete, ANC press statement following the occasion of the Republic of South Sudan's 9th July Independence Day celebrations, July 2011, http://www.anc.org .za/show.php?id=8805 [last accessed 16 April 2013].
100 Maite Nkoana-Mashabane, written reply to question 3630 (NW4409E), http://bit.ly/ zmKnlP [last accessed 16 April 2013].
101 GCIS, statement on the cabinet meeting of 9 November 2011, 10 November 2011, http://www.info.gov.za/speech/Dynamic Action?pageid=461&sid=23118&tid=48665 [last accessed 16 April 2013].
102 Catherine Grant, 'State visits as a tool of economic diplomacy: Bandwagon or business sense?' SAIIA Occasional Paper No. 87, July 2011, http://www.saiia.org.za/ occasional-papers/state-visits-as-a-tool -of-economic-diplomacy-bandwagon-or -business-sense.html [last accessed 16 April 2013].
103 Ibid.
104 Nomaxabiso Majokweni, 'Ibsa: What's in it for business?' *City Press*, 23 October 2011, http://bit.ly/x1lYFP [last accessed 16 April 2013].
105 Catherine Grant, 'State visits as a tool of economic diplomacy: Bandwagon or business sense?'
106 Interview with Catherine Grant, programme head of economic diplomacy at the South African Institute of International Affairs, September 2011.
107 Sekunjalo website, 'The history of our great land is an inspiration', http://www. sekunjalo.com/component/content/ article/13-timeline/39-the-history-of-our -great-land-is-an-inspiration [last accessed 16 April 2013].
108 Lionel Faull & Stefaans Brümmer, 'Tycoon pays for minister's guards', *Mail & Guardian*, 25 November 2011, http://bit.ly/ ztjePw [last accessed 16 April 2013].
109 Ibid.
110 SAPA, 'UAE court finds Karabus not guilty', *Independent Online*, 21 March 2013, http://www.iol.co.za/news/south-africa/ western-cape/uae-court-finds-karabus -not-guilty-1.1489906#.UVExgls9pUs [last accessed 16 April 2013].

CHAPTER 6: PARLIAMENT
1 See the Parliamentary Monitoring Group's website at www.pmg.org.za [last accessed 23 April 2013].
2 Anon., 'Top spy in R45m graft probe', *City Press*, 2 June 2012, http://bit.ly/17Uc6OZ [last accessed 23 April 2013].
3 For the most recent reports of parliamentary hearings on the NCACC, see 'National Conventional Arms Control Committee 2nd to 4th quarter 2011 performance report', 15 March 2012, http://bit.ly/17MctbA [last accessed 23 April 2013].
4 David Maynier, press statement, 'SA's dodgy arms sales to dictatorships', 2 August 2009, http://bit.ly/YJK0PR [last accessed 23 April 2013].
5 'South African arms exports, 2000–2009: A dossier', p. 9, http://bit.ly/11HXpbJ [last accessed 23 April 2013].
6 The report tabled in 2008 was, for example, the first for four years, according to Michael B. Bishku, 'South Africa and the Middle East', Middle East Policy Council, 2013, http://bit.ly/15Dpubg [last accessed 23 April 2013].

7   For the report, see 'Report of the
    Independent Panel Assessment of
    Parliament', 13 January 2009, http://bit.ly/
    YJe26c [last accessed 23 April 2013].
8   SAPA, 'Max Sisulu slams "poor quality"
    legislation', *Timeslive*, 29 May 2012, http://
    bit.ly/KCdUjs [last accessed 23 April 2013].
9   Parliament of South Africa, 'Oversight and
    accountability model: Asserting Parliament's
    oversight role in enhancing democracy',
    27 January 2009, http://bit.ly/ZFL7mT
    [last accessed 23 April 2013].

CHAPTER 7: THE ANC
1   Susan Booysen, *The African National
    Congress and the Regeneration of Political
    Power*, Johannesburg: Wits University
    Press, 2011.
2   Ngoako Ramathlodi, 'The big read: ANC's
    fatal concessions', *Times LIVE*, 1 September
    2011, http://www.timeslive.co.za/opinion/
    commentary/2011/09/01/the-big-read-anc
    -s-fatal-concessions [last accessed 24 June
    2013].
3   Booysen, *The African National Congress
    and the Regeneration of Political Power*.
4   Mcebisi Ndletyana, 'Policy incoherence:
    A function of ideological contestations?'
    in U. Pillay, G. Hagg & F. Nyamnjoy (eds),
    State of the Nation: South Africa 2012–2013,
    Cape Town: HSRC Press, 2013.
5   Ibid.
6   Stephen Ellis, *External Mission: The ANC in
    Exile, 1960–1990*, Johannesburg: Jonathan
    Ball, 2012.
7   Confidential dispatch by Ambassador
    Donald Gips, 30 December 2009, cited in
    Martin Plaut and Paul Holden, *Who Rules
    South Africa?* Johannesburg: Jonathan Ball,
    2012, pp. 69–70.
8   Affiliations as at 2012.
9   Bloomberg, 'ANC treasurer wants donations
    kept secret', *MoneyWeb*, 14 May 2013,
    http://m.moneyweb.co.za/moneyweb-south
    -africa/anc-treasurer-wants-donations-kept
    -secret [last accessed 24 June 2013].
10 Thabo Mbeki, '52nd national conference:
    Opening address and political report of
    ANC President Thabo Mbeki', 16 December
    2007, http://www.anc.org.za/show.php?id
    =2540 [last accessed 24 June 2013].
11 Ibid.

12 Ibid.
13 ANC, 'Organisational renewal: Building
    the ANC as a movement for
    transformation and a strategic centre of
    power', 10 April 2012, www.anc.org.za/docs/
    discus/2012/organisationalrenewalf.pdf
    [last accessed 24 June 2013].
14 Ibid., p. 17.
15 Ibid., p. 16.
16 Statement by Frene Ginwala, CASAC,
    21 January 2011, www.casac.org.za/?wpfb_dl
    =10 [last accessed 24 June 2013].
17 Mbeki, '52nd national conference: Opening
    address and political report of ANC
    President Thabo Mbeki'.
18 Natasha Marrian, 'Cosatu sashays around
    elephants in the room', *Mail & Guardian*,
    30 June 2011, https://groups.google.com/
    forum/#!msg/cosatu-daily-news/rgeRcg
    FGqVs/0UrDH5z10rcJ [last accessed
    24 June 2013].
19 Ibid.
20 Susan Booysen, 'The ANC circa 2012:
    Colossus in decline?' in John Daniel,
    Prishani Naidoo, Devan Pillay & Roger
    Southall (eds), *New South African Review 3:
    The Second Phase – Tragedy or Farce?*
    Johannesburg: Wits University Press, 2013.
21 Kenny Kunene, 'Kenny Kunene's letter to
    Zuma', *The Star*, 21 June 2013, www.iol.co.za/
    the-star/kenny-kunene-s-letter-to-zuma
    -1.1535280#.UcafgYwaySM [last accessed
    23 June 2013].
22 Pallo Jordan, 'Wanted: A president to
    restore the ANC's credibility', *Business Day*,
    11 October 2012.

CHAPTER 8: THE UNIONS
1   Anthony Sampson, *Anatomy of Britain
    Today*, London: Hodder & Stoughton, 1965.
2   Janet Munakamwe, 'The state of COSATU
    affiliates: The survey questionnaire report',
    NALEDI Organisational Renewal
    Programme, May 2009, p. 10, http://us-cdn
    .creamermedia.co.za/assets/articles/
    attachments/24164_state_of_cosatu_
    affiliates.pdf [last accessed 3 June 2013].
3   Sampson, *Anatomy of Britain Today*.
4   Ibid., p. 11.
5   COSATU, '11th COSATU congress
    secretariat report: 2nd draft for internal
    circulation', 24 August 2012, p. 6, http://www

.politicsweb.co.za/politicsweb/action/
media/downloadFile?media_fileid=2459
[last accessed 3 June 2013].

6   Ibid., pp. 16–17.
7   Ibid., p. 7, adapted.
8   Ibid., p. 7, adapted.
9   Ibid., p. 7, adapted.
10 'Adcorp employment index', April 2013,
    pp. 2–3, http://www.adcorp.co.za/
    Documents/Adcorp%20Employment%20
    Index%20-%20201305.pdf [last accessed
    3 June 2013].
11 SAPA, 'Trust in trade unions dropping',
    Moneyweb, 9 April 2013, http://www
    .moneyweb.co.za/moneyweb-south-africa/
    trust-in-trade-unions-dropping [last
    accessed 4 June 2013].
12 Ibid.
13 Munakamwè, 'The state of COSATU
    affiliates: The survey questionnaire report'.
14 Sakhela Buhlungu, A Paradox of Victory:
    COSATU and the Democratic
    Transformation in South Africa,
    Pietermaritzburg: UKZN Press, 2010.
15 COSATU, 'Findings of the COSATU
    workers' survey, 2012', http://www.COSATU
    .org.za/docs/reports/2012/final%20workers
    %20surveys%20results%20August%202012
    .pdf [last accessed 4 June 2013].
16 Adele, 'Sakhela Buhlungu's book on
    COSATU, A Paradox of Victory, launched
    at the Centre for the Book', Books LIVE,
    2 September 2010, http://ukznpress.
    bookslive.co.za/blog/2010/09/02/sakhela
    -buhlungus-book-on-cosatu-a-paradox-
    of-victory-launched-at-the-centre-for-the
    -book/ [last accessed 4 June 2013].
17 Buhlungu, A Paradox of Victory.
18 Adele, 'Sakhela Buhlungu's book on
    COSATU, A Paradox of Victory, launched
    at the Centre for the Book'.
19 Ibid.
20 Gavin Hartford, 'The mining industry strike
    wave: What are the causes and what are the
    solutions?' GroundUp, 10 October 2012,
    http://groundup.org.za/content/mining
    -industry-strike-wave-what-are-causes
    -and-what-are-solutions [last accessed
    4 June 2013].
21 Roger Southall & Edward Webster, 'Unions
    and parties in South Africa: Cosatu and the
    ANC in the wake of Polokwane', in Björn

Beckmann, Sakhela Buhlungu & Lloyd
    Sachikonye (eds), Trade Unions and Party
    Politics: Labour Movements in Africa,
    Cape Town: HSRC Press, 2010. Available
    at http://www.hsrcpress.ac.za/product.
    php?productid=2271&freedownload=1.
22 Richard Calland, Anatomy of South Africa,
    Cape Town: Zebra Press, 2006.
23 Verashni Pillay, 'Cosatu: The abused wife',
    Mail & Guardian, 14 June 2011, http://
    mg.co.za/article/2011-06-14-cosatu-the-
    abused-wife [last accessed 10 June 2013].
24 Mandy Rossouw, 'Cosatu conference
    "pains" ANC', Mail & Guardian,
    5 November 2010, http://mg.co.za/
    article/2010-11-05-cosatu-conference-
    pains-anc [last accessed 4 June 2013].
25 COSATU CEC, 'Statement of the COSATU
    central executive committee',
    22–24 November 2010, http://www.cosatu.
    org.za/show.php?ID=4309 [last accessed
    4 June 2013].
26 Staff reporter, 'Zuma and Cosatu: The end
    of the affair', Mail & Guardian,
    19 February 2010, http://mg.co.za/
    article/2010-02-19-zuma-and-COSATU
    -the-end-of-affair [last accessed 5 June
    2013].
27 COSATU secretary-general, 'Secretariat
    report to the 5th COSATU central
    committee 2011', June 2011, p. 57, http://www
    .COSATU.org.za/docs/reports/2011/
    secretariatreport.pdf [last accessed 4 June
    2013].
28 COSATU secretary-general, 'Secretariat
    report to the 11th COSATU national
    congress', September 2012, http://www
    .COSATU.org.za/show.php?ID=6535
    [last accessed 4 June 2013].
29 Carien du Plessis & SAPA, 'Shape up,
    Zuma warned', Pretoria News, 29 June 2011,
    http://www.iol.co.za/news/politics/shape-up
    -zuma-warned-1.1090498?ot=inmsa.
    ArticlePrintPageLayout.ot [last accessed
    5 June 2013].
30 Ibid.
31 COSATU secretary-general, 'Secretariat
    report to the 11th COSATU national
    congress'.
32 Ibid.
33 Ranjeni Munusamy, 'The week when Vavi
    of Troy faces his Achilles', Daily Maverick,

27 May 2013, http://www.dailymaverick.co
.za/article/2013-05-27-the-week-when-vavi
-of-troy-faces-his-achilles/ [last accessed
4 June 2013].

34 COSATU secretary-general, 'Secretariat
report to the 5th COSATU central
committee 2011', p. 10.

35 Ibid., p. 15.

36 Ibid., pp. 14–15.

37 Nickolaus Bauer, 'COSATU set to
"fumigate" ANC in 2012', *Mail & Guardian*,
20 December 2011, http://mg.co.za/article/
2011-12-20-COSATU-set-to-fumigate-anc-in
-2012 [last accessed 4 June 2013].

38 COSATU secretary-general, 'Secretariat
report to the 11th COSATU national
congress'.

39 Zwelinzima Vavi, 'Address to the National
Anti-Corruption Forum Summit, Sandton',
8 December 2011, http://www.cosatu.org.
za/docs/sp/2011/sp1208.html [last accessed
4 June 2013].

40 Ibid.

41 Matuma Letsoalo, 'Cosatu comes clean on
internal divisions', *Mail & Guardian*,
25 November 2011, http://mg.co.za/article/
2011-11-25-cosatu-comes-clean-on-internal
-divisions [last accessed 5 June 2013].

42 Hartford, 'The mining industry strike
wave: What are the causes and what are the
solutions?'

43 Ibid.

44 Ibid.

45 Rapule Tabane, 'Amcu a group of vigilantes
and liars, say alliance bosses', *Mail &
Guardian*, 17 May 2013, http://www.mg.co.za/
article/2013-05-17-00-amcus-no-union-its
-just-vigilantes-and-liars-say-alliance
-bosses [last accessed 5 June 2013].

46 Ibid.

47 Kwanele Sosibo & Phillip de Wet,
'Marikana: NUM and AMCU resort to
recruitment over a gun barrel', *Mail &
Guardian*, 17 May 2013, http://mg.co.za/
article/2013-05-17-00-marikana-num-and
-amcu-resort-to-recruitment-over-a-gun
-barrel [last accessed 5 June 2013].

CHAPTER 9: THE OPPOSITION

1 Jonathan Faull, 'DA charts future after
election fall-out', *Cape Times*, 26 November
2004.

2 Richard Calland, 'Ramphele is an unlikely
party animal', *Mail & Guardian*, 1 February
2013, http://mg.co.za/print/2013-02-01-00
-calland-ramphele-is-an-unlikely-party
-animal [last accessed March 2013].

3 Ibid.

4 Ebrahim Fakir and Waseem Holland,
'Changing voting patterns?' *Journal of
Public Administration* 46(3.1), September
2011, p. 1150.

5 Ibid., p. 1150.

6 Ibid., p. 1145.

CHAPTER 10:
THE TRADITIONAL LEADERS

1 Pierre de Vos, 'Affirming their own moral
inferiority', *Constitutionally Speaking*,
3 May 2012, http://constitutionallyspeaking
.co.za/affirming-their-own-moral
-inferiority/ [last accessed 27 May 2013].

2 Ibid.

3 Peter Ekeh, 'Individuals' basic security needs
and the limits of democracy in Africa', in
B. Berman, D. Eyoh & W. Kymlicka (eds),
Ethnicity and Democracy in Africa, Oxford:
James Currey Publishers, 1975.

4 Aninka Claassens, 'The Traditional Courts
Bill is a legal travesty', *Mail & Guardian*,
28 September 2012, http://mg.co.za/article/
2012-09-28-00-the-traditional-courts-bill
-is-a-legal-travesty [last accessed 27 May
2013].

5 Ibid.

6 Republic of South Africa, Traditional
Courts Bill (as introduced in the National
Council of Provinces (proposed section
76), on request of the minister of justice
and constitutional development;
explanatory summary of bill published in
Government Gazette No. 34850 of
13 December 2011) (Bill originally
introduced in National Assembly as
Traditional Courts Bill [B 15–2008], and
withdrawn on 2 June 2011), section 1(1),
p. 3, http://www.justice.gov.za/legislation/
bills/2012-b01tradcourts.pdf [last accessed
28 May 2013].

7 Ibid., section 10(2)(g), p. 8.

8 Pearl Sithole & Thamsanqa Mbele,
'Fifteen-year review on traditional
leadership: A research paper', Pretoria:
HSRC, 2008, http://www.hsrc.ac.za/en/

research-outputs/view/3680 [last accessed 28 May 2013].

9   Peter Delius, 'Contested terrain: Land rights and chiefly power in historical perspective', in A. Claassens & B. Cousins (eds), *Land, Power and Custom: Controversies Generated by South Africa's Communal Land Rights Act*, Cape Town: UCT Press, 2008.

10 Sithole & Mbele, 'Fifteen-year review on traditional leadership: A research paper'.

11 Christian Lund, 'Twilight institutions: Public authority and local politics in Africa', *Development and Change* 37(4), 2006, pp. 685–705.

12 Sithole & Mbele, 'Fifteen-year review on traditional leadership: A research paper'.

13 Pierre de Vos, 'Some thoughts of the rise of traditional leaders', *Constitutionally Speaking*, 8 May 2012, http://constitutionally speaking.co.za/some-thoughts-of-the-rise -of-traditional-leaders/ [last accessed 27 May 2013].

14 Lungisile Ntsebeza, 'Rural governance and citizenship in post-1994 South Africa: Democracy compromised?' Paper presented for the Department of Sociology, University of Cape Town, 2004, http://rmportal.net/library/content/ ntzebeza_paper.pdf/view [last accessed 27 May 2013].

15 Jacob Zuma, address at the official opening of the National House of Traditional Leaders, National Assembly, Cape Town, 3 June 2011, http://www.info. gov.za/speech/DynamicAction?pageid=461 &sid=18869&tid=34527 [last accessed 27 May 2013].

16 SABC, 'President Zuma encourages traditional leaders', 5 October 2011, http://www.sabc.co.za/news/a/59f8d50048 9497448067ed0573295752/President-Zuma -encourages-traditional-leaders-20111005 [last accessed 28 May 2013].

CHAPTER 11: THE JUDGES

1   Heidi Swart, 'Inside Mogoeng's house of God', *Mail & Guardian*, 23 September 2011, http://mg.co.za/article/2011-09-23-inside -mogoengs-house-of-god [last accessed 30 May 2013].

2   Such as the criteria advanced by Advocate Susannah Cowen in a very comprehensive and insightful paper commissioned by the DGRU, University of Cape Town: 'Judicial selection in South Africa', 2010, http:// www.dgru.uct.ac.za/usr/dgru/downloads/ Judicial%20SelectionOct2010.pdf [last accessed 30 May 2013].

3   As of the end of October 2012, only 70 out of a total of 247 sitting judges were women. This is a composition of 28 per cent, which is far from representative of our society. In the last three years (2010 to 2013), the JSC has interviewed a total of 231 candidates and appointed just 27 women. This problem is also present in the selection of acting judges, where appointments appear to favour male candidates over female candidates. This lack of acting appointments for females places them at a disadvantage when they are being interviewed for permanent positions, as there is a preference for appointing candidates who have had experience acting on the bench. The figures as of August 2012 from the Department of Justice show that of the 93 acting appointments, only 14 are female.

4   This account of Plasket's interview, and that of Justice Nigel Willis, draws on my own column published later that week: 'JSC's attitude opens door to conservatism', *Mail & Guardian*, 12 April 2013, http://mg .co.za/article/2013-04-12-00-jscs-attitude -opens-door-to-conservatism [last accessed 30 May 2013].

5   *Le Roux and Others v Dey*, CCT45/10 (2011) ZACC 4, at paragraph 185.

6   I would like to make it clear that this point refers to Mogoeng's academic writing rather than his industriousness on the bench itself. Indeed, his record on the Constitutional Court, both before and after he became chief justice, is similar to that of his three predecessors: 7 written judgments from 56 cases heard between appointment to the court and becoming chief justice; 5 from 46 after becoming chief justice. For Ngcobo, the figures are: 3 from 45, and 7 from 57. For Langa: 3 from 37, and 7 from 42. And for Chaskalson: 7 from 37, and 6 from 28.

NOTES | 483

CHAPTER 12: MONEY AND POLITICS

1 Steve Kretzmann, 'Chancellor House slammed by opposition parties as "unethical"', *West Cape News*, 23 February 2012, http://westcapenews.com/?p=3756 [last accessed 14 May 2013].

2 Setumo Stone, 'ANC "integrity body" may manage conflict of interest', *Business Day*, 14 July 2011, http://bit.ly/om3JfA [last accessed 14 May 2013].

3 Collette Schulz-Herzenberg, 'Trading public knowledge for private gain: Is the revolving door spinning out of control?' *PSC News: Reflections on an Ethical Public Service and Society*, November/December 2010, http://www.psc.gov.za/newsletters/docs/2010/PSC%20NEWS.pdf [last accessed 14 May 2013].

4 PSC, 'Fact sheet: Monitoring compliance with the requirements of the financial disclosure framework for the 2008/2009 financial year', 2009, http://bit.ly/11kmOYg [last accessed 27 May 2013].

5 Sellinah Nkosi, 'Management of gifts in the public service', PowerPoint presentation for round table with University of Pretoria, Burgers Park Hotel, Pretoria, 15 March 2011.

6 Terence Nombembe, 'Report of the Auditor-General to Parliament on a performance audit of entities that are connected with government employees and doing business with national departments', August 2008, http://www.agsa.co.za/Portals/1/85115%20Government%20employees.pdf [last accessed 14 May 2013].

7 Information Portal on Corruption and Governance in Africa, 'Who owns what?' database, July 2011, available at http://bit.ly/pCVeW6.

8 Mandy Rossouw & Sabelo Ndlangisa, 'Officials fume over tough new rules', *City Press*, 24 February 2013, http://www.citypress.co.za/politics/officials-fume-over-tough-new-rules/ [last accessed 14 May 2013].

9 Richard Calland, 'Lindiwe Sisulu: A plan to catch the lesser spotted filcher', *Mail & Guardian*, 1 February 2013, http://mg.co.za/article/2013-02-01-00-lindiwe-sisulu-a-plan-to-catch-the-lesser-spotted-filcher [last accessed 14 May 2013].

10 Niren Tolsi, 'Dlamini-Zuma report: Report puts KZN councillors in firing line', *Mail & Guardian*, 8 February 2013, http://mg.co.za/article/2013-02-08-00-report-puts-councillors-in-firing-line [last accessed 14 May 2013].

11 Government Gazette, No. 21399, Notice No. 41, Regulation 6853, http://bit.ly/UqTRJ2 [last accessed 14 May 2013].

12 Thuli Madonsela, Public Protector Report No. 1 of 2010/11, 'Report on an investigation into an alleged breach of section 5 of the Executive Ethics Code by President JG Zuma', http://bit.ly/nriphG [last accessed 14 May 2013].

13 Ibid.

14 Ibid.

15 Jacob Zuma, written reply to Question No. 3542 in Parliament, 10 December 2010, http://bit.ly/noMLtv [last accessed 14 May 2013].

16 Statement by the Presidency, 'Disclosure of interests by some members of the executive', 27 January 2011, http://bit.ly/qOaEYz [last accessed 14 May 2013].

17 Thuli Madonsela, Public Protector Report No. 1 of 2010/11.

18 Ibid.

19 Themba Maseko, 'Transcript: Post cabinet media briefing questions and answers', 6 May 2010, http://bit.ly/pKb3Jn [last accessed 14 May 2013].

20 Press release by Athol Trollip, 'No consequences for Zuma a sign of arrogance triumphing over principle', 6 May 2010, http://bit.ly/phZ6lZ [last accessed 14 May 2013].

21 Statement by Themba Maseko, 'Cabinet adopts interim sanctions applicable to members of cabinet who are found guilty of violating the Executive Members' Code of Ethics', 27 July 2010, http://bit.ly/qWo5l3 [last accessed 14 May 2013].

22 Jeff Radebe, reply to Question No. 3541 in Parliament, 26 November 2010, http://bit.ly/102pLAY [last accessed 14 May 2013].

23 Lynley Donnelly, 'Speaker refuses debate on Zuma Inc', *Mail & Guardian*, 19 August 2011, http://bit.ly/169VdSf [last accessed 14 May 2013].

24 Press statement by Athol Trollip, 'Business unusual: The DA's plan to address the rise of Zuma Inc.', 29 August 2011, http://bit.ly/pBoXqo [last accessed 14 May 2013].

25 Statement by the Presidency, 'President Zuma had declared all his interests', 29 August 2011, http://bit.ly/qXOShc [last accessed 14 May 2013].

26 Ibid.

27 Stefaans Brümmer & Sam Sole, 'State aided Zuma sugar mom', *Mail & Guardian*, 19 March 2010, http://bit.ly/13hIW7c [last accessed 14 May 2013].

28 Ibid.

29 Statement by Lionel Mtshali, 'IFP questions Zuma-linked Ithala appointment', 5 December 2008, http://bit.ly/q9kDNE [last accessed 14 May 2013].

30 CIPC records accessed from www.legalnet .co.za.

31 Companies and Intellectual Property Registration Office records show the company was registered on 2 September 2008 with the registration number 2008/021001/07, address 35 Roadhouse Crescent, Springfield Park, and a postbox in Saxonwold, Johannesburg.

32 'Aurora', *Carte Blanche* on MNet, producer: Adam Welz, 2 May 2010.

33 Bongani Mthethwa & Monica Laganparsad, 'Khulubuse Zuma: Lapping up the good life', *Business Times*, 17 April 2011, http://bit.ly/13hvrEm [last accessed 14 May 2013].

34 Nathi Mthethwa, reply to Question No. 1168 in Parliament, 24 May 2011, http://bit.ly/ nf6oAh [last accessed 15 May 2013].

35 SAPA, 'Vavi: Aurora debacle "greed at its best"', *Mail & Guardian*, 28 April 2011, http://mg.co.za/article/2011-04-28-vavi -aurora-debacle-greed-at-its-best [last accessed 15 May 2013].

36 NUM statement, 'ANC must give Khulubuse's donation to destitute Aurora workers', 12 April 2011, http://bit.ly/npgaoO [last accessed 15 May 2013].

37 Susan Shabangu, 'Appropriation Bill: Debate on vote no 32 – Mineral Resources', 1 June 2011, http://www.pmg.org.za/ node/27167 [last accessed 15 May 2013].

38 Stefaans Brümmer & Sam Sole, 'Zuma Inc's DRC oil coup (and the Tokyo factor)', 30 July 2010, http://bit.ly/YKFal7 [last accessed 15 May 2013].

39 Ibid.

40 Platform report, 'A lake of oil: Congo's contracts escalate conflict, pollution and poverty', May 2010, http://bit.ly/04xH3K [last accessed 15 May 2013].

41 Ibid., p. 6.

42 Stefaans Brümmer & Sam Sole, 'Zuma Inc's DRC oil coup (and the Tokyo factor)'.

43 Andreas Mehler, Henning Melber & Klaas van Walraven, *Africa Yearbook 5: Politics, Economy and Society South of the Sahara in 2008*, Leiden: Brill, 2009.

44 Stefaans Brümmer & Sam Sole, 'Zuma link in nephew's Korean deal', *Mail & Guardian*, 16 July 2010, http://bit.ly/nFZIFg [last accessed 15 May 2013].

45 Ibid.

46 John Robbie interview with Duduzane Zuma and Jagdish Parekh for Radio 702; reprinted in *The New Age*, 'The John Robbie interview on the Guptas and the media saga', 2 March 2011, http://bit.ly/ oVIPfn [last accessed 16 May 2013].

47 Editorial, 'Are the Guptas the new Shaiks?' *Mail & Guardian*, 9 July 2010.

48 John Robbie interview.

49 Ibid.

50 Ibid.

51 Michael Bleby, 'Manyi shifts balance of BMF, state roles', *Business Day*, 7 March 2011, http://bit.ly/np3xgM [last accessed 16 May 2013].

52 John Robbie interview.

53 Ibid.

54 Lindo Xulu, 'BEE baron: Duduzane Zuma owns less than you think', *Moneyweb*, 31 August 2010, http://bit.ly/pADoSB [last accessed 16 May 2013].

55 Lindo Xulu, 'BEE baron: The Guptas invited me to this deal', *Moneyweb*, 24 August 2010, http://bit.ly/rbueaA [last accessed 16 May 2013].

56 Stefaans Brümmer, 'Zuma Jnr heading for first billion', *Mail & Guardian*, 13 August 2010, http://amabhungane.co.za/ article/2010-08-13-zuma-jnr-heading-for -first-billion [last accessed 16 May 2013].

57 Lindo Xulu interview with Sandile Zungu, 'Special report podcast: Who is Sandile Zungu?' *Moneyweb*, 30 August 2010, http://bit.ly/oXQGdX [last accessed 16 May 2013].

58 John Robbie interview.

59 Statement by Shiva Uranium Ltd, April

2010, http://www.shivauranium.com/News
.html [last accessed 16 May 2013].
60 iThemba Governance and Statutory
Solutions (Pty) Ltd, http://www.
ithembaonline.co.za.
61 Statement by Shiva Uranium Ltd, op. cit.
62 Stefaans Brümmer & Sam Sole, 'Zuma
"meddled in mine buyout"', *Mail &
Guardian*, 14 May 2010, http://amabhungane
.co.za/article/2010-05-14-zuma-meddled
-in-mine-buyout [last accessed 16 May
2013].
63 Ibid.
64 Ibid.
65 Matuma Letsoalo, 'Veterans "helped" by
brothers', *Mail & Guardian*, 18 March 2011,
http://bit.ly/nZJJlU [last accessed 16 May
2013].
66 Matuma Letsoalo, 'Zuma Inc in row over
govt office tender', *Mail & Guardian*,
12 August 2011, http://bit.ly/nYrexQ
[last accessed 16 May 2013].
67 Ibid.
68 Ibid.
69 Matuma Letsoalo, 'More dodgy deals in
department of public works', *Mail &
Guardian*, 19 August 2011, http://mg.co.za/
article/2011-08-19-more-dodgy-deals-in
-department-of-public-works [last accessed
16 May 2013].
70 Ibid.
71 Ibid.
72 Ibid.
73 Ferial Haffajee, 'Political dynasties keep
the poor impoverished', *City Press*, 24 April
2010, http://www.citypress.co.za/
columnists/political-dynasties-keep-the
-poor-impoverished-20100424/ [last
accessed 16 May 2013].
74 Ibid.

CHAPTER 13:
THE CORPORATE BOARDROOMS
1 All data obtained from the IMF's World
Economic Outlook database at http://www
.imf.org/external/pubs/ft/weo/2012/02/
weodata/index.aspx [last accessed 18 April
2013].
2 Measures the deviation of the distribution
of income (or consumption) among
individuals or households within a country
from a perfectly equal distribution. A value

of 0 represents absolute equality
(everyone earns the exact same amount
of income) and a value of 100 absolute
inequality (one individual monopolises
all the wealth).
3 See http://data.worldbank.org/indicator/
SI.POV.GINI [last accessed 18 April 2013].
4 These figures are cited using World Bank
data at http://www.tradingeconomics.com/
south-africa/gini-index-wb-data.html.
The National Planning Commission's 2011
Diagnostic Report estimates that the top
20 per cent of income earners accrue
approximately 70 per cent of the national
wage, while the poorest 20 per cent earn
only 2.3 per cent; see http://www.npconline
.co.za/MediaLib/Downloads/Home/Tabs/
Diagnostic/Diagnostic%20Overview.pdf
[last accessed 18 April 2013].
5 Haroon Bhorat & Charlene van der
Westhuizen, 'Pro-poor growth and social
protection in South Africa: Exploring the
interactions', DPRU, April 2011, http://www
.npconline.co.za/MediaLib/Downloads/
Home/Tabs/Diagnostic/HumanConditions2
/Pro-poor%20Growth%20and%20
Social%20%20Protection%20in%20
SA%20v3%20Bhorat.ppt [last accessed
18 April 2013].
6 Thabo Mbeki, statement at the opening of
the debate in the National Assembly on
'Reconciliation and nation building',
29 May 1998, http://www.unisa.ac.za/
contents/colleges/docs/1998/tm1998/
sp980529.pdf [last accessed 18 April 2013].
7 National Planning Commission,
'Diagnostic overview', 2011, http://www
.npconline.co.za/MediaLib/Downloads/
Home/Tabs/Diagnostic/Diagnostic%20
Overview.pdf [last accessed 18 April 2013].
8 SAIRR, 'South Africa survey', 2012, p. 308,
http://www.sairr.org.za/services/
publications/south-africa-survey/
south-africa-survey-2012 [last accessed
18 April 2013].
9 Ibid., p. 288.
10 National Planning Commission,
'Diagnostic overview'.
11 SAIRR, 'South Africa survey', p. 293.
12 Ibid., p. 295.
13 All stats from World Federation of
Exchanges database at http://www.world

-exchanges.org/statistics [last accessed 18 April 2013].

14 Roger Southall, 'South Africa's fractured power elite', Wits University, 2012, p. 9, http://wiser.wits.ac.za/system/files/seminar/Southall2012_0.pdf [last accessed 18 April 2013].

15 Ibid., pp. 9–10.

16 Tables 13.1 and 13.2 have been adapted from those utilised by Roger Southall in his analysis of the JSE in 'South Africa's fractured power elite'. Data has been updated using indicators obtained directly from the JSE.

17 All stats from Chamber of Mines of South Africa 'Facts and figures' publications at http://www.bullion.org.za/content/?pid=71&pagename=Facts+and+Figures [last accessed 18 April 2013].

18 Jeanette Clark, 'SA platinum, gold mining electricity costs up $780m since 2007', Mineweb, 31 January 2013, http://www.mineweb.com/mineweb/content/en/mineweb-political-economy?oid=175591&sn=Detail [last accessed 18 April 2013].

19 For an interesting and accessible discussion of this, see Ed Cropley & Agnieszka Flak, 'Special report – Why South African mining's in decline', Reuters, 4 February 2011, http://uk.reuters.com/article/2011/02/04/uk-south-africa-mining-idUKLNE71303020110204 [last accessed 18 April 2013].

20 British American Tobacco news release, 'British American Tobacco obtains JSE listing', 28 October 2008, http://www.bat.com/group/sites/uk__3mnfen.nsf/vwPagesWebLive/DO7KTKZ2?opendocument&SKN=1 [last accessed 18 April 2013].

21 This table is adapted from Southall's 'South Africa's fractured power elite'. Data has been updated using information obtained from www.sharenet.co.za in February 2012.

22 Institute of Directors in Southern Africa, 'King Code of Governance Principles' (King III), 2009, http://african.ipapercms.dk/IOD/KINGIII/kingiiicode/ [last accessed 18 April 2013].

23 Institute of Directors in Southern Africa, 'Executive summary of the King Report on Corporate Governance' (King II), 2002, https://www.saica.co.za/Portals/0/documents/executive_summary_king11.

pdf [last accessed 18 April 2013]; an analysis by PricewaterhouseCoopers of the differences between King II and III can be obtained at https://www.saica.co.za/Portals/0/documents/PWC%20SteeringPoint%20KingIII.pdf [last accessed 18 April 2013].

24 Institute of Directors in Southern Africa, 'King Code of Governance Principles' (King III).

25 PricewaterhouseCoopers, 'Executive directors' remuneration practices and trends report', June 2011, https://www.pwc.co.za/en/assets/pdf/executive-directors-report-2011.pdf [last accessed 18 April 2013].

26 All fees obtained from PricewaterhouseCoopers, 'Non-executive directors' practices and fees trends report', January 2013, http://www.pwc.co.za/en_ZA/za/assets/pdf/ned-trends-report-jan-2013.pdf [last accessed 18 April 2013].

27 Market capitalisation is calculated by multiplying the number of shares by the value of each share at a specific time.

28 Market capitalisation data was obtained directly from the JSE via email correspondence on 30 January 2013. The details of directors were obtained from individual companies' websites and latest annual reports.

29 PricewaterhouseCoopers, 'Non-executive directors' practices and fees trends report'.

30 UK Government, 'Women on boards', February 2011, https://www.gov.uk/government/uploads/system/uploads/attachment_data/file/31480/11-745-women-on-boards.pdf [last accessed 18 April 2013].

31 PricewaterhouseCoopers, 'Non-executive directors' practices and fees trends report'.

32 SAIRR, 'South Africa survey', p. 294.

33 The PWC 'Executive directors' remuneration practices and trends report' calculates an even lower representation of black executive directors, at just 10 per cent.

34 See Mandhlaenkosi Nyirenda, 'Board composition in companies listed on the Johannesburg Securities Exchange', MBA dissertation, University of Pretoria, 10 November 2010, http://upetd.up.ac.za/thesis/available/etd-06182011-185630/

unrestricted/dissertation.pdf [last accessed 18 April 2013].

35 Matthew Andrews, 'Is black economic empowerment a South African growth catalyst? (Or could it be …)', Center for International Development at Harvard University Working Paper No. 170, May 2008, p. 67, http://www.hks.harvard.edu/var/ezp_site/storage/fckeditor/file/pdfs/centers-programs/centers/cid/publications/faculty/wp/170.pdf [last accessed 18 April 2013].

36 See 'Race 2012' table, https://www.saica.co.za/Portals/0/Members/documents/Race2012.pdf [last accessed 18 April 2013].

37 Matthew Andrews, 'Is black economic empowerment a South African growth catalyst? (Or could it be …)'.

38 Information Portal on Corruption and Governance in Africa (an initiative of the Institute for Security Studies Corruption and Governance Programme), 'Who owns what?' database, http://www.ipocafrica.org/index.php?option=com_coi&view=coiadvancedsearch&Itemid=105 [last accessed 13 May 2013].

CHAPTER 14: THE PROFESSIONS

1 Anthony Sampson, *Anatomy of Britain Today*, London: Hodder & Stoughton, 1965.

2 Data provided by the UCT Faculty of Commerce.

3 Data provided by the South African Institute of Chartered Accountants (SAICA).

4 SAICA press release, 31 May 2012, http://www.cacharter.co.za/displaycontent.asp?ContentPageId=1166&ContentPageName=Latest%20Press%20Release&Menu=7 [last accessed 20 May 2013].

5 All data provided by SAICA.

6 Tables in the accountants section were compiled using data provided by SAICA.

7 The word 'black' here is used inclusively.

8 This figure assumes the retirement of all CAs currently over the age of 60, and extrapolates forward the rate of change between the two youngest cohorts of CAs registered with SAICA.

9 A so-called bridging programme is intended to bring students from previously black tertiary institutions up to the standards of previously white universities. The Ugandan academic Mahmood Mamdani has stridently criticised their role in post-secondary education in South Africa, as perpetuating Bantu education.

10 Bridging programmes represent further opportunity cost and real cost in terms of time and money for students transferring from previously disadvantaged institutions. Candidates who are required to pass through bridging programmes prior to admission to accredited CTA institutions are further prejudiced in the job market as their undergraduate education is seen to be of an inferior quality compared to students passing out of the historically white universities. Clearly, expanding the 'throughput' for CTA from all educational institutions – if educational standards are maintained – will not only democratise the profession, but will serve as a further imperative to eroding the reputational glass ceilings and 'old res' or 'old varsity' ties that continue to stratify post-tertiary employment in the country.

11 SAICA press release, op. cit.

12 See Jonathan Faull, 'In praise of the South African Constitution', *Africa's a Country*, 16 February 2012, http://africasacountry.com/2012/02/16/praising-the-south-african-constitution/ [last accessed 20 May 2013].

13 This discussion of the legal profession draws extensively from an excellent 2007 paper by Shane Godfrey and Rob Midgley, 'Scarce and critical skills: The law profession', commissioned by the Department of Labour, https://www.labour.gov.za/downloads/documents/research-documents/Law_DoL_Report.pdf [last accessed 20 May 2013].

14 Tables in this section were compiled using data provided by the General Council of the Bar of South Africa (for advocates), and by the LSSA (for attorneys).

15 The legacy of the 'Coolie Act' of 1891 that prevented people of Indian descent from settling in the then independent Orange Free State and that was maintained through the apartheid period in varying incarnations until the lifting of influx controls in 1986 is evident in the complete

absence of attorneys of Indian descent registered with the Free State Law Society.

16 Niren Tolsi, 'Law's upper echelons still white men', *Mail & Guardian*, 17 May 2013, http://mg.co.za/article/2013-05-17-00-laws -upper-echelons-still-white-men [last accessed 20 May 2013].

17 The Grahamstown and Port Elizabeth components of the Bar together constitute the Eastern Cape Bar under the auspices of the General Council of the Bar of South Africa.

18 The extremely low representation of African advocates, and black advocates generally, at the Cape Bar is a matter of long-standing controversy, with Advocate Dumisa Ntsebeza consistently arguing that institutional racism prevents the ascendance of black advocates to the Cape Bar.

19 For a discussion on the legal issue and its background, see Pierre de Vos, 'Should we be conferring titles on advocates?' *Constitutionally Speaking*, 13 February 2012, http://constitutionallyspeaking.co.za/ should-we-be-conferring-titles-on -advocates/ [last accessed 20 May 2013].

20 Charl du Plessis, 'Top advocates still "SC" for now', *City Press*, 17 March 2013, http://www.citypress.co.za/news/sas-top -advocates-still-sc-for-now/ [last accessed 20 May 2013].

21 *Hoffmann v South African Airways*, 2001 (1) SA 1 (CC), paragraph 63.

22 This figure may be slightly inaccurate due to possible inconsistencies in how the judgments list counsels' names. If a lawyer was not known to the author, and was named differently (for example, due to spelling errors or different initials being used for a common surname), it is possible that the same advocate could have been counted twice. However, any such errors will not make a significant difference to the numbers listed.

23 *Hoffmann v South African Airways*, 2001 (1) SA 1 (CC), paragraph 63.

24 Member of the JSC until 2009.

CHAPTER 15: THE UNIVERSITIES

1 Shelagh Gastrow & Patric Tariq Mellet, 'Personal philanthropic giving amongst UCT alumni and the state of relations

between the University of Cape Town and UCT alumni globally', October 2002.

2 Anthony Sampson, *Anatomy of Britain Today*, London: Hodder & Stoughton, 1965, p. 221.

3 Ibid.

4 Department of Education, 'Report of the Ministerial Committee on Transformation and Social Cohesion and the Elimination of Discrimination in Public Higher Education Institutions', 30 November 2008, p. 9, http://bit.ly/zXZW7j [last accessed 20 May 2013].

5 Ibid.

6 Ibid., p. 11.

7 Ibid.

8 Available at http://bit.ly/14NXzja [last accessed 10 June 2013].

9 Murray Williams, 'Ramphele leaves UCT "changed"', *Argus*, 23 September 1999, http://bit.ly/10Pk4mC [last accessed 20 May 2013].

10 Sampson, *Anatomy of Britain Today*, p. 220.

11 Speech by Blade Nzimande, 'Response to the Humanities and Social Sciences (HSS) Charter Report', HSS Charter Conference, 29 March 2012, http://www.info.gov.za/ speech/DynamicAction?pageid=461&sid=2 6371&tid=63037 [last accessed 20 May 2013].

12 From SAIRR, 'South Africa survey', 2012, p. 496. Available at http://bit.ly/114D3Z6.

13 Ibid., p. 496.

14 Ibid., p. 494.

15 Adapted from Council on Higher Education, *VitalStats: Public Higher Education 2010*. Pretoria: Council on Higher Education, 2012, p. 51, http://bit.ly/ 17SSrRd [last accessed 20 May 2013].

16 Ibid., p. 13.

17 Moeketsi Letseka & Simeon Maile, 'High university drop-out rates: A threat to South Africa's future', *HSRC Policy Brief*, March 2008, p. 4, http://www.hsrc.ac.za/uploads/ pageContent/1088/Dropout%20rates.pdf [last accessed 20 May 2013].

18 Xolela Mangcu, 'UCT's senate is the problem', *Cape Times*, 20 February 2013, http://bit.ly/12ohllx [last accessed 20 May 2013].

19 Gastrow & Tariq Mellet, 'Personal philanthropic giving amongst UCT alumni and the state of relations between the

University of Cape Town and UCT alumni globally', October 2002.

20 For the record, I should state that I subsequently formally interviewed Mellet in order to capture the views that I quote in this chapter.

21 Data obtained from the Department of Education, *Education Statistics in South Africa at a Glance in 2001*, Pretoria: Department of Education, June 2003, http://www.education.gov.za/LinkClick.asp x?fileticket=4PlyFsOWgyc%3D&tabid=462 &mid=1326; and the Department of Basic Education, *Education Statistics in South Africa, 2009*, Pretoria: Department of Basic Education, November 2010, http://www.education.gov.za/LinkClick.asp x?fileticket=8RQsvgahSgA= [last accessed 20 May 2013].

22 Statistics South Africa, *Census 2011*, https://www.statssa.gov.za/census2011/ default.asp [last accessed 20 May 2013].

23 Adapted from Council on Higher Education, *VitalStats: Public Higher Education 2010*, p. 25.

24 Ibid., p. 26.

25 What is quite striking is that, although the field shares applicable to enrolments and graduates are relatively constant among most groups, the share of education for African graduates (32 per cent in 2010) is considerably greater than that for African enrolments (19 per cent in 2010). This drags up the general education share (graduates) for African students, which stood at 29.3 per cent in 2010. It seems that the share of B&C for African graduates is quite significantly lower than that for African enrolments (31.7 versus 26.4 per cent in 2010). While roughly 80 per cent of B&C enrolments were African in 2010, only 72 per cent of graduates were.

26 HSRC, 'Data-set for the Student Retention and Graduate Destination Study', Pretoria: Human Sciences Research Council, 2005.

27 Haroon Bhorat, Natasha Mayet & Mariette Visser, 'Student graduation, labour market destinations and employment earnings', in Moeketsi Letseka, Michael Cosser, Mignonne Breier & Mariette Visser, *Student Retention and Graduate Destination: Higher Education and Labour*

Market Access and Success, Cape Town: HSRC Press, 2010. Available at www. hsrcpress.ac.za.

28 Ibid., p. 116.

29 Ibid., p. 117.

30 Cape Higher Education Consortium, 2013, www.chec.ac.za.

31 Bhorat, Mayet & Visser, 'Student graduation, labour market destinations and employment earnings', p. 109.

32 Ibid.

33 Ibid., p. 119.

34 Ibid., p. 123.

CONCLUSION: ANATOMY OF A CRISIS

1 Udesh Pillay, 'Conclusion', in U. Pillay, G. Hagg & F. Nyamnjoy, *State of the Nation: South Africa 2012–2013*, Cape Town: HSRC Press, 2013.

2 Cited in Anthony Sampson, *Anatomy of Britain Today*, London: Hodder & Stoughton, 1965, p. 668.

3 Statistics South Africa, *South African Statistics, 2012*, Pretoria: Government Printer, 2012, section 6.2.8.

4 Multi-Level Government Initiative, 'Service delivery protests barometer 2: Provincial distribution of protests per year', 2013. Available at http://www.mlgi.org.za/ barometers/service-delivery-protest -barometer/service-delivery-protests -barometer-2-provincial-distribution-of -protests-per-year [last accessed 28 June 2013].

5 National Treasury, 'Budget review 2012', 22 February 2012, p. 37, http://www .treasury.gov.za/documents/national%20 budget/2012/review/Prelims%202012.pdf [last accessed 28 June 2013].

6 Multi-Level Government Initiative, 'Service delivery protests barometer 2'.

7 Multi-Level Government Initiative, 2013.

8 SAIRR, 2012, p. 276.

9 National Treasury, 'Local government budgets and expenditure review', 2011, http://www.treasury.gov.za/publications/ igfr/2011/lg/default.aspx [last accessed 08 July 2013].

10 See, for example, James Lorimer, 'Municipal managers and CFOs paid bonuses despite negative audit outcomes', DA press release, 20 September 2011,

http://www.da.org.za/newsroom.htm?action
=view-news-item&id=9798; and Gugu
Mbonambi, 'R6m bonuses for municipal
bigwigs', *The Mercury*, 4 October 2012,
http://www.iol.co.za/mercury/r6m-bonuses
-for-municipal-bigwigs-1.1396726#.URE_
AR2dfsY [both last accessed 28 June 2013].

11 Anthony Sampson, *Anatomy of Britain
Today*. p. xiii

12 Ibid. p. xiii

13 Brian Levy, 'Can islands of effectiveness
thrive in difficult governance settings?
The political economy of local level
collaborative governance', Policy Research
Working Paper 5842, World Bank,
October 2011.

14 Editorial, 'South Africa approaches tipping
point', *Business Day*, 10 June 2013,
http://www.bdlive.co.za/opinion/
editorials/2013/06/10/editorial-south-africa
-approaches-tipping-point [last accessed
28 June 2013].

**APPENDIX 2: CONSTITUTIONAL
COURT JUDGES**

1 All references to Chris Oxtoby are from
'Notes: New appointments to the
Constitutional Court', *The South African
Law Journal* 130(2), 2013.

2 All references to Pierre de Vos are from his
blog, *Constitutionally Speaking*, available
at http://constitutionallyspeaking.co.za.

3 Niren Tolsi, 'Attend Christian course,
Mogoeng tells judges', *Mail & Guardian*,
14 March 2012.

4 Verashni Pillay, 'Zuma's worst decision?'
Mail & Guardian, 17 August 2011.

5 SAPA, 'JSC records complaint against
Moseneke', *Mail & Guardian*, 1 November
2011.

6 Adrienne Carlisle, 'Judge Froneman says
"never again" to human rights violations
in SA', *Grocott's Mail*, 16 October 2009,
http://www.grocotts.co.za/froneman
[last accessed 21 June 2013].

7 Serjeant at the Bar, 'Traditional law denies
rights', *Mail & Guardian*, 28 March 2013.

8 Tony Leon, *On the Contrary: Leading the
Opposition in a Democratic South Africa*,
Johannesburg: Jonathan Ball Publishers,
2008.

9 Franny Rabkin, 'Gauntlett and Madlanga
seen as Constitutional Court frontrunners',
Business Day, 22 February 2013.

Index

Do you have any comments, suggestions or
feedback about this book or any other Zebra Press titles?
Contact us at **talkback@zebrapress.co.za**

*

Visit **www.randomstruik.co.za** and subscribe
to our newsletter for monthly updates and news